Lecture Notes
in Business Information Processing   321

More information about this series at http://www.springer.com/series/7911

Slimane Hammoudi · Michał Śmiałek
Olivier Camp · Joaquim Filipe (Eds.)

Enterprise Information Systems

19th International Conference, ICEIS 2017
Porto, Portugal, April 26–29, 2017
Revised Selected Papers

 Springer

Editors
Slimane Hammoudi
MODESTE/ESEO
Angers
France

Olivier Camp
MODESTE/ESEO
Angers
France

Michał Śmiałek
Warsaw University of Technology
Warsaw
Poland

Joaquim Filipe
INSTICC
Polytechnic Institute of Setúbal
Setúbal
Poland

ISSN 1865-1348   ISSN 1865-1356   (electronic)
Lecture Notes in Business Information Processing
ISBN 978-3-319-93374-0   ISBN 978-3-319-93375-7   (eBook)
https://doi.org/10.1007/978-3-319-93375-7

Library of Congress Control Number: 2018946628

Printed on acid-free paper

This Springer imprint is published by the registered company Springer International Publishing AG part of Springer Nature
The registered company address is: Gewerbestrasse 11, 6330 Cham, Switzerland

Preface

The present book includes extended and revised versions of a set of selected papers from the 19th International Conference on Enterprise Information Systems (ICEIS 2017), held in Porto, Portugal, during April 26–29, 2018.

ICEIS 2017 received 318 paper submissions from 43 countries, of which 12% are included in this book. The papers were selected by the event chairs and their selection is based on a number of criteria that include classifications and comments provided by the Program Committee members, the session chairs' assessment, and also the program chairs' global view of all the papers included in the technical program. The authors of selected papers were then invited to submit revised and extended versions of their papers having at least 30% innovative material.

The purpose of the 19th International Conference on Enterprise Information Systems (ICEIS) was to bring together researchers, engineers, and practitioners interested in advances and business applications of information systems. Six simultaneous tracks were held, covering different aspects of enterprise information systems applications, including enterprise database technology, systems integration, artificial intelligence, decision support systems, information systems analysis and specification, Internet computing, electronic commerce, human factors and enterprise architecture.

We are confident that the papers included in this book will strongly contribute to the understanding of some current research trends in enterprise information systems, including:

– Coupling and integrating heterogeneous data sources
– Social networks, Semantic Web, and ontology engineering
– Recommender systems and advanced applications of AI
– Business modeling and business process management
– Human–computer interaction and human factors
– Software engineering, distributed systems, and mobile computing

We would like to thank all the authors for their contributions and the reviewers for their hard work, which helped ensure the quality of this publication.

April 2017

Slimane Hammoudi
Michał Śmiałek
Olivier Camp
Joaquim Filipe

Organization

Conference Co-chairs

Olivier Camp   MODESTE/ESEO, France
Joaquim Filipe   Polytechnic Institute of Setúbal/INSTICC, Portugal

Program Co-chairs

Slimane Hammoudi   ESEO, MODESTE, France
Michal Smialek   Warsaw University of Technology, Poland

Program Committee

Alan Abrahams	Virginia Tech, USA
Manuel E. Acacio	Universidad de Murcia, Spain
Jose Alfonso Aguilar	Universidad Autonoma de Sinaloa, Mexico
Adeel Ahmad	Laboratoire d'Informatique Signal et Image de la Côte d'Opale, France
Emel Aktas	Cranfield University, UK
Patrick Albers	École Supérieure d'Électronique de l'Ouest, France
Eduardo Alchieri	Universidade de Brasilia, Brazil
Mohammad Al-Shamri	Ibb University, Yemen
Rainer Alt	University of Leipzig, Germany
Rachid Anane	Coventry University, UK
Andreas S. Andreou	Cyprus University of Technology, Cyprus
Plamen Angelov	Lancaster University, UK
Ruben Leandro Antonelli	Lifia, Universidad Nacional de La Plata, Argentina
Olatz Arbelaitz	Universidad del Pais Vasco, Spain
Oscar Avila	Universidad de los Andes, Colombia
Ramazan Aygun	University of Alabama in Huntsville, USA
Tamara Babaian	Bentley University, USA
José Ángel Banares Bañares	Universidad de Zaragoza, Spain
Cecilia Baranauskas	State University of Campinas - Unicamp, Brazil
Ken Barker	University of Calgary, Canada
Reza Barkhi	Virginia Tech, USA
Jean-Paul Barthes	Université de Technologie de Compiègne, France
Rémi Bastide	ISIS, CUFR Jean-François Champollion, France
Bernhard Bauer	University of Augsburg, Germany
Cristian Garcia Bauza	UNCPBA-PLADEMA-CONICET, Argentina
Orlando Belo	University of Minho, Portugal
François Bergeron	TELUQ-Université du Québec, Canada
Jorge Bernardino	Polytechnic Institute of Coimbra, ISEC, Portugal

Riccardo Martoglia	University of Modena and Reggio Emilia, Italy
Katsuhisa Maruyama	Ritsumeikan University, Japan
David Martins de Matos	L2F/INESC-ID Lisboa/Instituto Superior Técnico, Portugal
Wolfgang Mayer	University of South Australia, Australia
Rafael Mayo-García	CIEMAT, Spain
Jerzy Michnik	University of Economics in Katowice, Poland
Harekrishna Misra	Institute of Rural Management, India
Michele M. Missikoff	Institute of Sciences and Technologies of Cognition, ISTC-CNR, Italy
Lars Mönch	FernUniversität in Hagen, Germany
Francisco Montero	University of Castilla-La Mancha, Spain
Carlos León de Mora	University of Seville, Spain
João Luís Cardoso de Moraes	Federal University of São Carlos, Brazil
Fernando Moreira	Universidade Portucalense, Portugal
Edward David Moreno	Federal University of Sergipe, Brazil
Javier Muguerza	University of the Basque Country UPV/EHU, Spain
Pietro Murano	Oslo and Akershus University College of Applied Sciences, Norway
Leandro Alves Neves	Ibilce/São Paulo State University, Brazil
Vincent Ng	The Hong Kong Polytechnic University, SAR China
Ovidiu Noran	Griffith University, Australia
Bernardo Pereira Nunes	Pontifícia Universidade Católica do Rio de Janeiro, Brazil
Joshua C. Nwokeji	Gannon University, USA
Andrés Muñoz Ortega	Catholic University of Murcia, Spain
Carla Osthoff	Laboratorio Nacional de Computação Cientifica, Brazil
Mieczyslaw Owoc	Wroclaw University of Economics, Poland
Malgorzata Pankowska	University of Economics in Katowice, Poland
Rafael Stubs Parpinelli	Universidade do Estado de Santa Catarina, Brazil
Silvia Parusheva	University of Economics Varna, Bulgaria
Rafael Pasquini	Universidade Federal de Uberlândia, Brazil
Zbigniew Pastuszak	Maria Curie-Sklodowska University in Lublin, Poland
Luis Ferreira Pires	University of Twente, The Netherlands
Placide Poba-Nzaou	Université du Québec à Montréal, Canada
Fiona A. C. Polack	Keele University, UK
Michal Polasik	Nicolaus Copernicus University, Poland
Luigi Pontieri	National Research Council, Italy
Filipe Portela	University of Minho, Portugal
Naveen Prakash	IGDTUW, India
Daniele Radicioni	University of Turin, Italy
T. Ramayah	Universiti Sains Malaysia, Malaysia
Pedro Ramos	Instituto Superior das Ciências do Trabalho e da Empresa, Portugal

Konstantinos Rantos	Eastern Macedonia and Thrace Institute of Technology, Greece
Francisco Regateiro	Instituto Superior Técnico, Portugal
Ulrich Reimer	University of Applied Sciences St. Gallen, Switzerland
Nuno de Magalhães Ribeiro	Universidade Fernando Pessoa, Portugal
Ricardo Ribeiro	ISCTE-IUL and INESC-ID Lisboa, Portugal
Michele Risi	University of Salerno, Italy
Sonja Ristic	University of Novi Sad, Serbia
Sérgio Assis Rodrigues	Federal University of Rio de Janeiro, Brazil
Alfonso Rodriguez	University of Bio-Bio, Chile
Daniel Rodriguez	University of Alcalá, Spain
Luciana Alvim Santos Romani	Embrapa Agricultural Informatics, Brazil
Jose Raul Romero	University of Cordoba, Spain
Gustavo Rossi	Lifia, Argentina
Artur Rot	Wroclaw University of Economics, Poland
Francisco Ruiz	Universidad de Castilla-La Mancha, Spain
Rajaa Saidi	INSEA, Laboratoire Systèmes d'Information, Systèmes Intelligents et Modélisation Mathématique, Morocco
Luis Enrique Sánchez	Universidad de Castilla-La Mancha, Spain
Manuel Filipe Santos	University of Minho, Portugal
Jurek Sasiadek	Carleton University, Canada
Sissel Guttormsen Schär	University of Bern, Switzerland
Isabel Seruca	Universidade Portucalense, Portugal
Ahm Shamsuzzoha	Sultan Qaboos University, Oman
Markus Siepermann	TU Dortmund, Germany
Alberto Rodrigues Silva	IST/INESC-ID, Portugal
Sean Siqueira	Federal University of the State of Rio de Janeiro, Brazil
Seppo Sirkemaa	University of Turku, Finland
Hala Skaf-Molli	Nantes University, France
Michal Smialek	Warsaw University of Technology, Poland
Michel Soares	Federal University of Sergipe, Brazil
Janusz Sobecki	Politechnika Wroclawska, Poland
Chantal Soule-Dupuy	Université Toulouse 1, France
Rogéria Cristiane Gratão de Souza	São Paulo State University, Brazil
Marco Aurélio Spohn	Federal University of Fronteira Sul, Brazil
Clare Stanier	Staffordshire University, UK
Chris Stary	Johannes Kepler University of Linz, Austria
Hans-Peter Steinbacher	University of Applied Sciences Kufstein, Austria
Hiroki Suguri	Miyagi University, Japan
Reima Suomi	University of Turku, Finland
Jerzy Surma	Warsaw School of Economics, Poland
Zoltán Szabó	Corvinus University of Budapest, Hungary
Ryszard Tadeusiewicz	AGH University of Science and Technology, Poland
Tania Tait	Maringá State University and FEITEP, Brazil

Efthimios Tambouris	University of Macedonia, Greece
Mohan Tanniru	Oakland University, USA
Sotirios Terzis	University of Strathclyde, UK
Claudine Toffolon	Université du Maine, France
Leandro Tortosa	Universidad de Alicante, Spain
Dimitar Trajanov	Cyril and Methodius University, Skopje, Macedonia, The Former Yugoslav Republic of
Carolina Tripp	Universidad Autónoma de Sinaloa, Mexico
Theodoros Tzouramanis	University of the Aegean, Greece
Domenico Ursino	Università degli Studi Mediterranea Reggio Calabria, Italy
Mario Vacca	Italian Ministry of Education, Italy
José Ângelo Braga de Vasconcelos	Universidade Atlântica, Portugal
Michael Vassilakopoulos	University of Thessaly, Greece
Dessislava Vassileva	Sofia University St. Kliment Ohridski, Bulgaria
Jose Luis Vazquez-Poletti	Universidad Complutense de Madrid, Spain
Christine Verdier	LIG, Université Grenoble Alpes, France
Gualtiero Volpe	Università degli Studi di Genova, Italy
Vasiliki Vrana	Technological Educational Institute of Central Macedonia, Greece
Bing Wang	University of Hull, UK
Dariusz Wawrzyniak	Wroclaw University of Economics, Poland
Hans Weigand	Tilburg University, The Netherlands
Janusz Wielki	Opole University of Technology, Poland
Adam Wojtowicz	Poznan University of Economics, Poland
Mudasser Wyne	National University, USA
Hongji Yang	Bath Spa University, UK
Geraldo Francisco Donegá Zafalon	São Paulo State University, Brazil
Ewa Ziemba	University of Economics in Katowice, Poland
Eugenio Zimeo	University of Sannio, Italy

Additional Reviewers

María Luisa Rodríguez Almendros	University of Granada, Spain
Raouf Alomainy	University of Alabama in Huntsville, USA
Fadila Bentayeb	ERIC Lab, France
Claudia Cappelli	Universidade Federal do Estado do Rio de Janeiro, Brazil
Loredana Caruccio	University of Salerno, Italy
Andrés Cid-López	Corporación Nacional de Telecomunicaciones CNT EP, Ecuador
Luiz Manoel Rocha Gadelha Junior	National Laboratory for Scientific Computing, Brazil

Mahesh Juttu	University of Alabama in Huntsville, USA
Alexandre Maciel	University of Pernambuco, Brazil
Ana Patrícia Fontes Magalhães	Universidade Federal da Bahia, Brazil
Nikolaos Mallios	University of Thessaly, Greece
Alaa Marshan	Brunel University London, UK
George Mavrommatis	National Center for Public Administration and Local Government, Greece
Alexander Mera	PUC-Rio, Colombia
Asmat Monaghan	Royal Holloway, University of London, UK
Panagiotis Moutafis	University of Thessaly, Greece
Marcelo Z. do Nascimento	Federal University of Uberlândia, Brazil
Dario Di Nucci	Vrije Universiteit Brussel, Belgium
Stanislaw Osowski	Warsaw University of Technology, Poland
Fabio Palomba	University of Salerno, Italy
Maryam Radgui	INSEA, Laboratoire Systèmes d'Information, Systèmes Intelligents et Modélisation Mathématique, Morocco
Julio Cesar dos Reis	Institute of Computing, UNICAMP, Brazil
Bruno Warin	LISIC, France

Invited Speakers

Victor Chang	Xi'an Jiaotong-Liverpool University, China
Hermann Kaindl	TU Wien, Austria
Marco Brambilla	Politecnico di Milano, Italy
Christoph Rosenkranz	University of Cologne, Germany

Contents

Information Systems Analysis and Specification

Software Agents and Internet Computing

Human-Computer Interaction

Enterprise Architecture

Databases and Information Systems Integration

Towards a Framework for Aiding the Collaborative Management of Informal Projects

Luma Ferreira, Juliana Bezerra[✉], and Celso Hirata

ITA, São José dos Campos, Brazil
lumamaia@gmail.com, {juliana,hirata}@ita.br

Abstract. Informal projects, such as schoolwork and social meetings, are managed by groups in a collaborative way. Conventional management approaches are not suitable to deal with dynamism and decentralization required by informal projects. Although commonly used, communication tools alone are not sufficient for managing informal projects, due to a lack of coordination mechanisms and project awareness. Based on recommendations of cooperative work, motivation mechanisms and project management, we propose a framework to aid the collaborative management of informal projects. The framework consists of five guidelines regarding projects definition, activities' management, responsibility sharing, contribution recognition, and project visibility. We demonstrate that the proposed framework is practical by building a mobile application. Based on two case studies, we show that the framework assist management activities and also foster participation and recognition. We also discuss the use to the framework to analyze an existing tool in a way to identify weaknesses and improvements.

Keywords: General management · Informal systems · Technology
Collaborative management · Informal project · Collaboration · Incentives

1 Introduction

Project management is the discipline of planning, organizing, and managing resources to complete successfully goals and objectives of a specific project [23]. Without project management the project progress is uncertain and could be in jeopardy [30]. There are two management approaches to conduct projects: centralized and collaborative. Centralized management assumes a clear chain of command (hierarchy) to manage projects. In this case, specific responsibilities are in general assigned to roles, in which management is individually assigned and rarely shared. Collaborative management considers a self-organized structure where management responsibility is delegated among project members. Collaborative management is non-hierarchical and participative type of management [18, 19].

Regarding the nature of the projects, there are two types: formal and informal projects [16]. Formal projects due to their complexity generally are more rigorous in terms of management, requiring more detailing, effort and time in the planning and monitoring of activities [7]. Formal projects can be managed in a centralized way mainly in single

© Springer International Publishing AG, part of Springer Nature 2018
S. Hammoudi et al. (Eds.): ICEIS 2017, LNBIP 321, pp. 3–20, 2018.
https://doi.org/10.1007/978-3-319-93375-7_1

organizations or collaborative way in distributed or virtual organizations [19, 31]. Informal projects do not require formal processes of management, for example community projects, schoolwork, and social events such as birthday parties and open house meetings [24]. Informal projects are prone to both kinds of management, centralized or collaborative; being the collaborative the most adopted one. Collaborative informal projects have advantages as less bureaucracy, faster management of activities and more motivated and proactive members [22]. Our focus in this work is the collaborative management of informal projects.

In informal projects, members share responsibility for the results, and the success of the project depends on the participation, motivation and commitment of the members [12]. In general, the management of informal projects does not have specific support tools. Since informal projects are managed and executed collaboratively, there is growing use of communication tools, including email, text messages, instant messaging and social media [1, 13, 21]. Mobile applications such as WhatsApp and Facebook benefit the management and execution of informal projects, since the users are always connected and accessible [11, 17, 27, 29].

Communication tools are used to plan, monitor and control the activities in informal projects. Although the communication is an essential mechanism in collaboration, it does not suffice. Some problems are lack of support for coordination mechanisms, lack of awareness of project progress, difficulty to manage activities, and lack of motivation mechanisms [26]. So, other mechanisms need to be considered for a successful management of informal projects. On the other hand, using conventional management tools is not a solution. The main reason is that these tools bring intrinsic rigidity in management of centralized approaches and require detailed information for monitoring and control, which does not match the reality of informal projects that needs to be dynamic, flexible and decentralized [10].

We propose a framework to support the collaborative management of informal projects. The goal of the approach is to allow collaboration and enable an exchange of information according to the convenience of the project members, in a way to encourage the participation of members in project management. The approach is based on concepts, techniques, and recommendations of project management, cooperative work, and motivation mechanisms. The framework consists of five guidelines regarding projects definition, activities' management, responsibility sharing, contribution recognition, and project visibility.

The paper is organized as follows. Section 2 presents the background of our work. Section 3 describes the proposed framework to collaborative management of informal projects. Section 4 details the tool implemented according to the framework. Section 5 describes how we evaluate the proposed approach using the tool. Section 6 presents an analysis of an existent tool considering the observance of the framework guidelines. Finally, conclusions and future work are presented in Sect. 7.

2 Background

Existing research includes examples of informal groups, how groups are currently organized, how management occurs, what tools are used and the problems encountered.

Student work groups are an example of collaborative groups that develop informal projects, which correspond to projects in school or university. Research has been conducted to understand collaboration among students in a way to enhance students' experience and learning. Different platforms are used in experiments, such as Trac, ANGEL, Basecamp, Wiki, ClockingIT, and Moodle. Depending on project and context, combination of tools, development of new tool, or even adoption of specific tool are required [6, 15, 25, 32].

Research projects need to be managed as other projects and they have particularities. In general, research projects are collaborative effort, and involve members from universities and other organizations. In order to achieve success, these projects require freedom, flexibility, effective communication, shared power, shared knowledge, commitment and involvement of all project parties [5, 30]. Collaborative research projects present specific features and demand adaptations to existing project management approaches.

A more iterative and flexible project management is the Agile Project Management (APM), which aims to achieve better performance in projects, with less management effort, and higher levels of innovation and added value for the customer. APM theory recommends specific practices (e.g. product vision and sprints), roles (e.g. scrum master and agile mentor), and artifacts (e.g. backlog, and roadmap) [8, 9]. APM differs from collaborative management of informal projects in some aspects. Informal projects in general are not customer-oriented and do not necessarily require iterative process. A common element is the creation of the project plan collaboratively with shared responsibility.

The way people organize their day-to-day activities (including leisure, such as dinner and party) is through communication. Counts [10] creates a system that allows people to organize themselves into groups, and coordinate their leisure activities together. The system also provides an overview of what is happening in the groups. The proposal mainly provides mechanisms for creating groups and centralizing communication; however, there are no guidelines to help manage the group's activities.

The exchange of messages of 70 students at a university is investigated by Battestini et al. [1]. They collected nearly 60,000 text messages, including different mediums as SMS messages, emails, Facebook conversation, and online chats. Dominant topics were related to planning and coordination of events or activities together, such as meal times, rides, homework. The result emphasizes the lack of an approach for supporting management of informal projects.

Groups of students, conducting social activities as informal projects, were studied by Schuler et al. [26] in order to identify their challenges and problems during the collaborative management. Social activities were birthday parties, bachelor parties, reunions, barbecues, cinema sessions, football games, and lunches. Students used mainly communication via text messages, group messages (e.g. WhatsApp, e-mail), chat, phone calls and event systems (e.g. Facebook event and Google invite). The identified problems were decentralization, lack of focus and overhead of information in the conversations, which led to a lack of understanding and confusion about the details of the activity. Coordination occurred in a decentralized manner and information was distributed in different message flows. Although the researchers pointed out relevant challenges faced in the collaborative management of social activities, there was no suggestion for better support such management.

Donker and Blumberg [12] studied collaborative management and virtual teams, in order to identify management problems that make teams less effective. The main problem was the lack of interface between the project management tools and collaboration tools. They argue that it is needed to integrate information from both tools and also to define methods for managing collaborative processes. Such arguments are the motivation of our proposal.

Ferreira et al. [14] proposed an approach to assist collaborative management of informal projects. We extend their work by structuring a framework. The framework is composed by five guidelines. For each guideline, we add directives to better explain the guideline and to detail how it can be accomplished. We also discuss how to use the framework to analyze existent tools considering collaborative aspects. We assume that the analysis helps identifying improvements to better support collaborative management. In the next section, we present our proposal.

3   A Framework to Support Collaborative Management of Informal Groups

Three pillars support the proposed framework. They are: project management, cooperative work, and motivation mechanisms.

Our framework brings concepts from the project management discipline [23] in order to address planning, and monitoring and control of projects without requiring too much overhead. As informal project management requires a flexible approach, our framework specifically allows the creation of projects, group definition, definition of activities, time control, assignment of responsibilities, and workspace for monitoring and control.

The framework considers the main aspects regarding cooperative work, such as communication, coordination and cooperation [2, 4]. The aim is to provide effective communication, to enable cooperation and necessary coordination of members to carry out the management activities. Besides, the framework enables collaboration in the execution of project activities.

In a collaborative management, management should be carried out by the cooperation among participants in the project. So management must also be motivated, in a way that group members are encourage to participate. The idea is to avoid overhead of activities on few members, which can lead to dissatisfaction of them. All members should share responsibility for the management: any member can define project activities, deadlines, responsibilities, and even termination of activities.

In the framework, we opt to employ incentive mechanisms in order to encourage the participation of members through the needs of belonging, esteem and self-actualization [3, 20]. Belonging refers to the desire of social interaction or socialization in situations where one feels accepted. Esteem refers to the need to be recognized by others due to participation. Self-actualization is the need to maximize own potential, by developing skills and opening up new opportunities.

The framework is structured in five guidelines. A guideline is an indication or instruction that directs project members and the way that the management activities are performed. For each guideline, we highlight its importance and add ways as the guideline can be accomplished and further implemented in a tool. The tool has to aid not only the management activities but also to support the collaboration among the project members in a convenient and motivating manner. The subsections below describe the five guidelines of the framework.

3.1   Guideline 1: Definition of Project and Group

The basic definition of the project includes identification, purpose (objective) and duration. As a collaborative project, it is required to define the group by selecting the group members. In order to have an easier coordination and ensure individual motivation, it is important that all members be aligned with the objective of the project. So, the directives of Guideline 1 are:

(1a)   Any individual can create a project by describing its purpose and features (e.g. description and deadline).
(1b)   The project creator can invite members to participate of the project.
(1c)   Members who accept the invitation become part of the project group.
(1d)   Any member can at any time redefine the project features.
(1e)   Any member can at any time invite new members to the project group.

Incentive mechanisms are basically incorporated in the directives (1d) and (1e) above. By allowing everyone to have equal authority, it is understood that all members will share responsibilities, demoting the relevance of a possible 'owner' of the project. This incentive mechanism is related to belonging and esteem. For instance, to allow members to appoint new participants is a way to recognize the competence of members, which results in greater involvement and motivation.

3.2   Guideline 2: Definition and Management of Activities

As part of the management of project scope, the definition of the activities specifies the work to be performed in the project. Such definition happens not only in planning but also in execution and in response to the monitoring and control. During the project, new information must be considered and needs may change, which consequently affect activities definition. Therefore, activities' definitions can be changed any time. An activity can be excluded if it does not make sense for the scope of the project. A change can be performed by any member of the group. However, members have to be aware that activities must be completed to achieve the project goals. It is important that the information of activity status (such as change, completion and exclusion) be shared, so that everyone in the group can follow the progress of the project. So, the directives of Guideline 2 are:

(2a) Any member can create an activity, by defining its purpose and features (e.g. description and deadline).
(2b) Any member can redefine an activity, by changing its features.
(2c) Any member can exclude an activity.
(2d) Any member can complete an activity, by informing results.

Incentive mechanisms are considered in all directives above by the fact to allow any member at any time to have access to the activity definition and related actions (e.g. change, exclude and finish). This empowerment allows dynamism and flexibility, and also encourages members to participate in the project. Incentive mechanisms here are mainly related to belonging and self-actualization: a member feels that he/she belongs to the team when he/she can take action, as well as he/she can challenge himself/herself to perform better in the group.

3.3 Guideline 3: Sharing of Responsibility

A project has activities that need to be performed to reach the project completion and success. A way to increase the likelihood that the activity is performed is decentralizing responsibilities. For this, we assume that the members conduct their activities in a coordinated fashion. The idea is to encourage active participation of the members, fostering cooperation and proactive behavior. So the directives of Guideline 3 are:

(3a) One or more members can be responsible for an activity.
(3b) Any member can assign himself/herself voluntarily as responsible for an activity.
(3c) Any member can invite other to be responsible for an activity. This invitation is not of mandatory acceptance.
(3d) The responsible(s) for an activity can change during the project.
(3e) Any member can contribute to the activity development. There is no need to be responsible for a particular activity.

Incentive mechanisms are present in the directives above. The openness to a member to assume responsibility (directive 3b) is related to self-actualization as the member is faced to meet new challenges. To invite someone to be responsible (directive 3c) is related to incentive mechanisms of esteem, since the invitee can feel recognized and valued by the group and decide to contribute actively. The invitation becomes more accurate when members have knowledge of competences, skills and abilities of themselves. Directive 3e encourages members to participate actively in the activities, aiming to assist in planning, monitoring and control of activities. One way to capture contributions regarding activities is, for instance, to allow comments (textual or image attachments), which can be praise, criticism, suggestion or any other comment to assist in executing activities.

3.4 Guideline 4: Contribution Recognition

Contributions may happen at any time in a collaborative project management, and in various ways. For instance, members can suggest new activities or different perspectives about the development of existent activities. We believe that recognizing contributions is the key mechanism to the active participation of members in the project. Demonstrating recognition aims to encourage collaboration and ensures a conducive environment to the involvement of everyone in the project, which in turn raises the esteem of participants. According to the collaboration described in guidelines 1, 2 and 3, the directives of Guideline 4 are:

(4a) Any member can acknowledge new members in the project.
(4b) Any member can appreciate other member for inviting someone to participate in the project.
(4c) Any member can thank other member who created an activity or concluded an existent one.
(4d) Any member can congratulate other member who assumed responsibility for an activity.
(4e) Any member can appreciate other member for inviting someone to be responsible for an activity.
(4f) Any member can thank other member who contributed to an activity development.

Recognition can happen directly by thanking someone or issuing a positive comment about a contribution provided by a given member. A way to implement such directives is to use the mechanism of 'like', which allows members to demonstrate their satisfaction with a click on an icon that indicates positivism. To provide the opportunity to members to be recognized is seen as incentive mechanisms related to esteem, since the acquired visibility in the group and the feeling of prestige can encourage further participation in the project.

3.5 Guideline 5: Project Visibility Provision

Providing the project visibility allows the project members have access to everything that is happening. It is about giving transparency of the project management, facilitating monitoring and control and aligning the expectations of everyone with regard to project objectives. Members need to know what has to be done and what was done, since in order to cooperate, it is necessary to know when, where and how to cooperate. According to the collaboration described in guidelines 1, 2 and 3, the directives of Guideline 5 are:

(5a) A member should have access to a list of all projects that he belongs.
(5b) Members must have access to project activities, their responsible members, deadlines, and progress status information (e.g. open/closed and results).
(5c) Members should have access to interactions among members regarding the development of project activities.
(5d) Members need to be notified of interactions and changes in the whole project.

Providing visibility is an incentive mechanism that includes several motivations. For instance, a member can feel within the group once he knows everything that happens in the project. In addition, a member can feel prestige because his contributions are perceived and appreciated by the group. Activities' updates are performed concurrently by members usually in different locations. Therefore, updates have to be promptly made and visible to allow a proper coordination. This feature allows that the visibility provision be effective.

As seen, the framework is composed of generic guidelines. However, the guidelines per se are not practical. To be useful, guidelines should be structured into a systematic way to be followed. In what follows, we present a tool that implements the proposed guidelines in a systematic way.

4   Towards a Tool to Implement the Framework

We consider that the tool should allow members to collaborate according to the proposed guidelines in timely and convenient manner.

4.1   Tool Design and Implementation

A mobile application was developed to enable members perform the management activities collaboratively. We advocate that the tool should be a mobile application, since it enables members to perform the management activities collaboratively anywhere anytime. The advantages of mobile applications are convenience of use and mobility to the users.

The requirements are composed of prerequisites, functional requirements and non-functional requirements. As prerequisite, the Android platform was adopted. The system includes as front-end, smartphones and tablets with Android version 3.0 or later. Functional requirements describe the system functions. The functional requirements were defined in order to meet the guidelines proposed by the framework. In general, association of guideline directives to requirements is immediate. A non-functional requirement that deserves consideration is synchronization. The application must provide a synchronous interaction where information should be shared simultaneously, so we adopted the model WYSIWIS (What You See Is What I See).

Parse platform was used in our solution for data storage services, notifications, user management and client-server infrastructure. Parse allows developers to focus on building their applications without having to worry about managing servers and back-end infrastructure. The API Parse implicitly employs the client-cloud architecture, where the server is in the cloud. The server Parse is responsible for executing queries to the data. Parse is also responsible for sending and managing notifications to warn members of the interactions that occur in the project.

4.2   Tool Overview

The tool was developed taking into account the usability. The first interface (Fig. 1) of the tool shows all projects that the member participates and has a plus icon to create a new project. Next interfaces are shown considering a hypothetical project whose goal is to make a party (from now we call 'Farewell Party'). Figure 2 contains information of the considered project, including name, deadline and participants. Notice that individuals with 'checked' marks are the members that will conduct the project.

Fig. 1. List of projects in the developed tool [14].

Fig. 2. Project definition in the developed tool [14].

Entering in the project, the interface (Fig. 3) shows all activities defined to the project. For each activity, it is possible to see its identifier, responsible person's name (below the activity identifier), and deadline (besides the activity identifier). The status information is presented in the circle on the left of the activity identifier. Empty circle means open activity, while checked circle means closed activity. Color in the circle is related to the activity deadline: gray indicates that deadline is feasible; yellow indicates that deadline is near, and red indicates that deadline was missed. It is also possible to create new activities (plus icon); in this case, it will open the interface in Fig. 4.

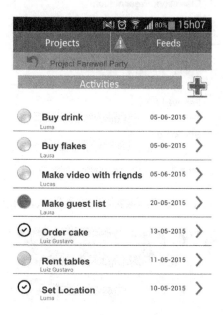

Fig. 3. List of project activities in the developed tool.

Given an activity, it is possible to access its information (Fig. 4). Clicking on 'edit', a member can change activity title, deadline and description. Clicking on 'Comment', a member can add new comments to help in developing the activity. All comments are shown in the activity interface and can be appreciated ('like' icon). Clicking on 'Finish', a member indicates that the activity terminated by adding its main results. Clicking on 'Responsible' icon, responsible members can be assigned (Fig. 5).

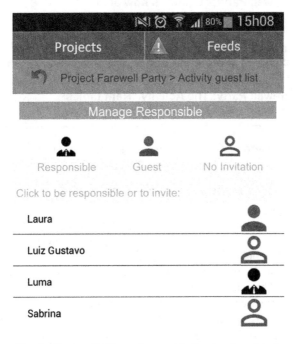

Fig. 4. Activity information in the developed tool.

Fig. 5. Responsibility assignment in the developed tool.

Interface in Fig. 5 shows the names of all project members. On the right of each name, there is an indication if the member is already responsible for the activity (e.g. 'Luma'); if the member was invited to be responsible for the activity (e.g. 'Laura'); or if the member has no direct responsibility on the activity (e.g. 'Sabrina'). A member assumes responsibility for an activity if he/she clicks on the icon associated to his/her name to change its status to 'responsible'. A member invites other to take responsibility for an activity if he/she clicks on the icon associated to other name to change its status to 'guest'.

The interface in Fig. 6 shows all notifications ('feeds') about the project. A notification is defined to each action that a member can perform in the project. The actions include inviting other member as responsible persons; assuming responsibility for an activity; completing an activity; and editing an activity. For each notification, a 'like' icon is associated in order to allow recognition of the member's contribution.

Fig. 6. Project notifications in the developed tool.

5   Evaluating the Framework to Support Groups

In order to assess if the framework proposed in Sect. 3 can meet the needs of groups with respect to the collaborative management of informal projects, we conducted two case studies using the tool described in Sect. 4.

In the first case study, we had with three participants, who are teenagers attending high school course. They chose a project that was schoolwork of History. In the second case study, there were seven participants, who were undergraduate students. The project of the second team was the definition of a programming exercise. Participants were between 15 to 24 years old. They decided their projects, but we limited the duration to two weeks.

Before the teams use the tool, we collected information regarding previous experiences of participants. We analyzed the groups' maturity with respect to the members' experiences with projects, communication tools and project management tools. Participants rated their experience using the levels: 'None', 'Little', 'Regular', 'Good' or 'Excellent'. Results are shown in Table 1. Experiences with projects were considered mostly as 'Good'. Experiences with communication tools were rated mostly as 'Excellent' or 'Good'. All participants also cited WhatsApp and half of them cited e-mail as the main used communication tools. Experiences with project management tools, such as 'Microsoft Project', were assessed mostly as 'Little' or 'None', which in turn indicate that most of the participants have not yet been presented to the project management tools.

Table 1. Background of participants.

	Experience with projects	Experience with collaborative tools	Experience with project management tools
None	0%	0%	30%
Little	10%	0%	50%
Regular	10%	10%	10%
Good	80%	30%	10%
Excellent	0%	60%	0%

The fact that all participants use as the primary way to manage their projects a communication tool, WhatsApp, strengthens the need of an approach to manage informal projects. The fact that the participants do not have experience with project management tools emphasizes that these tools are not disseminated or used to carry out the management of informal projects.

In order to verify whether the approach met the expectation to help groups in the collaborative management of their informal projects, participants assessed the same five statements (about how participants manage their informal projects) before and after using the tool. So we were able to compare previous experiences to tool experiences and reason about the framework support. For all the statements, respondents should answer using a scale from 0.2 to 1, where 0.2 means 'Strongly Disagree', 0.4 means Disagree, 0.6 means 'Neutral', 0.8 means 'Agree', and 1 means 'Strongly Agree' with the statement. Statements and results are shown in Table 2.

The results using the tool were always superior that those without the tool. The tool can aid in the three main groups of processes of project management: Project Planning, Project Execution, and Project Monitoring and Control. The main gain was perceived in the monitoring and control of activities. Other important results are regarding to participation and recognition, showing that, with the tool, members were encouraged to participate and they were recognized for their participations. Participants also stated that they were strongly satisfied when used the tool. Results then indicate that the proposed framework was able to meet the expectations to support the participation of members

Table 2. Gains with the tool that implements the framework.

Statement	Without the tool	With the tool
The used approach aided in Project Planning	0.76	0.93
The used approach helps in the Project Execution	0.73	0.93
The used approach aided in the Project Monitoring and Control	0.43	1
The used approach helps in the project recognition	0.68	0.93
The used approach helps in the project participation	0.78	0.97
I am satisfied with the used approach to manage my informal projects	0.60	0.96

in the collaborative management of informal projects and satisfy the participants with respect to the project management.

6   Analyzing an Existent Tool with Respect to the Framework

In this section we investigated an existent tool, Trello, with respect to the proposed framework. The idea is to verify if guidelines and related directives are presented in the tool, in order to identify gaps and improvements. Trello is a web-based project management application originally released in 2011. Its improved mobile version was released in 2014 [28]. We notice that our framework and Trello were proposed almost together coincidently. Below, we discuss about how Trello satisfies each framework guideline, explaining which directives are addressed by Trello features.

Trello has support for an individual to create project (directive 1a). It is a different approach for describing a project than that used in our tool (described in Sect. 4), mainly because Trello follows the kanban paradigm for managing projects. Projects are represented by boards, which contain lists (corresponding to task lists). Lists contain cards (corresponding to tasks). Cards are supposed to progress from one list to the next list (via drag-and-drop). It is possible to define members to participate in the project (directive 1b and 1c). Members can redefine the project features (directive 1d) and also invite new members to the project group (directive 1e). Due to the stated arguments, we claim that Guideline 1 (Definition of project and group) is satisfied.

In Trello, members can create an activity, which is in fact a card in a given board. For the activity, it is possible to define its characteristics, such as identifier, description and deadline (directive 2a). A checklist can also be created, associated to an activity, with the needed steps to develop the activity. Members can redefine an activity (directive 2b) and even exclude it (directive 2c). Members can also inform that an activity is completed (directive 2d), in this case, it is a common practice a project to have three board (named 'done', 'doing' and 'to do') and then move the activity from one board to another. We argue that Guideline 2 (Definition and management of activities) is satisfied.

More than one member can be responsible for an activity (directive 3a) in Trello. A member can select oneself as responsible for an activity (directive 3b). A member can also select other member to be responsible for an activity, and the invitee is free to continue or not as responsible (directive 3c). Activities can have different responsible members during their lifecycle (directive 3d). Members can add comments (textual or attachments) in an activity, in a way to contribute to the activity development (directive 3e). Due to the stated arguments, we claim that Guideline 3 (Sharing of responsibility) is satisfied.

Trello has a feature to allow members to vote on cards in a way to define priority among activities in the project. However, this feature can also be used when members desire to express satisfaction with some activities. In this case, it can be seen as an incentive mechanism, since the activity creator or responsible member become proud to contribute in that activity. Trello does not have other features related to support contribution recognition, for instance, there is no feature to acknowledge new members, and no feature to appreciate performance and attitude of other members. Considering the stated reasons, we argue that Guideline 4 (Contribution recognition) is not satisfied.

In Trello, members have access to projects that they participate, and they can monitor project activities and related information (responsible, deadlines, and progress). All conversation among members about activities is provided. Members can assign activities to be informed about changes and new interactions. Due to the stated arguments, we claim that Guideline 5 (Project visibility provision) is satisfied.

Our analysis shows that Trello follows all guidelines of the proposed framework, except Guideline 4 (Contribution recognition). The adherence between Trello and our framework explains Trello suitability to support management of informal projects. We believe that Trello has potential to support the collaborative management of informal projects that requires voluntary participation fully. It has just to add functionalities related to contribution recognition.

7 Conclusions

We proposed a framework to support the participation of members in the collaborative management of informal projects. The proposal embraces the fundamentals of project management, the needs of a cooperative work, and also the importance of motivation mechanisms. The objective of the framework is to assist and encourage the members in the management processes of informal projects. Encouragement is considered by using motivation mechanisms to incentive the participation and recognition of participants. Five guidelines structure the framework, considering the following aspects: the definition of project and group, the definition and management of activities, the sharing of responsibility, the contribution recognition, and the project visibility provision. Each guideline has specific directives to both ease its comprehension and orient its implementation.

We demonstrated that the proposed framework is practical by building a mobile application. Without a proper tool support, members would experience more difficulty to perform the management activities; they would be less aware of work performed by other members; and even they would not see recognition of their work. We conducted two case studies using the developed tool. Results showed that the tool helps in project planning and monitoring, while aiding satisfactorily project recognition and participation.

We used the framework to analyze Trello, an existent tool to manage projects. We identified that Trello lacks features related to the provision of contribution recognition. The support of contribution recognition involves mainly the design and implementation of motivation mechanisms, whose triumph depend on how the participants perceive and experience such mechanisms. Beyond to be a guidance to develop new tools, the proposed framework can also help to analyze existent tools in a way to identify weaknesses and improvements.

Results of the case studies are preliminary and limited, but they are also encouraging indications. More experiments must be made to improve the confidence in the initial findings. Experiments can be conducted in large groups, in order to verify the scalability of member participation. Others experiments need to have as participants more experienced professionals, who are more used to project management methodology and tools. Other types of project, such as formal and organizational projects, can benefit from the proposed guidelines. We believe that the basic condition to use our approach successfully is that management is decentralized, so members share responsibilities and must be motivated and committed to the project goals.

The framework can be improved with specific directives that need to be investigated before. Some directive to support hierarchy of groups and activities may be necessary if the group is large. New directives regarding recognition can be incorporated, depending on group commitment. Additional directives can be defined to deal with specific situations, such as redundant activities and overload of activities assigned to a specific member. Useful directives can deal with conflicts among members, in a way to identify and help members to solve them and come to decisions.

References

1. Battestini, A., Setlur, V., Sohn, T.: A large-scale study of text-messaging use. In: Proceedings of the 12th International Conference on Human Computer Interaction with Mobile Devices and Services. ACM (2010)
2. Beaudouin-Lafon, M.: Computer Supported Co-operative Work. Wiley, New York (1999)
3. Bezerra, J.M., Hirata, C.M., Randall, D.: A conceptual framework to define incentive mechanisms for virtual communities. J. Univ. Comput. Sci. **21**, 1107–1135 (2015)
4. Borgohoff, U.M., Schlichter, J.H.: Computer-Supported Cooperative Work. Springer, Heidelberg (2000). https://doi.org/10.1007/978-3-662-04232-8
5. Brocke, J.V., Lippe, S.: Managing collaborative research projects: a synthesis of project management literature and directives for future research. Int. J. Project Manag. **33**(5), 1022–1039 (2015)

6. Cajander, Å., Clear, T., Daniels, M., Edlund, J., Hamrin, P., Laxer, C., Persson, M.: Students analyzing their collaboration in an international open ended group project. In: Proceedings of the 39th IEEE Frontiers in Education Conference (FIE) (2009)

7. Carroll, J.M., Neale, D.C., Isenhour, P.L., Rosson, M.B., McCrickard, D.S.: Notification and awareness: synchronizing task-oriented collaborative activity. Int. J. Hum Comput Stud. **58**(5), 605–632 (2003)

8. Chin, G.: Agile Project Management: How to Succeed in the Face of the Changing Project Requirements. Amacon, New York (2004)

9. Conforto, E., Salum, F., Amaral, D., Da Silva, S.L., De Almeida, L.F.M.: Can agile project management be adopted by industries other than software development? Project Manag. J. **45**(3), 21–34 (2014)

10. Counts, S.: Group-based mobile messaging in support of the social side of leisure. Comput. Support. Coop. Work (CSCW) **16**(1), 75–97 (2007)

11. Dillman, D.A., Smyth, J.D., Christian, L.M.: Internet, Phone, Mail, and Mixed-Mode Surveys: The Tailored Design Method. John Wiley and Sons, Hoboken (2014)

12. Donker, H., Blumberg, M.: Collaborative process management and virtual teams. In: Proceedings of the 2008 International Workshop on Cooperative and Human Aspects of Software Engineering, pp. 41–43. ACM (2008)

13. Farnham, S., Keyani, P.: Swarm: hyper awareness, micro coordination, and smart convergence through mobile group text messaging. In: Proceeding of the 39th Annual Hawaii International Conference on System Sciences (HICSS). IEEE (2006)

14. Ferreira, L.M., Bezerra, J.M., Massaki, C.M.: An approach to collaborative management of informal projects. In: Proceeding of the 19th International Conference on Enterprise Information Systems (ICEIS), pp. 33–42 (2017)

15. François, A., Lanthony, A.: Work-in-progress: collaborative platform for systems engineering: active learning to train engineer students through projects. In: International Conference on Interactive Collaborative Learning (ICL) (2014)

16. Gulati, R., Puranam, P.: Renewal through reorganization: the value of inconsistencies between formal and informal organization. Organ. Sci. **20**(2), 422–440 (2009)

17. Ismail, S., Jamaludin, N.: Managing knowledge over social messaging application: the case of an event management project group. In: Proceedings of the 3rd International Conference on Computer and Information Sciences (ICCOINS) (2016)

18. Jansson, K., Ollus, M., Uoti, M., Riikonen, H.: Social and collaborative internet based project management. In: Proceedings of the IEEE International Technology Management Conference (ICE) (2009)

19. Jiang, Y., Kong, D.: Research of collaborative management of organization interface of large-scale engineering project. In: Proceedings of the International Conference on Information Technology and Applications (2013)

20. Kim, A.J.: Community Building on the Web: Secret Strategies for Successful Online Communities. Addison-Wesley Longman Publishing Co., Inc., Boston (2000)

21. Kowitz, B., Darrow, A., Khalsa, H., Zimmerman, J.: Gather: design for impromptu activity support utilizing social networks. In: Proceedings of the Designing Pleasurable Products and Interfaces (DPPI) (2005)

22. Lawson, B., Petersen, K.J., Cousins, P.D., Handfield, R.B.: Knowledge sharing in interorganizational product development teams: the effect of formal and informal socialization mechanism. J. Prod. Innov. Manag. **26**(2), 156–172 (2009)

23. PMI.: A Guide to the Project Management Body of Knowledge, 5th edn. PMI (2012)

24. Schatz, T.: Basic Types of Organizational Structure: Formal and Informal. In: Small Business (2016). http://smallbusiness.chron.com/basic-types-organizational-structure-formal-informal-982.html

25. Shen, A.X.L., Cheung, C.M.K., Lee, M.K.O., Wang, W.: The power of we: using instant messaging for student group project discussion. In: Proceedings of the 41st Annual Hawaii International Conference on System Sciences (2008)

26. Schuler, R.P., Grandhi, S.A., Mayer, J.M., Ricken, S.T., Jones, Q.: The doing of doing stuff: understanding the coordination of social group-activities. In: Proceedings of the SIGCHI Conference on Human Factors in Computing Systems, pp. 119–128. ACM (2014)

27. Shuai, H.H., Yang, D.N., Yu, P.S., Chen, M.S.: A comprehensive study on willingness maximization for social activity planning with quality guarantee. IEEE Trans. Knowl. Data Eng. **28**(1), 2–16 (2016)

28. Trello (https://trello.com)

29. Venkatesh, V., Thong, J.Y.L., Xu, X.: Consumer acceptance and use of information technology: extending the unified theory of acceptance and use of technology. MIS Q. **36**(1), 157–178 (2012)

30. Visser, D., Merwe, A.V., Gerber, A.: A comparison of project management in system and research projects. In: Proceedings of the IST-Africa Week Conference (2016)

31. Watfa, M., Todd, C.: Implications of virtual project management on project management processes. In: Proceedings of the Sixth International Conference on Innovative Computing Technology (INTECH) (2016)

32. Xiao, L.: An exploratory study of the effects of rationale awareness in project-based group activity. In: Proceedings of the 15th International Conference on Computer Supported Cooperative Work in Design (2011)

Using a Time-Based Weighting Criterion to Enhance Link Prediction in Social Networks

Carlos Pedro Muniz$^{(\boxtimes)}$, Ronaldo Goldschmidt, and Ricardo Choren

Computer Engineering Department, Military Institute of Engineering,
Pça Gen Tibúrcio 80, Rio de Janeiro, RJ 22290-270, Brazil
cptullio@gmail.com, {ronaldo.rgold,choren}@ime.eb.br

Abstract. Recently, the link prediction (LP) problem has attracted much attention from both scientific and industrial communities. This problem tries to predict whether two not linked nodes in a network will connect in the future. Several studies have been proposed to solve it. Some of them compute a compatibility degree (link strength) between connected nodes and apply similarity metrics between non-connected nodes in order to identify potential links. However, despite the acknowledged importance of temporal data for the LP problem, few initiatives investigated the use of this kind of information to represent link strength. In this paper, we propose a weighting criterion that combines the frequency of interactions and temporal information about them in order to define the link strength between pairs of connected nodes. The results of our experiment with weighted and non-weighted similarity metrics in ten co-authorship networks present statistical evidences that confirm our hypothesis that weighting links based on temporal information may, in fact, improve link prediction.

Keywords: Link prediction · Social networks · Temporal information

1 Introduction

Recently, social networks have attracted much attention from both scientific and industrial communities [1]. It tries to understand how the structures of large scale social networks evolve. These networks are usually denoted by graphs, where the nodes represent individuals (people, organizations, or other social entities) and the edges represent social relations and interactions (friendship, co-working, or information exchange) [2].

Social network evolution analysis tries to figure out the driving forces of network formation, and it is a challenge [3]. Assuming the nodes of a social network are fixed, network evolution is reflected by the edge generation among different nodes [4]. This is the goal of link prediction problem [5]: estimate the existent likelihood of an unobserved link using the of observed links in the network.

© Springer International Publishing AG, part of Springer Nature 2018
S. Hammoudi et al. (Eds.): ICEIS 2017, LNBIP 321, pp. 21–33, 2018.
https://doi.org/10.1007/978-3-319-93375-7_2

Link prediction has several applications, including recommending friends and products on online social networks and e-commerce websites, respectively [6]. Several link prediction methods have been proposed to solve the link prediction problem [5, 7–13]. According to [1], these methods can be classified into two main approaches: supervised and unsupervised. In the supervised approach, the original graph is converted to a binary classification problem and then learning algorithms, such as decision trees and neural networks, are used to build classification models [14]. In the unsupervised approach, similarity metrics compute scores to express some sort of compatibility degree between pairs of non-connected nodes (e.g. homophily, ties, degrees of separation, among others). Then a ranked list in decreasing order of scores is obtained and nodes from the pairs at the top of the list are more likely to connect [5].

The compatibility degree may also be considered when the nodes are connected. In this case, it is called link strength between nodes and consists of a numerical weight assigned to the edge that represents the corresponding connection. Higher (resp. lower) values of link strength indicate that the nodes are strongly (resp. weakly) linked. Most initiatives from the unsupervised approach to the link prediction problem do not take link strength into consideration. Yet, such information may be used to provide useful insights for link prediction. For example, two non-connected nodes strongly linked to their common neighbors are more likely to connect than the ones weakly linked to their common neighborhood.

Link strength is calculated by employing some weighting criterion. Usually, the adopted weighting criterion was the frequency of existing interactions between the nodes (F_i) [8, 9, 13]. Based on F_i, the link strength between nodes that interact frequently is higher than the link strength of those that occasionally connect. This criterion does not take into account other properties of the network evolution, such as the information about when the interactions occurred. Therefore, old and new interactions have the same influence in weight definition for link strength calculation. However, according to the Weak Ties social theory [15], recent interactions tend to stimulate the occurrence of new interactions in the network. Hence, recent connections should have higher influence in link strength calculation and, consequently, in link prediction.

In this article, we suggest that the combination of the frequency of interactions and temporal information for link strength calculation may improve link prediction. To further investigate the significance of the impact of temporal information in link prediction, we propose a diverse weighting criterion (FT_i) for link prediction.

The remainder of this paper is organized as follows. Section 2 presents the background of link prediction procedure. Section 3 reviews some relevant studies on unsupervised link prediction that use graph weighting. Section 4 presents the proposed approach, which illustrates the significance of the temporal information for link prediction. Section 5 shows some experimentation in which the proposed approach is compared with some baseline unsupervised weighted link prediction methods to investigate its performance. Finally, Sect. 6 concludes the paper and briefly explores directions for future research.

2   Link Prediction Procedure

We denote an homogeneous attributed multigraph G as (V, E), where V is the set of nodes and $E \subseteq V \times V$ is the set of undirected attributed (with at least one temporal information) interactions. We use u and v to indicate individual nodes and τ and t to denote a time-stamp.

In the above model, the goal of a link prediction approach is to foretell the adjacent multigraph $G_{\tau+1}$ at a next time-stamp $\tau + 1$. The usual procedure for an unsupervised approach to link prediction follows a sequence of steps [5]. The first step divides G into a training (G_{Trn}) and a test (G_{Tst}) subgraphs. G_{Trn} contains all edges created up to a given time-stamp t and G_{Tst} encloses all edges that are present in G after time-stamp t. E_{Old} expresses the set of edges in G_{Trn} and E_{New} denotes the set of edges that are in G_{Tst} but were not in G_{Trn}. In other words, E_{New} indicates the new interactions we are seeking to predict.

After the graph partition, there is the graph weighting step. In this step, artificial edges are created to connect nodes in G_{Trn}. Then, it is calculated a weight for each artificial edge, using a predefined rule.

Then, it is necessary to identify a `Core` set - the set of nodes that are more likely to connect. Social networks grow through the addition of nodes as well as edges, and it is not sensible to seek predictions for edges whose endpoints are not present in G_{Trn} [5]. Thus the `Core` set is defined to be all nodes incident to at least k_{Trn} edges in G_{Trn} and at least k_{Tst} edges in G_{Tst}. Parameters k_{Trn} and k_{Tst} are defined by the user and they typically depend on the average frequency of interactions in the network.

The fourth step is to produce a ranked list (L_p) in decreasing order of score, a proximity measure between pairs of nodes u and v ($u, v \in$ `Core`). There are several similarity metrics for score calculation (`score`: $V \times V \rightarrow \mathbb{R}$) (e.g. [8, 16–19]).

The last step is to evaluate the link predictor. In this step, we take the ranked list L_p of pairs and select the top n pairs with the highest likelihood to connect at a time-stamp posterior to t. The value of n is defined as:

$$n = |E_{New} \cap (Core \times Core)|$$

Then, we compare the performance of the link predictor to the performance of a baseline random predictor which simply randomly selects pairs of nodes that did not interact in the training subgraph. A random prediction is correct with probability expressed as:

$$P_{random} = \frac{|E_{New}|}{\binom{Core}{2} - |E_{Old}|}$$

The improvement factor of the link predictor over random is calculated as (where $E_{Correct}$ is the number of links correctly predicted by the link predictor):

$$Imp_{factor} = \frac{|E_{Correct}|/|E_{New}|}{P_{random}}$$

3   Related Work

Several approaches have been proposed for unsupervised link prediction and most of them are based on metrics that show proximity between nodes, which can be either semantic or topological [20]. In semantic metrics, the content of nodes are used to grade proximity. Topological metrics use the structure of the network to obtain proximity values. Common neighbours [21] and Adamic-Adar index [7] are similarity metrics traditionally used in LP. Both are described below.

Common Neighbors: *the number of neighbors that two given nodes have in common.*

$$CN(u, v) = |\Gamma(u) \cap \Gamma(v)|$$

Adamic-Adar: *a refinement of the common neighbors metric that takes neighbors with smaller degree into consideration more heavily.*

$$AA(u, v) = \sum_{z \in (\Gamma(u) \cap \Gamma(v))} \frac{1}{\log(|\Gamma(z)|)}$$

The graph weighting step does not belong to the original procedure for link prediction as defined by [5]. However, it has been used by the studies that consider link strength of connected nodes in order to predict new links (e.g. [9,24]). The work of Murata and Moriyasu [8] was the first work to propose the graph weighting step and the weighted versions of similarity metrics such as common neighbors and Adamic-Adar index. These weighted metrics are shown below [8].

Weighted Common Neighbors: *the average of weights associated to the links between two given nodes and their common neighbors.*

$$WCN(u, v) = \sum_{z \in (\Gamma(u) \cap \Gamma(v))} \frac{w(u, z) + w(v, z)}{2}$$

Weighted Adamic-Adar: *a refinement of the Adamic-Adar similarity metric that takes into account link weights.*

$$WAA(u, v) = \sum_{z \in (\Gamma(u) \cap \Gamma(v))} \frac{w(u, z) + w(v, z)}{2 * \log(\sum_{x \in \Gamma(z)} w(z, x))}$$

Other few works investigated the use of temporal information for the link prediction problem, most of them are based on the Weak Ties theory. In [25], the authors develop graph-based link prediction techniques that incorporate the temporal information contained in evolving social networks. The work proposes the incorporation of edge weights, possibly derived from temporal features, into the link prediction methods, such as the Adamic-Adar distance. In [26] the authors define a time-aware method based on the temporal path length of a network. This path length gives a global measure of how fast information spreads to all the nodes of the network by means of transitive connections between them.

4   Proposed Weighting Criterion

The FT_i weighting score is inspired by the Weak Ties theory, which states that the strength of a tie is a combination of the amount of time, intensity, intimacy and the reciprocal services that characterize the tie [15]. The idea is to combine data about the time and the frequency (intensity) of interactions. Therefore, recent interactions may have higher influence than old ones in link prediction inference.

The number of edges between two nodes is a topological information that describe the frequency of the interactions between this two nodes. The temporal information used in our proposal is inspired by the time score metric [10]. In this sense, the strength of a link varies over time. Links between two nodes that have not interacted with each other for a long time, with respect to the current time, become weaker. This weakness is depicted as a damping factor that increases as the difference between current time and the most recent interaction between two nodes decreases.

The temporal-topological weighting score for an interacting node pair u and v is thus defined as follows:

$$w^{FT_i}(u, v) = |E(u, v)| * \beta^k \tag{1}$$

In Eq. 1, β is an arbitrary damping factor $(0 < \beta \leq 1)$ to put more/less emphasis on the temporal influence and k is the difference between the current time and the time attribute from $e \in E(u, v)$ with the most recent time-stamp.

Consider the example depicted in Fig. 1. Restricting the weighting criterion to the number of interactions (F_i), the unsupervised link prediction methods reduce the weighting score to the frequency of existing interactions between nodes. In this sense, the weight scores for all three pairs of nodes are the same:

$$w^{F_i}(A, D) \equiv w^{F_i}(B, D) \equiv w^{F_i}(C, D) = 3.0$$

This means that their connections have the same importance in score calculation for link prediction. Therefore, the WCN and WAA measures for this example are:

$$WCN_{F_i}(A, B) \equiv WCN_{F_i}(A, C) \equiv WCN_{F_i}(B, C) = \frac{3 + 3}{2} = 3.0$$

$$WAA_{F_i}(A, B) \equiv WAA_{F_i}(A, C) \equiv WAA_{F_i}(B, C) = \frac{3 + 3}{2 * log(3 + 3 + 3)} \approx 3.85$$

On the other hand, if temporal information was taken into account as stated by the FT_i criterion, the most recent interactions would lead to higher weights and, hence, influence more in link prediction (in accordance with the Weak Ties theory). In the example, using FT_i criterion with current time $= 2016$ and $\beta = 0.8$, the weights would be:

$$|E(A, D)| = |E(B, D)| = |E(C, D)| = 3$$

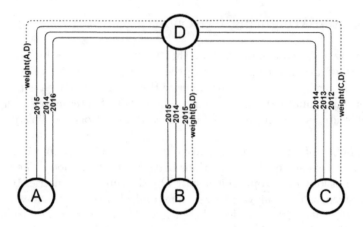

Fig. 1. An example of a co-authorship network.

$$w^{FT_i}(A, D) = 3 * 0.8^{(2016-2016)} = 3 * 1 = 3.0$$
$$w^{FT_i}(B, D) = 3 * 0.8^{(2016-2015)} = 3 * 0.8 = 2.4$$
$$w^{FT_i}(C, D) = 3 * 0.8^{(2016-2014)} = 3 * 0.64 = 1.9$$

$$WCN_{FT_i}(A, B) = (3 + 2.4)/2 = 2.7$$
$$WCN_{FT_i}(A, C) = (3 + 1.9)/2 = 2.45$$
$$WCN_{FT_i}(B, C) = (2.4 + 1.9)/2 = 2.15$$

$$WAA_{FT_i}(A, B) = (3 + 2.4)/(2 * log(7, 3)) \approx 3.12$$
$$WAA_{FT_i}(A, C) = (3 + 1.9)/(2 * log(7, 3)) \approx 2.83$$
$$WAA_{FT_i}(B, C) = (2.4 + 1.9)/(2 * log(7, 3)) \approx 2.49$$

Although the three pairs of nodes presented the same frequency of interactions (three connections each), with FT_i, the ones that interacted more recently received higher weights. Frequency of interactions was attenuated by the age of the most recent interaction between the nodes of each pair. The (A,D) pair presented the highest weight. In fact, the frequency of interactions between A and D suffered no attenuation because the nodes interacted in the current time (2016). On the other hand, frequencies of interactions between the nodes of the pairs (B,D) and (C,D) indeed suffered some attenuation. The last interaction between nodes C and D occurred in 2014 (age = 2 years). B and D last interacted in 2015 (age = 1 year). Hence, (C,D) weight attenuation was higher than the one suffered by (B,D) weight.

Therefore, according to the proposed approach, the pair (A,B) would be more likely to connect than the others. It presented higher similarity measures for WCN_{FT_i} and WAA_{FT_i}. Both nodes (A and B) interacted with their common neighbor (D) more recently than the other pairs did. It is important to emphasize that this result would be in line with the Weak Ties theory. Indeed, according to this theory, those recent interactions would stimulate the occurrence of a new interaction in the network, very possibly between nodes A and B.

5 Experiment

5.1 Data Sets

We have selected two versions of the same five co-authorship networks used in [5] to perform our experiments. The first version (papers from 1994 to 1999) covered the same interval of time used by [5]. That was very important to help us validate our implementation. The second version (papers from 2000 to 2005) covered the same period used by [10]. All networks were extracted from arXiv API[1]. Both versions of the networks were homogeneous attributed multigraphs where nodes and edges represent authors and papers, respectively. All networks contained one attribute in edges: the paper's year of publication.

5.2 Experimental Procedure

Our experiment extended the experiment presented by [28]. We followed the same procedure described in Sect. 2. Specific comments about each step are presented below:

Graph Partition: we divided each network in two three-year periods. Hence, each network with papers from 1994 to 1999 was partitioned in G_{Trn} [1994; 1996] and G_{Tst} [1997; 1999]. Similarly, networks with papers from 2000 to 2005 were split into networks G_{Trn} [2000; 2002] and G_{Tst} [2003; 2005].

Graph Weighting: we created artificial edges between nodes connected in G_{Trn}. Then we calculated ten weight values for each artificial edge. F_i was the weighting criterion used to calculate the first weight. FT_i was used to calculate the other nine weights. We ranged the values of the damping factor β from 0.1 to 0.9. Each value of β led to one of the nine weights.

Identification of Core: in order to identify the nodes that belong to the `Core` set, we considered k = 3. Hence, Core consisted of all active authors who had written at least 3 articles during the training period and at least 3 articles during the test period. Three reasons guided this decision: (a) Training and test periods' length of all networks was three years; (b) We considered that one year could be a reasonable frequency interval for paper publication; (c) It was the same value defined in [5], where similar experiments were performed.

Score Calculation: this step executed the similarity metrics (CN, AA, WCN and WAA) for each artificial edge in each network. In order to better present

---

[1] http://export.arxiv.org/api/.

the results, we used the acronyms WCN_{F_i} and WAA_{F_i} to represent the similarity metrics calculated with the weights produced by the F_i criterion. Acronyms $WCN_{FT_i(\beta)}$ and $WAA_{FT_i(\beta)}$ were used to represent the similarity metrics calculated with the weights produced by the proposed weighting criterion.

Performance Evaluation: the performances of CN, AA, WCN_{F_i}, WAA_{F_i}, $WCN_{FT_i(\beta)}$ and $WAA_{FT_i(\beta)}$ were compared to the performance of the random predictor. They represent the improvement factor of the corresponding metric over the random predictor.

5.3 Results

Tables 1 and 2 provide some statistics of the networks after the Identification of Core step. Tables 3 and 4 show each metrics performance on each network with respect to the improvement factor over the random predictor. An overall analysis reveals that no metric outperformed all the others in all networks and periods. Nevertheless, a closer analysis shows some interesting results.

In a simple and straightforward pairwise comparison of metrics, WCN_{FT_i} and WAA_{FT_i} outperformed WCN_{F_i} and WAA_{F_i} in six (60%) and eight (80%) out of ten networks, respectively. It is also important to emphasize that WCN_{FT_i} and WAA_{FT_i} outperformed WCN_{F_i} and WAA_{F_i} in four (80%) and five (100%) out of the five networks from the second version, respectively. We believe that it was due to the fact that those networks were more recent (2000 to 2005) and, hence, more complete and updated than the ones from the first version (1994 to 1999).

Table 1. Statistics about the 1st version of the networks used in the experiments - papers from 1994 to 1999 [28].

Network	Authors	Papers	Core	E_{New}
astro-ph	19864	21290	9616	2087
cond-mat	19289	21698	1336	723
gr-qc	5283	8299	390	137
hep-ph	12658	24294	1689	1950
hep-th	11229	20935	1192	767

Table 2. Statistics about the 2nd version of the networks used in the experiments - papers from 2000 to 2005 [28].

Network	Authors	Papers	Core	E_{New}
astro-ph	42771	50359	6197	37362
cond-mat	48298	51809	4437	7507
gr-qc	8939	13858	812	463
hep-ph	17750	31707	2476	8246
hep-th	14212	27444	1893	1293

Table 3. Improvement factor of similarity metric over the random predictor (1994–1999).

Similarity metric	Network				
	astro-ph	cond-mat	gr-qc	hep-ph	hep-th
$Rand_{Pred}$	0.23	0.11	0.18	0.14	0.11
CN	37.9	63.7	56.4	49.3	50.6
AA	36.9	66.2	56.4	53.5	62.6
WCN_{F_i}	27.9	64.9	**68.5**	44.8	**93.9**
WAA_{F_i}	40.0	**69.9**	64.4	47.5	**93.9**
WCN_{FT_i}	34.5	59.9	64.4	45.6	77.1
WAA_{FT_i}	**40.2**	67.4	**68.5**	**56.4**	77.1

Table 4. Improvement factor of similarity metric over the random predictor (2000–2005).

Similarity metric	Network				
	astro-ph	cond-mat	gr-qc	hep-ph	hep-th
$Rand_{Pred}$	0.20	0.08	0.14	0.27	0.07
CN	51.1	101.5	32.2	58.3	77.0
AA	52.8	111.1	42.9	59.6	75.9
WCN_{F_i}	50.2	106.2	45.9	61.2	83.4
WAA_{F_i}	52.5	116.3	50.5	61.7	83.4
WCN_{FT_i}	51.2	112.0	49.0	62.3	78.1
WAA_{FT_i}	**54.1**	**118.8**	**52.1**	**62.6**	**86.6**

Additionally, comparing the weighting criteria, FT_i outperformed F_i in seven (70%) out of ten networks. Five of those eight networks belong to the second version, reinforcing our theory about the completeness of the networks from that group. In one network, both criteria led to comparable results. F_i outperformed FT_i in just two networks. All the above mentioned results confirm the Weak Ties theory and our hypothesis that weighting links based on temporal information may improve link prediction.

Figures 2 and 3 present the average performance obtained by the FT_i parameter (damping factor) in the similarity metrics WCN and WAA in the two versions of the networks. For the first version of the network the best performances were achieved with $\beta = 0.4$ for both similarity metrics. The second version the best performances for WCN were achieved with $\beta = 0.2$ and WAA were achieved with $\beta = 0.6$.

In general, the differences of performance among the similarity metrics were not high. Hence, in order to check for statistical significance in those differences, we applied the Friedman test [27] with $\alpha = 0.05$ and null hypothesis stated as

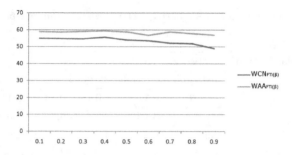

Fig. 2. Damping factor analysis - papers from 1994 to 1999 [28].

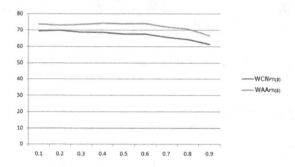

Fig. 3. Damping factor analysis - papers from 2000 to 2005 [28].

H_0: "the performance of the similarity metrics are statistically identical". In the test, we considered the six similarity metrics and the ten networks. The test rejected H_0, indicating a significant statistical difference among the metrics.

In order to better investigate the differences in performance of the similarity metrics, we decided to run a post-hoc test to compare the metrics with each other. The Nemenyi test [27] with $\alpha = 0.05$ was employed. We stated H_0 as "performances of metrics x and y are statistically identical". We run the test fifteen times, one for each pair of metrics. Five out of them revealed statistical difference. Table 5 summarizes the results of the test, pointing out the pairs of metrics where the difference occurred.

In 100% of the tests that presented significant differences, weighted similarity metrics outperformed the others (including the non weighted ones). It suggests that weighting graphs for LP as proposed by [8] may be a good providence indeed.

In 80% of the tests with significant differences, similarity metrics based on the combined weighting criterion FT_i outperformed the others. These results confirm our hypothesis that combining temporal and topological information can enhance unsupervised link prediction when it is based exclusively on topological data.

Another important aspect to be emphasized is that the Weighted Adamic Adar index (WAA) won 100% of the significant cases. It seems that the participants

Table 5. Results of the Nemenyi Test - pairs of similarity metrics that presented significant statistical differences of performance.

Case Id	Similarity metric performance	
	Higher	Lower
1	WAA_{F_i}	CN
2	WAA_{FT_i}	CN
3	WAA_{FT_i}	AA
4	WAA_{FT_i}	WCN_{F_i}
5	WAA_{FT_i}	WCN_{FT_i}

of the co-authorship networks employed in the experiment were restrictive when choosing their collaborators.

Finally, it is important to mention that the most prevalent winning similarity metric in the experiment was WAA_{FT_i}, indicating the good performance of WAA when combined with the proposed weighting criterion FT_i.

6   Conclusion and Future Work

Predicting whether a pair of nodes will connect in the future is an important network analysis task known as the link prediction problem. Several studies have been proposed to predict links in social methods. Some of them compute a compatibility degree (link strength) between connected nodes in order to get useful insights for link prediction. However, despite the acknowledged importance of temporal data for the link prediction problem, few initiatives investigated the use of this kind of information to represent link strength and its corresponding consequence in link prediction.

Inspired by the Weak Ties social theory, in this paper, we proposed a weighting criterion that combines the frequency of interactions and temporal information (FT_i) about them in order to represent the weights (link strength) between pairs of connected nodes in social networks. According to FT_i, recent interactions have higher influence than old ones in weight calculation and, consequently, in link prediction. Our experiment was performed over ten co-authorship networks previously used by many studies about link prediction. We compared the performances produced by the traditional similarity metrics weighted common neighbors (WCN) and weighted Adamic-Adar (WAA), combined with two weighting criteria: one was the proposed criterion (FT_i) and the other, state-of-art weighting criterion, was based just on the frequency of interactions (F_i). We also compared their performances with the ones produced by non-weighted similarity metrics such as common neighbors (CN) and Adamic-Adar index (AA). The results showed statistical evidences that WCN and WAA combined with FT_i outperformed WCN and WAA combined with F_i in most networks, confirming our hypothesis that weighting links based on temporal information may improve link prediction. The results also suggested that weighting graphs for LP as proposed by [8] may be a good providence: weighted versions of the similarity metrics outperformed the non-weighted ones in all cases.

As future work, we consider the formulation of a weighting criterion that combines temporal, topological and contextual data, simultaneously. It would also be interesting to evaluate the influence of our temporal based weighting criterion in the supervised approach to the link prediction problem. Experiments of our criterion with networks out of the context of co-authorship would be desirable too.

References

1. Wang, P., Xu, B., Wu, Y., Zhou, X.: Link prediction in social networks: the state-of-the-art. Sci. Chin. Inf. Sci. **58**(1), 1–38 (2015)
2. Hoefer, M.: Local matching dynamics in social networks. Inf. Comput. **222**(4), 20–35 (2011)
3. Borgatti, S.P., Mehra, A., Brass, D.J., Labianca, G.: Network analysis in the social sciences. Science **323**(5916), 892–895 (2009)
4. Wang, H., Hu, W., Qiu, Z., Du, B.: Nodes' evolution diversity and link prediction in social networks. IEEE Trans. Knowl. Data Eng. **29**(10), 2263–2274 (2017)
5. Liben-Nowell, D., Kleinberg, J.: The link-prediction problem for social networks. J. Am. Soc. Inf. Sci. Technol. **58**(7), 1019–1031 (2007)
6. Aiello, L.M., Barrat, A., Schifanella, R., Cattuto, C., Markines, B., Menczer, F.: Friendship prediction and homophily in social media. ACM Trans. Web **6**(2), 1–33 (2012)
7. Adamic, L.A., Adar, E.: Friends and neighbors on the Web. Soc. Netw. **25**(3), 211–230 (2003)
8. Murata, T., Moriyasu, S.: Link prediction of social networks based on weighted proximity measures. In: Proceedings of the IEEE/WIC/ACM International Conference on Web Intelligence, pp. 85–88 (2007)
9. Lü, L., Zhou, T.: Link prediction in weighted networks: the role of weak ties. Europhys. Lett. **89**(1), 18001 (2010)
10. Munasinghe, L., Ichise, R.: Time score: a new feature for link prediction in social networks. IEICE Trans. Inf. Syst. **E95.D**(3), 821–828 (2012)
11. Choudhary, P., Mishra, N., Sharma, S., Patel, R.: Link score: a novel method for time aware link prediction in social network. In: Prasad, D.N.H., Nalini, D.N. (eds.) Emerging Research in Computing, Information, Communication and Applications. Springer, New Delhi (2013)
12. Valverde-Rebaza, J., Valejo, A., Berton, L., de Paulo Faleiros, T., de Andrade Lopes, A.: A naïve bayes model based on overlapping groups for link prediction in online social networks. In: Proceedings of the 30th Annual ACM Symposium on Applied Computing, pp. 1136–1141 (2015)
13. Zhu, B., Xia, Y.: Link prediction in weighted networks: a weighted mutual information model. PLoS ONE **11**(2), e0148265 (2016)
14. Hasan, M.A., Chaoji, V., Salem, S., Zaki, M.: Link prediction using supervised learning. In: Proceedings of SDM 2006 Workshop on Link Analysis, Counterterrorism and Security, pp. 1–10 (2006)
15. Granovetter, M.S.: The strength of weak ties. Am. J. Sociol. **78**, 1360–1380 (1973)

16. Katz, L.: A new status index derived from sociometric analysis. Psychometrika **18**(1), 39–43 (1953)
17. Salton, G., McGill, M.J.: Introduction to Modern Information Retrieval. McGraw-Hill Inc, New York (1986)
18. Jeh, G., Widom, J.: SimRank: a measure of structural-context similarity. In: Proceedings of the Eighth ACM SIGKDD International Conference on Knowledge Discovery and Data Mining, pp. 538–543 (2002)
19. Hasan, M.A., Zaki, M.J.: A survey of link prediction in social networks. In: Aggarwal, C. (ed.) Social Network Data Analytics. Springer, Boston (2011). https://doi.org/10.1007/978-1-4419-8462-3_9
20. Gündoğan, E., Kaya, B.: A recommendation method based on link prediction in drug-disease bipartite network. In: Proceedings of 2nd International Conference on Advanced Information and Communication Technologies, pp. 125–128 (2017)
21. Newman, M.E.J.: Clustering and preferential attachment in growing networks. Phys. Rev. E **64**, 13 (2001)
22. Barabási, A.-L., Bonabeau, E.: Scale-free networks. Sci. Am. **288**(5), 50–59 (2003)
23. Tan, P.-N., Steinbach, M., Kumar, V.: Introduction to Data Mining. Pearson, New York (2005)
24. Zhao, J., Miao, L., Yang, J., Fang, H., Zhang, Q.-M., Nie, M., Holme, P., Zhou, T.: Prediction of links and weights in networks by reliable routes. Sci. Rep. **5**, 11770 (2015)
25. Tylenda, T, Angelova, R., Bedathur, S.: Towards time-aware link prediction in evolving social networks. In: Proceedings of the 3rd Workshop on Social Network Mining and Analysis, pp. 1–10 (2009)
26. Tang, J., Musolesi, M., Mascolo, C., Latora, V.: Temporal distance metrics for social network analysis. In: Proceedings of the 2nd ACM Workshop on Online Social Networks, pp. 31–36 (2009)
27. Demšar, J.: Statistical comparisons of classifiers over multiple data sets. J. Mach. Learn. Res. **7**, 1–30 (2006)
28. Muniz, C., Choren, Goldschmidt, R.: Using a time based relationship weighting criterion to improve link prediction in social networks. In: Proceedings of the 19th International Conference on Enterprise Information Systems - Volume 1, ICEIS, pp. 73–79 (2017)

Professional Competence Identification Through Formal Concept Analysis

Paula R. Silva[1]([⊠]), Sérgio M. Dias[2]([⊠]), Wladmir C. Brandão[1]([⊠]),
Mark A. Song[1]([⊠]), and Luis E. Zárate[1]([⊠])

[1] Pontifical Catholic University of Minas Gerais (PUC Minas), Belo Horizonte, Brazil
paula.raissa@sga.pucminas.br,
{wladmir,song,zarate}@pucminas.br
[2] Federal Service of Data Processing (SERPRO), Belo Horizonte, Brazil
sergio.dias@serpro.gov.br

Abstract. As the job market has become increasingly competitive, people who are looking for a job placement have needed help to increase their competence to achieve a job position. The competence is defined by the set of skills that is necessary to execute an organizational function. In this case, it would be helpful to identify the sets of skills which is necessary to reach job positions. Currently, the on-line professional social networks are attracting the interest from people all around the world, whose their goals are oriented to business relationships. Through the available amount of information in this kind of networks it is possible to apply techniques to identify the competencies that people have developed in their career. In this scenario it has been fundamental the adoption of computational methods to solve this problem. The *formal concept analysis (FCA)* has been a effective technique for data analysis area, because it allows to identify conceptual structures in data sets, through conceptual lattice and implications. A specific set of implications, know as proper implications, represent the set of conditions to reach a specific goal. So, in this work, we proposed a FCA-based approach to identify and analyze the professional competence through proper implications.

Keywords: Formal concept analysis · Proper implications
Professional competence · On-line social networks

1 Introduction

Currently, the job market has become increasingly competitive. The educational and technological advancements mean that companies are demanding that professionals are prepared to take positions. So, the people that are starting or rethinking their professional career have needed some guidance to become potential candidates for job openings. This guidance can be offered based on evidences obtained through prior knowledge about the job market. The prior knowledge base can be composed by the set of competences that people have developed

© Springer International Publishing AG, part of Springer Nature 2018
S. Hammoudi et al. (Eds.): ICEIS 2017, LNBIP 321, pp. 34–56, 2018.
https://doi.org/10.1007/978-3-319-93375-7_3

in certain positions. An interesting source of information for this purpose is the on-line professional social networks, because in these networks the people have made available their professional resume.

In increasingly interconnected world, the on-line social networks attend different people's interests and address the communication and information needs of several user groups [1]. In particular, there are on-line professional social networks focused on a specific group of users interest is oriented to business. One of the largest and most popular on-line professional social network is the *LinkedIn*, which has more than 500 millions users distributed in more than 200 countries and territories [2].

LinkedIn users can create their professional profiles, and to made available informations like skills, competences, and experience. They can also interact with each other, look for jobs, and another functionalities. Thus, *LinkedIn* provides a source of professional information that can be exploited by enterprise managers in different ways, like to find people with appropriate competences to fulfill specific positions. In addition, the size and diversity of user-generated content has created the opportunity to identify behavioral trends and user communities by computational methods. In this scenario, the *formal concept analysis (FCA)* presents itself as a technique that can be applied for this purpose.

FCA presents a mathematical formulation for data analysis, which identify conceptual structures from a data set [3]. It also presents an interesting unified framework to identify dependencies among data, by understanding and computing them in a formal way [4]. It is a branch of lattice theory motivated by the need for a clear formalization of the notions of concept hierarchy.

There are two ways to extract and represent knowledge from FCA: conceptual lattice and implications. In this work, we applied a particularly type of implications, know as *proper implications* [5]. We say that a proposition P logically implies a proposition Q $(P \rightarrow Q)$, if Q is true whenever P is true. The set of proper implications have a minimal left-hand side and only one item in right-hand side [5]. It has been applied when the need is to find the minimum conditions to lead a goal. In this article, the proper implications represent the set of minimum professional's skills (conditions) for achieve a job position (goal). For example, the proper implication $\{statistic, \ machine \ learning, \ databases\} \rightarrow \{data \ scientist\}$ represent a minimum set of skills which are necessary to be a data scientist.

Several authors have been applied FCA to address research problems related to *social networks analysis (SNA)*. Note that, there are other methods to retrieve knowledge from social networks. They are usually based on graph theory, clustering and frequent item-sets, which provide an approach to represent a social network through a formal way. Additionally, there are several FCA to SNA applications, such as ontology-based technique [6], social communities [7], network representation through concept lattice [8], contextual pre-filtering process and identifying user behavior through implications [9].

In this article, we proposed a FCA-based approach to identify professional competence through data from *LinkedIn*. First, we conceptually model a *LinkedIn* user profile according to the *model of competences* [10], because this model has more acceptance in industry and academia [11]. Second, as an input data set, our approach needs an incidence table (formal context) and a subset of proper implications are expected as an output. Lastly, a proper implication represent careers trajectories, by minimum professional's skills (conditions) for achieve a position (goal). These implications were extracted using our proposed algorithm named *PropIm*. The *PropIm* algorithm was proposed to extract proper implications with support greater than zero. It is important to note that this article is an extended version of [12].

The main contributions of this paper are: a professionals data set scraped from *LinkedIn*, a FCA-based approach, and experiments set for apply FCA to professional career analysis.

The structure of the article follows as: In Sect. 2, we present the preliminary definitions related to FCA. In Sect. 3, we report related work that applied FCA to social networks analysis. In Sect. 4, we present our FCA-based approach to SNA. In Sect. 5, we report experiments and results analysis. Finally, in Sect. 6, we present the conclusions and some proposals for future works.

2   Formal Concept Analysis

In this section, we introduce concepts related of formal concept analysis (FCA) reported on literature [13].

2.1   Formal Context

Formally, a formal context is a triple (G, M, I), where G is a set of objects (rows), M is a set of attributes (columns) and I are incidences. It is defined as $I \subseteq G \times M$. If an object $g \in G$ and an attribute $m \in M$ have a relationship I, their representation is $(g, m) \in I$ or gIm, which could be read as "object g has attribute m". When an object has an attribute, the incidence is identified and represented by "x". In the formal context shown in Table 1, rows are objects representing users, and the columns are professional skills and positions.

Given a subset of objects $A \subseteq G$ of formal context (G, M, I), there is an attribute subset of M common to all objects of A, even if empty. Likewise, given a set $B \subseteq M$, there is an object subset that shares the attributes of B, even if empty. These relationships are defined by derivation operations:

$$A' := \{m \in M | gIm \forall g \in A\} \tag{1}$$

$$B' := \{g \in G | gIm \forall m \in B\} \tag{2}$$

A formal context (G, M, I) is a clarified context, when $\forall\ g,\ h \in G$, from $g' = h'$ it always follows that and, correspondingly $m' = n'$ implies $m = n\ \forall\ m, n \in M$. The clarification process consists in maintaining one element (objects and attributes) from a set of equal elements eliminating the others. In this process, the number of objects and attributes can be reduced while retaining lattice form [3].

Table 1. Example context of an user's *LinkedIn* skills. The attributes are: a: networks, b: mobile application, c: software engineering, d: data bases, e: graphic processing, f: computer architecture, g: operational systems (Source: [12] p. 124).

	a	b	c	d	e	f	g
user 17	x	x		x	x		x
user 18			x	x			
user 19		x				x	x
user 20	x	x		x	x		
user 21			x	x			x
user 22		x				x	
user 23	x	x		x	x		x
user 24			x	x			

2.2 Formal Concept

From formal contexts we can obtain formal concepts, defined as pairs (A, B), where $A \subseteq G$ is called extension and $B \subseteq M$ and is called intention, and they must follow conditions $A = B'$ and $B = A'$ (Eqs. 1 and 2) [3].

Based on the formal context from Table 1, we generated the formal concept ({user 18, user 21, user 24}, {software engineering, data bases}), where elements of subset B are {software engineering, data bases}, that, by derivation (Eq. 2) yield subset A = {user 18, user 21, user 24}. This formal concept represents the subset of users (objects) who share skills in *software engineering* and *data bases*.

It is important to note that a formal concept corresponds to any aspect of the problem domain, represented by objects and attributes, in which exists some kind of comprehension and understanding.

2.3 Concept Lattice

With all formal concepts sorted hierarchically by order of inclusion $\subseteq$, we can build the concept lattice. Sorting must be done, so that, the concept (A_1, B_1) is considered less than or equal to (A_2, B_2) if and only if, $A_1 \subseteq A_2$ (equivalent to $B_2 \subseteq B_1$). In this case, the concept (A_1, B_1) is called sub-concept and the concept (A_2, B_2) super-concept. In Fig. 1 is shown an example of a concept lattice from the formal context in Table 1. It is important to note that concept lattice was built with the *Conexp*[1] software.

Generally the lattice is represented by a graph, in which the nodes are the formal concepts and the edges are the relationships among nodes. At the top of the graph there is a single node called *supremum*, whose extension is composed by all objects. The lower node is called *infimum*, whose intention contains the set of all attributes.

---

[1] Conexp: http://conexp.sourceforge.net/.

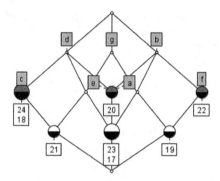

Fig. 1. Example of concept lattice (Source: [12] p. 125).

2.4   The Set of Implications

Given a formal context (G, M, I) or a concept lattice $\mathscr{B}(G, M, I)$, these can be extracted exact rules or approximate rules (rules with statistical values, for example, support and confidence) that express in a alternative way the underlying knowledge. The exact rules can be classified in implication rules and functional dependencies, while the approximation rules are divided in classification rules and association rules. It is particularly important in this work, to get the social networks users' behavior, consider exact rules. From now these rules are going to called only *implications*. Follows the definition of an implication [13]:

Definition 1. *Being a formal context whose attributes set is M. An implication is an expression $P \rightarrow Q$, which $P, Q \subseteq M$.*

An implication $P \rightarrow Q$, extracted from a formal context, or respective concept lattice, have to be such that $P' \subseteq Q'$. In other words: every object which has the attributes of P, it also have the attributes of Q.

Note that, if X is a set of attributes, then X *respects* an implication $P \rightarrow Q$ iff $P \not\subseteq X$ or $Q \subseteq X$. An implication $P \rightarrow Q$ *holds* in a set $\{X_1, \dots, X_n\} \subseteq M$ iff each X_i respects $P \rightarrow Q$; and $P \rightarrow Q$ *is an implication of the context* (G, M, I) iff it holds in its set of object intents (an object intent is the set of its attributes). An implication $P \rightarrow Q$ *follows from* a set of implications $\mathscr{I}$, iff for every set of attributes X if X respects $\mathscr{I}$, then it respects $P \rightarrow Q$. A set of implications $\mathscr{I}$ is said to be *complete* in (G, M, I) iff every implication of (G, M, I) follows from $\mathscr{I}$. A set of implications $\mathscr{I}$ is said to be *redundant* iff it contains an implication $P \rightarrow Q$ that follows from $\mathscr{I} \backslash \{P \rightarrow Q\}$. Finally, an implication $P \rightarrow Q$ is considered *superfluous* iff $P \cap Q \neq \emptyset$.

In social networks will be convenient that each implication represent a minimum behavior. For this, we will require that the complete set of implications $\mathscr{I}$ of a formal context (G, M, I) have the following characteristics, to be used as representative of the process:

- the right hand side of each implication is unitary: if $P \rightarrow m \in \mathscr{I}$, then $m \in M$;

- superfluous implications are not allowed: if $P \to m \in \mathscr{I}$, then $m \notin P$;
- specializations are not allowed, i.e. left hand sides are minimal: if $P \to m \in \mathscr{I}$, then there is not any $Q \to m \in \mathscr{I}$ such that $Q \subset P$.

A complete set of implications in (G, M, I) with such properties is the so called set of *proper implications* [5] or *unary implication system* (UIS) [14].

Definition 2. *Let $\mathscr{J}$ be the complete closed set of implications of a formal context (G, M, I). Then the set of* proper *implications $\mathscr{I}$ for (G, M, I) is defined as:* $\{P \to m \in \mathscr{J} \mid P \subseteq M \text{ and } m \in M \setminus P \text{ and } \forall Z \subset P : Z \to m \notin \mathscr{J}\}$.

Table 2. Proper implications extracted from formal context in Table 1 (Source [12] p. 125).

P	$\to$	m
{e} {b, d}	$\to$	{a}
{a} {e} {f}	$\to$	{b}
{d, g}	$\to$	{c}
{a} {c} {e}	$\to$	{d}
{a} {b, d}	$\to$	{e}

The Table 2 shows the set of proper implications, from the formal context example (Table 1). For example, in implication $b, d \to a$, the set P is composed by the set of attributes $\{b, d\}$, $m = \{a\}$ and $\to$ symbol represents the incidence. P and m are called as premise and conclusion. So the implication $b, d \to a$, can be read as the premise b, d implies in conclusion a. It is important to note that, the conclusion a can has more than one minimal premises. According to Definition 2, the premises $\{e\}$ and $\{b, d\}$ are minimal, and they can not be a subset of another premises that imply in a. For example, the implication $e \to a$ is a proper implication, but $e, g \to a$ is not a proper implication.

3   Related Works

Recently, several authors have applied FCA for social networks analysis [15–22]. These works have been motivated by the interest in understand and interpret social networks through mathematical formulation. The main subjects are social network representation as a concept lattice, community detection, concepts mining, ontology analysis and rule mining through implications.

In [23], the authors proposed knowledge-based model of influence applying FCA to compute minimal generators and closed sets directly from an implicational system, for obtain a structure of user's influence. The data was extracted from *Twitter* social network, it was transformed into a formal context and it was generated the Duquenne-Guigues basis. In [24], the author shows an approach to analyze a data base composed by internet's access logs. The authors apply the minimal set of implications and complex networks theories to identify substructures, that are not easily visualized with two-mode networks. In [25], the authors propose an FCA-based approach to build canonical models, which represents *Orkut* access' patterns. These papers resemble this work, because they also talks about how to map social networks in terms of objects and attributes, and extract knowledge through implications rules set.

As this work, in [26] the authors apply FCA to identify interaction patterns through data scraped from *LinkedIn*. They did not work with professional competencies and proper implications, like us, because their goal was classify users' behavior though their network interactions, and the knowledge was extracted from conceptual lattice.

Another authors like [27–29] have developed works related to behavior pattern mining in social networks using *LinkedIn* data. The main goals were identification of potential candidates for job positions, career path analysis and recommendation of professional skills. Even not applying FCA, these works were highlighted to show the importance of develop works related to professional social networks, as well as the solution of computational methods to optimize professional recruitment and development processes.

In general, the FCA has been applied to mining social media, because the FCA theory presents a formalism for the representation of network structure, behavior identification and knowledge extraction, through formal representation of problem domain from objects, attributes and their respective incidences.

The proposed approach in this work combines techniques of formal concept analysis, patter mining and model of professional competence. From the literature review process it was noticed that for the solution of problems related to the discovery of knowledge in on-line professional social networks, perhaps this approach is an unpublished work.

4   FCA-Based Approach

In this work, the problem of analysis and representation of professional profiles in social networks, can be grounded by building a conceptual model, that merge the social network with professional skills theory, and the transformation of this model to a formal context. After scraping and preprocess the data to a formal context, we can extract the set of implications to be analyzed. The Fig. 2 shows the methodology steps proposed to analyze *LinkedIn* social network through FCA.

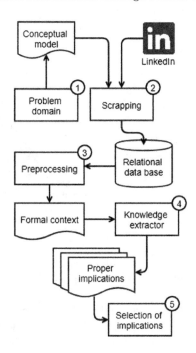

Fig. 2. Methodology based in FCA to SNA (Adapted from [12] p. 126).

4.1   Problem Domain

According to Fig. 2, the first step (1) was to construct the conceptual model according to the problem to be treated. In this case, the problem involves the characterization of a person as a professional. We adopted the *model of competence* [10], because this model has greater acceptance in both academic and business, since it seeks to integrate aspects related to this work, such as technical issues, cognition and attitudes [11]. A professional is characterized by his competence in accomplishing a certain purpose [10]. The competence is composed by three dimensions: *knowledge, attitudes* and *skill*. The dimensions are interdependent, because the behavior of a professional is determined not only by his *knowledge* but also by the *attitudes* and *skills* acquired over time. The *knowledge* dimension is linked to academic training and complementary courses. The *skill* dimension is related to a person's professional experiences. Finally, the *attitude* dimension is related to the way of people interact in their professional environment.

The conceptual model was built from the classification of categorical informations contained in *LinkedIn* users' pages. This classification process consisted in mapping the categories for the competency model dimensions. In this case the informations about academic education and complementary courses were attributed to the *knowledge* dimension. The information about professional experience were linked to *skill* dimension. The information related to the way of users

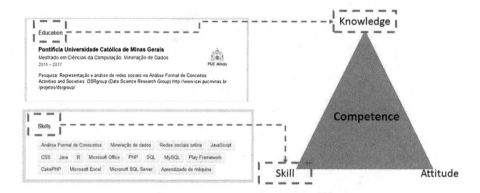

Fig. 3. Mapping LinkedIn informational categories.

interact in the social network has been attributed to the *attitudes* dimension. The Fig. 3 exemplifies how the categories were mapped into the model of competence dimensions.

As result, we obtained the conceptual model for characterize the professional profile from the model of competence (Fig. 4). In the conceptual model, the first labels' level is related to the concept of *competence*, at the second level there are the 3 dimensions related to the main concept, at the third level there are the 14 aspects that correspond to the *LinkedIn* sections, and at the fourth level there are 51 variables that correspond to fields that users can fill.

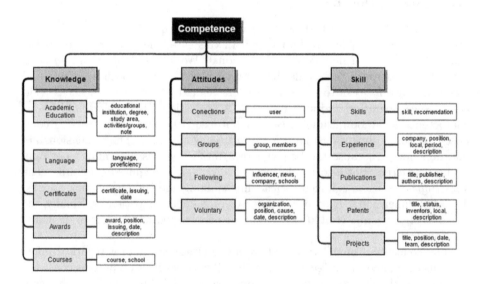

Fig. 4. Professional identification through model of competence (Source: [12] p. 127).

4.2   Scrapping

FCA techniques to social network analysis can yield insights into user behaviors, detecting popular topics, and discovering groups and communities with similar characteristics. So, a task of gathering the data on a specific subject is needed. In this case, the second step (2) of the methodology represents the Scraping component that is responsible for collecting the *LinkedIn* user data.

The collection process was divided into two phases. The first one selects the initial seeds, randomly two user profiles were selected. This amount of initial seed was considered satisfactory for the data collection process, due to the total of profiles obtained being sufficient for the study. It was defined that, as case study, the data would be collected from people of Belo Horizonte, Minas Gerais, Brazil and they must have at least graduate courses in the information technology (IT) area.

The second phase goal is collect the public profiles. As the *LinkedIn* does not provide an API (Application Programming Interface) to extract data directly from the server, an approach, known as open collection, has been adopted to extract data from users' public pages.

The Fig. 5 exemplifies the flow of data collection process. The process starts by accessing a seed. In the public profile there is a section denoted as "People also viewed" - a list with the 10 most similar profiles related to the visited profile [28]. The collector looks up these addresses and verifies which profiles meet the scope. Valid profiles are stored and each one becomes a new seed to extract new links, restarting the collection process until it reaches the stop criterion. The stopping criterion is based on the percentage of new profiles. Each iteration checks if 65% of the profiles were already in the database.

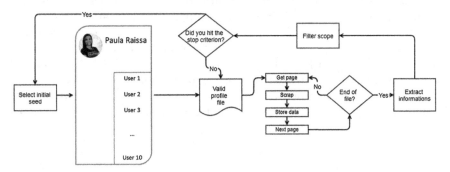

Fig. 5. Scraping *LinkedIn* profiles' process.

4.3   Preprocessing

The Preprocessing (3) component is responsible for pre-processing the data extracted in the previous step. In this work only the variables *skills* and *experience* were considered. However, in future works, the other dimensions will be included.

For the construction of the formal context, we considered, as attribute, each value of the *competence* and *experience* variables. Each user (professional of *LinkedIn*) is considered as an object. In the first version of the formal context, 4000 attributes and 1280 objects were detected. As such values are texts and *LinkedIn* allows users to fill the corresponding fields with a free text, some problems have been detected. In this case, it was necessary to create an ETL process (Extract Transform Load) to clean and transform the data, aiming to reduce the amount of attributes.

Table 3. Table of generic and specific terms.

Generic term	Specific term
Java	Java language
	JPA
	JSF
Software developer	Developer
	Programmer
	Program developer

The ETL process consists of two stages. In the first step, we applied basic procedures for string cleaning, like: UTF-8 encoding correction, accent removal, and standardization of all terms for the English language through Google Translate API[2]. In the second stage, we apply techniques to attribute reductions. Such reductions were based on terms with semantic relevance, in which the attributes *skill* and *experience* could be reduced. For example (Table 3), attributes as *JPA*, *JSF* were renamed to *java frameworks*; attributes as *developer, programmer, software developer, program developer* were renamed to *software developer*. The vague nouns or trademark terms, as *bachelor, engineer, accessibility, microsoft*, were removed, because they are not relevant to our study.

At the end of the preprocessing step, a formal context was created with 366 attributes and 970 objects, which 61 attributes are related to *experience* and 305 to *skills*.

4.4   Knowledge Extractor

The *Impec* [5] is the best-known algorithm for extracting proper implications from the formal context. This is due to the strategy that the algorithm adopts at the moment in which it finds the premises and their respective conclusions.

On the other hand, the strategy used by the algorithm is computationally inefficient and it can not be optimized or distributed. In some cases, only a few context attributes are interesting to be in the conclusion. The traditional algorithms only allow to generate the complete set, being necessary a step of filtering

---

[2] Translate API: https://cloud.google.com/translate/.

the rules to select to those whose attributes of interest appear as conclusion of the implications, occurring an unnecessary computational effort.

Based on the problems described above, an algorithm was proposed to generate the set of proper implications from the formal context. The algorithm allows that the set of proper implications can be extracted from the attributes of interest as the conclusion of implications. In general, the algorithm receives a formal context as input, finds the minimum premises for each conclusion by combining attributes, applies a pruning heuristic, and uses the derivation operators to validate the implications.

The pseudo-code of *PropIm* is given at Algorithm 1. The main objective is to find implications whose left side is minimal and the right side has only one attribute. The algorithm needs a formal context (G, M, I) as input, and its output is a set of proper implications. Line 1 initializes the set $\mathscr{I}$ with empty set. The following loop (Lines 2–17) looks at each attribute in the set M. We initially suppose that each attribute m can be a conclusion for a set of premises. For each m, we compute a left-hand side $P1$.

Input   : Formal context (G, M, I)
Output: Set of proper implications $\mathscr{I}$

```
1  𝓘 = ∅
2  foreach m ∈ M do
3  │   P = m″
4  │   size = 1
5  │   Pa = ∅
6  │   while size < |P| do
7  │   │   C = (P over size)
8  │   │   P_C = getCandidate(C, Pa)
9  │   │   foreach P1 ⊂ P_C do
10 │   │   │   if P1′ ≠ ∅ and P1′ ⊂ m′ then
11 │   │   │   │   Pa = Pa ∪ {P1}
12 │   │   │   │   𝓘 = 𝓘 ∪ {P1 → m}
13 │   │   │   end
14 │   │   end
15 │   │   size + +
16 │   end
17 end
18 return 𝓘
```

Algorithm 1. PropIm algorithm (Source: [12] p. 128).

To reduce the searching space, the algorithm finds the right side P for a left side m from a set of attributes common to m objects. After, it finds sets of possible premises for m based on P. The *size* counter determines the size of each premise, as the smallest possible size is 1 (an implication of type $\{b\} \rightarrow \{a\}$), it is initialized with 1 (Line 4).

A set of auxiliary premises Pa is used, where all valid premises found leading to m conclusion are stored (at Line 5 Pa is initialized as empty). In the loop, from Lines 6–16, the set of minimum premises is found and is bounded by $|P|$. In Line 7, the C set gets all combinations of size *size* from elements in P. In Line 8, the set of candidate premises is formed through the function *getCandidate* which will be described next.

Each candidate premise $P1 \subset P_C$ is checked to ensure if the premise $P1$ and the conclusion m results in a valid proper implication. Case $P1 \neq \emptyset$ and $P \subset P1'$, the premise $p1$ is added to the set of auxiliary premises Pa and $\mathscr{I} = \mathscr{I} \cup \{P1 \to M\}$.

A neighborhood search heuristic was implemented by the *getCandidate* function (Pseudo-code in Algorithm 2). The goal is to find, in the set of C combinations, all subsets B that do not contain some attribute that already belongs to some valid premise of Pa. It receives, as parameter, the sets C and Pa, and returns a set D of proper premises.

```
1  Function getCandidate (C, Pa)
2      D = ∅
3      foreach a ∈ A|A ⊂ Pa do
4          foreach B ⊂ C do
5              if a ∉ B then
6                  │  D = Pc \ B
7              end
8          end
9      end
10     return D
```

Algorithm 2. Function getCandidate (Source: [12] p.129).

Table 4 shows the steps of *PropIm* algorithm, on the example from Table 1. $\mathscr{I}$ contains initially $\emptyset$. The first value to m is a (first attribute from formal context) and m'' is the set of attributes $\{b, d, e, g\}$. The *size* of combination sets is 1, so $C = \{\{b\}, \{d\}, \{e\}, \{g\}\}$. Pa contains initially $\emptyset$, $C\backslash\emptyset$, so the set of attributes returned by the function *getCandidate* is $Pc = \{\{b\}, \{d\}, \{e\}, \{g\}\}$. For each subset of Pc, only the element $\{e\}$ attends the condition in Line 10 (Algorithm 1), because $\{e\}' = \{17, 20, 23\} \subset m'$. The set $\{e\}$ is added to Pa and the pair $\{e \to a\}$ is added to $\mathscr{I}$. When Pc is $\emptyset$ and *size* is $|P|$ the loop to $m = a$ is closed. So, the same steps happens for all attributes, from formal context, imputed to m.

From the formal context (G, M, I), after to apply the *PropIm* algorithm, we identified two subset of proper implications types with the following characteristics:

- The subset of proper implications, whose premises have common conclusions: $type\_\beta = \{P \to Q, S \to Q \in \mathscr{I} \mid \forall P, S, Q \subseteq M\}$. This type of implication represents that different conditions can imply in the same goal.
- The subset of implications, in which the same premise implies in different conclusions: $type\_\delta = \{P \to Q, P \to R \in \mathscr{I} \mid Q \neq R; \forall P, S, Q, R \subseteq M\}$. This subset shows that the premises can be shared by different conclusions.

Table 4. Example of *PropIm* algorithm execution (Source: [12] p. 129).

m	P	$size$	C	Pc	Pa	$\mathscr{I}$
a	{b, d, e, g}	1	{{b}, {d}, {e}, {g}}	{{b},{d}, {e}, {g}}	{{e}}	{{e→a}}
a	{b, d, e, g}	2	{{bd}, {be}, {bg}, {de}, {dg}, {eg}}	{{bd},{bg}, {dg}}	{{e}, {bd}}	{{e→a}, {bd→a}}
a	{b, d, e, g}	3	{{bde}, {bdg}, {beg}, {deg}}	∅	{{e},{bd}}	{{e→a},{bd→a}}
a	{b, d, e, g}	4	{{b, d, e, g}}	∅	{{e}, {bd}}	{{e→a},{bd→a}}
b	{a, d, e, f, g}	1	{{a}, {d}, {e}, {f}, {g}}	{{a},{d}, {e},{f},{g}}	{{a}, {e}, {f}}	{{e→a}, {bd→a}, {a→b}, {e→b}, {f→b}}
b	{a, d, e, f, g}	2	{{ad}, {ae}, {af}, {ag}, {de}, {df}, {dg}, {ef}, {eg}, {fg}}	{{dg}}	{{a}, {e}, {f}}	{{e→a}, {bd→a}, {a→b}, {e→b}, {f→b}}
b	{a, d, e, f, g}	3	{{ade}, {adf}, {adg}, {aef}, {aeg}, {afg}, {def}, {deg}, {dfg}, {efg}}	∅	{{a}, {e}, {f}}	{{e→a}, {bd→a}, {a→b}, {e→b}, {f→b}}
c	{d, g}	1	{{d}, {g}}	{{d},{g}}	∅	{{e→a}, {bd→a},{a→b}, {e→b}, {f→b}}
c	{d, g}	2	{{dg}}	{{dg}}	∅	{{e→a}, {bd→a}, {a→b}, {e→b}, {f→b}}

4.5   Selection of Implications

A relevant aspect in extracting implications is the possibility of to obtain all the relations existing among the attributes of a formal context. However, a large number of implications are generated, which makes it difficult for the end user to interpret them. One of the most important steps in the knowledge discovery process is to interpret the extracted information in a way that leads to a good understanding of the problem domain. In this case, there are several approaches that can be applied to selection, interpretation, and visualization of the set of implications. Examples include: evaluation measures, oracles, clusters, networks of implications, among others.

After extracting the set of proper implications, it was necessary to define a metric to evaluate such implications. The traditional metrics like support and confidence were not effective for this study, because the FCA is especially accurate and the extraction of the implications are based on logical operations on sets, which differs FCA of the traditional approaches of frequent patterns extraction. However, it is still necessary to define a measure that allows to classify the proper implications according to the proportion of objects represented by each implication.

In this article, we decided to evaluate the proper implications according to the relative frequency. The measure is like a local support and it was calculated according to the following equation: $\mathscr{F} = \dfrac{F_i}{F_p}$. At the equation $\mathscr{F}$ represents the relative frequency, F_i is the number of objects that respect the implication, and F_p is the number og objects that have the attribute of implication conclusion as incidence. For example: the implication $\{C\ language\} \to \{software\ engineer\}$ represents 31 objects (Fi), among 59 objects that have the attribute *software engineer* (implication conclusion) as incidence (Fp). So, the relative frequency of this implication is 0.52. To obtain the result in percentage we multiply the $\mathscr{F}$ value by 100, it generates value of 52% for the example mentioned above.

It is important to note that the relative frequency measure was adopted, because in this case the frequency represents the number of objects represented by the implication according to its class (implication conclusion). Thus, each job title is considered as a class and the sets of skills are evaluated separately for each job position. It makes that the relative frequency our local support be more relevant to evaluate this type of implication than the traditional support measure, which has to be calculated from the complete set of proper implications. For example: the implication $\{java\ frameworks\} \to \{software\ engineer\}$ has $\mathscr{F} = 75.56\%$, and global support equals 2.47%.

5   Experiments and Result Analysis

This section shows the procedures, adopted for running the experiments, and the analyses of results obtained based in proposed FCA-based approach. The experiments and results analysis were structured according to the two types of implications sets which were defined in Sect. 4.4. The interpretation of implications types β and δ shows how the competences developed by the professionals are related to job positions and how this information can help the people who need a specific position.

5.1   Obtaining Implications Type β

The implications subset of type β have the notation $type\_\beta = \{P \to Q, S \to Q \in \mathscr{I} \mid \forall P, S, Q \subseteq M\}$ and express different competence patterns (premises) which share the same job position (conclusion).

For testing and analyzing this implication type we selected 20 positions and their respective 180 skills, among the 61 positions identified in Sect. 4.3. In this case, the *PropIm* algorithm extracted 895 proper implications related to this reduced formal context. Figure 6, shows these proper implications as a graph representation (proper implications network). The central nodes are the positions and the edges represents the implications between premises (set of skills) and their conclusion (position). In this study case, the graph representation helps us to analyze the distribution among sets of skills and their respective positions.

The central nodes density represents the diversification of minimum sets of skills. The denser nodes represents positions which have more diversification of minimum sets of skills. For example, the highlighted node AD related to *administrative director* position have 163 minimal sets of skills. Generally, the *administrative director* function is manage the company resources, like human, technologies and financial resources. The specific skills of this professional can be different according to the company industry, because he have to develop

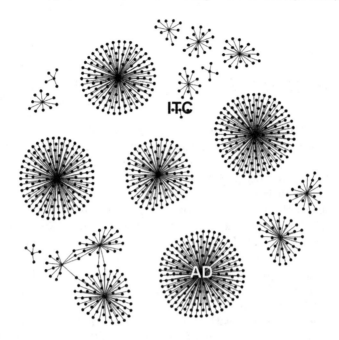

Fig. 6. Proper implications network (Source [12] p. 130).

business skills and know how about the company resources. It is expected that *administrative director* develop skills related to leadership, management, technology and communication. One of the proper implications which represents this professional profile is {*entrepreneurship, human resources, information management*} → {*administrative director*}. Another implication as {*assets management, it governance, leadership development, software development*} → {*administrative director*}, can represent a specific *administrative director* from companies focused on software development.

The central nodes with lower degree of incidence represent jobs positions that demand more specific sets of skills. This also indicates that there is not much variation among the requirements of the companies. For example the *ITC (IT consultant)* node have only 3 sets of skills related to it. An *IT consultant* duties can vary depending on the nature of company's project and client desires. However, in general, this professional has skills which combine IT and business knowledge. So, the proper implication {*ABAP*[3], *agile methodology, BI*[4]} → {*it consultant*} shows the common set of skills that the IT consultants have.

---

[3] ABAP: Advanced Business Application Programming.
[4] BI: Business Intelligence.

5.2   Obtaining Implications Type δ

The implications type δ have the notation $type\_\delta = \{P \rightarrow Q, P \rightarrow R \in \mathscr{I} \mid Q \neq R; \forall P, S, Q, R \subseteq M\}$ and represent competence patterns which the same set of skills (premise) result in two or more professional positions (conclusion). This characteristic can also be called as intersection among minimum sets of skills.

According to *Career Cast* research [30], the top 3 best jobs in *Information Technology* area is: data scientist, information security analyst and software engineer. From the set of proper implications, generated by *PropIm* algorithm, we filtered the *top 3* jobs positions, for analyze these jobs and identify the intersection among their skills.

Figure 7 shows the top 3 job positions and the intersections among their skills. The central nodes are the top 3 positions, according to *Career Cast* ranking [30]: P_1 (*data scientist*), P_2 (*information security analyst*) and P_3 (*software engineer*). The edges weight are the implication relative frequency. For example: the implication $\{C \, language\} \rightarrow \{software \, engineer\}$ represents 31 objects (Fi) among 59 objects that have *software engineer* as incidence (Fp). So, this implication relative frequency is 0.52. For obtain the result as percentage is only multiply by 100, generating the relative frequency percentage of 52% to this proper implication in *software engineer* set of implications. Therefore, the thicker edges represents implications with greater relative frequency. It is important to note that, we applied the relative frequency measure, because in this case, the frequency represents the significance of an implication inside its class. And the local significance is more relevant than the implication support in the complete proper implications set. For example, the implication $\{java \, frameworks\} \rightarrow \{software \, engineer\}$ has relative frequency of 75.56%, and its support is 2.47%. In this example, to analyze the relative frequency is more important than the implication support, because the specific objective is identify the conditions to reach a *software engineer* job. Is important to note that, in both cases the confidence is 100%.

Figure 7 shows the intersections between the minimal sets of skills, considering the top 3 jobs positions described above. In this case, the nodes P_1 and P_3 share four set of skills like $\{BI\} \rightarrow \{security \, analyst\}$ and $\{BI\} \rightarrow \{software \, engineer\}$. The nodes P_1 and P_2 share two set of skills, like the proper implications show: $\{agile \, methodology\} \rightarrow \{data \, scientist\}$ and $\{agile \, methodology\} \rightarrow \{information \, security \, analyst\}$. And, the nodes P_1 and P_3 share only one set of skills, on $\{active \, directory^5\} \rightarrow \{data \, scientist\}$ and $\{active \, directory\} \rightarrow \{software \, engineer\}$.

From these intersections, we observed that the greater the intersections amount between skills sets, more similar are the requirements to achieve a position. It would indicated possibilities to professional mobility among positions, when the set of skills (premises) implies in several different positions (conclusions). So a professional could have competence to assume different positions,

---

[5] Active directory: Microsoft tool kit for store and control information about network configurations.

Fig. 7. Top 3 jobs and their skills, where P_1 is *data scientist*, P_2 is *information security analyst* and P_3 is *software engineer* job position (Source: [12] p. 131).

because his skills could be applied to different jobs. For example, in recruitment and selection hiring process, this professional could be compatible with several job vacancy, therefore he could be more jobs opportunities. Another example is the case when a professional needs change jobs, his skills allow greater career mobility.

Figure 8 shows 4 positions that represents different hierarchical levels of IT career. The central nodes represent these 4 positions: P_1 (IT analyst), P_2 (IT coordinator), P_3 (IT manager) and P_4 (IT director). The other nodes represent minimal sets of skills, and edges represent implications. It is important to note that, edges weight was calculated using the relative frequency, previously described. From the figure we could observe that there are disjoint sets and there are not any intersections among positions. According to this hierarchy, P_1 and P_2 are positions related to the early career, while P_3 and P_4 are positions hierarchically superior. So, for P_1 was expected technical skills like in the proper implication {*.NET, automation systems*} → {*IT analyst*}. P_2 involves skills that represent the transition between technical and managerial level, like in the proper implication {*.NET, data base, ERP, it governance*} → *IT coordinator*. P_3 also involves skills related to hierarchical transition, but it was expected more managerial than technical skills, it could be expressed by the implication {*BPM*[6], *cloud computing, CRM*[7]} → *IT manager*. Finally, an IT director (P_4) have to develop managerial skills like was identified in implication {*assets management, BI, business management, consulting*} → *IT director*. Then, for the professional get a career advancement, he have to develop skills of different natures.

---

[6] BPM: Business process management.

[7] CRM: Customer relationship management.

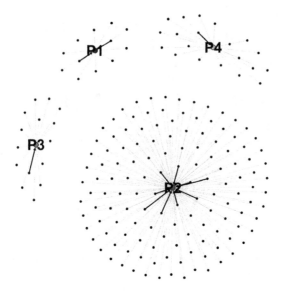

Fig. 8. IT career hierarchical levels, where P_1 to P_4 represents the following job positions: P_1 is *IT analyst*, P_2 is *IT manager*, P_3 is *IT coordinator* and P_4 is *IT director* (Source [12] p. 131).

6   Conclusion and Future Works

In this work our FCA-based approach was presented with the objective of identifying professional competencies. Specifically, one's own implications have been applied to identify the minimum sets of skills that are necessary to achieve a position. In this case, in the first place, the problem domain model was constructed in order to identify the variables that characterize a person as a professional, according to model of competence. Data were extracted from users of *LinkedIn* and techniques of data processing and transformation were applied to the formal context. Then, the *PropIm* algorithm was applied to extract the set of proper implications from formal context. Finally, graphs were constructed based on their own implications, and the relationships between premises and their respective conclusions were analyzed.

The main contributions of this article were:

– a FCA-based approach to obtain the set of proper implications, capable of representing the minimum conditions that imply in specific objectives;
– a relational database of profiles extracted from *LinkedIn*;
– two types of subsets of proper implications were defined and analyzed. These subsets of implications represent the diversity of competences required by the labor market (*type_β*), and the shared competences by different positions (*type_δ*).

As part of FCA-based approach, we propose the *PropIm* algorithm. The goal of *PropIm* algorithm is extract the set of proper implications. It was implemented applying pruning heuristics and scalable strategy. In future works the algorithm will be modified to run as a distributed application. The problem's order complexity to extract proper implications from formal context is $O(|M||\mathscr{I}|(|G||M| + |\mathscr{I}||M|))$. The proposed algorithm has exponential complexity, but the implemented strategy reduce the computational effort computing only implications with support greater than zero, and the pruning heuristic reduce the possibilities of attributes combinations into premises. Moreover, each conclusion from formal context can be processed separately without causing loss of information in the final set of proper implications.

Regarding the context of the work, the experiments answered the following questions:

– How to identify and represent professional competence?
– What are the relationships between competences and positions?

For the first question, the experiments the experiments allowed professional skills to be identified through proper implications. These implications represent the minimum set of characteristics that a professional could increase, when his goal is to achieve a job position. It is important to note that, when adopting the technique of minimum sets, the interest is to find the smallest set of objects that attend some condition. The number of objects for each condition, defines the relevance of the implication itself, by calculating the relative frequency, which was also called local support. By means of this calculation, the conditions could be classified as primary (the highest support, therefore most relevant), secondary (randomness) and specific (particularities).

For the second question, the relationships between competences and positions were defined by the subset of proper implications types (β and δ). These relationships were represented through a directed graph, which the nodes are sets of attributes and the edges represent the implications. The attribute sets are divided into two types, in which the source node is the premise and the destination node is the conclusion. It is important to note that we were only used graphs as an alternative representation, since they facilitate the visualization and analysis of the types of implications mentioned above. In general, the analyzes were based on the calculation of the degree of input of the nodes of the conclusion type (central nodes), and the degree of output of the nodes of the premise type. Through the in-degree, we identified the subset of proper implications named β, which represent the diversification of professional profiles required by the job market. Through the out-degree of nodes that represent the premises we could identify the intersections (implications type δ) which were shared among the skills sets and positions. These shared sets shows that the same skill set is a requirement for different positions, it allows the professional to be a potential candidate for different job opportunities. This also allows for greater job mobility if the person is looking for re-enter at the job market.

Despite the positive results obtained with the present work, it is also important to discuss the limitations of the proposed approach, ranging from problem modeling to the selection of implications. Such limitations and possible ways of solving them were discussed below.

As model of problem domain was built by mapping the sections of the *LinkedIn* for the *model of competence* [10], it is limited to the data provided by this social network, and by the interpretation given to the sections during the construction process. In future works, if there is any change in the *LinkedIn* sections, it will be necessary to adapt the model according to the platform changes. We also intend expand the experiments for all dimensions from the professional model of competence.

The data extraction process was performed from two initial seeds and the criterion of collector's stopping was based on the percentage of return of exclusive profiles. This percentage was chosen empirically, as well as the number of profiles used in the work, because it was necessary to define a set of data to analyze and extract the results. It is still necessary to improve the data extraction process in order to achieve, if possible, all profiles that belong to a problem scope.

At the data processing stage, the biggest limitation is that there is dependence on the domain expert. Therefore, such processes are susceptible to different interpretations, which would lead to different forms of attributes reduction, which could have an impact on results. In the future works, statistical or computational methods will be adopted to reduce the expert's dependence on the domain.

The algorithm was implemented sequentially and uses a traditional approach to the attributes combination. This causes an impact on the processing time of proper implications, which limits the amount of objects and attributes inserted in the formal context. As future work, another algorithms could be exploited, particularly those capable of obtaining the set of implications from concept or the subset of formal concepts as proposed by [31]. Moreover, we intend to implement the *PropIm* algorithm as a distributed application and compare several algorithms to extract proper implications from formal context. We also intent improve the selection of implications, and another measures will be tested and analyzed.

Finally, we intend to implement a web platform with this approach, to help professionals to increase their competencies in their professional resume and define career plans. In this platform the person can indicate the positions of interest and it will be returned the necessary competences to reach such position. It will also include a temporal analysis of career development, which may allow such plans to be traced in a dynamic approach.

Acknowledgement. The authors acknowledge the financial support received from the Foundation for Research Support of Minas Gerais state, FAPEMIG; the National Council for Scientific and Technological Development, CNPq; Coordination for the Improvement of Higher Education Personnel, CAPES. We would also express gratitude to the Federal Service of Data Processing, SERPRO.

References

1. Russell, M.A.: Mining the Social Web: Data Mining Facebook, Twitter, LinkedIn, Google+, GitHub, and More. O'Reilly Media Inc., Russell (2013)
2. LinkedIn: About LinkedIn (2017). Accessed 16 Aug 2017. https://press.linkedin.com/about-linkedin
3. Ganter, B., Stumme, G., Wille, R.: Formal Concept Analysis: Foundations and Applications, vol. 3626. Springer, Heidelberg (2005). https://doi.org/10.1007/978-3-540-31881-1
4. Codocedo, V., Baixeries, J., Kaytoue, M., Napoli, A.: Contributions to the formalization of order-like dependencies using FCA. In: Proceedings of the 5th International Workshop What can FCA do for Artificial Intelligence, CEUR-WS (2016)
5. Taouil, R., Bastide, Y.: Computing proper implications. In: Proceedings of the International Conference on Conceptual Structures - ICCS, Stanford, pp. 46–61 (2001)
6. Kontopoulos, E., Berberidis, C., Dergiades, T., Bassiliades, N.: Ontology-based sentiment analysis of Twitter posts. Expert Syst. Appl. **40**, 4065–4074 (2013)
7. Ali, S.S., Bentayeb, F., Missaoui, R., Boussaid, O.: An efficient method for community detection based on formal concept analysis. In: Andreasen, T., Christiansen, H., Cubero, J.-C., Raś, Z.W. (eds.) ISMIS 2014. LNCS (LNAI), vol. 8502, pp. 61–72. Springer, Cham (2014). https://doi.org/10.1007/978-3-319-08326-1_7
8. Cuvelier, E., Aufaure, M.-A.: A buzz and e-reputation monitoring tool for twitter based on Galois Lattices. In: Andrews, S., Polovina, S., Hill, R., Akhgar, B. (eds.) ICCS 2011. LNCS (LNAI), vol. 6828, pp. 91–103. Springer, Heidelberg (2011). https://doi.org/10.1007/978-3-642-22688-5_7
9. Neto, S.M., Song, M., Dias, S., et al.: Minimal cover of implication rules to represent two mode networks. In: IEEE/WIC/ACM International Conference on Web Intelligence and Intelligent Agent Technology (WI-IAT), vol. 1, pp. 211–218. IEEE (2015)
10. Durand, T.: Forms of incompetence. In: Proceedings Fourth International Conference on Competence-Based Management. Norwegian School of Management, Oslo (1998)
11. Brandão, H.P., Guimarães, T.A.: Gestão de competências e gestão de desempenho: tecnologias distintas ou instrumentos de um mesmo construto? Revista de Administração de empresas **41**, 8–15 (2001)
12. Silva, P., Dias, S., Brandão, W., Song, M., Zárate, L.: Formal concept analysis applied to professional social networks analysis. In: Proceedings of the 19th International Conference on Enterprise Information Systems, vol. 1, pp. 123–134. INSTICC, ScitePress (2017)
13. Ganter, B., Wille, R.: Formal Concept Analysis: Mathematical Foundations. Springer, Heidelberg (2012). https://doi.org/10.1007/978-3-642-59830-2
14. Bertet, K., Monjardet, B.: The multiple facets of the canonical direct unit implicational basis. Theor. Comput. Sci. **411**, 2155–2166 (2010)
15. Rome, J.E., Haralick, R.M.: Towards a formal concept analysis approach to exploring communities on the world wide web. In: Ganter, B., Godin, R. (eds.) ICFCA 2005. LNCS (LNAI), vol. 3403, pp. 33–48. Springer, Heidelberg (2005). https://doi.org/10.1007/978-3-540-32262-7_3
16. Snasel, V., Horak, Z., Kocibova, J., Abraham, A.: Analyzing social networks using FCA: complexity aspects. In: IEEE/WIC/ACM International Joint Conferences on Web Intelligence and Intelligent Agent Technologies, WI-IAT 2009, vol. 3, pp. 38–41 (2009)

17. Stattner, E., Collard, M.: Social-based conceptual links: conceptual analysis applied to social networks. In: IEEE/ACM International Conference on Advances in Social Networks Analysis and Mining (ASONAM), pp. 25–29 (2012)
18. Pedrycz, W., Chen, S.-M. (eds.): Social Networks: A Framework of Computational Intelligence, vol. 526. Springer, Cham (2014). https://doi.org/10.1007/978-3-319-02993-1
19. Krajči, S.: Social network and formal concept analysis. In: Pedrycz, W., Chen, S.-M. (eds.) Social Networks: A Framework of Computational Intelligence. SCI, vol. 526, pp. 41–61. Springer, Cham (2014). https://doi.org/10.1007/978-3-319-02993-1_3
20. Atzmueller, M.: Subgroup and community analytics on attributed graphs. In: Proceedings of the Workshop on Social Network Analysis using Formal Concept Analysis (2015)
21. Neznanov, A., Parinov, A.: Analyzing social networks services using formal concept analysis research toolbox. In: Proceedings of the Workshop on Social Network Analysis using Formal Concept Analysis (2015)
22. Soldano, H., Santini, G., Bouthinon, D.: Abstract and local concepts in attributed networks. In: Proceedings of the Workshop on Social Network Analysis using Formal Concept Analysis (2015)
23. Cordero, P., Enciso, M., Mora, A., Ojeda-Aciego, M., Rossi, C.: Knowledge discovery in social networks by using a logic-based treatment of implications. Knowl. Based Syst. **87**, 16–25 (2015)
24. Neto, S.M., Song, M.A., Dias, S.M., Zárate, L.E.: Using implications from FCA to represent a two mode network data. Int. J. Softw. Eng. Knowl. Eng. (IJSEKE) **1**, 211–218 (2015)
25. Jota Resende, G., De Moraes, N.R., Dias, S.M., Marques Neto, H.T., Zarate, L.E.: Canonical computational models based on formal concept analysis for social network analysis and representation. In: IEEE International Conference on Web Services (ICWS), pp. 717–720. IEEE (2015)
26. Barysheva, A., Golubtsova, A., Yavorskiy, R.: Profiling less active users in online communities. In: Proceedings of the Workshop on Social Network Analysis using Formal Concept Analysis (2015)
27. Li, L., Zheng, G., Peltsverger, S., Zhang, C.: Career trajectory analysis of information technology alumni: a LinkedIn perspective. In: Proceedings of the 17th Annual Conference on Information Technology Education. SIGITE 2016, New York, pp. 2–6. ACM (2016)
28. Xu, Y., Li, Z., Gupta, A., Bugdayci, A., Bhasin, A.: Modeling professional similarity by mining professional career trajectories. In: Proceedings of the 20th ACM SIGKDD International Conference on Knowledge Discovery and Data Mining, pp. 1945–1954. ACM (2014)
29. Lorenzo, E.R., Cordero, P., Enciso, M., Missaoui, R., Mora, A.: CAISL: simplification logic for conditional attribute implications. In: CLA (2016)
30. CareerCast: Jobs Rated Report 2016: Ranking 200 Jobs (2016). Accessed 12 Dec 2016. http://www.careercast.com/jobs-rated/jobs-rated-report-2016-ranking-200-jobs
31. Dias, S.M.: Redução de Reticulados Conceituais (Concept Lattice Reduction). Ph.D. thesis, Department of Computer Science of Federal University of Minas Gerais (UFMG), Belo Horizonte, Minas Gerais, Brazil (2016). (in Portuguese)

Data Quality Problems in TPC-DI Based Data Integration Processes

Qishan Yang[1(✉)], Mouzhi Ge[2], and Markus Helfert[1]

[1] Insight Centre for Data Analytics, Dublin City University, Dublin, Ireland
qishan.yang@insight-centre.org, markus.helfert@dcu.ie
[2] Faculty of Informatics, Masaryk University, Brno, Czech Republic
mouzhi.ge@muni.cz

Abstract. Many data driven organisations need to integrate data from multiple, distributed and heterogeneous resources for advanced data analysis. A data integration system is an essential component to collect data into a data warehouse or other data analytics systems. There are various alternatives of data integration systems which are created in-house or provided by vendors. Hence, it is necessary for an organisation to compare and benchmark them when choosing a suitable one to meet its requirements. Recently, the TPC-DI is proposed as the first industrial benchmark for evaluating data integration systems. When using this benchmark, we find some typical data quality problems in the TPC-DI data source such as multi-meaning attributes and inconsistent data schemas, which could delay or even fail the data integration process. This paper explains processes of this benchmark and summarises typical data quality problems identified in the TPC-DI data source. Furthermore, in order to prevent data quality problems and proactively manage data quality, we propose a set of practical guidelines for researchers and practitioners to conduct data quality management when using the TPC-DI benchmark.

Keywords: Data quality · Data integration · TPC-DI Benchmark
ETL

1 Introduction

The data warehouse, as an organization's data repository, is a subject-oriented, integrated, non-volatile and time-variant collection of data in support of management decisions [10]. A data warehouse may need an Extract-Transform-Load (ETL) system to collect and integrate data. A ETL system extracts data from data sources, enforces data quality standards, and conforms data, which gathers the separate sources and finally delivers data in data warehouses with a presentation-ready and unified format [11]. Even though a ELT system is invisible to end users as a black box, it could cost 70% of the resources in the data warehousing implementation and maintenance [11]. The process of the ETL can

© Springer International Publishing AG, part of Springer Nature 2018
S. Hammoudi et al. (Eds.): ICEIS 2017, LNBIP 321, pp. 57–73, 2018.
https://doi.org/10.1007/978-3-319-93375-7_4

be described by data integration (DI) which extracts, transforms and populates data into a data repository [14]. When building a data warehouse, a DI system is the bridge for the data migration from data sources to the destination.

The TPC-DI[1] is designed as the first benchmark to evaluate DI systems [14]. This benchmark provides the source and destination data models, data transformations and implementation rules. It allows people to evaluate DI systems in order to choose a suitable one that meets their requirements. It can also be leveraged to assess the performance of a legacy DI system for further improvements.

Data quality problems appear frequently in the stage of DI when extracting, migrating and populating data into data repositories. Data quality is considered an important aspect that influences the DI process [11]. Previous research indicates that understanding the effects of data quality is critical to the success of organisations [6]. Numerous business initiatives have been delayed or even cancelled, citing poor-quality data as the main reason. Most initial data quality frameworks consider that data quality dimensions are equally important [12]. More recently, as [5] states, it is necessary to prioritise certain data quality dimensions for data management. However, as far as we know, there is limited research on prioritising data quality dimensions and guiding the data quality management in the DI process. As far as we know, there is still no study that focuses on the data quality problems aligning with the TPC-DI benchmark.

Therefore, in this paper, we intend to find out which data quality dimensions are crucial to DI and also attempt to derive the guidelines for proactive data quality management in DI. The contributions of this paper are shown in three parts. The TPC-DI processes are investigated based on the data flow from different data sources to a data warehouse. Then we demonstrate some typical data quality problems which should be considered in the DI process. We specify these data quality problems and classify them into different data quality dimensions. Finally, in order to proactively manage data quality in DI, we derive a set of data quality guidelines that can be used to avoid data quality pitfalls and problems when using the TPC-DI Benchmark.

The remainder of the paper is organised as follows. Section 2 reviews the related work about data quality and DI. The processes of the TPC-DI benchmark is explained in Sect. 3. Section 4 describes a scenario used to conduct our research. Then we investigate the data quality problems in the DI process in Sect. 5 and classify these problems into different data quality dimensions in Sect. 6. Section 7 proposes the guidelines for data quality management in DI. Finally, Sect. 8 concludes the paper and outlines the future research.

2   Related Work

In order to manage data quality, Wang [22] proposes the Total Data Quality Management (TDQM) model to deliver high-quality information products.

---

[1] http://www.tpc.org/tpcdi/.

This model consists of four continuous phases: the definition, measurement, analysis and improvement. The measurement phase is critical as information quality cannot be managed without being measured effectively and meaningfully [1]. In order to measure data quality, data quality dimensions need to be determined. [9] investigates the data quality management in the process of the data warehousing aligned with a world-leading financial services company. A practically oriented concept is illustrated in order to manage the data quality in large data warehouse systems. It also shares experiences of developing a data quality strategy for data quality planning and controlling.

[16] lists possible data quality issues appearing in the different stages, such as the data source, DI and data profiling, data staging, ETL and database schema. 117 data quality problems are demonstrated. Nearly half of them (52) data quality flaws are contributed by the data source stage, 36 issues are derived from the stage of ETL tools, and rest occupies 29 data quality problems. Wang and Strong [23] use an exploratory factor analysis to derive 15 important data quality dimensions from initial 179 attributes, which are widely accepted in the following data quality research. Based on these proposed dimensions, data quality assessments are applied in different domains such as the Healthcare [21], Supply Chain Management [7], and Smart City Applications [8].

[4] declares the goal of the DI system which is to decrease the effort of users in acquiring high-quality answers. The DI system manages some procedures specifically in (1) revising or removing mistakes and missing data, (2) offering confident documented measures in data, (3) safekeeping the captured data flow of transactions, (4) calibrating and integrating multiple sources data, (5) structuring data for end-user tools [11]. Hence, the DI system is the foundational work of the data warehousing in order to provide synthesized, consistent and accurate data for further analysis.

Before the TPC-DI, there are some self-defined benchmarks, such as Efficiency Evaluation of Open Source ETL Tools [13] and the Data Warehouse Engineering Benchmark (DWEB) [3]. However, there is a lack of an industrial standardised ETL benchmark, which can be used to evaluate performances of ETL tools [24]. The TPC-DI is the first industrial benchmark to fill this gap regarding ETL evaluations [14]. It is released by the Transaction Processing Performance Council (TPC) which is a non-profit corporation founded to define transaction processing and database benchmarks.

Poess et al. [14] explain the components and characteristics of the TPC-DI, such as the source and target data models of a data warehouse, technical details for the generation of the data sets, the transformations of the DI workload, etc. The TPC-DI data comes from different data sources, which need to be integrated into a data warehouse. The data warehousing architecture and work flow are hierarchical and divided into the SUT (system under test) and out of SUT parts. The SUT part will be benchmarked, while the out of SUT is not covered in the process of evaluation. This standardised benchmark provides a standard specification for usage of the TPC-DI benchmark, in which 14 clauses are given to explain data sources, data warehousing schema, transformations, description of the system under test, execution rules & metrics, pricing etc. [18]. The code for data set generation can be downloaded and executed in JDK environment. The data set size can be controlled by configuring the scale factor parameter.

3   TPC-DI Processes

Since benchmarking is critical for DI evaluation [20], it is thus valuable to study how TPC-DI benchmark works. In this section, this benchmark is investigated from the process flow perspective.

3.1   Data Generation

DI processes of the TPC-DI benchmark usually begin from the data source files generated by DIGen which is built on top of the Parallel Data Generation Framework (PDGF). The capabilities of the PDGF are extended to create data sets with the specific characteristics required for this benchmark [18]. PDGF is implemented at the University of Passau, which is suitable for cloud scale data generation with highly parallel and very adaptable characteristics. This framework is configured using two XML files for data description and distribution, which facilitates the generation of different distributions of specified data sets. The implementation expends much effort on performance and extensibility. Hence, it is easily doable to generate new domains derived from PDGF [15]. This framework uses a peculiar methodology for the seed to exploit the pseudo random number generators in parallel. It keeps track of the random number sequences for each value in the data set, which gives this framework highly scalable ability on multi-core, multi-socket, and multi-node systems [14].

DIGen is a specific generator based on PDGF to create data sources and audit information for this benchmark. It is required to be executed in a Java environment and PDGF needs to be placed in the same directory [18]. There are some regulations for usage of DIGen according to the Standard Specification of the TPC-DI version 1.1.0 [19]: (1) The data source must be created using DIGen for this benchmark; (2) It is not allowed to modify DIGen; (3) The version of the specification and DIGen must match; (4) PDGF should be used; (5) Errors in a compliant DIGen version is deemed to be in compliance with the specification; (6) DIGen should be used to create the data source based on a minimum of Java SE 7; (7) Test sponsors need to ensure DIGen execution correctly in their environments; (8) The issue submission should contact the TPC administrator with the document including the exact issue and proposed fix.

3.2   Data Sources

According to [19], the data is comprised of five sources and a small number of reference files, which come from the online transaction processing (OLTP) database, Human Resource (HR) Database, Customer Prospect List, Financial Newswire

Table 1. The data sets.

System/Reference	File	Format	Historical	Incremental
OLTP	Account.txt	CDC		Y
	Customer.txt	CDC		Y
	Trade.txt	CDC	Y	Y
	TradeHistory.txt	CDC	Y	
	CashTransaction.txt	CDC	Y	Y
	HoldingHistory.txt	CDC	Y	Y
	DailyMarket.txt	CDC	Y	Y
	WatchItem.txt	CDC	Y	Y
HR DB	HR.csv	CSV	Y	
Represent List	Prospect.csv	CSV	Y	Y
FINWIRE	FINWIRE	Multi	Y	
Customer Management System	CustomerMgmt.xml	XML	Y	
Reference	Date.txt	DEL	Y	
	Time.txt	DEL	Y	
	Industry.txt	DEL	Y	
	StatusType.txt	DEL	Y	
	TaxRate.txt	DEL	Y	
	TradeType.txt	DEL	Y	

and Customer Management System. The OLTP database contains data for transactional information about securities market trading and the relevant entities. The HR Database manages data for the employees and their reporting hierarchy. The Prospect List is extracted daily from an external data provider. It includes customers of the brokerage and potential customers' name, contact and demographic information. The Financial Newswire contributes to the FINWIRE file for quarterly historical data feeding of the two dimension tables and a reference table: the DimCompany table, DimSecurity table and Financial table. The Customer Management System manipulates new and updated customer and account information. The reference file provides data or complementary information to support other tables. There are 18 files from these five sources and reference files, which are summarised and tabulated in Table 1 based on the TPC-DI standard specification [19]. After data is generated by DIGen, it will be sorted into three different directories: the Batch 1 for the historical load; the Batch2 for the Incremental Update 1; the Batch3 for the Incremental Update 2.

3.3 Data Warehouse

After data sources are generated, they are finally delivered into a data warehouse. This data warehouse is based on dimensional modeling with the ability to efficiently reply to business questions [19]. The fact tables and dimension tables are the fundamental components of a data warehouse. In this research, six fact tables, seven dimension tables and five reference tables are created to build this warehouse. Based on the document [19], the main relationships of these tables in this data warehouse are depicted in Fig. 1. As can be seen, tables are linked by foreign keys and most links are built between dimension tables and fact tables. For instance, the FactWatches table has relationships with three dimension tables (DimCustomer, DimSecurity and DimDate). However, there

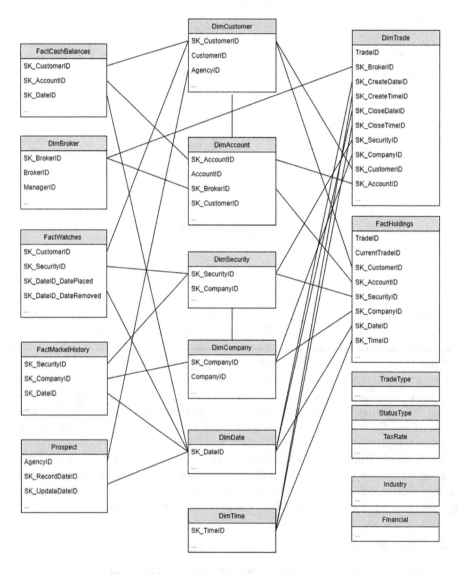

Fig. 1. The main relationships among tables.

are some links which appear among dimension tables, such as the link between the DimCustomer table and DimAccount table. Reference tables support other tables when more or detailed information is required. In addition, the DimTrade table can be seen as a dimension table or fact table depending on its functions in different situations.

3.4 Data Flow

The data flow in this research has several steps from the data generator to destination. After the data is generated by DIGen, it is delivered into the data staging area. This process is just the migration of data sources from outside to system under test (SUT) and no data transformations and cleansing operations are executed. After data is sent to the staging area, data quality issues should be solved before loading into the data warehouse. The data flow is depicted in Fig. 2. The data flow before the staging area is out of the testing scope, the rest of data flow is under the test for evaluations.

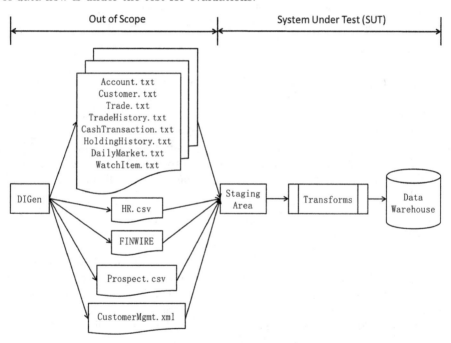

Fig. 2. The data flow.

4 Scenario

In order to investigate the data quality in DI aligned with the TPC-DI, a typical scenario is set up to frame our research. In practice, it is common to extract data firstly into flat files rather than transport data from data resources to a data warehouse directly. It is sometimes necessary to obtain or purchase external data from outside free data sources or third-party companies. In this case, a retail brokerage data warehouse is built and fed by using the TPC-DI data. During this process, some data quality problems appear in the process of DI, which are explained concretely in the following sections.

In our scenario, some tables are emphasised herein, since they are involved as the data quality issue examples. The DimCustomer dimension table stores customer records and DimAccount dimension table archives customers' account details. A new customer must accompany a new account, but existing customers can open more than one account. When analysing the key customers or trades via accounts, we need to obtain the records from DimTrade table, and join corresponding entities from DimCustomer and DimAccount tables. The DimCompany table contains companies' ID, name, CEO, address etc. The DimSecurity table incorporates securities issued by companies. The Financial table gathers all companies' financial data. All data for these three tables is fed by the FINWIRE files. When reviewing the market history or rating the companies from a finance perspective, the MarketHistory table would be retrieved, and the DimCompany, DimSecurity and Financial tables would be looked up to acquire information if necessary.

5   Data Quality Problems in Data Integration

In this section, we describe and define the data quality problems in the TPC-DI data sets when conducting this scenario. Some typical examples are given to describe these problems. Afterwards, we classify these problems into different data quality dimensions. Thus, we are able to identify which data quality dimensions are important for data quality management in DI aligned with the TPC-DI.

5.1   Missing Values

There are mainly two types of missing value problems in the DI processes. On one hand, the data in one field appears to be null or empty. We define this type of missing values as direct incompleteness, which means this can be directly detected by rule-based queries. On the other hand, the data can be missing because of the data operations such as data update. We define this type of missing values as indirect incompleteness. We describe the two types of missing values in details as follows.

The Missing Values in Fields. The Missing Values in fields indicate there is no non-null requirement or no compulsory values in some specific fields. In our scenario, the DimCompany table's data is obtained from FINWIRE files, some values are missing in the field of the FoundingDate which show the creation time of companies.

Even this field can be empty in the DimCompany table, but these missing values would influence the further data mining or data analysis (e.g. the company reputation assessment). The DimCompany table has a field named Sparting for standard & poor company's rating which would be influenced by values of the FoundingDate. So in this situation, if the missing values of the FoundingDate could be given or found, they might be leveraged to re-rate the value in the Sparting field.

The Updating Record with Missing Values. When updating some records, only new values are given to revise the old values, while other fields are missing because they are unnecessary to be updated. As a typical characteristic of the data warehouse, the update is not directly changing the old values of a record, instead, the data warehouse maintains and marks the old record as a legacy or inactive record and create a new record with a surrogate key for updating.

The records for updating may be nonuniform in the DimCustomer table. For example, some records only have new addresses, while some records only have emails, because they only need to update addresses or emails. A generalised example of these records is described in Table 2. Based on the characteristic of the data warehouse, when updating a record, a new record will be created and the legacy record will still be maintained rather than be deleted.

Table 2. The updating records with missing values.

Customer ID	Address	Email	Action type
56	XXX	X@X.X	New
56	YYY	NULL	Update
56	NULL	Z@Z.Z	Update

Updating these records could not be inserted into the dimension tables directly. Otherwise, errors may be thrown by a database system, because of inserting null or empty values into non-null-allowed fields.

5.2   The Conflict of Entities

In this paper, the definition of an entity is a record or object stored in a table. The reason why we differentiate the entity and record is that a record may contain several entities outside tables, while sometimes a record is an entity. The conflicts of entities mean that there is more than one valid or active record with the same identifier in a table. The records in tables need to agree with each other and avoid conflicts between them.

In our scenario, when inserting a record into the DimSecurity table, a lookup need to be conducted to check whether an ID already exists. If it is existed, the IsCurrent field of the old record should be modified to false or inactive firstly, and then the new record is inserted into the table. However, in order to speed up the process, caches and several threads may be leveraged for creating and updating operations in parallel. If operations of creating and updating a certain entity are allocated in different caches or threads, the updating could be executed before the creating. The lookup would return the "not exist" ID for updating. This may result in more than one record's IsCurrent shows active or true. But only a record should be active or true for an ID.

The situation above appears in our experiment when using big caches and several threads to load data. Some records would be active or true all the time even they have already been updated. If this issue is ignored or resolved improperly, some entities may have the same ID and active status but different surrogate keys. Conflicts occur when querying these entities with IDs.

5.3   Format Incompatibility

This issue appears frequently in the date format. Date format conflicts are mainly triggered by inconsistent date styles between the data resource and data warehouse.

In our scenario, the field of EffectiveDate means the effective date of a certain record. The date retrieved from the data source is the string with the format "YYYY-MM-DDTHH24:MI:SS" which includes the date and time split by the capital T. If the data warehouse is built in the Oracle database system as an example, the date format is "DD-Mon-YY HH.MI.SS.000000000 AM/PM" which shows different date and time formats compared with the format in the data source. Two formats of an EffectiveDate example in the data source and the Oracle data warehouse are given in Table 3.

Table 3. Examples of format incompatibility.

Date format	Place
2007-05-08T07:21:56	The date format in the data resource
07-MAY-08 07.21.56.000000000 AM	The date format in the data warehouse

If the original data with the different date format in the data source is inserted into the data warehouse without format transformations, an error would be thrown as the format violation. Therefore, the original date values need to be reformatted to match the date format in the data warehouse.

5.4   Multi-resource or Mixed Records

In raw data sources, a record may contain more than one table's entities. These entities in a record normally have referential or dependent relationships. For example, in the CustomerMgmt.xml, a record may contain two dimension tables' entities (DimCustomer and DimAccount tables). An account must belong to a certain customer and a customer could have more than one account (One-to-Many Relationship). For each record, there is a field named a Action Type, which shows the purpose of this record. When we insert a record to create or update a new account, the value of the Action Type is "New" or "UPDACCT" respectively. This record includes two entities which contain customer and account's information. Whereas, when we only update the customer information, the value of Action Type is "UPDCUST". In this case, the record only contains one entity. The Table 4 illustrates these three kinds of records.

Table 4. Examples of mixed records.

Customer ID	Account ID	Action type	Other customer info.	Other account info.
137	165	New	...	...
137	Null	UPDCUST	...	Null
137	165	UPDACCT	...	Null

As such, when carrying out the data operations, there are two options: (1) differentiating the entities then identifying the purpose; (2) identifying the purposes then differentiating the entities if necessary. We find that the option 1 is slower compared to the option 2, since some records do not need to be differentiated, but all purposes of records need to be identified.

5.5 Multi-table Files

In raw data sources, some files contain more than one table's records. This situation may happen when records in tables are collected from the one system. In the TPC-DI data sets, a file may contain three tables' data: CMP, SEC and FIN. The CMP records are related to the DimCompany table; the SEC is for the DimSecurty table; the FIN feeds the Financial table. Table 5 gives three examples of these types.

Table 5. Examples in multi-table files.

Posting date and time	Record type	Status	Other information
19860502-082315	FIN	NULL	Other financial information
19760713-103826	SEC	ACTV	Other Security information
19850826-113217	CMP	ACTV	Other Company Information

Based on types of records, the data extracted from this data source file can be divided into several branches. Each branch may have sub-branches for different purposes as they can be further split into different sub-branches (e.g. ACTV and INAC). Then there are several branches and sub-branches need to be considered in the process of loading data. If dependencies and links exist among these tables, the sequence of loading the data into tables needs to be prioritised as some tables may depend on other tables via foreign keys. If ignoring this sequence, errors would be triggered as the foreign keys are not found.

5.6 Multi-meaning Attributes

In data sources, an attribute or a field may allow containing different types of data which could have different meanings. It could be difficult to avoid ambiguities with improper differentiation.

In our scenario, a attribute named the CoNameOrCIK that may carry the company identification code (10 chars) or company name (60 chars). The Table 6 shows two records as examples from data sources. The first row uses a company identification code, while the second row uses a company name which may be encrypted. In the Financial table, there is an attribute called SK_CompanyID which is the primary key of the DimCompany table as well as the foreign key of the Financial table. Thus, when inserting a record into the Financial table, we could either use the company identification code or company name to look up the DimCompany table to find the primary key and then insert it into the Financial table as a foreign key.

Table 6. Examples of multi-meaning attributes.

Posting date and time	Record type	CoNameOrCIK
19790911-082315	FIN	18362001000000123456
19830512-091241	FIN	501026396HBGSKDFbFe bKiJHFLSJIEFgRjmqXd AQcnYFGETDHzRouxMx JHURQIjtVZu

If the company identification code and company name are very similar and hard to be identified, the program could not differentiate the meaning and type of a value. Errors could occur when loading these misunderstood or incorrect values into tables.

6   Classify Data Quality Problems

In order to facilitate the data quality management in DI, we classify these data quality problems into the classic data quality dimensions proposed by Wang and Strong [23]. The last two data quality problems are not totally fitted into proposed data quality dimensions and we propose new dimensions for the data quality problems, which are marked with *. The details is tabulated in Table 7.

Table 7. Data quality dimensions in data integration [25].

Data quality dimension	Data quality problem
Completeness	Missing value
Timeliness	Conflict of entities
Consistency	Format incompatibility
Operational Sequence*	Multi-Resource or Mixed records
	Multi-Table files
Uniqueness*	Multi-Meaning attributes

In the context of DI, not all data quality dimensions are equally important for data quality management in ID. We propose initially focusing on the dimensions of completeness, timeliness and consistency. This small set of dimensions not only point out the key focus of data quality management in DI but also provide a foundation for data cleansing in DI.

Moreover, some data quality dimensions need to be further refined. For example, representational consistency in DI is not enough. We need to align the definitions of the data rather than only align the names. Therefore the consistency can be further refined into syntactic, pragmatic and semantic levels.

Accuracy is always considered as one of the most important data quality dimensions in data quality management. However, in DI, it is usually lack of the ground truth for the data. Therefore, wrong value is not included in our data quality problems. As an initial step in data quality management, we recommend focusing on the tangible set of data quality dimensions.

Not all the data quality problems can be classified into classic data quality dimensions, especially the problems about the sequence of the data operations. A correct sequence of data operation can increase the process efficiency and avoid data quality errors. For example, we can identify different types of operations or use table dependencies to define the sequence of loading the data.

Furthermore, as Dakrory et al. [2] state that uniqueness is one of the important data quality dimensions in DI. We find that apart from the classic data quality dimensions, data uniqueness is a critical indicator to differ the data meaning in order to avoid possible data ambiguities.

7   Guidelines for Data Quality Management

In order to prevent these data quality problems in DI and proactively manage data quality, we propose the following guidelines to help researchers and practitioners to avoid data quality pitfalls and guide effective data quality management. Specifically, guideline 1 and 2 tackle the missing value problems; Guideline 3 can be used to prevent entity conflicts; Guideline 4 deals with format incompatibility; Guideline 5 is for optimising mixed records and multi-table files in DI and Guideline 6 intends to solve the problem of multi-meaning attributes.

To summarise the typical data quality problems in DI and the corresponding proactive actions, Table 8 is provided as an overview.

7.1   Guideline 1

In order to manage the possible effects of missing values, we can use business logic to derive the field dependency, then pay attention especially to the fields that are involved in the field dependency and meanwhile allow null or empty values.

There are certain fields that allow null or empty values in the data warehouse. Those fields may not cause errors in DI processes. But when these fields are used in the data analytics or some business operations, they may play as an independent variable and can be used to determine other fields or values. The Missing values would then cause a problem.

7.2   Guideline 2

In the data quality management for DI, the dimension of completeness should be further refined, since there can be direct incompleteness such as the missing value in a record or indirect incompleteness such as the missing value in the update process.

Completeness is one of the well-known dimensions in data quality management. Managing data completeness is especially important during DI, since it is usually a straightforward problem which can be foreseen, whereas in the meantime there might be certain incompleteness pitfalls that people will overlook. As the example given in the Sect. 5.1, when carrying out the update operation, the updated records can turn out to be incomplete without a lookup. Therefore, to deal with the indirect incompleteness caused by the update, it is necessary to look up and find the values that do not need to be updated.

7.3   Guideline 3

When both types of inserting and updating records appear in batch operations, the sequence of data operations in a batch can avoid entity conflicts.

Batch operations are typically used to speed up the data creation, read, update and deletion (CRUD) operations. In practice, distributed operations are also usually conducted in parallel to expedite the processing of data. Thus, for an entity, it is necessary to avoid update or deletion before the insert operation. One of the best practices is to separate the CRUD operations into different batches and rank them. Parallel operations could be conducted inside a separated batch.

7.4   Guideline 4

For DI, assuring format consistency in the syntactic (representational) level is not enough. Data format consistency between the data source and data warehouse should be aligned at a pragmatic level.

Table 8. The summary of guidelines [25].

Data quality problems	Guidelines	Proposed proactive actions for data integration
Missing values	Guideline1 Guideline 2	Field dependencies and indirect incompleteness caused by data operations should be specified
Conflict of entities	Guideline 3	The sequence of data operations in the batch needs to be properly designed to avoid entity conflicts
Format incompatibility	Guideline 4	Representational and pragmatic consistency should be both examined before ETL
Multi-Resource or Mixed records Multi-Table files	Guideline 5	The sequence of data operations can be optimised by firstly extracting the types of data operations and then differentiating the entities
Multi-Meaning attributes	Guideline 6	Data uniqueness should be included in the data quality management in data integration

Data format consistency cannot be confirmed only by the format name. With the same data format name (syntactic level), there might be different real usages or different definitions (pragmatic level). One of the prevalent format inconsistencies is the date format unconformity. Thus before carrying out DI, practitioners should especially look into what certain format means and whether the definitions of the format are aligned between the data source and data warehouse.

7.5 Guideline 5

Optimising the sequence of data operations can increase the efficiency of DI processes and avoid data quality problems.

In DI processes, data entities may be mixed together in a record. We recommend firstly to identify the purpose of this record, then separate the data entities if necessary. Moreover, when we load a data source with various tables, optimising the loading sequence can avoid the errors triggered by table dependencies.

7.6 Guideline 6

Data uniqueness is an important dimension in data quality management. Complete logic should be used to identify the data. In DI, regular expressions could be used to identify certain types of data. However, they are not always enough to differentiate the data. For example, when different letters or letter combinations have different meanings, it could be difficult for regular expressions to identify the meanings. Therefore, we recommend deriving a set of comprehensive conditional logic that can be used to categorise their semantics.

8   Conclusion

This paper investigates processes of DI allied with the TPC-DI benchmark. There is a set of typical data quality problems that may occur in the DI processes when using the TPC-DI. We define these problems and provide examples to demonstrate problem triggers and possible effects. These problems are further classified based on traditional data quality dimensions, which can be used to indicate that what data quality dimensions are important in DI. These dimensions can help researchers and practitioners to set the focus on data quality management, and reduce the cost and time to identify data quality dimensions. In addition, we propose a set of guidelines that can be used to avoid data quality problems when using the TPC-DI benchmark.

In the future, we will conduct experiments to examine which data quality dimensions can be improved and how to coordinate the trade-offs between the data quality dimensions. The different DI scenarios should be taken into account for further verifying the utility of the guidelines. In addition, as data is exploding and many organisations are building data warehouses in the context of Big Data, we will investigate DI and data quality problems allied with the TPC-DI in Big Data.

Acknowledgment. This publication is supported by the Science Foundation Ireland grant SFI/12/RC/2289 to Insight Centre for Data Analytics (www.insight-centre.org).

References

1. Batini, C., Scannapieco, M.: Erratum to: data and information quality: dimensions, principles and techniques. Data and Information Quality. DSA, p. E1. Springer, Cham (2016). https://doi.org/10.1007/978-3-319-24106-7_15
2. Dakrory, S.B., Mahmoud, T.M., Ali, A.A.: Automated ETL testing on the data quality of a data warehouse. Int. J. Comput. Appl. **131**(16), 9–16 (2015)
3. Darmont, J., Bentayeb, F., Boussaïd, O.: DWEB: a data warehouse engineering benchmark. In: Tjoa, A.M., Trujillo, J. (eds.) DaWaK 2005. LNCS, vol. 3589, pp. 85–94. Springer, Heidelberg (2005). https://doi.org/10.1007/11546849_9
4. Doan, A., Halevy, A., Ives, Z.: Principles of Data Integration. Elsevier, Amsterdam (2012)
5. Fehrenbacher, D., Helfert, M.: Contextual factors influencing perceived importance and trade-offs of information quality. Commun. Assoc. Inf. Syst. **30**(8) (2012)
6. Ge, M., Helfert, M., Jannach, D.: Information quality assessment: validating measurement dimensions and process. In: Proceedings of 19th European Conference on Information Systems, Helsinki, Finland (2011)
7. Ge, M., Helfert, M.: Impact of information quality on supply chain decisions. J. Comput. Inf. Syst. **53**(4), 59–67 (2013)

8. Helfert, M., Ge, M.: Big data quality-towards an explanation model in a smart city context. In: Proceedings of 21st International Conference on Information Quality, Ciudad Real, Spain (2016)

9. Helfert, M., Herrmann, C.: Introducing data quality management in data warehousing. In: Wang, R.Y. , Madnick, S.E., Pierce, E.M., Fisher, C.W. (eds.) Information Quality. Advances in Management Information Systems, vol. 1, pp. 135-150. M.E. Sharpe, Armonk, NY (2005)

10. Inmon, W.H., Strauss, D., Neushloss, G.: DW 2.0: The Architecture for the Next Generation of Data Warehousing: The Architecture for the Next Generation of Data Warehousing. Morgan Kaufmann, Massachusetts (2010)

11. Kimball, R., Caserta, J.: The Data Warehouse ETL Toolkit: Practical Techniques for Extracting, Cleaning, Conforming, and Delivering Data. Wiley, Hoboken (2011)

12. Knight, S.A., Burn, J.M.: Developing a framework for assessing information quality on the World Wide Web. Inf. Sci. Int. J. Emerg. Transdiscipl. 8(5), 159–172 (2005)

13. Majchrzak, T.A., Jansen, T., Kuchen, H.: Efficiency evaluation of open source ETL tools. In: Proceedings of the 2011 ACM Symposium on Applied Computing, pp. 287–294 (2011)

14. Poess, M., Rabl, T., Jacobsen, H.A., Caufield, B.: TPC-DI: the first industry benchmark for data integration. Proc. VLDB Endow. 7(13), 1367–1378 (2014)

15. Rabl, T., Frank, M., Sergieh, H.M., Kosch, H.: A data generator for cloud-scale benchmarking. In: Nambiar, R., Poess, M. (eds.) TPCTC 2010. LNCS, vol. 6417, pp. 41–56. Springer, Heidelberg (2011). https://doi.org/10.1007/978-3-642-18206-8_4

16. Singh, R., Singh, K.: A descriptive classification of causes of data quality problems in data warehousing. Int. J. Comput. Sci. Issues 7(3), 41–50 (2010)

17. Stvilia, B., Gasser, L., Twidale, M.B., Smith, L.C.: A framework for information quality assessment. J. Am. Soc. Inform. Sci. Technol. 58(12), 1720–1733 (2007)

18. TPC-DI. http://www.tpc.org/tpcdi/. Accessed 16 Dec 2016

19. TPC Benchmark DI: TPC Benchmark DI Stand Specification Version 1.1.0. Transaction Processing Performance Council (2014)

20. Vassiliadis, P.: A survey of extract-transform-load technology. Int. J. Data Warehous. Data Mining 5(3), 1–27 (2009)

21. Warwicka, W., Johnsona, S., Bonda, J., Fletchera, G., Kanellakisa, P.: A framework to assess healthcare data quality. Europ. J. Soc. Behav. Sci. 13(2), 1730 (2015)

22. Wang, R.Y.: A product perspective on total data quality management. Commun. ACM 41(2), 58–65 (1998)

23. Wang, R.Y., Strong, D.M.: Beyond accuracy: what data quality means to data consumers. J. Manag. Inf. Syst. 12(4), 5–33 (1996)

24. Wyatt, L., Caufield, B., Pol, D.: Principles for an ETL benchmark. In: Nambiar, R., Poess, M. (eds.) TPCTC 2009. LNCS, vol. 5895, pp. 183–198. Springer, Heidelberg (2009). https://doi.org/10.1007/978-3-642-10424-4_14

25. Yang, Q., Ge, M., Helfert, M.: Guidelines of data quality issues for data integration in the context of the TPC-DI benchmark. In: 19th International Conference on Enterprise Information System (2017)

Efficient Filter-Based Algorithms
for Exact Set Similarity Join on GPUs

Rafael David Quirino, Sidney Ribeiro-Junior, Leonardo Andrade Ribeiro[✉],
and Wellington Santos Martins

Instituto de Informatica, Universidade Federal de Goias (UFG), Alameda Palmeiras,
Quadra D, Campus Samambaia, 74001-970 Goiania, Goias, Brazil
{rafaelquirino,sydneyribeirojunior,laribeiro,wellington}@inf.ufg.br

Abstract. Set similarity join is a core operation for text data integration, cleaning, and mining. Most state-of-the-art solutions rely on inherently sequential, CPU-based algorithms. In this paper, we propose a parallel algorithm for the set similarity joins harnessing the power of GPU systems through filtering techniques and divide-and-conquer strategies that scale well with data size. Furthermore, we also present parallel algorithms for all data pre-processing phases. As a result, we have an end-to-end solution to the set similarity join problem, which receives input text data and outputs pairs of similar strings and is entirely executed on the GPU. Our experimental results on standard datasets show substantial speedups over the fastest algorithms in the literature.

Keywords: Advanced query processing
High performance computing · Parallel set similarity join · GPU

1 Introduction

In the last few decades, there have been substantial improvements in database systems, in part due to its commercial importance, usefulness and extensive testing throughout the years. And yet, managing complex data objects in these systems remains a challenge. In fact, many operations appropriate for simple objects are often ineffective for complex ones. As a prime example, operations based on equality tests, which are ubiquitously used in database management tasks, often cannot capture the subtle relations between complex objects. This observation highlights the need for similarity calculations on such data.

Set similarity join returns all pairs of data objects—represented by sets of features—from some data collection, for which the result of a similarity function is not less than a given threshold. The problem of efficiently evaluating set similarity joins has attracted growing attention over the years [1–8], as volume and complexity of data increase in the current Big Data era. It is both an important operation by itself, and as part of more advanced data processing tasks, including integration [9], cleaning [2], and mining of data [10].

© Springer International Publishing AG, part of Springer Nature 2018
S. Hammoudi et al. (Eds.): ICEIS 2017, LNBIP 321, pp. 74–95, 2018.
https://doi.org/10.1007/978-3-319-93375-7_5

Assessing the exact similarity between complex objects is costly. Thus, a naïve algorithm comparing all pairs of objects would be prohibitively expensive. Moreover, for textual data, the infamous *curse of dimensionality* becomes very apparent, since text data representations are often sparse and high-dimensional. Set similarity functions are very attractive in this context because predicates involving such functions can be equivalently expressed as a set overlap constraint. As a result, set similarity join is reduced to the problem of identifying set pairs with enough overlap.

In this scenario, it becomes clear that parallel solutions are welcome. Today, virtually all processors support parallelism through the use of multiple cores. Multi-core processing is a growing trend in the industry, and it has been followed by the so-called many-core architectures like GPUs (graphical cards used for general purpose computing). Many-core processors, also known as accelerators, have a large number of processing units—hundreds or thousands—but in the form of slower and simpler cores. Recent developments and the affordability of GPUs have made them attractive to scientists in many areas. GPUs are designed for massive multi-threaded parallelism and are inherently energy-efficient because they are optimized for throughput and performance per watt. However, GPUs have a different architecture and memory organization from traditional CPUs. Therefore, considerable parallelism (tens of thousands of threads) and an adequate use of its hardware resources are needed to fully exploit its capabilities. This fact imposes some constraints in terms of designing appropriate algorithms and new implementation approaches.

In this paper, we present *fgssjoin*, a fine-grained parallel algorithm for the set similarity join problem, which exploits state-of-the-art filtering techniques. The proposed parallel algorithm is based on a divide-and-conquer strategy and partitioning of the data set in blocks in such a way that all blocks are indexed and queried against all others, following an index-filter-verify cycle. This strategy ensures that any data set can be processed regardless of the GPU memory available. It also allows the skipping of some blocks from being queried against others for which no match could be generated. We provide a detailed description of the implementation of *fgssjoin*, which efficiently utilizes GPU resources. We experimentally evaluate *fgssjoin* on standard datasets. Our results show that our algorithm achieves significant speedups over the best sequential and parallel set similarity join algorithms and exhibits good scalability as the data size increases.

This article is an extended and revised version of an earlier conference paper [11]. As part of the new material, we include parallel algorithms and non-trivial, GPU-based implementations for all data pre-processing phases required by *fgssjoin*—in the previous version, this pre-processing was performed beforehand on the CPU. As a result, we now have an end-to-end solution to the set similarity join problem, which is entirely executed on the GPU.

The remainder of this paper is organized as follows. Section 2 covers related work. Section 3 defines the set similarity join problem and introduces important concepts. Section 4 presents an overview of the architecture and programming model of a GPU. Sections 5 and 6 describe our parallel algorithms and implementations respectively. Section 7 presents the experimental evaluation, while Sect. 8 concludes the paper.

2   Related Work

There is an extensive literature on efficiently answering set similarity joins [1–3,5–7,12]. Most proposals have focused on sequential, CPU-based algorithms—a comprehensive experimental evaluation of state-of-the-art techniques is presented by Mann et al. [13]. The *filtering-and-verification* framework is prevalently adopted by such algorithms: in the filtering phase, various filtering schemes are used to prune set pairs that cannot meet the similarity threshold; in the verification phase, the actual similarity computation is then performed on each of the remaining set pairs and those deemed as similar are sent to the output. Popular filtering schemes are *length-based filter* [1,12], *prefix filter* [1,2,6,7], and *positional filter* [5]. Verification can be optimized by employing a merge-like procedure that stops earlier on set pairs that do not satisfy the similarity constraint. Our proposed algorithm exploits all those optimizations on many-core architectures.

Another popular type of string similarity join employs constraints based on the edit distance, which is defined by the minimum number of character-editing operations—insertion, deletion, and substitution—to make two strings equal. As one can derive set overlap bounds from the edit distance [14], the filtering phase of our proposal can be readily used to substantially reduce the number of expensive distance computations; furthermore, edit distance also lends itself to efficient GPU implementation [15].

Lieberman et al. [16] presented a parallel similarity join algorithm for distance functions of the Minkowski family (e.g., Euclidean distance). The algorithm first maps the smaller input dataset to a set of space-filling curves and then performs interval searches for each point in the other dataset in parallel. The overall performance of the algorithm drastically decreases as the number of dimensions increases (see Fig. 5b in [16]) because every additional dimension requires the construction of a new space-filling curve. Thus, this approach can be prohibitively expensive on text data, whose representation typically involves several thousands of dimensions.

Approximate set similarity joins resort to data reduction techniques to speed up processing time. The most popular technique in this context is Locality Sensitive Hashing (LSH) [17], which is based on hashing functions that are approximately similarity-preserving. However, LSH-based algorithms may miss valid output pairs. In contrast, our approach always produces an exact result.

Cruz et al. [8] proposes an approximate set similarity join algorithm designed for GPU. The Jaccard similarity between two sets is estimated using MinHash [18], an LSH scheme for Jaccard. MinHash can be orthogonally combined with our algorithm to reduce set size and, thus, obtain greater scalability.

Recent work proposed to perform set similarity joins on the MapReduce framework [4,19]. In general, these proposals apply a partition scheme to send dissimilar strings to different *reducers* and, thus, avoid unnecessary similarity calculations; to some extent, the partition scheme plays the role of the filtering phase in sequential algorithms. Existing partition schemes are based on prefix filtering [4], symmetric set difference [19], and vertical partitioning [20]. We plan to investigate the integration of *fgssjoin* into a distributed platform to accelerate local computation in future work.

To the best of our knowledge, the *gSSJoin* algorithm, proposed by Ribeiro-Junior et al. [21], is the only existing GPU-based algorithm for exact set similarity join. Similarly to our approach, *gSSJoin* first builds an inverted index before performing similarity computations. However, *gSSJoin* does not employ any filtering technique to reduce the comparison space. We compare our proposal with *gSSJoin* in Sect. 7.

3   Background

In this section, we provide background material on the subject area. First, we present basic concepts and formally define the set similarity join problem. Then, we review various filtering techniques are reviewed. Finally, we provide a high-level description of a general set similarity join algorithm.

3.1   Basic Concepts and Problem Definition

In order to express text data as sets of features, we use the notion of *q-grams*, which are *tokens*[1] obtained by "sliding" a window of size q over the characters of a given string. For example, if we have two strings $s_1 = $ "Computation" and $s_2 = $ "Compilation", we have the following *2-gram* sets:

$$x = \{Co, om, mp, pu, ut, ta, at, ti, io, on\}$$
$$y = \{Co, om, mp, pi, il, la, at, ti, io, on\}$$

Applying the Jaccard similarity function (JS) to the strings above yields:

$$JS(x, y) = \frac{|x \cap y|}{|x \cup y|} = \frac{7}{10 + 10 - 7} \cong 0,538.$$

Definition 1 *(Set Similarity Join). Let U be a universe of features, C be a set collection where every set consists of a number of features from U, $Sim(x, y)$ be a similarity function that maps two sets from C to a number in $[0, 1]$ and γ be a number in $[0, 1]$ (called threshold). Set similarity join is the operation of defining the set S of all pairs of sets from C, for which $Sim(x, y) \geq \gamma$.*

3.2   Filtering Techniques

We focus on a general class of set similarity functions, for which the similarity predicate can be equivalently represented as a set overlap constraint. Specifically, we express the original similarity predicate in terms of an overlap lower bound (overlap bound, for short) [2].

---

[1] The terms feature and token are used interchangeably throughout the paper.

Table 1. Set similarity functions [11].

Function	Definition	Overlap(x,y)	[minsize(x), maxsize(x)]
Jaccard	$\dfrac{\lvert x \cap y\rvert}{\lvert x \cup y\rvert}$	$\dfrac{\gamma}{1+\gamma}(\lvert x\rvert + \lvert y\rvert)$	$\left[\gamma\lvert x\rvert, \dfrac{\lvert x\rvert}{\gamma}\right]$
Dice	$\dfrac{2\lvert x \cap y\rvert}{\lvert x\rvert + \lvert y\rvert}$	$\dfrac{\gamma(\lvert x\rvert + \lvert y\rvert)}{2}$	$\left[\dfrac{\gamma\lvert x\rvert}{2-\gamma}, \dfrac{(2-\gamma)\lvert x\rvert}{\gamma}\right]$
Cosine	$\dfrac{\lvert x \cap y\rvert}{\sqrt{\lvert x\rvert\,\lvert y\rvert}}$	$\gamma\sqrt{\lvert x\rvert\,\lvert y\rvert}$	$\left[\gamma^2\lvert x\rvert, \dfrac{\lvert x\rvert}{\gamma^2}\right]$

Definition 2 (Overlap Bound). *Let x and y be sets of features, Sim be a set similarity function, and γ be a similarity threshold. The overlap bound between x and y relative to Sim, denoted by $overlap(x,y)$[2], is a function that maps γ and the sizes of x and y to a real value, s.t. $Sim(x,y) \geq \gamma \Leftrightarrow \lvert x \cap y\rvert \geq overlap(x,y)$.*

This way, the similarity join problem can be reduced to a set overlap problem, in which we need to obtain all pairs (x,y) whose overlap is not less than $overlap(x,y)$. The set overlap formulation enables the derivation of size bounds. Intuitively, observe that $\lvert x \cap y\rvert \leq \lvert x\rvert$ whenever $\lvert y\rvert \geq \lvert x\rvert$, i.e., set overlap and thus similarity are trivially bounded by $\lvert x\rvert$. Exploiting the similarity function definition, it is possible to derive tighter bounds allowing immediate pruning of candidate pairs whose sizes are incompatible according to the given threshold.

Definition 3 (Size Bounds). *Let x be a set of features, Sim be a set similarity function, and γ be a similarity threshold. The size bounds of x relative to Sim are functions, denoted by $minsize(x)$ and $maxsize(x)$, that maps γ and the size of x to a real value, s.t. $\forall y$, if $Sim(x,y) \geq \gamma$ then $minsize(x) \leq \lvert y\rvert \leq maxsize(x)$.*

Therefore, given a set x we can safely ignore all sets whose size do not fall within the interval $[minsize(x), maxsize(x)]$, because they can not match with x according to the given threshold. Table 1 shows the overlap and size bounds of three of the most widely used similarity functions: Jaccard, Dice, and Cosine [1,5,12,22,23].

If we ensure that all sets in the collection have its features under the same total order O, we can combine overlap and size bounds to prune even more the comparison space through the *prefix filtering* technique. The idea is to derive a new overlap constraint to be applied only to subsets of the original sets. For any two sets x and y, under the order O, if $\lvert x \cap y\rvert \geq \alpha$ then the subsets consisting of the first $\lvert x\rvert - \alpha + 1$ elements of x and the first $\lvert y\rvert - \alpha + 1$ elements of y must share at least one element [1,2]. These subsets are called *prefix filtering subsets* and will be denoted by $pref(x)$. The exact prefix size is determined by $overlap(x,y)$, but it depends on each matching pair. Given a set x, the question is how to determine $\lvert pref(x)\rvert$ such that it suffices to identify all matches of x. Clearly, we have to take the largest prefix in relation to all y. The prefix formulation given

---

[2] For ease of notation, the threshold γ is omitted in the definitions of this section.

above tell us that the prefix size is inversely proportional to $overlap(x, y)$, and the former increases monotonically with y. Therefore, $|pref(x)|$ is largest when $|y|$ is smallest. The smallest possible size of y, such that the overlap constraint can be satisfied, is $minsize(x)$.

Definition 4 (Max-prefix). *Let x be a set of features. The max-prefix of x, denoted by $maxpref(x)$, is its smallest prefix needed for identifying $\forall y$ that $|x \cap y| \geq overlap(x, y)$. $|maxpref(x)| = |x| - \lceil minsize(x) \rceil + 1$.*

We can also impose an order in the whole collection. If we sort C by its sets sizes we can guarantee that x is only matched with y if $|y| \geq |x|$. In this case the size of $pref(x)$ can be reduced. Instead of using $maxpref(x)$ we can obtain a shorter prefix by using $overlap(x, x)$ to calculate the prefix size [3,5,23].

Definition 5 (Mid-prefix). *Let x be a set of features. The mid-prefix of x, denoted by $midpref(x)$, is its smallest prefix needed for identifying $\forall y \geq x$ that $|x \cap y| \geq overlap(x, y)$. $|midpref(x)| = |x| - \lceil overlap(x, x) \rceil + 1$.*

Further optimization is possible. We can sort each set by its features frequencies in the collection, in increasing order, which precipitates the least frequent ones to the prefixes, thus filtering out even more pairs (since less frequent ones are likely to have fewer matches). We can also exploit the positional information between common features in two sets, under the same order, to verify if the remaining features in both sets are enough to meet the given threshold [5].

3.3 General Algorithm

As already mentioned, most CPU-based set similarity join algorithms follow a filtering-and-verification framework. Additionally, an inverted index typically employed to quickly identify candidate set pairs. A high-level description of the framework is presented by Algorithm 1. An inverted list I_t stores all sets containing a token t in their prefix. The input collection C is scanned and, for each set r, its prefix tokens are used to find candidate sets in the corresponding inverted lists (lines 2–4). Each candidate s is checked using filters, such as positional [5] and length-based filtering [1] (line 5); if the candidate passes through, the actual similarity computation is performed in the refine step and r and s are added to the result if they are similar (line 6). Finally, r is appended to the inverted lists of its prefix tokens (line 7). An important observation is that Algorithm 1 is intrinsically sequential: sets, prefix tokens, and candidate sets are processed sequentially, while the inverted index is dynamically created.

Algorithm 1 is actually a self-join. Its extension to a binary join is trivial: we first index the smaller collection and then go through the larger collection to identify matching pairs.

Algorithm 1. General set similarity join algorithm.

    Input: A sorted set collection $\mathcal{C}$, a threshold τ
    Output: A set S containing all pairs (r, s) s.t. $Sim(r, s) \geq \gamma$
1 $I_1, I_2, \ldots I_{|\mathcal{U}|} \leftarrow \varnothing, S \leftarrow \varnothing$
2 **foreach** $r \in \mathcal{C}$ **do**
3   **foreach** $t \in pref_\beta(r)$ **do**
4   **foreach** $s \in I_t$ **do**
5   **if not** *filter* (r, s)
6              $S \leftarrow S \cup \textit{refine}(r, s)$
7        $I_t \leftarrow I_t \cup \{r\}$

8 **return** S

---

4 GPU Architecture and Programming Model

Next we provide a brief description of a GPU architecture and its corresponding programming model (cf. [24] for more details).

An abstracted architecture view of a GPU is illustrated in Fig. 1. This architecture is common to most GPUs currently available. The GPU architecture has two levels of parallelism, where P streaming multi-processors (SMs) are at the first level and p streaming processors (SPs) within each multi-processor. Thus a parallel program can be first divided into blocks of computation that can run independently on the P SMs (fat cores), without communicating with each other. These blocks have to be further divided into smaller tasks (threads) that execute on the SPs (thin cores), but with each thread being able to communicate with other threads in the same block. Each of these threads has access to a larger global memory as well as to a small but fast shared memory and registers.

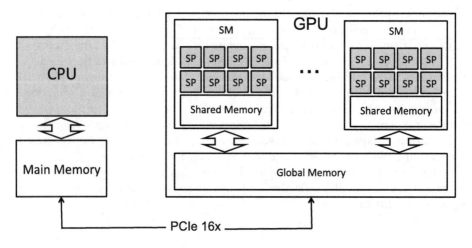

Fig. 1. GPU architecture [11].

The GPU consists of a Multiple SIMD (Single Instruction Multiple Data) processor. Each SIMD unit consists of a SM containing many SP cores. For any given clock cycle, each SP executes the same instruction, but operates on different data. The GPU supports thousands of light-weight concurrent threads and, unlike the CPU threads, the overhead of creation and switching is negligible. The threads on each SM are organized into groups that share computation resources such as registers and shared memory. A thread group is divided into multiple schedule units, called *warps*, that are dynamically scheduled on the SM.

Since the SPs work in a SIMD-like manner, if threads in a warp must perform different operations, such as going through branches, these operations will be executed serially, rather than in parallel. Additionally, if a thread stalls at a memory operation, the entire warp will be stalled until the memory access is performed. In this case the SM selects and switches to another available warp. The GPU global memory is typically measured in gigabytes of capacity. It is an off-chip memory and has both a high bandwidth and a high access latency. To hide the high latency of this memory, it is important to have more threads than the number of SPs and to have threads in a warp accessing consecutive memory addresses that can be easily coalesced. The GPU also provides a fast on-chip shared memory which is accessible by all SPs of an SM. The size of this memory is small but it has a low latency and it can be used as a software-controlled cache. Another important data movement channel is the PCIExpress connection, whereby CPU and GPU can exchange data between each other's address space but at a much slower speed.

The GPU programming model requires that part of the application runs on the CPU while the computationally-intensive part is accelerated by the GPU. The programmer has to modify his application to take the computation-intensive kernels and map them to the GPU. The general flow for a program consists of the following. First the program running on the CPU allocates memory to the GPU and copies data to this area. Then the GPU code (kernel function) is started on the GPU. The kernel executes its code in parallel on the GPU and copies the results back to the CPU main memory. A new iteration can take place or the CPU program can deallocate memory on the GPU and terminate.

A GPU program utilizes parallelism through the data-parallel SPMD (Single Program Multiple Data) kernel function. During implementation, the programmer can configure the number of threads to be used. Threads execute data parallel computations of the kernel and are organized in groups called *thread blocks*. Thread blocks are further organized into a grid structure. When a kernel is launched, the blocks within a grid are distributed to idle SMs.

Threads of a block are divided into warps, the schedule unit used by the SMs, leaving for the GPU to decide in which order and when to execute each warp. Threads that belong to different blocks cannot communicate explicitly and have to rely on the global memory to share their results. Threads within a thread block are executed by the SPs of a single SM and can communicate throught the SM shared memory. Furthermore, each thread inside a block has its own registers and private local memory and uses a global thread block index, and a local thread index within a thread block, to uniquely identify its data.

5 Parallel Set Similarity Join

In this section, we present our parallel algorithms to prepare de data (pre-process) and to solve the set similarity join problem exploiting various filtering techniques. We describe the three key phases, indexing, filtering and verification, and also our block partitioning strategy.

5.1 Pre-processing

All the following phases of the similarity join rely on a data transformation step performed on the input strings. First, we remove accents and convert all characters to lowercase. Then, we map all strings to sets of q-grams (tokens in our token-based approach), according to some specified q, which represents its features. An important point here is the observation that sets can not have repeating elements. To solve that we concatenate each q-gram with a numeric value representing its occurrence in the string. For instance, if we have the string "To be or not to be", its q-gram set will be { "to0", "o_0", "_b0", "be0", ..., "to1", "to_1", "_b1", "be1"}, with the first occurrence of "to" and "be" being different from the second.

A dictionary is created with only the distinct "tokens" (i.e., ids for the hash values) of the set collection. It is also necessary to create a frequency table. This table will serve some purposes. First, it is necessary in order to create the whole inverted index in the GPU memory, since we need to know the number of distinct features for the algorithm to work. Second, it is necessary to know the frequency of each token in the collection, because we will sort each set in increasing order of frequency (leaving the least frequent ones in the prefix of the set). Additionally, we also sort the whole collection in decreasing order of set cardinality.

All these procedures could be done by simple sequential algorithms based on hash tables. But since our proposal is to use many-core accelerators to improve performance, we need a new strategy. Hash tables are not well suited for GPUs, due to their irregular access patterns. For this reason, we developed an algorithm using primitive operations like sorting and prefix sums, which are optimized for many-core devices. This new algorithm enables fast pre-processing of data on the GPU, and completes our parallel end-to-end solution.

Algorithm 2 describes our approach to parallel pre-processing based on a series of parallel sorting and prefix-sum operations. We begin with the creation of a number of auxiliary arrays (lines 1–7). First, all sets are concatenated into an array T. The indexes of each element in T are then stored in a second array T_i. We sort both T and T_i simultaneously using some ordering, such as the lexicographical order of the q-grams strings. Specifically, sorting is performed on T and whenever some pair in T is swapped, we also swap the corresponding pair in T_i. As a result, two new arrays are created, T' and T_i'. We can easily derive each token frequency by simply scanning through T', thus generating table D (dictionary) with columns D_t (tokens) and D_f (frequencies). As in the previous step, an array D_i is created storing the indexes of elements in D. We then assigns

Algorithm 2. *Pre-processing.*

> **input** : The collection C of token sets.
> **output**: A new collection C' of sets, with tokens replaced by frequency sorted IDs.

1 Create array T by concatenating all sets from C;
2 Create array T_i with the indexes of T;
3 Sort T and T_i, based on T, generating arrays T' and T'_i, respectively;
4 Create array D_f by scanning T' and counting terms frequencies;
5 Create array D_i with the indexes of array D_f;
6 Sort arrays D_f and D_i, based on D_f, generating arrays D'_f and D_{pos}, respectively;
7 Create array T_{id};
8 **forall the** $i \in 0..|D|$, **in parallel do**
9 | $T_{id}[D_{pos}[i]] \leftarrow D'_i[i]$;
10 **end**
11 Perform a parallel exclusive prefix sum over D_f generating array D_{scan};
12 **forall the** $i \in 0..|D|$, **in parallel do**
13 | **forall the** $j in T_{scan}[i]..T_{scan}[i] + D_f[i]$ **do**
14 | | $T[T'_i[j]] \leftarrow T_{id}[i]$;
15 | **end**
16 **end**

an ID to each token in such a way that less frequent tokens have smaller IDs. To this end, another simultaneous sorting is performed, this time with the columns D, using D_f as the base (sort by frequency). This produces a new table (D') with columns D'_t, D'_f and D_{pos}, sorted by token frequency, where D_{pos} (which is D_i sorted according to D_f) represents the positions of each entry of D' in D (an index to D). Since we also have D'_i as the indexes of entries in D', the key is to use this new table to finally create the array T_{id}, which will contain each token's ID with the desired properties aforementioned. Now, we can simply scan through D' entries taking D_{pos} as index and D'_i as value for T_{id} (lines 8–9). Formally: $\forall\ 0 < i < |D| : T_{id}[D_{pos}[i]] \leftarrow D'_i[i]$.

Finally, we need to swap elements in T by their correspondent IDs in T_{id}. The problem is that we need a way to find the instance of each token in T in order to replace it by it's ID, i.e. we need an index. Now we perform an exclusive prefix-sum over D_f, thus creating array D_{scan}. Now, for each token in D, in parallel, we can assign it's tokens their IDs as follows. Use D_{scan} to find the start of each token in T' and D_f to know how much tokens we have for this term. Then, scan that portion of T'_i taking the indexes in T containing a certain term and replacing it by it's corresponding ID. Formally:

$$\forall\ 0 < i < |D|\ and\ \forall\ T_{scan}[i] < j < T_{scan}[i] + D_f[i] : T[T'_i[j]] \leftarrow T_{id}[i].$$

The idea is that we need a list of IDs such that their numerical values represents the frequencies of its associated tokens. So, for instance, ID 0 represents the least frequent token. Also note that we need our token sets to be sorted numerically, because some properties of the filtering algorithm demands that. Thats why we need to perform two sorts, one to ensure an order of tokens according

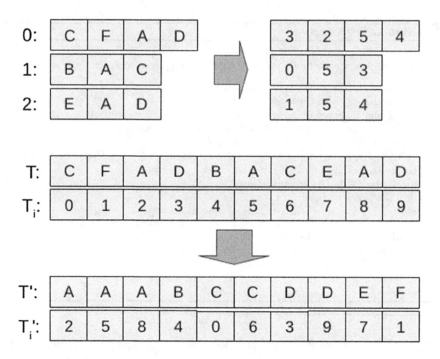

Fig. 2. First steps in the pre-processing algorithm. In this example we have 3 sets, with their tokens represented by capital letters. The first arrow represent the final conversion from tokens to frequency sorted IDs, e.g.'B' is the less frequent token in the 3 sets, thus receiving ID '0' and 'A' is the more frequent token, thus receiving ID '5'. The second arrow represent the process of simultaneous sorting of T and T_i using lexicographical order in T. The generated arrays T' and T_i' will serve as an index for the later replacing process.

to frequency, and one to enables us to have numerically sorted token sets while keeping the information of frequency for each token. This series of parallel sorts and prefix sums may seem over complicated, but their are necessary to ensure a good utilization of the GPU architecture. Performance requirements often steers us in the direction of more complicated, specific solutions (Fig. 3).

5.2 Indexing Phase

In state-of-the-art algorithms, the inverted index lists are dynamically created during the filtering process, which makes them inherently sequential algorithms: sets are sequentially probed against the index and the state of the lists in one iteration depends on their state in the previous iteration (recall Sect. 3.3). To avoid this issue, we need to create the entire inverted index statically before the filtering phase, as show in Fig. 4. In this way, we can perform probes independently, because the index is always complete.

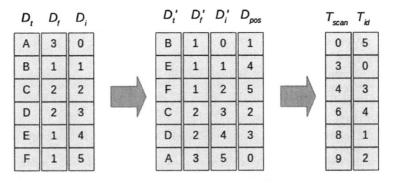

Fig. 3. Illustration of tables D and D' during execution of Algorithm 2. Table D is created by scanning through array T' from Fig. 2. Table D' is created by simultaneously sorting columns in D based on D_f. T_{scan} is the result of an exclusive prefix sum over D_f. Finally, each element in T_{id} is obtained by using D_{pos} as index and D_i' as value.

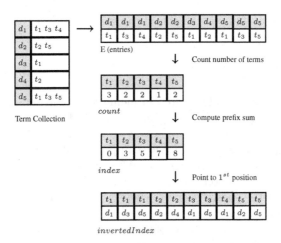

Fig. 4. Creating the inverted index [11].

Algorithm 3 describes our parallel algorithm to create the inverted index. We first concatenate all features from all sets in a unique array called E—note that V represents our dictionary (vocabulary). Let $e \in E$ be an entry that contains three fields: the set it belongs to, a feature and its positional information. Thus, the sets are reduced to an array of tuples (s_i, f_i, p_i). This will be important in the positional filtering step of the filtering algorithm. When creating the entries for the inverted index algorithm, we only add mid-prefix features to the array E. The concepts described in Sect. 3.2 allows us to use only max-prefix features from the sets to probe against mid-prefix features in the index, if we guarantee that matches will only occur between bigger probing sets and smaller indexed sets. We then calculate a count array, which counts the occurrence of each feature,

---

Algorithm 3. *DataIndexing(E)*.

---

input : Array of entries $E[0 .. |\mathcal{E}| - 1]$.
output: *count, index, invertedIndex*.

1 array of integers $count[0 .. |\mathcal{V}| - 1]$;
2 array of integers $index[0 .. |\mathcal{V}| - 1]$;
3 $invertedIndex[0 .. |\mathcal{E}| - 1]$
4 Initialize *count* array with zeros;
5 Count the occurrences of each token, in **parallel**, on the input and accumulates in *count*.
6 Perform an exclusive **parallel** prefix sum on *count* and store the result in *index*.
7 **forall the** $t \in E$, *in parallel* **do**
8 | Copy t to *invertedIndex*, according to *index* and update *index*.
9 **end**
10 **Return** the arrays: *count, index,* and *invertedIndex*.

---

and perform a prefix sum on it to obtain the starting indexes of each feature list in the inverted index.

5.3 Filtering Phase

With the entire inverted index stored in memory, we can set each processor to perform one probe (process one set) against the index, using only max-prefix features from the set. One problem is how to accumulate the scores (intersections) between all pairs of sets. Since we can potentially have all set pairs being candidates (specially for lower thresholds), we need "buckets" for all possible pairs of sets in the collection. Hence, we create an $n \times n$ matrix called b (the buckets to contain the partial scores), where n is the number of sets in our collection). It contains the partial intersection (i.e., ,partial scores) between probed and indexed sets, because only parts of the sets (the prefixes) are used in the process in this stage. After performing the filtering phase, we need to compact the content of the scores table to obtain only the positive scores, i.e., the candidate pairs. To this end, we create an additional $n \times n$ array, the *compacted_buckets* array. After the compaction, this array will contain the indexes of positive scores in the table. To reduce memory requirements ($n \times n$ array), we partition the data collection in blocks and, thus, we are be able to process collections of any size. Figure 5 illustrates the state of the memory after the filtering phase. Note that each row in the first matrix represents a set being queried against the index while each column represents an indexed set.

Algorithm 4 is similar to state-of-the-art filtering based algorithms in literature, but here it is executed by each GPU processor (core) for one probing set. Henceforth, we refer to a set being probed against the index as a *query*, and to a set in the index as a *source* (because they generate the index). For each query, the filtering algorithm has two loops, one to iterate on the max-prefix features of the query, and one to consult the sources in the inverted list corresponding to each feature. Then we test if the query id is smaller than the source id, i.e., we

f_0	f_1	f_2	f_3
S_0	S_0	S_0	S_1
S_2	S_1	S_1	S_2
	S_3	S_4	S_3
			S_3

S_0	f_0	f_1	f_2
S_1	f_1	f_2	f_3
S_2	f_0	f_3	
S_3	f_1	f_3	
S_4	f_2	f_3	

0	3	0	-1	0
0	-1	0	2	0
7	0	0	4	-1
2	-1	-1	0	0
0	-1	0	1	0

1	8	10	13	15
23	-	-	-	-
-	-	-	-	-
-	-	-	-	-
-	-	-	-	-

Fig. 5. Memory after the filtering phase, with inverted index, sets, the array b (buckets) of partial scores and its corresponding array of compacted buckets (with the indexes to the elements in b that have positive values), respectively. Since we have five sets in this example, our tables are 5×5. The numbers in the first table are the partial scores after the filtering phase. Negative (-1) numbers represents $-\infty$. The second table is a compacted version of the first; its values (i.e., the absolute indexes of the selected elements from the first table) represent the candidate pairs and are provided to the verification phase [11].

will only match set x with set y if $x.id < y.id$. This test avoids processing the same pair twice as well as ensures that query sets are bigger than the sources, since the whole collection is sorted in decreasing set cardinality order. When we obtain a match we test if the source is smaller than the query *minsize*. If it is, we can stop iterating on the current inverted index list, because each list is also sorted in decreasing order of set cardinality. Finally, only for pairs (buckets in *partial_scores*) not marked with $-\infty$, we test if the remaining features are enough to meet the threshold; note that $x.fpos$ is the positional information of the current feature in set x. If they are, we accumulate the score, if not we mark them with $-\infty$, so that they will not be considered anymore. In the end, array b will contain marked buckets, 0 buckets and positive ones, the former being compacted (their absolute indexes) in the array *compacted_buckets* (*cb* for short). The compacted indexes represent the pairs, since the bidimensional indexes of the matrix (which represents the ids of *query* and *source* sets) can be calculated from the absolute index. It is the resulting candidate pairs list, which will be passed to the verification phase, which is discussed next.

5.4 Verification Phase

The verification phase ultimately produces the final result. It simply consists in performing the remaining score calculation on each candidate pair to verify if there is enough overlap to qualify them as a match. This can be trivially processed in parallel by making each processor perform verification on one candidate pair. We can use the partial score to reduce a bit the overlap calculations. By comparing the last feature from the prefixes of the two sets in a candidate pair, we can start the overlap calculation in the position of the feature with the smaller id in its own set and in the beginning with the other. The initial value is the partial score of the candidate pair, because any match with prefix features

---

Algorithm 4. *Filtering*

---

      input : The collection of sets S, the inverted index I, the array of buckets b, a
               threshold τ
      output: The candidate pairs

1 Initialize b with zeros;
2 **for** *each set x in S, **in parallel*** **do**
3   **for** *each feature f in x's maxprefix* **do**
4   **for** *each set y in f's inverted list* **do**
5   **if** $x.id < y.id$ **then**
6   **if** $|y| < minsize(x)$ **then**
7                 $b[x.id][y.id] = -\infty$;
8   break;
9   **else**
10   **if** $b[x.id][y.id] \geq 0$ **then**
11                 $rem = min(|x| - x.fpos, |y| - y.fpos)$;
12                 $ps = b[x.id][y.id]$;
13                 $m = overlap(x,y)$;   /*τ omitted*/
14
15   **if** $ps + 1 + rem < m$ **then**
16                 $b[x.id][y.id] = -\infty$;
17   **else**
18                 $b[x.id][y.id] += 1$;
19   **end**
20   **end**
21   **end**
22   **end**
23   **end**
24 **end**
25 **end**

---

in this set was already calculated in the filtering phase. In each step of the overlap calculation, we also test if the remaining features are enough to meet the threshold, marking those which are not. Those not marked by this process form the result set, the similar pairs according to the threshold and the similarity function.

5.5   Block Partitioning and Optimization

The need for quadratic arrays in the filtering phase sets a limit for the size of the databases we can process. To solve this problem, we need to partition our search space into blocks that fit into the memory requirements. But then we must process this blocks in such a way that all sets are matched against each other. To achieve this we proceed similarly in the filtering phase, but we index the set's prefixes of one block, and use all the others before it to query its index. In this way we create an index-filter-verify cycle with the blocks, gradually aggregating the results, which can be flushed to the disk if approaching the memory limit. By using the previous blocks as queries, as shown in Fig. 6, we ensure that only bigger sets are queried against smaller ones in the index, since the collection is sorted in decreasing cardinality order. This fact also allows us to skip some blocks from being queried against others for which its first set's *maxsize* is smaller than the query block's last set. In such cases, it is guaranteed that no match can be obtained from the two blocks. This significantly improves performance for higher thresholds. Another consequence of block partitioning is the possibility of running in distributed memory systems, since we can process each probe/index block pair in one node in parallel, executing its own index-filter-verify calculations.

Algorithm 5. *Verification.*

---

input : The array of buckets b with partial scores, the array of compacted buckets cb with the indexes of the candidate buckets (with positive scores), the array of features f of each set and a threshold τ

output: The similar pairs list L

1 Initialize a list L;
2 **for** *each index idx in cb, in parallel* **do**
3 $\quad$ $x, y = calc\_indexes(idx)$;   /**x.id* < *y.id**/
4 $\quad$ $m = overlap(x, y)$;
5 $\quad$ $score = b[x.id][s.id]$;
6 $\quad$ $f1 = f[x.id][|maxpref(x)|]$;
7 $\quad$ $f2 = f[y.id][|midpref(y)|]$;
8 $\quad$ $p1, p2 = 0$;
9 $\quad$ **if** $f1 < f2$ **then**
10 $\quad\quad$ $p1 = |maxpref(x)|$;
11 $\quad$ **else**
12 $\quad\quad$ $p2 = |midpref(y)|$;
13 $\quad$ **end**
14 $\quad$ **while** $p1 < |x|$ *and* $p2 < |y|$ **do**
15 $\quad\quad$ $f1 = f[x][p1]$; $f2 = f[y][p2]$;
16 $\quad\quad$ **if** $(p1 == |x| - 1$ *and* $f1 < f2)$ *or* $(p2 == |y| - 1$ *and* $f2 < f1)$ **then**
17 $\quad\quad\quad$ *break*;
18 $\quad\quad$ **end**
19 $\quad\quad$ **if** $f1 == f2$ **then**
20 $\quad\quad\quad$ $score+ = 1$; $p1+ = 1$; $p2+ = 1$;
21 $\quad\quad$ **else**
22 $\quad\quad\quad$ $s = f1 < f2 ? x : y$; $p = f1 < f2 ? p1 : p2$;
23 $\quad\quad\quad$ $rem = |s| - p$;
24 $\quad\quad\quad$ **if** $rem + score < m$ **then**
25 $\quad\quad\quad\quad$ *break*;
26 $\quad\quad\quad$ **else**
27 $\quad\quad\quad\quad$ $p+ = 1$;
28 $\quad\quad\quad$ **end**
29 $\quad\quad$ **end**
30 $\quad\quad$ **if** $score \geq m$ **then**
31 $\quad\quad\quad$ include pair (x,y) in L;
32 $\quad\quad$ **end**
33 $\quad$ **end**
34 **end**

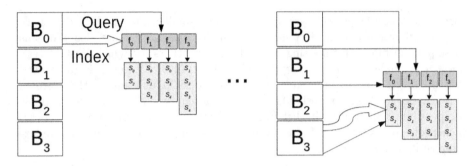

Fig. 6. The block processing scheme. "Query" means probing against the index, applying filtering schemes, and verifying selected candidates [11].

6   Implementation Details

In this section, we are going to give details about the implementation of the whole system, end-to-end, including pre-processing phase, indexing, filtering and verification.

6.1   Pre-processing Implementation Details

In order to execute the program, we need the data in a specific format. We gave our format the extension *.sets*, as they represent the sets obtained from the registers in the data set. The dataset must have each set in a line in the file. For simplicity, we are not dealing with neither multiple fields nor weighted features, although these features can be incorporated with a few changes. Our *.sets* format is a binary file with a header consisting of 12 bytes, encoding three unsigned integers (each with 4 bytes). The first represents the number of sets, the second represents the number of tokens (features), and the third the number of unique tokens in the dictionary. The header is followed by three arrays. The first two have their sizes equal to the number of sets (the first number in the header). The third array (*tkns*) has the size equal to the total number of tokens, i.e., all tokens from all sets are concatenated in one array. This format makes it easier to transfer the tokens to the GPU memory. All the sets are concatenated in one big array, thus we need to store the positions of each set in this array. The first array (*pos*) does just that, with each element *pos[i]* representing the position of set i in array *tkns*. The second array contains the size of each set.

Creating the token sets requires a few steps. First of all we need to convert the registers from the dataset (the strings) into sets of q-grams (our tokens). Then we need to create a dictionary where tokens and their frequencies are stored. Then, each term in the dictionary must be given an identification number in the range (0..*num_terms*) where *num_terms* represents the size of the dictionary. This is necessary for the parallel indexing algorithm to work. Finally we need to sort each set's tokens in increasing order of frequency, and the whole collection of sets in decreasing order of size. There are several kernels involved in this phase. The first one performs the pre-processing of the strings in the dataset (conversion to lowercase and removal of accents as well as multi-byte characters). The others are related to the primitive operations. We use the prefix sum implementation of the *Thrust* library from the CUDA toolkit. The sorting kernel is an adaptation of the *Bitonic Sort* algorithm. The output of this phase is the file with the format described above. It will be read by the similarity search program which will extract its sets.

6.2   Set Similarity Join Implementation Details

The set similarity join implementation consists of three main kernels together with other smaller kernels responsible for common parallel subtasks used by the main ones, such as parallel counting and prefix sum in the inverted index, creation and compaction in the filtering phase. The three main kernels are scheduled by the block processing function, which partitions the dataset into blocks and executes the block processing scheme (see Fig. 6). The block processing scheme executes the index-filter-verify cycle by calling their three associated kernels.

The kernel responsible for the creation of the inverted index is composed of three smaller kernels responsible for its steps: parallel counting, parallel prefix sum and parallel building of the index according to the count and prefix sum arrays. For the filtering algorithm, we create a single array in the GPU memory, the partial_scores array, with a number of elements equals to the square of the number of sets in one block (the number of all possible pairs for the block). We only allocate this array once, which is reused after each filtering execution to save the allocation time. We also allocate only once a compacted_buckets array of the same size of the partial_scores to store the result of the compactation. Of course, these arrays must be cleaned (set to 0) at each execution of the filtering-verification algorithms in the block processing scheme. The number of sets per block must be chosen in such a way that two times its squared value times the data type size used in partial_scores and compacted_buckets is less than the memory available in the GPU.

After the filtering kernel is executed, it fills the partial_scores array, and the compaction kernel can be called to fill the compacted_buckets array, as shown in Fig. 5. The result of the compaction is the absolute indexes of the positive elements in partial_scores. The indexes represent the pairs, since they can be derived from the absolute index. These indexes, i.e. the candidate pairs, as well as the partial_scores are passed to the verification kernel. It calculates the intersections (i.e., the final scores) between the candidate pairs, always checking if there is still enough features in the sets to meet the minimum overlap, according to the chosen similarity function. The pairs that pass the verification algorithm are pushed into a list, that is periodically flushed to the output file, where the actual similarity values are calculated. This is done by a concurrent thread which controls the stream of similar pairs from the verification algorithm to the output. This is usually not very significant for high thresholds as the portion of similar pairs is small, but for low thresholds it has a great impact in performance because we can have a lot of similar pairs in each block processing step. Besides enhancing performance, this approach produces results producing before having consumed all the input, thereby enabling the execution of our algorithm in a pipelined fashion. This behavior is of particular importance when set similarity join is not used as not as a standalone operator, but as part of a larger query.

We used a fixed number of thread blocks and of threads per block, which depends on to the specific GPU used. In order to ensure maximum utilization of the device, we used a technique called persistent threads. This technique allows one thread to be reused, thereby processing more than one data element when the number of elements to process is bigger than the number of threads sent to execution.

7   Experimental Evaluation

7.1   Experimental Setup

We tested two reference sequential algorithms, *allpairs* [3] and *ppjoin* [5], as well as a massively parallel algorithm *gssjoin* [21] and our parallel filter-based algorithm *fgssjoin*.

Our experiments were executed on a machine equipped with two Intel Xeon E5-2620, each with 6 processing cores (12 threads in hyper-threading) and 20 MB of cache memory, 16 GB of RAM memory and 4 Nvidia GTX Titan Black, each with 2880 processing cores and 6 GB of memory, although we only used one GTX Titan Black for our parallel implementation.

We used two standard databases: DBLP[3] (a collection of computer science article titles and authors), with 100 k registers, and IMDB[4] (a collection of movie titles, TV shows, etc), with 300 k registers, which are popular datasets used in previous work [13]. We pre-processed the data sets, removing accents and punctuation, and setting all characters to lowercase. Strings in both datasets were converted to sets of 2-grams and 3-grams. We conducted our experiments varying the threshold values from 0.5 to 0.9, in 0.1 increments. Our baseline comparison algorithms were executed on the Xeon processor, except gssjoin, which was also executed on the Gtx Titan Black.

7.2   Performance Analysis

We report execution runtimes with varying threshold values. Figure 7 shows the execution times obtained as we increase the threshold from 0.5 up to 0.9. As can be seen, our algorithm achieved considerable speedups of up to 25x faster than the leading sequential algorithm in literature. The best speedups were achieved when the datasets were tokenized with 2-grams. Of course the finer grained 2-grams requires more computational power, since there are fewer combinations of 2 characters and this leads to more matches and more candidate pairs in the filtering phase, consequently raising the load for the verification phase. Also,

---

[3] http://dblp.uni-trier.de.

[4] http://www.imdb.com.

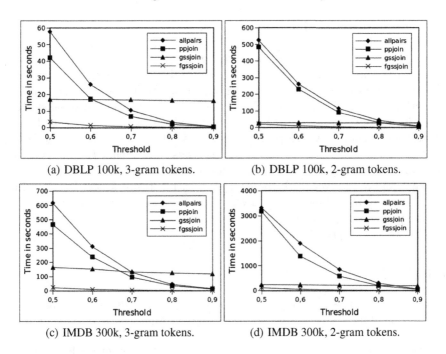

Fig. 7. Execution times on DBLP (100 k) and IMDB (300 k) for q = 2 and q = 3 [11].

we expect our algorithm to become even better as the size of the dataset grows. One caveat is that our algorithm relies on positional filtering, which is inherently sequential. Although it is very efficient in lowering the number of candidate pairs in the filtering phase, it imposes difficulties for some key optimization in many-core architectures. For example, it reduces memory coalescing, and hinders a higher degree of parallelism, e.g., parallelizing the tokens among processing units, instead of whole queries, in the filtering phase. Table 2 shows the best speedups achieved on each dataset over the 3 other algorithms used in the experiments; the corresponding threshold value is shown in parentheses. Note that, in contrast to the sequential algorithms, the speedups over gssjoin were achieved at the highest threshold value.

Table 2. Best speedups of fgssjoin over the other algorithms on each dataset, with corresponding threshold values [11].

Dataset	ppjoin	allpairs	gssjoin
DBLP, 2-gram	24.6x (0.8)	36.6x (0.8)	108.3x (0.9)
DBLP, 3-gram	12.4x (0.5)	17.1x (0.5)	132.7x (0.9)
IMDB, 2-gram	27.6x (0.6)	38.5x (0.6)	98.0x (0.9)
IMDB, 3-gram	21.0x (0.8)	27.5x (0.8)	127.1x (0.9)

8   Conclusions and Future Work

In this paper, we presented *fgssjoin*, a fine-grained parallel algorithm for exact set similarity join, which exploits state-of-the-art filtering techniques and divide-and-conquer strategies. We described an implementation of *fgssjoin* designed to efficiently utilize GPU resources. Furthermore, we also presented parallel algorithms for all data pre-processing tasks, thereby providing an end-to-end solution to the set similarity join problem, which is entirely executed on the GPU. Our experimental evaluation on standard datasets showed that *fgssjoin* achieves significant speedups over the fastest sequential and parallel algorithms in the literature and scales well with the data size. In future work, we plan to refine the use of shared/local memory as a way to increase locality and, hence, achieve greater speedups. We also plan to implement a multi-GPU version (to run on GPU clusters) and process larger datasets.

References

1. Sarawagi, S., Kirpal, A.: Efficient set joins on similarity predicates. In: Proceedings of the ACM SIGMOD International Conference on Management of Data, pp. 743–754 (2004)
2. Chaudhuri, S., Ganti, V., Kaushik, R.: A primitive operator for similarity joins in data cleaning. In: Proceedings of the 22nd IEEE International Conference on Data Engineering, p. 5 (2006)
3. Bayardo, R.J., Ma, Y., Srikant, R.: Scaling up all pairs similarity search. In: Proceedings of the 16th International Conference on World Wide Web, pp. 131–140 (2007)
4. Vernica, R., Carey, M.J., Li, C.: Efficient parallel set-similarity joins using MapReduce. In: Proceedings of the ACM SIGMOD International Conference on Management of Data, pp. 495–506 (2010)
5. Xiao, C., Wang, W., Lin, X., Yu, J.X., Wang, G.: Efficient similarity joins for near-duplicate detection. ACM Trans. Database Syst. **36**, 15 (2011)
6. Ribeiro, L.A., Härder, T.: Generalizing prefix filtering to improve set similarity joins. Inf. Syst. **36**, 62–78 (2011)
7. Wang, J., Li, G., Feng, J.: Can we beat the prefix filtering? An adaptive framework for similarity join and search. In: Proceedings of the ACM SIGMOD International Conference on Management of Data, pp. 85–96 (2012)
8. Cruz, M.S.H., Kozawa, Y., Amagasa, T., Kitagawa, H.: Accelerating set similarity joins using GPUs. T. Large-Scale Data Knowl. Cent. Syst. **28**, 1–22 (2016)
9. Doan, A., Halevy, A.Y., Ives, Z.G.: Principles of Data Integration. Morgan Kaufmann, Waltham (2012)
10. Leskovec, J., Rajaraman, A., Ullman, J.D.: Mining of Massive Datasets, 2nd edn. Cambridge University Press, Cambridge (2014)
11. Quirino, R.D., Ribeiro-Júnior, S., Ribeiro, L.A., Martins, W.S.: fgssjoin: a GPU-based algorithm for set similarity joins. In: Proceedings of the 19th International Conference on Enterprise Information System, pp. 152–161 (2017)
12. Arasu, A., Ganti, V., Kaushik, R.: Efficient exact set-similarity joins. In: Proceedings of the 32nd International Conference on Very Large Data Bases, pp. 918–929 (2006)

13. Mann, W., Augsten, N., Bouros, P.: An empirical evaluation of set similarity join techniques. PVLDB **9**, 636–647 (2016)
14. Gravano, L., Ipeirotis, P.G., Jagadish, H.V., Koudas, N., Muthukrishnan, S., Srivastava, D.: Approximate string joins in a database (almost) for free. In: Proceedings of 27th International Conference on Very Large Data Bases, pp. 491–500 (2001)
15. Chacón, A., Marco-Sola, S., Espinosa, A., Ribeca, P., Moure, J.C.: Thread-cooperative, bit-parallel computation of levenshtein distance on GPU. In: 2014 International Conference on Supercomputing, pp. 103–112 (2014)
16. Lieberman, M.D., Sankaranarayanan, J., Samet, H.: A fast similarity join algorithm using graphics processing units. In: Proceedings of the 24th IEEE International Conference on Data Engineering, pp. 1111–1120 (2008)
17. Indyk, P., Motwani, R.: Approximate nearest neighbors: towards removing the curse of dimensionality. In: Proceedings of the 13th Annual ACM Symposium on the Theory of Computing, pp. 604–613 (1998)
18. Broder, A.Z., Charikar, M., Frieze, A.M., Mitzenmacher, M.: Min-wise independent permutations. J. Comput. Syst. Sci. **60**, 630–659 (2000)
19. Deng, D., Li, G., Hao, S., Wang, J., Feng, J.: MassJoin: a mapreduce-based method for scalable string similarity joins. In: Proceedings of the 30th IEEE International Conference on Data Engineering, pp. 340–351 (2014)
20. Rong, C., Lin, C., Silva, Y.N., Wang, J., Lu, W., Du, X.: Fast and scalable distributed set similarity joins for big data analytics. In: Proceedings of the 33rd IEEE International Conference on Data Engineering, pp. 1059–1070 (2017)
21. Ribeiro-Júnior, S., Quirino, R.D., Ribeiro, L.A., Martins, W.S.: gSSJoin: a GPU-based set similarity join algorithm. In: Proceedings of the 31st Brazilian Symposium on Databases, pp. 64–75 (2016)
22. Li, C., Lu, J., Lu, Y.: Efficient merging and filtering algorithms for approximate string searches. In: Proceedings of the 24th IEEE International Conference on Data Engineering, pp. 257–266 (2008)
23. Xiao, C., Wang, W., Lin, X., Shang, H.: Top-k set similarity joins. In: Proceedings of the 25th IEEE International Conference on Data Engineering, pp. 916–927 (2009)
24. Kirk, D.B., Hwu, W.W.: Programming Massively Parallel Processors: A Hands-on Approach. Morgan Kaufmann, San Francisco (2010)

Experimenting and Assessing a Probabilistic Business Process Deviance Mining Framework Based on Ensemble Learning

Alfredo Cuzzocrea[1,2]([✉]), Francesco Folino[2], Massimo Guarascio[2], and Luigi Pontieri[2]

[1] DIA Department, University of Trieste, Trieste, Italy
alfredo.cuzzocrea@dia.units.it
[2] ICAR-CNR, Rende, CS, Italy
{francesco.folino,massimo.guarascio,luigi.pontieri}@icar.cnr.it

Abstract. *Business Process Intelligence* (BPI) and *Process Mining*, two very active research areas of research, share a great interest towards the issue of discovering an effective *Deviance Detection Model* (DDM), computed via accessing log data. The DDM model allows us to understand whether novel instances of the target business process are deviant or not, thus becoming extremely useful in modern application scenarios such as cybersecurity and fraud detection. In this chapter, we further and significantly extend our previous line of work that has originated, across years, an innovative ensemble-learning framework for mining business process deviances, whose main benefit is that of introducing a sort of *multi-view learning scheme*. One of the most relevant achievements of this extended work consists in proposing an alternative meta-learning method for probabilistically combining the predictions of different base DDMs, and putting all together in a conceptual system architecture oriented to support common *Business Process Management* (BPM) scenarios. In addition to this, we here envisage the combination of this approach with a deviance explanation methodology that leverages and extends a previous method still proposed by us in previous research. Basically, the latter method allows to discover accurate and readable deviance-aware trace clusters defined in terms of descriptive rules over both properties and behavioral aspects of the traces. We complement our analytical contributions with a comprehensive experimental assessment and analysis, even in comparison with a state-of-the-art DDM discovery approach. The experimental results we derive confirm flexibility, reliability and effectiveness of the proposed business process deviance mining framework.

1 Introduction

Business Process Intelligence (BPI) and Process Mining are active areas of research, which enjoy many relevant real-life applications.

S. Hammoudi et al. (Eds.): ICEIS 2017, LNBIP 321, pp. 96–124, 2018.
https://doi.org/10.1007/978-3-319-93375-7_6

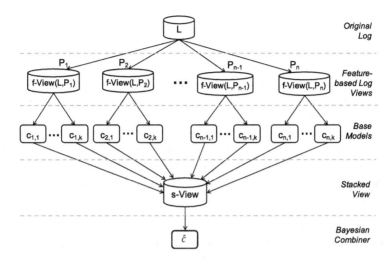

Fig. 1. Conceptual data-processing flow of the proposed approach: original data, transformed data and discovered DDMs [13].

A recent thread of research in this area concerns the problem of detecting deviant instances of a business process (a.k.a. "deviance mining"), i.e. instances that *deviate* from normal outcomes [5,11,36,38,42]. This problem is relevant in many application scenarios such as cybersecurity and fraud detection, and so forth. Essentially, the problem has been rephrased in the literature as a binary classification problem, where the class of all deviant process instances is to be discriminated from the one gathering all the other (normal) instances of the process under analysis. This problem has been faced by inducing a suitable classification model (named hereinafter *Deviance Detection Model*, or *DDM* for short), out of some flat representation of a historical log of process traces (labelled each as either deviant or normal). Such a model can be then applied to any new instance of the process to estimate whether it is a deviance or not.

In our opinion, the current literature in the field has not fully addressed a series of issues that are likely to arise in many real application scenarios. We discuss them in the following.

I1 First of all, most of the deviance mining approaches (including, in particular, [5,38,43]) rely on training a single DDM from a propositional view of the given log, where each trace is encoded into a fixed-length form by projecting the associated sequence of log events onto some given set of behavioral patterns (such as the *individual activities, maximal repeats, or tandem repeats* used in [5,38] and the experiments discussed in Sect. 6). As shown in [38] using multiple heterogeneous kinds of pattern can lead to higher classification accuracy. However, mixing all heterogeneous patterns into a single view is likely to produce a high-dimensional, sparse and redundant representation of the training instances. This calls for adopting some multi-view learning strategy (like the one proposed in [11]), capable of exploiting different complementary views of the given traces.

I2 In many real-life applications, analyzing a presumably deviant case is an expensive task. If equipping the detected deviant instances with a deviance probability score, this task could be focused on more suspicious instances. This capability could allow to use deviance prediction tools more flexibly and more effectively in real BPM systems.

I3 Deviance mining analysis must be often carried out in situations where the deviant instances are far less than normal ones. This is a case of "class imbalance" [28], which constitutes a challenge for most classifier induction approaches, conceived to maximize the overall accuracy without paying special attention to the minority (i.e. deviant, in our case) instances.

Some of these issues have been faced in previous works of ours [11,12], where an ensemble-learning approach was proposed that exploits multi-view learning to solve the deviance mining problem. This approach is summarized pictorially in Fig. 1. Basically, a number, say n, of complementary feature-based views of the given log L are produced, which provide each a vector-space encoding of both context properties and behavioral patterns of the traces in L. Two layers of deviation-detection models are induced from these views: *(i)* a collection of base models (learn by applying k different classifier-induction methods to one of the n views above), and *(ii)* a meta model, which integrates the predictions of the base models into a "high-order" deviance forecast. As explained in [11,12], the latter model deals with heterogeneous behavioral patterns at a higher level of abstraction, so effectively addressing the issue *I1*.

In order to deal with situations where deviant instances are far less than normal ones (issue *I3*), the learning procedure can be made integrate a re-sampling mechanism, in order to reduce the level of class imbalance.

In this chapter, we provide three novel contributions over [11,12], namely:

- two alternative Bayesian meta-learning methods for probabilistically combining the predictions of different base DDMs;
- a conceptual system architecture supporting the detection and analysis of deviances in a Business Process Management scenario; and
- a wide and comprehensive experimental analysis of algorithm HO-DDM-mine and of a state-of-the-art method [38].

Specifically, in our current approach the meta-learning task can take advantage of (a customized version of) one of the following methods for the induction of probabilistic classifiers: *AODE* [48] or *HNB* [52]. Notably, both these methods relax the assumption of attribute independence that underlies Naïve Bayes models—this assumption hardly holds, indeed, in our DDM learning setting, where several activities/patterns are likely to be correlated one another—with negligible additional costs in terms of computation time. This allows to associate any new process instance with a reliable estimate of the probability that it is deviant, thus addressing the delicate issue *I2*.

In addition to this, we here envisage the combination of this approach with a deviance explanation methodology that leverages and extends a previous method still proposed by us in previous research. Basically, the latter method allows to discover accurate and readable deviance-aware trace clusters defined in terms of descriptive rules over both properties and behavioral aspects of the traces.

The results of our empirical analysis confirmed the flexibility, reliability and effectiveness of the proposed deviance detection approach, and the improvement gained over its previous version.

The rest of the chapter is organized as follows. Section 2 introduces some basic concepts and notation on the kinds of Bayesian classifiers that are used in our approach to accomplish the meta-learning sub-task. The specific kind of overall DDM (named *High-Order Deviance Detection Model*, short HO-DDM) that is eventually returned by our approach is illustrated in Sect. 3. Section 4 then presents a conceptual system architecture for the detection and analysis of deviant process instances, in a BPM scenario, summarizes the induction algorithm for extracting a HO-DDM out a given set of historical log traces. Section 5 focuses the attention on the task of extracting readable deviance explanations (expressed in terms of conceptual deviance clusters) and describes a (sub-)system architecture for accomplishing this task. After discussing, in Sect. 6, the results of the experimental activities that we have conducted on a real case study, we draw a few concluding remarks in Sect. 8. This chapter extends [13], as it has been selected as one of the best papers of the conference.

2 Bayesian Models: Foundations, Definitions, Properties

As explained before, we want to probabilistically classify a process trace as either deviant or not, in order to equip the trace with a measure of confidence in the fact that it is really a deviance. In order to do this in a scalable way, we resort to two extensions of the popular Naïve Bayes method. Before presenting these methods in details, let us introduce some basic concepts and notation concerning Bayesian classifiers, in general, and Naïve Bayes models, in particular.

In general, *Bayesian classifiers* combine a-priori knowledge of the classes with new evidence gathered from data. Let us consider an instance space with $m + 1$ nominal attributes $X_1, \ldots, X_m, Y$, such that $m \in \mathbb{N}$, and a class attribute Y encoding the class label (if known) of any instance. For any attribute $Z \in \{X_1, \ldots, X_m, Y\}$, let $dom(Z)$ be the associated domain, and let $dom(Y) = \{c_1, \ldots, c_k\}$. Given an instance $\mathbf{x} = \langle x_1, \ldots, x_m \rangle$, where x_i is the value observed for attribute X_i, the classification problem amounts to estimating the class label $y \in dom(Y)$ for $\mathbf{x}$, based on some suitable classification model, previously extracted from (already classified) training instances.

In a hard classification setting, a Bayesian classifier computes $P(y|\mathbf{x})$ for each class $y \in dom(Y)$, and assigns $\mathbf{x}$ to the class associated with the with the highest probability, i.e., $y^* = \arg\max_{y \in dom(Y)} (P(y|\mathbf{x}))$. Clearly, $P(y|\mathbf{x}) = P(y, \mathbf{x})/P(\mathbf{x})$ and $\arg\max_{y \in dom(Y)} (P(y|\mathbf{x})) = \arg\max_{y \in dom(Y)} P(y, \mathbf{x})$. As $P(y, \mathbf{x}) = P(y) \cdot P(\mathbf{x}|y)$, this hard classification task amounts to finding $y^* \in dom(Y)$ such that: $y^* = \arg\max_{y \in dom(Y)} (P(y) \cdot P(\mathbf{x}|y))$.

For a fully probabilistic classification, every class membership probability can be estimated as:

$$P(y|\mathbf{x}) \approx \frac{P(y,\mathbf{x})}{\sum_{y' \in dom(Y)} P(y',\mathbf{x})} = \frac{P(y,\mathbf{x})}{\sum_{y' \in dom(Y)} P(y') \cdot P(\mathbf{x}|y')} \tag{1}$$

While the prior probability $P(y)$ can be derived from the sample frequencies in the training set, one should estimate the conditional probability $P(\mathbf{x}|y)$. In Naïve Bayes (NB) classifiers the latter task is accomplished by assuming that all the attributes are conditionally independent of one another, given the class label y. Under this hypothesis, for each $y \in dom(Y)$, it is $P(y,\mathbf{x}) = P(y) \cdot \prod_{i=1}^{m} P(x_i|y)$. Thus, the instance $\mathbf{x}$ is assigned to the class $y^* \in dom(Y)$ such that $y^* = \arg\max_{y \in dom(Y)} (P(y) \cdot \prod_{i=1}^{m} P(x_i|y))$. Any "soft" class membership probability $P(y|\mathbf{x})$ can be computed in a similar way.

NB classifiers work well in a wide range of applications [31]. However, in certain settings (like the one considered in this work), the attribute independence assumption is inappropriate [18,19]. Many efforts have been made in the literature to relax such an assumption, without making the probability distribution too complex and hard to induce. We next briefly illustrate two popular extensions of NB classifiers, namely AODE and HNB, which are both used in the current implementation of our approach.

2.1   The AODE Classifier

One-dependence estimators (ODEs) [41] generalize NBs by allowing each attribute to depend on one other attribute besides the class. A subclass of ODEs are SPODEs [29,50], where all the attributes can only depend on a single common one, the *super-parent* (in addition to the class). For example, for a SPODE with super-parent X_p, $P(y,\mathbf{x})$ is computed as follows:

$$P(y,\mathbf{x}) = P(y,x_p) \cdot P(\mathbf{x}|y,x_p) = P(y,x_p) \cdot \prod_{i=1}^{m} P(x_i|y,x_p)$$

SPODEs are typically combined into a sort of ensemble, in order to reduce the classification variance and ensure higher accuracy [48]. Clearly, if the data instances feature m attributes, at most m different SPODEs can be combined. The different SPODE models in such an ensemble are usually merged by computing an overall probability estimate for $P(y,\mathbf{x})$ as a linear combination of the probability estimates returned by all of these "base" models:

$$P(y,\mathbf{x}) = \sum_{j=1}^{m} w_j \cdot P_j(y,\mathbf{x}) = \sum_{j=1}^{m} w_j \cdot P(y,x_j) \cdot \prod_{i=1}^{m} P(x_i|y,x_j) \tag{2}$$

where $P_j(y,\mathbf{x})$ is the estimate of j-th SPODE for $\mathbf{x}$, and w_j is the weight given to the same SPODE.

The *Averaged One-Dependence Estimators* (AODE) [48] method adopts a simple combination strategy, which only considers the super-parents that appear in the training dataset more than a minimum support threshold $h \in \mathbb{N}$, and assigns uniform weights to all of their corresponding SPODEs. Hereinafter, we simply keep fixed $h = 1$—notice that the same choice has been made in the experiments described in Sect. 6. According to this strategy, $P(y, \mathbf{x})$ is eventually estimated as follows:

$$P(y, \mathbf{x}) = \frac{\sum_{j \in \mathcal{S}} P(y, x_j) \cdot \prod_{i=1}^{m} P(x_i | y, x_j)}{|\mathcal{S}|} \tag{3}$$

where $\mathcal{S}$ is the subset of values x_j that occur at least h times in the training set (and w_j is fixed to $1/|\mathcal{S}|$ for all x_j in $\mathcal{S}$).

In order to estimate, for each tuple $\mathbf{x} \in \mathbf{X}$ and each possible class label $y \in dom(Y)$, the probability $P(y|\mathbf{x})$, one can simply normalize the numerator in Eq. 3 over all the classes as follows:

$$P(y|\mathbf{x}) = \frac{P(y, \mathbf{x})}{\sum_{y' \in Y} P(y', \mathbf{x})} = \frac{\sum_{j \in \mathcal{S}} P(y, x_j) \cdot \prod_{i=1}^{m} P(x_i | y, x_j)}{\sum_{y' \in dom(Y)} \sum_{j \in \mathcal{S}} P(y', x_j) \cdot \prod_{i=1}^{m} P(x_i | y', x_j)} \tag{4}$$

2.2   The HNB Classifier

The basic assumption underlying a SPODE is that each attribute can only depend on another one (i.e. the super-parent), even though several other attributes might actually influence the former. This assumption is mitigated by averaging different SPODEs. By contrast, in the *Hidden Naïve Bayes* (*HNB* for short) model, each attribute x_i is assumed to be possibly influenced by a artificial "hidden" parent attribute, capturing the influence that all other attributes may have on x_i. In other words, each attribute x_i is allowed to depend on a hidden parent x_i^h ($\forall i = 1, \ldots, m$), in addition to the class y. Therefore, the probability $P(y, \mathbf{x})$ computed by an HNB can be written as:

$$P(y, \mathbf{x}) = P(y) \cdot \prod_{i=1}^{m} P(x_i | y, x_i^h) P(y) \cdot \prod_{i=1}^{m} \left(\sum_{j=1, j \neq i}^{m} w_{ij} \cdot P(x_i | y, x_j) \right) \tag{5}$$

where $\sum_{j=1}^{m} w_{i,j} = 1$.

Clearly, the hidden parent x_i^h for x_i is defined as a mixture of the weighted influences from all other attributes.

A key point in the construction of an HNB is the definition of the weights $w_{i,j}$ (for any i, j in $\{1, \ldots, m\}$). In the approach proposed in [52], any weight $w_{i,j}$ is computed on the basis of the *Conditional Mutual Information* $I_P(x_i, x_j | y)$ between x_i and x_j, which is defined as follows:

$$I_p(x_i, x_j | y) = \sum_{x_i, x_j, y} P(x_i, x_j, y) \cdot \log \frac{P(x_i, x_j | y)}{P(x_i | y) P(x_j | y)} \tag{6}$$

More specifically, for any $i, j \in \{1, \ldots, m\}$, it is:

$$w_{i,j} = \frac{I_p(x_i, x_j | y)}{\sum_{j=1, j \neq i} I_P(x_i, x_j | y)} \tag{7}$$

The posterior class-membership probability $P(y|\mathbf{x})$, for each tuple $\mathbf{x} \in \mathbf{X}$ and each possible class $y \in dom(Y)$, can be simply obtained as follows:

$$
\begin{aligned}
P(y|\mathbf{x}) = \frac{P(y, \mathbf{x})}{P(\mathbf{x})} &= \frac{P(y, \mathbf{x})}{\sum_{y' \in dom(Y)} P(y', \mathbf{x})} \\
&= \frac{P(y) \cdot \prod_{i=1}^{m} \left(\sum_{j=1, j \neq i}^{m} (w_{ij} \cdot P(x_i | y, x_j)) \right)}{\sum_{y' \in dom(Y)} \left(P(y') \cdot \prod_{i=1}^{m} \left(\sum_{j=1, j \neq i}^{m} (w_{ij} \cdot P(x_i | y', x_j)) \right) \right)}
\end{aligned} \tag{8}
$$

3   Models Supporting High-Order Deviance Detection

Our approach to the discovery of an HO-DDM relies on training multiple base learners on different feature-based views of a given log L. According to the processing flow depicted in Fig. 1, the approach founds on training multiple base learners on n different feature-based views of L, produced each according to a different list of behavioral patterns (like those used in [5,11,38], and in our experimentation).

Let $P_1, \ldots, P_n$ these pattern lists and $f\text{-}View(L, P_1), \ldots, f\text{-}View(L, P_n)$ be the feature-based views of L that are obtained by encoding the traces in L according to the patterns in $P_1, \ldots, P_n$, respectively. More precisely, for each P_i and each $\tau \in L$, the view $f\text{-}View(L, P_i)$ contains a tuple $f\text{-}View(\tau, P_i)$ that encodes all the context data of τ and the projection of τ onto the patterns of P_i. In particular, the correlation between τ and each pattern $p_j \in P_i$ is computed as the number of times that p_j occurs in τ. Further details can be found in [11].

By applying k different learning algorithms to all of these views, a list CL of $r = n \times k$ "base" DDMs is obtained. These multi-view base classifiers are made undergo a stacking-oriented meta-learning scheme, in order to integrate all of them into a single higher-level probabilistic DDM.

For the sake of notation, let PL be a list, of the same length as CL, of pattern lists such that $PL[q]$ is the specific list of patterns that was used to train the model $CL[q]$, for any $q \in \{1, \ldots, r\}$.[1]

Then the meta-learning task is performed on a meta-view $s\text{-}View(L, CL, PL)$ of log L that stores, for each trace $\tau \in L$, a tuple $s\text{-}View(\tau, CL, PL)$ having the same class label as τ, and featuring (as input attributes) both the predictions of all the DDMs in CL and the case/context attributes of τ. From $s\text{-}View(L, CL, PL)$ a probabilistic meta-classifier (one among HNB [52] and

---

[1] With regard to the labelling scheme of Fig. 1 (and assuming that the base DDMs appear in CL in the same left-to-right order as in the figure), it is $CL[q] = c_{i,j}$ iff $q = (i - 1) \times k + j$ and $PL[q] = P_i$ iff $i = \lfloor (q - 1)/k \rfloor + 1$.

$AODE$ [48]) is eventually induced, which can combine the predictions of all of the base DDMs in CL.

The final result of this learning procedure is a multi-view deviance detection model, named *High-Order Deviation Detection Model* (HO-DDM), which is formally defined below.

Definition 1 (HO-DDM). Let L be a log over some proper trace universe T, and $PROP(T)$ be the space of all the data attributes that are associated with the traces of T. Then, a *High-Order Deviance Detection Model* (HO-DDM) for L is a triple of the form $H = \langle CL, PL, \hat{c} \rangle$, where: *(i)* PL is a list of r pattern lists, for some $r \in \mathbb{N}$; *(ii)* CL is a list of r (base) DDMs such that, for each $i \in \{1, \ldots, r\}$, $CL[i]$ is a DDM, learn by using $f\text{-}View(L, PL[i])$ as training set, encoding a function of the form $CL[i] : PROP(T) \times \mathbb{R}^{|P_i|} \to \{0,1\}$, which maps the propositional representation $f\text{-}View(\tau, PL[i])$ of any trace $\tau \in T$ to a class label in $\{0,1\}$; and *(iii)* $\hat{c} : PROP(T) \times \{0,1\}^r \to [0,1]$ is a (meta) classifier providing an estimate for the probability that any trace τ in T is deviant, based on its ("stacking-oriented") representation $s\text{-}View(\tau, CL, PL)$.   □

In the current implementation of our approach, the predictions of all the discovered base DDMs in CL are combined using a probabilistic classifier $\hat{c}$, computed by applying one of the two Bayesian learning methods described in the previous section. When a novel trace τ is to be classified, each base model $CL[i]$ in the ensemble is applied to the vector-space representation $f\text{-}View(\tau, PL[i])$ of τ (produced according to the same list $PL[i]$ of patterns that was used to induce $CL[i]$). The predictions made of the models in CL are then combined into a single prediction by $\hat{c}$. Specifically, by providing the latter model with a propositional view of τ mixing the original data properties of τ (stored in $prop(\tau)$) and the predictions assigned to τ by the base models, the deviance probability score $\hat{c}(\tau)$ is eventually returned as output. A simple way to classify τ as deviant is to check whether $\hat{c}(\tau) > 0.5$—in this case to τ is assigned the label "1". For the sake of flexibility, we allow for fixing a lower deviance probability threshold $\gamma \in (0,1)$, so that any τ is deemed as deviant if and only if $\hat{c}(\tau) > \gamma$.

4   An Architecture for Supporting Deviance Mining and Analysis: Structure and Implementation

Figure 2 illustrates a conceptual system architecture supporting the detection and analysis of deviant process instances. Such a system, following a multi-layer structure, is meant to handle the whole flow of log-based process analysis, from the discovery of an HO-DDM out of historical (labeled) log data, to the detection of new deviant process instance, and the inspection and analysis of both the discovered models and detected deviances. The system is composed of four different layers: *Data/Model Repository*, *Deviance Mining*, *Model/Deviance Analysis*, and *User Interface*.

Essentially, the bottommost layer is responsible for storing both historical process logs and different kinds of views (namely f-Views and s-Views) extracted

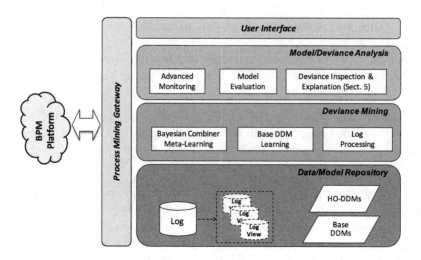

Fig. 2. System architecture for HO-DDM-mine[13].

from them, as well as the different kinds of models that compose our HO-DDMs. All the process mining and pre-processing methods implemented in the Deviance Mining layer are meant to support the induction of an HO-DDM out of historical log traces, annotated each with a Boolean deviance flag. The discovery of a HO-DDM from a given log L can be accomplished with the algorithm HO-DDM-mine proposed in [11], which is summarized in the following. Basically, the algorithm follows a two-phase computation strategy. In the first phase, a number of base classifiers are discovered by applying a given set of inductive learning methods to different views of L, obtained each by projecting the traces in L onto a different space of features. In the second phase, all of these base classifiers are combined into a single DDM, based on a meta-learning (stacking) procedure.

In more detail, the algorithm iterates over the following main steps:

1. Preliminary to the extraction of the patterns, in case log L is imbalanced, it can be made undergo an oversampling procedure, where each deviant trace in L is simply duplicated a certain number of times.
2. For each pattern family specified by the analyst (e.g., *individual activities*, *tandem repeats*, *maximal repeats* [5,11,38]), a list of relevant patterns of that family are extracted from L. The patterns that can be generated for each family are selected according to a frequency-based strategy, where the patterns with a high enough frequency in the log (or the q top frequent ones) are kept.
3. For each pattern list P of those that have been extracted in the previous step, the feature-based view $f\text{-}View(L, P)$ is materialized, and used as training set for discovering different base DDMs (using a different base learning algorithm for inducing each of the latter). As a result, a list CL of base DDMs is obtained, and an associated list PL of pattern lists (such that $PL[i]$ is the pattern list used to train $CL[i]$, for any position i in CL).

4. The discovered DDMs in CL are then combined into a single overall meta-classifier using a stacking strategy. To this end, the "stacked" view $s\text{-}View(L, CL, PL)$ is computed, and a meta-classifier $\hat{c}$ is induced from it, by applying one of the two alternative probabilistic learning methods (e.g., our customized versions of the methods AODE or HNB described in Sect. 2). The discovered combiner must be able to compute, for any "stacked" tuple $\mathbf{x} \in X$, an estimate $\hat{c}(\mathbf{x})$ of $\mathbf{x}$'s deviance probability (i.e. $\hat{c}(\mathbf{x}) \approx P(Y = 1|\mathbf{x})$) according to Eq. 4 or 8 This can be done efficiently by pre-computing a number of sufficient statistics, as described later on in this section.

All the discovered DDMs (be them base models or HO-DDMs) are made available to the Model/Deviance Analysis Layer, which can produce a series of evaluation measures, like those used in our experimentation to quantitatively assess the validity of our approach. The *Advanced Monitoring* module offers deviance-oriented runtime-support services, which include the notification of alert messages and the suggestion of countermeasures to be possibly undertaken when a deviant process instance is detected.

Finally, the *Deviance Inspection & Explanation* module is meant to allow the analyst to inspect and study single process instances detected as (mostly) deviant, and try to understand the causes of their abnormal behavior. In order to help the analyst recognise relevant, and general enough, deviance patterns, these basic per-instance analysis capabilities are extended with a powerful clustering-oriented pattern mining method, which are explained in detail in Sect. 5.

Details on the Discovery of a HO-DDM: *Statistics Underlying the Bayesian Combiners.* As explained previously, the Bayesian combiner $\hat{c}$ in any HO-DDM (cf. Definition 1) must return, for each "stacked" tuple $\mathbf{x} \in X$, an estimate $\hat{c}(\mathbf{x})$ of $\mathbf{x}$'s deviance probability (i.e. $\hat{c}(\mathbf{x}) \approx P(Y = 1|\mathbf{x})$) according to Eq. 4 or 8. Such an estimate is computed on the basis of the following (precomputed) statistics, which are all derived from $s\text{-}View(L, CL, PL)$ for all $i, j \in \{1, \ldots, m\}$, $x_i \in dom(X_i)$, and $x_j \in dom(X_j)$, and constitute the backbone of the combiner model $\hat{c}$:

- n_i is the number of values for attribute X_i;
- D (resp. N) is the number of deviant (resp. normal) tuples in $s\text{-}View(L, CL, PL)$;
- D_j (resp. N_j) is the number of deviant (resp. normal) tuples in $s\text{-}View(L, CL, PL)$ that feature the value x_j;
- D_{ji} (resp. N_{ji}) is the number of deviant (resp. normal) tuples in $s\text{-}View(L, CL, PL)$ that feature both values x_j and x_i;
- K is the number of tuples in $s\text{-}View(L, CL, PL)$ (all having a known value of the deviance label);
- K_j is the number of tuples in $s\text{-}View(L, CL, PL)$ for which the value of attribute X_j is known;
- K_{ji} is the number of tuples in $s\text{-}View(L, CL, PL)$ for which the values of both attributes X_i and X_j are known. $\square$

Notice that the counters above are sufficient to estimate every base probability of the form $P(y)$, $P(y, x_j)$ and $P(y, x_j, x_i)$. The latter, in turn, can be exploited to estimate every probability of the form $P(x_i|y)$ and $P(x_i|y, x_j)$—for each values x_j and x_i of the attributes X_j and X_i (with the former playing as super-parent), for $i, j \in \{1, \ldots, m\}$ and $y \in \{0, 1\}$—that are needed to compute $P(y|\mathbf{x})$ according to Eqs. 4 and 8. To make the estimation more robust, these base probabilities are computed by using the *Laplace estimation* method [48,52], as specified in the following: $P(Y = 1) = \frac{D+1}{K+2}$; $P(Y = 1, x_j) = \frac{D_j+1}{K_j+2 \cdot n_j}$; $P(Y = 1, x_j, x_i) = \frac{D_{ji}+1}{K_{ji}+2 \cdot n_i \cdot n_j}$; $P(Y = 0) = \frac{N+1}{K+2}$; $P(Y = 0, x_j) = \frac{N_j+1}{K_j+2 \cdot n_j}$; $P(Y = 0, x_j, x_i) = \frac{N_{ji}+1}{K_{ji}+2 \cdot n_i \cdot n_j}$; $P(x_i|Y = 1) = P(Y = 1, x_i)/P(Y = 1)$; $P(x_i|Y = 0) = P(Y = 0, x_i)/P(Y = 0)$; $P(x_i|Y = 1, x_j) = P(Y = 1, x_j, x_i)/P(Y = 1, x_j)$; $P(x_i|Y = 0, x_j) = P(Y = 0, x_j, x_i)/P(Y = 0, x_j)$.

5   Extending the Framework with Deviance Explanation Capabilities

Any HO-DDM returned by the discovery approach described so far can only be used to estimate whether new process traces are deviant or not. However, the analyst is provided with no explanation of typical and relevant deviance patterns. In order to overcome this limitation, we here envisage the combination of this approach with a deviance explanation methodology that leverages and extends the method proposed in [22]. Basically, this method can discover accurate and readable deviance-aware trace clusters defined in terms of descriptive rules over both properties and behavioral aspects of the traces.

More specifically, we associate each new trace analyzed with our system with the probabilistic classification it was given by the HO-DDM, and store all of these probabilistically labeled traces into a repository. Interpreting the numerical labels of these traces as respective deviance scores, the system is capable to extract a deviance-oriented conceptual clustering of the traces, which captures a number of easily-to-interpret relevant deviance scenarios.

5.1   A Propositional Deviation-Aware Log Encoding

For each trace τ in the given deviance-labelled log L and for each event attribute $A \in \mathcal{A}_\mathcal{E}$, we try to grasp a sufficiently general representation of the behavior captured by the sequence $abs_A(\tau)$ (i.e. by the sequence of event types extracted by using attribute A as an event abstraction function) by replacing the list of events of τ with two sets of behavioral attributes, which simply count as many times one specific value (resp., two specific values) of A appears (resp., appear one after the other) in the sequence. More formally:

Definition 2 (pEnc). Let L be a log, and let $\mathcal{A}$ and $\mathcal{A}_\mathcal{E}$ be the case attributes and the event attributes stored in L, respectively. For any event attribute A in $\mathcal{A}_\mathcal{E}$, let abs_A be the trace abstraction function replacing any trace $\tau \in L$ with the sequence $\langle A(\tau[1]), \ldots, A(\tau[len(\tau)]) \rangle$. Finally, let $\delta : L \to [0,1]$ be a deviance indicator defined over any trace τ of L, and computed by simply applying a discovered HO-DDM to τ. Then, the *Propositional Encoding* (short *pEnc*) of L w.r.t. δ, denoted by $pEnc(L, \delta)$, is a dataset that represents all of the traces of L in terms of both a set $X = \mathcal{A} \cup \mathcal{B} \cup \mathcal{B}_{pairs}$ of *descriptive attributes* and of a single *target attribute* Δ storing the deviance score that τ is given by δ. Besides the attributes (i.e. $\mathcal{A}$) originally stored in the log, X gathers two kinds of *behavioral* attributes, $\mathcal{B} = \{ \#[A = v] \mid A \in \mathcal{A}_{\mathcal{E}} \text{ and } v \in Dom(A) \}$ and $\mathcal{B}_{pairs} = \{ \#[A = u \to v] \mid A \in \mathcal{A}_{\mathcal{E}} \text{ and } u, v \in Dom(A) \}$ corresponding to basic kinds of execution schemes that may appear in a trace. Specifically, $pEnc(L, \delta)$ is a multi-set consisting of a tuple z_τ (also denoted by $pEnc(\tau, \delta)$) for each $\tau \in L$, such that:

- z_τ inherits the deviance score and all of the original data properties associated with τ, i.e. it holds both $\Delta(z_\tau) = \delta(\tau)$ and $A(z_\tau) = A(\tau)$ for each attribute $A \in \mathcal{A}$;
- each attribute $\#[A = v]$ in $\mathcal{B}$ associates z_τ with the number of times that the value v occurs in the abstract trace produced by applying A to the events in τ, i.e. $\#[A = v](z_\tau) = \mid \{ i \in \{1, \ldots, len(\tau)\} \mid \tau = abs_A(\tau) \text{ and } \tau[i] = v \} \mid$; and
- each attribute $\#[A = u \to v]$ in $\mathcal{B}_{pairs}$ maps z_τ to the number of times that the values u and v occur one after the other in the abstract trace produced by applying A to the events in τ, i.e. $\#[A = u \to v](z_\tau) = \mid \{ i \in \{1, \ldots, len(\tau)\} \mid \tau = abs_A(\tau) \text{ and } \tau[i] = u \text{ and } \tau[i + 1] = v \text{ and } i < j \} \mid$.   □

Each tuple $z \in pEnc(L, \delta)$ is hence provided with a number of descriptive properties (encoded by the attributes in X) and annotated with a deviance score (stored in Δ). In particular, the two subsets of behavioral attributes offer a condensed (abstract) view over the specific traces (i.e. sequences of multi-dimensional events) stored in L.[2]

5.2 Deviance-Aware Clustering: Problem Statement

The final goal of our deviance explanation methodology is to discover a number of interesting deviance-aware clusters for a given set of deviance-labelled log traces. For the sake of interpretability and explanation, we seek a conceptual clustering model encoded as a list of logical clustering rules. More precisely, using the contents of the view $Z = pEnc(L, \delta)$ as training data, we want to eventually extract a list of clusters, discriminated from one another by way of (conjunctive) propositional patterns over the descriptive attributes featuring in that view. The target attribute Δ (giving no contribution to the description of the clusters) is used to guide the learning process towards "interesting" clustering models, capable of separating well groups of traces with a high (average) levels of deviance. As above mentioned, this specific problem can be solved by envisaging the combination of the proposed approach with a deviance explanation methodology that leverages and extends the method proposed in [22].

---

[2] Similar encodings are used by recent process mining approaches [11,14,35] to obtain an abstract representation for a given log.

Pattern-Based Conceptual Clustering Models: Basics and Notation. The language we use for clustering rules is that of conjunctive propositional patterns, representing each a conjunction of one-attribute constraints (i.e. binary propositions)—this assumption is common in the fields of *Subgroup Discovery* (which is somewhat related to our work, as noticed in see Sect. 7) and of *Conceptual Clustering* [4].

More precisely, a *pattern* ϕ over a set X of attributes can be seen conceptually as a set $\phi = \{\xi_1, \ldots, \xi_m\}$, where, for $i \in \{1, \ldots, m\}$, ξ_i is a constraint of the form $\xi_i : Dom(A) \rightarrow \{\text{true}, \text{false}\}$, which imposes a condition on a single attribute $A \in X$, which restrict the range of values that it may take. Further details on the specific kinds of constraints considered in our approach are provided in Sect. 3.

Each pattern $\phi = \{\xi_1, \ldots, \xi_m\}$ encodes the following (combined) indicator function $\phi : Z \rightarrow \{\text{true}, \text{false}\}$, which maps each $z \in Z$ to the Boolean flag $\phi(z) = \xi_1(z) \wedge \ldots \wedge \xi_m(z)$.[3] The *cover* of ϕ over dataset Z, denoted by $cov(\phi, Z)$ is the multi-set of Z's tuples selected by ϕ (i.e. satisfying all of the constraints in ϕ): $cov(\phi, Z) = \{z \in Z \mid \phi(z) = \text{true}\}$. Since each trace τ in L corresponds to just one tuple $z_\tau = pEnc(\tau, \delta)$ in Z, we can easily extend the notion of cover to the log L, by defining the cover of ϕ over the log L, denoted by $cov(\phi, L)$, as the set of L's traces that have been mapped in Z to one of the tuples covered by ϕ, i.e. $cov(\phi, L) = \{\tau \in L \mid \phi(pEnc(\tau, \delta)) = \text{true}\}$.

Let us introduce the general form of clustering model employed in this work. Let L and Z be the given log and the associated propositional encoding (i.e. $Z = pEnc(L, \delta)$ w.r.t. some given deviance indicator δ). Let X be the complete set of descriptive attributes associated with (the propositional encoding of) each case in L. Then a *conceptual clustering model* for L (w.r.t. X) is a list $\mathcal{M} = [\phi_1, \ldots, \phi_k]$ of patterns over X (for some $k \in \mathbb{N}^+$), which encode each a different clustering rule. Similarly to a decision list (like those produced by certain rule-based classifiers and conceptual clustering methods), the model encodes a clustering function $clusterID_\mathcal{M} : L \rightarrow \{1, \ldots, k\}$ that partitions L into k disjoint clusters (assigned each a distinct label via a progressive numbering scheme). More precisely, for any trace $\tau \in L$ it is $clusterID_\mathcal{M}(\tau) = i$ iff i is the lowest cluster index in $\{1, \ldots, k\}$ such that $\phi_i(pEnc(\tau, \delta)) = \text{true}$. Finally, for any $i \in \{1, \ldots, k\}$, we denote by $cluster_\mathcal{M}(L, i)$ the i-th cluster produced by $\mathcal{M}$, which specifically consists of all the cases in L that are covered by ϕ_i and by none of the patterns that precede ϕ_i in the model, i.e. $cluster_\mathcal{M}(L, i) = \{\tau \in L \mid clusterID_\mathcal{M}(\tau) = i\} = cov(\phi_i, L) \setminus \bigcup_{j=1}^{i-1} cov(\phi_j, L)$. As the clustering model is required to define a complete partitioning of Z, we hereinafter assume that the last pattern in the list does not state any actual constraint (i.e. $\phi_k = \emptyset$), and that it hence acts like a sort of "immaterial" default rule, i.e. $\phi_k(z) = \text{true}$ for any $z \in Z$.

The Search Space: Deviance-Aware Clustering Models. In our deviance-centric setting, the discovered clustering models are expected to identify interesting groups of deviant traces, provided that there exist a list of propositional patterns

---

[3] With a little abuse of notation, we take the freedom of denoting both the pattern and the corresponding selector by the same symbol.

that allows to separate them from the remaining traces. Specifically, as formally stated later on, we want the former $k - 1$ patterns/rules of a clustering model to identify disjoint groups of deviant-enough traes capturing different scenarios for the occurrence of deviating behaviors, while simply putting all the remaining traces of L (representing either normal behavior or deviant ones that cannot be discriminated/explained through of the descriptive attributes in X) into the last cluster (equipped, indeed, with no real clustering rule).

To quantify the level of interestingness of a cluster (as representative of some relevant deviance scenario), we extend the notion of deviance indicator to clusters, by defining a function $\mathcal{I} : 2^L \rightarrow [0, 1]$ that maps any cluster $\hat{c}$ to a deviance score, which is computed as the average of those associated with $\hat{c}$'s cases, i.e. $\mathcal{I}(\hat{c}) = |\hat{c}|^{-1} \cdot \sum_{x \in \hat{c}} \delta(x)$.

In order to focus on significant and readable enough deviance-aware clustering models, we assume that the analyst can state three kinds of requirements, by fixing three different thresholds: (i) a lower bound γ for the deviance scores of the clusters, (ii) a minimal cluster size σ, and (iii) a maximal length $maxLen$ for the associated clustering rules (i.e. description patterns).

We are now in a place to formally define the specific kind of "deviance-aware" clustering models that constitute the search space for our inductive learning task.

Definition 3 (DACM). Let L and $\delta : L \rightarrow [0, 1]$ be a log and an associated deviance indicator, respectively, and let $Z = pEnc(L, \delta)$ be the propositional encoding implied by them. Let also X be the descriptive attributes associated with Z.

Let $\gamma \in [0, 1)$, $\sigma \in \mathbb{N}^+$ and $maxLen \in \mathbb{N}^+ \cup \{\infty\}$ be three thresholds encoding the three kinds of requirements mentioned above. Then, a *Deviance-Aware Clustering Model* (short DACM) $\mathcal{M}$ for L and δ w.r.t. γ, σ and $maxLen$[4] is a list of the form $\mathcal{M} = [\langle \phi_1, \hat{c}_1 \rangle, \ldots, \langle \phi_k, \hat{c}_k \rangle$ such that:

(i) $[\phi_1, \ldots, \phi_k]$ is a conceptual clustering model for L (where $\phi_k = \emptyset$);
(ii) for each $j \in \{1, \ldots, k\}$, it is $\hat{c}_j = cluster_{\mathcal{M}}(L, j)$;
(iii) for each $j \in \{1, \ldots, k-1\}$ it holds $\mathcal{I}(\hat{c}_j) > \gamma$, $|(\hat{c}_j)| \geq \sigma$ and $|\phi| \leq maxLen$;
(iv) for each $j \in \{1, \ldots, k\}$, is an event abstraction function of the form $\alpha_j : \mathcal{E} \rightarrow Dom(\alpha_j)$, meant to emphasize the differences in behavior (in terms of flows across the event classes in $Dom(\alpha_j)$) between the cases of $\hat{c}_j$ and the remaining ones;
(v) for each $j \in \{1, \ldots, k\}$, $AList_j$, is an ordered list of case attributes that have a significantly different distribution in $\hat{c}_j$ than in the rest of the log (the higher the difference, the earlier the attribute will feature in the list).   □

Notice that the constraints specified through γ, σ and $maxLen$ apply to all the clusters but the last (which is not meant, indeed, to represent a group of deviance cases).

---

[4] For better readability, we will omit $L, \delta, \gamma, \sigma$ and $maxLen$ when they are clear from the context.

Objective Function (to Maximize). Using γ as a minimal deviance level for individual cases, one can define the set $Dev(L, \gamma)$ of all the γ-*deviant* traces (i.e. traces having a deviance score higher than γ) that appear in the log: $Dev(L, \gamma) = \{\tau \in L \mid \delta(\tau) > \gamma\}$.

Let us introduce an ad-hoc measure (defined in [22]), for quantifying the degree of interestingness of any HO-DDM $\mathcal{M}$ discovered for a given log L w.r.t. some minimum deviance threshold $\gamma \in [0, 1)$:

$$Q(\mathcal{M}, L, \gamma) = \frac{\sum_{\tau \in Dev(L,\gamma)} w(\tau, L, \gamma) \cdot \mathcal{I}(cluster_{\mathcal{M}}(\tau))}{\sum_{\tau \in Dev(L,\gamma)} w(\tau, L, \gamma)} \qquad (9)$$

where $Dev(L, \gamma) = \{\tau \in L \mid \delta(\tau) > \gamma\}$ is the set of minimally deviant (i.e. γ-deviant) cases, while $w(\tau)$ is some weight assigned to any γ-deviant trace τ in $Dev(L, \gamma)$ based on its respective deviance rank (the lower the rank, the higher the weight)—remember that $\mathcal{I}(\hat{c})$ stands for the interesting score received by cluster $\hat{c}$ (here simply computed as the average deviation score of all the traces assigned to $\hat{c}$). For the sake of concreteness, in the rest of the chapter it is assumed that $w(\tau, L, \gamma) = |Dev(L, \gamma)| + 1 - rank(\delta(\tau))$, for any τ in L.

The discovery of an optimal DACM can be formally stated as follows.

Definition 4 (Problem DACM-mine). Given: A log L with an associated deviance indicator $\delta : L \rightarrow [0, 1]$; three thresholds $\gamma \in [0, 1)$, $\sigma \in \mathbb{N}^+$ and $maxLen \in \mathbb{N}^+ \cup \{\infty\}$.

Find: A HO-DDM $\mathcal{M} = [\langle \phi_1, c_1, \alpha_1, caseAttList_1 \rangle, \ldots, \langle \phi_k, c_k, \alpha_1, caseAttList_1 \rangle]$ for L and δ w.r.t. $\gamma, \sigma, maxLen$ such that $Q(\mathcal{M}, L, \gamma)$ is maximal, i.e. there is no other HO-DDM $\mathcal{M}'$ (for L and δ w.r.t. $\gamma, \sigma, maxLen$) such that $Q(\mathcal{M}', L, \gamma) > Q(\mathcal{M}', L, \gamma)$. $\square$

5.3   An Algorithm for Solving Problem DACM-mine

Solving the problem exactly is unfeasible in many real-life settings, as discussed in [22]. Figure 3 summarises a solution algorithm (still proposed in [22]), named HO-DDM-mine, that solves the problem heuristically in a two-phase way.

In the first phase, DACM-mine materializes the propositional encoding of each trace τ, obtained by projecting τ onto the sets $\mathcal{B}$ and $\mathcal{B}_{pairs}$ of behavioral attributes (as an abstract representation of the sequence of events associated with τ). In this phase, the original case attributes of τ can be extended with derived context information (e.g., workload indicators).

Steps 2–11 iteratively compute a list of clustering rules (i.e. description patterns), via a sequential covering scheme. Each iteration of the main loop (Steps 3–13) tries to extract the best possible clustering rule out of dataset Z (initially encoding all the cases in L) by way of function growClusteringRule. The instances covered by the discovered rule are removed from Z. This procedure is repeated until no further cluster $\hat{c}$ is found such that $\Delta(\hat{c}) > \gamma$. Before storing each discovered rule ϕ and the associated clusters of cases into a list M of (rule, cluster) pairs, the algorithm tries to optimize it heuristically through function

---

Input: Log L with associated sets $\mathcal{A}$ (resp., $\mathcal{A}_\mathcal{E}$) of case (resp., event) attributes, deviance indicator $\delta : L \to [0, 1]$, minimal deviance $\gamma \in [0, 1)$ and minimal size $\sigma \in \mathbb{N}^+$ for deviance clusters, and maximal length $maxLen \in \mathbb{N}^+$ for clustering rules (patterns).

Output: A HO-DDM model for L.

Method: Perform the following steps:

1 extendCaseAttributes$(L, \mathcal{A}_\mathcal{E})$; // materializes $\mathcal{B}$ and $\mathcal{B}_{pairs}$

2 $M := []$; $M' := []$; $Z := L$; continue := true;

3 **while** continue **do**

4    $\phi := \emptyset$; // starts with a dummy rule covering all the instances in Z

5    $\phi := $ growClusteringRule$(\phi, Z, \sigma, maxLen, \gamma)$;
   // observe that it is ensured $|cov(\phi, Z)| \geq \sigma$

6   **if** $\phi = \emptyset$ or $\Delta(cov(\phi_1, Z)) < \gamma$ **then** continue := false;

7   **else**

8       $\phi := $ prune&OptimizeRule$(\phi, cov(\phi, Z), \sigma, maxLen, \gamma)$;

9       $M.append(\langle \phi, cov(\phi, Z) \rangle)$; $Z := Z \setminus cov(\phi, Z)$;

10   **end**

11 **end**

12 $M.append(\langle \emptyset, Z \rangle)$; // adds the "default" rule and "normal" traces to M

13 $M := $ prune&OptimizeModel(M);

14 **for each** pair $\langle \phi, \hat{c} \rangle$ in M **do**

15   $\alpha := $ mineEventAbstraction$(\mathcal{A}_\mathcal{E}, \hat{c}, L)$;

16   $attrList := $ rankCaseAttributes$(\mathcal{A}, \hat{c}, L)$;

17   $M'.append(\langle \phi, \hat{c}, \alpha, attrList \rangle)$;

18 **end**

19 **return** M'

Fig. 3. Algorithm HO-DDM-mine.

prune&OptimizeRule. In particular, each constraint ξ is removed if the resulting (pruned) rule, say ϕ', does not decrease the deviance score of the cluster; otherwise, the function tries to replace ξ with a new constraint ξ', and confirms the modification if a better cluster is found than that specified by ϕ. A similar optimization procedure is applied iteratively to all the rules in the clustering model.

The second phase of the algorithm (Steps 14–19) provides each discovered cluster with an event abstraction model and a (ranked) list of characteristic case attributes, computed by functions mineEventAbstraction and rankCaseAttributes, respectively.

Further details can be found in [22].

5.4 A Comprehensive Architecture for Deviance Explanation

This subsection describes a system architecture that supports the induction of a DACM from a given log of deviance-labelled traces, possibly obtained by associating any originally unlabelled trace with the probabilistic deviance prediction provided by a HO-DDM (discovered as discussed in the previous sections).

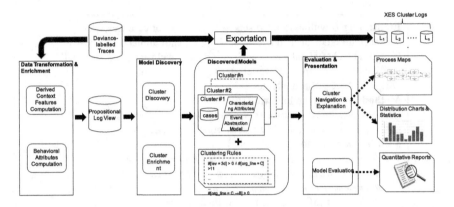

Fig. 4. Conceptual architecture of the developed extended prototype system.

This system architecture, depicted in Fig. 4, illustrates the main functionalities of a prototype system that is meant to support the recognition and explanation of relevant deviance groups, as an advanced capability of the *Deviance Inspection & Explanation* module of Fig. 2.

First of all, the cases in the given deviance-labelled log are passed trough the `Data Transformation & Enrichment` module for being encoded in the propositional form *pEnc* (cf. Definition 2) suitable for the next clustering phase. Basically, this is done with the help of two functional blocks: the *Derived Context Features Computation*, and the *Behavioral Attribute Computation*. The block *Derived Context Features Computation* enriches the set of original case attributes $\mathcal{A}$ in *pEnc* with some additional (derived) contextual features (e.g. environmental factors). Block *Behavioral Attributes Computation* completes the list of descriptive attributes for each case tuple in *pEnc* with the *behavioral attributes* $\mathcal{B}$ and $\mathcal{B}_{pairs}$ encoding the number of times a specific value (resp. two consecutive specific values) of an attribute $A \in \mathcal{A}_{\mathcal{E}}$ occur in each abstract trace, respectively. These propositional data instances are then saved into the repository "Propositional Log View" to make them available to the next `Model Discovery` module.

Module `Model Discovery` is meant to induce a (rule-based) conceptual clustering model `HO-DDM` (cf. Definition 3), and to provide the analyst with some additional information helping better explain it. In particular, the functional block *Cluster Discovery*, contained in it, implements the *PART I* (lines 2–15) of algorithm in Fig. 3, generating both the clusters $\{Cluster\#1, \ldots, Cluster\#n\}$, and the associated list of logical rules (i.e. *Clustering Rules*). The block *Cluster Enrichment* implements instead the second part of the algorithm (lines 16–20), where each cluster is further equipped with an ad-hoc event abstraction model, and with the list of its most characterizing context attributes.

The whole list of discovered logical clustering rules and all of the corresponding clusters of cases (each with its associated event abstraction models and list of characterizing context attributes) are saved into the data layer `Discovered`

Models for inspection and further analysis (supported by the Evaluation & Presentation module or by external process mining/analysis tools).

This latter module supports both the evaluation and the presentation of the HO-DDM model. Specifically, the block *Model Evaluation* provides the analyst with an analytic view (i.e. *Quantitative Reports*) about some quality metrics (including the *Interestingness* and *Explanation Complexity*) precisely tailored to our deviance detection setting (described in detail in the experimental section). The block *Cluster Navigation & Explanation* supplies the analyst with a series of visual tools like *Process Maps* and *Distribution Charts & Statistics*, offering an easy visual way to better comprehend what behavioral and/or context features most characterize the deviant clusters at hand.

Finally, the Exportation module receives both the original cases and the clustering rules discovered by the HO-DDM model, and exports the deviant clusters $\{L_1, \ldots, L_n\}$ (along with their relative event abstraction function) in the widely accepted format *eXtensible Event Stream* (XES) [46], allowing the analyst to further investigate them with any state-of-the-art process mining tools as *ProM* [46] or *Disco*[5].

6   Experimental Assessment and Analysis

The capability of our approach to effectively recognize deviant behaviors has been assessed by conducting a series of tests on a real-life log, storing information on the clinical pathways of gynecologic cancer patients within a Dutch hospital. This log was made available as a benchmark dataset for the *2011 BPI Challenge* [45]. Details on these datasets, omitted here for the sake of space, can be found in [11].

Different evaluation metrics exist in the literature for testing the effectiveness of classification models in the presence of a rare class. Carefully choosing these metrics is important since the usage of metrics that do not adequately account for the rarity of the minority class may easily lead to overestimating the accuracy of a classifier. Specifically, we used four metrics widely used over imbalanced data, i.e. *area under the ROC curve* (*AUC*) [6], the *G-mean* [30], *Precision* (*P*), and *Recall* (*R*) [7].

6.1   Experimental Settings

Testing our approach requires two key settings: (1) the kind of patterns used to project the log traces onto a vector space, and (2) the classifier-induction methods employed to derive, from such a feature-based representation of the traces, the base and combined models that compose the overall HO-DDM.

As concerns the former point, as a first family of behavioral patterns, denoted by IA (i.e. *individual activities*), we simply considered all the process activities in their own. In this case, for any trace, we regard each activity, say a, as an

---

[5] Available at https://fluxicon.com/disco/.

additional (pattern-oriented) feature of the trace, storing the number of times that a occurs in the trace. In order to produce more sophisticated representations of traces' behaviors, we also considered (as done in [5,38]) all the sequence-based patterns possibly capturing control-flow constructs (e.g., sub-processes, loops, and parallelism) ruling the behavior of the analyzed process: *tandem repeats* (TR), *alphabet tandem repeats* (ATR), *maximal repeats* (MR), and *alphabet maximal repeats* (AMR). When computing the *f-View* representation of a trace, we turned each of these patterns as a non negative integer attribute, storing the number of times the respective pattern occurred in the trace.

Similarly to [38], we considered the following heterogeneous families of patterns: *(i)* {IA}, i.e. individual activities used alone (producing a bag-of-activity representation of traces' structure); *(ii)* {IA,TR}, i.e. the combination of individual activities and of tandem repeats; *(iii)* {IA,ATR}, i.e. individual activities combined with alphabet tandem repeats; *(iv)* {IA,MR}, i.e. individual activities plus maximal repeats; *(v)* {IA,AMR}, i.e. individual activities plus alphabet maximal repeats.

For each pattern family, we used only a selection of those patterns that most frequently occur in the log (namely, 100 patterns of type {IA} and 250 patterns for each other pattern family). In addition, when HO-DDM-mine exploited the re-sampling to mitigate the skewness in the log, all the deviant (i.e. positive) traces in it were duplicated until a deviant-normal ratio of approximately 1:2 is reached.

As to the induction of base DDMs, we resorted to the following methods: the decision-tree learning method *J48* [40]; the *k-NN* procedure *IBk* (with $k = 10$); the multi-layer perception method (named hereinafter *ANN*) [51]; the *LibSVM* Support-Vector-Machines classifier [8] with an RDF kernel; and the rule-base classifier *JRip* [49].

For the induction of a probabilistic combiner model, we tested two alternative settings of algorithm HO-DDM-mine: one using an *AODE*-based classifier, and the other using an *HNB*-based classifier.

6.2   Experimental Results

A First Look a the Competitor's Results. Since the approach in [38] consists in applying each learning method to each distinct view of the log (generated according to one of the pattern families described in the previous subsection), it produces the 15 independent DDM models shown in Table 1—namely, $J48_{\{IA\}}$, ..., $J48_{\{IA+AMR\}}$, $IBk_{\{IA\}}$, ..., $IBk_{\{IA+AMR\}}$, $ANN_{\{IA\}}$, ..., $ANN_{\{IA+AMR\}}$— which should be compared with the ones discovered by our approach. However, it is easy to notice that the outcomes in Table 1 are almost all very close to one another, and no one single DDM can be clearly declared winning over its competitors in all the quality metrics simultaneously. For instance, the *AUC* value for the $IBK_{\{IA\}}$ model is 0.798, while that for $ANN_{\{IA+TR\}}$ is 0.795—this difference of less than 5% in their values reveals that they are practically equivalents to one another in terms of AUC performances. The same holds for the *G-Mean* of $J48_{\{IA+MR\}}$ (0.599), which is very close again to that of $IBk_{\{IA\}}$

Table 1. Prediction results obtained on the *BPIC11$_{CC}$* log when using different configurations of the (single DDM) competitor method [38]. All the values were computed by averaging the results of 5 trials, performed according to a 5 fold cross-validation scheme. For each metrics, the best outcome is reported in bold [13].

Alg.	Patterns	AUC	G-Mean	R	P	AvgRank	AvgRank_5%
IBk	{IA.AMR}	0.771±0.019	0.538 ± 0.049	0.321 ± 0.062	0.458 ± 0.106	9.00	2.75
	{IA.ATR}	0.782 ± 0.024	0.566 ± 0.062	0.362 ± 0.092	0.476 ± 0.108	4.25	1.50
	{IA.MR}	0.779 ± 0.020	0.538 ± 0.050	0.321 ± 0.062	0.456 ± 0.097	8.25	2.75
	{IA.TR}	0.772 ± 0.028	0.545 ± 0.111	0.351 ± 0.151	0.411 ± 0.076	9.00	2.25
	{IA}	**0.798 ± 0.034**	0.597 ± 0.043	0.397 ± 0.072	0.493 ± 0.084	**1.75**	**1.00**
ANN	{IA.AMR}	0.787 ± 0.023	0.451 ± 0.066	0.222 ± 0.076	0.468 ± 0.146	8.75	3.75
	{IA.ATR}	0.780 ± 0.020	0.470 ± 0.124	0.261 ± 0.172	0.409 ± 0.144	10.50	3.50
	{IA.MR}	0.777 ± 0.026	0.523 ± 0.201	0.360 ± 0.271	0.412 ± 0.082	8.75	2.25
	{IA.TR}	0.795 ± 0.038	0.512 ± 0.182	0.339 ± 0.227	0.417 ± 0.049	8.00	2.75
	{IA}	0.779 ± 0.037	0.426 ± 0.032	0.198 ± 0.028	0.359 ± 0.107	12.75	4.75
J48	{IA.AMR}	0.740 ± 0.066	0.587 ± 0.099	0.397 ± 0.139	0.459 ± 0.082	6.50	1.50
	{IA.ATR}	0.768 ± 0.019	0.570 ± 0.098	0.378 ± 0.134	0.425 ± 0.070	7.00	1.75
	{IA.MR}	0.746 ± 0.069	**0.599 ± 0.090**	**0.412 ± 0.128**	0.459 ± 0.086	5.00	1.50
	{IA.TR}	0.706 ± 0.062	0.458 ± 0.100	0.244 ± 0.105	0.370 ± 0.091	13.75	4.50
	{IA}	0.757 ± 0.044	0.561 ± 0.103	0.359 ± 0.138	**0.496 ± 0.042**	6.50	2.00
MAX		**0.798 ± 0.034**	**0.599 ± 0.090**	**0.412 ± 0.128**	**0.496 ± 0.042**	**1.75**	**1.00**

(0.597). Similar considerations can be easily spotted as well for the remaining metrics. In such a situation, choosing the most suitable competitor to run against HO-DDM-mine is not a straightforward task.

Summarizing the Competitor's Achievements. In order to enable an easier comparison of our approach to the alternative settings of the competitor approach presented above, we devised a method for summarizing the performances of the latter. More precisely, we defined three different criteria for choosing the best achievement of the competitor approach: *(i)* BEST_OF_BEST, *(ii)* BEST_AVG_RANK, and *(iii)* BEST_AVG_RANK_5%.

As to the BEST_OF_BEST row, it simply reports, for each evaluation method, the best value (i.e. the maximum) obtained by all of the different configurations of the approach in [38] in each single metric. To make clear which values are chosen, the best outcome in each column (i.e. performance metric) of Table 1 have been marked in bold. For the reader' convenience, these values are also explicitly reported in the row with the **MAX** label at the bottom of the same table. Clearly, it is important to point out that this row provides an overestimated evaluation of the competitor approach, which may not correspond to any actual configuration of it. In a sense, this row is a sort of upper bound for the performance of all the considered configurations of the competitor.

Thus, in order to provide a more realistic (yet concise) term of comparison, we defined a second criterion for a further competitor, denoted by BEST_AVG_RANK, aiming at meaningfully aggregating all the results obtained with the approach of [38] and reported in Table 1. The way this competitor is actually determined is explained in the following.

Let C be the set of all DDM models discovered by the tested methods, and $M = \{AUC, G\text{-}Mean, R, P\}$ be the set of metrics considered in our evaluation setting. For any model $c \in C$ and any metrics $m \in M$, let $score(c, m)$ be the value returned by evaluating m against c. Based on these values, we ranked the models in C over each metrics. More clearly, $rank(c, m) = 1$ (resp. $rank(c, m) = k$) iff c is the best (k-th best) performer according to metrics m. Considering all metrics equally important for assessing the quality of a DDM, we computed an overall average ranking score for each model $c \in C$ as follows:

$$AvgRank(c) = .25 \times (rank(c, AUC)$$
$$+ rank(c, G - Mean) + rank(c, R) + rank(c, P))$$

The BEST_AVG_RANK model, selected among all the other models discovered by (using different configurations of) the approach of [38], is the one reaching the highest value of the overall ranking score $AvgRank$.

Example 1. Let us consider the model $IBK_{\{IA\}}$, discovered with method IBk on individual-activities features (i.e., by using only the family IA of patterns) According to the values in Table 1, it can be easily noted that $rank(IBK_{\{IA\}}, AUC) = 1$ since $IBK_{\{IA\}}$ is scored higher than any other model on the AUC metric (i.e. it achieved the maximum score over the AUC column). By converse, $rank(IBK_{\{IA\}}, G\text{-}Mean) = 2$, since $IBK_{\{IA\}}$ is the second best performer according to the $G\text{-}Mean$ metric—the same holds also for the metrics R and P. As a final result, we obtain the overall rank-oriented score $AvgRank(IBK_{\{IA\}}) = .25 \times (1 + 2 + 2 + 2) = 0.25 \times 7 = 1.75$. According to this ranking criterion, the model returned by IBk on the IA-based log view is deemed as the best result of the approach in [38], namely BEST_AVG_RANK, with an average rank of 1.75. □

For the sake of comparison, the row of Table 2 marked as BEST_AVG_RANK reports the quality measures received by this model, as a second term of comparison for our approach.

The way the BEST_AVG_RANK competitor has been computed might be susceptible to criticisms due to numeric approximation problems possibly plaguing very close values. Indeed, it may happen that two models have performance scores so much close among them (i.e. under a certain approximation threshold z) that could be retained unfair assigning them different ranks. In order to preventively cope with such potential concerns, we considered a third evaluation strategy accounting as equivalent two models $c1, c2 \in C$ w.r.t. a given metric $m \in M$ if the difference between their values falls below a specified threshold z. More formally, this can be stated as in the following:

$$rank(c1, m) = rank(c2, m) \text{ iff}$$
$$|m(c1) - m(c2)| \leq z \times \min(m(c1), m(c2))$$

As a consequence of the definition above, a new rank $AvgRank\_z\%$ can be easily defined. Specifically, in our setting we considered as a reasonable approximation a threshold of 5% (i.e. $z = .05$), and then we selected the competitor BEST_AVG_RANK_5% (cf. last row of Table 2) according to the index $AvgRank\_5\%$.

Example 2. Let us focus again on the IBk_{IA} model, and let $z = .05$ be the threshold value used for alleviating the numeric approximation problem in our calculus. Based on Table 1, it results that $rank(IBK_{\{IA\}}, AUC) = 1$, as $IBK_{\{IA\}}$ performs better than any other approach over the metric AUC. However, under this new threshold-based setting, $rank(IBK_{\{IA\}}, G-Mean) = 1$, although the best performer w.r.t. the metric $G\text{-}Mean$ is $J48_{\{IA,MR\}}$. Indeed, $IBK_{\{IA\}}$ and $J48_{\{IA,MR\}}$ are ranked equally due to the fact that $|G\text{-}Mean(IBK_{\{IA\}}) - G\text{-}Mean(J48_{\{IA,MR\}})| = |0.597 - 0.599| = .002 \leq .05 \times min(0.597, 0.599) = .05 \times 0.597 = .03$. Similar considerations apply for metrics R and P. Therefore, we have that $AvgRank\_5\%(IBK_{\{IA\}}) = .25 \times (1+1+1+1) = 0.25 \times 4 = 1.00$. As a consequence, $IBK_{\{IA\}}$ is the best performer according to criterion $AvgRank\_5\%$, i.e. the **BEST_AVG_RANK_5%** model. Please, notice that, by pure chance, it incidentally coincides with the **BEST_AVG_RANK** model. □

Clearly, by the way it is computed, the performances of our competitor in its **BEST_OF_BEST** setting are always better than that in both the **BEST_AVG_RANK** and **BEST_AVG_RANK_5%** ones. Therefore, the comparative analysis carried out in the following is focused on the ("optimistic" for the competitor) **BEST_OF_BEST** scenario.

Comparing HO-DDM-mine's Results with the Best Ones of the Competitor. Table 2 reports the results obtained by algorithm HO-DDM-mine, compared with those of the proposed in [38]. For the sake of comparison, we used the same families of patterns and the same (or a slightly wider) set of classification methods as in [38], and turned the probabilistic classifications of HO-DDM-mine into deterministic ones, using a fixed deviance threshold $\gamma = 0.5$.

Table 2. Prediction results on the $BPIC11_{CC}$ log by HO-DDM-mine and selected configurations of the competitor method [38]. All the values were computed by averaging the results of 5 trials, performed according to a 5 fold cross-validation scheme. For each metrics, the best outcome is reported in bold [13].

Method	Bayesian combiner	Setting	AUC	G-Mean	Recall	Precision
Ours	HNB	RES+MORE_LEARNERS	**0.857 ± 0.051**	**0.740 ± 0.018**	**0.606 ± 0.041**	**0.745 ± 0.047**
		RES	0.822 ± 0.040	0.726 ± 0.030	0.592 ± 0.059	0.717 ± 0.044
		NO_RES	0.817 ± 0.024	0.652 ± 0.035	0.477 ± 0.055	0.505 ± 0.077
	AODE	RES+MORE_LEARNERS	0.853 ± 0.053	0.736 ± 0.022	0.598 ± 0.042	0.742 ± 0.049
		RES	0.819 ± 0.044	0.722 ± 0.047	0.584 ± 0.080	0.715 ± 0.047
		NO_RES	0.813 ± 0.026	0.648 ± 0.039	0.469 ± 0.056	0.502 ± 0.082
(Nguyen et al. [38])	-	BEST_OF_BEST	0.798 ± 0.034	0.599 ± 0.090	0.412 ± 0.128	0.496 ± 0.042
		BEST_AVG_RANK	0.798 ± 0.034	0.597 ± 0.043	0.397 ± 0.072	0.493 ± 0.084
		BEST_AVG_RANK_5%	0.798 ± 0.034	0.597 ± 0.043	0.397 ± 0.072	0.493 ± 0.084

Specifically, as far as concerns HO-DDM-mine, we tested three different configurations of it:

- NO_RES, where no re-sampling procedure is applied to the transformed log (in order to reduce the class imbalance ratio), and the same set of (base) inductive learning methods as in [38] (namely J48, IBk, ANN) are used;
- RES, using our basic oversampling scheme and the same battery of base classifiers as in the previous configuration (and in [38]);
- RES+MORE_LEARNERS, which uses the same oversampling setting as in configuration RES, while exploiting the classifier-induction methods implemented in our prototype system (i.e. J48, IBk, ANN, LibSVM, JRip) [23].

The three bottommost rows in the table report, as a term of comparison, the best scores obtained by all the settings of the competitor, and computed according to the three criteria (namely, BEST_OF_BEST, BEST_AVG_RANK, and BEST_AVG_RANK_5%) explained in the previous paragraph.

From the figures in Table 2, we can draw several interesting observations. First of all, HO-DDM-mine (irrespective of the kind of probabilistic combiner adopted), even in the basic NO_RES configuration, performs always better (over all the quality metrics) than the competitor [38], whatever configuration is used for the latter. This confirms the validity of using an ensemble-learning approach to the deviance detection problem. In particular, it is worth noticing that when allowed to induce an HNB combiner, algorithm HO-DDM-mine achieves better performances than its AODE-based version, despite the latter method make use of an ensemble of SPODEs (see Sect. 2.1) while HNB only adopts a single Bayesian model. This likely descends from the capability of HNB to effectively capture the inherent dependencies between the attributes in our *s-View* representation.

Performing a finer grain analysis, we can notice that the gain achieved by the HNB-based version of HO-DDM-mine over the approach in [38] in its basic configuration without re-sampling becomes even more marked when using a basic oversampling procedure (i.e. in the RES configuration). Specifically, even though the increment in terms of *AUC* is moderate (3.00%), we can observe a significant improvement for the metric *G-Mean* (21.20%), and a noticeable 44.56% (resp. 43.69%) achievement in terms of precision (resp. recall).

Further improvement is obtained by our approach (still equipped with HNB) when letting it use both the oversampling procedure and a broader range of base classifiers (i.e. configuration RES+MORE_LEARNERS)—actually, we only extended the learning methods used by our competitor with the insertion of *LibSVM* and *JRip*. Indeed, in this case, a gain of 7.39% (resp. 23.54%, 50.20%, 47.09%) is obtained in terms of *AUC* (resp. *G-Mean*, precision, recall) w.r.t. the overestimated BEST_OF_BEST configuration.

Notably, a similar trend in the results can be found for the version of HO-DDM-mine adopting AODE as combiner, and then it does not require any further supplementary discussion.

In summary, it seems that the combination of an oversampling method with our ensemble-learning strategy helps obtain higher improvements (w.r.t. the competitor supervised deviance-detection approach) than exploiting a wider range of base classifiers.

Benefits of Using Bayesian Combiners. In a further series of tests, we considered some variants of algorithm `HO-DDM-mine` where we tried the following meta-learning methods (for inducing the combiner model $\hat{c}$ of any `HO-DDM`) as an alternative to its native Bayesian classifiers: `AdaBoostM1`, `J48`, `JRip`, `Logistic`. The results of this experimentation are reported in Table 3. It is clear that both kinds of Bayesian combiner allow to achieve superior performances, over all the quality metrics, than these alternative methods. This is likely due to their capability of obtaining accurate and robust estimates of the class membership probability, despite the high degree of dependence between the attributes in the stacked view given as input to it.

7 Related Work

Log-Based Performance Analysis: Existing Tools. Existing BPI tools support the analysis of the whole business process with respect to typical performance measures such as cycle time, processing time and waiting time. Moreover, these tools show the distribution of performance measures by means of dashboards with graphics and aggregate statistics [26]. Nevertheless, some tools (e.g. Performance Analysis plugins of ProM [27] and Disco [26]) display the performance measures on top of a process model, for example by replaying the log on the process model [27,44] and calculating aggregate performance measures for each element in the process. In this case, process performances are studied in a "snapshot" manner, by taking as input an event log and extracting aggregate measures of interest such as *mean waiting time, processing time* or *cycle time.* Several commercial tools even allow an interactive analysis such as a "select/drill-down and explain". Selection is performed either on the base of performances (output variable) or of structural (organizational) and context-oriented (input variables) aspects. The aim is helping the analyst to understand what aspects affect the process-performances and, in this way, discovering bottlenecks and best practices. The paradigm of analysis in such tools is usually iterative and expert-driven, i.e. the analyst is called to manually search for that knowledge she/he is interested in and no explanation for it is provided by the system. The analyst studies the behavior of some performance measures and tries to extract insight about the distinguishing features characterizing the interesting instances on the basis of two typical kinds of interactions: *(i)* a workflow-oriented process map which contains the featuring tasks; and *(ii)* summary statistics for the different kinds of attributes.

The relevance of such interactive tools for identifying deviant instances is also acknowledged in the scientific community and algorithms/tools have been recently proposed to support effective and interactive analysis in the process mining field (e.g. [20]).

Outlier/Anomaly Detection and Explanation. The proposed approach has little similarities with those outlier/anomaly techniques that try to provide an explanation about the divergent behavior of an instance. The anomaly/outlier detection is a challenging issue, widely tackled in literature. In particular, some

Table 3. Prediction results on the $BPIC11_{CC}$ log by HO-DDM-mine (in the configuration RES+MORE_LEARNERS) when using different learning algorithms (as an alternative to our AODE-based and HNB-based Bayesian meta-classifiers) for the discovery of a combiner model. All the values were computed by averaging the results of 5 trials, performed according to a 5 fold cross-validation scheme. For each metrics, the best outcome is reported in bold [13].

Meta-algorithm	AUC	G-Mean	R	P
HNB	**0.857 ± 0.051**	**0.740 ± 0.018**	**0.606 ± 0.041**	**0.745 ± 0.047**
AODE	0.853 ± 0.053	0.736 ± 0.022	0.598 ± 0.042	0.742 ± 0.049
AdaBoostM1	0.811 ± 0.056	0.719 ± 0.039	0.579 ± 0.057	0.710 ± 0.070
J48	0.748 ± 0.057	0.724 ± 0.048	0.584 ± 0.065	0.718 ± 0.071
JRip	0.715 ± 0.029	0.693 ± 0.033	0.543 ± 0.040	0.676 ± 0.061
Logistic	0.789 ± 0.052	0.712 ± 0.033	0.570 ± 0.049	0.696 ± 0.042

outlier explanation approaches have been proposed to provide a human-readable description of the deviant behavior. [17,37] search simultaneously clusters of anomalous instances and attributes groups able to describe the anomaly. In [1], an outlier sub-population is given in input and compared with the inlier population in order to simultaneously characterize the whole exceptional sub-population. Anyway, these approaches assume that a normal behavior model is provided in input. By converse, we are interested to identify instances clusters which exhibit divergent values of some KPIs measures, independently of how much they look rare and hardly explainable w.r.t. to the background process model or normal instances.

Subgroup Discovery. Subgroup discovery goal is identifying descriptions of meaningful data subsets which exhibit a deviant behavior (w.r.t. a certain property of interest – aka target concept) when compared to that of the population [2]. This issue has been widely studied in the case of categorical target concepts (e.g. [32]), but its employing to the case of numerical targets is a challenging research topic and currently studied. The latter indeed paves the way to the exploitation of a broader variety of interestingness measures directly accounting for the distribution of a numerical target attribute [34].

Subgroup discovery methods allow to identify a set of interesting subgroups. However, due to multi-correlations between the independent variables, some of these subgroups can overlap significantly. Subgroup set selection is a critical issue for removing redundancy and improving the interestingness of the overall subgroup discovery result. For a wide discussion on the general task of diverse subgroup set discovery we refer the interested reader to [33], where different types of selection heuristics are proposed.

Basically, from a structural point of view, it is possible prevent the generation of totally useless patterns (already covered by other more informative ones), by restricting the search space to target-closed subgroups [25] (similar to the concept of condensed patterns) or to irrelevant subgroup hypotheses [24] (containing superfluous conditions, and similar to the concept of closed patterns). In absence of background knowledge, multi-correlations between independent variables can then be reduced by excluding overlapping subgroups. Therefore, common criteria for a best set of subgroups include a low overlap of the subgroups, a high coverage of their union, and a low number and high quality of the set of selected subgroups. In this context, the our approach is quite different compared with Subgroup Discovery techniques, we are interested to identify interpretable and not overlapping clusters which enable the analyst to understand the anomalous behavior suggesting a restricted number of accurate deviant behaviors clusters.

8 Conclusions and Future Work

Following our previous line of work that has originated, across years, an innovative ensemble-learning framework for mining business process deviances, whose main benefit is that of introducing a sort of multi-view-learning scheme, in this chapter we made substantial progress along this line by proposing an alternative meta-learning method for probabilistically combining the predictions of different base DDMs, and putting all together in a conceptual system architecture oriented to support common BPM scenarios. We have also envisaged the combination of this approach with a deviance explanation methodology that leverages and extends a previous method still proposed by us in previous research, and the corresponding extended architecture. Our analytical contributions have been complemented with a state-of-the-art DDM discovery approach. The experimental results we derive confirm flexibility, reliability and effectiveness of the proposed business process deviance mining framework. While our proposed approach is relevantly different from other multi-view learning approaches that do not follow an ensemble-based scheme (such as, e.g., [39,47]), it has clearly expressed flexibility, the reliability and the effectiveness, all being critical properties of next-generation BPM systems.

As regards future work, we following lines of research are actually followed by us: (i) combining of our ensemble learning approach with log-oriented clustering methods (e.g., [3,21]); (ii) studying the integration of intelligent data processing techniques (e.g., [9,10,15,16]) as to improve the overall effectiveness of our proposed framework.

References

1. Angiulli, F., Fassetti, F., Palopoli, L.: Discovering characterizations of the behavior of anomalous subpopulations. IEEE Trans. Knowl. Data Eng. **25**(6), 1280–1292 (2013)
2. Atzmueller, M.: Subgroup discovery - advanced review. Wiley Int. Rev. Data Min. Knowl. Disc. **5**(1), 35–49 (2015)
3. Bose, R.P.J.C., van der Aalst, W.M.P.: Trace clustering based on conserved patterns: towards achieving better process models. In: Rinderle-Ma, S., Sadiq, S., Leymann, F. (eds.) BPM 2009. LNBIP, vol. 43, pp. 170–181. Springer, Heidelberg (2010). https://doi.org/10.1007/978-3-642-12186-9_16

4. Blockeel, H., Raedt, L.D., Ramon, J.: Top-down induction of clustering trees. In: Proceedings of the 15th International Conference on Machine Learning (ICML 98), pp. 55–63 (1998)
5. Bose, R.P.J.C., van der Aalst, W.M.P.: Discovering signature patterns from event logs. In: IEEE Symposium on Computational Intelligence and Data Mining (CIDM 2013), pp. 111–118 (2013)
6. Bradley, A.P.: The use of the area under the ROC curve in the evaluation of machine learning algorithms. Pattern Recogn. **30**(7), 1145–1159 (1997)
7. Buckland, M., Gey, F.: The relationship between recall and precision. J. Am. Soc. Inf. Sci. **45**(1), 12–19 (1994)
8. Cortes, C., Vapnik, V.: Support-vector networks. Mach. Learn. **20**(3), 273–297 (1995)
9. Cuzzocrea, A.: Providing probabilistically-bounded approximate answers to non-holistic aggregate range queries in OLAP. In: Proceedings of ACM DOLAP 2005, pp. 97–106 (2005)
10. Cuzzocrea, A.: Accuracy control in compressed multidimensional data cubes for quality of answer-based OLAP tools. In: Proceedings of IEEE SSDBM 2006, pp. 301–310 (2006)
11. Cuzzocrea, A., Folino, F., Guarascio, M., Pontieri, L.: A multi-view learning approach to the discovery of deviant process instances. In: Debruyne, C., Panetto, H., Meersman, R., Dillon, T., Weichhart, G., An, Y., Ardagna, C.A. (eds.) OTM 2015. LNCS, vol. 9415, pp. 146–165. Springer, Cham (2015). https://doi.org/10.1007/978-3-319-26148-5_9
12. Cuzzocrea, A., Folino, F., Guarascio, M., Pontieri, L.: A robust and versatile multi-view learning framework for the detection of deviant business process instances. Int. J. Coop. Inf. Syst. **25**(4), 1–56 (2016)
13. Cuzzocrea, A., Folino, F., Guarascio, M., Pontieri, L.: Extensions, analysis and experimental assessment of a probabilistic ensemble-learning framework for detecting deviances in business process instances. In: Proceedings of ICEIS 2017, pp. 162–173 (2017)
14. Cuzzocrea, A., Folino, F., Guarascio, M., Pontieri L.: A multi-view multi-dimensional ensemble learning approach to mining business process deviances. In: Proceedings of the International Joint Conference on Neural Networks (IJCNN 2016), pp. 3809–3816 (2016)
15. Cuzzocrea, A., Furfaro, F., Saccà, D.: Enabling OLAP in mobile environments via intelligent data cube compression techniques. J. Intell. Inf. Syst. **33**(2), 95–143 (2009)
16. Cuzzocrea, A., Matrangolo, U.: Analytical synopses for approximate query answering in OLAP environments. In: Galindo, F., Takizawa, M., Traunmüller, R. (eds.) DEXA 2004. LNCS, vol. 3180, pp. 359–370. Springer, Heidelberg (2004). https://doi.org/10.1007/978-3-540-30075-5_35
17. Das, K., Schneider, J., Neill, D.B.: Anomaly pattern detection in categorical datasets. In: Proceedings of 14th International Conference on Knowledge Discovery and Data Mining (KDD 2008), pp. 169–176 (2008)
18. Domingos, P., Pazzani, M.J.: Beyond independence: conditions for the optimality of the simple Bayesian classifier. In: Proceedings of the 13th International Conference on Machine Learning (ICML 1996), pp. 105–112 (1996)
19. Domingos, P., Pazzani, M.J.: On the optimality of the simple Bayesian classifier under zero-one loss. Mach. Learn. **29**, 103–130 (1997)

20. van Dongen, B.F., de Medeiros, A.K.A., Verbeek, H.M.W., Weijters, A.J.M.M., van der Aalst, W.M.P.: The ProM framework: a new era in process mining tool support. In: Ciardo, G., Darondeau, P. (eds.) ICATPN 2005. LNCS, vol. 3536, pp. 444–454. Springer, Heidelberg (2005). https://doi.org/10.1007/11494744_25

21. Folino, F., Guarascio, M., Pontieri, L.: Mining predictive process models out of low-level multidimensional logs. In: Jarke, M., Mylopoulos, J., Quix, C., Rolland, C., Manolopoulos, Y., Mouratidis, H., Horkoff, J. (eds.) CAiSE 2014. LNCS, vol. 8484, pp. 533–547. Springer, Cham (2014). https://doi.org/10.1007/978-3-319-07881-6_36

22. Folino, F., Guarascio, M., Pontieri, L.: A descriptive clustering approach to the analysis of quantitative business-process deviances. In: Proceedings of 2017 Symposium on Applied Computing (SAC 2017), pp. 765–770 (2017)

23. Frank, E., Hall, M.A., Holmes, G., Kirkby, R., Pfahringer, B.: Weka-a machine learning workbench for data mining. In: Maimon O., Rokach L. (eds.) Data Mining and Knowledge Discovery Handbook, pp. 1305–1314. Springer, Boston (2009). https://doi.org/10.1007/978-0-387-09823-4_66

24. Gamberger, D., Lavrac, N.: Expert-guided subgroup discovery: methodology and application. J. Artif. Int. Res. **17**(1), 501–527 (2002)

25. Großkreutz, H., Paurat, D., Rüping, S.: An enhanced relevance criterion for more concise supervised pattern discovery. In: Proceedings of 18th International Conference on Knowledge Discovery and Data Mining (KDD 2012), pp. 1442–1450 (2012)

26. Günther, C.W., Rozinat, A.: Disco: discover your processes. In: Proceedings of 10th International Conference on Business Process Management (BPM 2012), pp. 40–44 (2012)

27. Hornix, P.T.: Performance analysis of business processes through process mining. Master's thesis, Eindhoven University of Technology, The Netherlands (2007)

28. Japkowicz, N., Stephen, S.: The class imbalance problem: a systematic study. Intell. Data Anal. **6**(5), 429–449 (2002)

29. Keogh, E.J., Pazzani, M.J.: Learning the structure of augmented Bayesian classifiers. Int. J. Artif. Intell. Tools **11**(40), 587–601 (2002)

30. Kubat, M., Holte, R., Matwin, S.: Learning when negative examples abound. In: van Someren, M., Widmer, G. (eds.) ECML 1997. LNCS, vol. 1224, pp. 146–153. Springer, Heidelberg (1997). https://doi.org/10.1007/3-540-62858-4_79

31. Langley, P., Iba, W., Thompson, K.: An analysis of Bayesian classifiers. In: Proceedings of 10th National Conference on Artificial Intelligence (AAAI 1992), pp. 223–228 (1992)

32. Lavrač, N., Kavšek, B., Flach, P., Todorovski, L.: Subgroup discovery with CN2-SD. J. Mach. Learn. Res. **5**, 153–188 (2004)

33. Leeuwen, M., Knobbe, A.: Diverse subgroup set discovery. Data Min. Knowl. Discov. **25**(2), 208–242 (2012)

34. Lemmerich, F., Atzmueller, M., Puppe, F.: Fast exhaustive subgroup discovery with numerical target concepts. Data Min. Knowl. Disc. 1–52 (2015)

35. Leontjeva, A., Conforti, R., Di Francescomarino, C., Dumas, M., Maggi, F.M.: Complex symbolic sequence encodings for predictive monitoring of business processes. In: Motahari-Nezhad, H.R., Recker, J., Weidlich, M. (eds.) BPM 2015. LNCS, vol. 9253, pp. 297–313. Springer, Cham (2015). https://doi.org/10.1007/978-3-319-23063-4_21

36. Lo, D., Cheng, H., Han, J., Khoo, S.C., Sun, C.: Classification of software behaviors for failure detection: a discriminative pattern mining approach. In: Proceedings of 15th International Conference on Knowledge Discovery and Data Mining (KDD 2009), pp. 557–566 (2009)
37. McFowland, E., Speakman, S., Neill, D.B.: Fast generalized subset scan for anomalous pattern detection. J. Mach. Learn. Res. $14(1)$, 1533–1561 (2013)
38. Nguyen, H., Dumas, M., La Rosa, M., Maggi, F.M., Suriadi, S.: Mining business process deviance: a quest for accuracy. In: Meersman, R., Panetto, H., Dillon, T., Missikoff, M., Liu, L., Pastor, O., Cuzzocrea, A., Sellis, T. (eds.) OTM 2014. LNCS, vol. 8841, pp. 436–445. Springer, Heidelberg (2014). https://doi.org/10.1007/978-3-662-45563-0_25
39. Nigam, K., Ghani, R.: Analyzing the effectiveness and applicability of co-training. In: Proceedings of the 9th International Conference on Information and Knowledge Management (CIKM 2000), pp. 86–93 (2000)
40. Quinlan, J.R.: C4.5: Programs for Machine Learning. Morgan Kaufmann Publishers Inc., San Francisco (1993)
41. Sahami, M.: Learning limited dependence Bayesian classifiers. In: Proceedings of the 2nd ACM SIGKDD of International Conference Knowledge Discovery and Data Mining (KDD 1996), pp. 334–338 (1996)
42. Suriadi, S., Ouyang, C., van der Aalst, W.M.P., ter Hofstede, A.H.M.: Root cause analysis with enriched process logs. In: La Rosa, M., Soffer, P. (eds.) BPM 2012. LNBIP, vol. 132, pp. 174–186. Springer, Heidelberg (2013). https://doi.org/10.1007/978-3-642-36285-9_18
43. Swinnen, J., Depaire, B., Jans, M.J., Vanhoof, K.: A process deviation analysis - a case study. In: Proceedings of 2011 Business Process Management Workshops, pp. 87–98 (2011)
44. van der Aalst, W., Adriansyah, A., van Dongen, B.: Replaying history on process models for conformance checking and performance analysis. Wiley Int. Rev. Data Min. Knowl. Disc. $2(2)$, 182–192 (2012)
45. van Dongen, B.F.: Real-life event logs - hospital log (2011)
46. Verbeek, H.M.W., Buijs, J.C.A.M., van Dongen, B.F., van der Aalst, W.M.P.: XES, XESame, and ProM 6. In: Soffer, P., Proper, E. (eds.) CAiSE Forum 2010. LNBIP, vol. 72, pp. 60–75. Springer, Heidelberg (2011). https://doi.org/10.1007/978-3-642-17722-4_5
47. Wang, W., Zhou, Z.H.: A new analysis of co-training. In: Proceedings of the 27th International Conference on Machine Learning (ICML 2010), pp. 1135–1142 (2010)
48. Webb, G.I., Boughton, J., Wang, Z.: Not so Naive Bayes: aggregating one-dependence estimators. Mach. Learn. $58(1)$, 5–24 (2005)
49. Witten, I.H., Frank, E.: Data Mining: Practical Machine Learning Tools and Techniques, Second Edition (Morgan Kaufmann Series in Data Management Systems). Morgan Kaufmann Publishers Inc., San Francisco (2005)
50. Ying, Y., et al.: To select or to weigh: a comparative study of linear combination schemes for superparent-one-dependence estimators. IEEE Trans. Knowl. Data Eng. $19(12)$, 1652–1665 (2007)
51. Zhang, G.P.: Neural networks for classification: a survey. IEEE Trans. Syst. Man Cybernet. Part C Appl. Rev. $30(4)$, 451–462 (2000)
52. Zhang, H., Jiang, L., Su, J.: Hidden Naive Bayes. In: Proceedings of AAAI, pp. 919–924 (2005)

Artificial Intelligence and Decision Support Systems

Triplet Markov Chains Based- Estimation of Nonstationary Latent Variables Hidden with Independent Noise

Mohamed El Yazid Boudaren[1]([⊠]), Emmanuel Monfrini[2],
Kadda Beghdad Bey[1], Ahmed Habbouchi[1], and Wojciech Pieczynski[2]

[1] Ecole Militaire Polytechnique, PO Box 17, 16111 Bordj El Bahri, Algiers, Algeria
boudaren@gmail.com
[2] TELECOM SudParis, CNRS, Université Paris-Saclay,
9 rue Charles Fourier, 91000 Evry, France

Abstract. Estimation of hidden variables is among the most challenging tasks in statistical signal processing. In this context, hidden Markov chains have been extensively used due to their ability to recover hidden variables from observed ones even for large data. Such models fail, however, to handle nonstationary data when parameters are unknown. The aim of this paper is to show how the recent triplet Markov chains, strictly more general models exhibiting comparable computational cost, can be used to overcome this shortcoming in two different ways: (i) in a firmly Bayesian context by considering an additional Markov process to model the switches of the hidden variables; and, (ii) by introducing Dempster-Shafer theory to model the lack of precision of prior distributions. Moreover, we analyze both approaches and assess their performance through experiments conducted on sampled data and noised images.

Keywords: Data segmentation · Hidden Markov chains
Nonstationary data · Signal processing · Triplet Markov chains

1 Introduction

Recovery of hidden variables is among the most challenging inverse problems in statistical signal processing. To this end, many Bayesian techniques have been proposed, particularly in the framework of hidden Markov chains (HMCs). This study, which extends the one presented in [1], tackles the problem of estimating hidden variables in nonstationary context in an unsupervised way. For this purpose, let $X = (X_1, .., X_N)$ and $Y = (Y_1, .., Y_N)$ be two stochastic processes where each X_n takes its values in $\Omega = \{\omega_1, .., \omega_K\}$ and each Y_n to $\mathbb{R}$. X is is hidden and is to be recovered from the observation $Y = y$. It is to say, the hidden sequence $x = (x_1, .., x_N)$, which is not directly accessible, is to be estimated based on the only observation $y = (y_1, .., y_N)$. Such estimation may be of interest in many fields covering image classification, image segmentation and image

© Springer International Publishing AG, part of Springer Nature 2018
S. Hammoudi et al. (Eds.): ICEIS 2017, LNBIP 321, pp. 127–144, 2018.
https://doi.org/10.1007/978-3-319-93375-7_7

change detection, in all of which one has to recover a hidden "process" from an observable one. In image classification for instance, one has to assign each pixel to one among a set of predefined set of classes. Image segmentation, which is considered here as illustrative application, is a derivative problem where classes are not known in advance. Thus, the observation y will be considered as a noisy version of x.

One among the most commonly considered HMCs is the independent noise-hidden Markov chain model, that will be simply denoted HMC along the remainder of this paper. According to such model, the link between x and y is expressed through the following joint probability distribution:

$$p(x,y) = p(x_1)p(y_1|x_1) \prod_{n=2}^{N} p(x_n|x_{n-1})p(y_n|x_n) \qquad (1)$$

The effectiveness of such models stems from their ability to estimate the realization of x, which is optimal "in average" among all the possible K^N ones, by means of some low-time-consuming Bayesian techniques such as maximum posterior marginals (MPM) [2] or maximum *a posteriori* (MAP) [3]. For further details, the reader may refer to [4] or [5] where both techniques are described. Another strength of HMCs relies in the fact that such estimation remains possible even in the unsupervised context, i.e. when the model parameters are unknown. Indeed, one can still estimate these latter thanks to some iterative but efficient algorithms such as expectation- maximization algorithm (EM) [2,6], its stochastic version (SEM) [7] or iterated conditional estimation (ICE) [8,9]. However, such algorithms assume the transition probabilities $p(x_n|x_{n-1})$ independent of the position n. The qualifier "Nonstationary" considered in this paper refers to the attempt to relax this simplifying assumption that turns out to be inappropriate in many situations. In the field of image processing for instance, one can mention image segmentation where the class-image, which is to be determined, may be too heterogeneous to be modeled through a stationary Markov chain, as shown by [10]. To overcome this inadequacy, the recent triplet Markov chains (TMCs) introduced by [11] have been used in both Bayesian and evidential context:

1. Lanchantin et al. [10] introduce an evidential Markov chain model by considering compound hypothesis instead of singletons in accordance with the Dempster-Shafer theory of evidence. Thus, the prior distribution is replaced by a belief function to overcome its unreliability. Afterward, the hidden evidential Markov chain (HEMC) is defined in an analogous manner to the HMC model.
2. In the switching hidden Markov chain (SHMC) proposed by [12], hidden data are considered stationary "per part" and an HMC is associated to each part. Moreover, the process governing the switches of the system is assumed to be Markovian.

The aim of this paper is twofold: (i) to show how TMCs are used according to the above mentioned contexts to achieve unsupervised estimation of nonstationary latent variable; and, (ii) to compare the performances of these two approaches, so far considered apart, to provide some answer to the following crucial question: when no *a priori* knowledge about data are available, which of the two approaches performs better?

The remainder of this paper is organized as follows: Sect. 2 summarizes the TMC model and describes the HEMC and SHMC models. Experimental results are provided and discussed in Sect. 3. Concluding comments and remarks end the paper.

2   Triplet Markov Chains for Nonstationary Data Modeling

Recently, there have been many attempts to go beyond the simplifying assumptions of HMCs in most of which, to our knowledge, the process X remains Markovian. Recently, these models have been generalized to PMCs [9,13] and TMCs [11] which offer more modeling capabilities while keeping the formalism simple enough to be workable. This section describes PMCs and TMCs, and reviews their use for nonstationary data modeling.

2.1   Pairwise Markov Chains

Let $X = (X_1, .., X_N)$ and $Y = (Y_1, .., Y_N)$ be two stochastic processes as in the previous section. The pairwise process $Z = (X, Y)$ is said to be a "Pairwise Markov chain" (PMC) if $Z = (X, Y)$ is a Markov chain. Its joint distribution is then written

$$p(z) = p(z_1) \prod_{n=2}^{N} p(z_n | z_{n-1}) \tag{2}$$

The transition probability can then be expressed as

$$p(z_n | z_{n-1}) = p(x_n | x_{n-1}, y_{n-1}) p(y_n | x_n, x_{n-1}, y_{n-1}). \tag{3}$$

Hence, setting $p(x_n | x_{n-1}, y_{n-1}) = p(x_n | x_{n-1})$ and $p(y_n | x_n, x_{n-1}, y_{n-1}) = p(y_n | x_n)$ for each $n = 2, .., N$, one finds again the HMC joint distribution of (1). The reader may refer to [12] for the proof. The noise distribution is then more complex in PMC and the hidden process X is no longer assumed Markovian. In spite of this generality, all Bayesian techniques remain workable and the performance in unsupervised segmentation is significantly better as shown by [9].

2.2   Triplet Markov Chains

Let $U = (U_1, .., U_N)$ be a discrete process where each U_n takes its values in a finite set $\Lambda = \{\lambda_1, .., \lambda_M\}$. The triplet process $T = (U, X, Y)$ is said to be a TMC if it is a Markov chain. Since both X and U are discrete finite, one can say setting $V = (U, X)$, that $T = (U, X, Y)$ is a TMC if and only if (V, Y) is a PMC. Hence, the Bayesian methods can still be used to estimate V from Y, which gives both X and U. The main interest of TMCs with respect to HMCs relies on the usefulness of the auxiliary process U to take some hard situations into account [10–12, 14–26].

2.3   Triplet Markov Chains Based-Estimation of Nonstationary Data Hidden with Independent Noise

In what follows, we summarize some TMC-related works that dealt with nonstationary data segmentation. [12] propose a "switching- HMC" to model switching data. According to such model, each portion of data can be modeled through an HMC with a different transition matrix. The aim of using the auxiliary process is then to consider the switches between such "unitary" models. Similarly, [27] define a "switching- PMC" in order to model switching data corrupted by more complex noise. For both previous models, U has been utilized to overcome the unreliability of the prior distribution $p(x)$. One potential application of these models is the texture segmentation problem where similar "switching-hidden Markov fields" have also been applied [14]. The situation where noise distributions $p(y_n|x_n)$ suffer from the same heterogeneity phenomenon has also been considered in the "jumping-noise HMC" introduced by [15]. Such model may be used to take light condition within an image into account or to model the fact that financial returns behave in a different way during a crisis. The same formalism has then been applied by [28] in triplet Markov fields context for PolSAR images classification.

An interesting link between triplet Markov models and theory of evidence [29] has also been established [30,31]. In fact, the use of Dempster-Shafer fusion (DS fusion) is unaffordable within HMC models since such a fusion destroys Markovianity. However, it has been shown in [30] that the fused distribution is a triplet Markov process and therefore, the different estimation procedures remain workable. Hence, in [10], authors propose a "hidden evidential Markov chain" (HEMC) to model nonstationary data. In this context, the unreliable prior distribution $p(x)$ is replaced by a belief function to model its lack of precision. In the same way, unsupervised segmentation of nonstationary images is considered in the PMC context [32]. Thus, DS fusion has been applied to model either sensor unreliability or data nonstationarity. [33] apply DS fusion to consider both situations at the same time. Evidential Markov chain formalism is also used to unify a set of heterogeneous Markov transition matrices [34].

It is worth pointing out that evidential hidden Markov models have been applied to solve other problems. [35] relax Bayesian decisions given by a Markovian classification of noisy images using evidential reasoning. [36] develop a method to prevent hazardous accidents due to operators' action slip in their use of a Skill-Assist. Recently, a second-order evidential Markov model is defined by [37]. Theory of evidence has also been applied in the Markov random fields context for image-related modeling problems [38–42]. Other applications of evidential Markov models also include data fusion and classification [43], power quality disturbance classification [44], particle filtering [45]. and fault diagnosis [46]. On the other hand, other potential applications of Bayesian triplet Markov models include complex data modeling [16,17,47], filtering [18,19], prediction [20], 3D MRI brain segmentation [21], SAR images processing [22–26]. Let us also mention that other Markov approaches have been successfully used to handle nonstationary data, particularly in the framework of "hidden semi-Markov models" [48].

In this study, we analyse the following classic problem from TMC viewpoint. Let us consider the HMC model defined by (1) and let us assume that the transitions $p(x_n|x_{n-1})$ depend on the position n. Considering data stationary, EM algorithm will give a fixed value to the transition probability defined on Ω^2, that may be considerably differ from the accurate varying $p(x_n|x_{n-1})$, which may result in poor performance. In the next sub-section, we show how the formalisms of SHMC and HEMC can be applied to remedy to this drawback. Even though both models belong to the TMC family, we will see that the meaning of the auxiliary U process in each model is quite different.

2.4   Evidential Triplet Markov Chains

This subsections describes the Hidden evidential Markov chains (HEMC) which is an evidential TMC that will be used to handle the estimation issue considered in this paper. Before we describe the HEMC model, let us first summarize some basics of the theory of evidence introduced by Dempster and reformulated by [29] and that will be needed for the purpose of this paper. Let us consider a "frame of discernment", also called "universe of discourse", $\Omega = \{\omega_1, ..., \omega_K\}$ and let $\mathcal{P}(\Omega)$ be the set of all its subsets. A mass function m is a function from $P(\Omega)$ to R^+ that fulfills:

$$p = \begin{cases} m(\emptyset) = 0 \\ \sum_{A \in P(\Omega)} P(A) = 1 \end{cases} \tag{4}$$

The mass function m defines then a "plausibility" function Pl from $\mathcal{P}(\Omega)$ to $[0, 1]$ by $Pl(A) = \sum_{A \cap B \neq \emptyset} m(B)$, and a "credibility" function Cr from $\mathcal{P}(\Omega)$ to $[0, 1]$ by $Cr(A) = \sum_{B \subset A} m(B)$. Also, both aforementioned functions are linked by $Pl(A) + Cr(A^c) = 1$. Furthermore, a probability function p can be considered as a particular case for which $Pl = Cr = p$.

When two mass functions m_1 and m_2 describe two pieces of evidence, we can fuse them using the so called "Dempster-Shafer fusion" (DS fusion), which gives $m = m_1 \oplus m_2$ defined by:

$$m(A) = (m_1 \oplus m_2)(A) \propto \sum_{B_1 \cap B_2 = A} m_1(B_1) m_2(B_2) \tag{5}$$

Finally, m is said "Bayesian" or "probabilistic" when, being null outside singletons, it defines a probability and we will say that it is "evidential" otherwise. One can then see that when either m_1 or m_2 is probabilistic, the fusion result m also is.

To establish a link between theory of evidence and the purpose of this study, let $(p_\theta)_{\theta \in \Theta}$ be a family of probabilities defined on $\Omega = \{\omega_1, \omega_2\}$, and let us define the following "lower" probability $\tilde{p}(\omega_n) = inf_{\theta \in \Theta} p_\theta(\omega_n)$. Let m be a mass function defined by $m(\{\omega_1\}) = \tilde{p}(\omega_1)$, $m(\{\omega_2\}) = \tilde{p}(\omega_2)$ and $m(\{\omega_1, \omega_2\}) = 1 - \tilde{p}(\omega_1) - \tilde{p}(\omega_2)$. The latter quantity models then the variability of the accurate probability p. Hence, it would be of interest to use this "fixed" value of evidential mass to run accurately algorithms such as EM while taking into account the unreliability of prior probabilities. This very key notion is exploited to define the HEMC.

Let us consider the following example to illustrate the interest of extending prior distributions using belief functions. First, we limit the frame to a blind context without spatial information.

Example: Let $\Omega = \{\omega_1, ..., \omega_K\}$ be a frame of discernment and suppose that our knowledge about the prior distribution $p(x)$ is $p_1 = p(x = \omega_1) \geq \varepsilon_1,...,$ $p_K = p(x = \omega_K) \geq \varepsilon_K$ with $\varepsilon = \varepsilon_1 + ... + \varepsilon_K \leq 1$. We can notice that ε measures the degree of knowledge of $p(x)$ in a "continuous" manner. Hence, for $\varepsilon = 1$, the distribution $p(x)$ is completely known, and for $\varepsilon = 0$, no knowledge about $p(x)$ is available. Let us assume that $p(y|x = \omega_1),..., p(y|x = \omega_K)$ are known, and let us consider the distribution $q^y = (q_1^y, ..., q_K^y)$ with $q_1^y = \frac{p(y|x=\omega_1)}{\sum_{i=1}^{K} p(y|x=\omega_i)}, \ ... \ , q_K^y = \frac{p(y|x=\omega_K)}{\sum_{i=1}^{K} p(y|x=\omega_i)}$.

One can assert that the Bayesian estimation of $X = x$ from $Y = y$ requires the knowledge of $p(x|y) \propto p(x)p(y|x)$ which is only partly known here. The crucial question would be how could one exploit this partial knowledge to achieve Bayesian classification? This is made possible by introducing the following mass function A on $P(\Omega)$: A is null outside $\{\{\omega_1\}, ..., \{\omega_K\}, \Omega\}$ and $A[\{\omega_1\}] = \varepsilon_1,$ $... , A[\{\omega_K\}] = \varepsilon_K, A[\Omega] = 1 - (\varepsilon_1 + ... + \varepsilon_K) = 1 - \varepsilon$. The DS fusion of A with $q^y = (q_1^y, ..., q_K^y)$ gives a probability p^* defined on Ω by $p^*(\omega_i) = \frac{(\varepsilon_i + 1 - \varepsilon)q_i^y}{\sum_{j=1}^{K}(\varepsilon_j + 1 - \varepsilon)q_j^y}$.

Consequently, the use of p^* allows one to use the partial knowledge of $p(x)$ to estimate X. Perfect knowledge of $p(x)$ corresponds to $\varepsilon = 1$ and hence, we have $p^*(x) = p(x)$. The situation where $\varepsilon = 0$ implies that $p^*(x) = q^y(x)$, which corresponds to the maximum likelihood classification.

The next step is to introduce the spatial information. A mass m defined on $P(\Omega^N)$ is said to be an evidential Markov chain (EMC) if it is null outside $[P(\Omega)]^N$ and if it can be written

$$m(U) = m(U_1)m(U_2|U_1) \cdots m(U_N|U_{N-1}) \tag{6}$$

Let us now introduce the observable process Y. For this purpose, the conventional Markov chain within the HMC model is replaced by the EMC given by (6) to take the nonstationary aspect of the data into account. In fact, the main link between classical Bayesian restoration and Dempster-Shafer theory is that the evaluation of the posterior distribution can be seen as a DS fusion of two probabilities [30]. Thus, extending the latter to mass functions, one extends the posterior probabilities and thus, one extends the frames of Bayesian computation. In the Markovian context, It has been established that the DS-fusion of the prior mass (EMC) m_1 given by (6) with the likelihood mass given by $m_2(x) \propto p(y|x) = \Sigma_{n=1}^{N} p(y_n|x_n)$ is the posterior distribution $p(x|y)$ defined by $p(x,y)$ which is itself a marginal distribution of a TMC $T = (U, X, Y)$ where each U_n takes its values from $P(\Omega)$. Such TMC is called HEMC. For further details, the reader may refer to [10,30] where proofs and different estimation procedures are extensively described.

2.5 Bayesian Triplet Markov Chains

This subsection is devoted to the description of the switching hidden Markov chains (SHMC), which is a Bayesian TMC considered of the purpose of this study. To this end, let $T = (U, X, Y)$ be a TMC where each U_n takes its values from a finite set of auxiliary classes $\Lambda = \{\lambda_1, .., \lambda_M\}$. T is called an SHMC if its transition probability is given by

$$p(t_n|t_{n-1}) = p(u_n|u_{n-1})p(x_n|x_{n-1}, u_n)p(y_n|x_n) \tag{7}$$

Hence, the transition probabilities depend on the realization of the auxiliary process U. Furthermore, the auxiliary process, which models the regime switches, is assumed to be Markovian. Therefore, neighboring sites tend to belong to the same auxiliary class. Such modeling has been successfully applied in texture images segmentation in HMC [12], PMC [27] and HMF [14] contexts.

To model nonstationary data, SHMC model considers each stationary part of the data apart by assigning a different set of parameters (transition probabilities) to each part. Partitioning data into different stationary parts is achieved as part of the unsupervised segmentation process. However, let us mention that the number of "stationarities" M is assumed to be known in advance. Notice that, setting $M = 1$, one finds again the conventional HMC. This shows the greater generality of the SHMC over the HMC. The conventional parameter estimation algorithms such as EM and the Bayesian MPM restoration have been extended to the SHMC context. Indeed setting $V = (U, X)$, one can write $T = (V, Y)$ which is a classic HMC. For further details, the reader may refer to [12] where the theoretical fundaments of the model are presented.

2.6 Bayesian Vs. Evidential TMCs

In what follows, we briefly discuss the difference between both Bayesian and evidential TMCs from purely theoretical viewpoint. In the evidential TMC model (HEMC), the auxiliary process U aims at modeling the lack of precision of prior information by also considering compound hypotheses. Hence, rather than making hard decisions that may be erroneous, HEMC takes uncertainty into account. On the other hand, the Bayesian TMC model (SHMC) only supports reliable information; however, it offers the opportunity to assign a different set of parameters to different data parts assumed locally stationary. To summarize, the main difference between both models relies in their perception of data: while the evidential TMC perceives data as unreliable through the weakening mechanism provided by Dempster-Shafer theory, the Bayesian TMC considers data stationary per part.

3   Experiments

In this section, we propose to assess the performance of both HEMC and SHMC for unsupervised segmentation of nonstationary data. For this purpose, we consider three sets of experiments considered in [1]. The first set is concerned with data sampled according to switching transition matrices. More explicitly, transition matrices are chosen randomly from a predefined set of matrices. The second set deals with images sampled according to randomly varying transition matrices where the priors vary linearly or sinusoidally according to pixel position. Finally, the third set considers two binary class-images that are noised using some white Gaussian noise.

For all experiments, unsupervised segmentation is performed using MPM according to: K-means, S-HMC model (for values of M ranging from 1 to 5) and HEMC model. All segmentations are assessed in terms of overall error ratios. Please notice that the conventional HMC model is itself the S-HMC having $M = 1$. Hence, the performance of all approaches are assessed with respect to the classic HMCs as well. For both S-HMC and HEMC, parameters are estimated through EM algorithm (100 iterations). The average results obtained on 100 experiments per subset are reported.

3.1   Unsupervised Segmentation of Switching Data Corrupted by Gaussian White Noise

Let $T = (U, X, Y)$ be a SHMC with $T = (T_n)_{n=1}^N$ where $N = 4096$, U_n takes its values from $\Lambda = \{\lambda_1, \lambda_2, \lambda_3\}$, X_n takes its values from $\Omega = \{\omega_1, \omega_2\}$ and Y_n from R. Accordingly, u_1 is sampled via a uniform draw from the set Λ whereas the next realizations of U are sampled using the transition matrix

$$Q = \begin{pmatrix} 0.998 & 0.001 & 0.001 \\ 0.001 & 0.998 & 0.001 \\ 0.001 & 0.001 & 0.998 \end{pmatrix}.$$

Similarly, x_1 is sampled by a uniform draw from the set Ω whereas the next realizations of X are sampled using the transition matrix A_m corresponding to the realization $u_n = \lambda_m$ as specified in (7):

$$A_1 = \begin{pmatrix} 0.99 & 0.01 \\ 0.01 & 0.99 \end{pmatrix}, A_2 = \begin{pmatrix} 0.5 & 0.5 \\ 0.5 & 0.5 \end{pmatrix},$$

$$A_3 = \begin{pmatrix} 0.01 & 0.99 \\ 0.99 & 0.01 \end{pmatrix}.$$

Finally, the realizations of Y are sampled through the Gaussian densities $\mathcal{N}(0, 1)$ and $\mathcal{N}(2, 1)$ associated with ω_1 and ω_2 respectively.

The quantitative performance metrics of different models are reported in Table 1 (set A).

As one can see from the results obtained, SHMC performs better than HEMC; particularly for actual values of M or even higher ones. This is due to the fact that data were sampled according to SHMC. In fact, SHMC searches for the best regularization that fits each part of the data (for a given number of stationarities M); whereas the HEMC model adopts a unique regularization along all the data sequence while considering a weakening mechanism to reach a good trade-off between *a priori* and likelihood information.

3.2 Unsupervised Segmentation of Randomly Varying Data Corrupted by Gaussian White Noise

Let $Z = (X, Y)$ be a nonstationary HMC with $Z = (Z_n)_{n=1}^N$ where $N = 4096$, X_n takes its values from a discrete finite set Ω and Y_n from $\mathbb{R}$. The joint distribution of Z is given by (1), whereas the transition probabilities $p(x_n|x_{n-1})$ are given by

$$A_n = \begin{pmatrix} \delta_n & \frac{1-\delta_n}{2} & \frac{1-\delta_n}{2} \\ \frac{1-\delta_n}{2} & \delta_n & \frac{1-\delta_n}{2} \\ \frac{1-\delta_n}{2} & \frac{1-\delta_n}{2} & \delta_n \end{pmatrix}.$$

For this series of experiments, we consider two different forms of the parameter δ_n and two different sets Ω, which gives 4 subsets. More explicitly, for subsets B.1 and B.3, we have $\delta_n = \frac{n}{N}$ whereas for subsets B.2 and B.4, we have $\delta_n = \frac{3}{4} + \frac{1}{4}\sin(\frac{n}{5})$. On the other hand, we have $\Omega = \{\omega_1, \omega_2\}$ for subsets B.1 and B.2 and $\Omega = \{\omega_1, \omega_2, \omega_3\}$ for subsets B.3 and B.4. Finally, the distributions $p(y_n|x_n)$ associated with ω_1, ω_2 and ω_3 are the Gaussian densities $\mathcal{N}(0, 1)$, $\mathcal{N}(2, 1)$ and $\mathcal{N}(4, 1)$ respectively.

For visualization purpose, some results obtained on subsets B.1, B.2, B.3 and B.4 have been converted to images via the Hilbert-Peano scan, and are illustrated in Figs. 1, 2, 3 and 4 respectively [1]. Average error ratios are also provided in Table 1 (Subsets B.1–B.4) [1].

Overall, both SHMC and HEMC outperform K-means and HMC on all datasets B1–B4.

For the considered data, the parameter δ_n is varying along the data sequence. When δ_n varies gradually, the data may still be partitioned into homogeneous parts. When δ_n varies sinusoidally, however, such partitioning may be unfeasible. The HEMC can still handle such situation thanks to its weakening mechanism. In particular, such mechanism is applied in sites for which the value of δ_n is too low and hence the likelihood information is to be considered rather than the unreliable *a priori* ones.

Indeed for subsets B.1 and B.3, where the parameter $\delta_n = \frac{n}{N}$ increases gradually from 0 towards 1 along the data sequence, the SHMC divides the data into M "homogeneous" parts with a different transition matrix per each, to achieve MPM segmentation and outperforms hence the HEMC performance. In fact, it is possible to check from the SHMC-based estimate of the auxiliary process U in Figs. 1 and 3 how the SHMC partitions the data into $M = 3$ (Figs. 1(h) and 3(h)), $M = 4$ (Figs. 1(j) and 3(j)) and $M = 5$ (Figs. 1(l) and 3(l)).

In subsets B.2 and B.4, on the other hand, the parameter $\delta_n = \frac{3}{4} + \frac{1}{4}\sin(\frac{n}{5})$ is of sinusoidal form, and for such fluctuating transition matrix, it is hard to

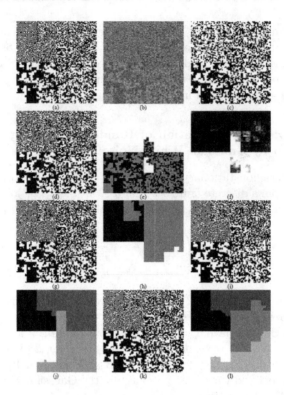

Fig. 1. Unsupervised segmentation of sampled nonstationary data (subset B.1) [1]. (a) class-image $X = x$. (b) Noised image $Y = y$. (c) HMC based segmentation, error ratio $\tau = 26\%$. (d) HEMC based segmentation, error ratio $\tau = 11.9\%$. (e) HEMC based estimate of U. (f) conditional weakening coefficient $\alpha = 1 - \sum_{k=1}^{K} p(x_n = \omega_k | y)$. (g) SHMC (M = 3) based segmentation, error ratio $\tau = 10.7\%$. (h) SHMC (M = 3) based estimate of U. (i) SHMC (M = 4) based segmentation, error ratio $\tau = 10.6\%$. (j) SHMC (M = 4) based estimate of U. (k) SHMC (M = 5) based segmentation, error ratio $\tau = 10.4\%$. (l) SHMC (M = 5) based estimate of U.

partition the sequence of data into M homogeneous parts and hence, SHMC performs relatively bad.

Still, the HEMC makes it possible to handle this kind of data thanks to its weakening mechanism. Indeed, notice that the smaller is the value of parameter δ_n, the more intense is the weakening and vice versa as shown in Fig. 2(g) and (h) in which a zoom on the first 1024 values of the parameter δ_n and the associated conditional weakening coefficient $\alpha_n = 1 - \sum_{k=1}^{K} p(x_n = \omega_k | y)$ respectively are depicted. This is due to the fact that for low values of parameter δ_n, the observation information is more important than the prior information, and hence, the weakening is intense in such sites.

Fig. 2. Unsupervised segmentation of sampled nonstationary data (subset B.2) [1]. (a) class-image $X = x$. (b) Noised image $Y = y$. (c) HMC based segmentation, error ratio $\tau = 12.6\%$. (d) HEMC based segmentation, error ratio $\tau = 12\%$. (e) HEMC based estimate of U. (f) conditional weakening coefficient $\alpha_n = 1 - \sum_{k=1}^{K} p(x_n = \omega_k|y)$. (g) 1024 first values of conditional weakening coefficient α_n. (h) 1024 first values of parameter δ_n. (i) SHMC (M = 4) based segmentation, error ratio $\tau = 12\%$. (j) SHMC (M = 4) based estimate of U. (k) SHMC (M = 5) based segmentation, error ratio $\tau = 12\%$. (l) SHMC (M = 5) based estimate of U.

3.3 Unsupervised Segmentation of Binary Class-Images Corrupted by Gaussian White Noise

Let us consider the nonstationary class-images "Nazca" (sets C.1 and C.2, Fig. 5) [1] and "Zebra" (sets C.3 and C.4, Fig. 6) [1], of size 128×128 and 256×256 respectively. Let $Z = (X, Y)$ be a nonstationary HMC with $Z = (Z_n)_{n=1}^{N}$. Images are converted to 1D-sequences via Hilbert-Peano scan as done by [9]. We then have a realization x with $\Omega = \{\omega_1, \omega_2\}$ where ω_1 and ω_2 corresponds to black pixels and white ones respectively. For sets C.1 and C.3 (resp. sets C.2 and C.4), noisy images are obtained by drawings from the Gaussian noise densities $\mathcal{N}(0, 1)$ and $\mathcal{N}(2, 1)$ (resp. $\mathcal{N}(0, 1)$ and $\mathcal{N}(1, 1)$) associated to ω_1 and ω_2 respectively.

Some obtained segmentation results are illustrated in Figs. 5 and 6. On the other hand, average error ratios are provided in Table 1 (Subsets C.1–C.2). The

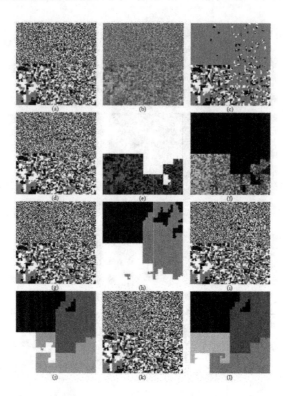

Fig. 3. Unsupervised segmentation of sampled nonstationary data (subset B.3) [1]. (a) class-image $X = x$. (b) Noised image $Y = y$. (c) HMC based segmentation, error ratio $\tau = 44.5\%$. (d) HEMC based segmentation, error ratio $\tau = 17.4\%$. (e) HEMC based estimate of U. (f) conditional weakening coefficient $\alpha = 1 - \sum_{k=1}^{K} p(x_n = \omega_k|y)$. (g) SHMC (M = 3) based segmentation, error ratio $\tau = 16.8\%$. (h) SHMC (M = 3) based estimate of U. (i) SHMC (M = 4) based segmentation, error ratio $\tau = 16.7\%$. (j) SHMC (M = 4) based estimate of U. (k) SHMC (M = 5) based segmentation, error ratio $\tau = 16.5\%$. (l) SHMC (M = 5) based estimate of U.

interest of this series of experiments relies in the fact that the realization of the hidden process is no longer sampled.

Models provide comparable results with a slight supremacy of SHMC, which is may be due to the possibility of partitioning each image into homogeneous regions. HEMC assigns the image regions having a lot of details to the compound auxiliary class $\{\omega_1, \omega_1\}$ to reduce the regularization in such regions. On the other hand, given a value of M, the SHMC classifies the image into M "auxiliary" classes sharing similar properties; the regularization within each auxiliary class is similar to the HMC one.

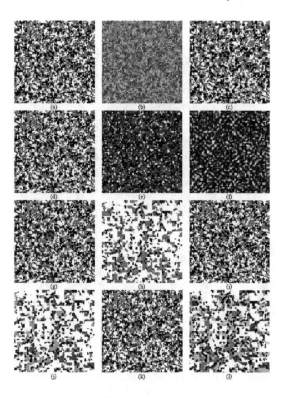

Fig. 4. Unsupervised segmentation of sampled nonstationary data (subset B.4) [1]. (a) class-image $X = x$. (b) Noised image $Y = y$. (c) HMC based segmentation, error ratio $\tau = 17.5\%$. (d) HEMC based segmentation, error ratio $\tau = 12\%$. (e) HEMC based estimate of U. (f) conditional weakening coefficient $\alpha = 1 - \sum_{k=1}^{K} p(x_n = \omega_k|y)$. (g) SHMC (M = 3) based segmentation, error ratio $\tau = 12.3\%$. (h) SHMC (M = 3) based estimate of U. (i) SHMC (M = 4) based segmentation, error ratio $\tau = 12.3\%$. (j) SHMC (M = 4) based estimate of U. (k) SHMC (M = 5) based segmentation, error ratio $\tau = 12.2\%$. (l) SHMC (M = 5) based estimate of U.

3.4   Discussion

For all datasets, SHMC and EHMC always provide better results than conventional HMC. On the other hand, the supremacy of both models over the blind K-means clustering shows the interest of considering the prior information, even when fluctuating, in the segmentation process. While both models exhibit comparable performance in general, Bayesian TMC turned to be better-suited when the number of "stationarities" is beforehand known. Evidential TMC, on the other hand, seems a good option where such information are not available; thanks to the weakening mechanism that overcomes the lack of precision of the prior knowledge by searching at each site the best weight balance between *a priori* and observation information.

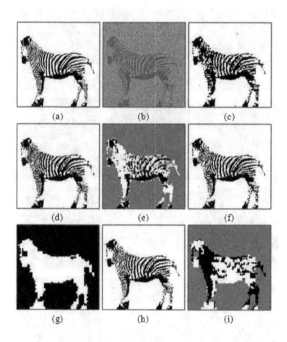

Fig. 5. Unsupervised segmentation of "Zebra" image [1]. (a) class-image $X = x$. (b) Noised image $Y = y$. (c) HMC based segmentation, error ratio $\tau = 6\%$. (d) HEMC based segmentation, error ratio $\tau = 3.6\%$. (e) HEMC based estimate of U. (f) SHMC ($M = 2$) based segmentation, error ratio $\tau = 3.7\%$. (g) HEMC ($M = 2$) based estimate of U. (h) SHMC ($M = 3$) based segmentation, error ratio $\tau = 3.3\%$. (i) HEMC ($M = 3$) based estimate of U.

Table 1. Average error ratios (%) of unsupervised segmentation of nonstationary data [1].

Set	K-means	HEMC	SHMC				
			M=1	M=2	M=3	M=4	M=5
A	15.5	10.2	15.8	11.4	**5.9**	**5.9**	6
B.1	26.1	11.4	25.5	11	10.5	10.4	**10.3**
B.2	16	**12**	12.7	12.1	12.1	**12**	**12**
B.3	21.7	17.6	45.1	17.8	16.7	**16.5**	**16.5**
B.4	21.2	**12**	17.6	12.2	12.2	12.3	12.2
C.1	27	5	13.3	5.2	4.9	5.2	**4.8**
C.2	38.7	**11**	15.4	16.4	14.6	14.1	14.9
C.3	26.1	3.7	6	3.7	**3.3**	**3.3**	**3.3**
C.4	38.5	8.2	12.3	8.1	7.7	**7.6**	7.7

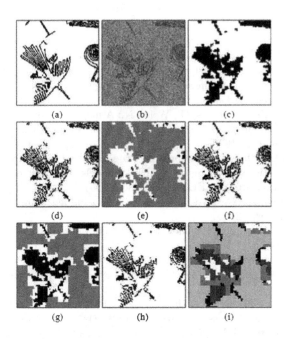

Fig. 6. Unsupervised segmentation of "Nazca" image [1]. (a) class-image $X = x$. (b) Noised image $Y = y$. (c) HMC based segmentation, error ratio $\tau = 13.2\%$. (d) HEMC based segmentation, error ratio $\tau = 4.9\%$. (e) HEMC based estimate of U. (f) SHMC (M = 3) based segmentation, error ratio $\tau = 4.9\%$. (g) HEMC (M = 3) based estimate of U. (h) SHMC (M = 7) based segmentation, error ratio $\tau = 4.7\%$. (i) HEMC (M = 7) based estimate of U.

4 Conclusions

Wa have shown in this paper how the recent TMCs can be used to estimate hidden variables in nonstationary data context. More explicitly, we considered both Bayesian and evidential versions of TMCs. The illustrative application for performance evaluation was unsupervised image segmentation where estimation of hidden process leads to segmentation. Experiments have been conducted on three sets of nonstationary data obtained in different manners. TMCs estimation quality has been assessed with respect to conventional models through the error ratio metric (τ). Overall, the results obtained showed that both considered TMCs significantly outperform standard HMCs. The supremacy of one model over another depends on the kind of data. An interesting future direction would be to tackle the model selection problem in order to determine the best-suited model (model choice, number of stationarities,...) for a given set of data using some criteria such as the Bayesian information criterion (BIC) as done in [12]. A potential application of the current study would be to combine both models as done in Markov field context [49,50].

142 M. E. Y. Boudaren et al.

References

1. Boudaren, M.E.Y., Monfrini, E., Bey, K.B., Habbouchi, A., Pieczynski, W.: Unsupervised segmentation of nonstationary data using triplet Markov chains. In: ICEIS 2017: 19th International Conference on Enterprise Information Systems. vol. 1., pp. 405–414. Scitepress (2017)
2. Baum, L.E., Petrie, T., Soules, G., Weiss, N.: A maximization technique occurring in the statistical analysis of probabilistic functions of Markov chains. Ann. Math. Stat. **41**(1), 164–171 (1970)
3. Forney Jr., G.D.: The viterbi algorithm. Proc. IEEE **61**, 268–278 (1973)
4. Rabiner, L.: A tutorial on hidden Markov models and selected applications in speech recognition. Proc. IEEE **77**, 257–286 (1989)
5. Cappé, O., Moulines, E., Rydén, T.: Inference in hidden Markov models, vol. 6. Springer, New York (2005)
6. McLachlan, G., Krishnan, T.: The EM algorithm and extensions, vol. 382. Wiley, New Jersey (2007)
7. Celeux, G., Chauveau, D., Diebolt, J.: Stochastic versions of the EM algorithm: an experimental study in the mixture case. J. Stat. Comput. Simul. **55**, 287–314 (1996)
8. Delmas, J.P.: An equivalence of the EM and ICE algorithm for exponential family. IEEE Trans. Signal Process. **45**, 2613–2615 (1997)
9. Derrode, S., Pieczynski, W.: Signal and image segmentation using pairwise Markov chains. IEEE Trans. Signal Process. **52**, 2477–2489 (2004)
10. Lanchantin, P., Pieczynski, W.: Unsupervised restoration of hidden nonstationary Markov chains using evidential priors. IEEE Trans. Signal Process. **53**, 3091–3098 (2005)
11. Pieczynski, W., Hulard, C., Veit, T.: Triplet Markov chains in hidden signal restoration. In: International Symposium on Remote Sensing, International Society for Optics and Photonics, pp. 58–68 (2003)
12. Lanchantin, P., Lapuyade-Lahorgue, J., Pieczynski, W.: Unsupervised segmentation of randomly switching data hidden with non-Gaussian correlated noise. Signal Process. **91**, 163–175 (2011)
13. Pieczynski, W.: Pairwise Markov chains. IEEE Trans. Pattern Anal. Mach. Intell. **25**, 634–639 (2003)
14. Benboudjema, D., Pieczynski, W.: Unsupervised statistical segmentation of nonstationary images using triplet Markov fields. IEEE Trans. Pattern Anal. Mach. Intell. **29**, 1367–1378 (2007)
15. Boudaren, M.E.Y., Monfrini, E., Pieczynski, W.: Unsupervised segmentation of random discrete data hidden with switching noise distributions. IEEE Signal Process. Lett. **19**, 619–622 (2012)
16. Boudaren, M.E.Y., Monfrini, E., Pieczynski, W., Aissani, A.: Phasic triplet Markov chains. IEEE Trans. Pattern Anal. Mach. Intell. **36**, 2310–2316 (2014)
17. Blanchet, J., Forbes, F.: Triplet Markov fields for the classification of complex structure data. IEEE Transactions on Pattern Anal. Mach. Intell. **30**, 1055–1067 (2008)
18. Ait-El-Fquih, B., Desbouvries, F.: Bayesian smoothing algorithms in pairwise and triplet markov chains. In: IEEE/SP 13th Workshop on Statistical Signal Processing, pp. 721–726. IEEE (2005)
19. Ait-El-Fquih, B., Desbouvries, F.: Kalman filtering in triplet Markov chains. IEEE Transactions on Signal Process. **54**, 2957–2963 (2006)

20. Bardel, N., Desbouvries, F.: Exact Bayesian prediction in a class of Markov-switching models. Methodol. Comput. Appl. Probab. **14**, 125–134 (2012)
21. Bricq, S., Collet, C., Armspach, J.P.: Triplet Markov chain for 3D MRI brain segmentation using a probabilistic atlas. In: 3rd IEEE International Symposium on Biomedical Imaging: Nano to Macro, pp. 386–389. IEEE (2006)
22. Gan, L., Wu, Y., Liu, M., Zhang, P., Ji, H., Wang, F.: Triplet Markov fields with edge location for fast unsupervised multi-class segmentation of synthetic aperture radar images. IET Image Process. **6**, 831–838 (2012)
23. Wang, F., Wu, Y., Zhang, Q., Zhang, P., Li, M., Lu, Y.: Unsupervised change detection on SAR images using triplet Markov field model. IEEE Geosci. Remote Sens. Lett. **10**, 697–701 (2013)
24. Zhang, P., Li, M., Wu, Y., Gan, L., Liu, M., Wang, F., Liu, G.: Unsupervised multi-class segmentation of SAR images using fuzzy triplet Markov fields model. Pattern Recognit. **45**, 4018–4033 (2012)
25. Zhang, P., Li, M., Wu, Y., Liu, M., Wang, F., Gan, L.: SAR image multiclass segmentation using a multiscale TMF model in wavelet domain. IEEE Geosci. Remote Sens. Lett. **9**, 1099–1103 (2012)
26. Wu, Y., Zhang, P., Li, M., Zhang, Q., Wang, F., Jia, L.: SAR image multiclass segmentation using a multiscale and multidirection triplet markov fields model in nonsubsampled contourlet transform domain. Inf. Fusion **14**, 441–449 (2013)
27. Boudaren, M.E.Y., Monfrini, E., Pieczynski, W.: Unsupervised segmentation of switching pairwise Markov chains. In: 2011 7th International Symposium on Image and Signal Processing and Analysis (ISPA), pp. 183–188. IEEE (2011)
28. Liu, G., Li, M., Wu, Y., Zhang, P., Jia, L., Liu, H.: Polsar image classification based on wishart TMF with specific auxiliary field. IEEE Geosc. Remote Sens. Lett. **11**, 1230–1234 (2014)
29. Shafer, G.: A mathematical theory of evidence, vol. 1. Princeton University Press Princeton, Princeton (1976)
30. Pieczynski, W.: Multisensor triplet Markov chains and theory of evidence. Int. J. Approx. Reason. **45**, 1–16 (2007)
31. Soubaras, H.: On evidential Markov chains. In: Foundations of reasoning under uncertainty, pp. 247–264. Springer, Heidelberg (2010)
32. Boudaren, M.E.Y., Monfrini, E., Pieczynski, W.: Unsupervised segmentation of nonstationary pairwise Markov chains using evidential priors. In: EUSIPCO, Bucharest, pp. 2243–2247. IEEE (2012)
33. Boudaren, M.E.Y., Monfrini, E., Pieczynski, W., Aïssani, A.: Dempster-Shafer fusion of multisensor signals in nonstationary Markovian context. EURASIP J. Adv. Sig. Proc. **2012**, 134 (2012)
34. Boudaren, M.E.Y., Pieczynski, W.: Unified representation of sets of heterogeneous Markov transition matrices. IEEE Trans. Fuzzy Syst. **24**, 497–503 (2016)
35. Foucher, S., Germain, M., Boucher, J.M., Benie, G.B.: Multisource classification using ICM and Dempster-Shafer theory. IEEE Trans. Instrum. Meas. **51**, 277–281 (2002)
36. Yoji, Y., Tetsuya, M., Yoji, U., Yukitaka, S.: A method for preventing accidents due to human action slip utilizing HMM-based Dempster-Shafer theory. In: Proceedings of the IEEE International Conference on Robotics and Automation 2003, ICRA 2003, vol. 1, pp. 1490–1496. IEEE (2003)
37. Park, J., Chebbah, M., Jendoubi, S., Martin, A.: Second-Order belief hidden Markov models. In: Cuzzolin, F. (ed.) BELIEF 2014. LNCS (LNAI), vol. 8764, pp. 284–293. Springer, Cham (2014). https://doi.org/10.1007/978-3-319-11191-9_31

38. Pieczynski, W., Benboudjema, D.: Multisensor triplet Markov fields and theory of evidence. Image Vis. Comput. **24**, 61–69 (2006)
39. Le Hégarat-Mascle, S., Bloch, I., Vidal-Madjar, D.: Introduction of neighborhood information in evidence theory and application to data fusion of radar and optical images with partial cloud cover. Pattern Recognit. **31**, 1811–1823 (1998)
40. Tupin, F., Bloch, I., Maître, H.: A first step toward automatic interpretation of SAR images using evidential fusion of several structure detectors. IEEE Transactions on Geosci. Remote Sens. **37**, 1327–1343 (1999)
41. Boudaren, M.E.Y., Pieczynski, W.: Dempster-Shafer fusion of evidential pairwise Markov chains. IEEE Trans. Fuzzy Syst. **24**, 1598–1610 (2016)
42. An, L., Li, M., Boudaren, M.E.Y., Pieczynski, W.: Evidential correlated gaussian mixture Markov model for pixel labeling problem. In: Vejnarová, J., Kratochvíl, V. (eds.) BELIEF 2016. LNCS (LNAI), vol. 9861, pp. 203–211. Springer, Cham (2016). https://doi.org/10.1007/978-3-319-45559-4_21
43. Fouque, L., Appriou, A., Pieczynski, W.: An evidential Markovian model for data fusion and unsupervised image classification. In: Proceedings of the Third International Conference on Information Fusion, FUSION 2000, vol. 1. IEEE (2000). TUB4-25
44. Dehghani, H., Vahidi, B., Naghizadeh, R., Hosseinian, S.: Power quality disturbance classification using a statistical and wavelet-based hidden Markov model with Dempster-Shafer algorithm. Int. J. Electr. Power Energy Syst. **47**, 368–377 (2013)
45. Reineking, T.: Particle filtering in the Dempster-Shafer theory. Int. J. Approx. Reason. **52**, 1124–1135 (2011)
46. Ramasso, E.: Contribution of belief functions to hidden Markov models with an application to fault diagnosis. In: Proceedings of the IEEE International Workshop on Machine Learning for Signal Processing, pp. 1–6 (2009)
47. Habbouchi, A., Boudaren, M.E.Y., Aïssani, A., Pieczynski, W.: Unsupervised segmentation of markov random fields corrupted by nonstationary noise. IEEE Signal Process. Lett. **23**, 1607–1611 (2016)
48. Lapuyade-Lahorgue, J., Pieczynski, W.: Unsupervised segmentation of hidden semi-Markov non stationary chains. In: Bayesian Inference and Maximum Entropy Methods in Science and Engineering (AIP Conference Proceedings Volume 872), vol. 872, pp. 347–354. Citeseer (2006)
49. Boudaren, M.E.Y., An, L., Pieczynski, W.: Unsupervised segmentation of SAR images using Gaussian mixture-hidden evidential Markov fields. IEEE Geosci. Remote Sens. Lett. **13**, 1865–1869 (2016)
50. Boudaren, M.E.Y., An, L., Pieczynski, W.: Dempster-Shafer fusion of evidential pairwise Markov fields. Int. J. Approx. Reason. **74**, 13–29 (2016)

Detection and Explanation of Anomalous Payment Behavior in Real-Time Gross Settlement Systems

Ron Triepels[1,2]([✉]), Hennie Daniels[1,3], and Ronald Heijmans[2]

[1] Tilburg University, Warandelaan 2, Tilburg, The Netherlands
r.j.m.a.triepels@uvt.nl
[2] De Nederlandsche Bank, Westeinde 1, Amsterdam, The Netherlands
[3] Erasmus University, Burg. Oudlaan 50, Rotterdam, The Netherlands

Abstract. In this paper, we discuss how to apply an autoencoder to detect anomalies in payment data derived from an Real-Time Gross Settlement system. Moreover, we introduce a drill-down procedure to measure the extent to which the inflow or outflow of a particular bank explains an anomaly. Experimental results on real-world payment data show that our method can detect the liquidity problems of a bank when it was subject to a bank run with reasonable accuracy.

Keywords: Anomaly detection · Autoencoders · Payment behavior
Real-Time Gross Settlement systems

1 Introduction

Financial Market Infrastructures (FMIs) play an important role in our economy as they facilitate the settlement and clearing of financial obligations. An FMI that does not function properly can potentially destabilize our entire economy. These systems therefore have to live up to high internationally accepted standards, called Principles for FMIs (PFMIs) [10]. Real-Time Gross Settlement (RTGS) systems are a class of FMI that have recently received considerable attention due to their central position in the FMI landscape.[1] RTGS systems are specialist funds transfer systems used mainly by commercial banks. Key features of RTGS systems are that they settle payments immediately when banks have sufficient liquidity on their accounts (real time) and on a one-to-one basis (gross). Once the payments have been processed they are final and irrevocable.

To guarantee the smooth processing of payments, FMI operators need to manage liquidity risk in RTGS systems. Liquidity risk refers to the risk of payments not being settled at the expected time because of insufficient liquidity at the paying bank [7]. The causes of this insufficient liquidity could include inadequate liquidity management by participants, delayed incoming payments (because of technical

---

[1] Many FMIs settle their positions in an RTGS system.

© Springer International Publishing AG, part of Springer Nature 2018
S. Hammoudi et al. (Eds.): ICEIS 2017, LNBIP 321, pp. 145–161, 2018.
https://doi.org/10.1007/978-3-319-93375-7_8

problems or liquidity problems at the paying bank), and unexpected large outgoing payments initiated by a bank's clients. When the liquidity position of a bank becomes critical to the point where payment obligations can no longer be fulfilled, liquidity problems can quickly propagate to many other banks due to contagion effects [2]. In the worst case, this can lead to a gridlock, with many banks all waiting for the other to make the first payment [3].

During the processing of payments, RTGS systems generate many data about the liquidity flows of banks. These payment data constitute a valuable source of information to identify potential liquidity risk. By analyzing payment data, we can obtain insight into the way banks manage their liquidity. For example, it has been shown that banks tend to recycle payments to decrease their liquidity requirement throughout the day [4,13]. Moreover, banks also change their liquidity management during times of financial stress. After the collapse of Lehman Brothers, banks in the British RTGS system (CHAPS) initiated payments at a considerable slower pace [5]. For FMI operators, it is important to detect such anomalies. Anomalous payment behavior is a key indicator of financial stress and a signal of potential liquidity risk [23]. When anomalous payment behavior emerges, FMI operators should identify it immediately and take appropriate countermeasures.

An interesting research question is whether we can detect anomalous payment behavior automatically by applying unsupervised anomaly detection on payment data. Anomaly detection deals with the problem of detecting patterns in a set of data that do not conform to expected behavior [9]. In the case of unsupervised anomaly detection, the goal is to identify anomalous patterns in unlabeled data, i.e. without having examples of the anomalies to be detected. The application of anomaly detection on payment data is promising. Sophisticated anomaly detection methods can be applied to analyze large sets of payment data and detect cases of anomalous payment behavior. The anomalies these methods detect may help FMI operators to conduct their activities more efficiently.

Anomaly detection is already applied in many financial domains. For example, stock exchanges apply anomaly detection to stock market data to detect trades that violate securities laws. Specific models have been designed to detect cases where brokers do not act in the best interest of their clients [18], manipulate stock prices [24], or use information that is not disclosed to the general public [14]. Credit card companies also apply anomaly detection to credit card data to detect suspicious spending patterns and warn card holders of potential credit card fraud. Many models have been proposed for this purpose including neural networks [19,29], Bayesian networks [29], self-organizing maps [31,38], association rules [32], and hidden Markov models [34].

In this paper, we discuss how an autoencoder can be applied to detect anomalous payment behavior in the payment data of an RTGS system. An autoencoder is a feed-forward neural network that learns features of data by compressing them to a lower dimensional space, and accordingly, reconstructing them back in the original space. Moreover, we introduce a drill-down procedure to measure the extent to which anomalies can be explained by the inflow and outflow of a particular bank.

Based on this drill-down procedure, we evaluate the performance of our method on real-world payment data. We do this by determining how well our method can identify the liquidity problems of a commercial bank when it was subject to a bank run. The evaluation shows that our method detects the liquidity problems of the bank with reasonable accuracy.

Our work relates to many existing methods in the literature. Risks in FMIs are commonly identified by determining whether a set of risk indicators cross certain thresholds, see e.g. [6,23]. Usually, these risk indicators are based on network measures that measure changes in the topology of the underlying payment network of FMIs [17,28,30,33]. Another approach to identify risks in FMIs is by means of simulations, see e.g. [12,22,25,27]. Simulations allow studying the impact on FMIs when they would operate under very different conditions. For example, simulations are applied to measure the impact on the solvency of banks when one or more banks would start to delay their payments [3]. In contrast to these methods, our work is, to the best of our knowledge, the first application of anomaly detection on the payment data of an RTGS system.

2   Anomaly Detection in RTGS Systems

In this section, we describe the main concepts of the methodology for anomaly detection in RTGS systems. We introduce the notation and definitions used throughout this paper (Sect. 2.1), define an autoencoder (Sect. 2.2), and discuss how an autoencoder can be applied to detect anomalous payment behavior (Sects. 2.3 and 2.4).

2.1   Notation and Definitions

We use the same notation as in [36]. Let $\mathcal{B} = \{b_1, \ldots, b_n\}$ be a set of n banks that initiate payments to each other in an RTGS system. Furthermore, let $\mathcal{T} =< t_1, \ldots, t_m >$ be an ordered set of m time intervals, where $t_1 = [\tau_0, \tau_1)$, $t_2 = [\tau_1, \tau_2)$, and so on. We assume that the time intervals are consecutive and of equal duration. They might, for example, represent the operating hours of the settlement system.

The liquidity that the banks transmit to each other is recorded. Let $a_{ij}^{(k)} \in [0, \infty)$ be the total amount of liquidity that bank b_i sends to b_j at time interval t_k. We also call $a_{ij}^{(k)}$ a liquidity flow. Moreover, let $\mathbf{A}^{(k)}$ be a liquidity matrix.

Definition 1 (Liquidity Matrix). *Liquidity matrix $\mathbf{A}^{(k)}$ is a n by n matrix of aggregated liquidity flows between banks in time interval t_k, i.e.:*

$$\mathbf{A}^{(k)} = \begin{bmatrix} a_{11}^{(k)} & \cdots & a_{1n}^{(k)} \\ \vdots & \ddots & \vdots \\ a_{n1}^{(k)} & \cdots & a_{nn}^{(k)} \end{bmatrix} \tag{1}$$

The diagonal elements of $\mathbf{A}^{(k)}$ have a special interpretation. Each $a_{ii}^{(k)}$ denotes the total amount of liquidity that bank b_i transfers between its own accounts in time interval t_k.[2] The inflow vector $\mathbf{a}_{i\leftarrow}^{(k)}$ and outflow vector $\mathbf{a}_{i\rightarrow}^{(k)}$ of bank b_i are defined as:

Definition 2 (Inflow Vector). *Inflow vector* $\mathbf{a}_{i\leftarrow}^{(k)}$ *is a n-dimensional column vector containing the incoming liquidity flows from all banks* $\mathcal{B}$ *to bank* b_i *in time interval* t_k*, i.e.:*

$$\mathbf{a}_{i\leftarrow}^{(k)} = [a_{1i}^{(k)}, \ldots, a_{ni}^{(k)}]^T \tag{2}$$

Definition 3 (Outflow Vector). *Outflow vector* $\mathbf{a}_{i\rightarrow}^{(k)}$ *is a n-dimensional row vector containing the outgoing liquidity flows from bank* b_i *to all banks* $\mathcal{B}$ *in time interval* t_k*, i.e.:*

$$\mathbf{a}_{i\rightarrow}^{(k)} = [a_{i1}^{(k)}, \ldots, a_{in}^{(k)}] \tag{3}$$

$\mathbf{a}_{i\leftarrow}^{(k)}$ and $\mathbf{a}_{i\rightarrow}^{(k)}$ are respectively the i-th column and i-th row of $\mathbf{A}^{(k)}$. For analysis purposes, we vectorize $\mathbf{A}^{(k)}$ to $\mathbf{a}^{(k)}$. We also call $\mathbf{a}^{(k)}$ a liquidity vector.

Definition 4 (Liquidity Vector). *Liquidity vector* $\mathbf{a}^{(k)}$ *is a* n^2*-dimensional column vector consisting of the columns of* $\mathbf{A}^{(k)}$ *vertically enumerated, i.e.:*

$$\mathbf{a}^{(k)} = [a_{11}^{(k)}, \ldots, a_{n1}^{(k)}, \ldots, a_{1n}^{(k)}, \ldots, a_{nn}^{(k)}]^T \tag{4}$$

2.2   Autoencoder

An autoencoder is a feed-forward neural network that is trained to reconstruct the input layer at the output layer. It does this by processing the input through a hidden layer in which a set of neurons form a compressed representation of the input in a lower dimensional space. The architecture of a classic three-layered autoencoder is depicted in Fig. 1.

Suppose $\mathbf{x} = [x_1, \ldots, x_n]^T$ is an n-dimensional feature vector. An autoencoder can be defined by an encoding function $\mathbf{h} = \phi(\mathbf{x})$ and decoding function $\hat{\mathbf{x}} = \psi(\mathbf{h})$. The encoding function takes $\mathbf{x}$ as input and encodes it in l-dimensional space by processing it through the hidden layer:

$$\phi(\mathbf{x}) = f^{(l)}(\mathbf{W}_1 \mathbf{x} + \mathbf{b}_1) \tag{5}$$

where, $\mathbf{W}_1$ is a l by n matrix of weights, $\mathbf{b}_1$ is a vector of l bias terms, and $f^{(l)}(\mathbf{x}) = [f(x_1), \ldots, f(x_l)]$ is a set of activation functions that are applied to $\mathbf{x}$ element-wise. Potential functions for f are the linear (identity) function, sigmoid function or hyperbolic tanh function. The result of the encoding $\mathbf{h} = [h_1, \ldots, h_l]$ is a vector of l hidden neuron activations forming an under-complete hidden

---

[2] A feature of many RTGS systems is that banks may initiate payments on behalf of other banks. This is known as tiering, see e.g. [1]. Payments settled between indirect participants in the settlement system via the same direct participant are recorded as internal payments of the direct participant.

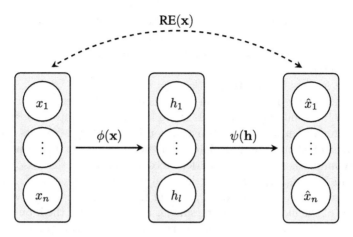

Fig. 1. The architecture of a classic three-layered autoencoder. The input layer (left) is compressed to an under-complete hidden representation in the hidden layer (middle) and reconstructed at the output layer (right). The reconstruction error made by the network is estimated by comparing the original input with the reconstructed input at the output layer.

representation of $\mathbf{x}$. The decoding function takes $\mathbf{h}$ as input and reconstructs it back in n-dimensional space by processing it through the output layer:

$$\psi(\mathbf{h}) = g^{(n)}(\mathbf{W}_2\mathbf{h} + \mathbf{b}_2) \tag{6}$$

where, $\mathbf{W}_2$ is a n by l matrix of weights, $\mathbf{b}_2$ is a vector of n bias terms, and $g^{(n)}(\mathbf{x})$ is a set of activation functions. The result of the decoding $\hat{\mathbf{x}} = [\hat{x}_1, \ldots, \hat{x}_n]$ is a vector of n outputs forming a reconstruction of $\mathbf{x}$.

The parameters $\Theta = \{\mathbf{W}_1, \mathbf{W}_2, \mathbf{b}_1, \mathbf{b}_2\}$ of the autoencoder are estimated from a set of m feature vectors $\mathcal{X} = \{\mathbf{x}^{(1)}, \ldots, \mathbf{x}^{(m)}\}$. We can do this by minimizing the Mean Reconstruction Error (MRE). The reconstruction error of a single feature vector $\mathbf{x}^{(i)}$ can be defined as:

$$\text{RE}(\mathbf{x}^{(i)}) = ||\hat{\mathbf{x}}^{(i)} - \mathbf{x}^{(i)}||_2^2 \tag{7}$$

where $||\mathbf{x}||_2^2$ is the ℓ_2-norm of $\mathbf{x}$. Accordingly, the problem of minimizing the MRE of all m feature vectors in $\mathcal{X}$ with respect to parameters Θ can be defined as:

$$\Theta^* = \arg\min_{\Theta} \frac{1}{m} \sum_{i=1}^{m} \text{RE}(\mathbf{x}^{(i)}) \tag{8}$$

$$= \arg\min_{\Theta} \text{MRE}(\mathcal{X}) \tag{9}$$

The MRE is minimized when the reconstructed $\hat{\mathbf{x}}^{(i)}$ is as close as possible to the original $\mathbf{x}^{(i)}$ for each $\mathbf{x}^{(i)} \in \mathcal{X}$. Usually, the MRE is minimized by gradient descent in conjunction with back-propagation to efficiently calculate all gradients during the optimization procedure [8,37]. In this case, the parameters are iteratively updated proportional to the negative gradient of the MRE with respect to the parameters. This process is repeated until the parameters converge to a configuration for which the MRE is (locally) minimized.

The quality of the reconstruction depends on the number of neurons in the hidden layer. If the number of neurons is too low, then the autoencoder may not be able to provide an accurate reconstruction of the feature vectors. Whereas, if the number of neurons is too high, then the autoencoder may approximate the identity mapping and achieve perfect reconstruction. In this case, it simply copies feature vectors from the input layer to the output layer.

To prevent an autoencoder from learning the identity mapping, we need to limit the size of the hidden layer to be smaller than the size of the input layer and output layer. In this way, an autoencoder is forced to compress feature vectors to an under-complete hidden representation. Achieving a good reconstruction is difficult when the feature vectors are entirely random and do not have any structure. However, if they do have structure, some input features for example are dependent, and an autoencoder might then learn features of these dependencies in the hidden layer to achieve a better reconstruction.

2.3 Anomaly Detection Task

An autoencoder can be applied for anomaly detection [11,21,35]. The general approach is to train an autoencoder from a set of training data, and accordingly, determine how well the network can reconstruct a set of test data that it has not seen before. We apply a similar approach to detect anomalous payment behavior in payment data.

Let $\mathcal{D} = \{\mathbf{a}^{(1)}, \ldots, \mathbf{a}^{(m)}\}$ be a set of m historic liquidity vectors derived from the payment data of an RTGS system. The liquidity vectors are assumed to be independent and identically distributed (iid). We train an autoencoder on $\mathcal{D}$ to learn features of the way banks normally manage their liquidity. Each time a new liquidity vector $\mathbf{a}^{(k)}$ arrives, it is reconstructed by the autoencoder and classified as anomalous or non-anomalous. $\mathbf{a}^{(k)}$ is classified as anomalous if the reconstruction error is higher than a certain threshold value $\zeta > 0$. Otherwise, $\mathbf{a}^{(k)}$ is classified as non-anomalous. ζ needs to be determined by a domain expert or can be estimated empirically from $\mathcal{D}$. A good heuristic is to set ζ two standard deviations above the MRE of $\mathcal{D}$, or to choose ζ so that a certain percentage of the training vectors in $\mathcal{D}$ are classified as anomalous.

Autoencoders have several appealing properties which make them a good choice to model liquidity vectors. First, they do not make any explicit assumption about the distribution of liquidity vectors except that they are iid. Second, they can handle the high dimensionality of liquidity vectors well. Third, they allow calculating the contribution of each liquidity flow to the overall reconstruction error. This property can be used to explain anomalies.

2.4   Explanation of Anomalies

The reconstruction error can be further analyzed to determine whether the error can be explained by the inflow or outflow of a particular bank. Given Eq. 7, the reconstruction error of a liquidity vector can be defined as:

$$\text{RE}(\mathbf{a}^{(k)}) = ||\hat{\mathbf{a}}^{(k)} - \mathbf{a}^{(k)}||_2^2 \tag{10}$$

where $\hat{\mathbf{a}}^{(k)}$ is the reconstructed liquidity vector at time interval t_k. $\text{RE}(\mathbf{a}^{(k)})$ is the reconstruction error aggregated over all liquidity flows between the banks in the settlement system. It measures the extent to which the configuration of the payment system as a whole is anomalous. A useful property is that we can express $\text{RE}(\mathbf{a}^{(k)})$ in terms of the inflow or outflow of each individual bank:

$$\text{RE}(\mathbf{a}^{(k)}) = \sum_{i=1}^{n} ||\hat{\mathbf{a}}_{i\leftarrow}^{(k)} - \mathbf{a}_{i\leftarrow}^{(k)}||_2^2 = \sum_{i=1}^{n} \text{RE}(\mathbf{a}_{i\leftarrow}^{(k)}) \tag{11}$$

$$= \sum_{i=1}^{n} ||\hat{\mathbf{a}}_{i\rightarrow}^{(k)} - \mathbf{a}_{i\rightarrow}^{(k)}||_2^2 = \sum_{i=1}^{n} \text{RE}(\mathbf{a}_{i\rightarrow}^{(k)}) \tag{12}$$

where $\hat{\mathbf{a}}_{i\leftarrow}^{(k)}$ and $\hat{\mathbf{a}}_{i\rightarrow}^{(k)}$ are respectively the reconstructed inflow and outflow of bank b_i at time interval t_k. The relative contribution of the inflow of each bank to the overall error is:

$$\mathbf{c}_{\leftarrow}^{(k)} = [\frac{\text{RE}(\mathbf{a}_{1\leftarrow}^{(k)})}{\text{RE}(\mathbf{a}^{(k)})}, \dots, \frac{\text{RE}(\mathbf{a}_{n\leftarrow}^{(k)})}{\text{RE}(\mathbf{a}^{(k)})}] \tag{13}$$

where, $\mathbf{c}_{\leftarrow}^{(k)}$ is a n-dimensional row vector, $(\mathbf{c}_{\leftarrow}^{(k)})_i \in [0,1]$ is the relative contribution of the inflow of bank b_i to the overall reconstruction error at time interval t_k, and $\sum_{i=1}^{n}(\mathbf{c}_{\leftarrow}^{(k)})_i = 1$. Similarly, for the outflow we have:

$$\mathbf{c}_{\rightarrow}^{(k)} = [\frac{\text{RE}(\mathbf{a}_{1\rightarrow}^{(k)})}{\text{RE}(\mathbf{a}^{(k)})}, \dots, \frac{\text{RE}(\mathbf{a}_{n\rightarrow}^{(k)})}{\text{RE}(\mathbf{a}^{(k)})}] \tag{14}$$

In case we find an anomaly on the system-level, i.e. $\text{RE}(\mathbf{a}^{(k)}) > \zeta$, we can estimate $\mathbf{c}_{\leftarrow}^{(k)}$ and $\mathbf{c}_{\rightarrow}^{(k)}$ and perform a drill-down of the reconstruction error to the level of individual banks to obtain an explanation of the anomaly.

3   Experimental Setup

We conducted a series of experiments on real-world payment data to determine how well an autoencoder can detect anomalous payment behavior. In this section, we elaborate on the characteristics of the payment data (Sect. 3.1), the pre-processing of the data (Sect. 3.2), and the implementation of three autoencoder variants (Sect. 3.3).

3.1 Payment Data

We used real-world payment data extracted from TARGET2. TARGET2 is the largest RTGS system in the European Union for both domestic and cross-border euro-denominated payments.[3]

The data reflect the financial activities within the Dutch part of the settlement system (TARGET2-NL). It includes approximately 3.6 million domestic customer payments which were settled between September 2008 and October 2009 among the twenty most actively participating banks.[4] Customer payments are payments that are initiated by banks on behalf of their customers. They reflect activities such as transfers of funds, purchases of assets, credit extensions, or debt repayments, among indirect participants of the settlement system. The data is of particular interest because it spans a short period of time in which one of the banks was subject to a bank run. Our goal is to determine whether our method can identify the liquidity problems of the bank in this period.

We aggregated the payment data over 3,055 time intervals that each spanned one operational hour and derived the corresponding liquidity vectors. The liquidity vectors were partitioned into separate sets for training and evaluation purposes. The parameters of the autoencoders were estimated from a training set. This set contained 2,148 liquidity vectors corresponding to ten months (November 2008 until August 2009). A holdout set containing 463 liquidity vectors corresponding to the first two months (September and October 2008) was set aside to optimize the number of neurons of the autoencoders. Finally, the autoencoders were evaluated on a test set which contained 444 liquidity vectors corresponding to the final two months (September and October 2009).

3.2 Normalization of Liquidity Flows

It is important to normalize liquidity vectors before modeling them in an autoencoder. Liquidity flows across banks have different magnitudes depending on the size of the sending and receiving bank. These differences in magnitude may cause large liquidity flows to dominate the reconstruction. Moreover, from a technical point of view, providing unnormalized data to a gradient-based learning machine can significantly slow down its convergence rate [26].

To deal with these issues, we rescaled liquidity flows by an exponential transformation to reduce their highly skewed distribution. Accordingly, we normalized all non-zero liquidity flows to have zero mean and unit variance by z-normalization:

$$\tilde{a}_{ij}^{(k)} := \begin{cases} \frac{a_{ij}^{(k)} - \bar{a}_{ij}}{\sqrt{s_{ij}^2 + \epsilon}} & \text{if } a_{ij}^{(k)} > 0 \\ 0 & \text{otherwise} \end{cases} \tag{15}$$

---

[3] For a more detailed description of TARGET2, see [15,16].

[4] The extent to which banks actively participated in the settlement system was based on the number of payments that they initiated each month.

where, $\bar{a}_{ij}$ and s_{ij}^2 are respectively the sample mean and variance of the liquidity flows between bank b_i and b_j estimated from the training set, and ϵ is a small constant added for numerical stability. Normalized $\tilde{a}_{ij}^{(k)}$ is the number of standard deviations $a_{ij}^{(k)}$ deviates from the average liquidity flow $\bar{a}_{ij}$. In case $\tilde{a}_{ij}^{(k)} = 0$, then there is no liquidity flow between bank b_i and b_j in time interval t_k, i.e. $a_{ij}^{(k)} = 0$, or the flow equals the average, i.e. $\tilde{a}_{ij}^{(k)} = \bar{a}_{ij}$.

3.3   Implementation

We implemented three autoencoders. We will refer to the autoencoders as AE-L, AE-S and AE-T. All networks have linear activations for the output layer but different activations for the hidden layer. AE-T has linear activations for the hidden layer, whereas AE-S and AE-T have respectively sigmoid and tanh activations for the hidden layer. The parameters of the networks were randomly initialized according to the heuristic proposed by [20]. Stochastic gradient descent in conjunction with back-propagation was in turn applied to estimate the parameters from the training set. This procedure was performed for 200 iterations through the training set with a fixed learning rate of 0.001.

The number of neurons was optimized by a grid search. During the search, a set of autoencoders having a different number of neurons $l \in \{10, 20, \ldots, 400\}$ in the hidden layer were estimated from the training set. The MRE of the networks was evaluated on the holdout set. We determined the optimal number of neurons by looking for the point where adding more neurons did not yield a considerably better reconstruction of the holdout set.

4   Results

In this section, we present the results of our evaluation. We discuss the outcome of the grid search (Sect. 4.1), provide an overview of the system-level anomalies found by our method in the test set (Sect. 4.2), and provide an explanation of the anomalies on the level of individual banks (Sect. 4.3).

4.1   Grid Search

The results of the grid search are depicted in Fig. 2. The figure shows the relationship between the number of neurons and the corresponding MRE of the networks estimated on the holdout set. Initially, the MRE sharply decreased when increasing the number of neurons. Then, after sufficient neurons were added to the networks, it started to saturate. At this point, the networks captured the most important dynamics of the liquidity vectors, and the MRE did not decrease much further. The optimal configuration for the networks was approximately 220 neurons. Given this configuration, AE-L reconstructed the holdout set the best with an MRE of about 0.28, followed by AE-T with an MRE of 0.60, and finally AE-S with an MRE of 1.10.

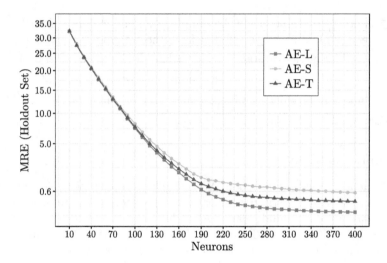

Fig. 2. The MRE (on square root scale) of AE-L, AE-S, and AE-T estimated on the holdout set while having a different number of neurons in the hidden layer.

4.2 Anomalies in the Test Set

We applied AE-L to detect anomalies in the test set. Figure 3 depicts the reconstruction error of the network for each liquidity vector. The dashed line represents anomaly threshold ζ. The threshold was set two standard deviations above the MRE of AE-L on the training set. Liquidity vectors having a reconstruction error equal or higher than this threshold are considered anomalous. The labels on the time axis highlight the particular time intervals when this happens.

The reconstruction error fluctuated strongly over time with short periods in which several liquidity vectors were classified as anomalous. We will take a closer look at the anomalies in three such periods (the highlighted areas A, B, and C in Fig. 3). We do this by performing a drill-down of the reconstruction error to the individual bank level. This drill-down provides some insight into the type of anomalies the network detected and whether these relate to financial stress.

4.3 Explanation of Anomalies in Period A, B, and C

Figure 4 depicts the drill down of the reconstruction error for period A. The figure visualizes two matrices, $[(\mathbf{c}_{\leftarrow}^{(2663)})^T, \ldots, (\mathbf{c}_{\leftarrow}^{(2723)})^T]$ and $[(\mathbf{c}_{\rightarrow}^{(2663)})^T, \ldots, (\mathbf{c}_{\rightarrow}^{(2723)})^T]$, on respectively the top and bottom. Each element of the matrices corresponds to a bank at a particular time interval. The color of the element indicates the extent to which the reconstruction error can be attributed to the inflow or outflow of the bank at the given time interval. The highlighted columns represent the time intervals at which the reconstruction error crossed the anomaly threshold. These columns are of particular interest for our analysis. If a highlighted column contains a colored element, especially an orange or red one, then this implies that the anomaly can be

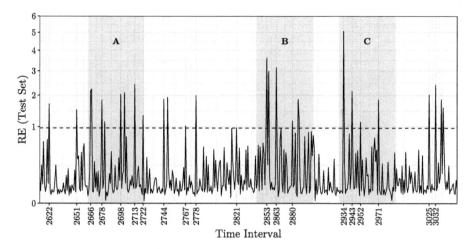

Fig. 3. The reconstruction error (on square root scale) of AE-L for each liquidity vector in the test set. The dashed line represents the anomaly threshold. The labels on the time axis highlight the cases when the anomaly threshold is crossed. Notice: some labels are deliberately removed to make the remaining labels more readable.

explained well by the element. Colored elements outside the highlighted columns are of less interest, because in these cases there is generally not much error to be explained.

According to the drill-down, all anomalies in period A can be explained by an unusual inflow and outflow of a particular pair of banks. Consider the anomaly at time interval 2267. It can be explained by an unusual outflow of bank 14 and inflow of bank 20. However, no successive anomalies related to the same banks are detected in the next few hours. Based on this observation, we believe that these anomalies are not related to financial stress. Instead, we suspect that they are caused by exceptions in the day-to-day business of the banks' customers. They might, for example, be caused by a company buying very expensive machinery that suddenly creates an unusually large liquidity flow between the banks of the company and the manufacturer. If the paying bank were to have indeed faced financial stress, then this would also have affected other liquidity flows of the bank around the same time interval.

The anomalies detected in period B can be explained differently (see the drill-down of the error in Fig. 5). Several anomalies were detected shortly after each other which all can be explained by an anomalous outflow of one bank (bank 6) and inflow of several other banks (bank 7, 9 or 20). Bank 6 was a relatively small Dutch commercial bank that provided mortgages, consumer loans, savings, and insurance products to individuals. Around time interval 2834, it became subject to a commercial bank run in which many of its depositors withdrew their savings from the bank. During the time intervals that followed, more than 600 million euro was withdrawn and transferred to another bank. Eventually, around time interval 2955, the bank was declared bankrupt due to ongoing liquidity issues.

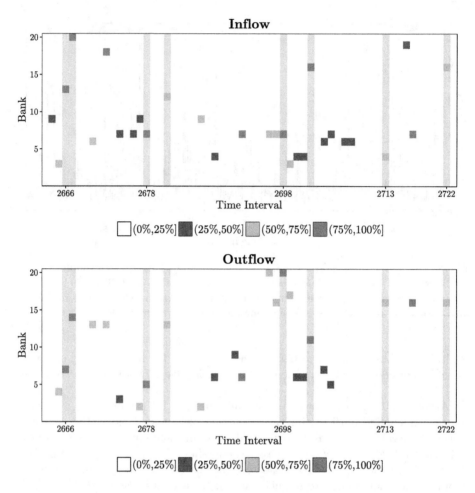

Fig. 4. The drill-down of the reconstruction error for period A. Each anomaly can be explained by an unusual inflow and outflow of a different pair of banks.

The timing of the anomalies does, however, not quite resemble a pattern that we would expect for a bank run. During a bank run, a bank typically needs to deal with a continuous outflow of payments which increase in size as the bank run gains momentum. Therefore, we also expect to find a sequence of consecutive liquidity vectors whose reconstruction error increases over time. In our analysis, we detected only a few anomalies with relatively large gaps between them.

We identified two explanations for these gaps. First, the bank run did not follow a typical trajectory. Instead, the outflow of bank 6 was high initially but then decreased during the bank run. Moreover, there were also several time intervals in which no outgoing payments were settled at all. This is likely due to the fact that the bank's website was difficult to reach at the time and many depositors were unable to access their savings. Also, after time interval 2905,

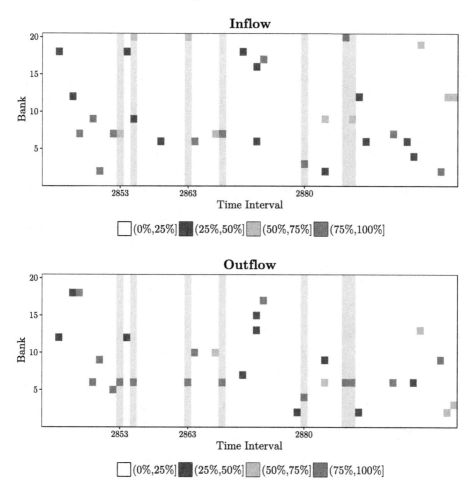

Fig. 5. The drill-down of the reconstruction error for period B. Nearly all anomalies can be explained by an unusual outflow of one bank (bank 6) and the inflow of several other banks (bank 7, 9 or 20). During this period, bank 6 was subject to a bank run in which many customers redraw their deposits at the bank.

access to the savings accounts was entirely blocked due to the liquidity problems of the bank. Second, AE-L was over-fitting some liquidity flows. For example, bank 6 had often liquidity flows to bank 1, 15, and 17 in the training set. During the bank run in the test set, these liquidity flows changed quite drastically but could be well reconstructed by AE-L, although the network was not trained to do so. As a result, AE-L failed to detect anomalies in these liquidity flows.

The anomalies in period C can be similarly explained to the anomalies in period A (see the drill-down of the reconstruction error in Fig. 6). Most anomalies can be explained by an unusual inflow and outflow of a pair of banks. No related anomalies

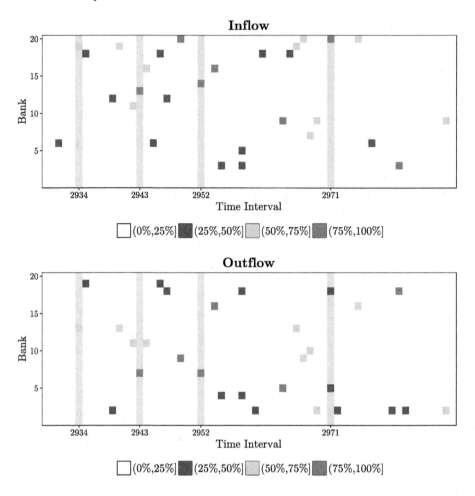

Fig. 6. The drill-down of the reconstruction error for period C. Most anomalies can be explained, similarly as in period A (see Fig. 4), by an unusual inflow and outflow of a specific pair of banks.

are detected shortly afterward. Therefore, we believe that these anomalies are also due to exceptions in the business of the banks' customers.

5   Conclusions

Based on our results, we conclude that an autoencoder can detect anomalous payment behavior reasonably well. Liquidity vectors can be compressed to a much lower dimensional space and reconstructed back to the original space while preserving their most important dynamics. The reconstruction error made by an autoencoder after performing these transformations has shown to be, to some extent, an indicator of anomalous payment behavior.

In our experiments, our base model (AE-T) correctly identified the anomalous outflow of bank 6 at the time the bank was subject to a bank run. However, the network also missed several anomalies because it severely over-fitted some liquidity flows of the bank. We recognize that this is a deficiency of our method and aim to address it in future research.

Moreover, in future research, we also plan to address some limitations of our anomaly detection method. First, we assumed that liquidity flows are identically distributed, which is not a realistic assumption. The business strategy or customer base of a bank is likely to change over time which ultimately impacts its liquidity flows. It is important to deal with the non-stationary nature of liquidity flows to ensure that our method keeps producing reliable results. Second, we assumed that liquidity vectors are independent, while dependencies between liquidity flows are likely to exist over time. Incorporating these dependencies might further improve our method.

Acknowledgements. We would like to thank Ron Berndsen and Richard Heuver for their helpful suggestions and feedback.

References

1. Adams, M., Galbiati, M., Giansante, S.: Liquidity Costs and Tiering in Large-Value Payment Systems (2010)
2. Allen, F., Gale, D.: Financial contagion. J. Polit. Econ. **108**, 1–33 (2000)
3. Bech, M., Soramäki, K.: Gridlock resolution and bank failures in interbank payment systems. In: Leinonen, H. (ed.) Liquidity, Risks and Speed in Payment and Settlement Systems - A Simulation Approach, Proceedings from the Bank of Finland Payment and Settlement System Seminars 2005, pp. 149–176 (2005)
4. Becher, C., Galbiati, M., Tudela, M.: The timing and funding of CHAPS sterling payments. Econ. Policy Rev. **14**, 113–133 (2008)
5. Benos, E., Garratt, R., Zimmerman, P.: Bank Behaviour and Risks in CHAPS Following the Collapse of Lehman Brothers (2012)
6. Berndsen, R., Heijmans, R.: Risk Indicators for Financial Market Infrastructure: From High Frequency Transaction Data to a Traffic Light Signal. De Nederlandsche Bank Working Paper No. 557 (2017)
7. BIS: Real-time Gross Settlement Systems (1997)
8. Bottou, L.: Stochastic learning. In: Bousquet, O., von Luxburg, U., Rätsch, G. (eds.) ML -2003. LNCS (LNAI), vol. 3176, pp. 146–168. Springer, Heidelberg (2004). https://doi.org/10.1007/978-3-540-28650-9_7
9. Chandola, V., Banerjee, A., Kumar, V.: Anomaly detection: a survey. ACM Comput. Surv. (CSUR) **41**(3), 15:1–15:58 (2009)
10. CPSS: Principles for Financial Market Infrastructures: Disclosure Framework and Assessment Methodology. Bank for International Settlements (2012)
11. Dau, H.A., Ciesielski, V., Song, A.: Anomaly detection using replicator neural networks trained on examples of one class. In: Dick, G., Browne, W.N., Whigham, P., Zhang, M., Bui, L.T., Ishibuchi, H., Jin, Y., Li, X., Shi, Y., Singh, P., Tan, K.C., Tang, K. (eds.) SEAL 2014. LNCS, vol. 8886, pp. 311–322. Springer, Cham (2014). https://doi.org/10.1007/978-3-319-13563-2_27

12. Diehl, M.: The use of simulations as an analytical tool for payment systems. In: Alexandrova-Kabadjova, B., Martinez-Jaramillo, S., Garcia-Almanza, A., Tsang, E. (eds.) Simulation in Computational Finance and Economics: Tools and Emerging Applications, pp. 29–45. IGI Global (2012)
13. Diehl, M.: Measuring free riding in large-value payment systems: the case of TARGET2. J. Financ. Mark. Infrastruct. **1**(3), 31–53 (2013)
14. Donoho, S.: Early detection of insider trading in option markets. In: Proceedings of the Tenth ACM SIGKDD International Conference on Knowledge Discovery and Data Mining, pp. 420–429. ACM (2004)
15. ECB: Information Guide for TARGET2 Users (2010)
16. ECB: TARGET anual report 2011 (2012)
17. Embree, L., Roberts, T.: Network Analysis and Canada's Large Value Transfer System (2009)
18. Ferdousi, Z., Maeda, A.: Unsupervised outlier detection in time series data. In: 22nd International Conference on Data Engineering Workshops (ICDEW 2006), pp. 51–56. IEEE (2006)
19. Ghosh, S., Reilly, D.L.: Credit card fraud detection with a neural-network. In: 1994 Proceedings of the Twenty-Seventh Hawaii International Conference on System Sciences, vol. 3, pp. 621–630. IEEE (1994)
20. Glorot, X., Bengio, Y.: Understanding the difficulty of training deep feedforward neural networks. In: AISTATS, vol. 9, pp. 249–256 (2010)
21. Hawkins, S., He, H., Williams, G., Baxter, R.: Outlier detection using replicator neural networks. In: Kambayashi, Y., Winiwarter, W., Arikawa, M. (eds.) DaWaK 2002. LNCS, vol. 2454, pp. 170–180. Springer, Heidelberg (2002). https://doi.org/10.1007/3-540-46145-0_17
22. Heijmans, R., Heuver, R.: Preparing simulations in large value payment systems using historical data. In: Alexandrova-Kabadjova, B., Martinez-Jaramillo, S., Garcia-Almanza, A., Tsang, E. (eds.) Simulation in Computational Finance and Economics: Tools and Emerging Applications, pp. 46–68. IGI Global, Hershey (2012)
23. Heijmans, R., Heuver, R.: Is this bank ill? the diagnosis of doctor TARGET2. J. Financ. Mark. Infrastruct. **2**(3), 3–36 (2014)
24. Kim, Y., Sohn, S.Y.: Stock fraud detection using peer group analysis. Expert Syst. Appl. **39**(10), 8986–8992 (2012)
25. Laine, T., Korpinen, K., Hellqvist, M.: Simulations Approaches to Risk, Efficiency, and Liquidity Usage in Payment Systems. IGI Global (2013)
26. LeCun, Y.A., Bottou, L., Orr, G.B., Müller, K.-R.: Efficient backprop. In: Montavon, G., Orr, G.B., Müller, K.-R. (eds.) Neural Networks: Tricks of the Trade. LNCS, vol. 7700, pp. 9–48. Springer, Heidelberg (2012). https://doi.org/10.1007/978-3-642-35289-8_3
27. Leinonen, H., Soramäki, K.: Optimising Liquidity Usage and Settlement Speed in Payment Systems. In: Leinonen, H. (ed.) Liquidity, risks and speed in payment and settlement systems - a simulation approach, Proceedings from the Bank of Finland Payment and Settlement System Seminars 2005, pp. 115–148 (2005)
28. León, C., Pérez, J.: Assessing financial market infrastructures' systemic importance with authority and hub centrality. J. Financ. Mark. Infrastruct. **2**, 67–87 (2014)
29. Maes, S., Tuyls, K., Vanschoenwinkel, B., Manderick, B.: Credit card fraud detection using Bayesian and neural networks. In: Proceedings of the 1st International Naiso Congress on Neuro Fuzzy Technologies, pp. 261–270 (2002)
30. Pröpper, M., van Lelyveld, I., Heijmans, R.: Network dynamics of TOP payments. J. Financ. Mark. Infrastruct. **1**(3), 3–29 (2013)

31. Quah, J.T., Sriganesh, M.: Real-time credit card fraud detection using computational intelligence. Expert Syst. Appl. **35**(4), 1721–1732 (2008)
32. Sánchez, D., Vila, M., Cerda, L., Serrano, J.M.: Association rules applied to credit card fraud detection. Expert Syst. Appl. **36**(2), 3630–3640 (2009)
33. Squartini, T., van Lelyveld, I., Garlaschelli, D.: Early-warning signals of topological collapse in interbank networks. Sci. Rep. **3**(3357), 1–9 (2013)
34. Srivastava, A., Kundu, A., Sural, S., Majumdar, A.: Credit card fraud detection using hidden Markov model. IEEE Trans. Dependable Secur. Comput. **5**(1), 37–48 (2008)
35. Tóth, L., Gosztolya, G.: Replicator neural networks for outlier modeling in segmental speech recognition. In: Yin, F.-L., Wang, J., Guo, C. (eds.) ISNN 2004. LNCS, vol. 3173, pp. 996–1001. Springer, Heidelberg (2004). https://doi.org/10.1007/978-3-540-28647-9_164
36. Triepels, R., Daniels, H., Heijmans, R.: Anomaly detection in real-time gross settlement systems. In: Proceedings of the 19th International Conference on Enterprise Information Systems - Volume 1: ICEIS, pp. 433–441. INSTICC, ScitePress (2017)
37. Werbos, P.J.: Applications of advances in nonlinear sensitivity analysis. In: Drenick, R.F., Kozin, F. (eds.) System Modeling and Optimization. LNCIS, vol. 38, pp. 762–770. Springer, Heidelberg (1982). https://doi.org/10.1007/BFb0006203
38. Zaslavsky, V., Strizhak, A.: Credit card fraud detection using self-organizing maps. Inf. Secur. **18**, 48 (2006)

Quality of Care Driven Scheduling of Clinical Pathways Under Resource and Ethical Constraints

Christophe Ponsard[1]([✉]), Renaud De Landtsheer[1], Yoann Guyot[1],
François Roucoux[2], and Bernard Lambeau[3]

[1] CETIC Research Center, Charleroi, Belgium
{christophe.ponsard,renaud.delandtsheer,yoann.guyot}@cetic.be
[2] Grand Hôpital de Charleroi, Charleroi, Belgium
francois.roucoux@ghdc.be
[3] Enspirit, Sombreffe, Belgium
blambeau@gmail.com

Abstract. Currently, hospitals have to face a growing number of patients under an increasing pressure of profitability. In this context, clinical pathways provide a more efficient organisation of the complex multidisciplinary workflows involved. They also support the timely decision making required for meeting strict treatment constraints for patients within limited hospital resources. However, implementing clinical pathways is challenging because of the variety of constraints that must be met simultaneously for a large pool of patients. In this paper we propose a decision support for driving clinical pathways primarily based on care quality indicators, so the patient health has always the priority. We demonstrate how constraint-based local search techniques can (1) support real-world chemotherapy pathways, (2) efficiently react to a variety of adverse events, such as unexpected delays or partial drug deliveries, and (3) address ethical concerns related to the fairness of resource allocation. Our claim is supported by an extensive validation on a series of scenarios of different size, load and complexity.

1 Introduction

In Western countries, due to progress in medical care and ageing of the population, hospitals have to manage increasingly complex and multidisciplinary medical procedures over a growing pool of patients. In the worst case, this results in a decrease in the quality of care received by patients, which does not always match the recommended care process yet prescribed. A survey of 30 pathologies ranging from osteoarthritis to breast cancer, observed that, on average, half of the patients received the recommended medical care [1].

In order to reduce the variability in clinical processes and improve the care quality, a level of standardisation was proposed through clinical (or care) pathways. A clinical pathway is defined as a multi-disciplinary specification of the treatment process required by a group of patients presenting the same medical

© Springer International Publishing AG, part of Springer Nature 2018
S. Hammoudi et al. (Eds.): ICEIS 2017, LNBIP 321, pp. 162–186, 2018.
https://doi.org/10.1007/978-3-319-93375-7_9

condition with a predictable clinical course [2]. It describes concrete treatment activities for patients having identical diagnoses or receiving the same therapy.

This standardization results usually in less delays, higher quality assurance and reduced costs. Because of their strong process orientation, clinical pathways also maintain a global view on the patient's overall journey, instead of individual doctors having a view exclusively limited to their medical speciality [3].

The use of clinical pathways have been reported as successful in many therapies, such as arthroplasty [4] and breast cancer [3]. Clinical pathways in oncology involve a precise description of the therapeutic workflow and all its ancillary activities. Such a partial workflow about the chemotherapeutic aspect of a treatment is illustrated in Fig. 1. Of course, implementing clinical pathways requires involvement. A number of success factors have been reported, like continued clinician acceptance, top management support and a dedicated team of case managers, nurses and paramedical professionals [5].

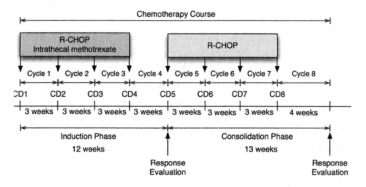

Fig. 1. A typical chemotherapy workflow [6].

On the IT side, the computerization of workflows, guidelines, and care pathways is also reported as a key step for process-oriented health information systems [7]. This allows these processes to be managed by hospital information systems or in dedicated workflow management systems. Such autonomous workflow management systems can indeed use clinical workflows as a process model description [8]. A key component in this evolution is to provide efficient tools to support the scheduling of these workflows. While scheduling the pathway of a single patient or scheduling the activities of a specific medical department are not that difficult, scheduling a large pool of patients in an hospital with limited resources raises a lot of trade-off concerns [9]. Ideally, such concerns should not impact the quality of care of individual patient. Moreover, basic ethical principles state that every patient deserves optimal care regardless of his medical condition or prognosis. Given that the patients flow is continuous and that a number of unforeseen events require postponing or adaptation of treatment sessions, schedules need to be adjusted on the go. These adjustments should of course comply with already confirmed appointments. The observed practice is that treatment scheduling still usually rely on human-operated manual tools such as spreadsheets or scheduling templates [10].

Our research targets the problem of scheduling treatment appointments in clinical pathways. In order to ensure care quality over a large pool of patients within available resources, care quality indicators are driving our scheduling algorithms. A key design choice of our approach is to rely on Constraint-Based Local Search (CBLS), a technique known for its ability to scale on large scheduling problems [11]. It can also efficiently deal with on-line problems, i.e. provide new schedules in reaction to changes in some patient constraints.

In our previous work, we have already explained the problem of dynamically scheduling care pathways involving multiple patients, presented our general approach and our tool architecture [12]. This paper significantly extends our previous work by performing a deeper validation which was only illustrated on a typical medium scale scenario. In this work, we present a larger set of validation scenarios covering large scale validation and the analysis of specific degraded cases such as unavailability, no-show (patient not attending a confirmed appointment) and partial deliveries. As our previous work was mostly focusing on breast cancer, this work also considers a larger sets of oncological pathways, e.g. breast cancers, brain cancers, lymphoma ... for which a key treatment quality indicator called RDI (Relative Dose Intensity) has been defined [13]. The availability of the RDI for these treatments, and its proven correlation with survival rates, enables us to quantify the enforcement of time constraints, so that corrective actions might be considered in case of a deviation. In order to support this extended validation work, our simulation framework was also extended. An updated and more detailed description of our simulator is given.

This paper is organised as follows. In Sect. 2, we present domain background about chemotherapy pathways and technical background on constraint-based local search. Section 3 gives a clear statement of the problem tackled in the paper. Section 4 discusses key design aspects of the solution while Sect. 5 details its implementation. An extended presentation of the validation framework is presented in Sect. 6 while the result of our validation campaign is presented in Sect. 7. Some related work is discussed in Sect. 8 and finally Sect. 9 concludes and highlights our future work.

2   Background

This section first presents the problem domain of chemotherapy pathways before introducing local search frameworks, and then focusing on the necessary vocabulary of CBLS framework used in the remaining of the paper, based on the OscaR.cbls engine.

2.1   Chemotherapy Pathways

The typical workflow for a chemotherapy is a sequence of drugs deliveries or cures, typically administered in day hospital. Each cure is followed by a resting period at home that can last for a few days to a few weeks. A minimal interval between cures is required because chemotherapy drugs are toxic agents. Typical secondary effects are fatigue, pain, mouth and throat sores. Consequently, the body needs some time to recover between two drugs deliveries. When following the ideal treatment protocol, the number of cancerous cells are progressively reduced, hopefully to reach a full healing or cancer remission as shown in Fig. 2a.

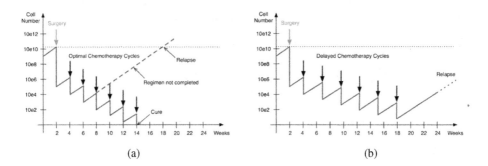

(a)   (b)

Fig. 2. (a) Optimal chemotherapy cycles (b) Delayed chemotherapy cycles [6].

If for some reason, chemotherapy cures do not closely follow the intended periodicity or if doses are significantly reduced, the treatment efficiency may be suboptimal. In such conditions, cancerous cells may multiply again, which can result in a cancer relapse as shown in Fig. 2b.

In order to measure the quality of chemotherapeutic cares, a quantifiable indicator called the "Relative Dose Intensity" (RDI) [13] was defined. It captures both the fact that the required dose is administered and the timing of the delivery, on a scale from 0% (no treatment) to 100% (total conformance).

$$RDI = \frac{planned\_dose}{delivered\_dose} \times \frac{real\_duration}{planned\_duration}$$

Medical literature has shown, for a number of cancers, that the relapse-free survival is strongly correlated with the RDI. For instance, for breast cancer, a key threshold value is 85% as illustrated in Fig. 3 [14]. Hence this indicator can be seen has a gauge that should be carefully managed across the whole clinical pathway.

2.2   Local Search Frameworks

Local search frameworks aim at making the development of algorithmic local search solutions much simpler than traditional coding. To this end, they provide different degrees of implementation support, from problem modelling to the elaboration of a search procedure. We use such a framework to develop a schedule optimizer for clinical pathways.

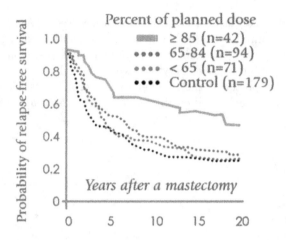

Fig. 3. Probability of relapse-free survival vs. RDI [14].

Among the general local search frameworks, EasyLocal++ is a well known and representative one that requires a dedicated model to be developed from scratch using ad-hoc algorithms. It mainly provides support for declaring the search procedure [15]. It does not provide as much assistance in the development of a model as a CBLS framework would. Notably it does not allow the developer to package efficient global constraints that can be instantiated on demand.

Besides OscaR, the framework we have used and described in the next section, there are a few tools supporting constraint-based local search specifically:

- Comet is the seminal system for constraint-based local search [11]. It features a differentiation facility that is not implemented in OscaR.cbls. OscaR.cbls relies rather on partial propagation to provide a comparable efficiency. Besides, differentiation as provided by Comet cannot handle intricate models where constraints are posted on variables controlled by invariants. Comet is a proprietary system available under a commercial licence.
- LocalSolver is a commercial solver implementing CBLS. It supports boolean and floating point variables. It does not require the user to specify neighbourhoods or meta-heuristics [16].
- Kangaroo provides a partial propagation feature that is more selective than OscaR.cbls [17].

2.3   CBLS, the OscaR Way

Among the different solvers, OscaR.cbls was selected. Since this contribution has been done in the context of the OscaR.cbls tool, we further introduce the basic concepts of CBLS using the vocabulary of OscaR.cbls.

As usual in local search, solving a problem involves specifying a *model* and a *search procedure*.

The *model* is composed of *incremental variables* (integers and sets of integers at this point), and *invariants* which are incremental directed constraints maintaining one or more output variables according to the atomic expressions they implement (e.g. Sum: the sum of inputs). *Constraints* are special invariants that maintain their violation as an output variable. They are Lagrangian relaxations of their specification. Besides, they also maintain some information about which variable causes the violation.

The *search procedure* is expressed using *neighbourhoods*, which can be queried for a *move*, given the current state of the model, an acceptance criterion, and an objective function. *Combinators* are a set of operators on neighbourhoods that combine them and incorporate several metaheuristics, so that a complex search strategy can be represented by a composite neighbourhood totally expressed in a declarative way [18]. A library of combinators is available for specifying standard metaheuristics (e.g. simulated annealing, restart, hill climbing), for managing solutions (e.g. when to save the current state, or restore a saved state), and for expressing stop criteria.

In order to set up the floor for designing a scheduling solution, we give details on how the model is represented and updated during the search.

The *data structure* behind a model is a graph, called the *propagation graph*, which we can approximate to a directed acyclic graph, where the nodes are *variables* and *invariants*. Variables have an associated type and implement specific algorithms related to their type. Invariants have specific definitions, and implement this definition mostly through incremental algorithms. Edges in the graph represent data flows from variables to listening invariants and from invariants to controlled variables. The directed acyclic graph starts with input (a.k.a. decision) variables, and typically ends at a variable whose value is maintained to be the one of the objective function. Figure 4 illustrates a propagation graph for a simple warehouse location problem.

In such engine, *propagation* is about propagating updates along the propagation graph in such a way that a node is reached at most once by the update wave, and only if one of its inputs has changed and if needed by the model update. OscaR.cbls manages this wave by sorting the nodes based on the distance from the decision variables. The propagation is coordinated through a dedicated heap that aggregates nodes at the same distance in a list. This offers a slightly better time complexity than the classical approach based on topological sort initially presented in [11].

The search starts from an initial solution and explores the specified neighbourhood. Each neighbour solution is examined by modifying the input variables, and querying the objective function of the model which is updated through propagation.

During propagation, variables *notify* each invariant listening to them about their value change. For integer variables, a notification carries a reference to the variable, and the old and new value of the variable. For set variables, it

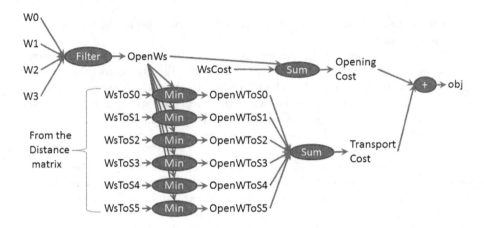

Fig. 4. Propagation graph on a warehouse location problem [19].

carries a reference to the variable, the old value of the variable, the new value of the variable, and both the set of values that have been added and removed from the variable. All values transmitted by variables, through notification or through queries to the variables are immutable, to make the implementation of algorithms in invariants easier.

3   Problem Statement

The problem considered here is to continuously optimize the scheduling on an evolving set of patients following a specific chemotherapy process as described in Sect. 2. The goals of the scheduling optimization are the following:

- maintain the best quality of care (i.e. achieve the best RDI) by avoiding delay for all the patients in the pool.
- meet the resources constraints: available treatment rooms and nurses.
- respect service opening days (weekends, holidays) and hours.
- take into account strong unavailabilities of patients, when known.
- when possible, distribute the workload evenly over time to avoid work peaks.

When entering his chemotherapy pathway, a patient can be given an indicative optimal schedule based on what is known at that time. However the global scheduling can be impacted by many events such as:

- the cancellation of treatment delivery, because of patient no-shows or medical no-go (e.g. too low white blood cells detected in last blood test),
- the delivery of a partial dose, due to degraded condition induced by chemotherapy toxicity,
- other patients entering and leaving the pathway.

These events are communicated by different actors to the system (e.g. nurses monitoring the drugs delivery, doctors checking the patient condition, administrative staff registering the arrival or non-attendance of a patient).

To maintain optimality, the occurrence of such events will trigger a re-scheduling. Consequently, the considered scheduling is an *on-line problem* which should meet the following additional constraints:

- the recorded past is of course irreversible: this makes any deviation to the ideal care delivery schedule hard to reverse.
- confirmed appointments for other patients should preferably not be changed because it requires administrative work and can induce a cascading effect.

A key actor in charge of activity re-planning is the administrative nurse. She is frequently in contact with the patient and acts as a relay between the patient and the system. She is also in charge of negotiating and confirming the future treatment delivery dates between the patient and the system:

- in the ideal case, all dates initially computed are respected.
- in case of problems in the patient's pathway, the patient schedule is adapted. This can impact the schedules of other patients. This is not important if the schedule shift is minor and concerns dates that are not yet confirmed.
- if the patient wants to delay a treatment delivery, the system shall estimate the impact of such delay in terms of degradation of the chances of healing. This degradation shall be reported to the patient, e.g. by strongly insisting on the importance to comply with the proposed date if a good RDI is compromised.

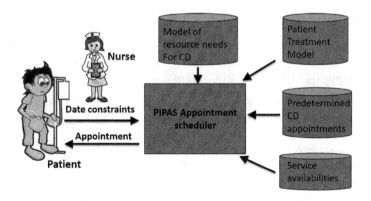

Fig. 5. Problem context diagram [12].

Figure 5 gives a complete contextual view of the information flow between the patient and the scheduling system and the information the system need an access to. This includes two kind of models which are used to configure the system: a model of the needs for Chemotherapy Deliveries (CD) and the treatment model.

The former will capture all the required resources needs (i.e. room time, staff intervention, pharmacy, etc.) while the later give a workflow description of care pathway. In addition, instance level information is required to run one or possibly several care pathways simultaneously: the CD appointments and the services availabilities which may follow a specific pattern but with exceptions (like public holidays).

4   Solution Design

In this section, we first propose a global architecture for the scheduling solution and then consider the more tricky problem of specifying a fair objective function.

4.1   Global Scheduling vs. First Come First Serve

Our approach is about scheduling the care of all patients together in such a way that some global time constraints are enforced. The actual situation in most day hospitals is that patients are scheduled on a first-come first-serve basis. With such a policy, in case of resource shortage (beds, nurses), the treatment of a patient might be postponed by some days. For some patients, such a delay can result in great harm in terms of chance of healing.

In contrast, our solution avoids resource shortage by smartly spreading over time the start date of the chemotherapy pathways. However, if resources were still limited, the system will smartly select patients to postpone by limiting the impact on their time constraints and thus their RDI.

4.2   Proposed Architecture

An agile prototype-based approach was applied to design our scheduling solution. The architectural design of our solution quickly evolved towards the agent-based architecture depicted in Fig. 6 and composed of the following agents:

- the *Orchestrator* is the central agent. It ensures that the system behaviour is consistent with the input received and that the information generated by the system is dispatched to the end user.
- the *User interface* captures relevant patient information and gives comprehensive views over the pathways at different levels of detail.
- the *Simulator* is used for validation purpose (see Sect. 5).
- the *Persister* is in charge of managing the state information about the patients involved in the clinical pathways. It provides a domain representation to the orchestrator and relies on a relational database for persistent storage.
- the *Oncoplanner* is responsible for proposing solutions matching the domain constraints sent by the Orchestrator when a change requires to compute an updated solution. It relies on the OscaR.cbls framework.

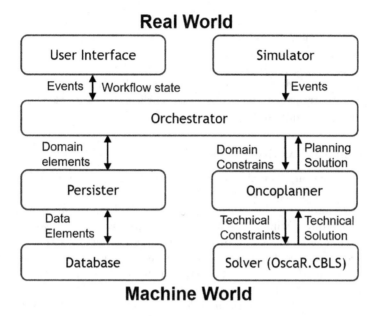

Fig. 6. Global architecture [12].

This architecture has the following benefits:

- it ensures a clear separation between the real world (user side) and the computer world.
- it allows one to plug different kinds of user interfaces easily: first, a basic command line user interface, and later a web-based one using the same communication protocol.
- it also enables to easily integrate a full environment simulator which can play complex scenarios that are able to test the system under high stress.
- it provides good integration capabilities with hospital systems, e.g. to retrieve information from available databases through specific agents.

In this architecture, the scheduler can also work as a background service constantly trying to improve the solution in the open future (i.e. beyond all confirmed appointments), while the orchestrator can take care of reporting when some change occurs in the real world. In case a change makes the current computation irrelevant, the orchestrator can ask the scheduler to stop his work and launch a new computation based on the updated constraints.

We started with a simplified model combining the chemotherapy workflows models resulting from a rigorous analysis process [20], resource constraints and possible interfering events. An appointment scheduler was developed along with key companion tools such as a scenario repository, a graphical interface to manage appointments and a simulator of patient-related events. This greatly made easier the validation described in Sect. 6. The following features were progressively addressed to reach a model that is now realistic enough to consider a validation at day hospital:

- simple resource model, expressed in bed/nurse hours evolving to a finer grained model where each nurse/bed is explicitly allocated.
- service opening days and hours.
- treatment plans, modelled as sequences of steps (day of cure, resting periods) parameterized with doses, durations and involved resources.
- constraints on treatment plan instances: earliest/latest start date, patient unavailability, set appointment (past or confirmed).

4.3   Modelling the Objective Function

The objective function to maximize is the global RDI over the pool of patients. We have developed two global criteria:

A first criterion was to maximize the minimal RDI among all patients. It is implemented by minimizing the schedules makespan among all patients using *iFlatRelax* [21]. The schedule of a patient is an interleaving of appointments and resting periods, followed by a "stub" activity at the end. This stub is needed because all patients do not start their treatment at the same time. That stub activity enables us to consider their treatment duration instead of reasoning on their ending date. This criteria may look fair but patients with the highest "healing chances at start" (e.g. with no dose reduction) could be considered as "neglected".

A second criterion was to maximize the summed RDI. This can be modelled as a tardiness problem, i.e. overshot of a given point in time (patient dependent) multiplied by a constant. This problem is widely studied and was solved using a task swapping neighbourhood starting from a solution provided by *iFlatRelax* because it was tightly packed and computed very quickly.

5   Implementation of Agents

The implementation of the architecture detailed in the previous section relies on web services technologies: our agents communicate through a RESTful protocol relying on the JSON format for exchanging the required information. This section highlight key implementation issues of the agents, except for the simulator which is detailed in Sect. 6.

5.1   Scheduler Agent

A strong requirement was to cope with large patient sets, typically involving hundreds of patients simultaneously at various stages of their own clinical pathway. In order to scale to such size, we used local search-based approaches, mainly *iFlatRelax* for scheduling, and in a later phase, *BinPacking* for day-level reasoning. Both algorithms were implemented using the CBLS engine of OscaR [19, 22]. They are further described in the next subsections.

Based on this techniques, our prototype is able to schedule chemotherapy appointments over roughly five hundred of patients in a few seconds and supports interactive adjustments.

Iterative Flattening-Relaxation Search. The algorithm implemented in our prototype is the one already presented in our previous report, namely: the iFlatRelax. This algorithm has been improved with the following new features:

- The possibility to define non-moveable tasks, that is: tasks that already have a given date. We need to represent these, because some appointments of treatments might already be fixed, and we do not want them to be moved, since they were communicated to the patient.
- The possibility to define forbidden zones for some activities, that is: a set of points in time where the activity cannot take place. The activity is henceforth moved forward in time until a proper position is found. We will use this feature to represent patient unavailability.
- A more flexible model of resources, that will enable us to represent bin-packing resources, as mentioned in the next section.

Bin Packing. Beds and nurses need to be modelled as they are in the real world: a patient needs to occupy a bed for a certain amount of time, and more beds allocated for a patient will not reduce his time spent in a specific bed. The consequence is that we cannot represent the bed resources as a single integer value in terms of "bed hours" available in a certain day. Instead, we need to model beds as done in a bin packing problem: each bed is a bin whose size is the duration of the day, and each patient of the day must be put in a bed selected among the available ones. This allocation shall comply to the fact that the sum of duration of each patient occupying the same bed is lower or equal to the duration of the day. Patients will occupy the same bed in sequence, of course.

We therefore needed to represent a so-called "bin packing resources" exhibiting this behaviour. A bin packing resource in a scheduling problem is a resource divisible into bins of given size. Each activity using this resource declares a certain amount of usage. The activities using the same resource at the same time must be scheduled in proper bins, so that the sum of each activity using the same bin do not exceed the capacity of that bin.

So far, we have developed a model of the bin-packing problem, and a solver for bin-packing problems. We still need to integrate this solver into our scheduling engine.

5.2   Persister Agent

The persister agent provides a service-based implementation of the normalised conceptual model depicted in Fig. 7.

It can also be considered as a domain specific language for clinical pathways and is composed of the following concepts:

- *Patient*: models the information about patients treated and monitored by the tool.
- *TreatmentPlan*: captures a reusable treatment template which is composed of one or more *SchemaSteps*, either *RestStep* or *DeliveryStep*.

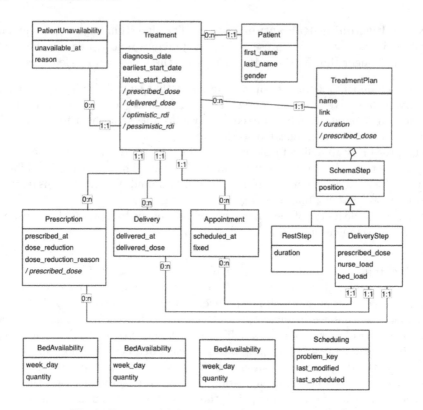

Fig. 7. Data model for a chemotherapy pathway [12].

- *Treatment*: captures a processing instance, for a given patient. It involves a number of monitored events such as *Prescription*, *Delivery* and *Appointment*. These are linked to drug injection steps through *DeliveryStep*.
- *PatientUnavailability*, *NurseAvailability*, and *BedAvailability* respectively capture the availability of beds, nurses and patients for the scheduling of appointments.

5.3   Agenda-Based User Interface Agent

The user interface is a browser-based HTML/JavaScript application interacting with the orchestrator. It is implemented using AngularJS. The interface is depicted in Fig. 8. It provides the following end-user visualisation and control capabilities:

- visualisation of the clinical pathways of the whole set of patients, allowing to spot the past chemotherapy deliveries (in green), the future deliveries with a distinction between the confirmed ones (in yellow - the scheduler will not alter them but the nurse could move them provided the patient is in the loop) and unconfirmed ones (in blue - these can be moved by the scheduler until they become confirmed). Service and patient unavailabilities are also displayed in red. The current day is represented with a vertical red line. The visualisation supports different granularity scales (day, week, months) as well as some filters like hiding the hours or days when the service is closed.

- Control over the pool of patients. This includes registration time operation for encoding a new patient and specific characteristics of his workflow instance (earliest start date, regimen periodicity and duration, target dose, etc.). It also allows to manage agenda related information like specific unavailabilities and confirmation status of next delivery (which means it cannot be moved by the scheduler). Although a specific UI is provided, a web-service interface is available for enabling the integration with agenda systems already deployed inside the hospital.
- Encoding of delivery related information, e.g. partial dose delivery, cancellation, no-show, ... This is simply done by clicking on a specific event instance.

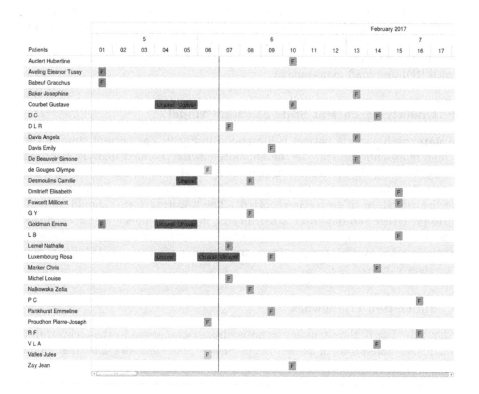

Fig. 8. Agenda user interface [12]. (Color figure online)

6   Validation

6.1   Validation Approach

Validation of care pathways in a real day hospital environment will be considered in advanced research phases. Until now we used a simulation-based approach because it helps to understand the system behaviour over long periods and under stressed conditions that are difficult to experience in the real world. It also has the ability to step inside processes and provide a good understanding of problematic scenarios. In order to enable an earlier validation, we designed the simulator with the following capabilities:

- Providing a reactive and complete user interface, giving a good user experience about the key characteristics of our algorithms like the quality of the solutions, the speed of recalculation, and the ability to take into account complex events such as no-show, partial dose, report, ...
- Integrating an environment simulator able to generate flows of planned and unforeseen events that are experienced by the targeted hospital services and that can be used to consolidate the required indicators proving the value of our tool, especially in relation to the quality of care in terms of compliance with RDI and load management.

6.2   Underlying Patient State Machine Model

The state machine for a patient is illustrated in Fig. 9. The current state of the machine represents the state of the appointment for the next delivery required for the patient by his/her treatment plan: between treatment deliveries, it should be in an "Appointment fixed" state and just after the delivery it should be in a "Delivered" state (if correctly reported). The "Waiting state" should only be transitory: either the day after a delivery or in case of no-show. Those states should be tracked in order to make sure their duration is minimised. The simulator generates events covering those transitions with given probabilities, e.g. for no-show events.

6.3   Simulation Framework

As shown by Fig. 6, the simulator agent is directly connected to the orchestrator through the same protocol as the user interface. The simulator has three main components detailed hereafter.

The "driver" Component is responsible for simulating the interactions a user would normally have with the orchestrator using the UI. It relies on exactly the same communication protocol (JSON via HTTP) as the UI. It takes as input a description of the scenario which is expressed using a specific Domain Specific Language (DSL) developed in Scala and which includes the keywords detailed in

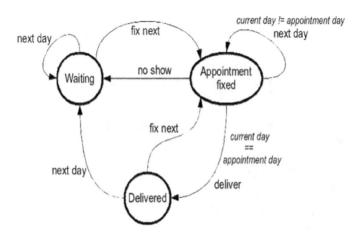

Fig. 9. Possible patient states and transitions [12].

Listing 1. All those keywords are commands expressed within a context containing the simulation driver component and the current planning state. Each command triggers a new scheduling operation that respects the constraints stated earlier in the problem statement and tries to optimise the RDI of all patients.

Listing 1. DSL for care pathways scenarios.

```
// pause simulation until next action in control panel
def pause

// slow down the simulation with specified delay (in ms)
def sleep(sleepDuration: Int = 10000)

// enroll a list of patients with the default protocol
def enrollDefaultTP(patients: List[(String, String)])

// enroll a specific patient with a specific protocol
def enroll(patients: List[(String, String, Option[String])])

// indicate a patient will not be available at a specific day
def unavailableInDays(nbDaysFromNow: Int = 0)
                     (firstName: String, lastName: String)

// confirm next delivery for the specified patient
def fixNext(firstName: String, lastName: String)

// confirm next delivery for each patient
def fixAllNext

// confirm next delivery for each patient if set today
def fixAllToday
```

```
// no-show event for the specified patient
def noShow(firstName: String, lastName: String)

// delivery event (possibly partial)
def deliver(firstName: String, lastName: String,
            dose: Float = 1.0f)

// deliver full dose to all patients of today
def deliverAll

// move simulation time to the next day
def nextDay
```

As example, Listing 2 gives a short typical scenario. On the first day, four patients are enrolled with the default protocol. Some unavailabilities are also specified and then the first appointments on the resulting schedule are confirmed. On the next day it starts delivering and confirming next appointments.

Listing 2. Simple simulation scenarios expressed in our DSL.

```
enrollDefaultTP(List(("Gustave", "Courbet"),
                      ("Rosa", "Luxembourg"),
                      ("Josephine", "Baker"),
                      ("Jean", "Zay"))),
unavailableInDays(4)("Gustave", "Courbet"),
unavailableInDays(5)("Gustave", "Courbet"),
unavailableInDays(4)("Rosa", "Luxembourg"),
fixAllNext,

nextDay,
deliverAll,
fixAllNext,
...
```

The "control Panel" Component gives control over the running simulation, i.e. ability to play, pause, restart a scenario. Two running modes are available:

1. step-by-step mode. This mode enables to have a deep understanding of a specific run. It can also be used to introduce specific events manually using the usual user interface.
2. fully automated mode, running at machine speed. This mode relies on the generation of events based on probability distributions. It can be used to spot specific problems and also to assess the performance over a large number of runs using a Monte-Carlo process.

The "KPI Component" is a component collecting and displaying the evolution of key performance indicators (KPIs), such as RDIs and service load (including resources like nurses and beds). An example of KPI display is depicted in

Fig. 11. In addition to graphical widget enabling to follow the evolution of the main KPI during the simulation, a larger set of KPI are also logged in a CSV format enabling to easily analyse them off-line, e.g. using a spreadsheet or more elaborated data analysis software. The persister agent also offers a full repository that can be easily queried to find more elaborated information.

7   Validation Results

7.1   Investigated Scenarios

Several simulation sessions were organised both with the technical team and with oncology practitioners involving three hospitals (UCL/Cancer Institute, Grand Hospital of Charleroi and UZ Leuven). The following scenarios were investigated with a FEC chemotherapy protocol composed of six occurrences of a three weeks cycle time in a service running only during the week days. We also only focused on the bed capacity by allocating a non-limiting nurse capacity. We considered two kinds of service:

- one toy service with a 3 bed capacity per day, i.e. 15 beds per week and 45 beds theoretical full pathway capacity over a 3 week period (i.e. 45 patients if full day patients). This is a small unit not of realistic size but it was useful for keeping first learning sessions shorter
- a realistic service with a 10 bed capacity per day, i.e. 50 beds per week, 150 beds theoretical pathway capacity. This is a typical configuration in units of our partner hospitals.

The following set of scenarios covering both normal and exceptional cases were investigated:

1. regular enrolment over time within service capacity
2. regular enrolment until overloading service
3. unbalanced load that can result in a problem to cope with peaks
4. special cases like injection of unavailabilities, partial deliveries for a specific patient

The solver was allowed a computation time of 2 s. This timing was selected because:

- benchmarking showed the quality is already quite good within this time bound.
- it is compatible with interactive use of the solver, e.g. when looking for the next appointment with the patient.
- to avoid slowing down the simulation. Actually in real use, the solver can be used during idle time to improve solution.

Typical run times range from a few minutes for short scenarios to a few hours. The longest run was a 4 months scenario on the 10 bed service and lasted after about 4 h. In the following section we present two type of figures: global pathway view at a specific time and temporal evolution of key figures like number of patients, minimum RDI and bed load.

7.2   Scenario 1 - Progressive Load on Toy Service

In order to simulate this scenario we consider a simplified protocol composed of
4 deliveries with only one week of rest period. This means that patients will start
leaving the pathway after 4 weeks. With a patient injection rate of 4 patients per
week the service should stabilise around 16 patients. Figure 10 gives an overview
of the system after 5 weeks. It visually shows the renewal is well managed through
the general diagonal structure of the pathway.

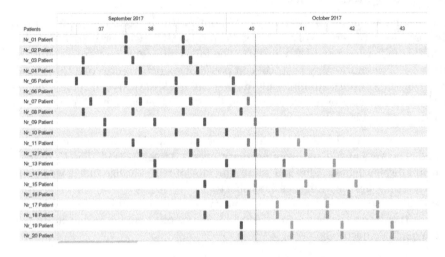

Fig. 10. Pathway overview of a long run simulation on toy service.

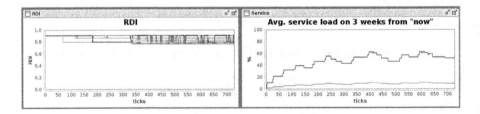

Fig. 11. Pathway KPIs for a long run simulation on toy service.

Figure 11 confirms the good stability of the system: the minimal RDI is kept
constant as well as the foreseen load over the next weeks. Note some RDI are
only 80% but the explanation lies in the larger sensitivity given the smaller rest
period and number of cycles.

7.3   Scenario 2 - Regular Enrolment Until Overloading Service

The scenario is to regularly introduce new patient at a rate that will overload the system after some time. For the toy service, an average of 1 patient is introduced per day, meaning the full capacity is reached after 45 days. For the real size system 15 patients are introduced per week which will saturate the system after 10 weeks. The temporal evolution show a quite similar behaviour for both the toy and real size system (see Fig. 12). Before reaching saturation, the minimum RDI is quite stable around 95% which is excellent. Once reaching the full capacity, the scheduler has no choice that starting to delay some patient which immediately result in an RDI degradation. Note that after one week overloading, the minimal RDI has already reached the key 85% threshold. This means that the occurrence of overload should be closely monitored and anticipated as much as possible to avoid it, e.g. by opening extra rooms or redirecting some patients to other services. Finally note that at the saturation point the reported load is not the full capacity (e.g. 80% for toy system), due to the fact that treatment time is actually less than one day but the availability is not enough to fit an extra patient.

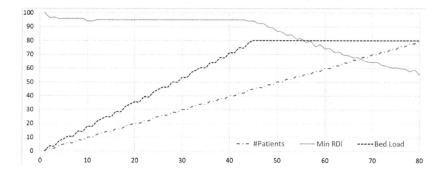

Fig. 12. Long run simulation on toy service.

7.4   Scenario 3 - Dealing with Peak

The peak scenario considers first a regular rate and then a higher rate of limited duration (1 week) which is over the service capacity. This scenario is run on the same simplified protocol used in scenario 2 because of its larger sensitivity.

The patient peak is easy to spot at day 15 of the temporal evolution shown on Fig. 13 by the change in patient rate and load. There is also an impact on the RDI which is reduced by a few percent. As the peak occurred at the end of a cycle, there is also a danger of cascading impact on the next week when first second cycle patients come back. In this case however globally the impact is within control. However the longer the peak, the bigger the degradation, moreover the impact can also have some echoes in the next cycles as the scheduler will try to respect a minimal rest period for the maximal number of patients.

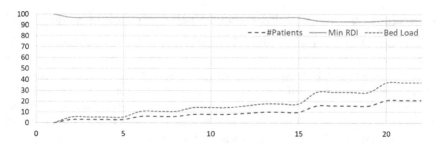

Fig. 13. Scheduler behaviour in the presence of peak.

7.5 Scenario 4 - Copying with Unavailabilities

In this scenario, we consider the effect of a patient not available over a few days that impact a delivery. This is typically the case a the beginning of the treatment which should start as soon as possible. We introduce an unavailability of 4 days and simultaneously introduce other patient. The result depicted at Fig. 14 shows that the patient is scheduled immediately after its period of unavailability while other patient are scheduled at other time. Of course there is still an impact on the RDI (see red curve on insert in Fig. 14) but this impact is minimised. Note the impact is quite significant and that is why any unavailability impacting a planned delivery should be detected and the patient warned about the impact.

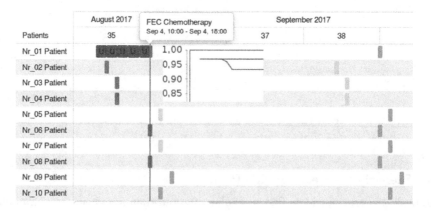

Fig. 14. Scheduler behaviour in the presence of unavailability. (Color figure online)

The scheduler reacts in a similar way of a no-show or partial dose. Due to the limited space, those simulations are not elaborated further here.

7.6 Discussion

The outcome of our simulation campaign is quite positive. It shows the good capability of our scheduler to simultaneously ensure quality of care and a smart use of resources. The RDI is kept under control in normal circumstances and also has a minimal impact in case of deviation events or limited peaks. Of course, this can result in some decrease over time as the result of minor delays or partial doses delivered due to chemotherapy toxicity but those can be kept within bounds. The service load is also exhibiting a smooth curve meaning that appointments can be evenly dispatched over time.

Of course under sustained high load conditions, the system cannot cope anymore and will tend to uniformly degrade the quality of care for all the patients involved. The simulation shows the impact can quickly become significant which means that the load should be carefully monitored. The fact that the scheduler is working many weeks ahead of times gives very good predictability and should enable the service to anticipate such problems.

The prototype also raised ethical concerns, such as the capacity of the tool to choose to favor some patients rather than others in case of resource shortage. Our conclusion is that the system should report such situations ahead of time to allow the day hospital team to take corrective measures, like a transient increase of staffing. In order to keep the medical team in control, the developed graphical display was also a huge practical improvement. Some interesting feature such as the visualization of allocation windows ensuring a good RDI level definitely helped oncologists and nurses in charge of appointments updates.

8   Related Work

A complete literature review on integrated hospital scheduling problems, including pathways, was recently published by [9]. Although concepts such as clinical pathways or diagnosis related groups have been around for more than 20 years, the study reveals that most of the relevant work is quite recent. Besides progress in methods and tooling, the main trigger factor is that hospitals are facing the necessity to break barriers across services for dealing with the performance and capacity challenges they have to face. Currently, off-line scheduling approaches are more often reported than on-line methods because hospitals want to provide the best possible solutions which are related to the largest possible exploration of the state space. This rules outs methods which are mostly based on (meta-) heuristics. However very good (and in some cases optimal) results of using local search for outpatient scheduling has been reported in the literature [23] and are confirmed by the quality of our simulation results. A key point is that our CBLS engine ensures fast exploration of the search space, resulting in a good coverage. Moreover our design also allows the system to continue optimizing the time horizon for appointments not yet confirmed to patients and thus without strong time constraints.

A methodology to design appointment systems for outpatient clinics and diagnostic facilities that offer both walk-in and scheduled service is presented in [24]. The proposed schedule has two levels: a global level stating the number of appointments per day and a day level detailing when each appointment should be scheduled on a given day. Each level is managed by a specific model and the two models are connected by an algorithm. Our approach also proposes two levels with a coarser granularity at the global level (e.g. we consider global bed-hours availabilities) while at the day level a fine grained model is used (i.e. we assign patient to available beds). Our current validation is however currently limited to the global level.

Scheduling has also been successfully applied in other hospital areas. In radio-therapy, several approaches of operation research ranging from strategic capacity management to operational scheduling levels are reported in [25]. It highlights that many improvements regarding the waiting times and resource utilization can be achieved. A substantive attention is also devoted to the scheduling of the operation room because it accounts for up 40% of resource costs in a hospital. However it differs from oncology pathways by a far more important level of unpredictability. Reported results shows that about 30% more patients can be scheduled than in actual practice and the operating room utilization rate is increased by 20% [26].

Multiple algorithms and software tools to generate qualitative surgery schedules on the tactical and operational level are also reported in [27]. This work actually also shows a wider impact on the whole hospital, since these operation rooms are interrelated to many other departments or organizational problems like nurse scheduling or bed levelling. It also points out the necessity of a good visualization capabilities because they help health managers to have good insights and they also guide them in testing different scenarios.

Regarding the computer tools used, the observed practice is often still the manual use of basic tools such as spreadsheets or scheduling templates [10].

9   Conclusion

This paper presented an extended validation of our scheduling approach for clinical pathways. In such system, a large number of deliveries, e.g. for chemotherapy, must be adequately planned to comply with strict time constraints of a large pool of patients under limited resources. Missing a deadline means treatments are spaced too much, which directly affects their efficiency. On the other side, if the deadline is too anticipated, treatments are too close in time, with the risk of side effects on the patient or partial delivery.

In contrast with the current state of practice which is still often close to a "first come, first served" allocation, our scheduling approach is global and is driven by the goal of constantly maximising the care quality measured using clinically validated indicators such as the RDI. Through the combined use of a scalable open source CBLS scheduling engine, a web-based visualisation and an efficient simulation environment, we were able to conduct an in-depth validation campaign. Our validation covered medium size scenarios focusing on the study of specific behaviours (e.g. to specific adverse events) to large real size scenarios over large periods of time and including different load types.

The result of our validation is that our scheduler can definitely support the medical actors in their work. It can operate under quite high loading (i.e. reaching the maximum number of patients per day) while preserving the care quality indicators with respect to acceptable thresholds. The process is also fair for the patients, event those more constrained. Or course, the system cannot handle high loading situations where resources are lacking. However, such cases can be anticipated a few cycles in advance and the system can then serve as a medium-term management board which can drive resources allocation (e.g. longer opening times, more nurses hired, ...) or trigger the redirection of new patients to other services. Under this mode, the system has not any ethical responsibility in operating in a degraded mode where he would have to start degrading the care quality of some patients.

The next step of our research is to continue to raise the maturity of our prototype in order to be able to conduct an on-site validation. A major request is to achieve finer tasks management, i.e. within each day. This requires to rework our algorithms to integrate the bin packing solver into the scheduling engine and be able to efficiently combine the optimisations performed at both levels. Other operational deployment constraints also have to be met, such as the need to integrate with the existing electronic patient record and agenda systems.

Acknowledgements. This research was partly funded by the Walloon Region by the PIPAS (nr. 1017087) and PRIMa-Q (nr. 1610088) projects. We thanks UCL/Cancer Institute, Grand Hospital of Charleroi and UZ Leuven for their valuable feedback.

References

1. McGlynn, E.A., et al.: The quality of health care delivered to adults in the United States. N. Engl. J. Med. **348**, 2635–2645 (2003)
2. Campbell, H., Hotchkiss, R., Bradshaw, N., Porteous, M.: Integrated care pathways. Br. Med. J. **316**, 133–137 (1998)
3. van Dam, P.A., et al.: A dynamic clinical pathway for the treatment of patients with early breast cancer is a tool for better cancer care: implementation and prospective analysis between 2002–2010. World J. Surg. Oncol. **11**, 70 (2013)
4. Walter, F., et al.: Success of clinical pathways for total joint arthroplasty in a community hospital. Clin. Orthop. Relat. Res. **457**, 133 (2007)
5. Choo, J.: Critical success factors in implementing clinical pathways/case management. Ann. Acad. Med. Singap. **30**(Suppl. 4), 17–21 (2001)
6. Roucoux, F., et al.: Pipas - optimal piloting of care pathways. Final Report, Université catholique de Louvain (2014)
7. Gooch, P., Roudsari, A.: Computerization of workflows, guidelines, and care pathways: a review of implementation challenges for process-oriented health information systems. J. Am. Med. Inform. Assoc. **18**, 738–748 (2011)
8. Mauro, C., et al.: From medical processes to workflows: modeling of clinical pathways with the unified modeling language. In: International Conference on Health Informatics (HealthInf), Valencia, Spain, vol. 161, pp. 9–10 (2010)
9. Marynissen, J., Demeulemeester, E.: Literature review on integrated hospital scheduling problems. Technical report 555258, KU Leuven, Faculty of Economics and Business (2016)
10. Ahmed, Z., Elmekkawy, T., Bates, S.: Developing an efficient scheduling template of a chemotherapy treatment unit: a case study. Australas. Med. J. **4**, 575–88 (2011)

11. Van Hentenryck, P., Michel, L.: Constraint-Based Local Search. MIT Press, Cambridge (2009)
12. Ponsard, C., Landtsheer, R.D., Guyot, Y., Roucoux, F., Lambeau, B.: Decision making support in the scheduling of chemotherapy coping with quality of care, resources and ethical constraints. In: Proceedings of the 19th International Conference on Enterprise Information Systems, ICEIS 2017, Porto, Portugal, 26–29 April 2017
13. Lyman, G.: Impact of chemotherapy dose intensity on cancer patient outcomes. J. Natl. Compr. Cancer Netw. 7(1), 99–108 (2009)
14. Piccart, M., Biganzoli, L., Di Leo, A.: The impact of chemotherapy dose density and dose intensity on breast cancer outcome: what have we learned? Eur. J. Cancer 36, 4–10 (2000)
15. Di Gaspero, L., Schaerf, A.: EASYLOCAL++: an object-oriented framework for the flexible design of local-search algorithms. Softw. Pract. Exp. 33, 733–765 (2003)
16. Benoist, T., Estellon, B., Gardi, F., Megel, R., Nouioua, K.: Localsolver 1.x: a black-box local-search solver for 0-1 programming. 4OR 9, 299–316 (2011)
17. Newton, M.A.H., Pham, D.N., Sattar, A., Maher, M.: Kangaroo: an efficient constraint-based local search system using lazy propagation. In: Lee, J. (ed.) CP 2011. LNCS, vol. 6876, pp. 645–659. Springer, Heidelberg (2011). https://doi.org/10.1007/978-3-642-23786-7_49
18. De Landtsheer, R., Guyot, Y., Ospina, G., Ponsard, C.: Combining neighborhoods into local search strategies. In: Amodeo, L., Talbi, E.-G., Yalaoui, F. (eds.) Recent Developments in Metaheuristics. ORSIS, vol. 62, pp. 43–57. Springer, Cham (2018). https://doi.org/10.1007/978-3-319-58253-5_3
19. OscaR Team: OscaR: Operational Research in Scala (2012). https://bitbucket.org/oscarlib/oscar
20. Damas, C., Lambeau, B., van Lamsweerde, A.: Analyzing critical decision-based processes. IEEE Trans. Softw. Eng. 40, 338–365 (2014)
21. Michel, L., Hentenryck, P.V.: Iterative relaxations for iterative flattening in cumulative scheduling. In: 14th International Conference on Automated Planning & Scheduling (ICAPS) (2004)
22. De Landtsheer, R., Ponsard, C.: Oscar.cbls: an open source framework for constraint-based local search. In: Proceedings of ORBEL'27 (2013)
23. Kaandorp, G.C., Koole, G.: Optimal outpatient appointment scheduling. Health Care Manag. Sci. 10, 217–229 (2007)
24. Kortbeek, N., et al.: Designing cyclic appointment schedules for outpatient clinics with scheduled and unscheduled patient arrivals (2011)
25. Vieira, B., et al.: Operations research for resource planning and-use in radiotherapy: a literature review. BMC Med. Inform. Decis. Mak. 16, 149 (2016)
26. Barbagallo, S., et al.: Optimization and planning of operating theatre activities: an original definition of pathways and process modeling. BMC Med. Inform. Decis. Mak. 15, 38 (2015)
27. Demeulemeester, E., Sermeus, W., Beliën, J., Cardoen, B.: Clinical pathways and operations management: it takes two to tango. Rev. Bus. Econ. Lit. LII, 451–470 (2007)

Information Systems Analysis and Specification

Strategies to Foster Software Ecosystem Partnerships – A System Dynamics Analysis

George Valença[1] and Carina Alves[2(✉)]

[1] Departamento de Computação, Universidade Federal Rural de Pernambuco, Recife, Brazil
george.valenca@ufrpe.br
[2] Centro de Informática, Universidade Federal de Pernambuco, Recife, Brazil
cfa@cin.ufpe.br

Abstract. Software ecosystems originate in the idea of business ecosystems, as a collection of relationships among actors in an economic community. They represent the current functioning of the IT industry, in which companies co-create innovations and extend their solutions by means of partnerships. This research investigates the driving factors of relationships in a software ecosystem. To address this goal, we performed multiple case studies of two emerging software ecosystems formed by Small-to-Medium Enterprises. Based on evidence from twenty-seven interviews conducted with eight companies, we analysed the main facilitators and barriers for their partnerships to thrive. We used System Dynamics method to identify cause-effect relations among these factors. The resulting dynamic models enabled us to map key factors and interactions to propose four strategies that promote software ecosystems health. We believe that practitioners can benefit from this synthesis by understanding the facilitators to reinforce and barriers to restrain, as a means to catalyse the success of their networks. In addition, we demonstrate for researchers the utility of System Dynamics to provide a diagnostic of relevant scenarios.

Keywords: Software ecosystems · Partnerships · System dynamics · Strategies

1 Introduction

Software ecosystems figure among the most recent and relevant trends in IT industry. A software ecosystem is as a set of businesses functioning as a unit and interacting with a shared market for software and services, together with the relationships among them [1]. They involve the interdependence and interrelation to external partners and stakeholders with which a software company collaborates and competes [2]. Software ecosystems promote the idea of coopetition, when companies embrace competitive collaborations and start to co-evolve their products in a hub of local and/or global market [3]. Software vendors gradually share their customers and get access to new segments. As partners, they start to base their business on the other as the relationship becomes mutually beneficial for both sides [4].

By defining partnerships to engage in this networked setting, companies acquire new skills, share features and clients, and divide R&D costs [5]. Moreover, they can cope

© Springer International Publishing AG, part of Springer Nature 2018
S. Hammoudi et al. (Eds.): ICEIS 2017, LNBIP 321, pp. 189–211, 2018.
https://doi.org/10.1007/978-3-319-93375-7_10

with financial, time and knowledge constraints [6]. Successful examples of software ecosystems include Apple's iPhone and the range of complementary apps developed by third-party players available at Apple Store, Eclipse open source ecosystem, among other platforms in the IT industry. The increasing growth of software ecosystems confirms that firms co-existing in the same market have recognised their need to cooperate to survive in a turbulent environment.

This paper reports on exploratory multiple case studies of software ecosystems on a birth stage and formed by Small-to-Medium Enterprises (SMEs). The tight relationships among these companies result from frequent joint projects to integrate their ERP software solutions and services. On the one hand, SMEs must cope with limited financial and human resources. On the other hand, they have flexible organisational structure and motivation to explore innovative business models. These aspects direct the way SMEs define partnerships and position themselves in a software ecosystem.

Our motivation was to investigate the factors that affect positively and/or negatively the evolution of partnerships among SMEs establishing a software ecosystem. We achieved this goal by adopting System Dynamics (SD) method [7] to analyse the factors that nurture and/or hamper the partnerships. The contribution of our study lies in describing these factors and presenting diagrams expressing causal relations among them. Besides, we present strategies that enable software companies to understand what drives the healthy evolution of their ecosystems.

This paper is organised as follows. Section 2 describes the conceptual background of the research. Section 3 details the research method. Section 4 presents systemic diagrams by adopting System Dynamics. Section 5 uses the diagnostic of the partnerships to delineate strategies that companies can adopt to foster the evolution of the software ecosystems, in light of literature in the field. Section 6 discusses issues related to the use of System Dynamics. Finally, Sect. 7 presents final considerations.

2   Conceptual Background

2.1   Software Ecosystems

Partnerships differ from more general business relationships due to firms' degree of mutual commitment, respect, trust and influence; communication behaviour that involves transparency and information sharing; and tendency towards joint problem solving; among other properties [8]. They are the seed of a **software ecosystem** by allowing external actors to customise or complement the features of existing products, and provide technical services [9]. This network changes the dominant logic of doing business via integrated manufacturing, in-house R&D and direct sales. Partners focus on innovative business models, which define novel ways for a firm to collaborate with external agents and for them to create and capture value from the network [10].

Manikas and Hansen [11] proposed a broader and common **classification** of software ecosystem. In *proprietary* ecosystems, the source code and other artefacts produced are protected and new players usually need to be certified to participate in the network. Popular examples are the Apple iOS, Microsoft Dynamics CRM and SAP ecosystems. In their turn, *free or open-source* software ecosystems have actors who participate independently from receiving revenues from their activity and whose certification is generally flexible. Eclipse ecosystems belong to this category. Recently, Manikas [12] introduced the type *hybrid*, which concerns ecosystems that support both proprietary and open-source contributions. We consider this definition, which classifies the studied cases as proprietary ecosystems.

The **actors** of a software ecosystem have different roles and responsibilities. Manikas and Hansen [11] provide an overview of the most common actors in a software ecosystem, which includes *keystone, niche player, external developer* or *third party developers, vendor* or *reseller, customer* and *user*. The *keystone* has a critical function, since it guarantees the well-functioning of the ecosystem. This player is responsible for running the software platform, creating and applying rules, processes and business procedures, setting and monitoring quality standards, and orchestrating actors' relationships. In their turn, *niche players* are also central to the ecosystem, as companies that use the platform to develop or add components (e.g. apps) to it, producing functionality that customers require. They create or enhance capabilities that differentiate them from other participants. Their importance lies in complementing keystone work and influencing decision-making in ecosystem management.

All actors are committed to a certain degree to ensure their own **health** as well as their partners' health in the ecosystem. Hence, ecosystem prosperity represents their own prosperity. Hartigh and colleagues [13] argue the health of an ecosystem is a way of assessing its strength at a specific moment. Iansiti and Levien [14] propose a classification inspired on biological ecosystems to define health as the extent to which an ecosystem as a whole is durably creating opportunities for its members and those who depend on it. The three measures of health are *productivity, robustness* and *niche creation. Productivity* indicates the ecosystem ability to transform inputs into products and services. Number of applications in an App Store is a means to assess the productivity of an ecosystem. *Robustness* indicates the ecosystem capacity to deal with interferences and competition pressure. The survival rate of ecosystem members is a possible metric to assess this aspect. Finally, *niche creation* represents the opportunities in the ecosystem. It fosters diversity by creating valuable resources and niches. The number of new players around the platform is a way to assess niche creation.

The health of a software ecosystem must encompass its three **dimensions** [13]. The *business* dimension involves elements such as the marketplace, entry barriers and customer base. The *technical* dimension addresses technological and architectural issues such as the common software platform and integrated solutions. Finally, the *social* dimension considers interfirm relationships, promotion and skills, for instance.

By measuring the health of an ecosystem, it is possible to monitor its maturity. According to Moore [15], business ecosystems evolve according to a four-phase **life-cycle**: *birth, expansion, leadership* and *self-renewal*. Once a software ecosystem in associated with an evolutionary phase, it is possible to understand how it will move and direct the changes. The studied software ecosystems are in a birth stage, resulting from the strengthening of multiple, bi-lateral alliances among complementors. During birth phase, software firms focus on evolving the core of their products while relying on partners to develop complements or extensions such as specific modules. Multiple complementors co-create value by combining their solutions to treat market demands.

2.2 System Dynamics

System Dynamics provides understanding about the structure and functioning of systems in which we are embedded. By using this approach to represent relationships among important factors from a given context, it is possible to identify patterns, cycles and consequences of such relationships. SD supports the definition of high-leverage policies for sustained improvement. However, the effectiveness of this approach depends on the ability of researchers to reflect and comprehend the reality under study. System behaviour is represented by graphical schemes combining reinforcing and balancing cycles formed by variables from studied phenomena. Reinforcing loops are the engine of growth. They can be virtuous (situations that reinforce in desired directions) or vicious (situations that start badly and grow worse). Balancing loops maintain the status quo of a context. Many loops also contain delays, which are consequences that will occur in the long term [7].

These schemes can be related to one or more generic system archetypes (Fig. 1), i.e. known patterns of system behaviour representing specific combination of virtuous reinforcement and balancing cycles. They are a rich technique to analyse a past situation or forecast specific scenarios by identifying potential traps and mitigating risks of occurrence. Each archetype has a script that guides the interpretation of the context explored [7]. The selection of an archetype depends on how the related script properly describes the studied scenario. This is done by identifying contextual variables that hold cause and effect relations that fit the archetype script. According to Braun [16], there are ten system archetypes: *Limits to Growth (aka Limits to Success), Shifting the Burden,* Eroding Goals, *Escalation, Success to the Successful, Tragedy of the Commons, Fixes that Fail, Growth and Underinvestment, Accidental Adversaries,* and *Attractiveness Principle* [16]. Figure 1 shows how these system archetypes interact with each other. The characteristics of the scenario included in the scheme (e.g. *"but I think my growth leads to your decline"*, *"but my fix is your nightmare"*, etc.) are also means to guide to the selection of one or more archetypes for a studied phenomenon.

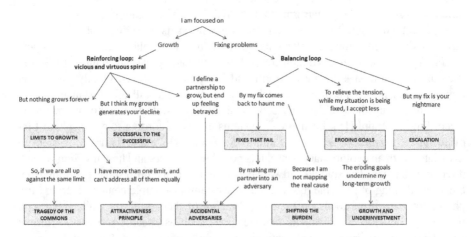

Fig. 1. Interaction among system archetypes – based on Braun [16].

3   Research Method

Our multiple case studies examined the main drivers of partnerships among SMEs in a software ecosystem. We translate this goal in three research questions (RQ):

- RQ1 – What are the facilitators and barriers of partnerships among software companies participating in a software ecosystem?
- RQ2 – How the facilitators and barriers factors interact with each other?
- RQ3 – Which strategies can support the health of the software ecosystem in light of these factors?

To address these research questions, we performed 2 case studies (Case Study I – CSI and Case Study II – CSII) composed of 5 and 3 software companies, respectively. We purposefully selected them in order to obtain information-rich cases to investigate the phenomenon of software ecosystem partnerships in depth [17].

3.1   Case Companies

In CSI, we investigated 5 partner firms from Recife, Brazil, here called Company A, Company B, Company C, Company D and Company E (Table 1). These firms integrate their products in frequent joint projects, which are started by one or more partners. By strengthening their relationships, the partners have gradually created a software ecosystem formed by the integrated software systems developed by these complementary companies. We initiated our study analysing the partnership between Company A and Company B. Preliminary interviews enabled us to identify other relevant players: Company C, which is partner of Company A and Company B; and Company D, which is partner of Company B. We then mapped Company E, as partner of Company D.

Table 1.   Overview of Companies A, B, C, D and E [18].

Company	Solutions
Company A	ERP with 5 modules focused on retail chains and distributors
Company B	ERP with 15 modules for several niches (healthcare, logistics etc.)
Company C	Information system with 3 modules for pharmacies
Company D	10 information systems for hospitals
Company E	Web portal for electronic quotations

CSII involved 3 software firms operating in Recife and São Paulo, Brazil, here named as Company F, Company G and Company H (Table 2). They build a software ecosystem in which Company F is the keystone and the main responsible for sharing business deals with partner companies. We started CSII by exploring the partnership between Companies F and G, which involves the integration of complementary healthcare solutions. In addition, we mapped the partnership between Company F and Company H, which is critical to maintain the products of Company F.

Table 2. Overview of Companies F, G and H [18].

Company	Solutions
Company F	ERP solutions with 60 modules for hospitals and healthcare market
Company G	20 information systems for laboratories
Company H	Services to revamp software systems in diverse markets

3.2 Data Collection

We undertook open-ended and semi-structured interviews to map the factors that enable and inhibit a partnership in a software ecosystem, which we name as facilitators and barriers. We interviewed twenty professionals in CSI (Table 3) and seven professionals in CSII (Table 4). The participants played both technical and managerial roles in the companies. One author conducted and transcribed the twenty-seven interviews. The transcripts were later analysed with the other author to reach an agreed understanding about the collected data and discuss the findings.

Table 3. Participants from CSI – Initial Data Collection [18].

Company	Job function
Company A	Project Manager, Business Analyst, System Analyst
Company B	Project Manager, Product Manager, Release Manager, Integration Team Leader, Business Analyst, System Analyst (2), Tester
Company C	Services Manager, Project Manager, Business Analyst
Company D	Product Manager, Project Manager, Solutions Architect, System Architect, System Analyst
Company E	Operations and Deployment Director

Table 4. Participants from CSII – Initial Data Collection [18].

Company	Job function
Company F	Sales Director, Marketing Manager, Product Owner, Business Analyst, System Analyst
Company G	Marketing Manager
Company H	Operations Director

3.3 Data Analysis

We started data analysis by searching for barriers and facilitators in interviews discourse. We mapped factors that were common to both cases to represent key drivers of partnerships. These factors were considered variables in System Dynamics method [7]. We listed and crossed them in a table to examine causal relations among them. Once we identified a possible relation in such causal matrix, we inserted a code d or i to indicate that the variable in the line caused the variable in the column in a directly (d) or inversely (i) proportional form, respectively. We also labelled each relation with the values 1 and 3 to indicate standard weights related to causal relations intensity. If no relation was remarked, the cells were left blank. We crossed the factors considering interviews evidence and our interpretation of the facts.

We subsequently reordered the variables in the resultant matrix by values in two final columns: *sum weight of causes* and *sum weight of effects*. Hence, we could order the variables by what can be understood as their 'systemic power'. This is useful to identify potential leverage factors to the performance of the partnerships. Then, we created SD models to represent the variables and correspondent relations. We considered the most relevant variables, i.e. those with greater systemic power in the matrix. By selecting variables with high values of influence, we also avoided the complexity explosion that would result from a large number of contextual variables and relationships in the models. The subsequent step was the identification of a subset of variables considered as critical, based on our interpretation and interviewees' opinions. The resultant model presents the barriers and facilitators to describe the dynamics of the studied context in a graphical form. It denotes leverage points and causal cycles that contribute to or limit the healthy evolution of the ecosystem.

In a final step, we discussed the SD models via confirmatory interviews with the studied firms. We interviewed 5 professionals in CSI and 1 professional in CSII (Table 5). Participants considered their knowledge about the business and partnerships established to assess the suitability of the relations among the prioritised factors. During this process, we asked participants (i) whether the diagram represented the appropriate elements (factors and relations), and (ii) whether there were other elements to include. As a result, we performed some punctual refinements in SD models.

Table 5. Participants from CSI and CSII – DS Models Evaluation.

Company	Job function
Company A	Project Manager
Company B	Operations Director
Company C	Configuration Manager, Innovation Manager
Company D	Project Manager
Company F	Sales director

4 Systemic View of Facilitators and Barriers in Partnerships

In Sect. 4.1, we present the facilitators and barriers that influence the partnerships among companies of CSI and CSII. Section 4.2 describes the SD models generated for our multiple case study. The models present a synthesised view of facilitators and barriers identified in the partnerships of studied companies. Given the fact that firms of CSI and CSII share similar contextual factors (e.g. size, geographical location, ERP application domain, types of partnerships), we opted to conduct an integrated analysis of facilitators, barriers and the resulting systemic archetypes of CSI and CSII.

4.1 Facilitators and Barriers

This section answers RQ1 by describing a set of facilitators and barriers for the studied companies to thrive in their software ecosystems. Facilitators (F) are factors that can contribute to the creation and growth of partnerships. Our analysis of CSI and CSII revealed the following seven facilitators:

- **F1 – Personal and Geographical Proximity**

  Companies' physical proximity promotes joint projects among them: *"since it (Company B) was near, we took the software from Company B"*, cited the software architect from Company D. In particular, companies that operate in the same region understand the specific needs of this market. Hence, geographically and personally close firms often become relevant partners.

  The joint projects start with strict professional relationships among staff of partners companies (e.g. managers in an integration project). Once these interactions evolve to more personal relationships, the companies can benefit from a good communication channel and professionals that aim to leverage the partnership. The arguments of the marketing manager from Company G illustrate this scenario: *"since we worked very well (and) I know several people from Company F, we will try to grow this partnership; the communication channel facilitates a lot; the partnership flows very well"*.

  It means that the closer personal relationship between staff of partner companies catalyses their collaboration, as the services manager from Company C detailed: *"I 'hit the door' of Company A to talk to the president to seek business opportunities"*. Their personal relations facilitate the execution of projects: *"communication (with Company B) flows well since this team worked together in other projects; it emerged a friendship outside the firm; this helps a lot"*, argued Company A project manager.

- **F2 – Respectful Attitude**

  Companies that keep a respectful attitude are fostering their partnership. The marketing manager from Company G highlighted the relevance of a good conduct: *"these are companies that always respected each other, which is very important; Company F never mentioned anything (related to paying) a commission; they are very professional and Company G never offered anything to them"*. The companies appreciate such attitude of a partner, which increases the trust on the other company.

- **F3 – Mutual Trust**

Trust results from the close relationship of the firms, sometimes a personal proximity of their members. It is seen as a premise for a partnership to emerge, as cited by the innovation manager from Company C: *"to establish a partnership, you already trust the partner; you already have confidence, you know he is responsible; it is a premise for you to establish a partnership"*.

The commercial director from Company F also argued the dependence kept by partners requires full reliability: *"(we must have) total trust, because they hold key knowledge of the code"*. The trust factor increases with actions that favour joint projects, such as promptly treating systems integration problems. The project manager from Company A clarified the relevance of trust: *"I'd rather have a less competent but reliable partner than a super competent but unreliable one"*.

- **F4 – Openness for Technical and Business Negotiation**

Flexibility for business and technical negotiations is a critical factor for a partnership to succeed, because companies must guarantee a win-win approach. Companies mentioned positive experiences with partners who were open to discuss technical and business issues. The marketing manager from Company G discussed this fact: *"there is this technical part, when we can integrate (our systems) very well; (where) people get (access to) the necessary channels and are available to help us at any time"*.

The project manager from Company D exemplified the impact of this factor in a relationship: *"the partner approached us with interest and humility; (another) partnership did not evolve because the partner was inflexible"*. The commercial director from Company F also stressed the importance of easily negotiating commercial issues with partners: *"any integration that I do consumes time with maintenance, installation, or a failure; (so) it is fair that part of it (payment) is reverted to me; there are firms that are very open; others (are) inflexible; this is very bad"*.

Openness for negotiation is a common trend among SMEs: *"when there is the possibility to negotiate is because they are firms of the same size; in general, there is (openness for negotiation)"*, declared the operations director from Company B.

- **F5 – Effective Communication**

Good communication is essential for an integration project to succeed and thereby for a partnership to evolve. It is important to establish adequate communication channels and ensure the right people are available to have technical or business discussions with a partner. For instance, Company F maintains an integration team, which has a wider view of the integrations between its healthcare solutions and other systems. The marketing manager from Company G explains such facilitator: *"we have much trouble to get to the person who will develop the integration; this is something that really makes it (integration) difficult; the (partnership of) Company G with Company F works because of the right channels; it is the best (communication channel) we have (with a partner)"*.

- **F6 – Perceived Quality of Products and Services**

The quality of products and services is a criterion considered by companies to select a partner, given the relevance of quality for client satisfaction. For instance, Company

D considers the quality of a partner team and services as a premise to establish a new partnership. The project manager of the firm illustrated this situation: *"in addition to off the field factors like 'whether a partner has a qualified team, (we analyse) whether his services desk is good'"*.

The companies assess the quality of a system from another vendor as an indicator to invest in a new partnership. *"A partner would hardly be invited if beforehand we knew that he would not satisfy (our quality criteria)"*, cited Company F business analyst. The marketing manager from Company G explained the relevance of this factor: *"they recommend us because they know they will not have problems in the integration; they will recommend a firm to stay in their client; if it is a bad firm, which gives many problems, the system crashes; it is worse for them"*. Low quality solutions can affect the reputation of a company as a supplier, as described by the commercial director from Company F: *"the quality of the product, its acceptance in the market and how much it adds value (to mine)…; we need to choose well our partners since (they) will, in a way, influence our (system) routines and reputation"*.

- **F7 – Availability of Standards/Technologies to support Systems Integration**

By defining or adopting integration standards, partners facilitate their collaboration, as illustrated by the software architect from Company D: *"the 'Integrator' has helped and now HL7 (international standards for data transfer between healthcare systems) will help even more"*. A common integration infrastructure reduces mismatches among products and rework in joint projects. *"One of the main gains we will have (with integration technology) is to prevent us from redeveloping integrations whenever someone knocks our door"*, argued the project manager from Company D. One partner may develop the integration infrastructure or it may emerge as a joint creation: *"we are aligning what one has with what the other has, what one may add… Company C can contribute with definitions, Company B with human resources, etc."*, explained the release manager from Company B.

The following paragraphs present nine Barriers (B) of studied partnerships. These factors are the opposite view of facilitators: they weaken companies' relationships and disturb their joint projects. Hence, barriers may reduce the health of their ecosystems.

- **B1 – Inefficiency to handle Integration Problems**

The non-involvement of a firm in the analysis of system integration problems strongly weakens a partnership: *"(another) partnership did not evolve (because) the partner was uncompromising and did not resolve (the issue)"*, explained the project manager from Company D. Given the fuzzy boundary among integrated systems, firms may try to convince the partner that the problem is originated in his system: *"the partner often shifts the issue to the other (company)"*, declared the team leader from Company B. Others simply prioritise other projects, as reported by the project manager from Company A: *"sometimes the partner has more critical issues in another project and leaves (ours) behind"*. This is common in the context of SMEs, which are often overwhelmed, handling demands of multiple clients with limited resources. Such low attention may also happen because the partner does not see the client as strategic: *"sometimes partners do not give attention since (the client) is not in their top customer base"*, cited the services manager from Company C.

When the client is not aware that multiple vendors are providing the solution or simply does not understand their duties in a joint project, it is hard to know who to blame and appeal. Handling integration issues demands a clear definition of roles and responsibilities among partners. However, a partner may refuse such responsibility.

To avoid client dissatisfaction, some firms take the duties of a partner not to jeopardise their reputation. Company F currently treats this issue by managing customer support, as described by the commercial director: *"we concentrate the support within our firm and meet specific demands by contacting the customers"*. The lack of support reduces companies' trust in a partner, who is no longer recommended to clients. *"Our manager asks not to contact Company B; we try to solve the issue here; nowadays we do not recommend Company B"*, cited the systems analyst from Company D.

- **B2 – Unavailability of a Professional to manage Systems Integration**

The absence of a permanent employee responsible for the integrated solution is a problem, as described by the product manager from Company B: *"I change part of the process, but this brings a big risk, because you do not have someone in charge of the whole (integration)"*. Defining a professional as the 'owner of the integration' facilitate negotiations and alignment of products, according to the services manager from Company C: *"we do not have this guy, which would be the focal point; such confusion and discussions would be minimised; (he would be in charge of) communication and sharing of information"*. The duties of an integration owner include the identification of evolution needs due to market demands and analysis of impact of product changes in integrations. However, they cannot afford his salary without a running project: *"There must be someone paying him, (but) we are project-oriented"*, cited the services manager from Company C.

- **B3 – Weak Commercial/Prices Alignment**

The commercial alignment of the firms is critical for a partnership to evolve: *"this is crucial, because if partner price is not feasible for the deal, we have to look for another (product)"*, argued the operations director from Company B. Partners who define high price weaken negotiations with clients. *"(Product) price affect negotiations; we have to talk to partner board to lower costs; it hinders some partnerships"*, argued Company E's operations and deployment director. This attitude leads to gradual replacement of these SMEs in the ecosystem or the development of the complementary system by the other company: *"we normally sell with the software from Company B, but their cost may turn the proposal expensive; if we had a financial module, it would cheapen the (final) system"*, explained the system analyst from Company D. The high prices asked by Company G might derail their partnership. *"We are pressuring Company G to lower prices because they are moving the market away; if we do not reach a consensus, I would opt for another partner"*, cited him.

Similarly, a vendor from Chile required a high price to include its system in a joint project, which increased the final price of the proposal and made Company F rethink this partnership. *"I chose to use an ERP that was already adapted to Chile, (but) it made my offer very costly; we negotiate, but it is hard"*, argued the commercial director. Due to the partner's size and position in the Chilean market, Company F was dependent on its system. The partner had bargaining power. *"It is a world-class player much bigger than us; we can have a policy to reduce (our prices), but they (decide) and said 'my price is this'; it is better (to align with smaller partners)"*, added him.

- **B4 – Poor Strategic Alignment of Products**

Strategic alignment of products is necessary for partnerships to thrive. *"It is very difficult to reconcile strategies and portfolios; but it is also very difficult to survive without (it)"*, declared the product manager from Company D. The project manager from Company D reinforced this fact: *"lack of synchronisation is very negative"*. As the scope of systems integration grows, the dependence between products increases, as the system analyst from Company B cited: *"the conflict is: I'm evolving and I can damage something there, or there may be a need and we are eliminating for disuse"*.

So far, studied firms have not formally aligned product strategies (e.g. roadmaps, releases) and are not prepared to jointly evolve the systems: *"one thing that makes the partnership fragile is that when I do my strategic planning, I do it independently of them"*, cited Company B operations director. The challenge to ensure such alignment stem from the fact that firms attempt to manage partnerships and parallel demands with restricted resources: *"it is difficult to (align releases) since the partner has things going on outside partnerships"*, explained the innovation manager from Company C.

The well-functioning of a product integration must be ensured during the lifetime of the systems from different vendors, which demands a technical and strategic alignment. However, such convergence may not be perceived in partners' daily operation, as argued by the commercial director from Company F: *"in all partnerships/integrations we had, there is a great and natural difficulty: I have a product evolving with a great speed and the partner cannot follow it"*. Product strategic alignment is essential in ecosystems, when there is a great mutual dependence between firms. *"In a simple integration, I do not have to make roadmap alignment with him (partner); with Company H, which has a framework that needs to evolve over time, if we do not evolve together, we go anywhere; some partnerships are for survival"*, argued him. The same occurs with technologies: *"another issue is the technological misalignment between products; (it is easy to integrate) when technology is adherent"*.

- **B5 – Overlap between Features offered by the Company and Potential Partners**

Studied firms prioritise fully complementary vendors; as such partnership does not require scope negotiation (i.e. decide which feature will be provided, in case it is available in both systems). The commercial director from Company F explained this fact: *"(a problem emerges) when there is a conflict of interests; when (partner's) product is competing with our (solution); it is forbidden to do this"*. If a vendor offers a system in the same domain of interest of the firm, it has reduced chances to become a partner. In this case, there may be punctual collaborations: *"in some situations we can even establish an isolated partnership, but we do not define the partnership in a fixed form (which) can be used in any (client) environment"*, cited him.

Company F aims to keep its independence on partners in specific areas: *"some areas are reserved for us; we do not facilitate"*. When the area is strategic, the firm develops the feature instead of searching for a partner. This attitude stems from the possibility that a partner has to decrease the envisaged market share of Company F: *"the main restriction (for a partnership) is if it (system) enters an area in which I offer or want to offer solutions; the firm kills my chance to grow in this market"*.

- **B6 – Differences in Working Practices**

Some partners have very different working practices. *"We have releases almost every fortnight; the partner says 'I can only (deliver it) in 3 months'; it is another pace"*, cited Company A project manager. This situation poses challenges to joint development: *"if I tell him (partner client) I deliver it (feature) in 6 months, he says it is ok; if I tell (it to) him (retailer client), he send me away"*, stated the services manager from Company C. Hence, Company C has slower deliveries with Company B: *"it has to do with culture; this was the difficulty with Company B; all happened very methodically"*, added him. Even the evolution of technologies is affected, according to the operations and deployment director from Company E: *"sometimes we are well ahead of partners; we want them to evolve and sometimes (their processes) are too rigid"*.

- **B7 – Limited authority over Partner's Development Team**

The lack of authority of a firm over the partner's team is an issue faced by firms in joint projects. *"You have to manage a team (in charge of) another system, from another firm over which you have no authority; it is too complicated"*, argued the project manager from Company B. The project manager from Company A detailed this fact: *"when you take on this role (project manager), it has the dependence (on partners since) you do not have all that strength in other (software) factories"*.

Partners can restrict the access to their teams, even in collaborative projects. In general, the teams only follow orders from their own firms, in a weak functional matrix: when a project manager leads the joint project, he must negotiate with managers from partners to forward demands. *"I have power over my team, but I cannot impose (anything) to that of Company B"*, detailed the project manager from Company A.

- **B8 – Low Availability of Financial and Human Resources**

A firm with restricted financial and human resources may hamper the development of partnerships, as it involves several operational costs (e.g. travels) and strategic investments (e.g. innovation projects). In such cases, a firm is seen as unprepared for the collaboration, according to the commercial director from Company F: *"if the partner has no capacity to invest in systems integrations and products, it compromises (the relationship) as he (partner) cannot work with you"*. As SMEs, partners usually face big restrictions of financial and human resources, affecting joint projects. *"It (Company B) suffers from lack of resources and I cannot move on"*, argued Company A's project manager. Firms that can invest in joint projects support partnerships.

- **B9 – Short Expertise in Integration Projects**

Although systems integration seems a common practice for studied companies, in some situations they lack such expertise, which may harm a new partnership. The business analyst from Company F explained this fact: *"the firm with which we will make the integration may already have the (integration) know-how, the experience of doing this, which we (may) not have, maybe not at the same level"*. Inexperienced and immature companies may affect the success of integration projects.

4.2 System Dynamics Models

We answer RQ2 by presenting SD models that analyse interactions among previous facilitators and barriers. Figure 2 shows a SD model for the ecosystems from CSI and CSII. It is formed by a network of causal relations among 6 facilitators (blue) and 6 barriers (red). We neutralised their names by eliminating adjectives and/or adjusting the nouns. For instance, we altered the barrier *inefficiency to handle integration problems* to *effectiveness to handle integration problems*, removing its negative form.

The colours of the factors indicate how they are perceived in the studied context. This was a means to simplify the analysis of causal relations and avoid inappropriate logical comparisons. The model represents factors that already exist (e.g. *perceived quality of products and services*) and those that lack in practice (e.g. *commercial/prices alignment*). The arrows associating the factors indicate the influence they may have on each other: the factor from which an arrow leaves tends to promote the one in which the arrow arrives. For instance, *commercial/prices alignment* promotes *strategic alignment of products strategies and technologies*. However, since both are in red, one shall interpret it as *weak commercial/prices alignment* reinforces the poor *strategic alignment of products strategies and technologies*.

We highlight the most critical factors in circles (relationships among them are also detached with thick arrows), i.e. *commercial/prices alignment, effectiveness to handle systems integration issues, personal and geographical proximity, strategic alignment of products, openness for technical and business negotiation, perceived quality of products and services*, and *mutual trust*. These factors were obtained from interview evidence, such as the arguments of the project manager from Company A about a partner inefficiency to handle integration problems: *"this (occurrence of issues in the integration) happens a lot; it is the biggest difficulty when we have a partner"*.

The commercial director from Company F also confirmed this fact: *"this (inefficiency to treat integration problems) is an important challenge"*. Another example lies in the opinion of the operations director from Company B regarding the poor alignment of prices among partners: *"this (lack of commercial alignment) happens and we have to negotiate before (presenting a proposal to the client); because if it is not feasible we have to search for another solution; this is vital for a partnership"*.

From the SD model in Fig. 2, we perceive the virtuous reinforcing loop RF 1, which leads partners to effectively perform the joint projects. The *openness for technical and business negotiations* favours the *availability of standards or technologies to support systems integration* among partners, which can contribute to partners' *efficiency to*

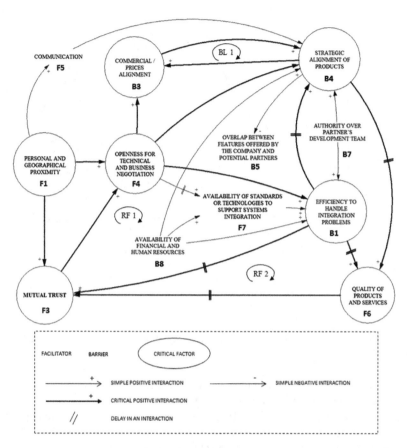

Fig. 2. SD model representing positive and negative interactions among barriers and facilitators [18].

handle integration problems. This factor will further leverage their *mutual trust* and facilitate future negotiations. A wider view of this cycle is the virtuous reinforcing loop RF 2, which includes the factor perceived *quality of products and services* by clients and partners. This factor results from partners' *efficiency to handle systems integration problems* and fosters their *mutual trust.* However, results from the simple balancing cycle BL 1 may affect RF 2: the weak *commercial/prices alignment* reduces the already weak *strategic alignment of products.*

In Fig. 3, we describe another representation of the barriers and facilitators. This specific view translates a system archetype called Accidental Adversaries (AA). The AA illustrates a situation in which two actors start a relationship aiming at capitalising their power and reducing their weaknesses. It considers that a healthy collaborative environment supports a goal that cannot be achieved by parties individually. However, issues arise when one or both parties take actions they consider reasonable but that end up suppressing partner's success. These harmful actions foster a sense of antipathy and

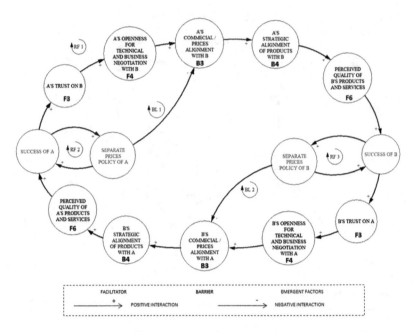

Fig. 3. Accidental Adversaries system archetype representing interactions among barriers and facilitators [18].

may even turn partners into adversaries. This scheme synthesises some challenges that partners face in the studied software ecosystems.

In the AA archetype presented in Fig. 3, the names of the factors were adjusted to represent the systemic action between two given partners in the ecosystem. We also created four variables (in grey) that were inferred from the situation at hand. In short, the outermost virtuous reinforcing cycle RF 1 is a virtuous loop that promotes the evolution of partnerships. In their turn, the virtuous reinforcing cycles RF 2 and RF 3 mean individualistic actions that bring unintentional consequences that ultimately create the balancing cycles BL 1 and BL 2. These loops hold back the virtuous cycle of the partnerships (RF 1), as negative situations that restrict partnerships prosperity.

Braun [16] describes three prescriptive actions in case AA is identified in a given context. The author suggests that the parties must revisit the original opportunity that brought them together into a collaborative relationship. In this case, partner firms could recognise their mutual dependence, with complementary capabilities that must combined to address customer demands. Another suggestion is to use the AA archetype to map the origins of adversarial attitudes. In the studied scenario, the separate price policy of the firms is a barrier, as it hampers a partner to close a deal. By fostering their commercial alignment, partners enable the recurrence of joint projects. This shall increase companies' confidence in partnerships prosperity. It is then likely to observe an increase in the strategic alignment of products, denoting the shared vision of the collaborative effort. This may ultimately foster the quality of products and services offered to clients. Therefore, according to previous diagrams, once firms are open for negotiations, they leverage ecosystem health and mutual success as vendors.

5   Strategies to Foster Software Ecosystem Partnerships

Based on the former SD models and considering guidelines from the literature, we derive strategies to guarantee a healthy collaboration among partners, enabling the evolution of the software ecosystem. Hence, we address RQ3.

The first strategy (S1) is related to the business dimension of the software ecosystem. It treats the barriers *poor strategic alignment of products* (B4*), overlap between features offered by the company and potential partners* (B5) and *limited authority over partner's development teams* (B7).

- **S1 – Partners must Align Products Strategies to sustain Systems Integration**

In a software ecosystem, a SME must try to align its business models with that of partners. If this firm has a power position, it may even succeed in putting partners onto its desired path. Hence, the firm may lead others to want what it envisages [19]. In some cases, studied SMEs jointly analyse their commercial models (e.g. prices, sales process). However, this is an informal initiative of directors with closer relationships. Firms such as Companies A and C are trying to promote the alignment of their product portfolios by sharing market intelligence with partners. This practice attaches partners to the ecosystem by fulfilling their business expectations. It also implicitly directs ecosystem participants.

Nowadays, software companies are expected to provide an overall view of their products evolution and decision-making about future product releases [20]. By following this trend and opening product roadmaps, partners embrace the mutual dependence that is required in an ecosystem. They start to give up the right of independently defining new features and share this privilege with others. Hence, studied firms shall enable ecosystem partners to influence changes in roadmaps regularly. If the product roadmaps in the ecosystem are not correctly aligned, partners can have major problems, e.g. integration mismatches, solutions mutually competing and reduced co-innovation [21]. For instance, there may be conflicts related to features functioning or removal of features due to supposed disuse by a system from a partner company. To integrate their products properly, partners should make joint decisions regarding upcoming features.

Although a firm may gain the right to act as integration coordinator in a specific collaboration project, it does not exert sufficient control over partner teams. Hence, the coordinating firm faces challenges to align product releases of multiple vendors and treat integration conflicts. Partners can address this barrier by adopting a technical orchestration strategy that enables them to hold a new right: to access a partner development team. By gaining authority over each other's teams, a firm can plan future product releases aligned with product evolutions from other ecosystem participants.

The strategic alignment of integrated solutions guarantees their correct operation and ultimately fosters the success of a firm, as shown in the archetype in Fig. 3. Such alignment contributes to ecosystem *robustness*, since the increased *quality of products and services* (F6) reinforces the expertise of the firms and the notion that the ecosystem can survive from the changes of the environment.

To treat the barriers *inefficiency to handle integration problems* (B1) and *poor strategic alignment of products* (B4), partner firms should also invest in the creation of a common software platform. This gives rise to the strategy S2, which explores the technical dimension of the software ecosystem.

- **S2 – SMEs Forming an Ecosystem can jointly Develop a Software Platform**

To address the challenges inherent to the integration of several products, partners can evolve their specific integration mechanisms towards a common platform. This infrastructure may consist of services, tools and technologies that ecosystem members can use to combine features or services [22]. Companies shall thereby evolve from a "productisation" to a "platformisation" approach [23]. Such strategic action enable suppliers to address resource constraints and offer new features, fostering a vibrant and potentially larger ecosystem around the platform.

Initially, the SMEs shall discuss how this platform will be offered and managed. Since the creation of this infrastructure represents an extra cost not funded by clients, partners could opt for a shared development and maintenance of the platform. An option could be to evolve one firm's platform. However, negotiations and disputes around integration technologies may occur due to advantages that firms perceive in having platform ownership, e.g. become a keystone and control its influence in the ecosystem [24].

The software platform can enhance firms' expertise and performance by supporting the creation of valuable synergies for clients [14]. The platform can increase the *productivity* of the software ecosystem by enabling firms to build and integrate solutions more naturally. In addition, it supports *niche creation* by enabling partners to develop complementary innovations, putting new functions into operation and increasing technology diversity [25].

Communication (F5) is a key factor for software companies to deal with the barrier poor *strategic alignment of products* (B4) in their partnership. In light of that, we propose the following strategy S3, which is associated with the social dimension of the software ecosystem.

- **S3 – Partners must Develop Effective Ecosystem Communication Channels**

Our studies revealed that partners must improve their communication capabilities, since this process is still unstructured and immature. Their challenge lies in defining centralised and continuous communication channels. For instance, the manager of a joint project among the SMEs has great difficulty to interact with partners' teams. We observed that communication tends to be rich during the peak of product integration projects. Then, it gradually decreases and suddenly resumes as problems emerge. We also noticed problems in the distribution of information among partners: integration and functional requirements that are not informed; artefacts that are not shared; problems that last to be solved; and feature releases that are not reported to partners.

According to Jansen et al. [1], one of the challenges in a software ecosystem is indeed to build common and efficient communication channels, which enable the orchestration of partners. To address this issue, Fricker [26] recommends the use of traceability, audit trails and computer-supported collaborative work. These are means to increase knowledge sharing and management among players in the ecosystem. Ecosystem players can guarantee effective interchange of information by informing each other about product technological advances and upcoming features. This practice support the creation of complementary solutions, which is essential to strengthen ecosystem *productivity* as well as *niche creation*.

A final strategy proposed to the studied software ecosystems targets the balancing cycle BL 1, which may affect the positive cycle RF 2 in the SD model presented in Fig. 2. It means that the weak *commercial/prices alignment* (B3) will reinforce the poor *strategic alignment of products* (B4). To treat these critical factors, we elaborate the strategy S4, which addresses the business dimension of the software ecosystem.

- **S4 – Partners must Agree on a Revenue Model for the Software Ecosystem**

Studied companies argued that some partnerships might not evolve due to mismatches in their commercial strategies. In particular, some companies believe that they can define prices independently of partners. This situation makes the integration of products hard or even unfeasible due to incompatible prices. It reveals a lack of commercial alignment (maybe due to a reluctance to perform commercial negotiations) that jeopardise the growth of partnerships. There is an increasing dependence and need for convergence, demanding partners to align their strategies and business models, among other efforts to sustain the emerging ecosystem [27].

A revenue model consists of one or more revenue streams, which define the way to get compensation from a good or service provided [28]. For instance, in the case of software as a service, the client normally pays a subscription fee [29]. In an ecosystem formed by big players such as Apple or Google, the keystone is responsible for defining the revenue model(s) adopted in the network, with which external agents must be aligned. In the studied ecosystems, partners can negotiate revenue models that are more suitable for their context. They must ensure a win-win approach with an egalitarian revenue model. This strategy will prevent the migration of partners to other networks, which could decrease ecosystem *robustness*. It shall also support *niche creation* by fostering innovative businesses [15].

6 Discussion

The previous sections deeply analysed the factors affecting partnerships in an ecosystem. We showed that SD is an insightful tool for understanding and dealing with the complexity of business situations, contributing to organisational learning. It enables firms to generate very intuitive and high level causal models. In addition, researchers and practitioners can go further into their details and even simulate the studied reality. However, SD has some challenges related to models' creation and interpretation.

Concerning models creation, an option is to **start from a 'clean table' and answer central questions**. In this research, we asked '*what are the goals for the partnership from different views?*' and '*what are the facilitators and barriers to achieve these goals?*', for instance. This information may be available in existing documentation (e.g. documented processes, project reports). However, it is important to **go beyond gathering superficial factors that translate the functioning of the studied reality**. It is a means to obtain a systemic perspective and deeply understand the context. This can be done by involving case participants in SD modelling efforts. While communicating their interpretation of the problem, new insights may emerge and improve models development.

Too much information gathered may entail complex models. The more one try to include realism and details, the more time spent in explaining an SD model. To tackle this problem, an option is to **define several abstraction levels of an SD model**. These different levels can be related to different types of iterations (positive and negative) or different stakeholders involved in the modelling phases (factors according to the roles interviewed), for instance. They can also reflect different parameters of the software ecosystem, e.g. actors (factors related to the keystone or third party developers) or dimension (social, technical, business).

The identification of a proper systemic archetype is a key issue. This is a tricky part of SD models creation because there are no formal steps to select one among the existing archetypes. The researcher must initially **develop a generic cause-effect model by interrelating facilitators and barriers**. Then, he/she must **compare the resultant model with the set of systemic archetypes** proposed by Senge and Kurpius [7]; i.e. perceive in one or more archetype the tendencies occurring in the studied reality. To reduce the subjective nature of this step, the researcher shall **assess the results with participants**.

Finally, **historical data is a means to calibrate the SD models**. For instance, the interviews only provided us with a snapshot of the context, which may not be sufficient to build sophisticated models. In case we gained access to longitudinal data about the factors, we could show variations in their interactions and identify patterns. This would allow us to present dynamic models and predict changes. This kind of historical analysis can be performed in future studies.

7 Conclusion

In a software ecosystem, partner firms co-create value by building a collaborative network around their products. To guarantee the success of the ecosystem, these partners must manage a set of positive and negative factors that affect their relationships. Once understanding these factors and their interactions, companies can derive strategies that leverage the facilitators while restraining the barriers. In this paper, we presented a multiple case study of two software ecosystems. By considering data collected from companies engaging in emerging ecosystems, we could build cause-effect models that represent the interactions among the facilitators and barriers of the partnerships. We also proposed strategies that can support promote ecosystem health.

7.1   Implications for Research and Practice

We believe the findings presented in this paper are applicable to other emerging ecosystems built by SMEs. Both the SD models (mainly the Accidental Adversaries archetype) and the strategies elaborated on top of them may guide the decisions made by ecosystem actors. This is critical for the emerging software ecosystems, which do not result from an initial strategic action of a big software player/keystone, but rather from a collaborative process of exploration among partners [30]. Hence, this preliminary stage can be rather challenging.

From a research perspective, we highlight that our results address the fact that small to medium firms do not rely on a vast literature about their operation. In spite of the market relevance of SMEs, which represent 95% of business organisations worldwide, the majority of academic research does not consider their specific needs in the context of software development [31, 32]. To enrich this contribution, we invite researchers to assess our results and determine how closely their contexts match that of the case studies.

7.2   Threats to Validity

We considered the guidelines from Wohlin et al. [33] and Merriam [34] for assessing the validity of this research. We describe the threats to validity as follows.

- The *construct validity* involves gathering operational measures that reflect the research questions. During interviews, we explicitly asked participants about the facilitators and barriers of the partnerships, enabling us to 'measure the right thing'.
- The *internal validity* aims to ensure that research findings are valid according to the notion of reality of qualitative paradigm. To strengthen our interpretation, we considered a wide dataset formed by the transcripts of twenty-seven interviews. In addition, we had our results examined by an expert in System Dynamics, who also clarified some steps of the procedure.
- The *conclusion validity* aims to ensure the consistency of results, i.e. they derive from collected data. We addressed this issue via confirmatory interviews with the companies, when we discussed the SD models, which represent our main findings.
- Finally, the *external validity* involves the extent to which the findings are valid to other situations. In this case, we consider the notion of notion of transferability, providing rich descriptions of the factors and SD models so that the reader can define how closely their situations match the studied context.

7.3   Future Work

In future work, we plan to conduct additional studies of software ecosystems in different evolution phases, raised by other types of actors (e.g. big players), following other business models (e.g. open/community-oriented networks), etc. By changing these characteristics, we believe it is possible to identify varied set of factors and SD models, allowing a further generalisation of findings.

References

1. Jansen, S., Finkelstein, A., Brinkkemper, S.: A sense of community: a research agenda for software ecosystems. In: 31st International Conference on Software Engineering, pp. 187–190 (2009)
2. Olsson, H.H., Bosch, J.: Collaborative innovation: a model for selecting the optimal ecosystem innovation strategy. In: 42nd Euromicro Conference on Software Engineering and Advanced Applications (SEAA), pp. 206–213 (2016)
3. Popp, K.M.: Mergers and Acquisitions in the Software Industry: Foundations of due Diligence. BoD–Books on Demand (2013)
4. Hanssen, G.K.: A longitudinal case study of an emerging software ecosystem: implications for practice and theory. J. Syst. Softw. **85**(7), 1455–1466 (2012)
5. Bosch, J.: From software product lines to software ecosystems. In: 13th International Software Product Line Conference, pp. 111–119 (2009)
6. Khalil, M.A.T., Dominic, P.D.D., Kazemian, H., Habib, U.: A study to examine if integration of technology acceptance model's (TAM) features help in building a hybrid digital business ecosystem framework for small and medium enterprises (SMEs). Front. Inf. Technol., 161–166 (2011)
7. Senge, P.M., Kurpius, D.: The fifth discipline: the art and practice of the learning organization (1993)
8. Mohr, J., Spekman, R.: Characteristics of partnership success: partnership attributes, communication behavior, and conflict resolution techniques. Strat. Manag. J. **15**(2), 135–152 (1994)
9. Cusumano, M.A.: The Business of Software: What Every Manager, Programmer, and Entrepreneur Must Know to Thrive and Survive in Good Times and Bad. Simon and Schuster, New York (2004)
10. Weiblen, T.: Opening Up the Business Model: Business Model Innovation through Collaboration, Ph.D. thesis. University of St. Gallen (2015)
11. Manikas, K., Hansen, K.M.: Software ecosystems – a systematic literature review. J. Syst. Softw. **86**(5), 1294–1306 (2013)
12. Manikas, K.: Revisiting software ecosystems research: a longitudinal literature study. J. Syst. Softw. **117**, 84–103 (2016)
13. Hartigh, E., Tol, M., Visscher, W.: The health measurement of a business ecosystem. In: European Chaos/Complexity in Organisations Network Conference (2006)
14. Iansiti, M., Levien, R.: Strategy as ecology. Harvard Bus. Rev. **82**(3), 68–81 (2004)
15. Moore, J.F.: Predators and prey: a new ecology of competition. Harvard Bus. Rev. **71**(3), 75–83 (1993)
16. Braun, W.: The system archetypes. System, p. 27 (2002)
17. Coyne, I.T.: Sampling in qualitative research. Purposeful and theoretical sampling; merging or clear boundaries? J. Adv. Nurs. **26**(3), 623–630 (1997)
18. Valença, G., Alves, C.: We need to discuss the relationship: an analysis of facilitators and barriers of software ecosystem partnerships. In: 19th International Conference on Enterprise Information Systems, pp. 17–28 (2017)
19. Yoffie, D.B., Kwak, M.: With friends like these: the art of managing complementors. Harvard Bus. Rev. **84**(9), 88–98 (2006)
20. Suomalainen, T., et al.: Software product road mapping in a volatile business environment. J. Syst. Softw. **84**(6), 958–975 (2011)
21. Jansen, S., Peeters, S., Brinkkemper, S.: Software ecosystems: from software product management to software platform management. In: IW-LCSP@ICSOB, pp. 5–18 (2013)

22. Isckia, T., Lescop, D.: Open innovation within business ecosystems: a tale from Amazon.com. Commun. Strat. **74**, 37–54 (2009)
23. Artz, P., van de Weerd, I., Brinkkemper, S., Fieggen, J.: Productization: transforming from developing customer-specific software to product software. In: Tyrväinen, P., Jansen, S., Cusumano, M.A. (eds.) ICSOB 2010. LNBIP, vol. 51, pp. 90–102. Springer, Heidelberg (2010). https://doi.org/10.1007/978-3-642-13633-7_8
24. Harland, P.E., Wust, S.: Strategic, brand and platform requirements for an interactive innovation process in business ecosystems. In: International Conference on Engineering, Technology and Innovation, pp. 1–9 (2012)
25. Hyrynsalmi, S., et al.: Wealthy, healthy and/or happy – what does 'ecosystem health' stand for? In: International Conference of Software Business, pp. 272–287 (2015)
26. Fricker, S.: Requirements value chains: stakeholder management and requirements engineering in software ecosystems. In: Wieringa, R., Persson, A. (eds.) REFSQ 2010. LNCS, vol. 6182, pp. 60–66. Springer, Heidelberg (2010). https://doi.org/10.1007/978-3-642-14192-8_7
27. Dittrich, Y.: Software engineering beyond the project – sustaining software ecosystems. Inf. Softw. Technol. **56**(11), 1436–1456 (2014)
28. Hyrynsalmi, S., Suominen, A., Mäkilä, T., Järvi, A., Knuutila, T.: Revenue models of application developers in android market ecosystem. In: 3rd International Conference of Software Business, pp. 209–222 (2012)
29. Popp, K.M.: Hybrid revenue models of software companies and their relationship to hybrid business models. In: Third International Workshop on Software Ecosystems, pp. 77–88 (2011)
30. Attour, A., Barbaroux, P.: Architectural knowledge and the birth of a platform ecosystem: a case study. J. Innov. Econ. Manag. **1**, 11–30 (2016)
31. Colomo-Palacios, R., Biró, M., Messnarz, R.: Special issue on software and service improvement in the scope of SMEs. Softw. Qual. J. **24**(3), 485–487 (2014)
32. World Trade Organization (WTO). World Trade Report 2016 – Levelling the Trading Field for SMEs (2016)
33. Wohlin, C., Runeson, P., Höst, M., Ohlsson, M.C., Regnell, B., Wesslén, A.: Experimentation in Software Engineering. Springer, Heidelberg (2012). https://doi.org/10.1007/978-3-642-29044-2
34. Merriam, S.B.: Qualitative Research: A Guide to Design and Implementation. Jossey-Bass, San Francisco (2009)

Task-oriented Requirements Engineering for Personal Decision Support Systems

Christian Kücherer$^{(\boxtimes)}$ and Barbara Paech

Institute for Computer Science, Heidelberg University, Im Neuenheimer Feld 205,
69120 Heidelberg, Germany
{kuecherer,paech}@informatik.uni-heidelberg.de

Abstract. [**Context and motivation**] In decision-making, executives are supported by Personal Decision Support Systems (PDSSs) which are information systems providing a decision- and user-specific data presentation. PDSSs operate on current data with predefined queries and provide a rich user interface (UI). Therefore, a Requirements Engineering (RE) method for PDSSs should support the elicitation and specification of detailed requirements for specific decisions. However, existing RE approaches for decision support systems typically focus on ad-hoc decisions in the area of data warehouses. [**Question/problem**] Task-oriented RE (TORE) emphasizes a comprehensive RE specification which covers stakeholders' tasks, data, system functions, interactions, and UI. TORE allows for an early UI prototyping which is crucial for PDSS. Therefore, we explore TORE's suitability for PDSSs. [**Principal ideas/results**] According to the Design Science methodology, we assess TORE for its suitability for PDSS specification in a problem investigation. We propose decision-specific adjustments of TORE (DsTORE), which we evaluate in a case study. [**Contribution**] This paper is an extended version of previously published work. The contribution of this paper is fourfold. First, the suitability of the task-oriented RE method TORE for the specification of a PDSS is investigated as problem investigation. Second, the decision-specific extension of TORE is proposed as the DsTORE-method. DsTORE allows identifying and specifying details of decisions to be supported by a PDSS, utilizing a number of artifacts. Third, strategic information management is used as the example task for the evaluation of DsTORE in a case study. All interview questions used in the design science cycle are given. Experiences from the study and the method design are presented. Fourth, the evaluation of the developed system prototype is presented along with the questionnaire we used, showing the utility and acceptance.

Keywords: Decision Support System · DSS · Personal DSS
Requirements specification · Task-oriented requirements engineering
TORE

© Springer International Publishing AG, part of Springer Nature 2018
S. Hammoudi et al. (Eds.): ICEIS 2017, LNBIP 321, pp. 212–238, 2018.
https://doi.org/10.1007/978-3-319-93375-7_11

1 Introduction

Today, data warehouses (DW) are standard technology for decision support in companies. They are a specific form of Decision Support Systems (DSSs) that represent a subgroup of information systems. As discussed in a recent overview by Hosack et al. [1], there is a large variety of DSSs and an extensive history of research on DSSs. This research is ongoing and incorporates new trends such as social media or mobile computing [2]. Similarly, there is a growing field of research focusing on the development methodologies for DSS. Saxena [3] presents a very early development methodology which emphasizes the understanding of decision tasks and prototyping. In a more recent review, Gachet and Haetten-schwiler investigate early and widely acknowledged development processes of DSSs [4], focusing on either decisions or system engineering or both. They also emphasize the importance of an evolutionary approach that considers both, organizational and technical issues. In the same vein, Arnott [5] presents a business intelligence development approach starting from a fundamental understanding of senior executives' behavior. We are interested in Personal DSSs (PDSSs, introduced in detail in Sect. 2.2) which are small-scale systems supporting decision-making of a single or a small group of executives with an exactly defined set of supported decisions [6]. While the early approaches to DSS provide a general framework, they do not describe a detailed requirements engineering method. Whilst retaining the emphasis on these methodologies, we take the task-oriented requirements engineering (RE) approach TORE [7,8] as our basis to develop a detailed RE method for PDSSs. TORE has proven useful for information systems and it supports a refinement of requirements concerning all system details up to the user interface (UI), and thus to early prototyping. However, it has not yet been applied to PDSSs.

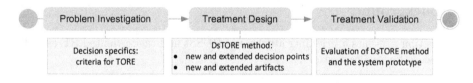

Fig. 1. General method according to design science [9].

With this recent scholarly background in mind, the overall Research Question (RQ) of this paper is: *How can TORE be extended to support the RE of a PDSS?.* We follow the design science cycle described by Wieringa [9] to answer this RQ, illustrated in Fig. 1. In the *problem investigation*, we evaluate TORE's suitability to support the RE for PDSSs. In the *treatment design*, we propose a decision-specific adaptation of TORE (DsTORE). Finally, we evaluate DsTORE in the *treatment validation*.

Enhancements to the ICEIS'17 Paper

This paper presents an extended and enhanced version of our task-oriented RE method for personal decision support systems [10]. The main additional benefit of the presented extensions are that the method can be applied more easily by other researchers or analysts. More details are given to ease the understanding and reuse of the method (extension 1–3), and the evaluation is more comprehensive (extensions 4):

1. We present the interview questions for problem investigation.
2. In [10] we used the CIO task project management as a detailed example for the treatment design. In this paper we use another CIO task IT strategy as an example.
3. We provide more details and artifacts created with DsTORE for the task IT strategy: (a) an overview of all subtasks to gain a better understanding of the task, (b) the workspace model, (c) the data source model.
4. We present the results of the CIO's system prototype evaluation along with the questionnaire for the treatment validation.

This paper is structured as follows. Section 2 introduces PDSSs, presents the case for this study, and offers a brief overview of TORE. Section 3 discusses related work on RE for DSSs. The summary of the problem investigation of TORE's support for the RE of PDSSs is presented in Sect. 4. The treatment design DsTORE is presented in Sect. 5. The treatment validation is described in the form of a case study in Sect. 6. The results of the problem investigation and the case study are discussed in Sect. 7, where we also present the lessons that we have learned. The threats to validity are discussed in Sect. 8. Finally, the paper is concluded in Sect. 9 by sketching some ideas of future work.

2   Background

This section presents a brief introduction of PDSSs and task-oriented RE as well as the case for our case study.

2.1   Decisions and Decision Knowledge

A decision can be defined as a choice that is made between multiple alternative courses of action, and which in turn leads to a desired objective [11]. Alternatives have implications and decision-making requires knowledge. For example, the prioritization of projects (choice) results in the precedence of one project over others (alternatives) based on the project's importance, benefit for operations, or the estimated budget (knowledge). *Structured decision problems* have defined criteria in order to make the decision: They have known alternatives and implications, and require specific types of knowledge. By contrast, *unstructured decision problems* are by their nature unexpected, have unstable context and unknown alternatives, possess unknown criteria, and rely on situations in which

Table 1. Operational and decisional systems. (Left three columns acc. [12,13], except the rows *structure of data* and *predefined decisions*).

	Operational	Decisional	PDSS
Objective	Busin. operation	Busin. analysis	Specific busin. decisions
Main functions	Daily operations (OLTP)	DSS (OLAP)	Decision-specific UI data presentation, reporting
Decisions	n/a	Un-, semi-, structured	Semi-, structured
Usage	Repetitive, predef	Innovative, Unexp	Repetitive, predef.
Design orientation	Functionality	Subject	Subject
Kind of users	Clerk	Executives	Executives
Number of users	Thousands	Hundreds	One to ten
Accessed tuples	Hundreds	Thousands	Hundreds
Data sources (dsrc)	Isolated	Integrated	Heterogeneous, isolated
Structure of dsrc	Structured	Structured	Un- and structured
Granularity	Atomic	Summarized	Atomic and summarized
Time coverage	Current	Historical	Current and historical
Access (work units)	Simple transact	Complex queries	Simple queries
Size	MB/GB	GB/TB/Petabytes	MB

no or an incomplete level of knowledge is available [11]. *Semi-structured decision problems* are in between. Decision knowledge is taken from a *data source*, persisting data for future access via interfaces or file access. Examples of data sources are databases or documents such as spreadsheets and text documents. A data source is described through data source format, location, and content. For example, a project list used by an executive can be described by a spreadsheet (format), a uniform resource locator (URL) (location), and a list of projects (content). A text document contains unstructured data, whereas the structured data of a spreadsheet follows a formal definition of data types. Thus, data sources of structured data are typically databases, while semi-structured data is held in spreadsheets, and unstructured data in text-documents.

2.2   Personal Decision Support Systems

In general DSSs support all kinds of decisions. Salinesi et al. [13] provide a comparison of operational information systems (IS) and DW (called decisional IS) which is adapted in [12]. DSSs in general cover a broad range of different system types and incorporate a variety of different techniques such as decision models or artificial intelligence [14,15]. The specifics of Personal DSSs have been described by Arnott [6]. He summarizes that PDSSs are developed for a single or a small group of managers with the goal to improve the process and outcome of decision-making. The scope of a PDSS is the support of one or a small number of decision tasks, where often semi-structured data based on spreadsheets are used. The fact that PDSSs are small-scale systems refers to the supported small number of users and features and requirements. To distinguish PDSSs from DSSs in general, we add a third column to Table 1. The *objective* of PDSSs is to support

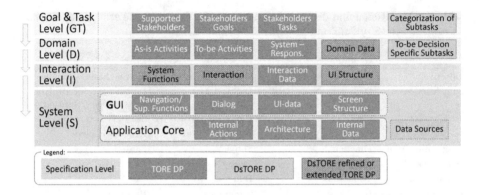

Fig. 2. Decision points of the TORE framework [7] and PDSS-specific extensions.

decision-making within a defined context. Its *main function* is to provide specific and predefined information for structured and semi-structured decisions in an overview UI or as a report to executives. In a similar way to DW, the primary *users* are executives, who access heterogeneous and isolated *data sources* at runtime. In contrast to DW, this usage is repetitive and predefined and the amount of accessed data is not extensive. In summary, the data of PDSSs are complex, while their usage is simple.

2.3   Task-oriented Requirements Engineering

Task-orientation focuses on the RE process and helps to deliver software that satisfies user needs [7]. As a conceptual framework, TORE provides a conceptual model for RE and has been successfully applied in a number of IS development projects of different problem domains [8]. Important aspects of the requirements specification are determined in each of TORE's 18 Decision Points (DPs), which are grouped into four levels of abstraction, as shown on the left part of Fig. 2. Note that TORE's DPs are different from *decisions* in the context of DSSs. The goal & task level focuses on stakeholders, goals, and tasks. Tasks are often activities within larger business- or management-processes, but the latter of these is outside of the focus of TORE. The domain level accommodates as-is and to-be activities which refine the tasks by subtasks that contribute to the completion of a stakeholder's task. Further, this level contains system responsibilities (often called system features) and domain data. The interaction level determines how stakeholders will be supported in their to-be-activities by the system. Finally, the system level determines UI details and infrastructure including the system architecture. TORE does not fix or prescribe artifact types for documentation of the DPs. In particular, it is not necessary to have a separate artifact for every DP, as lower-level DPs contain decisions for corresponding higher-level DPs. Several artifact types have often been used, as is shown in Table 2 by their relation to the DP. The artifact type **task description** according to Lauesen's Task&Support [16] describes stakeholders' tasks. **Subtask templates** are used to describe the DPs As-is and To-be-activities.

Table 2. TORE decision points and supported artifact types relevant for this study [7]. Rows marked in grey are introduced in Sect. 5.

Level	Decision Point	Artifact
Goal & task	Stakeholders Tasks	Task description
Domain	As-is activities, To-be activities	Subtask template
Domain	Domain Data	UML class diagram, ER diagram
Domain	Categorization of subtask	Task description
Domain	To-be decision specific subtask	Decision specific subtask template
Interaction	UI Structure	workspace model
GUI	UI Data	UI Prototype, Virtual window
GUI	Screen Structure	UI Prototype, Virtual window

The DP **Domain Data** is described with an unified modeling language (UML) class diagram or entity relationship diagram, containing domain entities and their relationships. The **workspace model** shows the navigation between workspaces for DP UI Structure, where **workspaces** group system functions. **Virtual windows** [16] describe the DP Screen Structure by a high-level grouping and structuring of the UI data, in order to illustrate the information needs of tasks early on in the RE process. The **UI Prototype** refines the virtual window with the navigation functions and dialogue and documents the DP UI Data, Dialog and Navigation Functions.

2.4   The Case and Its Context

The case was selected on the basis of availability and was provided by the research project Semantic Network of Information Management in Hospitals (SNIK)[1] [17]. The project team develops, among other things [18], a dashboard for the CIO of a hospital called CIO-Navigator (CION). The CIO is the head of the Information Management (IM) Department and is responsible for the successful provisioning of IT services, thus for decision-making in strategic, tactical, and operational IM. His/her role is located at executive level. Currently, the main CIO needs to collect distributed and scattered information in several systems and documents for individual decisions, as illustrated in Fig. 3. By the use of CION, we enable the CIO to navigate current data of the IM department and provide him/her with the relevant set of information required for decision-making of a predefined set of recurring issues. According to the characteristics presented in Table 1, CION is a PDSS.

During the design science cycle, different parts of the case were studied. The problem was investigated using TORE with the example of the CIO-tasks project management and change management. The purpose of the task project management is to align and monitor running projects as well as to prioritize planned projects. The purpose of the task change management is to assess, prioritize,

---

[1] www.snik.eu.

Fig. 3. Integration aspect of CION.

and plan favored changes of existing IT services. For treatment validation a case study was performed which applied DsTORE to the CIO-tasks project management and change management as well as IT strategy. The purpose of the task IT strategy is to define the strategic goals of the IM department on a five-year scale and assess the adherence of these strategic goals. Due to resource constraints, the system prototype was implemented for the first two tasks only.

3   Related Work

For related work, we first discuss two papers that provide an overview of RE for DSSs and then we discuss goal-oriented RE approaches for DSSs.

Garcia et al. [12] present a comprehensive mapping study of 27 articles related to RE for DSS. Although the title suggests DSSs, the search terms and the identified literature focus on DW. The authors conclude that there is a gap in the process of creating the design of a DSS in a methodical manner. In particular the business needs gain too little attention during the RE process. They propose to elicit business needs from stakeholders by asking "what do you do and why?". Another overview by Salinesi and Gam [13] (not covered by Garcia et al.) provides a comprehensive discussion of 15 RE approaches for DSSs, all of which are DW-specific. They found three families of methodological processes. (1) Data-driven approaches which are focused on the structure of data sources to design multi-dimensional schemas. However, these approaches do not cover decision specifics. (2) Requirement-driven approaches which focus on decision makers' requirements. The weakness of these approaches is that the availability of data sources is not treated sufficiently so that user requirements may not be realizable. (3) Mixed-driven approaches are a combination of (1) and (2). Both overviews again confirm the necessity to understand the needs of businesses and stakeholders.

As the approaches of both overview papers focus on DW, they support in particular the specification of DW data schema, data marts for DWs, and DW-specific ETL (extract, transform, load) processes, which are not important for PDSSs. The presented RE approaches do not provide a detailed task-oriented guideline for PDSS development.

There are several goal-oriented RE approaches for DSS. Again they focus on DW. They share the importance of the business and decision focus, but focus on decision specifics for DW such as key performance indicators [19] or business strategy and indicators [20, 21]. Giorgini, Rizzi and Garzetti propose with GRAnD [22] a goal-oriented method which connects a decisional model with a source schema. While this method provides a detailed analysis of the goals and decisions, it does not provide guidance for the UI design and early prototyping with the user.

Altogether, we did not find a RE method for DSS in general and PDSS in particular, providing guidance for a seamless transition from the business level to UI details.

4   Problem Investigation

The problem investigation, explained in detail in [10], is based on the CIO task project management for the development of CION and is summarized here. The pre-assessment of the tasks and data of the IM department by a combined task- and system analysis [23] revealed several CIO tasks. With the CION dashboard, the CIO wants to gain a transparent view of the operative and tactical data of the IM department [24]. In a semi-structured interview (duration 2:15 h.) with the CIO, we refined our understanding of TORE's DP Stakeholders Tasks and Domain Data wrt decisions. We performed a document analysis based on screenshots, several spreadsheets and text documents provided by the CIO to understand their decision specifics.

The problem investigation showed that TORE's DP can capture a large amount of relevant requirements, although some details of the CIO's decisions cannot be captured explicitly. We identified five decision-specific pieces of information (I_n) which must be included in a decision-supporting extension of TORE: I_1: *Distinction of decisions from conventional subtasks.* As decision-subtasks are particularly relevant for PDSS specification, they must be distinguished from conventional subtasks. I_2: *Detailed description of decision-relevant data.* The documentation of decision subtasks with a standard subtask template does not show explicitly the required data for decision making. It is necessary to document (a) details how certain data is calculated and (b) which information influences the decision exactly. I_3: *Decision-specific rules to choose from alternatives.* It is essential to understand the rules of the choice between alternatives, if there are any. I_4: *Support of decision-specific patterns in data for tables and summary fields.* A typical spreadsheet used by the CIO for decision making is illustrated in Fig. 4. The spreadsheet shows the project list, which provides an overview of planned and running projects. In the first row the headlines are printed in bold. The spreadsheet shows properties from project entities, such as the project ID, title, description, planned start and estimated human resources (HR) effort, and from budget entities, such as the planned and assigned budget. The budget is related to another spreadsheet containing the department's yearly budget. A summary row - the lower row in Fig. 4 - contains a sum of the column planned budget, assigned budget and estimated human resources effort of the shown projects. There are two decision specifics in this spreadsheet: First, there are combinations of entity/attribute pairs from several entities in rows

Prio	Project ID	Title	Description	Planned start	Planned budget	Assigned budget	HR
1	15-1	Server Virt.	Migration ...	Q3/2015	120.000 €	90.000 €	260
3	16-17	Letter softw.	Update phy...	Q4/2016	15.000 €	0 €	25
2	16-3	Service Mngr	Add KPI ...	Q2/2016	80.000 €	50.000 €	65
Σ	Projects total: 3		Year 2016		215.000 €	140.000 €	350

Fig. 4. Fragment of the decision-specific spreadsheet `project list`.

(e.g. project.ID, budget.assigned_budget). Second, one row typically contains computed data such as sums or any other kind of condensed data of columns (e.g. the planned budget of all projects, the number of ongoing projects). It is important to model these decision-specific data patterns explicitly in the domain data model. I_5: *Relation between content, format, and URL for data sources.* Decisions require information that might be distributed over different types of files such as spreadsheets or text-documents. Their content and format is an important input for system design decisions. Therefore, it is necessary to document and understand these data sources by a detailed description of the content in terms of entities, the format and the URL.

5   DsTORE - Treatment Design

The design of the DsTORE method addresses the design problem: *Improve the TORE method by decision-specifics I_1-I_5 with the goal to gain a comprehensive and structured specification for PDSSs.* This section presents a short introduction of DsTORE as a TORE enhancement based on the example of the task IT strategy. At this stage, we first introduce new decision-specific DPs with related artifact types (cf. the right side of Fig. 2). In some cases, we adapt DPs, indicated as dashed DPs in Fig. 2. DsTORE uses the same artifact types as TORE. There are two extended artifact types (i) the subtask description and (ii) the domain data model, and one new simple data source model.

5.1   Goal and Task Level

The new decision-specific DP **Categorization of subtasks** fulfills I_1 and enforces the identification of subtasks which *are* decisions. For categorization, the presence of alternatives to choose from and the verb or substantive of the subtask, indicating a decision, are used.

Subtasks can be a *decision* or a *conventional subtask*. For the IM domain, we use a non-exhaustive model encompassing 7 categories and distinguish objects or situations (x) and subjects(y). In other domains, the categorization scheme needs to be populated differently. Decisions are **A**pproval of x, **E**valuation of x or y, and **P**rioritization of x. Conventional subtasks are **M**onitoring of x, **D**ocumentation of x, **C**ommunication of x to y, and **S**upport of x or y. Table 3 shows the identified subtasks of IT strategy and their categorization. We explain the subtasks of Table 3 in brief and emphasize the respective decisions. The task IT strategy

Table 3. The subtasks of task IT strategy.

ID	Sub task	Category
1	Creation of strategic information management plan	
1a	Approval of IT strategy stakeholder	Approval
1b	Prioritization of future fields of activities for IT strategy	Prioritization
1c	Perform workshop	Communication
1d	Evaluation of workshop results	Evaluation
1e	Documentation of IT actions	Documentation
1f	Prioritization of IT actions	Prioritization
1g	Presentation of strategic information management plan	Communication
2	Use of strategic information management plan	
2a	Prioritization of projects	Prioritization
2b	Evaluation of change request	Evaluation
2c	Prospective/Retrospective justification for departments finances	Evaluation
2d	Evaluation of security-criticality of projects	Evaluation
2e	Use of strategic information management plan for funding applications	Support
2f	Evaluation of strategic information management plan adherence	Evaluation

consists of two groups: (i) subtasks 1a–1g related to the creation of the strategic information management plan (strategic IM plan) and (ii) subtasks 2a–2f related to the use of the strategic IM plan: A first step in the creation of the strategic IM plan is to define the stakeholders (subtask 1a) who are involved in the definition of IT actions which fulfill strategic hospital goals. As the CIO needs to choose, nominate, and finally *approve* a small group of IT strategy stakeholders, subtask 1a is a decision. As the CIO wants to direct possible IT actions into a certain direction, he prioritizes an initial set of activity fields (subtask 1b). This *prioritization* in subtask 1b is the decision about the activities' importance. Then a workshop is held with the nominated IT strategy stakeholders and the CIO in subtask 1c where the participants discuss ideas, how the future fields of activities can be realized in the IM department. From the workshop results, the CIO distills (evaluates) a set of IT actions in subtask 1d which fulfill the strategic hospital goals. This involves the decision about the correctness and completeness of IT actions. Afterwards, the CIO *documents* the identified IT actions in subtask 1e into the *strategic IM plan* document, which is a normal subtask. In the next step, the CIO *prioritizes* the identified IT actions of the strategic IM plan in subtask 1f, which involves the decision about their importance. Finally, the *strategic IM plan* is presented to the boards of directors in subtask 1g, which is a communication task and does not involve a decision. Projects are prioritized according to their contribution to defined IT actions in subtask 2a, which is a decision about the level of contribution to IT actions. During the evaluation of change requests in subtask 2b, their contribution or possible conflict to IT actions are considered, which involves the decision whether the change request involves a conflict or a contribution to an IT action. The departments' budgets are evaluated prospectively resp. retrospectively in subtask 2c wrt. the strategic IM plan. This is the decision to what extent certain expenses contribute to IT actions. As security is one of the high priority IT actions, all projects are evaluated wrt. their contribution to security since security critical projects are prioritized higher than others. The decision in subtask 2d is about the security criticality of projects. In subtask 2e, the IT actions contained in the strategic IM plan are used for the writing of funding applications or research project proposals to assure that all important strategic IM aspects are considered. Finally, the adherence to the strategic IM plan is evaluated in subtask 2f to identify achieved or neglected IT actions. The adherence of the strategic IM plan involves the decision to what extent an IT action is fulfilled or not.

5.2   Domain Level

Decision-related subtasks are specified in the DP **To-be decision-specific subtasks** and are documented with the decision-specific subtask template. The *decision-specific subtask template* extends TORE's subtask template to define the semantics for decision artifacts and fulfills I_2 and I_3. It covers details of a decision in five structured fields, which are marked yellow in Fig. 5. The field *category* contains the category of the subtask as classified in DP Categorization

ID: Subtask	IT strategy 2f: Evaluation of strategic IM plan adherence		
Category	Evaluation		
Actor I Supp.Act.	CIO I Information management board, project manager		
Contribution	Exoneration from fulfillment of strategic information management plan, collection of lessons learned		
Cause	Biannual evaluation; creation of new strategic information management plan; review or evaluation meeting with IT strategy board		
Description	The IT strategy board evaluates the achievement of planned IT actions. A recommendation of action is given, if postulated IT actions are neglected.		
Pre condition	Existing project status reports with relation to IT actions.		
Combined Data	**Entity**	**Attribute**	
	IT action	project, degree of fulfillment	
	Project	budget, status	
	Project list	(all)	
Computed Data	**Entity**	**Attribute**	**Computation**
	Project	overall cost	sum of single expenses
	IT action	overall cost of projects	sum of all contributing projects overall costs
Post condition	evaluation of strategic IM plan is done		
Info out	**Entity**	**Attribute**	
	IT action	degree of fulfillment	
	exoneration protocol	exoneration of CIO	
	exoneration protocol	recommendation for neglected IT actions	
Rules	– none given –		

Fig. 5. Decision subtask IT strategy 2f: Evaluation of strategic IM plan adherence.

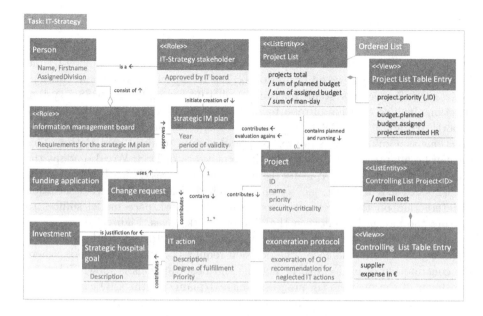

Fig. 6. Part of the domain data model for IT strategy.

of subtasks. *Combined data* expresses necessary decision- and/or stakeholder-specific data with entity/attribute pairs. Data aggregations, e.g. of time or spatial data often used for decision-making, are documented by *computed data* and indicated by '/' for derived attributes in the Domain Data Model (cf. Fig. 6). Details of the computations, such as add, subtract, etc., are documented in the column `computation`. The result of the decision is documented in the field *Info-out*, again with entity/attribute pairs. *Rules* describe which alternative will be chosen by the decision maker and under which circumstances. The notation can be textual or formal, as is appropriate. Decisions require specific domain data which is defined in the extended DP **Domain Data** which uses additional stereotypes. The entities and attributes need to be consistent with those of the decision-specific subtasks. The decision-specific spreadsheets, as presented in the problem investigation (cf. Sect. 4), are modeled in the domain data in Fig. 6 with UML stereotypes. Lists, such as the project list (cf. Fig. 4), are modeled by the stereotype <<ListEntity>>. The <<ListEntity>> is related to the listed entities and to a <<View>> entity which captures combined attributes. As an example, the `project list` (cf. Figure 4) is modeled in the domain data model in Fig. 6. Similarly, the domain data model contains the project specific controlling list `Controlling List Project<ID>`. This list holds the computed attribute `overall cost` which is calculated by summing up the individual expenses of the project. The list rows are modeled by the class <<View>> `Controlling List Table Entry`, holding the attributes supplier and expense.

5.3   Interaction Level

In the DP *system functions*, TORE focuses on the to-be system functions. DSSs have a limited range of typical system functions, cf. Holsapple [14], and Power [25]. Therefore, we add criterion I_6: the RE specification should consider typical PDSS-specific system functions explicitly. Examples of PDSSs' system functions include creation of reports, navigation to data sources, and document export. We adapt the DP to use a decision-specific predefined set of system functions as a guidance to support completeness and to avoid gold plating. This set can be adapted according to the different types of DSS. We also adapt the DP Interaction which is typically described by use cases. Since PDSSs provide a dashboard-like UI with one screen for each decision, a detailed description of interaction on this level is not necessary. The workspace model suffices to capture the navigation between the different workspaces. Figure 7 shows as an example the workspace model for the decision task IT strategy 2f: the evaluation of strategic IM plan adherence. The decision requires only one workspace, where the contribution of projects to IT actions and hospital goals is shown. Then by the status of the projects (in progress/finished/planned), the CIO can estimate the achievement of the IT actions, and thus assess the whole strategic IM plan. The CIO needs to view the strategic IM plan. This function is an instance of the PDSS function *navigation to data sources*. When the CIO needs to adjust details of the projects (status, budget, or planned start), s/he needs to navigate to the workspace of the project management task 3a (described in [10]).

5.4   System Level

The DP UI-Data and Screen Structure is documented with a Virtual Window. Figure 8 shows the Virtual Window of the subtask *Evaluation of strategic IM plan adherence*. It shows the arrangement of the decision-specific subtask's data. For the subtask 2f (cf. Table 3 and Fig. 5), it is essential for the CIO to see an overview of the IT actions defined in the last strategic IM plan along with the details of contributing projects. In particular, the financial aspects of the project are interesting, which also relates to subtask 2c: retrospective justification of departments finances. The IT actions are related visually to the strategic hospital

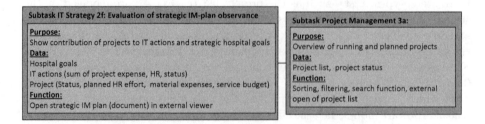

Fig. 7. The workspace model of subtask IT strategy 2f.

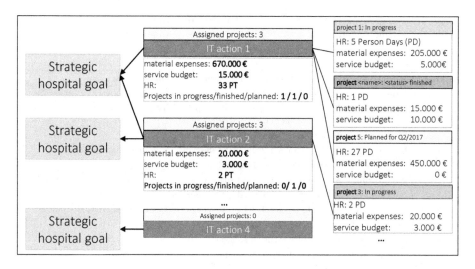

Fig. 8. The virtual window for subtask Evaluation of strategic IM plan adherence.

goals. With this information presented in one view, the CIO is able to evaluate which IT actions are fulfilled to what degree.

On the system level, there is a new DP **Data sources**. In TORE, data sources are left to software design. As argued in I_5 the consideration of data sources in DsTORE is important. Data source description can be captured in a simple table with the rows *entities*, *format*, and *location*, as shown in Fig. 9. All entities in this description are related to entities in the DP domain data model. In the example model, it is shown that the strategic IM plan is a (text-)document located on a specific URL on the sharepoint server.

entity	format	location
strategic IM plan	document	http://intranet.sharepointServer/2015/strategic plan.docx
project list	excsl/csv	http://filesrv1/2016/pwl.xlsx
controlling list project	excsl/csv	http://intranet.sharepointServer/2017/controllingList.xlsx

Fig. 9. The data source model task IT strategy.

6   Case Study: Treatment Validation

This section describes the design and results of the two-phase case study to evaluate the treatment design DsTORE. The case and its context is described in Sect. 2.4.

Table 4. Overview of the case study's activities, duration, and effort to create or modify the artifacts (indicated by ↳). (T=Telephone), Duration in [h:mm].

ID	Dur.	Activity	Decision point / Description

ID	Dur.	Activity	Decision point / Description
Tasks of treatment validation Phase 1: project management, change management				
1	1:20	Interview	Categor. of Subtasks, To-be Decision Specific Subtask, UI Structure
↳	56:00	Engineering	Artifacts for act. 1: Task description, decision-specific subtask, workspace model, virtual window
2	1:20	Interview	System Functions, Interaction Data
↳	15:00	Engineering	Artifacts for act.2: function description, domain data model
3	T1:30	Interview	System Functions, Interaction Data, UI Data
↳	23:00	Engineering	Artifacts for act.3: workspace model, domain data model, virt. window
4	1:45	Interview	To-be activities, Domain data, Screen Structure
↳	12:00	Engineering	Artifacts for act.4: UI prototype, workspace model, virtual window
5	–	Developm	Development of system prototype (~12 months á 40 h.)
6	1:00	Presentation	System prototype in software
Tasks of treatment validation Phase 2. Task: IT strategy				
7	1:30	Interview	Stakeholders Tasks, Categorization of Subtasks, To-be Decision Specific Subtasks, Domain Data, Interaction Data
↳	3:00	Engineering	Artifacts for act.7: Task description, decision-specific subtask, domain data model
8	1:30	Interview	To-be Decision Specific Subtasks, Interaction Data
↳	4:00	Engineering	Artifacts for act.8: decision-specific subtask, domain data model
9	T0:45	Evaluation	Eval.: interviews, artifacts, system prototype
10	1:00	Evaluation	Interview with CIO for evaluation of system prototype based on questionnaire (cf. Appendix A.3)
11	–	Evaluation	Questionnaire for resulting activities triggered by RE (cf. Appendix A.4)

6.1   Design

The research objective is to identify the extent to which DsTORE supports the RE of PDSSs. The *object of study* is the application of the DsTORE method. Therefore, we raise *RQ.1: How well does DsTORE support the specification of requirements for a PDSS?* In **phase one** we re-visited the tasks project management and change management (already investigated in the pre-assessment), but now using DsTORE artifact types for specification. Missing information was additionally elicited. We used four semi-structured interviews (activity 1–4) to elicit the requirements with DsTORE, as shown in Table 4. DPs visited are: Categorization of subtasks, As-is and to-be, To-be decision-specific subtasks, UI Structure, System functions, Interaction data, and Screen Structure. Table 4 also shows which artifacts have been created or modified after the elicitation in activities 1–4 and 7–8. For each artifact, the time needed for its creation or refinement is given, including an internal review and a review with the stakeholder. The task descriptions of project management and change management were taken from the problem investigation. All other artifacts were newly created.

Table 5. Metrics of data collection for the case study - treatment validation.

Goal	Metric	Description of metrics
Efficiency	m1	Time taken for the creation of artifacts
	m2	Number & Duration of interview sessions in total
Usability	m3	Stakeholder's feedback to the interviews
	m4	Stakeholder's feedback to the artifacts
	m5	Requirements engineer's feedback
Utility	m6	Stakeholder's acceptance of the system prototype

The following two DPs were not relevant: The DP Navigation/Supporting Functions was not relevant, since no supporting functions were necessary. The DP Dialog was not relevant, since the dashboard does not support complex dialogues. All system DPs were refined during the implementation of the system prototype in activity 5, where two students implemented a system prototype in .NET which integrates into SharePoint. We presented this system prototype to the CIO in activity 6 and let the CIO himself evaluate the system prototype as part of activity 10. In **phase two**, we investigated the CIO task IT strategy with *activity 7–8*. The DPs Stakeholders Task, Categorization of subtasks, To-be decision-specific subtasks, Decision-specific domain data, and Interaction data have been visited in activity 7. In activity 8 we refined the requirements of the DPs To-be decision-specific subtasks, and Interaction data.

We performed the data analysis for both phases after all interviews. To answer RQ.1, we used a Goal Question Metric approach (GQM) [26]. We study the following effects of the application of DsTORE (see [9] for similar distinctions): the **efficiency** in terms of the time taken for artifact creation and the interviews (m1 and m2), the **usability** in terms of the ease of use of the artifacts and the process for the stakeholder (m3 and m4) and the requirements engineer (m5), and the **utility** in terms of the value of the outcome for the stakeholder (m6). The data for these metrics was collected in a semi-structured interview (activity 9). Table 5 summarizes the metrics used to answer RQ.1.

6.2 Results for the RE Phase

The creation of artifacts (m1) took 106 h in phase one and 7 h in phase two, cf. Table 4. Four interviews with a duration of approx. 7 h were conducted (m2) in phase one, and two interviews with a duration of 3 h in phase two. The CIO liked the interviews of both phases and rated the semi-structured execution of the interviews as good (m3), since it gave him room to discuss ideas. He suggested two improvements: the provisioning of an RE-process description with a graphical sequence upfront, and the consultation of other departments' experts in some situations. The CIO found it sometimes difficult to provide all relevant decision information. It would have helped, if he had had a prepared description of decisions before the RE phase. The meeting minutes and the correction iteration was good and helpful for the CIO. The interview preparation and the review was difficult due to time restrictions. Especially for phase two, the CIO rated the identification of decisions overall as good. For the task IT strategy, the CIO rated the description of decision-related information as difficult. He did not consider the definition of the IT strategy as a decision, although the interview had identified 5 decisions. The CIO's feedback to the artifacts (m4) is summarized in Table 6.

The CIO's perception of the artifacts did not change between phase one and two. All decision-specific information was contained in the artifacts. The CIO perceived the *task description* as important, and easy to understand and comment on. However, he considered the *Categorization of Subtasks* as difficult to understand and comment on. Once the categorization was done, the CIO understood its importance. Initially, the CIO did not see the importance of the *Decision-specific Task Description*, and hence, rated the understanding as difficult but easy to comment on. After the first review of this description, he rated them as important. He perceived the description of complex processes (such as decisions) as challenging. The CIO rated the description of *data sources* as very easy to understand, but difficult to comment on (and fill in), since he was not aware of detail knowledge about URLs. The CIO perceived the *workspace model* as a complex and overloaded representation and rated it as difficult to understand and comment on. He recommends to hide workspace details and focus on the navigation between them. The *UI Prototype* gives the most detailed description of the system-to-be and allows to check whether the UI contains the necessary information. It was rated as very easy to understand and comment on and as a very important artifact. The requirements engineer rated (m5) the detailed understanding of the artifact types and their relations to each other as very important to structure the interviews. The requirements engineer needs to understand the RE process to choose an appropriate sequence of DPs to visit and

Table 6. Metrics and CIO's artifact rating (• difficult, ○ easy, ○○ very easy, ++ very important, + important, - less important).

Artifact type	Simplicity		Import.
	Underst	Comment	Underst
Task description	○	○	+
Categorization of subtasks	•	•	+
Decision specific task description	•	○○	+
Data sources	○○	•	++
Workspace model	•	•	+
Virtual windows	○○	○	++
UI Prototype	○○	○○	++

artifacts to create. During the RE phase, s/he must keep all artifacts consistent, which is challenging. The DsTORE artifacts enabled a detailed understanding of the decisions. The specification was extremely helpful to guide the developers during the implementation of the prototype, in particular the knowledge of the required data and their origin.

During the system prototype evaluation (presented in the next Sect. 6.3), the CIO mentioned that the RE phase triggered some changes related to the investigated tasks. We wanted to understand them in more detail and therefore asked the CIO which activities and task changes he started after the RE phase of problem investigation and treatment design. The questionnaire we used is presented in Appendix A.4. The CIO started the following activities, which also impact decisional data.

(1) The project planning was consolidated. Previously separated yearly lists with running and waiting projects have been joined together in one continuous project list. Filter criteria help to work with this list.
(2) The project websites containing their status have moved to a dedicated project server, which affects the data source model.
(3) The financial controlling list will be migrated to SharePoint.
(4) He plans to evaluate and introduce a contract management tool.
(5) He plans to integrate the change management documentation from SharePoint into the IT-service management tool SCSM.

Regarding his tasks, there are no changes compared to the interview. However, in the future it could be necessary to change workflows which will affect subtasks. The decision specific information for subtasks has not been changed so far.

6.3   Results of the System Prototype Evaluation

We used an additional GQM scheme for the evaluation of the system prototype wrt. acceptance, usability and utility, shown in Table 7. A screen shot of the system prototype UI for the task project management is shown in Fig. 10. As the hospital's default language is German, the system prototype follows this restriction.

The CIO mentioned five positive properties (p.m1): (a) it was easy for the CIO to understand the tool (b) CION is the central place to gain an overview of data in an aggregated form (c) CION meets the idea of a dashboard (d) is modularized and extendable (e) quick filtering is helpful. As negative properties, the CIO mentioned the following three (p.m2): (a) the system prototype was extremely slow (b) the results were only partially comprehensible based on the limited test data (c) the drill down into the data needs further consideration. The CIO stated (p.m3) that he likes the system prototype *well*. As missing properties (p.m4), the CIO enumerated some issues: (a) the change request overview needs to contain the last comment of the change history. (b) There is no advantage in displaying the department's budget along with the change details. Show it on a separate page. (c) It is sufficient to show material expenses and service

Table 7. Metrics of system prototype evaluation (Question refers to Appendix A.3).

Goal	Metric	Description of metrics	Question
Acceptance	p.m1	Stakeholder's feedback on positive system prototype properties	C.1
	p.m2	Stakeholder's feedback on negative system prototype properties	C.1
	p.m3	Stakeholder's rating of liking	C.5
	p.m4	Missing properties in general	C.2
	p.m5	Identified errors and problems	C.2
	p.m6	Requested improvements by stakeholder	C.8
	p.m7	Stakeholder's rating of usability	C.3
Usability	p.m8	Stakeholder's feedback to positive usability properties	C.3
	p.m9	Missing properties wrt. usability	C.3
Utility	p.m10	Stakeholder's rating of utility	C.4
	p.m11	Likelihood of future use	C.7
	p.m12	Obstacles to future use	C.7
	p.m13	Degree of compliance with given requirements	C.6

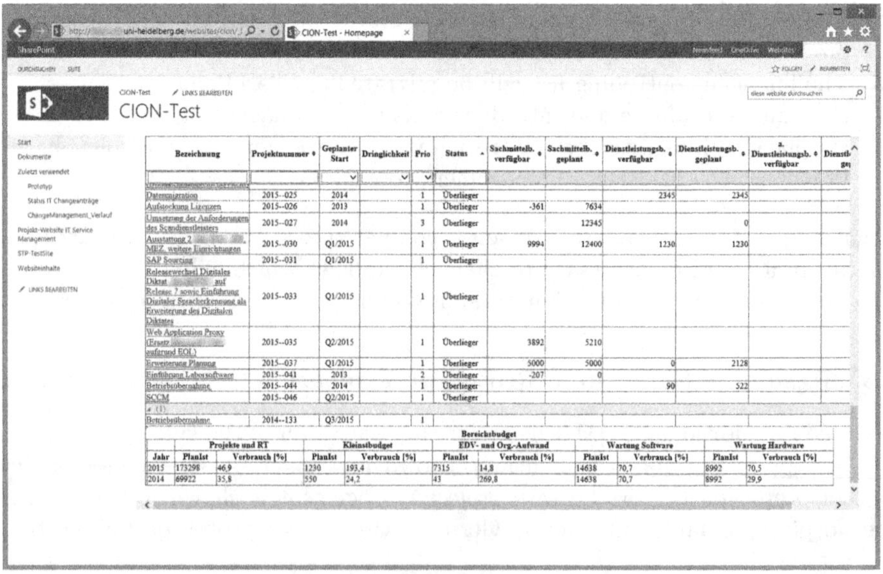

Fig. 10. The developed software prototype in a browser.

budget for change requests. **(d)** Show the planned and available budget for material expenses and service budget. **(e)** the departments budget should be on top of the page project overview. Some minor issues in p.m4 were missing buttons, change of labels, open pages in new tab. The CIO identified two errors wrt. navigation (p.m5): **(a)** return from project detail page to overview results in a redirection to the start page. **(b)** horizontal scrolling is unusual. The CIO requested one improvement (p.m6), that is, separate budget to a different page (already mentioned as missing property, cf. p.m4)). The usability of the system prototype (p.m7) was rated *well* by the CIO. The mentioned positive usability property (p.m8) was the easiness of navigation between different CIO tasks. The CIO stated no concrete missing properties wrt. usability (p.m9), but assumed that the observed problems might be related to test data. For future development it seems important to the CIO whether the focus of CION is to gain an overview or an in-depth view. The CIO rated the utility of the system prototype as (p.m10) *useful* and stated that he *maybe* will use the system prototype in the future (p.m11). Possible obstacles for of future use are (p.m12): (**o.1**) the availability of all data necessary for decisions (**o.2**) the hospital's ability to continue the development of the software (**o.3**) the existence of defined responsibilities (**o.4**) a proof of operational safety. The CIO stated that his expectations formed by the requirements specification (p.m13) were *well* fulfilled. Further comments of the CIO were:

1. The RE led to some changes in the division. In particular during the conversations, he gained some ideas for the restructuring of data.
2. The invested time was beneficial.
3. The lessons learned are the major value of the project.
4. For the CIO it is still unclear to what extend the dashboard will integrate data from the system environment. Possibly there is more to do.

6.4 Summary

The CIO liked the semi-structured execution of interviews and rated the identification of decisions as overall good. All decision-specific information was contained in the artifacts and thus, the DsTORE artifacts enabled a detailed understanding of the decisions. The CIO likes the system prototype well, although there are some minor missing properties and problems in navigation. The CIO rated the system prototype as well usable and useful. His expectations of the system prototype documented in the requirements specification was well fulfilled. Therefore RQ.1 can be answered as follows: DsTORE supports the specification of requirements for a PDSS adequately. It allows for an early and continuous stakeholder feedback, emphasizes the decision-specific data, and decision-specific UI prototyping.

7   Discussion

In this section, we discuss the results of the DsTORE evaluation and possible improvements to DsTORE, as well as lessons learned during the method adaptation.

Discussion of DsTORE. The *problem investigation* shows that TORE as a structured RE framework provides the basis for the specification of a PDSS. This is not surprising as PDSSs share some properties with ISs (cf. Table 1). The missing decision-specifics are provided by DsTORE. Small adaptations in DsTORE help to understand decisions and to gain a detailed specification of all PDSS aspects. The *treatment validation* shows that DsTORE is accepted by the stakeholder and the requirements engineer, although there is potential for improvement.

The effort of 106 h to create the artifacts is very high, but decreased significantly in phase two based on the prior experience. Four interviews with 7 h and two interviews with 3 h is a reasonable effort. Based on the CIO's feedback, the semi-structured interviews are adequate to elicit requirements and allow a creative discussion. The results show that the CIO views atomic decisions as part of larger business- or management processes as important to him. It therefore appears interesting to study the relations of tasks and their atomic decisions to management processes. The CIO rated only the workspace model as less important for him. We used the workspace model to structure the virtual windows. In the future, the workspace model might be used only by the requirements engineer while the structure is discussed with the stakeholder directly in the virtual windows. The CIO's rating emphasizes the importance of the data sources and the UI. The CIO's suggestions do not concern the DPs, but rather the execution of the interviews, which can easily be improved. E.g. decisions can be identified on the task level with the CIO without specifying details, and can then be detailed with external experts. The latter can also supply the data source details. The categorization of subtasks can be done initially by the requirements engineer and presented to the CIO for review. The artifacts' consistency can be improved by a yet to define tool support. Both, CIO and requirements engineer, missed a RE-process description covering activities and artifacts. This can easily be provided in the future.

Discussion of the System Prototype. The evaluation of the system prototype shows its usability and usefulness for the CIO, who overall likes the system prototype *well*. In particular his expectations of the system prototype formed by the requirements specification were *well* fulfilled. The evaluation shows also some deficits of the system prototype. The deficits related to navigation, the negative and missing properties can be changed in the system prototype with little effort. Some deficits are directly related to the test system and its data, and are nonexistent in a productive system environment. The reasons why the CIO *maybe* will use the system prototype (cf. p.m12 in Sect. 6.3 and Table 7) can be mitigated by the following selective measures: Missing data (cf. o.1 in Sect. 6.3) obviously can neither be provided by CION nor can they be used with CION. It is up to the CIO or a responsible project manager to adapt departments' organizational structures to capture unavailable but relevant data for future use. However, during the RE phase we saw that most of the data is available as scattered or unstructured data, which increases effort, but principally allows a use in CION. The obstacles wrt. the hospital's ability to further develop the software (cf. o.2 in Sect. 6.3) and undefined responsibilities (cf. o.3) can be mitigated by a skilled staff member who is responsible for the software and continuous development. This person needs an initial training and can use a provided system documentation. A simple system structure and easy build and deployment process is also essential to support the hospital in further development. The proof of operational safety (cf. o.4 in Sect. 6.3) is the most difficult one, since it targets possible side effects to the existing IM services. As CION is a prototype, there is certainly additional effort necessary to turn it into a product and then to prove the operational safety. We minimized possible side effects with two facts. First, the system prototype is realized as a SharePoint extension, avoiding any new infrastructure. Second, the prototype accesses the data sources at run-time in a read only mode to avoid any file or process locks.

Also of interest are the activities triggered by RE. During the interviews, we queried and captured details of decisions and their related data. As a result of these interviews, the CIO realized existing weaknesses and possible improvements. This is an important aspect of RE: Activities such as system assessments and data governance which emphasize deficits in data or system structure explicitly, are often neglected. The RE for a system like CION incorporated a system analysis and the interviews, which triggered possible improvements.

Lessons Learned. The following sequence is helpful for creating some of the artifacts of DsTORE. (1) task and subtask (2) detailed decision description (3) domain data model (4) workspace model (5) virtual windows (6) UI prototype. A template for the naming of subtasks should be used, i.e. <verb | nominalized verbs><object>. Synonyms for similar verbs should be avoided. During the elicitation of the to-be decision-specific subtask description, it is important to continuously ask the stakeholder which data exactly is necessary for this decision. It is important to distinguish explicitly between domain entities and attributes, as this is not done directly by the stakeholder. The specification of rules is often awkward, especially when they are complex, or have not been formulated previously. It was helpful for us to assure that attributes of rules can be mapped to the domain data model. It is worth the effort to assemble the results of the decision description into virtual windows as early as possible.

General Experiences with Method Adaptation. During the *treatment design* we developed several further artifact types, which we finally discarded or simplified, so that they could fit into DsTORE artifact types. The design science process helped to structure the adaptation of TORE into problem identification, specific adaptations, and their evaluation. It forced us to create explicit justifications for the adaptations. Further, it forced us to collect explicit feedback from the stakeholders involved in the method execution. It is important to discuss the adaptations with independent experts not involved in the method execution.

8   Threats to Validity

The threats to validity are structured according to Runeson et al. [27]. **Construct validity** considers whether the study measures what it claims. The artifact types of DsTORE were not yet fixed during phase 1. As all DsTORE DPs as presented in Sect. 5 were applied in treatment validation, we believe that the DsTORE artifact types that have been temporarily used and discarded do not distort the final results. **Internal validity** considers causal relations of investigated factors, i.e. effects of unknown factors that influence an investigated factor.

Training obviously affected the effort and the opinion of the stakeholders. The effort decreased between the case studies, owing to training effects of the requirements engineer and CIO. We asked the CIO about his opinion in activity 9, after he had gained experience. The system test and the implementation of the results of the case study, phase two, might change the evaluation. However, we consider this as unlikely. **External Validity** describes the generalizability of the findings and the transfer of study results to other cases. The case studies are based on a single case only. The case study involved only one person. DsTORE is specific to PDSSs and the transferability to other DSS types is unclear. **Reliability** considers the influence of the specific researcher and indicates threats to validity for a repetition of the study. The main threat to reliability is that the first author (as requirements engineer) had much influence on the development and process of the case study, in particular during the interviews and the data analysis. We mitigated this by continuous discussions with the 2nd researcher.

9   Conclusion

In this study, we presented a *problem investigation* where we evaluate the ability of task-oriented RE to support the specification of PDSS, DsTORE as the *treatment design* which extends TORE to support requirements engineering for PDSS, and a *case study* that evaluates DsTORE in the case of a PDSS, in order to show its basic feasibility. We identified five decision specifics, which a method for PDSSs specification needs to consider: (1) distinct decisions from subtasks, (2) detailed description of decision relevant data, (3) decision specific rules, (4) decision specific patterns in spreadsheet data, (5) relation between content, format and URL for data sources. With DsTORE, we created a specification for a CIO dashboard to navigate in current data for predefined and reoccurring decisions. The specification comprises decisions within the tasks project- and change-management and IT strategy.

The results are encouraging to continue with the following future work: First, we will consolidate the improvements of DsTORE as we have sketched above. Second, as data play a prominent role, we will explore how an ontology can support the RE process. In carrying out this last aspect, we rely on the SNIK domain ontology [18] for IM in hospitals. We want to elaborate, how this knowledge can be used in combination with DsTORE to further improve the requirements elicitation and specification. Fourth, we believe that it would be interesting to investigate whether and how the presented approach also supports the specification of other types of DSSs.

Acknowledgements. We thank the involved CIO for his time and motivated collaboration and the SNIK project team for their intensive cooperation. This work was supported by DFG (German Research Foundation) under the Project SNIK: Semantic Network of Information Management in Hospitals, Grant no. 1605/7-1 and 1387/8-1.

A   Appendix

A.1   Interview Questions Used in the Problem Investigation

To assure an appropriate set of questions used in interviews of the problem investigation, we followed five goals: G1: Create a set of detailed user task descriptions with existing problems for the CIO specifically. G2: Determine existing deficits in currently used tools for the execution of user tasks. G3: Understand the CIO's expectations wrt. system functions and characteristics of CION. G4: Understand the information and their relation necessary to execute the user tasks. G5: Elicit existing data sources for system integration. The following questions have been asked for each user task project management and change management, except for question 10 which is not user task specific.

1. Which subtasks, data, systems and interfaces are related to the execution of the task <x> in the current state? (G1, as-is)
2. How do you imagine the future support of CION during the task <x>? Which activities and subtasks play a role during the task execution? Which data are important for the task execution? (G2, G3, G4, G5, to-be)
3. Which information, tools and computation or aggregation are you missing in the current tool-landscape for the execution of task <x>? (G2, as-is)
4. Which data shall be presented for task <x>? (G4, to-be)
5. Which system functions shall be provided by CION to edit data or information? (G3, to-be)
6. To what extent is configurability important for CION to interpret the data? (G3, to-be)
7. What are your expectations regarding the composition (manual or automatic) and presentation of these data? (G1, to-be)
8. Who provides you currently with the necessary data to execute task <x> and which data are these? (G4, G5, as-is)
9. Who are you reporting to about the analysis results of CION to task <x> and in which form are they? (G3, G5, to-be)
10. In your opinion: Is CION a dashboard, a data warehouse or a tool to create data relations? (G3, to-be)

A.2   Interview Questions Used in the Treatment Validation

The goal of treatment validation is a better understanding of the decision subtasks of project management, change management and IT strategy. We used the extended subtask template (cf. Fig. 5) to fill in each attribute together with the CIO.

1. What is the decision-outcome?
2. What information is necessary to make the decision?
3. Which combined and computed data is necessary to make the decision?
4. What are possible rules for the decision-making?

A.3   Questionnaire for System Prototype Evaluation

This questionnaire helped us to evaluate the existing software prototype of CION. We are interested in your opinion about the tested browser based CION.

1. What do you particularly like about the current software prototype?
   | free text |

2. What are you missing in the current software prototype?
   | free text |

3. How do you rate the user friendliness of the software prototype?
   ☐ very good   ☐ good   ☐ neither..nor   ☐ suboptimal   ☐ bad
   | free text for reasons |

4. How do you rate the utility of the software prototype (5 item lickert scale, additional free text for reason).
   ☐ very useful   ☐ useful   ☐ neither..nor   ☐ less useful   ☐ hardly useful
   | free text for reasons |

5. How do you like the software prototype overall?
   ☐ very well   ☐ well   ☐ neither..nor   ☐ partly   ☐ not at all
   | free text for reasons |

6. To what extent are your expectations formed by the requirements documents (task descriptions, UI prototype) fulfilled by the software prototype?
   ☐ very well   ☐ well   ☐ neither..nor   ☐ partially   ☐ not at all
   | free text for reasons |

7. Would you use the software prototype in the future?
   ☐ in any case ☐ maybe ☐ not sure ☐ rather not ☐ under no circumstances
   | free text for reasons |

8. How would you change or improve the prototype? Any further comments?
   | free text |

A.4   Questionnaire for Resulting Activities Triggered by RE

Resulting activities in the CIO's division:

1. We are interested in the activities and ideas you initiated after the interviews: Which activities did you initiate to change or improve the situation in the information management department based on the interviews?
   | free text |

2. We are interested in changes on tasks and subtasks you initiated after the interviews:
   (a) Which documents and spreadsheets were changed?
   | free text |

(b) Have tasks (also decisions) or subtasks been changed?

    free text

(c) Has the information needed to make decisions changed?

    free text

References

1. Hosack, B., Hall, D., Paradice, D., Courtney, J.: A look toward the future: decision support systems research is alive and well. J. Assoc. Inform. **13**, 315–340 (2012)
2. Gao, S.: Mobile decision support systems research: a literature analysis. J. Decis. Syst. **22**, 10–27 (2013)
3. Saxena, K.B.C.: Decision support engineering: a DSS development methodology. In: Proceedings of the 24th Annual Hawaii International Conference on System Sciences (HICSS 1991), vol. 3, pp. 98–107 (1991)
4. Gachet, A., Haettenschwiler, P.: Development processes of intelligent decision-making support systems: review and perspective. In: Gupta, J.N.D., Forgionne, G.A., Manuel Mora, T. (eds.) Intelligent Decision-making Support Systems. Decision Engineering, pp. 97–121. Springer, London (2006). https://doi.org/10.1007/1-84628-231-4_6
5. Arnott, D.: Senior executive information behaviors and decision support. J. Decis. Syst. **19**, 465–480 (2010)
6. Arnott, D.: Personal decision support systems. In: Burstein, F., Holsapple, C. (eds.) Handbook of Decision Support Systems 2. International Handbooks Information System, pp. 127–150. Springer-Verlag, Heidelberg (2008). https://doi.org/10.1007/978-3-540-48716-6_7
7. Paech, B., Kohler, K.: Task-driven requirements in object-oriented development. In: do Leite, J., Doorn, J.H. (eds.) Perspectives on Software Requirements. The Springer International Series in Engineering and Computer Science, vol. 753, pp. 1–25. Kluwer Academic, Boston (2004). https://doi.org/10.1007/978-1-4615-0465-8_3
8. Adam, S., Doerr, J., Eisenbarth, M., Gross, A.: Using task-oriented requirements engineering in different domains experience of application in research and industry. In: Proceedings of 17th IEEE International Requirements Engineering Conference (RE 2009), pp. 267–272 (2009)
9. Wieringa, R.J.: Design Science Methodology for Information Systems and Software Engineering. Springer, Heidelberg (2014). https://doi.org/10.1007/978-3-662-43839-8
10. Kücherer, C., Paech, B.: A task-oriented requirements engineering method for personal decision support systems - a case study. In: 19th International Conference on Enterprise Information Systems (ICEIS 2017) (2017)
11. Holsapple, C.W.: Decisions and knowledge. In: Burstein, F. (ed.) Handbook on Decision Support Systems 1. International Handbooks Information System, pp. 21–53. Springer, Heidelberg (2008). https://doi.org/10.1007/978-3-540-48713-5_2
12. García, S., Romero, O., Raventós, R.: DSS from an RE perspective: a systematic mapping. J. Syst. Softw. **117**, 488–507 (2016)
13. Salinesi, C., Gam, I.: How specific should requirements engineering be in the context of decision information systems? In: Proceedings of the Third International Conference on Research Challenges in Information Science, RCIS 2009, Fez, Morocco, pp. 247–254. IEEE (2009)

14. Holsapple, C.W.: DSS Architecture and Types. In: Burstein, F. (ed.) Handbook on Decision Support Systems 1. International Handbooks Information System. Springer, Heidelberg (2008). https://doi.org/10.1007/978-3-540-48713-5_9
15. Arnott, D., Pervan, G.: A critical analysis of decision support systems research. J. Inf. Technol. **20**, 67–87 (2005)
16. Lauesen, S.: User Interface Design. Pearson/Addison-Wesley, Harlow, Munich (2005)
17. Jahn, F., Schaaf, M., Paech, B., Winter, A.: Ein semantisches Netz des Informationsmanagements im Krankenhaus. In: Informatik 2014, Volume LNI P-232, pp. 1491–1498 (2014)
18. Schaaf, M., Jahn, F., Tahar, K., Kücherer, C., Winter, A., Paech, B.: Entwicklung und Einsatz einer Domänenontologie des Informationsmanagements im Krankenhaus. In: Informatik 2015, Volume LNI P-246 of Lecture Notes in Informatics, Cottbus, Germany (2015)
19. Pourshahid, A., Johari, I., Richards, G., Amyot, D., Akhigbe, O.S.: A goal-oriented, business intelligence-supported decision-making methodology. Dec. Anal. J. **9**, 1–36 (2014)
20. Barone, D., Topaloglou, T., Mylopoulos, J.: Business intelligence modeling in action: a hospital case study. In: Ralyté, J., Franch, X., Brinkkemper, S., Wrycza, S. (eds.) CAiSE 2012. LNCS, vol. 7328, pp. 502–517. Springer, Heidelberg (2012). https://doi.org/10.1007/978-3-642-31095-9_33
21. Topaloglou, T., Barone, D.: Lessons from a hospital business intelligence implementation. In: Proceeding from CAiSE 2015, pp. 19–33 (2015)
22. Giorgini, P., Rizzi, S., Garzetti, M.: GRAnD: a goal-oriented approach to requirement analysis in data warehouses. Decis. Support Syst. **45**, 4–21 (2008)
23. Ammenwerth, E., Haux, R., Knaup-Gregori, P., Winter, A.: IT-Projektmanagement im Gesundheitswesen, 2nd edn. Schattauer, Stuttgart (2015)
24. Kücherer, C., Jung, M., Jahn, F., Schaaf, M., Tahar, K., Paech, B., Winter, A.: System analysis of information management. In: Informatik 2015, volume LNI P-246, pp. 783–796 (2015)
25. Power, D.J.: What are the features of a document-driven DSS? Technical report, DSS News (2011). Accessed 08 Aug 2016
26. Van Solingen, R., Basili, V., Caldiera, G., Rombach, H.D.: Goal question metric (GQM) approach. In: Marciniak, J.J. (ed.) Encyclopedia of Software Engineering. Wiley, Hoboken (2002)
27. Runeson, P., Höst, M.: Guidelines for conducting and reporting case study research in software engineering. Empirical Softw. Eng. **14**, 131–164 (2009)

Feature Model as a Design-pattern-based Service Contract for the Service Provider in the Service Oriented Architecture

Akram Kamoun[1(✉)], Mohamed Hadj Kacem[1], Ahmed Hadj Kacem[1], and Khalil Drira[2]

[1] National School of Engineers of Sfax, University of Sfax, Sfax, Tunisia
{akram.kamoun,mohamed.hadjkacem}@redcad.org, ahmed.hadjkacem@fsegs.rnu.tn
[2] Université de Toulouse, CNRS, Toulouse, France
khalil@laas.fr

Abstract. In Service Oriented Architecture (SOA), many feature modeling approaches of Service Provider (SP) have been proposed, notably: the two widely used service contracts WSDL and WADL. By studying these approaches, we found that they suffer from several problems, notably: they only work for specific communication technologies (e.g., SOAP or REST) and they do not explicitly model SOA Design Pattern (DPs) and their compounds. One major benefit of using a DP or a compound DP is to develop SPs with proven design solutions. In this paper, in order to overcome these problems, we propose an approach that integrates Software Product Line (SPL) techniques in the development of SPs. Essentially, we propose a Feature Model (FM), which is the defacto standard for variability modeling in SPL, for the feature modeling of SP. This FM, named FM_{SP}, is designed as a DP-based service contract for SP that models different features including 16 SOA DPs and their compounds that are related to the service messaging category. Its objective to enable developers to generate fully functional, valid, DP-based and highly customized SPs for different communication technologies. Through a practical case study and a developed tool, we validate our FM_{SP} and demonstrate that it reduces the development costs (effort and time) of SPs.

Keywords: Service oriented architecture · Service provider
Service contract · Design pattern · Feature model
Software Product Line

1 Introduction

Service Oriented Architecture (SOA) is an architectural model that represents a distributed computing platform by considering services as the essential means through which a solution logic is implemented [9]. A service consists of a set of capabilities (i.e., operations) that are implemented in a Service Provider (SP)

© Springer International Publishing AG, part of Springer Nature 2018
S. Hammoudi et al. (Eds.): ICEIS 2017, LNBIP 321, pp. 239–264, 2018.
https://doi.org/10.1007/978-3-319-93375-7_12

and can be invoked by different Service Consumers (SCs). One of the main objectives of SOA is to promote loose coupling, reusability and interoperability of SCs and SPs. The latter can be customized to implement different features. In this paper, we focus on modeling the SP features notably the ones of services, capabilities, SOA Design Patterns (DPs) [10], and the three communication technologies Simple Object Access Protocol (SOAP), REpresentational State Transfer (REST) and Middleware Oriented Messaging (MOM) [5,14].

DPs are appropriate and proven design solutions that have been introduced by veteran problem solvers for specific problems in certain contexts. In the practice, it is frequent to implement a compound DP that represents a composition of a set of DPs that are applied together in order to solve a complex problem [10].

In the literature, many SP feature modeling approaches have been proposed [1,6,8,11,15,17,20–22,26,29,30] notably the two widely used service contracts: Web Services Description Language (WSDL) [6] and Web Application Description Language (WADL) [17]. These service contracts are represented with XML documents, with different notations, through which the features of the communication technologies SOAP and REST are modeled, respectively. It is important to note that the service contract represents a core part and one of the fundamental design principles in SOA [9]. Erl [9] says: *"the service contract represents a core part of a service's architecture and is a focal point during the service design process to the extent that a principle is dedicated to its customization"*. By studying these SP feature modeling approaches, we identify that they suffer from several problems, as follows:

[P.1] explicitly modeling the SOA DPs and compound DPs is not considered. This makes difficult the development of DP-based and complex SPs with proven design solutions. It should be noted that developing valid SOA DPs and compound DPs is not a straightforward and easy task and requires a solid core of expert knowledge [28]. Schmidt *et al.* [28] said: *"combining several patterns into a heterogeneous structure is complicated"*;

[P.2] only a limited set of features has been modeled. This prevents the development of complex SPs;

[P.3] there is a lack of solutions to generate fully functional SPs. The main reason is that, as reported by Parra and Joya [26] and Fantinato *et al.* [11], the features (e.g., input and output data) of capabilities and services are not modeled;

[P.4] there is a lack of solutions that model SP features independently of communication technologies. This is important to be able to generate SPs that support different communication technologies. For example, the features modeled in the service contracts WSDL and WADL are dependent on the SOAP and REST communication technologies, respectively;

[P.5] some communication technologies do not offer service contracts, notably the MOM. In this case, it would be not possible to benefit from the advantages of using service contracts;

[P.6] developing many separated service contracts can be needed to develop a SP. For example, if a given service in the SP supports the SOAP and

REST communication technologies, then this service should be implemented and accompanied with the two different service contracts WSDL and WADL, respectively. This can decrease the governance of the SP and can make difficult for SP developers to implement SP features. Also, it can make difficult for SC developers to discover the features that are offered by the SP (e.g., to discover the supported communication technologies of SP);

[P.7] each SP feature modeling approach (e.g., WSDL and WADL) uses its own notation even to model the same features (e.g., input and output data features). This can lead to misinterpretation and difficulty to understand SP features, and reduces the efficiency of the reusability design principle [9] in the SP feature modeling.

In order to overcome these problems, we introduce in this paper, an approach that uses Software Product Line (SPL) [27] techniques for the feature modeling and the mass-customization of SPs in SOA. Essentially, we propose a Feature Model (FM) [7], named FM_{SP}, that is designed as a DP-based service contract for the SP feature modeling. This FM expresses 72 features including 16 SOA DPs that are related to the service messaging category (see chapter "Service Messaging Patterns" in [10]). This category provides various techniques for processing and coordinating data exchanges between services. One of the main challenges tackled in this work is to design this FM_{SP} in a way that it ensures deriving valid compounds of these 16 SOA DPs and valid SPs accordingly. The objective of the proposed FM_{SP} is to enable developers to generate fully functional, valid, DP-based and highly customized SPs for different communication technologies (SOAP, REST and MOM).

The contribution proposed in this paper extends our earlier work [23], which has been published as a conference paper in *ICEIS'2017*. Principally, we extend the earlier proposed FM_{SP} with other 26 features, we introduce some revision and enhancements to it to be able to derive more complex SPs, and we discuss it in more details. The objectives of these newly added features are twofolds. First, they allow to generate more complex SPs. In particular, we add modeling the `Messaging metadata DP` [10] which is an essential DP for the other modeled DPs. Second, they take into consideration all the required information that must be discovered by SC developers in order to develop SCs which can communicate correctly with all the possible SPs that can be derived from FM_{SP}.

The rest of this paper is structured as follows. In Sect. 2, we provide a brief overview of the FM. In Sect. 3, we introduce our approach including our FM_{SP}. In Sect. 4, we evaluate our approach through a practical case study. In Sect. 5, we discuss some related works. This paper is concluded in Sect. 6.

2   A Brief Overview of the Feature Model

One increasing trend in application development is the need to develop multiple and customized applications instead of just a single individual application. The main reason is that, because of the cost and time constraints, it is not possible for developers to realize a new application from scratch for each new project, and so software reuse must be increased. The Software Product Line (SPL) [27] offers software reusing solutions to these not quite new, but increasingly challenging, problems to enable the mass-customization of applications. It relies on the variability modeling of the application artifacts (e.g., source code and design) to be able to generate customized applications. The variability consists in the ability of an artifact to be customized or configured in a particular context. The Feature Model (FM) [7] is the defacto standard for variability modeling in SPL. Its objective is to model the legal combination of the SPL features to generate customized applications.

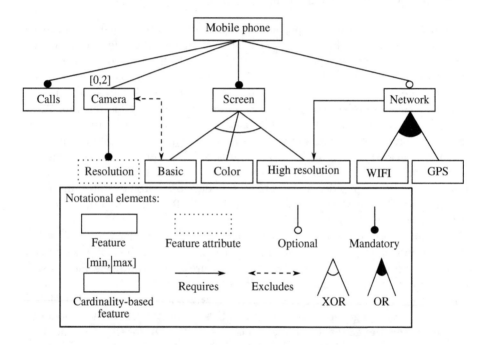

Fig. 1. Example of a feature model for mobile phone.

In Fig. 1, we present an example of a FM for mobile phone. The structure of the FM is a rooted tree of features that can be defined through different notational elements. Many FM metamodels [7,24] have been proposed in the literature that offer different notational elements. We rely on the FM metamodel of Czarnecki et al. [7] because its notational elements fit well and are necessary in our work. In Fig. 3, we present these notational elements that will be briefly presented in the following. The *feature* can be either *mandatory* or *optional*. The *feature attribute* allows to add an attribute value to specify extra-functional information for features. The *cardinality-based feature* [*min, max*] defines the lower and upper bounds of instances of a given feature. In our example, a mobile phone can have from 0 to 2 instances of the feature `Camera`. Each instance has the mandatory feature attribute `Resolution` that must be valued by the developer in order to set the camera resolution. The feature constraints *"requires"* and *"excludes"* permit to define inclusion and exclusion constraints between features. The *feature group XOR* $[1,1]$ allows selecting exactly one out of its child features which can be called as alternative exclusive features. The *feature group OR* $[1,n]$ allows selecting one or many of its child features which can be called as alternative inclusive features.

In order to derive and generate a customized application from a FM, a developer needs to derive a model that is a specialization of this FM. Specialization is a refinement process that allows the elimination of some variability information from a FM. Czarnecki *et al.* [7] introduce several specialization ways, such as: refining a cardinality-based feature $[min, max]$, selecting a required feature, deselecting an unwanted feature and assigning a feature attribute value. If all the variability of the derived model has been resolved by the developer (i.e., all of its features are mandatory), then this model is called Application Model (AM).

3   Contribution

In this section, we present our contribution. First, we present an overview of our approach. Second, we provide its benefits. Third, we lead a rigorous discussion of the features and constraints that have been modeled in the proposed FM_{SP}.

3.1   Approach Overview

In order to overcome the problems that have been enumerated in the introduction **P.1**, **P.2**, **P.3**, **P.4**, **P.5**, **P.6** and **P.7**, we propose an approach that consists in developing an SPL, named SPL_{SP}, for the feature modeling and the mass-customization of SPs. In Fig. 2, we introduce an overview of our approach including its implementation steps that will be presented in the following.

In the **first step**, the SPL developer realizes a FM, named FM_{SP}, for the SP feature modeling. In this FM, we propose that anything that is required to develop SPs is modeled as a feature. For example, services, capabilities, communication technologies and Design Patterns (DPs) are modeled as features. In Fig. 3, we present the proposed FM_{SP} which will be discussed in detail in Sect. 3.3. This FM is design to be a DP-based service contract for SP. It models 72 SP features including 16 SOA DPs [10] and the three communication technologies SOAP, REST and MOM. In Table 1, the descriptions of all of these features are presented and the DPs are illustrated with a color. We recall that the 16 studied DPs are related to the service messaging category (see chapter "Service Messaging Patterns" in [10]). The objective of the proposed FM_{SP} is to enable developers to generate fully functional, valid, DP-based and highly customized SPs. We recall that this FM_{SP} extends our earlier work [23] as mentioned in the introduction. Also, some contents of Table 1 have been reused from this same earlier work.

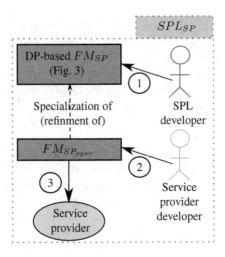

Fig. 2. Approach overview.

Developing SOA DPs and valid compound DPs is not a straightforward and easy task and requires a solid core of expert knowledge [28]. Mathematically, there exist 2^{16} compound DPs that represent the existence or the non-existence of the 16 studied DPs. However, not all of these compound DPs are valid. For example, in order to use the `Event-driven messaging` DP, it is necessary to use in conjunction the `Service callback` DP (see Table 1). Hence, if a given compound DP includes the `Event-driven messaging` DP but omits the `Service callback` DP, then this compound DP is invalid. One of the main challenges tackled in this work is to identify and model the valid compound DPs in our FM_{SP}. In this context, it is crucial to identify and model the constraints between DPs in FM_{SP} (see Sect. 3.3). We note that Erl [10] presents several relationships between these DPs. However, he illustrates them in many dispersed and not standardized diagrams. This makes difficult to properly identify their constraints.

In the **second Step**, in order to derive a SP, a developer needs to specialize (i.e., refine) a FM, named $FM_{SP_{spec}}$, from FM_{SP} (essentially by selecting and deselecting features). The $FM_{SP_{spec}}$ has two objectives. The *first objective* is allowing to define the features that the SP developer wants to implement in his/her SP. The *second objective* is permitting SC developers to discover the optional features offered by the SP. For example, let us suppose that the feature `Direct authentication` DP (see Table 1) is modeled as optional in $FM_{SP_{spec}}$ and in the SP accordingly. In this context, the SC developers can discover from $FM_{SP_{spec}}$ that they have the choice to provide or not credentials authentication, to use this feature, when developing their SCs to be able to communicate with this SP.

In our previous work [23], in order to derive a SP, we have proposed to instantiate an AM from FM_{SP}. This allows certainly to consider the *first objective*. However, the *second objective* cannot be respected because an AM can only contain mandatory features (i.e., cannot include optional features). This is why we propose, in this paper, to refine a FM ($FM_{SP_{spec}}$) from FM_{SP} in order to respect these two objectives.

In the **third Step**, an automatic model to code transformation operation will transform $FM_{SP_{spec}}$ to the required SP. Afterwards, the SP developer can manually adapt the generated SP to implement his/her application requirements (e.g., defining the business logic of the SP).

In our approach, we propose, as a *principle*, that the $FM_{SP_{spec}}$ of the SP can be downloaded by the SC developers. The goal is to allow these developers to discover the supported features of this SP in order to implement SCs that can communicate correctly with it. In this context, our FM_{SP} is designed to include all the required features that must be discovered by SC developers so they can realize SCs which can communicate correctly with all the possible SPs that can be derived from this FM. To implement this *principle*, the FM_{SP} that has been proposed in [23] has been extended with other features which will be discussed in Sect. 3.3. We note that this *principle* is widely used by the service contracts WSDL [6] and WADL [17].

3.2   Benefits

Our FM_{SP} is designed to overcome the problems that have been enumerated in the introduction: **P.1**, **P.2**, **P.3**, **P.4**, **P.5**, **P.6** and **P.7**. We present in the following the benefits of our FM_{SP} and which problems they consider:

1. it relies on the FM notation which permits to efficiently model the features and complex constraints of the SP. Also, its graphical presentation can be easily interpreted to identify the features and constraints of SP. By using the FAMILIAR tool [4], we calculate that our FM_{SP} permits to derive a capability in the SP with 372904 different possible configurations. In order to derive a SP including its capabilities, a developer only needs to have basic knowledges about the features of FM_{SP} and to select the required ones in line with the constraints of this FM. This facilitates the mass-customization of SPs (considering Problems **P.2**, **P.3**, **P.4**, **P.5**, **P.6** and **P.7**);
2. it includes the required features and constraints to generate fully functional, valid, DP-based and highly customized SPs. This reduces the development costs (effort and time) of SPs (considering Problems **P.2**, **P.3**, **P.4**, **P.5** and **P.7**);
3. it is designed as a DP-based service contract for SP which is generic and independent of the communication technologies. It can be considered as a reference model [12] which reflects the variability of practical SP features (considering Problems **P.1**, **P.2**, **P.3**, **P.4**, **P.5**, **P.6** and **P.7**);
4. it models 16 DPs and their corresponding constraints. This permits to easily identify and derive only valid compound DPs. By using the FAMILIAR tool [4], we have calculated that FM_{SP} permits to derive 790 valid compound DPs from 2^{16} possible ones (considering Problem **P.1**);

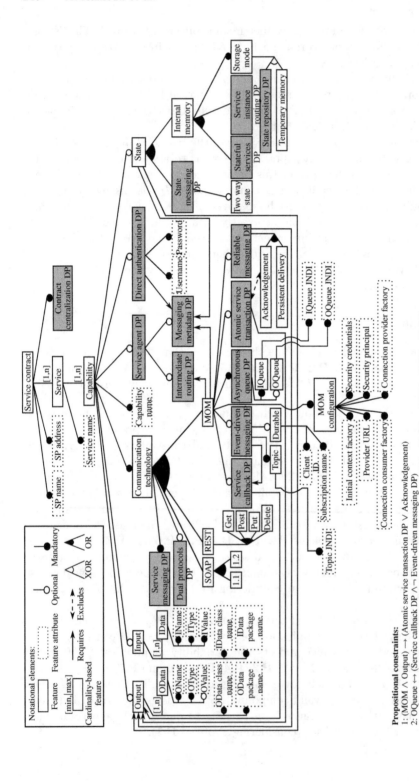

Fig. 3. Feature model for the service provider FM_{SP} (design pattern features are colored).

Propositional constraints:

1: (MOM ∧ Output) ⟶ (Atomic service transaction DP ∨ Acknowledgement)

2: OQueue ⟷ (Service callback DP ∧ ¬ Event-driven messaging DP)

3: Dual protocols DP ⟷ ((MOM ∧ REST) ∨ (MOM ∧ SOAP) ∨ (REST ∧ SOAP) ∨ (MOM ∧ REST ∧ SOAP))

5. many benefits can be enumerated when expressing DPs as features in our FM_{SP}. DPs are introduced by veteran problem solvers in order to provide appropriate and proven design solutions. A DP shows the right level of abstraction to describe a certain solution in a generic context, i.e., independently of the programming languages and platforms. It also has a major benefit of providing a common language which it is understandable by the developers instead of using terminologies related to a certain context. For example, simply saying the Event-driven messaging DP [10] is more efficient and easier than to explain it in details. Hence, integrating DPs in our FM_{SP} allows to ensure that the SPs that can be derived are based on proven solutions (considering Problems **P.1**, **P.2**, **P.3**, **P.4**, **P.5**, **P.6** and **P.7**).

3.3   Feature Model for the Service Provider FM_{SP}

In Fig. 3 and Table 1, we present our FM_{SP} and descriptions of its features. In this table, we highlight the feature attributes which represent the values that need to be given by the developer to derive a SP. Also, we propose to classify the features of FM_{SP} into several categories that are presented in the first column of this table. This help to better understand and interpret the proposed FM_{SP}. In the following subsections, we discuss in detail one-by-one the features and constraints of each category, notably the ones of the modeled 16 DPs. It is important to note that these features and constraints have been identified from theoretical and practical conducted studies that are essentially based on these works [2,9,10,14,18,19].

Service Provider Information Features. The feature Service contract represents the root of FM_{SP}. The feature attributes SP name and SP address need to be valued by the SP developer to specify the name and address of his/her SP. The values of these feature attributes will allow the SC developers to realize SCs that can communicate correctly with this SP.

We express the feature Contract centralization DP as mandatory for two reasons. First, the FM_{SP} is designed as a centralized service contract that models the SP features. Second, this FM will be used by SCs as the sole entry point to discover the features supported by the SP in order to correctly communicate with it. Implementing this DP permits to avoid developing different and separated service contracts to model the SP features which can be problematic as shown in Problems **P.6** and **P.7** in the introduction.

Services and Capabilities Features. The cardinality-based feature Service $[1, n]$ allows the developer to implement 1 to n instances of services in his/her SP. Each instance has a name that is modeled by its child feature attribute Service name. It also has a cardinality-based feature Capability $[1, n]$. The latter allows the developer to implement 1 to n instances of capabilities in each service instance. The other features of FM_{SP} are modeled as child features to

Table 1. Descriptions of the features of FM_{SP} (design pattern features are colored).

Category	Feature name	Feature attribute	Description
	Service contract	-	Root feature
SP information	Contract central-ization DP	-	Gathering the SP features within the service contract so it will be used by the SC as the sole entry point to communicate with the SP
	SP name	+	Name of the SP
	SP address	+	Address of the SP
	Service $[1, n]$	-	Services of the SP
	Service name	+	Name of a given service
	Capability $[1, n]$	-	Capabilities of a given service
	Capability name	+	Name of a given capability
	Input	-	Input data of a given capability
	IData $[1, n]$	-	Gathering the input data features
	IName	+	Name of a given input data
	IType	+	Type of a given input data (e.g., String)
	IValue	+	An input value that will be given by the SC to invoke a given capability
Service and capability	IData class name	+	Name of the class that encapsulates the input data names and types
	IData package name	+	Name of the package that includes the input data classes
	Output	-	Output data of a given capability
	OData $[1, n]$	-	Gathering the output data features
	OName	+	Name of a given output data
	OType	+	Type of a given output data
	OValue	+	Output value of a given capability that will be returned to the SC
	OData class name	+	Name of the class that encapsulates the output data names and types

(Continued)

Table 1. (*Continued*)

OData package name	+	Name of the package that includes the output data classes	
Service messaging DP	-	Using a messaging-based communication between the SC and SP to remove the need of persistent connections (e.g., remote procedure call binary connections) and to reduce coupling requirements	
Dual protocols DP	-	Configuring a given capability to support two or more communication technologies. This allows to accommodate different application requirements	
Communication technology	-	Gathering communication technologies	
REST	-	REST communication technology	
Get	-	HTTP get method for REST	
Post	-	HTTP post method for REST	
Put	-	HTTP put method for REST	
Delete	-	HTTP delete method for REST	
SOAP	-	SOAP communication technology	
1.1	-	SOAP version 1.1	
1.2	-	SOAP version 1.2	
MOM	-	Middleware Oriented Messaging (MOM) communication technology	
MOM configuration	-	Gathering the MOM configuration information	
Initial context factory	+	Initial context that is required to access to the MOM via a Java Naming and Directory Interface (JNDI)	
Provider URL	+	MOM address that is required to access to this MOM	
Connection provider factory	+	Object name that encapsulates a set of MOM connection configuration parameters that will be used by the SP to access to this MOM	
Connection consumer factory	+	Object name that encapsulates a set of MOM connection configuration parameters that will be used by the SC to access to this MOM	
Security credentials	+	Username that is required to access to the MOM	
Security principal	+	Password that is required to access to the MOM	

(Communication)

Table 1. (*Continued*)

Asynchronous queue DP	-	Deploying an intermediary MOM allowing the SP and SC to asynchronously communicate and to independently process messages by remaining temporally decoupled
IQueue	-	Input queue that implements the `Asynchronous queue DP` to handle the asynchronous incoming SC messages
OQueue	-	Output queue that implements the `Asynchronous queue DP` to handle the asynchronous outgoing SP messages
IQueue JNDI	+	A JNDI that allows to discover, look up and communicate with `IQueue`
OQueue JNDI	+	A JNDI that allows to discover, look up and communicate with `OQueue`
Event-driven messaging DP	-	Asynchronously sending the response messages of the publisher (i.e., SP), when ready, to its corresponding subscribers (i.e., SCs) through the MOM
Service callback DP	-	Redirecting the SP response messages to a callback address that can be different of the requester SC address
Topic	-	Topic that implements the `Event-driven messaging DP`
Topic JNDI	+	A JNDI that allows to discover, look up and communicate with `Topic`
Atomic service transaction DP	-	Treating a group of the SP response messages as a single work unit. The latter is wrapped in a transaction with a rollback feature that resets all actions and changes if the exchanging messages fails
Reliable messaging DP	-	Adding a reliability mechanism to the SP response messages in order to ensure message delivery. This mechanism relies on acknowledging the SP messages and persisting them in a data store
Persistent delivery	-	Persisting the SP messages in a data store so they are not lost if the MOM fails. Therefore, we ensure that the SP messages are delivered to the SC
Acknowledgement	-	The MOM acknowledges the SP about its messages that have been received by the SC
Durable	-	A durable MOM stores the messages of the publisher (i.e., SP) for the subscribers (i.e., SCs) if the latter disconnect. Hence, we ensure that, upon reconnecting, the subscribers will receive all these messages
Client ID	+	An identifiant that must be given by the SC to use the feature `Durable` of MOM

Security and reliability

Table 1. (*Continued*)

	Subscription name	+	A subscription name that must be given by the SC to use the feature `Durable` of MOM
	Direct authentication DP	-	Requiring that the SCs must provide authentication credentials (username and password) to invoke a capability
	Username	+	A username that must be given by the SC for authentication
	Password	+	A password that must be given by the SC for authentication
Agent	Service agent DP	-	Deferring some logic (e.g., logging messages) from services to event-driven programs to reduce the size and performance strain of services
	Intermediate routing DP	-	Dynamically routing messages through a service agent that relies on an intermediary routing logic
	Messaging metadata DP	-	Supplementing the messages headers, through service agents, with metadata in order to share activity-specific logic between SC and SP.
	State	-	Gathering techniques that handle the state data of capabilities
	Internal memory	-	Storing the state data in the SP internal memory
	Stateful services DP	-	Managing and storing state data by intentionally stateful utility services
	Service instance routing DP	-	Allowing a given SC to communicate with the same instance of a given service to retain its state
	Storage mode	-	Gathering the modes of how the state data are stored
State	Temporary memory	-	Storing the state data in a temporary memory in the SP
	State repository DP	-	Deferring storing state data from a temporary memory to a state repository in the SP. The objective is to alleviate services from having to unnecessarily retain state data in memory for extended periods
	State messaging DP	-	Delegating the storage of state data to the SP response messages instead to the SP internal memory. The objective is the same as the `State repository DP`
	Two way state	-	Configuring both the SP and SC to delegate the storage of state data in their outgoing messages

each capability instance. Hence, it would be possible to configure the variability of each capability instance differently and independently. In FM_{SP}, each capability can be configured with 372904 different possible configurations, in particular, with different 790 valid compounds of the 16 modeled DPs.

Each capability has a name that is modeled by the feature attribute `Capability name`. The optional features `Input` and `Output` and their children permit to model the information about the input and output data of each capability. If these features have been omitted by the developer when deriving a given capability in his/her SP, then this capability will not accept any input data from SCs and will not return any result. In this case, the signature of this capability will be: `void capabilityName()`.

The cardinality-based features `IData` $[1, n]$ and `OData` $[1, n]$ specify the count of the input and output data of each capability. These features contain in particular the feature attributes `IValue` and `OValue`, respectively. The sole objective of the mandatory feature attribute `IValue` is to inform the SCs that they must provide an input value in the body of their request messages to invoke a given capability. The optional feature attribute `OValue` gives the choice to the SP developer to specify a static result of capabilities. In fact, capabilities often have dynamic results that are defined in the business logic of capabilities. In this case, the feature attribute `OValue` can be omitted by the developer when deriving his/her SP. However, this feature attribute can be useful to test if a given capability, with a given configuration, can be invoked correctly by SCs.

To implement a SP, it is important to permit the SP capabilities to take and return objects (classes instances) as input and output data. In this context, the classes that encapsulate these data need to be implemented as serializable so their objects can be included in the SP and SC messages. We note that the use of serializable classes is widely supported by the programming languages, like Java and C#. In the other hand, to implement a SC that can communicate correctly with this SP, these classes must be also implemented in this SC by using the same names and packages that have been defined in the SP [16]. In this context, as a requirement, the class and package names that are defined in the SP must be discovered by the SC developers. This requirement has been taking into consideration by modeling the mandatory feature attributes `IData class name`, `OData class name`, `IData package name` and `OData package name` in FM_{SP}. The values of these feature attributes must be defined by the SP developer to derive a valid SP and to allow SC developers to discover them.

Communication Features. The SC needs to send a request message to the SP in order to invoke a capability. If this capability returns a response message, then the communication type is called two-way. Otherwise, it is called one-way. In FM_{SP}, selecting or omitting the feature `Output` when deriving a SP will induce using the two-way or one-way communication types, respectively.

In FM_{SP}, we model the feature `Service messaging` DP as mandatory because the three modeled communication technologies `SOAP`, texttt`REST` and `MOM` are messaging-based, and the modeled DPs are related to the service messaging category (see chapter "Service Messaging Patterns" in [10]). Erl [10] reports that this DP is one of the most fundamental DPs because it permits to promote the loose-coupling and interoperability design principles [9] by reducing the coupling requirements between the SC and SP.

The feature `Dual protocols` DP requires that a given capability must support two or more communication technologies and vice-versa. The third propositional constraint defined in FM_{SP} implements this requirement. Our FM allows to implement a capability that can support the communication technology `SOAP` with versions `1.1` or `1.2` or both. Also, a capability can be implemented to support the communication technology `REST` with one or more HTTP methods. This allows to accommodate different application requirements for each capability.

The features `SOAP` and `REST` rely on a synchronous communication for the message exchanging between the SC and SP. The problem of the synchronous communication is that it forces processing overhead in SC and SP because they must wait and continue to consume resources (e.g., memory) until they finish the message exchanging [10]. To overcome this problem, the asynchronous communication is used as a solution which is implemented through the feature `MOM` in our work. In this context, because the DP features `Service callback` DP, `Asynchronous queue` DP and `Event-driven messaging` DP are dedicated for an asynchronous communication, we define them as child features of the feature `MOM`.

In the `MOM`, the SC messages are always carried on by an asynchronous queue that reflected by the feature `IQueue` which is an implementation of the feature `Asynchronous queue` DP [14]. This is the reason why we define these features `IQueue` and `Asynchronous queue` DP as mandatory in FM_{SP}. The feature `Asynchronous queue` DP can be configured with two different ways when deriving a SP. The first way consists in selecting the feature `Asynchronous queue` DP in conjunction with the feature `Service callback` DP and omitting the feature `Event-driven messaging` DP. In this case, the SC and SP messages will be handled by two different asynchronous queues that are modeled respectively by the features `IQueue` and `OQueue`. The second way consists in selecting the feature `Asynchronous queue` DP and omitting the features `Service callback` DP and `Event-driven messaging` DP. In this case, all SC and SP messages are handled by the same asynchronous queue that is modeled with the feature `IQueue`. These two ways are taken into account in our work by modeling `OQueue` as an optional feature, by defining the second propositional constraint in FM_{SP} and by modeling a "requires" constraint from the feature `Service callback` DP to the feature `Output`.

In order to implement the feature `Event-driven messaging` DP, we rely on the asynchronous topic [14] which is reflected by the feature `Topic`. The latter is used to asynchronously redirect the response messages of the SP to its SC callback addresses. To permit this redirection, we define, in FM_{SP}, a "requires" constraint from the feature `Event-driven messaging` DP to the feature `Service callback` DP.

We model the child features attributes of the feature MOM configuration, and the feature attributes IQueue JNDI, OQueue JNDI and Topic JNDI as mandatory in FM_{SP} for two reasons. First, they must be valued to implement a MOM in the SP. Second, they represent all the required information that must be discovered by SCs so they can communicate with the MOM of the SP.

Security and Reliability Features. It is common to use the features Atomic service transaction DP and Reliable messaging DP in conjunction with the MOM to implement a reliable asynchronous communication [10]. Hence, we express these features as children of the feature MOM. Since the MOM communication technology ensures a loosely coupled and an asynchronous communication between the SC and SP, then it should inform the SC and SP if their outgoing messages have been successfully received. In this context, the MOM should use either the features Acknowledgement or Atomic service transaction DP [10], [14]. This requirement is considered in our work by defining these two features as mutually exclusive and by defining the first propositional constraint in FM_{SP}.

The features Atomic service transaction DP and Reliable messaging DP can be only applied for the SP response messages, i.e., for the two-way communication type (see Table 1). Thus, we define "requires" constraints from these features to the feature Output.

In FM_{SP}, the feature MOM can be configured to support the feature Durable. The latter has the Client ID and Subscription name as mandatory child feature attributes. Their sole objective is to inform the SCs that they must value them in their request messages to use the feature Durable.

The objective of feature attributes Username and Password is to inform the SCs that they must provide a username and a password, as metadata, in their request messages to invoke a given capability when using the Direct authentication DP. In this context, we define a "requires" constraint from the feature Direct authentication DP to the feature Messaging metadata DP in FM_{SP}.

Agent Features. The DP features Intermediate routing DP and Messaging metadata DP are implemented through a service agent as shown in Table 1. Thus, we define them as optional child features of the feature Service agent DP in FM_{SP}.

In contrast of SOAP and REST, the SC request messages which are dedicated to MOM do not explicitly contain information about the capability and service that the SC wants to invoke. As a consequence, it would be not possible to invoke the required capability and service. As a solution, we propose, to implement the feature Intermediate routing DP which exploits the metadata (Messaging metadata DP) presented in the SC request messages to dynamically routing these messages to the required capability and service. To support this dynamic routing, we define, in our FM_{SP}, "requires" constraints from the feature MOM to the features Intermediate routing DP and Messaging metadata DP.

From our study on SOA DPs [10], we notice that the four features Service callback DP, Event-driven messaging DP, Atomic service transaction DP and Reliable messaging DP require the feature Messaging metadata DP. This requirement is already considered in our FM_{SP} because (1) we have already defined these four features as optional children to the feature MOM and we have already defined a "requires" constraint from the feature MOM to the feature Messaging metadata DP.

State Features. Erl [10] reports that the service state DPs State messaging DP, Service instance routing DP, Stateful services DP and State repository DP can be implemented in conjunction in the SP. This requirement is implemented in our FM_{SP} by defining these DPs as alternative inclusive features.

In one hand, the feature State messaging DP works by delegating the storage of state data to the SP messages, as *metadata*. In the other hand, the features Stateful services DP and Service instance routing DP work by supplementing the SP messages with a specific identifier (session or service instance identifiers) for each SC, as *metadata*. These identifiers need to be incorporated in the SC messages so the SP can use them to manage correctly the state of their corresponding SCs. In this context, as a requirement, the three features State messaging DP, Stateful services DP and Service instance routing DP need to rely on the features Messaging metadata DP and Output to be able to supplement the SP messages with *metadata*. In order to implement this requirement, given that these three features are modeled as alternative inclusive children of the feature State in FM_{SP}, we define "requires" constraints from the feature State to the features Messaging metadata DP and Output.

4   Evaluation

In order to show the merits and evaluate our approach including our FM_{SP} (see Figs. 2 and 3) in practice, we propose to use the case study of the Integrated Air Defense (IAD) (see Fig. 4 [23]). The IAD is a command and control compound of geographically dispersed force elements already in peace time as well as in crisis. In Fig. 4, we illustrate 17 force elements which are grouped into three main forces: ground force (command and control system, radars, anti-aircrafts and infantry), air force (drones, helicopters and jet aircrafts) and maritime force (aircraft carriers and submarines). These force elements communicate with services to achieve their missions. One main requirement must be satisfied to realize this IAD case study:

IAD Requirement. *Each of the 17 force elements illustrated in the IAD case study is a SP that is responsible to implement its own features.*

As illustrated in the introduction (see Problems **P.1**, **P.2**, **P.3**, **P.4**, **P.5**, **P.6** and **P.7**), the SP feature modeling approaches that have been proposed in the literature [1,6,8,11,15,17,20–22,26,29,30] notably the SOA traditional service

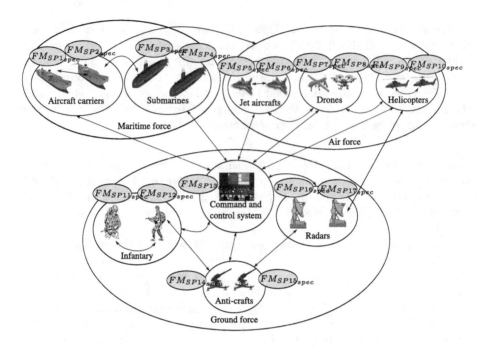

Fig. 4. Case study of the integrated air defense.

contracts WSDL [6] and WADL [17] suffer from several problems to develop SPs. This prevents to efficiently realize **IAD Requirement**. In order to overcome these problems and to efficiently realize **IAD Requirement**, we propose deriving for each SP of the 17 IAD force elements a specific $FM_{SP_{spec}}$ (e.g., see Fig. 5) from our FM_{SP} (see Fig. 3). For example, in Fig. 4, the $FM_{SP13_{spec}}$ includes the SP features of the command and control system force element.

Using our FM_{SP} has several benefits as mentioned in Sect. 3.2 notably it facilitates the mass-customization of SPs. This is important especially when we have numerous SPs to develop which it is the case of our IAD case study (17 SPs to develop). Pohl *et al.* [27] show, from empirical investigations, that developing a SPL allows to reduce the development costs of systems if there are more than three or four systems to develop which it is our case (17 systems).

In fact, Erl [10] reports that the U.S. Department of Defense (DoD) has decided to plan and manage its business IT (Information Technology) via an architectural approach based upon SOA. The IAD system presented in Fig. 4 is a part of the DoD's business IT. He also reports that due to the scale, complexity and diversity of the DoD's business IT, the DoD developed a strategy with guiding principles which relies on the SOA DPs [10]. In this context, because our FM_{SP} relies on the SOA DPs, it can help to contribute to develop this DoD's business IT.

In Fig. 5, we present an example of a derived $FM_{SP_{spec}}$ from FM_{SP} for the command and system IAD force element (see Fig. 4). It is possible that this

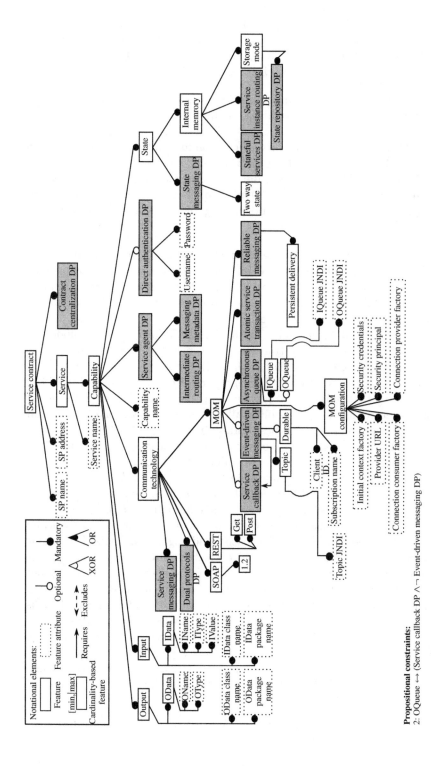

Fig. 5. Example of a derived feature model of a service provider $FM_{SP_{spec}}$ from FM_{SP} (design pattern features are colored).

$FM_{SP_{spec}}$ contains different services and capabilities (see Fig. 3). For the sake of simplicity, we derive this $FM_{SP_{spec}}$ to contain a single `Service` which it is composed of a single `Capability`. The latter has a single `Input` data and a single `Output` data. Overall, it contains 66 features, notably:

- features that forms a valid compound of the modeled 16 DPs;
- features that define the information about the SP and its `Service` and `Capability`;
- features that define the variability of the communication technologies that can be used by SCs to invoke the `Capability`. We note that the `SOAP` version `1.2`, `REST` with the HTTP methods `Get` and `Post`, and `MOM` have been selected;
- optional features like the `Direct authentication` DP, `Service callback` DP and `Event-driven messaging` DP that can be used or not by SCs to invoke the `Capability`.

The values of the feature attributes defined in $FM_{SP_{spec}}$ are given in Table 2. Some feature attributes allow to define information about the SP, its capability and service, and the MOM configuration, like `SP address`, `Capability name` and `Provider URL`. Some others are dedicated to be valued by SCs in order to invoke the SP capabilities like `IValue`.

We developed a tool [3] that relies on the Apache Velocity[1] tool (a model-to-code template engine) in order to transform a given $FM_{SP_{spec}}$ to the artifacts of the corresponding SP. Our tool relies on Java EE technologies. It generates SPs based on the Enterprise Service Bus (ESB) Switchyard [2]. The latter is a recent free software ESB that relies on the service component architecture [25] which is a technology-neutral assembly capability allowing the composition of services in SPs. It includes different technologies, notably the HornetQ [14] to implement the feature `MOM`, Apache CXF [5] to implement the features `SOAP` and `REST`, and Apache Camel [19] to implement DPs. These technologies are integrated on demand in the generated SP depending on the features of $FM_{SP_{spec}}$. Our tool also relies on the SPL tool FAMILIAR [4] to develop and manage the FM_{SP} and $FM_{SP_{spec}}$ (e.g., to check that $FM_{SP_{spec}}$ is a specialization of FM_{SP}).

From the $FM_{SP_{spec}}$ illustrated in Fig. 5, our tool succeeds to automatically generate a fully functional, valid, DP-based and highly customized SP. This generated SP has been successfully deployed in the JBoss Java server without any further manual interventions. It should be noted that the SP developer needs to manually adapt the generated SP to implement his/her application requirements (e.g., defining the business logic of the SP). The generated SP is composed of 334 Java code instructions and five XMLs[2]. These XMLs permit to configure the SOAP and MOM communication technologies and to configure the ESB Switchyard. The time required to derive the $FM_{SP_{spec}}$ (see Fig. 5) and generate its corresponding SP is one minute. By using the SOA traditional service contracts WSDL and WADL, and by relying on the tools that are offered

---

[1] http://velocity.apache.org.
[2] https://github.com/MSPL4SOA/MSPL4SOA-tool/tree/master/generated_SPs_SCs/conf/sp.

Table 2. The values of the feature attributes of $FM_{SP_{spec}}$ that is illustrated in Fig. 5.

	Feature attribute	Value
	SP name	SP_command
	SP address	http://localhost:8080/SP_command
	Service name	Personal
	Capability name	login
	IName	id
	IType	String
SP information, service and capability	IData class name	Session
	IData package name	SP_command.input
	OName	isLogged
	OType	Boolean
	OData class name	SessionResponse
	OData package name	SP_command.output
	Initial context factory	org.jboss.naming.remote.client.InitialContextFactory
	Provider URL	remote://localhost:4447
	Connection provider factory	ConnectionFactory
MOM configuration	Connection consumer factory	RemoteConnectionFactory
	Security principal	guest
	Security credentials	guest_PassWorD
	IQueue JNDI	SP_command_in_queue_Personal_login
	OQueue JNDI	SP_command_out_queue_Personal_login
	Topic JNDI	SP_command_topic_Personal_login
	IValue	It needs to be valued in the SC
	Username	It needs to be valued in the SC
SC	Password	It needs to be valued in the SC
	Client ID	It needs to be valued in the SC
	Subscription name	It needs to be valued in the SC

by the ESB Switchyard, we require more than 20 min to develop the same SP and we need many manual interventions. Hence, we can say that using our FM_{SP} reduces the development costs (effort and time) of SPs.

In order to ensure that all the possible SPs, including the possible 790 compound DPs, that can be derived from our FM_{SP} are valid and fully functional, we implement in our tool [3] an automatic test functionality that generates all the possible SPs from FM_{SP}. These generated SPs have been successfully deployed in the JBoss Java server without errors and any further manual interventions. Hence, we can assume that these SPs are valid and fully functional.

5   Related Work

In the literature, many works have been proposed to model the features and variability of SP and DPs [1,6,8,11,15,17,20,26,29,30]. In Table 3, we present these works and compare them with our approach notably with our FM_{SP} (see Fig. 3) by relying on the following criteria:

- which feature modeling approach is used?
- do the SP features are modeled?
- do the modeled features include the required information that need to be discovered by the SC developers in order to realize SCs that can communicate correctly with a given SP?

Table 3. Comparing our approach notably our FM_{SP} with related works (Generic: modeling more than two communication technologies; OOP: Object Oriented Pattern; DREP: Distributed Real-time and Embedded Pattern).

Work	Feature modeling approach	SP	SC	SOA Communication tech. Features	Variability	Design pattern Single	Compound	Type	Generated code
WSDL [6]	XML	+	+	SOAP	+	-	-	-	Fully
WADL [17]	XML	+	+	REST	+	-	-	-	Fully
Wada et al. [30]	FM	+	-	+ (n/a)	+	-	-	-	Semi
Fantinato et al. [11]	FM	+	-	SOAP	+	-	-	-	Semi
Ed-douibi et al. [8]	EMF	+	-	REST	+	-	-	-	Semi
Parra and Joya [26]	FM	+	-	Generic	-	-	-	-	Semi
Kajsa and Návrat [20]	FM	-	-	-	-	+	-	OOP	Semi
Street Fant et al. [15]	FM	-	-	-	-	+	+	DREP	-
Seinturier et al. [29], [1]	FM	+	-	Generic	+	-	-	-	Semi
Our approach	FM	+	+	Generic	+	+	+	SOA	Fully

– which communication technologies are modeled?
– does the variability of the communication technology features is modeled?
– do the DP features are modeled?
– does modeling compound DPs is considered?
– which DP type is modeled?
– does the code generation is supported. If it is the case, does the generated code is semi or fully functional?

From this table, we can notice that, in contrast with the related works, our FM_{SP} supports all the criteria. To summarize, it permits to generate fully functional, valid, DP-based and highly customized SPs for different communication technologies (i.e., generic) while modeling the required features that need to be discovered by the SCs to communicate correctly with these SPs. In the following, we discuss the related works presented in this table by highlighting their major contributions and showing how they can be used to extend and enhance our FM_{SP} for potential future works.

WSDL [6] and WADL [17] are two widely used service contracts that model the SP features of the communication technologies SOAP and REST, respectively. Our FM_{SP} is designed to extend these service contracts so it would be possible to generate DP-based SPs for different communication technologies.

Wada *et al.* [30] propose a FM that models SP non-functional features. Although their FM includes communication features, it does not explicitly specify which communication technologies are supported. This is why we put the symbol "+ (n/a)" in Table 3. Their FM can be used to extend our FM_{SP} in order to support SP non-functional features.

Parra and Joya [26] propose a FM that expresses the SOAP, REST and EJB communication technology features. However, in contrast with our FM_{SP}, their FM does not model the variability of these communication technology features, i.e., it does not model their possible configurations. As an instance, the HTTP methods (post, get, put and delete) that can be used by REST and the versions of SOAP are not modeled. Fantinato *et al.* [11] elaborate a FM that models the features of the communication technology SOAP. These two FMs [26], [11], as reported by their authors, need to be extended with the features (e.g., input and output data) of capabilities and services of SP so they can generate fully functional SPs. This has been considered in our FM_{SP}.

Seinturier *et al.* [29],[1] propose a FM to model the features of their FraSCAti tool. The latter is a component framework and an implementation technology providing runtime support for the service component architecture [25] in SOA. Our FM_{SP} has a higher level of abstraction than their FM because it is based on generic SOA DPs that are independent to the implementation technologies. Their FM can be used in conjunction with ours to be able to generate highly customized SPs dedicated for specific implementation technologies.

Ed-douibi *et al.* [8] introduce EMF data models that are dedicated to express the features of the communication technology REST. These models can be used to extend our FM_{SP} with more REST features (e.g., security features).

Kajsa and Návrat [20] introduce a FM that models the features of the object oriented DPs [13]. The goal is to enable generating, on demand, the code of a specific DP. The advantage of our FM_{SP} is that it allows to generate the code of DPs and also of compound DPs.

Street Fant et al. [15] elaborate a FM that expresses the features of a set of distributed real-time and embedded DPs. For each DP, they elaborate UML diagrams (collaboration, interaction, component and state machine diagrams) to identify its variability and behavior. The objective is to generate customized DPs and compound DPs with customized diagrams. In our work, we focus on generating the code of SOA DPs rather than generating their UML diagrams. Their work can be useful in our approach to generate customized diagrams for SOA DPs.

6   Conclusion

In this paper, we have proposed an approach that consists in developing a Software Product Line (SPL) for the mass-customization of Service Provider (SP) in Service Oriented Architecture (SOA). Essentially, we have introduced a Feature Model (FM), named FM_{SP}, for the SP feature modeling. Its objective is to enable developers to generate fully functional, valid, DP-based and highly customized SPs for different communication technologies while modeling the required features that need to be discovered by the SCs to communicate correctly with these SPs. Our FM_{SP} is designed as a DP-based service contract for SP that models 72 features. In particular, it includes the features of the three communication technologies Simple Object Access Protocol (SOAP), REpresentational State Transfer (REST) and Middleware Oriented Messaging (MOM). It also includes the features of 16 SOA DPs that are related to the service messaging category. It is important to note that our FM_{SP} allows to derive only valid compounds from these DPs which is crucial to drive valid SPs. Based on the features and constraints that are modeled in FM_{SP}, we have calculated that it permits to derive 790 valid compound DPs from 2^{16} possible ones. Also, we have calculated that our FM_{SP} expresses 372904 possible configurations that can be used to derive a highly customized capability in the SP.

We have demonstrated through a practical case study and a developed tool, that our FM_{SP} is valid and permits to reduce the development costs (effort and time) of SPs. We have also shown the efficiency of our FM_{SP} compared with some SP feature modeling approaches that have been proposed in the literature, notably the two widely used service contracts Web Services Description Language (WSDL) and Web Application Description Language (WADL).

In future research, we plan to extend our FM_{SP} by other features, especially with security DPs, in order to generate more complex and secured SPs. Currently, we are working on developing an SPL, including a FM, that is dedicated for Service Consumer (SC). The objective is to enable SC developers to generate fully functional, valid, DP-based and highly customized SCs that can communicate correctly with all the possible SPs that can be derived from our FM_{SP}.

References

1. Feature model of FraSCAti. http://frascati.ow2.org/doc/1.4/ch12s02.html
2. Switchyard tool. http://switchyard.jboss.org
3. MSPL4SOA tool (2017). https://mspl4soa.github.io
4. Acher, M., Collet, P., Lahire, P., France, R.B.: FAMILIAR: a domain-specific language for large scale management of feature models. Sci. Comput. Program. **78**(6), 657–681 (2013)
5. Balani, N., Hathi, R.: Apache CXF Web Service Development. Packt Publishing, Birmingham (2009)
6. Chinnici, R., Moreau, J.J., Ryman, A., Weerawarana, S.: WSDL 2.0 (2007). https://www.w3.org/TR/wsdl20
7. Czarnecki, K., Helsen, S., Ulrich, E.: Staged configuration through specialization and multilevel configuration of feature models. Softw. Process Improv. Pract. **10**(2), 143–169 (2005)
8. Ed-douibi, H., Izquierdo, J.L.C., Gómez, A., Tisi, M., Cabot, J.: EMF-REST: generation of RESTful APIs from models. In: Proceedings of the 31st Annual ACM Symposium on Applied Computing (SAC 2016), Pisa, Italy, pp. 1446–1453 (2016)
9. Erl, T.: SOA Principles of Service Design. Prentice Hall, Upper Saddle River (2007)
10. Erl, T.: SOA Design Patterns. Prentice Hall, Upper Saddle River (2009)
11. Fantinato, M., Felgar, D.M.B., Maria, D.I.: WS-contract establishment with QOS: an approach based on feature modeling. Coop. Inf. Syst. **17**(03), 373–407 (2008)
12. Galster, M., Avgeriou, P., Tofan, D.: Constraints for the design of variability-intensive service-oriented reference architectures - an industrial case study. Inf. Softw. Technol. **55**(2), 428–441 (2013)
13. Gamma, E., Helm, R., Johnson, R., Vlissides, J.: Design Patterns: Elements of Reusable Object-Oriented Software. Addison-Wesley, Redwood City (1995)
14. Giacomelli, P.: HornetQ Messaging Developer's Guide. Packt Publishing, Birmingham (2012)
15. Gomaa, H., Street Fant, J., G Pettit IV, R.: A pattern-based modeling approach for software product line engineering. In: Proceedings of the 46th Hawaii International Conference on System Sciences (HICSS 2013), Maui, Hawaii, USA, pp. 4985–4994, January 2013
16. Goncalves, A.: Begining Java EE 7. Apress, New York (2013)
17. Hadley, M., Sun Microsystems: WADL (2009). https://www.w3.org/Submission/wadl
18. Hohpe, G., Woolf, B.: Enterprise Integration Patterns: Designing, Building, and Deploying Messaging Solutions. Addison-Wesley, Boston (2004)
19. Ibsen, C., Anstey, J.: Camel in Action. Manning Publications Corporation, New York (2011)
20. Kajsa, P., Návrat, P.: Design pattern support based on the source code annotations and feature models. In: Proceedings of the 38th International Conference on Current Trends in Theory and Practice of Computer Science on SOFtware SEMinar (SOFSEM 2012), Špindlerův Mlýn, Czech Republic, pp. 467–478, January 2012
21. Kamoun, A., Hadj Kacem, M., Hadj Kacem, A.: Feature model for modeling compound SOA design patterns. In: Proceedings of the 11th ACS/IEEE International Conference on Computer Systems and Applications (AICCSA 2014), Doha, Qatar, pp. 381–388, November 2014

22. Kamoun, A., Hadj Kacem, M., Hadj Kacem, A.: Multiple software product lines for software oriented architecture. In: Proceedings of the 25th IEEE International Conference on Enabling Technologies: Infrastructure for Collaborative Enterprises (WETICE 2016), Paris, France, pp. 56–61, June 2016

23. Kamoun, A., Hadj Kacem, M., Hadj Kacem, A., Drira, K.: Feature model based on design pattern for the service provider in the service oriented architecture. In: Proceedings of the 19th International Conference on Enterprise Information Systems (ICEIS 2017), Porto, Portugal, pp. 111–120, April 2017

24. Kang, K.C., Lee, H.: Variability modeling. In: Capilla, R., Bosch, J., Kang, K.C. (eds.) Systems and Software Variability Management: Concepts, Tools and Experiences, pp. 25–42. Springer, Heidelberg (2013). https://doi.org/10.1007/978-3-642-36583-6_2

25. Laws, S., Combellack, M., Feng, R., Mahbod, H., Nash, S.: Tuscany SCA in Action. Manning Publications Corporation, New York (2011)

26. Parra, C., Joya, D.: SPLIT: an automated approach for enterprise product line adoption through SOA. Internet Serv. Inf. Secur. **5**(1), 29–52 (2015)

27. Pohl, K., Böckle, G., Van Der Linden, F.: Software Product Line Engineering. Springer, Heidelberg (2005). https://doi.org/10.1007/3-540-28901-1

28. Schmidt, D.C., Stal, M., Rohnert, H., Buschmann, F., Henney, K., Meunier, R., Sommerlad, P., Kircher, M.: Pattern-Oriented Software Architecture (POSA), vol. 1–5. Wiley (1996–2007)

29. Seinturier, L., Merle, P., Rouvoy, R., Romero, D., Schiavoni, V., Stefani, J.B.: A component-based middleware platform for reconfigurable service-oriented architectures. Softw. Pract. Exp. **42**(5), 559–583 (2012)

30. Wada, H., Suzuki, J., Oba, K.: A feature modeling support for non-functional constraints in service oriented architecture. In: Proceedings of the 4th IEEE International Conference on Services Computing (SCC 2007), Salt Lake City, Utah, USA, pp. 187–195, July 2007

A Method and Programming Model for Developing Interacting Cloud Applications Based on the TOSCA Standard

Michael Zimmermann$^{(\boxtimes)}$, Uwe Breitenbücher, and Frank Leymann

Institute of Architecture of Application Systems,
University of Stuttgart, Stuttgart, Germany
`zimmerml@iaas.uni-stuttgart.de`

Abstract. Many cloud applications are composed of several interacting components and services. The communication between these components can be enabled, for example, by using standards such as WSDL and the workflow technology. In order to wire these components several endpoints must be exchanged, e.g., the IP addresses of deployed services. However, this exchange of endpoint information is highly dependent on the (i) middleware technologies, (ii) programming languages, and (iii) deployment technology used in a concrete scenario and, thus, increases the complexity of implementing such interacting applications. In this paper, we propose a programming model that eases the implementation of interacting components of automatically deployed TOSCA-based applications. Furthermore, we present a method following our programming model, which describes how such a cloud application can be systematically modeled, developed, and automatically deployed based on the TOSCA standard and how code generation capabilities can be utilized for this. The practical feasibility of the presented approach is validated by a system architecture and a prototypical implementation based on the OpenTOSCA ecosystem. This work is an extension of our previous research we presented at the International Conference on Enterprise Information Systems (ICEIS).

Keywords: Development method · Programming model
Orchestration · Interaction · Communication
Automated deployment · TOSCA

1 Introduction

Cloud computing is of vital importance for realizing modern IT systems by enabling automated deployment and management of applications [18]. Cloud properties, for example, scalability, pay-on-demand pricing, or self-service enables developers building flexible and automated cloud applications. These cloud applications typically consists of multiple components, which need to be

© Springer International Publishing AG, part of Springer Nature 2018
S. Hammoudi et al. (Eds.): ICEIS 2017, LNBIP 321, pp. 265–290, 2018.
https://doi.org/10.1007/978-3-319-93375-7_13

able to communicate with each other. Therefore, one of the most important issues from an application developer's perspective is to orchestrate and wire these different components. Also regarding connected sensors and actuators in the field of Internet of Things (IoT), the services and devices need to be wired—often IoT integration middleware technologies are used for this purpose [11].

However, this orchestration and wiring mainly depends on the technologies used to realize the application as well as its components. Thus, dependent on these technologies, different information need to be exchanged during the automated deployment of the overall application in order to enable the communication between the components. For example, consider a component which is hosted on a public cloud platform implementing a graphical user interface that presents data from physical devices, such as measured temperature data. In order to enable this component presenting any data from a device, it needs to be wired with this device measuring the data as well as the software running on this device. Therefore, the endpoint information of the component implementing the graphical interface needs to be exchanged with the devices during the automated deployment of the overall application. Such endpoint information required for the communication between components of such *composite applications* are, for example, URLs of services, IP addresses, and required credentials [37].

Unfortunately, the exchange of these endpoint information mainly depends on technologies, such as the middleware, the programming languages, and the deployment technology used to implement and deploy the application and its components. Therefore, the exchange of these information requires the usage of custom written code, which limits the portability of the application and increases the complexity of implementing the components. Although available technologies, for example, WSDL [32], service buses [9], or orchestration and deployment technologies such as Docker Compose[1] enable to describe and abstract the communication between different components, the composition of multiple heterogeneous technologies is still an open issue. Furthermore, a programming model easing the implementation of interacting components or a method describing the systematically development of such applications is missing.

In this paper, we tackle these issues by presenting a TOSCA-based programming model and a corresponding development method that ease the implementation of interacting components of automatically deployed applications. The main idea of our approach is to abstract endpoint handling of interacting components by using the identifiers and interface descriptions from TOSCA models and by utilizing a service bus, which is integrated in the deployment runtime. This work is an extension of our previous research [37] presented and published at the *International Conference on Enterprise Information Systems (ICEIS)*. While our previous work already covered the TOSCA-based programming model and the required TOSCA extension, we extend these concepts in this work by a systematic development method that supports developers in applying the programming model. Moreover, we show how code generation capabilities can be used to automate some steps of the method. The practicable feasibility of our approach

---

[1] https://docs.docker.com/compose/.

is validated by providing a system architecture and prototypical implementation following our programming model and supporting the presented method.

Before we present our extension and new contribution in Sect. 7, we first recap our previous research [37] to provide a comprehensive overview: Sect. 2 discusses different state-of-the-art approaches for automating the orchestration and wiring of components and illustrates the existing problems and limitations we tackle in this work. We introduce the TOSCA standard for modeling and managing cloud applications in Sect. 3. Section 4 presents our TOSCA-based programming model, which enables abstracting the communication between components and the endpoint handling during deployment. Our TOSCA extension to enable the modeling of operations implementing business operations is presented in Sect. 5, which we also adapted in this extended version. In Sect. 6 the corresponding communication concepts implemented as service bus are presented. Section 7 presents the new contribution of this extended paper in the form of a method for modeling and developing TOSCA-based cloud applications following the presented programming model. The validation of our approach by implementing a prototype is presented in Sect. 8. Finally, Sect. 9 discusses related work and Sect. 10 presents our conclusion as well as planned future work.

2   Problem Statement

In this section, different state-of-the-art approaches for automating the orchestration and wiring of components using existing technologies are discussed. Moreover, based on the discussed approaches the problems taking place when utilizing them are discussed, such as the required exchange of endpoint information.

Of course, the issue of automatically wiring components of applications in which all components are deployed and operated using only one technology can be solved by using a single composition technology, such as Docker Compose[2] or Kubernetes[3]: Typically such technologies provide built-in wiring and orchestration capabilities that must be considered when implementing a component. For example, by propagating environment variables to containers or by placing and sharing configuration files, which are used by a component to connect to another one [8]. However, in composite cloud applications consisting of multiple heterogeneous components typically multiple technologies have to be combined, especially if physical devices are involved in IoT scenarios [7]. Unfortunately, this also requires to combine multiple invocation mechanisms, protocols, and endpoint exchange mechanisms. Thus, this leads to custom code binding a component to an invoked component as well as its implementation if no *service bus* [9] or—in case of cyber-physical scenarios—*IoT middleware* [11] is used for abstraction.

Accordingly, for the interaction of (micro)services the calling service needs to know the endpoint of the other service to enable their communication. The service bus concept solves this issue from a communication layer perspective.

---

[2] https://docs.docker.com/compose/.

[3] http://kubernetes.io/.

However, if a concrete target service shall be invoked, at least its unique identifier (*ID* in the following) is required and must be contained in the message sent to the bus. In case of an IoT middleware, such as a message broker, typically the ID of the topic to which a device publishes must be known by sender and receiver. However, the exchange of such IDs is technically similar to the exchange of endpoints of the invoked components, for example, URLs of the deployed components. Thus, an appropriate exchange mechanism is required nevertheless which approach is used. Typically such information is required during deployment time of a component to tell it to which other components (or to which service bus) it shall connect[4]. However, a standardized approach for (i) automatically exchanging arbitrary kinds of endpoint information between components which they require to communicate with each other and (ii) exchanging IDs to enable components to invoke a certain component via a service bus is missing. Therefore, typically this kind of information is handled in an application-specific manner during the deployment time of the overall application by using manually created configuration scripts and similar approaches. For instance, if a component is implemented as script, environment variables are typically used to pass this kind of endpoint information. This kind of exchange is used, e.g., in a work of Wettinger et al. enabling the unified invocation of scripts implementing management operations [34]. Furthermore, often configuration files need to be updated, for example, as shown by da Silva et al. in an IoT deployment scenario [28]. However, all these issues are reflected in the implementations of components, thus, limiting the application's portability since the used technologies and their exchange mechanisms need to be considered.

To sum up, despite service-orientation, standards such as WSDL, service buses and the workflow technology, providing common means for enabling the interaction between components, their *automated deployment and wiring* is still a technology-dependent issue. Furthermore, this issue itself highly depends on the used (i) middleware technologies, (ii) programming languages, and (iii) deployment technologies. Thus, it results in an increase of the complexity of implementing components as well as orchestrating them leading to custom written code. The problems occurring when using state-of-the-art wiring approaches, for instance, establishing a direct communication between two components or applying a service bus instead, are illustrated by means of an exemplary IoT-Cloud scenario in the next section.

2.1 Motivating Scenario

In Fig. 1 a typical IoT-Cloud scenario describing the wiring of components is depicted. In the illustrated scenario, the *Python 3 App* running on a Raspberry Pi measures temperature data that shall be sent to the *Java 7 App*, which is responsible for storing and displaying this data. To enable the *Python 3 App* to send the measured temperature data to the *Java 7 App*, after the automated

---

[4] This is a general requirement for deploying composite applications. Of course, this does not apply to hard-wired scenarios, which are not the focus of this work.

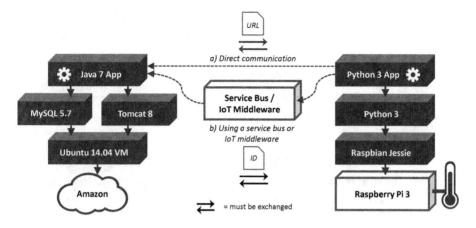

Fig. 1. Two state-of-the-art orchestration variants of an IoT-Cloud scenario [37].

provisioning of all shown components the *Python 3 App* requires additional end-point information. The figure illustrates two possibilities to connect the components: (i) a direct communication and (ii) a communication via a central service bus. However, both variants require exchanging endpoint information: Either the *Python 3 App* needs to know (i) an endpoint (e.g. an URL) of the *Java 7 App* in case of a direct communication, or (ii) some kind of ID specifying the *Java 7 App* in case of using the service bus. Furthermore, in case of the service bus, the *Java 7 App* must be first registered at the bus to make itself known. Even when using a standard such as WS-Addressing[5], some information requires to be exchanged before a connection can be established initially. Thus, resulting in custom code written for each component in order to accomplish the initial exchange of the required endpoint information. However, since this binds the components to the used orchestration technology, in particular, to its endpoint exchange mechanism, this limits the portability of components. Furthermore, because of multiple error sources, additional effort and expertise is required for implementing and debugging components. In order to address these issues, we present a standards-based programming model to abstract the communication between heterogeneous components and proprietary endpoint exchange mechanisms in this paper.

3   The TOSCA Standard

Because the following concepts are based on TOSCA, we introduce the TOSCA standard in this section to provide a comprehensive background. The OASIS standard *Topology and Orchestration Specification for Cloud Applications (TOSCA)* [3,22,23] enables to describe the required infrastructure resources,

---

[5] https://www.w3.org/TR/ws-addr-core/.

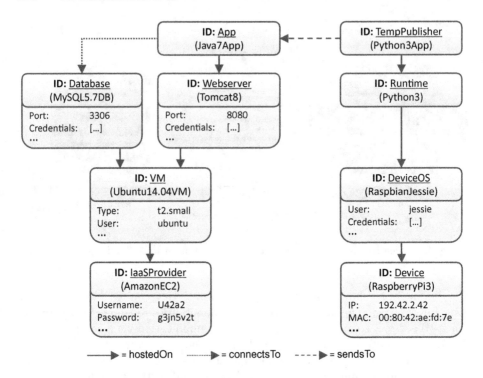

Fig. 2. Exemplary TOSCA topology template (Extension of [37]).

the components, as well as the structure of a cloud application in an interoperable and portable manner. Moreover, TOSCA supports to define the operations required for managing an application. Thus, TOSCA enables the automated provisioning as well as management of cloud applications. The structure of a cloud application is defined in a *topology template*. Figure 2 shows such a template modeling the motivating scenario described in Sect. 2.1 following the visual notation VINO4TOSCA [6]. A topology template is a graph consisting of nodes and directed edges. The nodes of the graph are called *node templates* and represent components of the application, for example, an Apache Tomcat, a MySQL-Database, a virtual machine, or a cloud provider. Edges connecting the nodes are called *relationship templates* and allow to model the relationships between the components. For example, *"hosted on"* is a relation specifying that a component is hosted on another component, *"depends on"* specifies that a component has dependencies to another component, and *"connects to"* specifies that a component needs to connect to a database, for instance.

In order to support reusability, TOSCA enables the specification of *node types* and *relationship types* defining the semantics of the node and relationship templates. For example, *properties*, such as passwords, user names, or the port of a web server, as well as available *management operations* of a modeled component are defined within the types. Management operations are bundled in *interfaces* and enable the management of components. For example, usually a component node provides an "install" operation in order to install the component, while a hypervisor or cloud provider node typically provides a "createVM" operation in order to create a new virtual machine. The artifacts, which implement the management operations, are called *implementation artifacts* and are implemented, for instance, as a web service packaged as a WAR file or just as a simple SH script. Besides implementation artifacts, additionally TOSCA defines *deployment artifacts* representing the artifacts implementing the business logic of the nodes. For example, a deployment artifact could be a WAR file implementing the Java application that should be provisioned on the VM of our motivating scenario.

To create or terminate instances of a topology template and to enable the automated management of applications, so-called *management plans* can be specified in TOSCA models. Management plans are executable workflow models implementing a certain management functionality. For example, they define which management operations need to be executed in order to achieve a higher level management goal, such as to provision a new instance of the entire application or to scale out a component. TOSCA does not specify a particular process modeling language for the definition of plans, however, recommends to use a workflow language such as the standardized *Business Process Execution Language (BPEL)* [21] or the *Business Process Model and Notation (BPMN)* [24][6].

Furthermore, TOSCA also specifies a portable and self-contained packaging format, which is called *Cloud Service Archive (CSAR)*. All artifacts, type definitions, the topology template, management plans, as well as all additional files required for automating the provisioning and management are packaged into the CSAR. Such a CSAR can be processed and executed automatically by all standard-compliant *TOSCA Runtime Environments*, such as OpenTOSCA [2], and thus ensuring the application's portability as well as interoperability.

4   TOSCA-based Programming Model

In this section, our TOSCA-based programming model is presented as described in our previous work (Zimmermann et al. [37]). The main goal of the programming model is to completely abstract (i) the communication between components as well as (ii) any endpoint handling during deployment. Therefore, it allows to program the invocation of operations provided by other components in almost the same manner as they would be available locally.

In Fig. 3 the concept of the programming model is illustrated. The upper half of the figure shows a simplified deployment model of the motivating scenario as TOSCA topology template. The left side of the template shows the *Java 7 App* component with ID *App* and its underlying stack, which is hosted on the Amazon cloud. Moreover, the description of the interface *TempManagement* and its

---

[6] We also developed a TOSCA-specific workflow modeling extension called BPMN4TOSCA [14,16] that eases developing management plans.

operation *updateTemp* to update a temperature value with the input parameter *val* is illustrated. The right side of the template shows the stack of the *Python 3 App* component with ID *TempPublisher*, which shall be hosted on a physical *Raspberry Pi 3*. The main function of the *TempPublisher* component is to send the measured temperature data to the *Java 7 App* component by invoking its operation *updateTemp*. The lower half of the figure illustrates the physical deployment of this template. For example, the temperature sensor connected to the *Raspberry Pi 3* is depicted in this physical deployment view. The left side outlines an exemplary pseudo code implementation of the *updateTemp* operation, while the right side illustrates the simplified implementation of the *TempPublisher*.

The main idea of our proposed TOSCA-based programming model is to enable the invocation of operations offered by other components only based on information contained in the TOSCA topology template. Therefore, to program an invocation, the TOSCA ID of the component to be invoked is used as object in the code while the desired operation is called as usual in object-oriented programming. For instance, the code of the *TempPublisher* component contains the invocation of the operation *updateTemp* of the TOSCA node template having the ID *App* (`App.updateTemp(val)`). Thus, although the component *App* is hosted on the Amazon cloud and the component *TempPublisher* is hosted on a physical device, the operation *updateTemp* can be used within the *TempPublisher* component as it would be a locally available method. Therefore, all relevant wiring

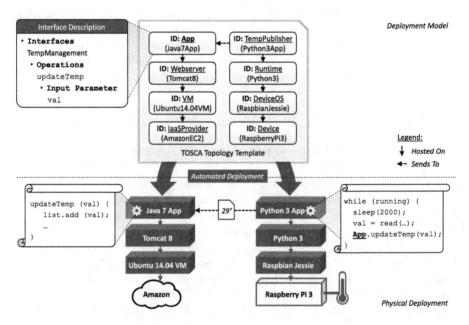

Fig. 3. TOSCA-based programming model based on the simplified motivating scenario [37].

aspects are abstracted and no programming for endpoint handling or to connect to a service bus is required. Moreover, all TOSCA IDs of the components are specified within the topology template and are, therefore, well-known. Thus, discovering components and establishing a connection to enable the communication between components requires no exchange of IDs at all.

5   TOSCA Extension for the Programming Model

In order to realize our programming model, the operations implementing the business logic of an application must be defined in the corresponding TOSCA model. However, since this is not supported by TOSCA out of the box, in this section, a TOSCA-extension to define *business operations* of applications modeled using TOSCA is presented. Thus, we extend TOSCA by an *Interface Definition Language (IDL)* for business operations in this section[7]. We first differentiate business operations from management operations, which can be already modeled in TOSCA, in order to ease the understanding.

5.1   Application Interfaces

In Sect. 3 the fundamentals of the TOSCA standard were presented. Moreover, we outlined that management operations provided by node templates are implemented by implementation artifacts. They can be realized using any arbitrary technology such as a simple shell script, a WAR file exposing a web service, or more sophisticated technologies such as Chef recipes [30] or Ansible playbooks [19]. These management operations enable to automate arbitrary management tasks of cloud applications and are orchestrated by management plans. However, nodes of course can also have operations implementing the business logic of the corresponding component. In our motivation scenario, for instance, the Java component *Java 7 App* provides the operation *updateTemp* in order to update the temperature data to be displayed (cf. Sect. 2.1). However, this business operation cannot be modeled using standard TOSCA elements. But since they are required to realize our new programming model, we extend TOSCA node types by a modeling schema for business operations. Listing 1.1 shows how application interfaces and business operations can be defined using the extension.

```
1  <NodeType name="xs:NCName">
2    <ot:ApplicationInterfaces>
3      <Interface name="xs:NCName">
4        <Operation name="xs:NCName">
5          <documentation/> ?
6          <InputParameters>
7            <InputParameter name="xs:string" type="xs:string"
8                            required="yes|no"?/> +
9          </InputParameters> ?
```

---

[7] This section is based on our previous work but extends it by a schematic overview of the extension and a schematic description of the generated code-skeletons [37].

```
10              <OutputParameters>
11                <OutputParameter name="xs:string" type="xs:string"
12                           required="yes|no"?/> +
13              </OutputParameters> ?
14            </Operation> +
15          </Interface> +
16      </ot:ApplicationInterfaces> ?
17 </NodeType>
```

Listing 1.1. TOSCA extension for specifying application interfaces containing business operations.

We extended the TOSCA metamodel of node types by an *ApplicationInterfaces* element following the schema of the TOSCA *ManagementInterfaces* element [23]. Thus, within the *ApplicationInterfaces* element, the elements originally specified for defining management operations can be reused: *Operation*, *InputParameter*, and *OutputParameter*. However, an *Operation* contained in an *ApplicationInterfaces* element specifies a business operation and not a management operation. Our extension enables the communication between components contained (i) in one topology template as well as the communication between components contained (ii) in different templates, and thus also enables other applications to utilize the provided operations.

```
1 class [interfaceName] {
2
3   /**
4    * [documentation]
5    */
6   static [operationName]([InputParameter1],[InputParameter2],...) {
7     // TODO generated method stub
8     return [OutputParameter]
9   }
10 }
```

Listing 1.2. Abstract generated code-skeleton.

Based on this extension, a code-skeleton (Listing 1.2) can be generated (We detail this in Sect. 6.2). Moreover, we show in Sect. 7.3 an example of such a definition and a generated code-skeleton for the motivation scenario.

5.2   Bindings

In order to technically enable callers, for example a service bus, invoking the specified business operation, binding information are required. Therefore, these information, for example, regarding the invocation style or application-specific invocation properties, need to be specified by the application developer in the TOSCA model of the corresponding operation so that they are available during runtime. The following XML listing (Listing 1.3) shows an example of such binding information based on the motivating scenario, thus, the schema is straightforward.

```
1 <ot:ApplicationInterfacesBinding>
2   <ot:Endpoint>/TempApp</ot:Endpoint>
3   <ot:InvocationType>JSON/REST</ot:InvocationType>
4   <ot:ApplicationInterfaceInformations>
5     <ot:ApplicationInterfaceInformation name="TempManagement"
6         class="org.temp.TempManagement"/>
7   </ot:ApplicationInterfaceInformations>
8 </ot:ApplicationInterfacesBinding>
```

Listing 1.3. Binding information for an application interface [37].

The presented binding information need to be defined in the artifact template referenced by the deployment artifact implementing the business operations, which are defined in an application interface of the corresponding node template. Again, a node template represents a component of an application within a TOSCA topology template, whereas a deployment artifact represents an artifact implementing the business logic of such a component (cf. Sect. 3). For example, a WAR file, which implements the Java application that should be provisioned in the cloud. Therefore, these defined binding information together with our TOSCA extension described in Sect. 5.1 enable specifying the offered business operations of a component as well as how they have to be invoked in detail.

Of course, instead of using such a custom artifact template for binding business operations, accepted standards, such as the Web Services Description Language (WSDL) [32] can also be used to describe the provided functionality of web services. A WSDL file enables to bind the signature of an operation, i.e., the name and the input and output parameters, to information about how this operation can be invoked, such as the endpoint and the supported communication protocol. However, in [34] Wettinger et al. presented a similar TOSCA-based approach to define such binding information within an artifact template for management operations. Thus, for sake of consistency, we decided to additionally support this custom definitions of binding information within an artifact template, too. Therefore, our approach supports both, (i) a binding definition as already used within another TOSCA-based approach as well as (ii) standards such as WSDL. In case of using WSDL, the interface and operations specified within the TOSCA model should correspond to the information defined in the WSDL file. Thus, our presented approach enables to use all the proven and established tooling possibilities for WSDL, for example, automated top-down code generation.

6   System Architecture

Since there was no possibility to define operations implementing business logic using TOSCA without our extension, no tool support exists enabling the communication (i) between components within one TOSCA topology template as well as (ii) between components of different TOSCA topology templates. Thus, in this section, we present a system architecture for TOSCA runtimes that utilizes a service bus supporting our extension of the TOSCA standard. We already presented this system architecture in our previous work [37] and recap it to ease understanding the method introduced in Sect. 7.

6.1   Overview

Figure 4 illustrates our proposed system architecture in a simplified manner, only depicting components of TOSCA runtimes that are required for realizing our new programming model. Of course, several other components are also required, for instance, a component for interpreting the model, etc. A comprehensive overview on different TOSCA runtime architectures can be found in [22].

The central component of the concept is a service bus, which is integrated in the TOSCA runtime[8]. This service bus provides a unified and generic interface for *incoming* invocation requests of business operations provided by components. This interface can be realized, for instance, as RESTful interface supporting synchronous operation invocations with a single HTTP request or asynchronous invocations via resource polling. But also other communication protocols, such as a SOAP interface supporting WS-Addressing [33] or a plugin-based implementation are possible. Depending on the implementation of the interface, also a proxy may be used for the implementation of the component in order to ease the communication with the service bus, e.g., to handle asynchronous callbacks.

In order to support the invocations of different types, such as SOAP/HTTP, the service bus also contains a plugin system for executing *outgoing* invocation requests. For enabling the invocation of the business operations of components, the service bus must determine invocation-relevant properties, for example, the IP address of a deployed component providing the corresponding operation.

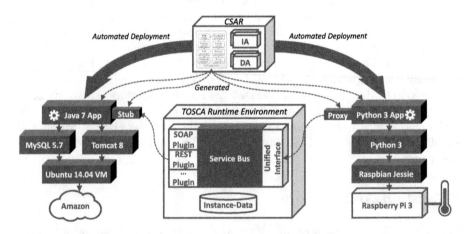

Fig. 4. Simplified system architecture of a TOSCA runtime supporting the presented programming model by a service bus [37].

---

[8] Of course, other kinds of middleware may also be used similarly for realizing our programming model, e.g., a messaging middleware. This is part of our future work.

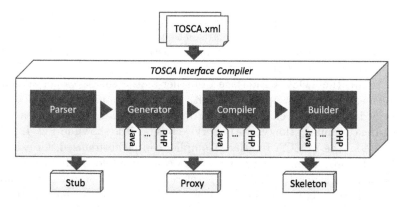

Fig. 5. Overview of the TOSCA interface compiler.

Thus, the service bus is integrated with other components of the TOSCA runtime in order to be able to access such stored information about application instances, for example, gathered information during the provisioning of the application.

To process incoming messages from the bus, the code implementing the communication part of the invoked component needs to understand these messages. This can be achieved by (i) manually programming against a communication protocol offered by the bus, (ii) using a generic stub for an existing plugin, or (iii) using a *TOSCA Interface Compiler* to generate compatible stubs and proxies out of the TOSCA model. While the first and second possibility require manual implementation, we introduce TOSCA Interface Compilers in the next subsection.

6.2 TOSCA Interface Compiler

In order to ease implementing the communication part of a component, our approach enables the generation of a client-proxy and a server-stub able to communicate with the service bus. Since all required information about the business operations, such as their parameters and binding information are contained in the TOSCA model, similarly to generating code out of WSDL files, our approach supports this, too, in order to ease the implementation of interacting components.

The basic architecture of the TOSCA Interface Compiler component is depicted in Fig. 5. As input the TOSCA Interface Compiler gets the TOSCA files defining the operations implementing the business logic of an application. Then, the *Parser* component parses the TOSCA definition files and searches them for containing node types with specified application interfaces and operations. After that, the *Generator* component generates a client-proxy, a server-stub, or a code-skeleton, depending on the users selection. After the generation of the code, depending on the programming language, for example in case of Java the generated code needs to be compiled. This is done in the *Compiler* component. In the last step, again depending on the programming language, the *Builder* component finally builds the artifact to be ready to be provisioned. For example in case of Java, a JAR file is build based on the compiled *.class-files created by the Compiler component of the TOSCA Interface Compiler.

As a result, the TOSCA Interface Compiler assists the developer (i) during the implementation of an application with the generation of code-skeletons of the specified operations (cf. Sect. 7.4) and (ii) to generate a stub and a proxy enabling the communication with the service bus, as it is shown in Fig. 4. Before the generation, the TOSCA Interface Compiler can be customized, for example, to choose the programming language of the component for including required libraries, etc. If a separate WSDL file is referenced instead of using our binding definition (cf. Sect. 5.2), also the top-down approach for code generation using any WSDL tool can be used. Therefore, our approach complements existing code generation tools and enables their efficient usage during development.

7   A Method for Developing and Deploying Interacting TOSCA-based Cloud and IoT Applications

In this section, we present the major new contribution of this extended paper in the form of a method for systematically developing and deploying TOSCA-based applications following the presented programming model. Furthermore, we explain the general advantages of this new method and show how code generation can be utilized in order to speed up the development of TOSCA-based applications.

7.1   Motivation for the Method

Model-driven software development (MDSD) is an important factor in software engineering as it enables, for example, to speed up the development time of an application by generating code [29]. However, for the modeling of complex and distributed cloud or IoT applications, several different models are required. For example, models describing the single components of the application, models defining the relations and dependencies between different components, as well as models describing the required infrastructure resources for the application and its components. Therefore, either the modeler needs to be an expert in all these different model languages and model types, or several modelers with diverse expertise are required. Also, an automation of the entire development and deployment process – from the beginning of the modeling, to the implementation, to the deployment of the application – would be difficult to realize. Furthermore, the orchestration of a cloud application consisting of already existing cloud applications is cumbersome if different model types and languages or no models at all are used. Therefore, our approach allows to model all of the previously described aspects combining the development as well as the deployment steps.

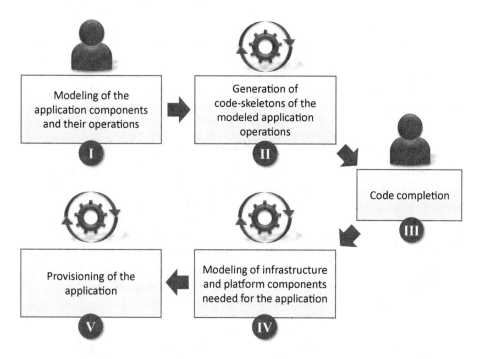

Fig. 6. Method for the development of a TOSCA-based cloud application.

7.2   Overview of the Method

As stated in Sect. 3, the TOSCA standard enables the modeling of the components, the structure, relations and management operations out of the box. As a reminder, the management operation are responsible for the management of a cloud application, for example to install an Apache HTTP Server on a virtual machine. For our approach, we extended the TOSCA standard by so called *application operations*, which are the business operations the cloud application itself implements and provides. Thus, the application operations are not invokable before the cloud application was successfully deployed (with help of the management operations). Altogether, our extension enables the modeling of cloud applications, their structure, the required components and infrastructure nodes, the installation procedure, the offered management as well as application operations uniformly with TOSCA. Thus, our approach not only enables the automated provisioning of the cloud application but also increases the development speed by means of code generation functionalities. Our novel method is composed of five steps to develop a TOSCA-based application and is illustrated in Fig. 6.

In the first step, the components of the application as well as the operations of the application are modeled by the application modeler using TOSCA. In the second step, the code-skeletons based on the previously modeled application operations are generated using the code-skeleton generator. In the third step, the code-skeletons generated in the previous step are completed manually with business logic by the programmer. In the fourth step, the infrastructure and platform components required for the execution of the application are modeled using default TOSCA elements. In the fifth and last step, the modeled and implemented application is deployed automatically by using a TOSCA runtime. The single steps of the method are explained in detail in the following.

7.3   Modeling of the Application Components and their Operations

In the first step, the application modeler models the components of the application as well as the application operations using TOSCA. The components can be modeled using the default TOSCA constructs. Also, already existing TOSCA-based topology models can be reused. Additionally, all application operations implementing business logic, which the application itself should provide, need to be defined within the new *ApplicationInterfaces* element introduced in Sect. 5. Since this is a manual task, using an existing TOSCA modeling tool, like for example Winery [15], can be very helpful for accomplishing this task.

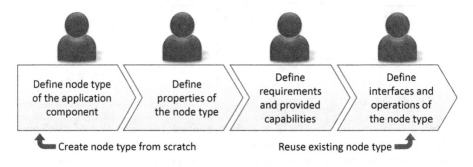

Fig. 7. Required steps for modeling an application component.

In this first step of our method, node type definitions are required to model the topology. For every component of the application, in general the following issues must be considered regarding existing node type definitions that can be reused directly and definitions that must be modified or created from scratch: Either (i) just an existing node type can be reused as it already specifies and implements all required application interfaces, (ii) an available node type already specifies everything required for deployment and only missing application interfaces and binding information must be added, or (iii) the node type needs to be modeled completely from scratch. All three possibilities are depicted in Fig. 7: If a suitable node type already exists, these steps can be ignored. If a complete new node type must be modeled, the modeler first needs to specify the type of the component, for example, that it is a Java application as well as the name of the application. Furthermore, all properties, such as port or password and username needs to be defined for the new component type. Moreover, defining requirements and provided capabilities enables the automatically completion of the application topology model in step 4 (cf. Sect. 7.6). Afterwards, the application interfaces and operations this component should provide are specified using the *ApplicationInterfaces* element. If an already available node type – which is modeled by only using the default TOSCA structures – should be reused in this method, only the interfaces and operations need to be added to the model. Thus, existing node types can be easily reused in the presented method by using the inheritance mechanism of TOSCA that allows to create subtypes of node types that inherit their semantics but allow to extend them.

Listing 1.4 shows the node type of the *Java 7 App* component from the motivation scenario offering the application operation *updateTemp* in order to store and display received temperature data. The temperature value is specified via the input parameter *val*[9]. Based on the shown example defining the provided operation, the input and optional output parameters, as well as documentations, a code-skeleton can be generated in the next step.

```
1  <NodeType name="Java7App">
2    <ot:ApplicationInterfaces xmlns:ot="http://opentosca.org">
3      <Interface name="TempManagement">
4        <Operation name="updateTemp">
5          <documentation>
6            Updates the temperature
7          </documentation>
8          <InputParameters>
9            <InputParameter name="val" type="xs:int"/>
10         </InputParameters>
11       </Operation>
12     </Interface>
13   </ot:ApplicationInterfaces>
14 </NodeType>
```

Listing 1.4. Example of the TOSCA extension for specifying application interfaces containing business operations [37].

7.4   Generation of Code-Skeletons of the Modeled Application Operations

The second step is the generation of code-skeletons based on the previously modeled topology, which includes all node type definitions as well as their application interfaces and operations. Depending on the code-skeleton generator implementation, code for any arbitrary programming language can be generated, for example, as Java or PHP application. Thus, no restriction regarding the used programming language are made for the application developer as our programming model enables an abstract and technology independent modeling of the application components. Since this step can be automated, the developer of the application is supported and, therefore, the development time can be significantly decreased. In Sect. 8, we describe our prototypical implementation of this step that enables the automated generation of code skeletons.

---

[9] Output parameters can be specified the same way.

```
1 class TempManagement {
2
3   /**
4    * Updates the temperature
5    */
6   static void updateTemp(int val) {
7     // TODO generated method stub
8   }
9 }
```

Listing 1.5. Generated code-skeleton in Java [37].

```
1 procedure GenerateCodeSkeleton(ToscaDefinition)
2  for every NodeType used in the TopologyTemplate
3   for every ApplicationInterface
4    if Code-Skeleton must be generated for this ApplicationInterface
5     createClass(interfaceName)
6     for every ApplicationOperation
7      createMethod(operationName, inputParams, outputParams, doc)
8     end for
9    end if
10   end for
11  end for
12 end procedure
```

Listing 1.6. Pseudocode algorithm showing the basic functionality for generating code-skeletons.

Listing 1.5 shows an example of a generated code-skeleton based on the defined application operations presented in Listing 1.4. The basics of the TOSCA Interface Compiler component have been discussed already in Sect. 6.2. For generating the code-skeletons the TOSCA Interface Compiler checks for every found node type if it has defined application interfaces as well as operations. The simplified pseudocode-algorithm for this is shown in Listing 1.6.

Of course, the code-skeleton is generated depending on the defined programming language. Thus, the TOSCA Interface Compiler is based on a plugin-mechanism so that it can be easily extended in order to add support for additional programming languages. Moreover, the TOSCA Interface Compiler also enables the developer to specify for which application interfaces code-skeletons need to be generated as possibly code already exists in the form of a deployment artifact that implements the interface. Especially, if suitable node types are reused without any change in step 1 of the method, no code-skeletons must be generated for these node types that already provide complete implementations. We discuss more details about how this step can be realized in the scope of our prototypical validation based on the OpenTOSCA ecosystem presented in Sect. 8.

7.5 Code Completion

In the third step, the code-skeletons generated in the previously step need to be completed with the business logic. Since at this step business knowledge is needed, this step needs to be done manually by the application developer. However, because of the generated code-skeletons, the code is already prestructured and only the pure business logic needs to be implemented. Furthermore, since also stubs and proxies can be generated abstracting the communication between different components, the programmer can focus completely on the implementation of the business logic and does not need to take care of communication or messaging at all. Of course, this step needs to be repeated for every component a code-skeleton was generated and, thus, should be implemented.

7.6 Modeling of Infrastructure and Platform Components Required for Deploying and Executing the Application

In the fourth step, the infrastructure and platform components required for the execution of the application need to be modeled using the default TOSCA elements. Again, already existing TOSCA-based topology models can be reused in this step. Furthermore, there is other work [35] enabling to generate TOSCA modeling artifacts from various other existing technologies, such as DevOps artifacts, for example, Chef cookbooks or Juju charms. Thus, already proven solutions can be reused in TOSCA again significantly simplifying the development, modelling, and implementation of the required platform and infrastructure components.

Based on the requirements defined in step 1 (cf. Sect. 7.3) the application topology model can be automatically completed by finding existing suitable components providing matching capabilities [13]. For example, a Java application packaged as WAR might define that a web server is required in order to successfully provision it. Thus, if an Apache Tomcat is modeled with defined capabilities matching this requirement, these both components can be connected automatically—for example by using the approach presented by Hirmer et al., which has been integrated in Winery [13]. Likewise this can be done for other components too, for example, that a virtual machine node must be hosted on a infrastructure component such as a hypervisor or a cloud provider. Besides the fully automated completion, also a semi-automatically completion is possible: If several components are matching the requirements of a component, the modeler can decide which one should be used in the model. Also, instead of single components, entire topology fragments can be selected for completing the topology. The topology completion is depicted in Fig. 8. If this modeling task needs to be done manually – since no suitable components can be found automatically – existing modeling tools such as the Winery can support the modeler in this step. However, in this case the modeler needs some domain-specific knowledge about, for example, which components can and should be hosted on which components or what other dependent components are required in the model. Also the fragment-based completion is supported by Winery [36].

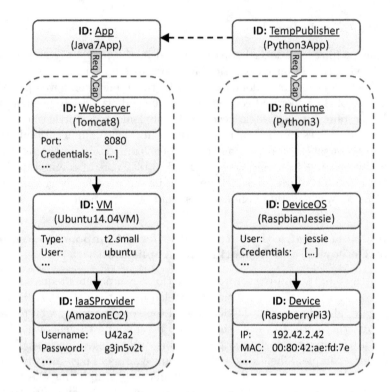

Fig. 8. Automatically completion of the application topology based on specified requirements and capabilities.

7.7   Provisioning of the Application

The fifth and last step is the provisioning of the modeled application with help of a TOSCA runtime environment. In this step, first the modeled infrastructure and platform components, such as virtual machines or web servers, are installed and configured and afterwards the application itself is installed. Since the corresponding topology model was created beforehand, this step only needs to be triggered manually but afterwards runs fully automatically. Thus, by using the integrated service bus, no components need to be configured or connected manually in order to be able to communicate with each other. In Sect. 8, the modeling tool Winery [15], the open-source TOSCA runtime environment OpenTOSCA [2], as well as the self-service portal Vinothek to start the provisioning [5] are introduced, which provide the basis for our prototype described in the next section.

8   Validation

In order to validate the practical feasibility of the presented concepts we implemented a prototype, which is integrated in the OpenTOSCA open-source toolchain. Furthermore, in this section, we show how the steps presented in the previous section can be realized using this toolchain.

In order to implement our prototype, we extended the *OpenTOSCA Ecosystem*[10], which consists of: (i) the graphical TOSCA modeling tool *Winery*[11] [15], (ii) the *OpenTOSCA container*[12] [2], and (iii) the self-service portal *Vinothek* [5]. An overview of the ecosystem is depicted in Fig. 9. Using Winery the topology template of the application can be modeled and all files can be packaged into a CSAR. The OpenTOSCA container can use the resulting CSAR as input, interprets the containing files, and deploys the modeled application[13]. The self-service portal Vinothek is used in order to trigger the provisioning of the application. It provides a graphical, web-based end user interface. The tools mentioned in this section are all available as open-source implementations. Therefore, our developed and integrated prototype provides an open-source end-to-end toolchain, which supports the modeling, provisioning, management, orchestration, and communication of TOSCA-based cloud applications. More technical details about the prototypical implementation of the service bus and how the programming model has been realized can be found in the original paper [37]. In the following, we want to focus on how this toolchain supports our new method proposed in this extended work for modeling and developing TOSCA-based applications.

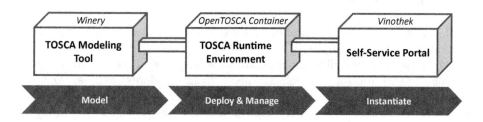

Fig. 9. Overview of the OpenTOSCA ecosystem.

The first step of the method presented in the previous section is the modeling of the application components and their operations. This step can be realized using Winery, which is a standard-compliant modeling tool for TOSCA. Winery provides a graphical modeling editor for creating Node Types, Relationship Types, and other TOSCA-specified artifacts as well as entire topology models. Furthermore, Winery enables the export of CSARs containing all files required for deploying and managing the modeled application. Thus, Winery supports the modeler of the application components by providing a graphical modeling tool. Therefore, the modeler does not need to write TOSCA definition files in

---

[10] For testing, instructions to automatically deploy the ecosystem can be found at http://install.opentosca.org.

[11] https://projects.eclipse.org/projects/soa.winery.

[12] https://www.github.com/OpenTOSCA.

[13] Details about this deployment can be found in Breitenbücher et al. [4].

XML himself. For the second step, the generation of code-skeletons of the previously modeled application components, the TOSCA Interface Compiler (cf. Sect. 6.2) can be used. It supports the generation of code-skeletons for different programming languages. For completing the generated code-skeletons any preferred IDE can be used. The fourth step of the method – modeling of the infrastructure and platform components as well as completing the topology – can be realized by using Winery again. It supports the creation of new infrastructure or platform nodes as well as the completion of the application topology manually, semi-automatically, as well as fully automatically based on the concepts of Hirmer et al. [13] and Zimmermann et al. [36]. After that, the final CSAR containing the complete topology model as well all required artifacts and files can be exported. The last step is the provisioning of the modeled application. Therefore, the exported CSAR can be consumed by the OpenTOSCA Container. After the CSAR was processed successfully by the OpenTOSCA Container, the application is available to be provisioned. In the Vinothek, all installed applications are offered. Therefore, using the Vinothek the application can be selected, required information, for example, credentials for a cloud provider added and the provisioning of a new instance of the modeled application be started.

9   Related Work

In this section, our discussion about related work, which we already discussed partially in Sect. 2 is completed. Regarding the dynamic and flexible invocation of web services, there is different work available [10,17,20]. However, their works do not consider topology modeling aspects using standards such as TOSCA. Regarding TOSCA-related work, a concept as well as a prototype enabling the invocation of operations through a unified interface was proposed by Wettinger et al. [34]. However, they only consider the invocation of management operations, which are already supported by the TOSCA standard, and do not consider the invocation of operations implementing the business logic of an application.

In [12] Happ et al. present limitations of the publish-subscribe pattern, for example implemented in the widely accepted IoT protocol MQTT, for the area of IoT. They argue, for example, that a potential publisher of sensor data respectively the used topic can not be easily discovered. Moreover, they argue that the standard is missing details about the messaging reliability. Therefore, this leads to custom solutions and implementations, which results in incompatible applications. Thus, in their work they provide a concept improving the discovery and reliability. However, standards to describe the structure of an application such as TOSCA are not considered in their work.

Occurring problems when integrating different custom components and technologies were already discussed in related work. In [7] Breitenbücher et al. argue, that because most of the available web services and APIs of vendors and cloud providers are not standardized, existing solutions cannot integrate them. Therefore, they provide an approach to integrate provisioning and configuration technologies. However, they do not consider the invocation of business operations through a unified interface, but only focus on management technologies.

In the field of container-based orchestration, there is related work [1,27,31] available. They discuss orchestration approaches using containers and advantages using container technologies such as Docker Compose[14], Docker Swarm[15] and Kubernetes[16] in the cloud in general. For example, these technologies enable to transfer and reuse containers between different cloud providers. However, they do not consider the orchestration of non-containerized components.

The general approach of generating a stub from an interface definition for enabling the invocation of a remote method as a local invocation is similar to other approaches such as Java-RMI [26] and CORBA [25]. However, since we use web service technologies, for example, HTTP and XML our approach is agnostic regarding the underlying technology. Furthermore, since we use HTTP in our prototype we have no issues with firewalls blocking the traffic.

10   Conclusion

In this paper, we presented a programming model for enabling the unified communication of components of automatically deployed applications (cf. Sect. 4). Therefore, we extended the Topology and Orchestration Specification for Cloud Applications (TOSCA) in order to define business operations of components in a technology-agnostic manner, as presented in (cf. Sect. 5). Moreover, we described a system architecture of an automated deployment and orchestration system utilizing an integrated service bus supporting our programming model (cf. Sect. 6). Furthermore, we presented a generic method for systematically modeling and developing TOSCA-based applications following our proposed programming model (cf. Sect. 7). In order to validate our concepts, we implemented a prototypical service bus and integrated it in the OpenTOSCA toolchain (cf. Sect. 8). Based on the motivation scenario illustrated in Sect. 2.1, we also showed how the proposed method can be applied using the OpenTOSCA toolchain.

In order to support a wider range of IoT scenarios following our programming model, we plan to integrate other middleware components, such as a message broker in future work. Furthermore, in order to improve the performance of our approach, we plan to eliminate the centralized service bus by realizing our approach in a decentralized manner. We also plan in future work to investigate other middleware technologies for enabling and coordinating the communication between components using TOSCA, for example, by utilizing a tuple space.

Acknowledgements. This work was partially funded by the BMWi project *SmartOrchestra* (01MD16001F).

---

[14] https://www.docker.com/products/docker-compose.
[15] https://www.docker.com/products/docker-swarm.
[16] http://kubernetes.io/.

References

1. Bernstein, D.: Containers and cloud: from LXC to docker to kubernetes. IEEE Cloud Comput. **1**(3), 81–84 (2014)
2. Binz, T., Breitenbücher, U., Haupt, F., Kopp, O., Leymann, F., Nowak, A., Wagner, S.: OpenTOSCA – a runtime for TOSCA-based cloud applications. In: Basu, S., Pautasso, C., Zhang, L., Fu, X. (eds.) ICSOC 2013. LNCS, vol. 8274, pp. 692–695. Springer, Heidelberg (2013). https://doi.org/10.1007/978-3-642-45005-1_62
3. Binz, T., Breitenbücher, U., Kopp, O., Leymann, F.: TOSCA: Portable Automated Deployment and Management of Cloud Applications. Advanced Web Services, pp. 527–549. Springer, New York (2014)
4. Breitenbücher, U., Binz, T., Képes, K., Kopp, O., Leymann, F., Wettinger, J.: Combining declarative and imperative cloud application provisioning based on TOSCA. In: International Conference on Cloud Engineering (IC2E 2014). pp. 87–96. IEEE, March 2014
5. Breitenbücher, U., Binz, T., Kopp, O., Leymann, F.: Vinothek - A self-service portal for TOSCA. In: Proceedings of the 6th Central-European Workshop on Services and their Composition (ZEUS 2014), pp. 69–72. CEUR-WS.org, February 2014
6. Breitenbücher, U., Binz, T., Kopp, O., Leymann, F., Schumm, D.: Vino4TOSCA: a visual notation for application topologies based on TOSCA. In: Meersman, R., Panetto, H., Dillon, T., Rinderle-Ma, S., Dadam, P., Zhou, X., Pearson, S., Ferscha, A., Bergamaschi, S., Cruz, I.F. (eds.) OTM 2012. LNCS, vol. 7565, pp. 416–424. Springer, Heidelberg (2012). https://doi.org/10.1007/978-3-642-33606-5_25
7. Breitenbücher, U., Binz, T., Kopp, O., Leymann, F., Wettinger, J.: Integrated cloud application provisioning: interconnecting service-centric and script-centric management technologies. In: Meersman, R., Panetto, H., Dillon, T., Eder, J., Bellahsene, Z., Ritter, N., De Leenheer, P., Dou, D. (eds.) OTM 2013. LNCS, vol. 8185, pp. 130–148. Springer, Heidelberg (2013). https://doi.org/10.1007/978-3-642-41030-7_9
8. Burns, B., Grant, B., Oppenheimer, D., Brewer, E., Wilkes, J.: Borg, Omega, and Kubernetes. Commun. ACM **59**(5), 50–57 (2016)
9. Chappell, D.A.: Enterprise Service Bus. O'Reilly, USA (2004)
10. De Antonellis, V., Melchiori, M., De Santis, L., Mecella, M., Mussi, E., Pernici, B., Plebani, P.: A layered architecture for flexible web service invocation. Softw. Pract. Exp. **36**(2), 191–223 (2006)
11. Guth, J., Breitenbücher, U., Falkenthal, M., Leymann, F., Reinfurt, L.: Comparison of IoT platform architectures: a field study based on a reference architecture. In: Proceedings of the International Conference on Cloudification of the Internet of Things (CIoT 2016). IEEE, November 2016
12. Happ, D., Wolisz, A.: Limitations of the Pub/Sub pattern for cloud based IoT and their implications. In: 2nd International Conference on Cloudification of the Internet of Things (CIoT 2016). IEEE, November 2016
13. Hirmer, P., Breitenbücher, U., Binz, T., Leymann, F., et al.: Automatic topology completion of TOSCA-based cloud applications. In: GI-Jahrestagung, vol. P-251, pp. 247–258. GI, September 2014
14. Kopp, O., Binz, T., Breitenbücher, U., Leymann, F.: BPMN4TOSCA: a domain-specific language to model management plans for composite applications. In: Mendling, J., Weidlich, M. (eds.) BPMN 2012. LNBIP, vol. 125, pp. 38–52. Springer, Heidelberg (2012). https://doi.org/10.1007/978-3-642-33155-8_4

15. Kopp, O., Binz, T., Breitenbücher, U., Leymann, F.: Winery – a modeling tool for TOSCA-based cloud applications. In: Basu, S., Pautasso, C., Zhang, L., Fu, X. (eds.) ICSOC 2013. LNCS, vol. 8274, pp. 700–704. Springer, Heidelberg (2013). https://doi.org/10.1007/978-3-642-45005-1_64

16. Kopp, O., Binz, T., Breitenbücher, U., Leymann, F., Michelbach, T.: A domain-specific modeling tool to model management plans for composite applications. In: Proceedings of the 7th Central European Workshop on Services and their Composition, ZEUS 2015, pp. 51–54. CEUR Workshop Proceedings, May 2015

17. Leitner, P., Rosenberg, F., Dustdar, S.: Daios: efficient dynamic web service invocation. Internet Comput. IEEE **13**(3), 72–80 (2009)

18. Leymann, F.: Cloud computing: the next revolution in IT. In: Proceedings of the 52nd Photogrammetric Week, pp. 3–12. Wichmann Verlag, September 2009

19. Mohaan, M., Raithatha, R.: Learning Ansible. Packt Publishing, Birmingham (2014)

20. Nagano, S., Hasegawa, T., Ohsuga, A., Honiden, S.: Dynamic invocation model of web services using subsumption relations. In: Proceedings of the International Conference on Web Services (ICWS 2004), pp. 150–156. IEEE, July 2004

21. OASIS: Web Services Business Process Execution Language (WS-BPEL) Version 2.0. Organization for the Advancement of Structured Information Standards (OASIS) (2007)

22. OASIS: Topology and Orchestration Specification for Cloud Applications (TOSCA) Primer Version 1.0. Organization for the Advancement of Structured Information Standards (OASIS) (2013)

23. OASIS: Topology and Orchestration Specification for Cloud Applications (TOSCA) Version 1.0. Organization for the Advancement of Structured Information Standards (OASIS) (2013)

24. OMG: Business Process Model and Notation (BPMN) Version 2.0. Object Management Group (OMG) (2011)

25. OMG: CORBA 3.3. Object Management Group (OMG) (2012)

26. Oracle: Java Remote Method Invocation - Distributed Computing for Java (2010). http://www.oracle.com/technetwork/java/javase/tech/index-jsp-138781.html

27. Pahl, C.: Containerisation and the PaaS cloud. IEEE Cloud Comput. **2**(3), 24–31 (2015)

28. da Silva, A.C.F., Breitenbücher, U., Képes, K., Kopp, O., Leymann, F.: Open-TOSCA for IoT: Automating the deployment of IoT applications based on the mosquitto message broker. In: Proceedings of the 6th International Conference on the Internet of Things (IoT 2016), pp. 181–182. ACM, November 2016

29. Stahl, T., Voelter, M., Czarnecki, K.: Model-driven software development. Technology, Engineering, Management. Wiley, Chichester (2006)

30. Taylor, M., Vargo, S.: Learning Chef. A Guide to Configuration Management and Automation. O'Reilly, Sebastopol (2014)

31. Tosatto, A., Ruiu, P., Attanasio, A.: Container-Based orchestration in cloud: state of the art and challenges. In: Ninth International Conference on Complex, Intelligent, and Software Intensive Systems (CISIS 2015), pp. 70–75. IEEE (Jul 2015)

32. W3C: Web Service Definition Language (WSDL) Version 1.1. World Wide Web Consortium (2001)

33. W3C: Web Services Addressing (WS-Addressing). World Wide Web Consortium (2004)

34. Wettinger, J., Binz, T., Breitenbücher, U., Kopp, O., Leymann, F., Zimmermann, M.: Unified invocation of scripts and services for provisioning, deployment, and management of cloud applications based on TOSCA. In: Proceedings of the 4th International Conference on Cloud Computing and Services Science (CLOSER 2014), pp. 559–568. SciTePress, April 2014
35. Wettinger, J., Breitenbücher, U., Leymann, F.: Standards-based DevOps automation and integration using TOSCA. In: Proceedings of the 7th International Conference on Utility and Cloud Computing (UCC 2014), pp. 59–68. IEEE, December 2014
36. Zimmermann, M., Breitenbücher, U., Falkenthal, M., Leymann, F., Saatkamp, K.: Standards-based function shipping - how to use TOSCA for shipping and executing data analytics software in remote manufacturing environments. In: Proceedings of the 21st IEEE International Enterprise Distributed Object Computing Conference (EDOC 2017). IEEE, October 2017
37. Zimmermann, M., Breitenbücher, U., Leymann, F.: A TOSCA-based programming model for interacting components of automatically deployed cloud and IoT applications. In: Proceedings of the 19th International Conference on Enterprise Information Systems (ICEIS), pp. 121–131. SciTePress, April 2017

Security Requirements and Tests
for Smart Toys

Luciano Gonçalves de Carvalho[1,2]([⊠]) and Marcelo Medeiros Eler[1]([⊠])

[1] School of Arts, Sciences and Humanities,
University of São Paulo, São Paulo, Brazil
{luciano.carvalho,marceloeler}@usp.br
[2] FATEC Mogi das Cruzes,
São Paulo State Technological College, São Paulo, Brazil

Abstract. The Internet of Things creates an environment to allow the integration of physical objects into computer-based systems. More recently, smart toys have been introduced in the market as conventional toys equipped with electronic components that enable wireless network communication with mobile devices, which provide services to enhance the toy's functionalities and data transmission over Internet. Smart toys provide users with a more sophisticated and personalised experience. To do so, they need to collect lots of personal and context data by means of mobile applications, web applications, camera, microphone and sensors, for instance. All data are processed and stored locally or in cloud servers. Naturally, it raises concerns around information security and child safety because unauthorised access to confidential information may bring many consequences. In fact, several security flaws in smart toys have been recently reported in the news. In this context, this paper presents an analysis of the toy computing environment based on the threat modelling process from Microsoft Security Development Lifecycle with the aim of identifying a minimum set of security requirements a smart toy should meet, and propose a general set of security tests in order to validate the implementation of the security requirements. As result, we have identified 16 issues to be addressed, 15 threats and 22 security requirements for smart toys. We also propose using source code analysis tools to validate seven of the security requirements; three test classes to validate seven security requirements; and specific alpha and beta tests to validate the remaining requirements.

Keywords: Smart toy · Security requirement · Security test
Internet of Things

1 Introduction

The Internet of Things (IoT), a pervasive and ubiquitous network that allow the interconnectivity of real-world objects, is a set of technologies which includes Machine-to-Machine communication (M2M), Machine-to-Human communication (M2H), Radio Frequency Identification (RFID), Location-Based Services (LBS), Lab-on-a-Chip (LOC) sensors, Augmented Reality (AR), robotics and vehicle telematics [1]. According to Gartner [2], "8.4 billion connected things will be in use worldwide in 2017" and

© Springer International Publishing AG, part of Springer Nature 2018
S. Hammoudi et al. (Eds.): ICEIS 2017, LNBIP 321, pp. 291–312, 2018.
https://doi.org/10.1007/978-3-319-93375-7_14

"will reach 20.4 billion by 2020". According to IDC [3], worldwide investments and business on Internet of Things (IoT) can reach $1.4 Trillion in 2021.

The IoT creates a suitable environment to allow the integration of physical objects into computer-based systems aiming at improving efficiency, accuracy and reduced human intervention in several domains. Computer-based systems can control and retrieve information from physical objects, hence information security has become one of the key concerns in IoT networks, specially when confidential data is involved.

Smart toys, which are fundamentally used by children, are examples of real-world objects that can be part of IoT networks which require special measures with respect to information security. A smart toy is a combination of three components: a conventional physical toy equipped with sensors and electronic components to enable network communication; a mobile device that provides the physical part with mobile services; and a mobile application to interact with the physical toy.

This special association between the physical toy and a mobile device has been called toy computing by Rafferty and Hung [4]. Therefore, a physical toy with embedded technology to communicate, sense and/or interact with the external environment, is a smart object in the IoT. To avoid any misunderstanding, in this paper we consider smart toys those that fall in the field of toy computing, which has an association between a physical toy and a mobile device and application. We don't refer to toys that are intended to help children to become smarter (e.g. puzzles) or toys with electronic parts that reacts to environment stimuli and even learn patterns based on user data and interaction (electronic toys).

Historically, security and safety have been of a great concern for toy manufacturers. For instance, traditional toys are designed to target specific age ranges: toys which can be disassembled in small pieces are only suitable for older children (e.g. 4+), and such information must be clearly displayed for parents to know if they are appropriate for their children. Consequently, smart toys manufacturers must also design products with safety and security requirements in mind.

By their nature, smart toys may manipulate confidential data such as private information and localisation, for example. In conventional systems, users may allow third parties to access their location or even confidential information for marketing or customization purposes, for example. Children, however, are considered vulnerable users that may not be able to make informed decisions when it comes to sharing confidential data.

Parental control mechanisms can mitigate relevant privacy issues, however they cannot avoid attacks that compromise other security properties. A simple search for smart toys security issues on any search engine can reveal how they are vulnerable to attacks. For instance, relevant sources such as Newsweek [5], Forbes [6], Fortune [7], Motherboard [8] and PCWorld [9] have reported security flaws in smart toys: information leakages (bio information, photos), toys used as spies, and outsiders interacting with children via a smart toy. Such flaws may be a threat even to the children safety since they can provide confidential information (e.g. location) and children can even unrestrictedly follow instructions given by the toy.

In fact, in July of 2017, the threats that come from the lack of security in smart toys provoke the Federal Bureau of Investigation (FBI) in the USA to raise an alert for families on the risks such toys can bring to their homes [10]. According to them, many toys sporting cloud-backed features such as speech recognition or online content hosting "could put the privacy and safety of children at risk due to the large amount of personal information that may be unwittingly disclosed". One of the reasons behind these issues is that "security safeguards for these toys can be overlooked in the rush to market them and to make them easy to use".

Unfortunately, few policies have been disclosed regarding security policies for smart toys so far. In general, solutions for specific flaws are disclosed only after a security issue is revealed. Although security solutions for IoT are available, as the Industrial Security Appliances (ISA) and Cisco ASA from CISCO Systems, they are very expensive and for more complex infrastructures. Policies and requirements have been also proposed to assure the security of mobile services and applications [11–13], nonetheless, defining such policies and requirements for smart toys requires a separate investigation since they usually run in a less secure environment, e.g. with few security controls.

A smart toy is a more vulnerable device than a mobile application because smart toys have an actual physical toy (a simpler device than a smartphone or a tablet, controlled by the mobile application) that may also collect, manipulate and store information. Moreover, it has network features to communicate with the mobile device and other computational systems, which increases the attack surface. The fact that smart toys are basically used by children makes it even more challenging, since the security policies must comply with children rights and specific acts of each country or state.

In this context, it is imperative that specific policies, regulations and requirements for smart toys be devised to assure the safety and security of their users. Researchers have been working in this specific subject [14–16], however, they have only addressed security issues restricted to privacy and confidentiality problems that, while very important, are not the only ones.

In previous work [17], we used a Security Requirements Engineering approach from Microsoft called Security Development Lifecycle (SDL) and a threat modelling tool to analyze the three components of a smart toy and their interaction aiming at identifying issues, threats and security requirements for a typical toy computing scenario. We have identified 12 issues based on specific regulations (COPPA [18] and PIPEDA [19]), 15 threats and 20 security requirements.

This paper extends our previous work by further discussing basic concepts behind toy computing, including up to date examples and security flaws reported; by taking into account the General Data Protection Regulation (GDPR) of the European Parliament and the Council of the European Union [20] during the requirements phase; and by executing the phases Verification and Implementation of the SDL process, whose results indicate security tests in order to check, in a high level, whether security requirements were implemented.

Taking into consideration the GDPR, the number of the security issues increased to 16, the number of threats remained the same and the number of the security requirements increased to 22, compared to previews work. In order to verify the accomplishment of the security requirements, we proposed the utilization of the source code analysis tools, responsible to verify 7 security requirements, 3 test classes to verify 7 security requirements and specific alpha (6) and beta (2) tests to verify the others.

The remainder of this paper is organized as follows. Section 2 shows the basic concepts of smart toys and toy computing. Section 3 presents the concepts related to security requirements. Section 4 discusses the related work. Section 5 presents the threats, the requirements identified and the security tests as well the procedure used to identify them. Finally, concluding remarks and future directions are presented in Sect. 6.

2 Smart Toys and Toy Computing

Technology evolution has been significantly changing the way people perform almost all day-by-day activities, including leisure and work activities. Not surprisingly, it has also changed the ways children play with their toys. Recently, the growing interest for technological gadgets from people of all ages has promoted the development of high tech toys, also known as smart toys.

According to Hung et al. [21], a smart toy is a device consisting of a physical toy component that connects to one or more toy computing services to facilitate gameplay in the Cloud through networking and sensory technologies to enhance the functionality of a traditional toy. A smart toy can also use camera, microphone and various other sensors to capture voice, record videos and photos, track location and to store personalized information [21]. A smart toy can be considered an Internet of Thing which can collect contextual data on the context of the user (e.g., time of day, location, weather, etc.) and provide personalized services to enhance user's experience.

Smart toys are in general composed of three parts: a conventional physical toy (such as a car or a doll) equipped with electronic components, sensors, and software which enable wireless communication with other computational systems via Wi-Fi, Bluetooth, Near Field Communication (NFC); a mobile device that provides the smart toys with mobile services to enhance their functionalities; and a mobile application that interacts with the physical toy. Figure 1 shows an illustration of this environment including the user.

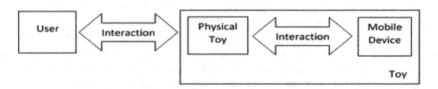

Fig. 1. Toy computing environment [16].

Rafferty and Hung [4] refer to this field of study as toy computing, which associates the physical computation (embed systems and sensors in a traditional toy) with mobile services. Table 1 shows a comparison among traditional toys, electronic toys and smart toys.

Table 1. Toys comparison.

	Traditional	Electronic	Smart
Interaction	Mechanical	Mechanical Sensor	Mechanical Sensor Visual Auditory Wireless
Data collection	No	Yes Limited	Yes
Data sharing	No	Yes Limited	Yes
Data storage	No	Yes Internal	Yes External
Processing capabilities	No	Yes Limited	Yes
Network capabilities	No	Yes Limited	Yes
Controlled by Mobile Devices	No	No	Yes

Note: Adapted from Rafferty and Hung [15].

2.1 Smart Toys Samples

Following we present an overview of a few smart toys available in the marketing aiming at providing illustration of the smart toys capabilities and specially how vulnerable they can become. The first example is called CloudPets, which consist in a stuffed pet with built in capabilities and associated mobile services. Parents, relatives or friends can record and send messages using the CloudPets App from anywhere in the world. A parent or guardian gets the message on their CloudPet App and then approves it and delivers it wirelessly to the CloudPet. When the CloudPet has a message, its heart blinks. When the child squeezes its paw, the message plays. Children can also record a message by squeezing the CloudPet's paw. The message goes wirelessly to the nearby device. From there, it can be delivered to a contact network anywhere in the world!

The Tech Recon Hammer Head and Tech Recon Havoc are high performance blasters developed by Tech 4 Kids that along with a mobile device and a mobile application provide users with a realistic battle field game experience. Figure 3 presents the Havoc model of this smart toy. The mobile application uses the GPS technology provided by the mobile device to track the users in real time. It also allows users to communicate via voice message using Wi-Fi or 3G technology.

The Mattel Fisher-Price interactive learning smart toys with voice and image recognition features are capable to collect data to adapt to create personalized playing. Figure 4 shows the Smart Toy® Bear. Through the mobile app and a Wi-Fi connection, the smart toy gets updates and the parents can unlock bonus activities (Fig. 2).

Another Mattel smart toy, the Hello Barbie is a doll equipped with a microphone, speaker and a speech recognition feature, allowing a two-way conversation when connected to a Wi-Fi network. A mobile app is required for account set up and allow

Fig. 2. CloudPets toy scheme: parents, relatives and friends can send messages via mobile services that can be played by the stuffed pet.

Fig. 3. Tech Recon Hammerhead and Tech Recon Havok (Adapted from www.tekrecon.com).

Fig. 4. Smart toy bear (Adapted from http://fisher-price.mattel.com).

parents to listen child's conversation with the toy. To improve conversation, the toy store conversations and sent them to a server in the Internet.

My friend Cayla, a smart toy doll, and I-QUE Intelligent Robot, both from Genesis Toys, are smart toys able to answer several questions and, to improve user experience, connects to the Internet through a mobile device. Figure 5 shows I-QUE environment.

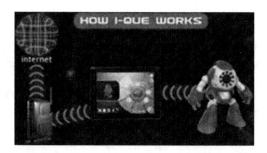

Fig. 5. I-QUE intelligent robot (Adapted from http://ique-robot.co.uk/).

2.2   Security Flaws

Most of the smart toys uses cameras, microphone and different sensors to collect, observe or infer personal information to provide customers with more personalized game experiences. The data collected by the physical part of the smart toy are sent to a mobile device and/or a server through a wireless network. The mobile application of the smart toy running in the mobile device, in turn, gets mobile services provided by Internet servers.

Data collection may be a problem when appropriate security controls are missing because private information could be exposed in a data leakage. A quick search over the internet for security issues in smart toys will reveal security flaws such as private information leakages and outsiders interacting with children via a smart toy, for example.

Spiral Toys, the CloudPets manufacturer, left customer data of its CloudPets brand on a database that wasn't behind a firewall or password-protected. The exposed database contained data on 821,396 registered users, 371,970 friend records (profile and email) and 2,182,337 voice messages. The voice messages were not in the database, but they were stored in an Amazon S3 bucket that doesn't require authentication. Moreover, customers used weak passwords making it trivial to log into their accounts and listen to the saved messages. One of the biggest concern in this context is that someone may be able to use disclosed information to send inappropriate messages to children and to gather information on families, friends, which may put children safety in risk.

Genesis Toys, which makes the Cayla and I-QUE products, was accused by consumer groups in the US, among other things, of collecting children's personal data [22]. It was possible to connect to the toys from any mobile device through Bluetooth. The data exchange between physical toy and mobile device can be easily intercepted. The Hello Barbie doll app, for example, could automatically connect to unsecured Wi-Fi networks and reveal confidential information [9]. Some Internet servers may fail to authenticate users and expose data and profiles. A Smart Toy® Bear vulnerability in the backend systems enabled attackers to access private information.

As this specific market grows, so does the concerns around the security of smart toys, especially because they are massively used by children. Children are considered vulnerable and most of the times incapable of making informed or rational decisions, that is why they are usually covered by specific acts and children's rights depending on the country or state they live. In general, children do not understand the concept of privacy and the children do not know how to protect themselves online, especially in a social media and Cloud environment. Moreover, children may disclose private information to smart toys and not be aware of the possible consequences and liabilities [21].

In such a scenario, it is urgent a proper investigation of the possible threats and security requirements a smart toy should meet to assure a reasonable level of security for its users.

3   Security Requirements

Requirements Engineering (RE) is the process of collecting, analysing, specifying and designing system requirements. Systems requirements are descriptions of the functionalities that a system must provide and its related constraints [23]. They can be classified as functional requirements, when they refer to the features a system must have, usually related to business rules, and non-functional requirements, usually related to constraints over the systems functions such as Service Level Agreement (SLA), for example.

Smart toy makers has the challenge of understanding customer needs, constraints and trends in this area in order to increase their market share and even provide customers with different products. However, they must also have a better understanding of the implications of all features each smart toy product are build with in order to take specific measures to assure their users' security and safety. Therefore, in this context, security requirements analysis plays a key role in the development process, since users usually stop using products they don't feel safe with, specially when it is a threat to their children.

Security requirements aim at assuring the confidentiality, integrity and availability of a system, which are the fundamental principles behind information security along with privacy and non-repudiation. Security requirements are usually referred as non-functional requirements as they represent system constraints which may be implemented in many ways. But they may also be classified as functional requirements when they must provide authentication, for example.

Unfortunately, software engineers are not usually trained to concern about security requirements, even in critical domains. Consequently, for a long time, systems were developed almost exclusively to meet functional requirements and almost no attention was given to security requirements. Security issues were basically met by means of security patches released after the discovery of a vulnerability [24]. Nowadays, much more attention has been given to security requirements as the number of security incidents has been growing across the time. Figure 6 shows the number of security issues reported to the United States Federal Agencies.

The process of identifying, analyzing and documenting requirements is known as Requirements Engineering. Handling security requirements demands specific knowledge and practices, thus some authors classified the process of managing security requirements as Security Requirements Engineering (SRE). There are several SRE approaches found in the literature and used in industrial level, such as Comprehensive, Lightweight Application Security Process (CLASP), Security Quality Requirements

Number of reported incidents

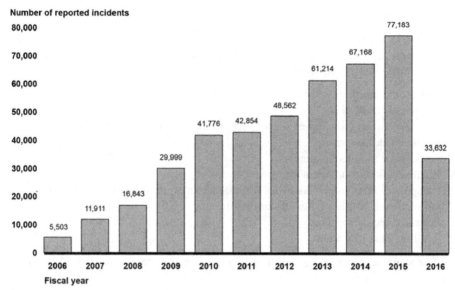

Source: GAO analysis of United States Computer Emergency Readiness Team and Office of Management and Budget data for fiscal years 2006-2016.

Fig. 6. Security incidents report [25].

Engineering (SQUARE), and the Security Development Lifecycle (SDL) from Microsoft, for example. Following, we present the details of such approaches.

3.1 CLASP

CLASP is composed of several security-related activities that can be integrated into any software development process, in order to build a security requirements set. Security requirements are formulated according to the following steps [26]:

1. Identify system roles and resources.
2. Categorize resources into abstractions.
3. Identify resource interactions through the lifetime of the system.
4. For each category, specify mechanisms for addressing each core security services.

The requirements specifier, an important role in that process, is responsible for detailing security relevant business requirements, determining protection requirements for the architectural resources, and specifying misuse cases. Misuse cases describe actors' undesirable behaviour [27].

The main activities related to requirements elicitation and performed by the requirements specifier are [28]:

- Specify operational environment.
- Identify global security policy.
- Identify resources and trust boundaries.
- Detail misuse cases.

3.2   SQUARE

SQUARE is a process that aims to integrate security concerns into the systems development life cycle. This process consider nine steps in order to elicit, categorize and prioritize security requirements, as follow [29]:

1. Agree on definitions.
2. Identify security goals.
3. Develop artifacts to support security requirements definition.
4. Perform risk assessment.
5. Select elicitation techniques.
6. Elicit security requirements.
7. Categorize requirements as to level (system, software, etc.) and whether they are requirements or other kinds of constraints.
8. Prioritize requirements.
9. Requirements inspection.

The steps related to SRE are from 5 to 9, but the steps from 1 to 4 are very important to the success of this process [29]. It is important to note that crucial artifacts, such as misuse case scenarios and diagrams, and attack trees, are created or assembled in the step 3 in order to assist the requirements elicitation process in the step 6. SQUARE can be used either to an under development system or to a released one.

3.3   SDL

Microsoft Trustworthy Computing SDL [30, 31] stands for security software development and it has the main following phases and its security mandatory tasks:

1. Requirements: security requirements establishment, quality gates and bug bars definition and documentation (set security and privacy minimum levels), and security and privacy risk analysis;
2. Design: design requirements establishment, attack surface analysis and threat modelling;
3. Implementation: approved tools utilization, insecure functions disable and static analysis execution;
4. Verification: dynamic analysis and fuzzing tests execution, and attack surface review;
5. Release: incident response plan elaboration, final security review execution and software release.

The SDL foresees its use in conjunction with both conventional and agile software development processes [31].

Requirements identification will occur in the first two phases. In the requirements phase, minimum security and privacy quality levels are established through quality gates and bug bars whereas in the design phase, security and privacy design specification is built, which describe the security and privacy features that will be exposed directly to the user.

During the design phase, performing a threat modeling is considered a critical activity, since it is a systematic process for identifying threats and vulnerabilities. The following steps are essential in threat modeling:

1. Diagram: system decomposition with Data Flow Diagrams (DFD).
2. Identify threats: system threat identification using the STRIDE (Spoofing, Tampering, Repudiation, Information disclosure, Denial of service and Elevation of privilege) approach.
3. Mitigate: address each threat identified.
4. Validate: validate the whole threat model.

Microsoft have developed the SDL Threat Modeling Tool to provide guidance on creating and analyzing threat models.

4 Related Work

Ng and his colleagues [14], aware about security and privacy issues in the toys and mobile apps union, present in their work two main security and privacy concerns: location history and data tracking, and encryption and data security. Mobile devices connected to Internet through a mobile data plan or a Wi-Fi network are susceptible to different forms of attacks (denial of service, man in the middle, spoofing, etc.). These devices usually log location history that, when it is sent over the Internet, could be intercepted, exposing motion patterns and the real time individual location.

In order to provide security and privacy, the communications must use secure protocol to ensure identities and data encryption in the data exchange. Rafferty and her colleagues through a formal privacy threat model, developed by them and inspired by well-known threat modelling techniques, have investigated privacy requirements for toy computing [31]. The analyses consider a threat architecture, illustrated in Fig. 7, and they are performed in five (5) steps:

1. Architecture overview: architectural perspective of the toy computing application.
2. Assets and data flow: assets identification and application decomposition.
3. Privacy threats: privacy threats identification and mapping.
4. Methods of attack: privacy threat trees determination and misuse case scenarios creation.
5. Privacy requirements and Controls: privacy requirements and control proposal.

According to the toy computing nature and threat architecture, privacy are affected by the following:

- Child's Identity: identity is associated with collected data.
- Location Data: collection of location data and probably association with identities.
- Networking Capabilities: collected data sharing over a network.

As a result, they have compiled six (6) privacy rights (privacy requirements):

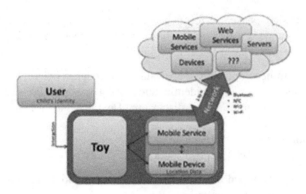

Fig. 7. Threat architecture [31].

- The right for a parent/guardian to request restrictions on the use or disclosure of private information of their child.
- The right for a parent/guardian to access, copy, and inspect collected records on their child.
- The right for a parent/guardian to request deletion of their child's private data records, or correction if records are inaccurate.
- The right for a parent/guardian to request acknowledgements through a communication channel when private information of their child is collected.
- The right to file complaints to toy company.
- The right to find out where the child's private data has been shared for purposes other than a game.

Although these work addresses security issues for smart toys, they are restricted to privacy and confidentiality problems that, while very important, are not the only ones.

Rafferty and her colleagues also proposed a privacy rule conceptual model where parents/legal guardians are the owners of their child's data and provide consent to share the data collected through access rules [16].

5   Security Requirements and Tests for Smart Toys

In order to contribute to the smart toy computing area, the main goal of this paper is to perform an analysis on typical smart toys environments and architectures to provide researchers, developers and manufacturers with a list of possible threats, security requirements and high level tests to validate the implementation of the requirements.

To achieve our goals, we used the phases Requirements and Design from the Microsoft SDL process in order to identify generic security requirements that could be used to develop any smart toy. We also used the threat modeling tool provided by Microsoft. Moreover, we followed the Implementation, Verification and Release phases from the SDL process to devise security tests check whether the security requirements have been proper implemented.

In the following subsections we present the execution of the SDL process considering as underlying architecture a typical toy computing environment: a physical toy controlled by mobile applications running in mobile devices and using mobile services.

5.1 SDL Requirements Phase

The basic features provided by smart toys are gathered based on user requirements and market trends. However, when it comes to information security, specially related to children, laws and regulations are important sources of requirements. Hence, during the Requirements phase, the main sources of information used to define the security requirements were laws and regulations the toy industry must comply with.

As smart toys are massively used by children, the first law we used to gather issues related to children information security was the Children's Online Privacy Protection Act (COPPA) [18], from the USA. From this law we identified the following issues that should be addressed:

I1. Provide notice about information collection, use and disclosure practices.
I2. Obtain parental consent for personal information collecting, using and disclosing.
I3. Not promote unnecessary personal information disclosure.
I4. Protect personal information confidentiality, integrity and availability.
   In general, personal and confidential information must be protected. Therefore, The Personal Information Protection and Electronic Documentation Act (PIPEDA) [18] was also considered during our analysis. It defines the following issues to be addressed:
I5. Provide the same protection level for third party information processing.
I6. Implement procedures to protect personal information.
I7. Document the purposes for which personal information is collected.
I8. Obtain individual consent for the personal information collection, use or disclosure.
I9. Specify the type of personal information collected.
I10. Retain personal information only as long as necessary.
I11. Maintain personal information accurate, complete and up-to-date as is necessary.
I12. Protect personal information against loss or theft, unauthorized access, disclosure, copying, use, or modification.
   Another important source of information to extract security issues is the General Data Protection Regulation (GDPR) of the European Parliament and the Council of the European Union [20]. The relevant security issues direct applied to the toy computing environment are:
I13. The request for consent must be given in an intelligible and easily accessible form.
I14. Breach notification is mandatory and data processor are required to notify their customers.
I15. Data erasure of personal data, cease the further dissemination of the data and halt processing of the data for third parties.
I16. Inclusion of data protection from the onset of the designing of systems.

COPPA, PIPEDA and GDPR address many important security aspects that may cover most issues concerning children information security policies. However, there may be other relevant issues in this context that are relevant to other countries or regions. In that case, a tailored analysis should be performed including specific regulations and laws in order to raise all security issues for smart toys and children information. Such a specific analysis is important to make sure that the threat modelling activity is able to identify all threats and then all relevant security requirements.

5.2   SDL Design Phase

We performed the design phase analysis based on the toy computing general architecture presented in Fig. 1. Moreover, we have also considered the threat architecture presented in Fig. 7. Following the SDL process, the result of this phase is presented in Fig. 8, which presents a context diagram; Fig. 9, in which a DFD level 0 is presented; and Fig. 10, which shows a DFD level 1.

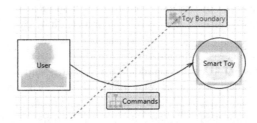

Fig. 8. Toy computing context diagram.

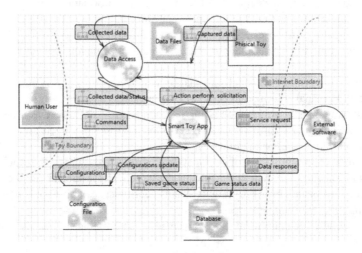

Fig. 9. Level 0 smart toy processes.

Although it is possible to continue to detail processes through lower level DFD, this strategy no longer contributes significantly to the understanding of the toy computing environment.

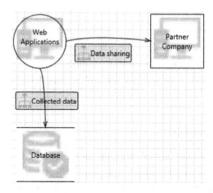

Fig. 10. Level 1 external software processes.

5.3   Threats

The threats identified, through threat modeling technique supported by STRIDE [31] are:

T1. Spoofing:
    T1.1. The children is not playing, but the attacker (insider), who wants to discover confidential information.
    T1.2. An attacker is using another mobile device to control the toy (Bluetooth parallelization).
    T1.3. The mobile service provider is fake.

T2. Tampering:
    T2.1. Modification of the configuration file of the mobile device (loads a configuration file not suitable for the user).
    T2.2. Modification of the information exchanged through network communication between the components (physical toy x mobile device x access point/router).
    T2.3. Modification of the database in the mobile device (changes the game points, user's actions history etc.).

T3. Repudiation:
    T3.1. User denies purchases of services, accessories etc.

T4. Information disclosure:
    T4.1. Disclosure of personal information stored in the database.
    T4.2. Disclosure of information used to request mobile services (localisation, context data etc.).
    T4.3. Disclosure of information stored in the mobile device (photos, video, text messages etc.).

T5. Denial of Service:
    T5.1. A service inserts enough information in the database to reach the full capacity of the mobile device storage system.
    T5.2. More than one device sends commands to the physical toy making it not able to provide the correct answer.
    T5.3. An attacker denies access to mobile services through the access point.

T6. Elevation of privilege:

> T6.1. An attacker watches the data exchanged by the network communication between the mobile device and the toy, then changes it to access the toy.
> T6.2. An attacker watches the data exchanged by the network communication between the mobile device and the mobile services, then changes it to access the mobile services.

5.4   Security Requirements

The requirements analysis, the attack surface analysis and the threat modelling were useful to identify a minimum security requirements set for smart toys in a toy computing that addresses the sixteen raised issues and fifteen threats. This set of requirements is presented as follows:

SR01. The smart toy app must provide notice of what information it collects and the further use and disclosure practices.

SR02. The smart toy app must provide an specific interface in order to identify user age and obtain user consent before the personal information collection and manipulation; in the case of child user, obtain verifiable parental consent and parental consent review.

SR03. The smart toy app must not ask for more personal information in order to continue its operation.

SR04. The smart toy app must authenticate users.

SR05. Communication between physical toy and mobile device must use a protocol that allow authentication and authorization mechanisms.

SR06. Mobile services providers must own digital certificates allowing identity verification.

SR07. Configuration file integrity must be maintained and verified in every mobile app play session.

SR08. Every communication in toy computing environment must use cryptographic mechanisms.

SR09. The Database Management Systems (DBMS) must provide user authentication.

SR10. The DBMS must provide security mechanisms against to external modification of stored data.

SR11. The smart toy app must request authentication renew before every financial transaction.

SR12. The DBMS must provide data encryption feature or allow data encryption by third-party tools.

SR13. The smart toy app must encrypt personal information accessed from others apps inside the same mobile device.

SR14. The mobile app must not access unnecessary files from others mobile apps inside the same mobile device.

SR15. The mobile app must monitor and limit database growth.

SR16. The physical toy must not accept commands from mobile devices outside the current play session.

SR17. Every communication must use secure protocol with cryptographic mechanisms.

SR18. The smart toy app must show the privacy police when required.

SR19. The smart toy must delete every unnecessary personal information collected.

SR20. The smart toy must maintain personal information accurate, complete and up-to-date as is necessary.

SR21. The smart toy app must notify users about security breach and enable updates.

SR22. The smart toy development and updates must consider well-known security principles.

Table 2 presents which security requirement addresses witch security issues ant threats.

5.5 SDL Implementation Phase

During the implementation, developers must take into account the security requirements identified in previous stages. It is important to keep in mind each requirement along with the issues and threats they refer to. That way, developers can implement the suitable security mechanisms to prevent any security issue while the smart toy is in the operation environment. Table 3 presents which security requirements can be verified with their respective security flaw.

It is important that well known and established development practices are used at this stage to detect security issues. Source code analysis tools must be used to identify

Table 2. Security requirements versus issues and threats.

Security requirement	Issues and/or Threats
SR01	I1 and I8
SR02	I2, I8 and I13
SR03	I3
SR04	T1.1
SR05	I4, I12 and T1.2
SR06	I4, I5, I12, T1.3
SR07	I4, I12, T2.1
SR08	I4, I5, I6, I12 and T2.2
SR09	I4, I12 and T2.3
SR10	I4, I12 and T2.3
SR11	T3.1
SR12	I4, I6, I12 and T4.1
SR13	I4, I6, I12 and T4.2
SR14	I4, I12 and T4.3
SR15	I4 and T5.1
SR16	I4 and T5.2
SR17	I4, I6, I12, T6.1 and T6.2
SR18	I7 and I9
SR19	I10 and I15
SR20	I11
SR21	I14
SR22	I16

well-known security flaws at the code level. These sort of security tools, also referred to as Static Application Security Testing (SAST) tools, automatically find security flaws by the inspection of the source code for occurrences of bug patterns. A list of SAST tools can be found in [32].

Table 3. Security requirements versus security flaws.

Security requirements	Security flaw
SR04	absence of user authentication mechanisms
SR05, SR08 and SR17	weak protocols utilization
SR09	weak authentication
SR13	sensitive data exposure
SR22	several security flaws

5.6   SDL Verification Phase

In this phase, more specialized security testing is required to ensure that the code application meets the established security requirements according. In order to include all possible tests, each security requirement must be validated by a class of tests [32], as follow:

- Authentication tests: digital identity verification.
- Testing for weak cryptography: sensitive data protection verification.
- Configuration and deployment management testing: deployed configuration (network, application platform etc.) verification.

Table 4 presents which class of tests applies to each security requirement at this stage of the process.

Table 4. Class of tests versus security requirements.

Security requirement	Class of tests
SR06	Authentication tests
SR07, SR10 and SR12	Testing for weak cryptography
SR14, SR15 and SR19	Configuration and deployment management testing

5.7   SDL Release Phase

The security requirements SR01, SR02, SR03, SR11, SR16, SR18, SR20 and SR 21 cannot be fully validated during development time. Therefore it can only be applied when a new release is coming out. The recommendation is that such requirements be validated during operational tests, namely alpha and beta tests. Following we present in high level which activities could be performed to validate each requirement.

In this phase, alpha tests are able to verify the accomplishment of the following security requirements:

- SR01: an informed human user must use the application to find the required notice.
- SR02: an informed human user must use the application to find the required interface.
- SR03: an informed human user must use all the resources of the smart toy without informing any extra personal information.
- SR11: an informed human user must face an authentication interface before access any paid resource.
- SR16: an informed human user must send commands to the toy during a play session of another user.
- SR18: an informed human user must request access to the privacy police and get it at any time.

Beta tests are able to verify the accomplishment of the following security requirements:

- SR20: an end user must check the accuracy, completeness and actuality of his/her data.
- SR21: an end user must check whether the application warns about security breaches and enable updates.

5.8 Discussion

The 22 security requirements identified in this study address most of the security issues found in any software products, including smart toys: confidentiality, integrity, availability, privacy, non-repudiation and authenticity. By analyzing the security problems presented by the Smart Toy® Bear, Hello Barbie, Cayla and I-QUE Intelligent robot, among others, all presented in earlier sections in this paper, it is possible to realize the effectiveness of the security achieved when the proposed security requirements are met.

Security flaws in the Smart Toy® Bear caused by the use of unsecured application programming interfaces (APIs) [6, 7] allowed attackers access personal information and send commands to the physical toy. These problems could be avoided by the implementation of the security requirements SR04, SR05, SR06, SR07, SR08, SR12, SR16 and SR17. Several vulnerabilities were uncovered in the Hello Barbie doll like communications interception, personal information disclosure and connection to unsecured Wi-Fi network [9]. These problems could be avoided by the implementation of the security requirements SR05, SR06, SR07, SR08, SR12 and SR17. The Cayla doll and I-QUE Intelligent Robot, among other problems, allowed an attacker ask children personal information and unauthorized Bluetooth connections from any near mobile device [22]. These security issues are solved by the implementation of the security requirements SR03, SR04 and SR05.

The security requirements identified in this work cover the whole toy computing environment. Therefore, future advances in the development of smart toys that comply with this environment can also benefit from this list of security requirements. The tests presented are a useful resource to identify mistakes in security solutions applied to accomplish the security requirements. The results of this work can also serve as a basis for the elaboration of security policies, since toy manufacturers usually only have privacy policies, which are less comprehensive, besides evidencing the need to formally deal with information security, which can be translated in the creation of future security standards to be met by the toy industry.

6   Concluding Remarks

The Internet of Things has been changing the way people use technology and interact with physical real world objects equipped with network technology. Toys have been around in the humanity for quite a long time and have recently been transformed into an IoT object as well. As such, beyond the natural concern regarding information security in this context, the fact that smart toys are in general used by children brings many other concerns for manufacturers and specially parents or guardians. Children are considered vulnerable by most of the children related laws and regulations around the world. In fact, most of the time they are not able to perceive situations of risk and tell the difference between situations in which they should or should not provide confidential information.

In this paper we presented the main concepts behind smart toys and how they have been a target of cybernetic attacks. We presented several examples of vulnerabilities exploited by attackers. To contribute to this specific field we presented an analysis performed on the toy computing environment using the Microsoft SDL process and its threat modelling tool to identify the main vulnerabilities, threats and consequently the minimum security requirements that every smart toy should meet. We believe the implementation of the requirements identified in this paper can minimize the number of vulnerabilities and prevent most cyberattacks that may expose users to potentially harmful situations. Moreover, we presented the relationship between each security requirement with each issue and possible threat in this context. Furthermore, we discussed aspects of the development process that should be taken into account when developing smart toys so the security requirements can be implemented and validated to increase the confiability in such products reducing the risk of attacks.

Even though it is hard to prevent cybernetic attacks, the list of 22 security requirements presented in this paper is important to allow the developers to plan how the security mechanisms will be implemented during the development life cycle of the smart toys, whereas the tests proposed are an attempt to measure the effectiveness of the security solutions. As each new smart toy may have different characteristics and even electronic components or architectures, enlarging the surface attack and the potential threats, each new smart toy will require a proper security requirements elicitation and analysis in order to ensure that any new security requirements can be identified and later included in the general list of security requirements for smart toys with their respective security tests. Also, different countries may have different laws and regulations when it comes to information security in children related technology. Understanding such aspects of each country is important to identify and implement security requirements to comply with the legislation of each target marketing. We believe the set of features of each smart toy release or version can be handled as product lines whose security features may vary according to the target marketing.

It is known that most of vulnerabilities in software systems come from the users rather than the technology itself.

Therefore, smart toys manufacturers should provide parents and guardians with information on which measures parents or guardians should take to ensure the security and safety of their children.

Moreover, it should be clearly stated for which ages the toy is appropriate for, which are the security measures the manufacturers have taken to implement security mechanisms, what are the risks involved and what parents should do when they are suspicious of any security issue.

References

1. CISCO Homepage. https://www.cisco.com/c/en/us/about/security-center/secure-iot-proposed-framework.html. Accessed 10 Sep 2017
2. Gardner Homepage. http://www.gartner.com/newsroom/id/3598917. Accessed 10 Sep 2017
3. IDC Homepage. https://www.idc.com/getdoc.jsp?containerId=prUS42799917. Accessed 10 Sep 2017
4. Rafferty, L., Hung, P.C.K.: Introduction to toy computing. In: Hung, P.C.K. (ed.) Mobile Services for Toy Computing. ISCEMT, pp. 1–7. Springer, Cham (2015). https://doi.org/10.1007/978-3-319-21323-1_1
5. Newsweek Homepage. http://www.newsweek.com/internet-connected-teddy-bear-leaks-2-million-voice-recordings-parents-and-561969. Accessed 13 Sep 2017
6. Forbes Homepage. http://www.forbes.com/sites/thomasbrewster/2016/02/02/fisher-price-hero-vulnerable-to-hackers/#359130c71cfe. Accessed 8 Dec 2016
7. Fortune Homepage. http://fortune.com/2016/02/02/fisher-price-smart-toy-bear-data-leak/. Accessed 8 Dec 2016
8. Motherboard Homepage. https://motherboard.vice.com/en_us/article/bmvnjz/hacked-toy-company-vtech-tos-now-says-its-not-liable-for-hacks. Accessed 13 Sep 2017
9. PCWorld Homepage. http://www.pcworld.com/article/3012220/security/internet-connected-hello-barbie-doll-can-be-hacked.html. Accessed 12 Dec 2016
10. Internet Crime Compliant Center (IC3) homepage. https://www.ic3.gov/media/2017/170717.aspx. Accessed 17 Sep 2017
11. Biswas, D.: Privacy policies change management for smartphones. In: IEEE International Conference on Pervasive Computing and Communications Workshops, pp. 70–75 (2012)
12. Zapata, B., Niñirola, A., Fernández-Alemán, J., Toval, A.: Assessing the privacy policies in mobile personal health records. In: 36th Annual International Conference of the IEEE Engineering in Medicine and Biology Society, pp. 4956–4959 (2014)
13. Nagappan, M., Shihab, E.: Future trends in software engineering research for mobile apps. In: IEEE 23rd International Conference on Software Analysis, Evolution, and Reengineering (SANER), vol. 5, pp. 21–32 (2016)
14. Ng, G., Chow, M., Salgado, A.L.: Toys and mobile applications: current trends and related privacy issues. In: Hung, P.C.K. (ed.) Mobile Services for Toy Computing. ISCEMT, pp. 51–76. Springer, Cham (2015). https://doi.org/10.1007/978-3-319-21323-1_4
15. Rafferty, L., Fantinato, M., Hung, P.C.K.: Privacy requirements in toy computing. In: Hung, P.C.K. (ed.) Mobile Services for Toy Computing. ISCEMT, pp. 141–173. Springer, Cham (2015). https://doi.org/10.1007/978-3-319-21323-1_8

16. Rafferty, L., Hung, P., Fantinato, M., Peres, S., Iqbal, F., Kuo, S., Huang, S.: Towards a privacy rule conceptual model for smart toys. In: Proceedings of the 50th Hawaii International Conference on System Sciences, HICSS (2017)
17. Carvalho, L., Eler, M.: Security requirements for smart toys. In: Proceedings of the 19th International Conference on Enterprise Information Systems (ICEIS 2017), vol. 2, pp. 144–154 (2017)
18. Canadian Public Works and Government Services: Personal Information Protection and Electronic Documents Act (2000)
19. United States Federal Trade Commission Homepage. http://www.coppa.org/coppa.htm. Accessed 27 Nov 2016
20. The European Parliament and the Council of the European Union: Regulation (EU) 2016/679 of the European Parliament and of the Council. Regulations, Official Journal of the European Union (2016)
21. Hung, P.C.K. (ed.): Mobile Services for Toy Computing. ISCEMT. Springer, Cham (2015). https://doi.org/10.1007/978-3-319-21323-1
22. BBC News homepage. http://www.bbc.com/news/technology-38222472. Accessed 12 Dec 2016
23. Sommerville, I.: Software Engineering, 9th edn. Pearson, Boston (2011)
24. Tondel, I., Jaatun, M., Meland, P.: Security requirements for the rest of us: a survey. IEEE Softw. **25**(1), 20–27 (2008)
25. United States Government Accountability Office homepage. https://www.gao.gov/products/GAO-17-440T. Accessed 17 Sep 2017
26. Viega, J.: Building security requirements with CLASP. In: Proceedings of the 2005 Workshop on Software Engineering for Secure Systems—SESS 2005, 15–16 May, St. Louis, MO, USA (2005)
27. Sindre, G., Opdahl, A.: Eliciting security requirements with misuse cases. Requir. Eng. **10**(1), 34–44 (2005)
28. IDA homepage. https://www.ida.liu.se/~TDDC90/literature/papers/clasp_external.pdf. Accessed 16 Nov 2016
29. US-CERT homepage. https://www.us-cert.gov/bsi/articles/best-practices/requirements-engineering/square-process. Accessed 3 Nov 2016
30. Lipner, S.: The Trustworthy computing security development lifecycle. In: Proceedings of the 20th Annual Computer Security Applications Conference (ACSAC 2004). IEEE (2004)
31. Microsoft homepage. http://www.microsoft.com/sdl. Accessed Feb 2017
32. Open Web Application Security Project (OWASP) homepage. https://www.owasp.org/index.php/Source_Code_Analysis_Tools. Accessed 17 Sep 2017
33. Open Web Application Security Project (OWASP) homepage. https://www.owasp.org/index.php/OWASP_Testing_Guide_v4_Table_of_Contents. Accessed 17 Sep 2017

An Approach for Semantically-Enriched Recommendation of Refactorings Based on the Incidence of Code Smells

Luis Paulo da Silva Carvalho[1](✉), Renato Lima Novais[2](✉),
Laís do Nascimento Salvador[3], and Manoel Gomes de Mendonça Neto[3]

[1] Federal Institute of Bahia, 3150 - Zabele, Vitoria da Conquista, Bahia, Brazil
`luispscarvalho@gmail.com`, {`luiscarvalho,renato`}`@ifba.edu.br`
[2] Federal Institute of Bahia, 39 - Canela, Av. Araújo Pinho, Salvador, Bahia, Brazil
[3] Federal University of Bahia,
Av. Ademar de Barros, s/n, Ondina, Salvador, Bahia, Brazil
{`laisns,manoel.mendonca`}`@ufba.br`

Abstract. Code smells are symptoms of bad decisions on the design and development of software. The occurrence of code smells in software can lead to costly consequences. Refactorings are considered adequate resources when it comes to reducing or removing the undesirable effects of smells in software. Ontologies and semantics can play a substantial role in reducing the interpretation burden of software engineers as they have to decide about adequate refactorings to mitigate the impact of smells. However, related work has given little attention to associating the recommendation of refactorings with the use of ontologies and semantics. Developers can benefit from the combination of code smells detection with a semantically-oriented approach for recommendation of refactorings. To make this possible, we expand the application of our previous ontology, **ONTO**logy for **C**ode sm**Ell** **AN**alysis (ONTOCEAN), to combine it with a new one, **O**ntology for **SO**ftware **RE**factoring (OSORE). We also introduce a new tool, our **RE**factoring **RE**commender **SYS**tem (RESYS) which is capable of binding our two ontologies. As a result, refactorings are automatically chosen and semantically linked to their respective code smells. We also conducted a preliminary evaluation of our approach in a real usage scenario with four open-source software projects.

Keywords: Ontology · Semantic · Refactoring · Recommendation
Code smells

1 Introduction

Code smells are metaphors used to describe bad effects of certain design and implementation choices. Such bad effects reflect on difficulties of comprehending and maintaining the software [7,8]. Long method is an example of code smell

© Springer International Publishing AG, part of Springer Nature 2018
S. Hammoudi et al. (Eds.): ICEIS 2017, LNBIP 321, pp. 313–335, 2018.
https://doi.org/10.1007/978-3-319-93375-7_15

that refers to methods that are too long and have many variables, parameters, or conditional tests. For instance, long methods are hard to read and reuse [10]. A software engineer can exploit instances of code smells found in software to improve the source code. In this case, developers can revise methods detected as long methods to reduce their sizes and complexities. Thus, it is important for developers to know about how to apply adequate refactorings in such situations.

Counsell *et al.* [11] define refactoring as a change made to software in order to improve its structure without changing the program's semantic. The authors also point out the advantages of refactoring: (a) it reduces the complexity and increases the comprehensibility of the code; (b) it contributes to make the maintenance of software relatively easy which represents both a short-term and long-term benefit. Refactoring-related operations can be time-consuming when performed manually, so it is important to seek ways to automate them [15]. According to Fowler [17], code smells found in a software project can reveal refactoring opportunities. A natural way to recommend refactorings can be based on the incidence of smells in the source code of software systems.

While developing the ONTOCEAN, we noticed that related work usually bases the analysis of software projects on syntactic operations. As a consequence, the advantages of the intrinsic semantic properties of software projects are not taken into account. Moreover, related work has given little attention to associating semantics with the recommendation of refactorings. For instance, other areas of software engineering [5,6] have already exploited Semantic Recommendation [14], but we were not able to find any related work that attempted to bring such approach into refactorings recommendation.

In our previous work [9], we developed an ontology to support the management of code smells in software. Our **ONTO**logy for **C**ode sm**E**lls **AN**alysis (ONTOCEAN) can be used to: (a) represent information about smells and (b) manage the impact of smells on software projects. We added axiomatic rules to ONTOCEAN with the purpose of retrieving instances of smells mined from the source code of software projects. According to the criteria stored in the rules, semantic reasoners can retrieve and present the instances of code smells. However, ONTOCEAN lacks resources to enable the recommendation of refactorings considering the occurrence of smells.

With the purpose of supporting the semantic recommendation of refactorings, we expand the purpose of ONTOCEAN by associating it with a new ontology. Our **O**ntology for **SO**ftware **RE**factoring (OSORE) encapsulates classes to represent refactorings. For instance, the 'Decompose Conditional' (DC) is a refactoring that can be used to refactor methods of classes affected by the 'Long Method' smell [17]. DC aims at reducing the complexity of conditional expressions which is a common cause of long methods. We have embedded information about refactorings, such as DC, into OSORE with the intention to use it as catalog for ONTOCEAN, *i.e.*, OSORE contains a repository of refactorings which is used to populate ONTOCEAN with ontological instances of refactorings. Later on, software engineers and developers can benefit from the recommendations to increase the quality of software projects they work on. By associating ONTOCEAN with OSORE we have provided ways to make semantically-enriched recommendations of refactoring possible.

On the interest of basing the recommendation of refactorings on a semantically-oriented approach, we broadened the requirements defined in our prior work [9]. Table 1 contains information about the new requirements.

Table 1. Requirements for a semantically-enriched recommendation of refactorings.

Req. id	Description
REQ 1	The catalog of refactorings stored in OSORE must be able to provide recommendations for code smells embedded in instances of ONTOCEAN
REQ 2	Recommendations must precisely locate the item of the software (*e.g.*, method, class) which each refactoring is applicable to
REQ 3	The approach must indicate how the refactoring can be applied to fix parts of the source code that have been affected by code smells

Requirement **REQ 1** ensures that all code smells found in the instances of ONTOCEAN will be semantically linked to refactorings stored in OSORE. The code smells mapped into ONTOCEAN can refer to either methods (*e.g.*, Long Method) or entire classes (*e.g.*, God Class) of a software. We must take advantage of such feature and link each refactoring to the respective method or class it applies to (then fulfilling requirement **REQ 2**). The intention is to enable developers to spot the components of the software systems that contain smells and bind them to the correct refactoring(s). Adding classes to OSORE to represent templates for the refactorings can fulfill Requirement **REQ 3**. The templates are code samples that show how to use the refactorings. Fowler has documented the templates [17] and viewing them can be helpful for developers. They will know how to implement the refactoring.

The fulfillment of the aforementioned requirements enabled us to realize the following contributions: (a) combining a new ontology, OSORE, with our previous one, ONTOCEAN. Such combination enables the recommendation of refactorings suited for code smells; (b) embedding of functionalities into a new tool to enable the recommendation of refactorings through the automatic binding of classes from OSORE to those of ONTOCEAN; and (c) performing the analysis of the recommendations for real software projects in order to spot ways to improve our approach.

The rest of this paper is organized as follows: Sect. 2 describes the method we used in our studies. OSORE, our new ontology, is detailed in Sect. 3. Section 4 presents our new tool, the **RE**factoring **RE**commender **SYS**tem (RESYS), that uses ONTOCEAN and OSORE to recommend refactorings. We use RESYS to evaluate our approach in Sect. 5. Section 6 presents our conclusions and future work.

2   Study Methodology

To fulfill the aforementioned requirements, we defined and followed the activities shown in Fig. 1. 'Activity 1' has the purpose of acquiring knowledge about the state of art in areas that can contribute to our goals. We focused on two types of related work:

1. Efforts in mapping code smells onto adequate refactorings – as we developed our new ontology (OSORE), we used the mapping to link each type of code smell to its respective refactorings. We present our mapping, extracted from related work and embedded in OSORE, in Sect. 3.1;
2. Efforts in defining architectural principles and practices for semantically-oriented recommendations. We analyzed such efforts to elicit desirable characteristics for our recommending system. Then, we used the elicited information to conceptualize and implement the **RE**factoring **RE**commender **SYS**tem (RESYS). More detail can be found in Sect. 4.

After we familiarized with refactorings, we embedded them into our new ontology, OSORE, as proposed in 'Activity 2'. During the fulfillment of 'Activity 3', we created a new tool to enable the use of OSORE in combination with ONTOCEAN: RESYS. 'Activity 4' and 'Activity 5' aimed at evaluating the application of our approach in the detection of code smells ('Activity 4') and recommendation of refactorings ('Activity 5').

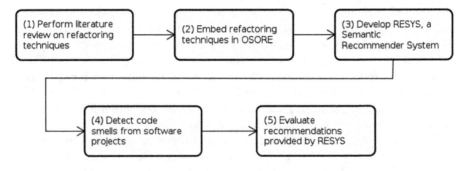

Fig. 1. Study's method.

3   An Ontology for SOftware REfactoring (OSORE)

In this section, we present OSORE: an **O**ntology for **SO**ftware **RE**factoring. It contains classes that can be used to represent refactorings. The main purpose of OSORE is to propose refactoring techniques after code smells are detected and stored in instances of ONTOCEAN. We have achieved this by linking the ontological classes of ONTOCEAN (code smells) to the classes of OSORE (refactorings).

Figure 12 shows our schema of ontologies. 'A' points to the classes of ONTO-CEAN. 'B' highlights the classes that were added to OSORE. The 'Refactoring' class encapsulates attributes of refactoring techniques. Each 'Refactoring' has a 'Template'. The 'Template' class represents an example (*e.g.*, a source code sample) of the refactoring technique. For instance, 'DC' is an instance of 'Refactoring'[1]. It represents the 'Decompose Conditional' refactoring. 'DCTemplate' is an instance of 'Template' and it contains two excerpts of source code. The first excerpt shows an example of source code affected by the Long Method smell. The second excerpt shows the source code refactored by DC. 'DC' is semantically linked to 'LMInstance', which is an instance of a Long Method smell. Thus, by associating 'DC' with instances of Long Method we are semantically representing that 'DC' is suited to refactor this type of smell. One key feature of OSORE is the use of the object property, 'refactoredBy', which binds the instances of classes that represent smells (stored in ONTOCEAN) to their respective refactoring techniques (instances of refactorings from OSORE) (Fig. 2).

Another important part of OSORE is the representation of refactoring templates. Each template gives developers a hint about how to apply a refactoring technique. Taking DC as an example, the source code excerpt bellow illustrates the body of a method detected as a long method [17]:

```
...
if (date.before (SUMMER_START) || date.after(SUMMER_END))
  charge = quantity * _winterRate + _winterServiceCharge;
else charge = quantity * _summerRate;
...
```

As the number of conditional statements is used to detect instances of long method from the source code, DC proposes encapsulating statements in other methods to prevent this type of smell from happening. The following fragment of source code [17] shows the result of the application of DC:

```
...
if (notSummer(date))
  charge = winterCharge(quantity);
else charge = summerCharge (quantity);
...
```

We have added all refactoring templates mentioned from this point (DC included) to OSORE as instances of the 'Template' ontological class. Figure 3 shows an instance of DC's refactoring template. 'A' points to the template's instance 'DCTemplate'. 'B' shows pieces of source code that represent the 'before' and 'after' the application of DC.

---

[1] 'DC' is used as an example to illustrate the representation of refactorings, but OSORE contains other ones. The full schema of OSORE's ontological classes and instances can be found at the end of this paper.

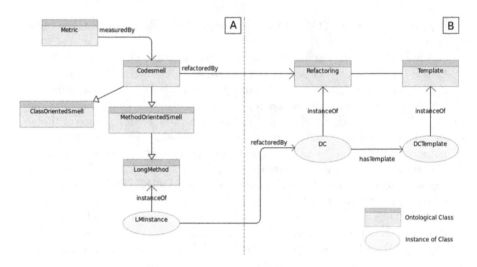

Fig. 2. Ontology for **SO**ftware **RE**factoring (OSORE).

3.1   OSORE's Catalog of Refactoring Techniques

We performed an exploratory study to collect information about refactoring techniques. In specific, we focused on studies that have either: (a) proposed taxonomies for software refactoring or (b) experimented with the techniques suited to mitigate the effects of smells. We used the information collected from the studies to create a catalog of refactoring techniques which we embedded in OSORE.

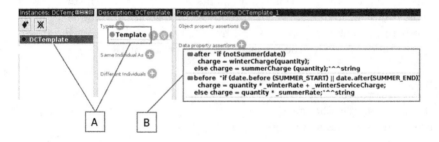

Fig. 3. Template showing 'before' and 'after' the application of DC

Each refactoring technique has been mapped onto a specific set of code smells that our mining tool, **O**ntology-Oriented **C**ode sm**E**ll **AN**alyzer (OCEAN)[2] [9], is capable of detecting. Table 2 describes the smells [1,10,17].

---

[2] We used OCEAN in our previous work to automate the detection of code smells.

Table 2. Detectable code smells.

Code smell	Description
God Class	Long and complex class that centralizes the intelligence of the system
Brain Method	Long and complex method that centralizes the intelligence of a class
Brain Class	Complex class that accumulates intelligence by brain methods
Long Method	A method that is too long or has many variables, parameters or conditional statements
Data Class	Class that contains data but not behavior related to the data
Feature Envy	When a method makes too many call to other classes to obtain data or to access functionalities

Table 3. OSORE's catalog of refactorings.

Code smell	Refactorings
Long Method	Extract Method (EM), Replace Temp With Query (RTWQ), Introduce Parameter Object (IPO), Preserve Whole Object (PWO), Decompose Conditional (DC), Replace Method With Method Object (RMWMO), Consolidate Conditional Expression (CCE)
Data Class	Move Method (MM), Encapsulate Field (EF), Encapsulate Collection (ECo), Hide Method (HM), EM
God Class	Extract Interface (EI), Extract Sub Class (ESubC), Replace Data With Object (RDWO), Extract Hierarchy (EH), Extract Super Class (ESupC), Move Field (MF), MM, Pull-up Field (PF), Pull-up Method (PM), Replace Conditional With Polymorphism (RCWP)
Feature Envy	EM, MM, PM, MF
Brain Method	EM, RMWMO, RCWP, MM
Brain Class	Extract Class (EC), EM

We considered the refactorings described by Fowler [17] as a natural path to follow since several related studies have adopted his findings. Our catalog of refactorings, detailed in Table 3, reflects this preference once all refactorings mentioned by related work [10–13] were originally defined by Fowler.

OSORE's catalog is not exhaustive. More refactorings can be added to the ontology as further investigations may prove that other ones are fit to fix defective source code. We have paired refactorings with the code smells that OCEAN is capable of detecting. Consequently, the list of smells and related refactorings is likely to grow in the future as we expand our detection/recommending strategies.

4   RESYS: A Semantic Recommender System Based on OSORE

In the interest of evaluating the application of OSORE (in association with ONTOCEAN) we decided to create a Recommender System (RS). Our recommender, **RE**factorings **RE**commender **SYS**tem (RESYS), has the intention to furnish recommendations of refactorings for software engineers and developers. RESYS relies upon ONTOCEAN to take instances of code smells mined from software projects as input. As a result, RESYS must provide information about adequate refactorings stored in OSORE. RESYS enables software specialists to find instances of code smells and to count on ways to reduce the negative impact of smells in software systems.

RS can be defined as a program that recommends suitable items (products or services) to users by evaluating user's interest in an item based on information about the items, the users, and the interactions between items and users [2]. A refactoring recommendation system, such as RESYS, fits into this definition. Refactorings are the suitable items offered to users. The users, software engineers and developers, have an interest in refactorings which they can use to improve the quality of the source code of programs.

RESYS is a specific type of RS. Among all types of RS, there are those characterized by the incorporation of semantic knowledge: the Semantic Recommender Systems (SRS). The addition of semantics to a RS aims at improving the quality of the recommendations [14]. As the information acquires semantic meaning, its representation, interpretation, searching, sharing and reuse is enhanced [3]. RESYS is a SRS in the sense that it is based on an ontology-oriented approach to semantically enrich the knowledge about the relationship between code smells and refactorings.

4.1   An Architecture for RESYS

Before creating RESYS we investigated about possible software architectures appropriate for the development of SRS. In specific, we wanted to know the architectural design decisions that are important to take in consideration.

Codina and Ceccaroni [14] presented an architectural design based on a service-oriented recommendation engine. The authors claim that their approach is abstract enough to allow its application under varied contexts of use. Such a feature is granted by the input of domain-specific ontologies into the engine. We found another candidate architecture in [3]. The architecture is also based on a service-oriented approach to enable the creation of e-learning recommending systems. Ouni *et al.* [4] developed a multi-objective refactoring recommendation approach to introduce design patters and fix code smells in software (MORE). MORE's purpose is closely aligned with RESYS's: recommendation of refactorings. Although the authors do not explicitly classify MORE as a SRS, it uses semantic constraints to propose design patterns and refactorings for an analyzed software.

The architecture of RESYS reflects the main characteristics from the afore-mentioned SRS: (a) it relies upon the use of ontologies to process information about recommendations, and (b) it is a service-oriented architecture (SOA). As shown in Fig. 4, RESYS manipulates both ONTOCEAN and OSORE using the Java OWL API[3]. The targeted architecture takes an instance of ONTOCEAN as input and produces a new one in which the classes that represent smells are mapped onto those in OSORE that represent refactorings. The instances of ONTOCEAN are the same that we produced in our previous work [9]. The instances of ONTOCEAN are populated by the addition of refactorings that can revert a software artifact from being affected by smells. To add SOA's features to RESYS we used the Java Jersey API[4].

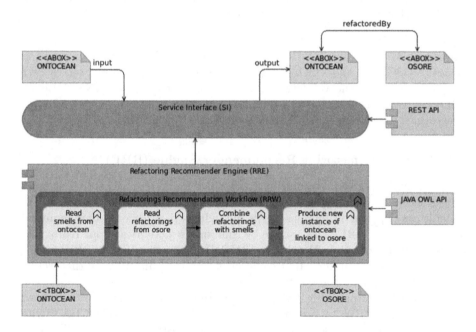

Fig. 4. The architecture of RESYS.

RESYS encapsulates two main modules: (a) a Service Interface (SI) and (b) a Refactorings Recommender Engine (RRE). SI is the entry point through which client applications input instances of ONTOCEAN into RESYS. RRE is respon-sible for the addition of refactorings in the instances of ONTOCEAN. We have achieved this by the executing the routines of our Refactorings Recommendation Workflow (RRW) (illustrated in Fig. 4). The routines are defined as follows:

---

[3] http://owlapi.sourceforge.net/.

[4] https://jersey.github.io/.

1. **Read Smells from ONTOCEAN** – RESYS depends on Java OWL API to read information about smells from ONTOCEAN. The instances of smells are used to select the most suitable refactorings.
2. **Read Refactorings from OSORE** – RESYS also counts on the Java OWL API to read OSORE in order to retrieve refactorings. OSORE is used as a repository of information about refactorings.
3. **Combine Refactorings with Smells** – after retrieving instances of smells (from ONTOCEAN) and refactorings (from OSORE) this routine combines both into a new ontology, *i.e.*, refactorings are mapped onto respective smells (as described in Table 3).
4. **Produce New Instance of ONTOCEAN Linked to OSORE** – the mapping between smells and refactorings is stored in a new instance of ONTOCEAN that is semantically linked to OSORE.

We replicate the approach of our previous work [9]. We automated the production of A-Boxes[5] from T-Boxes[6] ontologies. Our T-Boxes are composed of both ONTOCEAN and OSORE. ONTOCEAN's T-Box ontology serves as a template to enable the validation and processing of ONTOCEAN's A-Boxes. OSORE's T-Box is also used as a template, but with a different purpose: to link refactorings to the instances of smells stored in ONTOCEAN.

4.2 RESYS' Refactoring Recommender Engine (RRE)

We designed RESYS to recommend refactorings for code smells stored as ontological classes (*i.e.*, individuals) in ONTOCEAN. The recommendation of the refactorings depends on binding smells individuals to other ones that represent refactorings in OSORE. This is done by running the activities of our **Refactorings Recommendation Workflow (RRW)** as shown in Fig. 4. RRW is part of RRE. As RRE is an important component of our architecture, in this section we provide more details about it.

For didactic purpose, Fig. 5 illustrates a communication diagram that shows how RRE uses RRW to propose refactorings by uniting ONTOCEAN with OSORE. OCEAN mines software projects into new instances of ONTOCEAN (as describe in our previous work [9]). The instances of ONTOCEAN can be input into RESYS to initiate the recommendation workflow (activity '1' of the diagram). RRE is dependant on two components that are capable of manipulating the ontologies: **OceanConnector** and **OsoreConnector**. The recommendation begins by reading all refactorings-related individuals from OSORE (performed by the activity '2'). Each refactoring has been mapped onto the specific set of smells they are applicable to (as described in Table 3). As the smells are retrieved from ONTOCEAN (activity '3') the mapping is used to recommend adequate refactorings (activity '4'). The output of the recommendations is stored as links between a new instance of ONTOCEAN (generated by activity '5') and OSORE.

---

[5] Assertional Box.
[6] Terminological Box.

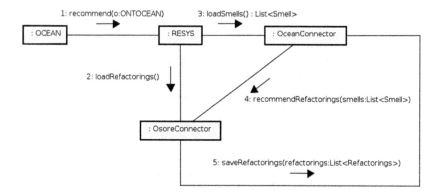

Fig. 5. RESYS' Refactoring Recommender Engine (RRE).

5 Scenario Examples of Usage and Analysis

This section describes how we evaluated OSORE and RESYS to propose refactorings to code smells stored in instances of ONTOCEAN. The intention was to simulate a real usage scenario in which RESYS processes code smells detected from software projects and creates a new instance of ONTOCEAN which is linked to the refactorings stored in OSORE.

We focused on the refactorings recommended to software projects presented in Table 5. Our main purpose was twofold: (a) we wanted to check if the refactorings were recommended to their respective instances of code smells, as described in Table 3; and (b) we wanted to evaluate if the semantic binding between our two ontologies, ONTOCEAN and OSORE, has fulfilled the requirements detailed in Table 1.

We expanded the tests to evaluate our approach on projects that were not taken in consideration by our previous work [9]. We tested our approach on the two software projects we used before, JUnit[7] and Log4j[8], and added two new ones: Google-Guava[9] and DbFit[10]. Table 4 lists the software projects which RESYS recommended refactorings to. The tag numbers (third column in Table 4) refer to the specific versions of the software systems that were analyzed. Such versions correspond to stable releases of each software project.

We executed OCEAN to mine the projects and to detect instances of code smells from the source code. One important remark: OCEAN can detect smells through different versions of software projects, *i.e.*, OCEAN seeks occurrences of code smells through all commits obtained from specific tags and/or branches of the targeted software systems. Consequently, as OCEAN mines the software projects all the historical data containing the occurrences of code smells are

---

[7] https://github.com/junit-team.
[8] https://github.com/apache/log4j.
[9] https://github.com/google/guava.
[10] https://github.com/dbfit.

Table 4. Evaluated software projects.

Soft. project	Description	Tag/Version
JUnit	API that automates unitary tests of software	R5.0.0-M1
Google-Guava	Core libraries used by several Google's projects: collections, caching, primitives support, concurrency libraries, common annotations, string processing, I/O, and so forth	v8.0
DbFit	A testing framework that supports test-driven development of database code	v3.1.0
Log4j	A library that adds logging routines to programs	v1.2.9

stored in ONTOCEAN. Accordingly, as RESYS recommends refactorings, the recommendations will date back to the first instances of code smells attached to a particular tag/version. Table 5 summarizes the instances of code smells and refactorings for the software projects we analyzed.

Table 5. Code smells and refactorings per software Project.

Software project	Long method	God class	Data class	Brain method	Brain class	Feature envy	Number of recommendations
JUnit	290	134	21	1	0	23320	73304
Google-Guava	627	179	1	20	0	10532	37661
DbFit	317	126	0	12	0	3135	12794
Log4j	1147	199	28	161	67	2747	18818

Figure 6 shows the refactorings recommended for the God Classes mined from Google-Guava's source code (pointed by 'A'). 'B' highlights the refactorings that can mitigate the bad effects of this type of code smell. The 'refactoredBy' object property binds each instance of smell (stored in ONTOCEAN) to the refactorings (stored in OSORE). This link between our two ontologies evidences that **REQ 1** was accomplished. The 'hasMeasured' object property points to the metrics (and their values) which were used to detect the instances of smells (indicated by 'C'). 'D' informs the location of the code smell, *i.e.*, the physical location of the class that was recognized as a God Class. Thus, **REQ 2** is fulfilled.

As we managed to evaluate ONTOCEAN in our prior work [9] we proposed that developers who have introduced instances of smells in software projects[11] should be trained in adequate programming techniques to prevent further decay in the quality of the source code. We are positive that allowing developers to grow knowledgeable about such techniques can prevent smells from being inserted in

---

[11] We called such developers 'code smells propagators'.

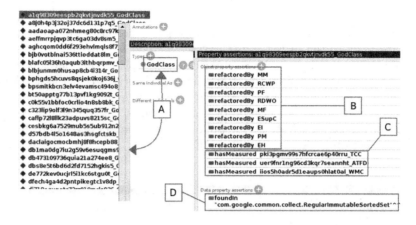

Fig. 6. Accessing refactorings recommended for code smells.

software projects. By linking OSORE's classes (the ones that represent refactorings) to ONTOCEAN's smells we are providing an initial guideline for developers about good practices that can be applied in the making of software systems. Figure 7 contains an example of refactorings recommended for a Log4j's developer who introduced an instance of Feature Envy in the source code. 'A' points to the email of the developer[12]. 'B' is the type of smell which was added by the developer (Feature Envy). 'C' highlights the refactorings he/she can use to remove the smell. 'D' is the location of the smell (the class and method that has been affected by the Feature Envy smell).

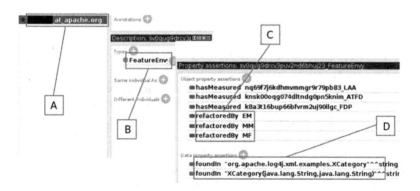

Fig. 7. Accessing the refactorings recommended for a developer.

---

[12] The name of the developer was blurred out for privacy.

After having found out the smells he/she introduced the developer can also consult the template of the refactorings. Considering, for instance, the instance of Feature Envy shown in Fig. 7, the Extract Method (EM) refactoring is recommended. Figure 8 displays the before and after templates that developers can consult to learn how to apply the refactoring. 'A' indicates that the developer is visualizing the template of the EM refactorings. 'B' points to an example of source code prior to the application of EM. 'C' shows how the source code is expected to be refactored as EM is applied. By allowing developers to browse proposed refactorings, we have fulfilled **REQ 3**.

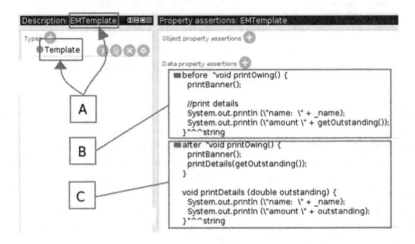

Fig. 8. Accessing the template of a code smell.

5.1   Using SPARQL to Detail Data Analysis

Querying data is important in the context of semantically-oriented approaches. It provides mechanisms via which users and applications can interact with ontologies and data [16]. For instance, applications can use the data shown in Fig. 8 as long as they are able to extract such data from the instances of ONTOCEAN. To evaluate of previous work [9] we relied on rule-based axioms to select the data. We now experiment with SPARQL[13] to automate the retrieval of refactorings. As SPARQL resembles SQL we believe that it is more intuitive for programmers who create applications that extracts data from ontologies.

The following SPARQL query retrieves the refactorings recommended for a developer who committed God Classes to Google-Guava project[14]:

---

[13] https://www.w3.org/TR/sparql11-overview/.

[14] All prefixes of referenced ontologies has been shortened to better fit in article's page.

```
1SELECT ?committer ?datetime ?location ?refactoring
2WHERE {
3   ?committer repo:hasCommited ?commit .
4   ?commit repo:datetime ?datetime .
5   ?commit ocean:hasIntroduced ?codesmell .
6   ?codesmell rdf:type smells:GodClass .
7   ?codesmell ocean:foundIn ?location .
8   ?codesmell ocean:refactoredBy ?refactoring .
9 FILTER regex(str(?committer), "*identification*of*committer").
10}
11 ORDER BY DESC (?datetime)
```

Considering a particular 'committer' specified in the filter (line #9), the query finds all instances of code smells that he/she has added to Google-Guava. The 'hasIntroduced' object property (line #5) is used to bind all the instances of 'commit' that were sent by the 'committer' and that have introduced instances of smells in the software. In line 6 we constrain the search to refactorings that are fit to deal with God Classes. The 'foundIn' object property (line #7) retrieves the location of the smell (*i.e.*, the class that has been detected as a God Class). The 'refactoredBy' object property (line #8) lists all possible refactorings which can mitigate the effects of the smell or even remove it. As ONTOCEAN may contain many instances of God Classes that were introduced through the evolution of Google-Guava, we have ordered by the date-and-time, new instances first (line #11).

Executing the query will retrieve a list of refactorings for a developer who has introduced God Classes in the project. Figure 9 shows the result of querying the data using Protege IDE[15]. The first column of the resultset shows the name of the developer to whom refactorings will be recommended. The second column informs the datetime the instance of God Class was added to the source code. The third column shows the name of the class which were detected as God Class. The fourth column indicates the recommended refactorings.

committer	datetime	location	refactoring
at_google.com_at"2010-10-29 02:48:00"	"com.google.common.collect.Iterables"	ESupC
at_google.com_at"2010-10-29 02:48:00"	"com.google.common.collect.Iterables"	RDWO
at_google.com_at"2010-10-29 02:48:00"	"com.google.common.collect.Iterables"	PM
at_google.com_at"2010-10-29 02:48:00"	"com.google.common.collect.Iterables"	PF
at_google.com_at"2010-10-29 02:48:00"	"com.google.common.collect.Iterables"	MF
at_google.com_at"2010-10-29 02:48:00"	"com.google.common.collect.Iterables"	MM
at_google.com_at"2010-10-29 02:48:00"	"com.google.common.collect.Iterables"	EH
at_google.com_at"2010-10-29 02:48:00"	"com.google.common.collect.Iterables"	EI
at_google.com_at"2010-10-29 02:48:00"	"com.google.common.collect.Iterables"	RCWP

Fig. 9. Querying refactorings recommended for a developer.

---

[15] http://protege.stanford.edu/.

SPARQL is also capable of fetching information about the templates of a refactoring (as depicted in Fig. 8). The following query retrieves templates of all refactorings recommended for God Classes:

```
12  SELECT ?refactoring ?codesmell ?before ?after
13  WHERE {
14    ?refactoring osore:hasTemplate ?template .
15    ?refactoring osore:applicableTo ?codesmell .
16    ?template osore:before ?before .
17    ?template osore:after ?after .
18    FILTER regex(str(?codesmell), "GodClass") .
19  }
```

The query filters the resultset to only include refactorings that are applicable to God Classes (line #18). The 'applicableTo' object property (line #15) ensures that only refactorings that are mapped to this type of smell is fetched. As we are also interested in the refactorings' templates (line #14), the query also contains instructions to retrieve the 'before' and 'after' source code samples (lines #16 and #17). This type of query consults OSORE directly with no need of involving an instance of ONTOCEAN. In this case, we want to emphasize that OSORE is logically independent of ONTOCEAN and shows potential to be combined with any other resource to indicate refactorings for smells.

Figure 10 shows the resultset obtained from the execution of the previous query. The first column shows the refactorings. The second column confirms that the query retrieved only templates for God Classes. The third and fourth column show the before and after code sample of the template.

refact...	codesm...	before	after
MF	"GodClass"	public class Class1 { aField; } public class Clas	"public class Class1 { aField; } pu
RDWO	"GodClass"	public class Order { String customer; }"^^<ht	"public class Order { Customer c
EH	"GodClass"	public class BillingScheme { public void proces	"public interface BillingScheme {
ESupC	"GodClass"	public class Department { double getTotalAnn	"public class Party { double getT
MM	"GodClass"	public class Class1 { aMethod(); } public class	"public class Class1 { } public cla
RCWP	"GodClass"	double getSpeed() { switch (_type) { case EUF	"public abstract class Bird { dou
PM	"GodClass"	public class Employee { } public class Salesm:	"public class Employee { getNam
PF	"GodClass"	public class Employee { } public class Salesm:	"public class Employee { String n
EI	"GodClass"	public class ProcessController { public void do.	"public interface ControllerInterfa

Fig. 10. Querying templates for refactorings.

5.2   Ranking and Precedence of Refactorings

In this section we use SPARQL statements to analyze the incidence and the relationships between the different types of refactorings. The statement bellow ensures that only the commits that introduced smells are taken into account (lines #22 and #23). Line #24 links the instances of smell to the recommended refactorings. Figure 11 translates the resultset obtained from the statement as a timeline of refactorings. The 'ORDER BY' instruction (line #26) sorts the resultset by the datetime of selected commits.

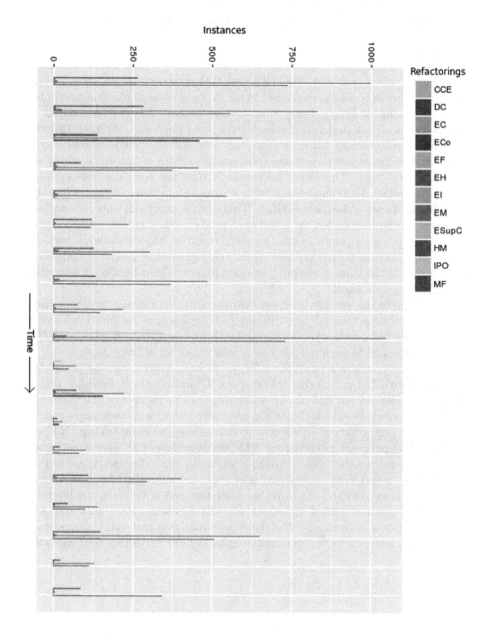

Fig. 11. Incidence of refactorings through time (Log4j).

```
20 SELECT ?datetime ?codesmell ?refactoring
21 WHERE {
22   ?commit repo:datetime ?datetime .
23   ?commit ocean:hasIntroduced ?codesmell .
24   ?codesmell ocean:refactoredBy ?refactoring .
25 }
26 ORDER BY ?datetime
```

Figure 11 shows that EM, MF, DC, and MM stand out as the most recommended refactorings. They are related to the types of code smells that abounded from the mining of Log4j: Long Method and Feature Envy. The analysis of Google-Guava, JUnit, and DbFit revealed the same phenomenon. Analyzing the tendency of refactorings through time can help software engineers to decide about optimal strategies to manage code smells and the refactorings which are fit to mitigate them. Therefore, we conclude that the semantic relationships between the refactorings can benefit from a 'priority' property: **refactoring 'R' hasPriority Low—Medium—High**. This new property can rank refactorings after they are recommended for a software project. Ranking the recommended refactorings to higher priorities may have an educative impact on developers. As soon as they are instructed on how to fix the problematic pieces of code they may not repeat the inadequate programming practices that tend to produce the most common code smells.

In addition to the 'priority' property we also want to evaluate the intersection between refactorings through time. Taking EM, for instance, as shown in Table 3, it is applicable to fix code artifacts affected by both Long Method and Data Class smells. In case EM is recommended as a refactoring for a Long Method 'M' of a Data Class 'C' and as a refactoring for 'C' as well, developers may preferably experiment with EM refactoring 'M' and not 'C' in first place. Perhaps, prioritizing the application of EM on 'M' will contribute to remove or attenuate the effects of the smell found in 'C'. As a consequence, the recommendation can be refined by adding a 'precede' property to our ontologies: **refactoring 'R1' on location 'L1' precede refactoring 'R2' on location 'L2'**. To evaluate such possibility we rely on the next SPARQL statements. Both statements are similar as they select refactorings (lines #31 and #41) recommended for instances of code smells (lines #33 and #43). As we are interested in knowing the intersection between method-related and class-related refactorings lines #29 and #39 filters the datasets accordingly. The datetime (lines #34 and #44) is important to determine the exact frames of time the instances of refactorings intersect with each other.

```
27 SELECT ?type ?refactoring ?location ?datetime
28 WHERE {
29    ?type rdfs:subClassOf smells:MethodOrientedSmell .
30    ?codesmell rdf:type ?type .
31    ?codesmell ocean:refactoredBy ?refactoring .
32    ?codesmell ocean:foundIn ?location .
33    ?commit ocean:hasIntroduced ?codesmell .
34    ?commit repo:datetime ?datetime .
35 }
36 ...
37 SELECT ?type ?refactoring ?location ?datetime
38 WHERE {
39    ?type rdfs:subClassOf smells:ClassOrientedSmell .
40    ?codesmell rdf:type ?type .
41    ?codesmell ocean:refactoredBy ?refactoring .
42    ?codesmell ocean:foundIn ?location .
43    ?commit ocean:hasIntroduced ?codesmell .
44    ?commit repo:datetime ?datetime .
45 }
```

Table 6 summarizes the quantity of intersections between refactorings recommended for method-oriented and class-oriented smells. Each intersection represents the instances of the same refactoring which was recommended for a method 'M' and for a class 'C', considering that 'M' is encapsulated in 'C'. The third column of the table informs the types of smells involved in the intersection (pairs composed of a method-oriented and a class-oriented smell). The data points to the fact that mapping the precedence of refactorings shows potential to refine the recommendations. For instance, the application of MM to fix the instances of Feature Envy may precede its application to mitigate the instances of Data Class. As a consequence, RESYS will be capable of optimizing the work of developers as they manage to remove smells from software projects.

Table 6. Intersection of refactorings.

Refactoring	Number of intersections	Code smells
MM	1043	Feature Envy, Data Class
EM	693	Long Method, Data Class
MF	864	Feature Envy, God Class
RCWP	138	Brain Method, God Class

We must investigate further the addition of semantic relationships to base the priority and precedence of refactorings. The investigation will provide us the necessary certainty to use these new features to refine the OSORE's semantics and the recommending mechanisms of RESYS.

6   Conclusion and Future Work

The presence of code smells in software can reveal opportunities for recommendation of refactorings. Developers can benefit from refactorings to either attenuate or remove the bad effects of code smells. To this, it is important to bind the instances of code smells with their respective refactoring. In this context, we reused our previous ontology, ONTOCEAN, and created a new one, OSORE, to present a new approach that uses semantic information to support the recommendation of refactorings.

As we evaluated ONTOCEAN in our previous work [9], we pointed out that we limited our effort to representing code smells and making use of inferring mechanisms. We also mentioned that we wanted to investigate further the advantages of using ontologies in a semantic-oriented approach to automate services for developers. We have now fulfilled this by associating ONTOCEAN with OSORE, and developing RESYS to make semantic recommendation of refactorings possible. Developers may take advantages of our approach to improve the quality of the source code of software systems by applying fitting refactorings.

As for our initial requirements, they were fulfilled as described in Table 7.

Table 7. Fulfillment of requirements for a semantically-enriched recommendation of refactorings.

Req. id	How was it fulfilled?
REQ 1	We investigated related work that experimented with refactorings. The refactorings were mapped onto the code smells they are able to mitigate. The mapping was added to OSORE to allow the recommendation of refactorings for the smells stored in instances of ONTOCEAN
REQ 2	ONTOCEAN already has all ontological classes that are necessary to indicate the precise location of the code smells. As we linked the refactorings represented in OSORE to the smells it became possible to spot the recommended refactorings
REQ 3	The catalog of refactorings stored in OSORE also includes a collection of templates to illustrate how each refactoring can be applied

The combination of ONTOCEAN and OSORE in association with RESYS shows potential, if it is considered that: (a) information about refactorings are represented as ontological classes and such classes are bound to others that represent code smells; (b) ontologies provide a natural way to navigate through the linked data, so that a developer can view the refactorings that were recommended for the instances of code smell found in a software project; (c) a recommender system like RESYS can automate the binding between our two ontologies, avoiding the need for manual indication of refactoring opportunities.

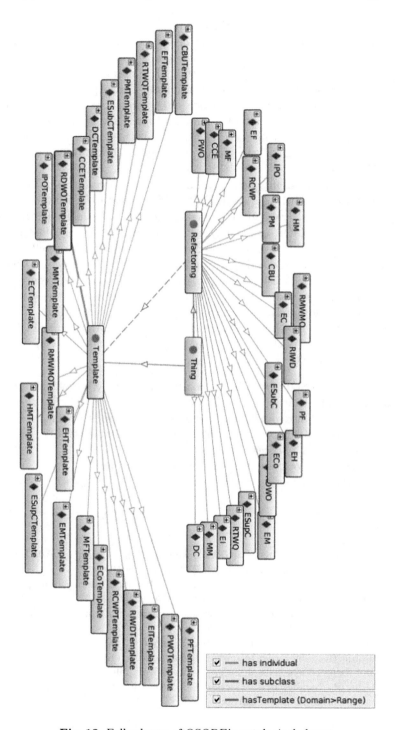

Fig. 12. Full schema of OSORE's ontological classes.

During the evaluation of both this study and our previous one [9], we did not conduct any validation with the help of software developers. Therefore, we have limited our conclusions to the findings revealed by the tests we performed on the software projects analyzed in Sect. 5. It is mandatory to evaluate our ontologies and tools under a formal experiment. The experiment will enable us to estimate the actual degree in which our approach is actually applicable and can be extrapolated to a broader context of use. However, we are confident that the analysis described in Sect. 5.2 has revealed new contributions for the semantic recommendation of refactorings. Our approach and others can benefit from our findings.

Considering the possibility of expanding our set of ontologies and the functionalities of our tools, it is also desirable to add new features with the intention of supporting other tasks related to the management of code smells. For instance, software engineers and developers may not feel inclined to either adopt the recommended refactorings or consider a particular instance of code smell harmful. In this case, our approach could count on mechanisms to represent and process information about the decisions developers make in face of the occurrence of code smells in software projects. Such mechanisms would then be used to refine the detection of code smells and the recommendation of refactorings.

We encourage the replication of our tests and use/adaption of ONTOCEAN, OSORE, and RESYS. With this purpose, we have made the following available for download and use[16]:

1. ONTOCEAN + OSORE's set of ontologies (all the analyzed software projects included). Available at:
   https://www.dropbox.com/s/zyjl7m4ixu3kehr/ontologies.zip?dl=0
2. The source code of our previous tool, OCEAN. Available at:
   https://github.com/luispscarvalho/ocean.git
3. The source code of our new tool, RESYS. Available at:
   https://github.com/luispscarvalho/resys.git

References

1. Vidal, S.A., Marcos, C., Díaz-Pace, J.A.: An approach to prioritize code smells for refactoring. J. Autom. Softw. Eng. **23**(3), 501–532 (2016)
2. Lu, J., Wu, D., Mao, M., Wang, W., Zhang, G.: Recommender system application developments: a survey. Decis. Support Syst. **74**, 12–32 (2015)
3. Fraihat, S., Shambour, Q.: A framework of semantic recommender system for e-Learning. J. Softw. **10**(3), 317–330 (2015)
4. Ouni, A., Kessentini, M., Ó Cinnéide, M., Sahraoui, H., Deb, K., Inoue, K.: MORE: a multi-objective refactoring recommendation approach to introducing design patterns and fixing code smells. J. Softw. Evol. Process **29**(5), (2017)
5. Montuschi, P., Lamberti, F., Gatteschi, V., Demartini, C.: A semantic recommender system for adaptive learning. IEEE IT Professional **17**(5), 50–58 (2015)

---

[16] Details about how to use our ontologies and tools can be found at: https://github.com/luispscarvalho/resys/wiki.

6. Espín, V., Hurtado, M.V., Noguera, M.: Nutrition for elder care: a nutritional semantic recommender system for the elderly. Expert Syst. **33**(2), 201–210 (2016)
7. Yoshida, N., Saika, T., Choi, E., Ouni, A., Inoue, K.: Revisiting the relationship between code smells and refactoring. In: 24th International Conference on Program Comprehension (ICPC), pp. 1–4. IEEE Press (2016)
8. Emden, V., Leon, M.: Java quality assurance by detecting code smells. In: 9th Working Conference on Reverse Engineering, pp. 97–106. IEEE Press (2002)
9. Carvalho, L.P.S., Novais, R., Salvador, L.N., Mendonça, M.: An ontology-based approach to analyze the occurrence of code smells in software. In: 19th International Conference on Enterprise Information Systems (ICEIS), Portugal (2017)
10. Meananeatra, P., Rongviriyapanish, S., Apiwattanapong, T.: Using software metrics to select refactoring for long method bad smell. In: 8th Electrical Engineering/Electronics, Computer, Telecommunications and Information Technology (ECTI) Association of Thailand, Thailand, pp. 492–495 (2011)
11. Counsell, S., Hassoun, Y., Loizou, G., Najjar, R.: Common refactorings, a dependency graph and some code smells: an empirical study of Java OSS. In: Proceedings of the 2006 ACM/IEEE International Symposium on Empirical Software Engineering (ISESE), Brazil, pp. 288–296 (2006)
12. Fontana, F.A., Mangiacavalli, M., Pochiero, D., Zanoni, M.: On experimenting refactoring tools to remove code smells. In: Scientific Workshop Proceedings of the XP2015, Finland, pp. 7:1–7:8 (2015)
13. Rodriguez, A., Longo, M., Zunino, A.: Using bad smell-driven code refactorings in mobile applications to reduce battery usage. In: Simposio Argentino de Ingeniería de Software (ASSE), Rosario (2015)
14. Codina, V., Ceccaroni, L.: Taking advantage of semantics in recommendation systems. In: 13th International Conference of the Catalan Association for Artificial Intelligence, Amsterdam, The Netherlands, pp. 163–172 (2010)
15. Hamza, H., Counsell, S., Hall, T., Loizou, G.: Code smell eradication and associated refactoring. In: Proceedings of the 2nd Conference on European Computing Conference, Malta, pp. 102–107 (2008)
16. Kollia, I., Glimm, B., Horrocks, I.: SPARQL query answering over OWL ontologies. In: Antoniou, G., Grobelnik, M., Simperl, E., Parsia, B., Plexousakis, D., De Leenheer, P., Pan, J. (eds.) ESWC 2011. LNCS, vol. 6643, pp. 382–396. Springer, Heidelberg (2011). https://doi.org/10.1007/978-3-642-21034-1_26
17. Fowler, Ma., Kent, B.: Refactoring: Improving the Design of Existing Code. Addison-Wesley Professional, Reading (1999)

Software Agents and Internet Computing

A Scoring Method Based on Criteria Matching for Cloud Computing Provider Ranking and Selection

Lucas Borges de Moraes and Adriano Fiorese[(✉)]

Department of Computer Science, Santa Catarina State University, Joinville, Brazil
lucasborges1292@gmail.com, adriano.fiorese@udesc.br

Abstract. Cloud computing has become a successful service model for hosting and elastic on demand distribution of computing resources all around the world, using the Internet. This cornerstone paradigm has been adopted and incorporated not only in all major known service providers IT companies (e.g., Google, Amazon, etc.), but also triggered a competitive race at the creation of new companies as providers of cloud computing services. Although this increase on the companies offering cloud computing services is beneficial to the client, on the other hand it challenges the clients' ability to choose among those companies the most suitable to attend their requirements. Therefore, this work proposes a logical/mathematical scoring method to be used to rank and select among several cloud computing provider candidates the most appropriate to the user. This method is based on the analysis of several criteria comprising performance indicators values required by the user and associated with every cloud computing provider that is able to attend the user's requirements. The proposed method is composed of a three stages algorithm that evaluates, scores, sorts and selects different cloud providers based on the utility of their performance indicators according to the values of the performance indicators required by the users. In order to illustrate the proposed method's operation, example of its utilization is provided.

Keywords: Cloud computing provider · Performance indicator
Selection method · Ranking · Matching

1 Introduction

The evolution of information society brought the need of efficient, affordable and on-demand computational resources. The evolution of telecommunications technology, especially computer networks, provided a perfect environment for the rise of cloud computing. Cloud computing has shown a new vision of service delivery to its customers. It became a differentiated paradigm of hosting and distribution of computer services all over the world via Internet.

Cloud computing abstracts to the user the complex infrastructure and internal architecture of the service provider. Thus, to use the service, the user don't

© Springer International Publishing AG, part of Springer Nature 2018
S. Hammoudi et al. (Eds.): ICEIS 2017, LNBIP 321, pp. 339–365, 2018.
https://doi.org/10.1007/978-3-319-93375-7_16

need to perform installations, configurations, software updates or purchase specialized hardware [1]. On this way, the cloud computing model has brought the benefit of better use of computing resources [2]. In addition to being a convenient service, it is easily accessible via the network and it is only charged for the time that is used [2,3]. In this model all computing resources that the user needs, can be managed by the cloud provider [2].

The success of cloud computing paradigm is currently noticeable and it has been adopted in major IT companies like Google, Amazon, Microsoft and Salesforce.com and has become a good source of development/investment both in the academy and industry [4,5]. This success led to the rising of a large number of new businesses such as cloud computing infrastructure providers. With the increasing amount of new cloud providers the task of choosing and selecting which cloud providers are the most suitable for each user's need has become a complex process. The process of measuring the quality of each provider and compare them is not trivial, as there are usually many factors involved, many criteria to be studied and checked out throughout the process.

Measuring the quality and performance of a cloud provider (called Quality of Service or simply QoS) can be made using various strategies. One well-known strategy is numerically and systematically to measure the quality of each provider's performance indicators (PIs), reaching a certain value or score. Thus, providers can be ranked and the provider that offer the higher score is theoretically the most appropriate provider to that user.

The research questions that this study aims to investigate and answer are:

- What are and what kind of PIs are used to describe cloud computing providers?
- How to utilize these PIs to systematically measure the quality of each provider for each user?

The answer to the second question is obtained through the method to be specified in this work, that is, how to use the different data types (numbers, classes, subclasses) collected from each cloud provider and stored in different PIs to score a finite list of different providers according to the needs and requirements demanded by every possible consumer of resources of these cloud service providers. Each cloud computing service consumer is an user of the proposed method. The consumer can have x different requirements, wishing the w best ranked cloud providers based on expected values for m PIs of interest.

The developed method is a logical/mathematical algorithm able to select the w more suited providers for each specific user, scoring and ranking each provider. This process is based on the utility of each user's interest PIs for each available provider. The utility of each PI is calculated based on their type (quantitative or qualitative), the nature of the behaviour of its utility function (Higher is Better or HB; Lower is Better or LB; Nominal is Best or NB [6]), the desired/expected value by the user (indicated through the input expression) and the value of its competitors (other providers to be analyzed by the method).

Therefore, this work aims to propose a simple, intuitive (logical) and agnostic method with high generality and high dimensionality, that is, flexible and applicable to any PIs that may exist, regardless of its type (quantitative or qualitative) for n generic providers with m generic PIs, where n and m can grow indefinitely.

This paper is organized as follows: Sect. 2 presents and discusses different PIs found in the studied literature to qualify cloud computing providers. Section 3 presents related works to the selection, scoring and ranking of cloud providers based on indicators. Section 4 presents and discusses the proposed method that scores and ranks the different cloud providers based on user's interest PIs. Section 5 illustrates an example, with hypothetical data, that represents an application of the proposed method, in order to validate it and to demonstrate its operation presenting the results. Finally, Sect. 6 presents the final considerations.

2   Performance Indicators for Cloud Computing Providers

This section aims to expose and clarify some performance indicators (PIs) used to evaluate and qualify the different cloud computing providers. Indicators are tools that allow a synthesized gathering information for a particular aspect of the organization using metrics that are responsible for quantifying (assigning a value) the study of objects to be measured. In general, the indicators can be classified into two categories [6]: Quantitative (discrete or continuous) and qualitative (ordered or unordered).

- **Quantitative.** They are those states, levels or categories that can be expressed numerically, and can be worked algebraically. The numerical values assigned can be discrete or continuous. Examples of discrete quantitative indicators are: number of processors, amount of RAM (Random Access Memory), disk block size, etc. Example of continuous quantitative indicators are: response time, weight, length of an object, area of a land, etc.
- **Qualitative.** Also called categorical indicators. These indicators have distinct states, levels or categories that are defined by an exhaustive and mutually exclusive set of subclasses, which may or may not be ordered. The ordered subclasses have a perceptible logical graduation among their subclasses, giving the idea of a progression between them. Examples of ordered qualitative PIs: security level (low, medium, high), frequency of use of a service (never, rarely, sometimes, often, always), etc. The unordered subclasses do not have the idea of progression, e.g.: type of computer service (processing, storage, connectivity), research purpose (scientific, engineering, education), etc.

We can also classify PIs according to the behavior of its utility function [6]. This means how useful (effective benefit) the PI becomes when its numerical value increases or decreases. There are three possible classifications [6]:

- **HB (*Higher is Better*).** Users and/or system managers prefer the highest possible values for that indicator. For instance: System throughput, amount of resources (money, memory, materials, etc.), availability of a service, etc.;

- **LB (*Lower is Better*).** Users and/or system managers prefer the lowest possible values for this indicator. For instance: Response time, delay, costs, etc.;
- **NB (*Nominal is Best*).** Users and/or system managers prefer specific values. Higher and lower values are undesirable. A particular value is considered the best. The system load is an example of this feature. A very high system utilization is considered bad to users because it generates high response times. On the other hand, a very low utilization is considered bad by system managers since the resources are not being used (idle).

For the cloud computing paradigm we have a especial set of PIs called key performance indicators (KPIs) defined at Service Measurement Index (SMI). The SMI was developed by the Cloud Service Measurement Index Consortium (CSMIC) [7] and represents a set of KPIs that provide a standardized method for measuring and comparing cloud computing services. It also provides metrics and guidelines to help organizations measure cloud-hosted business services the also serves as a framework that provides a holistic view of the quality of service required by cloud computing consumers. The SMI is a hierarchical structure whose upper level divides the measurement space into seven categories and each category is optimized by four or more attributes (subcategories). The seven major categories are [7]: accountability, agility, service assurance, financial, performance, security and privacy, usability.

Figure 1 depicts a mental map that displays and classifies several PIs that can be used for evaluation and monitoring of cloud computing service providers according technical literature [8–12]. The PIs presented do not represent an exhaustive list of all existing PIs. They form a portion of the indicators most often found in scientific papers studied. These PIs can be quantitative (integer or real numbers), qualitative (represented by a category or a set of them - simple categorical or compound categorical) and/or may even fall into both types (can appear as quantitative or qualitative). It is important to note that PIs with boolean values were classified as qualitative (at the proposed method they will be treated as unordered qualitatives with only two categories). The selection method proposed in this work is agnostic, that is, its user can use any PI that he wishes (since its present for at least one provider registered in the database of the method), not limited to those listed in this Section.

3   Related Works

This section presents related works already developed by other authors to rank and select cloud computing providers based on indicators.

Sundareswaran and others [10] proposed a new brokerage architecture in the cloud, where brokers are responsible for selecting the appropriate service for each user/ customer. The broker has a contract with the providers, collecting their properties (performance indicators), and with consumers, collecting their service requirements. It analyzes and indexes the service providers according to the similarity of their properties. When the broker receives a cloud service

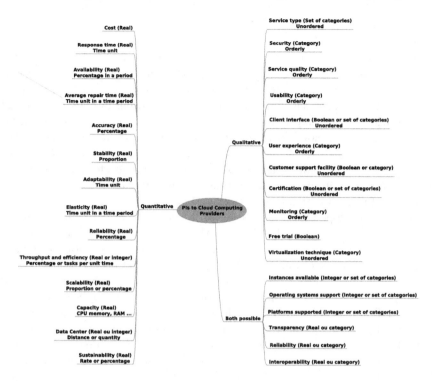

Fig. 1. Classification of different PIs for cloud computing providers.

selection request the broker will search the index to identify an ordered list of candidate providers based on how well they meet the needs of users.

The authors [11] specify a framework to quantify the efficiency of different cloud computing providers through the Quality of Service metrics (QoS). Based on that, the proposed framework ranks cloud computing providers. The framework divides the QoS metrics into two categories: application dependent metrics (reliability, availability, security, data center, cost, operating systems support, platforms supported, service response time, throughput and efficiency) and user dependent metrics (reputation, client interface, free trial, certification, sustainability, scalability, elasticity and user experience).

A framework called "SmiCloud" is presented in [9]. It is responsible for measuring the quality of service (QoS) of cloud providers and ranking them based on that calculated quality. The quality is directly related to the values of each metric of the Service Measure Index (SMI) [7] classified into functional and nonfunctional. The work uses the Analytical Hierarchical Process (AHP) [13] in the calculation of the quality and ranking of providers.

The framework developed in [12] presents an expectation of QoS metrics (also based on SMI) that the every cloud provider should have. This expectations are then used by a cloud broker that assists selecting the most appropriate ones. That framework uses a voting method that takes into account the user requirements for ranking cloud providers.

The work developed in [14] proposes an evaluation model that verifies the quality and the status of service provided by cloud providers. The data is obtained by cloud auditors and is viewed via a heat map ordered by the performance of each provider, showing them in descending order of overall quality of service provided. This map represents a visual recommendation aid system for cloud consumers and cloud brokers. The main metrics are again based on the SMI: availability (divided in uptime, downtime and interrupt frequency), reliability (divided in load balancing, MTBF, recoverability), performance (latency, response time and throughput), cost (per storage unit and per VM instance) and security (authentication, encryption, and auditing).

The work developed in [15] presents a broker based architecture for select the more suitable cloud provider based on the measurement of quality of service of each cloud provider and prioritize them based on the needs of each request to the broker. The key elements of the approach are: the broker, the requester (cloud provider consumer), and a list with n cloud providers. Selection involves three steps: Identify the appropriate criteria for the request, by identifying the necessary KPIs present in the SMI, evaluating the weight of each of these criteria using the AHP method, and ranking of each provider using the Technique for Order Preference by Similarity to Ideal Solution (TOPSIS), used to select the alternative which are closest to the ideal solution and farthest from negative ideal solution.

A cloud service provider ranking model based on service delivery measurements and user experience is proposed in [16]. In this work, in order to rank and select the appropriate cloud service provider, an intuitionistic fuzzy group decision making is used, which can include both measurable and non-measurable factors.

The work developed in [17] presents an approach concerning Hypergraph based Computational Model (HGCM) for ranking cloud service providers. This work uses an HGCM based technique called Minimum Distance-Helly Property (MDHP) to evaluate the cloud service providers. To accomplish that, authors exploit the relationship between metrics from the Service Measurement Index (SMI) coping with the cloud users requirements. The results show scalability regarding the algorithms developed.

Authors from this work have already contributed in the cloud computing providers ranking field. A shorter version of this work [18] proposes a deterministic scoring method, and consequently a ranking system model, based on cloud providers' performance indicators comprising users needs and requests.

4   The Proposed Scoring and Ranking Method

This section aims to present and discuss the proposed cloud service providers selection method. The following subsections expose how the method works, presenting a method overview, its inputs and outputs, steps and mechanisms for calculating the score and ranking of each cloud provider.

4.1   Method Overview

Figure 2 depicts the two preconditions necessary to the method usage. The first precondition is related with the method's Database composition and its feeding. In this case, the database is composed of all n possible cloud computing providers and their M PI names and value records.

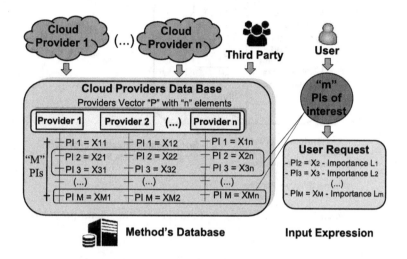

Fig. 2. Preconditions to the proposed method.

This database will be fed by cloud computing providers themselves or third party agents. For all the effects this database can be seen as a list of cloud providers candidates to be choosen by an user. The second precondition is the user request, that is composed by the names, values and eventually other attributes of all m user's desired PIs, plus how many ranked cloud providers the user wants to receive back as a result from the method.

Figure 3 presents an overview of the selection method to be described in this Section. The database of cloud provider candidates and their performance indicators can be fed indirectly through websites such as "Cloud Harmony" (https://cloudharmony.com) or through cloud providers by their own (e.g: Amazon) or it can be consolidated by third parties.

Data input (Inputs) corresponds to a list P with n different candidates (cloud providers), each one with M different PIs (whose values are known), and an input expression (generated by the user of the method) containing m PIs of interest (subset of the known M PIs) and the priority level of each one. This priority level is set by the method's user according the classification adopted in the proposed method. The initial cloud providers list P will be filtered, at the first step of the method, based on the input expression and at the end it will have n' elements (with $n \geq n'$). If $n' = 0$, there is none available compatible provider to the user, so the method interrupts the process with an error message; if $n' = 1$, there is

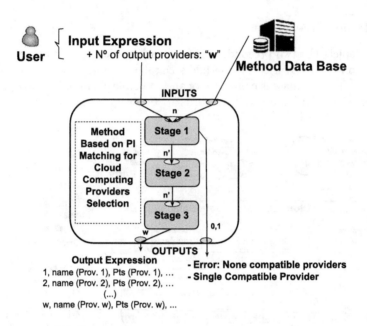

Fig. 3. Overview of the matching method for selecting cloud providers.

only a single compatible provider, which will be returned to the user; however, if $n' > 1$ the method proceeds along to another stage to rank providers. The expected output data (Outputs), except the special conditions mentioned, is a list with the cloud providers better scored by the method. The proposed method is divided into three main stages:

1. Stage 1: Elimination of incompatible cloud providers to the user.
2. Stage 2: Evaluation and scoring of interest PIs for each priority level.
   (a) Score quantitative PIs.
   (b) Score qualitative PIs.
3. Stage 3: Calculation of the final score for each cloud provider, ranking them and return results to the user.

4.2 Stage 1 – Elimination of Incompatible Cloud Providers

In this Stage, a filter is applied on the list of initial cloud computing provider candidates (P). This filter cleans out all incompatible (concept discussed further) cloud providers, generating a new list P' with n' different providers.

This filter can be applied since we have created the classification of PIs' priority levels presented in Fig. 4. Each PI can be classified as essential or non-essential by method's user. The non-essential PIs have different priority levels, which can vary between levels "High" and "Low". In order to simplify this work, it was adopted only one intermediate level of priority, named "Medium".

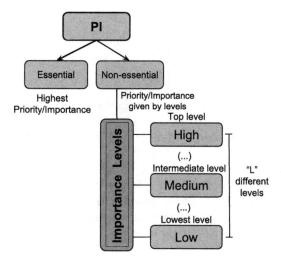

Fig. 4. Classification of priorities of the PIs in the proposed method. (Source [18]).

An essential PI has the highest priority/importance for the customer (user) and consequently to the proposed method. It indicates that if the specific value entered in the Input expression is not satisfied, the user cannot achieve their goals. This makes it a criterion of elimination. Thus, a provider that does not attend all essential PIs will be automatically deleted from the list P of valid candidates (compatible providers) because it is incompatible to that user in question.

On the other hand, if a non-essential PI is not attended, it does not incapacitate the user to achieve their goals. But, it can jeopardize them. How much it could be jeopardized (seriously or very little) is directly related to the priority level of the PI, set by the user. Do not attending a very high level PI means that the user will be seriously impaired in achieving their goals. On the other hand, do not attending a minimum priority level PI implies that the negative impact will be virtually imperceptible. The optional PIs can be automatically classified with minimum priority level.

In this work, it will be considered incompatible, the cloud provider that does not attend all the user's essential PIs. The concept of incompatibility and, in general, the scores of cloud providers, are based on the premise of attending/matching the desired PIs values (made available in the input expression by the user). However, what means a particular PI j attends a specific y value desired/required by the user? The answer to this question depends on the type of the PI and the behavior of the utility function of j. Thus, if j is quantitative, there are three possible classifications for the behavior of its utility function: HB (Higher is Better), LB (Lower is Better) or NB (Nominal is the best) [6].

Thus, given a quantitative PI j that stores the value x (number) and j belongs to the cloud provider i, if j attends the value y, specified by the user, then we can conclude that:

$$x \text{ attends } y \text{ then } \begin{cases} x \geq (y - t_j) \text{ if } j \in HB \\ x \leq (y + t_j) \text{ if } j \in LB \\ x = (y \pm t_j) \text{ if } j \in NB \end{cases} \quad (1)$$

where t_j represents a certain tolerance regarding x, that is, a deviation from the desired value y tolerated by the user. Comprising the proposed method, the default tolerance value is zero, but it can be adjusted by the user via input expression.

Meanwhile, if the PI j is qualitative, it can be ordered or unordered [6]. If it is unordered, the rule is simple: if x is the value that the user specify (y), then the PI j is attended, otherwise it is not. However, if PI j is ordered each value (category or class) has a certain relationship with the others, scaling from a lower level to a higher level. If the user specifies a low level value, a higher level value can also satisfy, it depends on the PI in question. An example of this are the qualitative PIs security and quality of service with values: "low", "medium" and "high" [10]. If the PI is quality of service and the user specify the value "medium", the value "low" would not be appropriate, but the value "high" would be equally good, or even better. For the PI security level this isn't always true, because a very high degree of security can be harder to work and this may impair the user's work. Thus, higher and/or lower level values (categories) than the desired category y can also satisfy the user. Therefore, to solve this problem an ontology, similar to the one in [6], was created in order to indicate if an ordered qualitative PI has tolerances for categories below and/or above the desired category.

- **Higher is Tolerable (HT).** Categories above of the desired one are tolerable;
- **Lower is Tolerable (LT).** Categories below of the desired one are tolerable;
- **Higher and Lower are Tolerable (HLT).** Categories above and below of the desired one are both tolerable;

These tolerances can be set by the user via input expression. If nothing is informed, the default used is NB. Thus, given a qualitative PI j, which stores the value x (category), and j belongs to the provider i, if j attends the value y, specified by the user, then we can conclude that:

$$x \text{ attends } y \text{ then } \begin{cases} x = y \text{ if j is unordered OR } j \in NB \\ x \geq y \text{ if j is ordered AND } j \in HT \\ x \leq y \text{ if j is ordered AND } j \in LT \\ \text{j is ordered AND } j \in HLT \end{cases} \quad (2)$$

In any case of PI j, whether quantitative or qualitative, whose value x does not satisfy Eq. 1 or Eq. 2, respectively, it is said that j doesn't attend the value of y, specified by the user. Therefore, taking into account the PI attending premise and the incompatibility concept, at the end of this initial stage it will remain a list of candidate cloud providers containing only those compatible ones with the requirements of essential PIs to be selected.

4.3   Stage 2 – Evaluation and Scoring Interest PIs to Each Priority Level

This second stage aims to score each provider individually, according to the utility (real benefit) of each one of its PIs. The higher the utility value associated with the PI, the higher the score. The utility is influenced by the value specified by the user (desired one) and also regarding the best value (bigger utility) among all candidate providers for that specific PI.

This stage will receive the list P', with the n' filtered providers from the previous stage. Each provider presents values for the m user's interest PIs, which can be quantitative or qualitative. Each one of these PIs has a priority level associated with that is set by the user in the input expression. Thus, if L is the number of different available priority levels and m_l the amount of PIs with the lth level of priority, the score (Pts_l) for the ith provider is given by Eq. 3.

$$Pts_l(i) = \frac{\sum_{k=1}^{m_l}(Pts(PI_k))}{m_l} \tag{3}$$

That is, the score of the lth priority level is the simple arithmetic average of the individual scores for each PI_k with the same priority level l, whether the PI is quantitative or qualitative. This stage ends when all the L levels are scored for each of the n' available providers. For example, in this work we considered four priority levels $(L = 4)$: "Essential" (always maximum level), "High", "Medium" and "Low". Thus, each provider i will always have four scores at the end of this stage; one for each priority level. Regardless of the priority level, the individual score $(Pts(PI_k))$ for a quantitative and a qualitative PI is calculated in different ways.

Scoring Quantitative PIs. The score of a PI j of a provider i, will be 0 if its numerical value x doesn't attend the numerical value y, specified by the user. If the value is attended, it will be scored in proportion to how useful (utility) this value is compared to all other compatible providers available in the candidates list (given by a constant). The evaluation function of a quantitative PI is shown in Eq. 4. It always returns a normalized real number between 0 and 1 ($\forall\ value(j), y, X_{max}, X_{min} \geq 0$ and $C_1, C_2, t > 0$).

$$Pts(j) = \begin{cases} 0, & \text{if } value(j) \text{ doesn't attend } y \\ C_1 + C_2 * \frac{value(j)-y}{X_{max}-y}, & \text{if } j \in HB \\ C_1 + C_2 * \frac{y-value(j)}{y-X_{min}}, & \text{if } j \in LB \\ C_1 + C_2 * \frac{t-|y-value(j)|}{t}, & \text{if } j \in NB \end{cases} \tag{4}$$

Where the real constants (empirical parameters) C_1 and C_2 belong to the normalized open interval between $]0,1[$, and $C_1 + C_2 = 1$, mandatory. The number X_{max} is the highest value among all other n providers in the list P' for that

PI j; as well as X_{min} is the lowest value and t is the maximum tolerated distance (number) from the optimum point (y) for a NB PI (since that PI attends y, that is, belongs to the interval $[y - t; y + t]$). The value of t can be configured by the user.

The same happens with the coefficients C_1 and C_2. They can be tuned according the user understanding of how to weight the PI attending and how proportionally attended is the PI regarding the same PI on other providers. The constant C_1 weighs the score given the desired minimum match (including the tolerances associated with the PI, if any) between the value in the provider (x) and the value that the user wants (y), based on the PI type under analysis (HB, LB or NB). The constant C_2 weighs the score given to how much this PI value excels the desired minimum, that is, the value x is, in practice, better than the desired value y. It is noteworthy that the first coefficient (C_1) must be greater than the second one (C_2), because it is not interesting to weight more how better a PI is comprising its value in other cloud providers, in prejudice of the attending the user desired value. Also, it is essential that $C_1 + C_2 = 1$.

For this work, it was initially adopted $C_1 = 0.7$ and $C_2 = 0.3$. Thus, to the fact that a quantitative PI attends the value y (desired by the user), it is given a score of 0.7 (70% of the total score). The other 0.3 (30% of the total score) comes from how well ranked this PI is among all other competitors in the list of compatible candidate providers (P'). If the PI has the best value among all, the evaluation returns 1. If it has the lowest (but still attends the given value y) then $Pts(j)$ is 0.7. Summing up, if PI does not attend the value y, then evaluation returns 0, otherwise it returns a value between 0.7 and 1. Thus, when $j \in HB$, the higher its value, the closer to 0.3 will be the second term of the sum in Eq. 4. When $j \in LB$, the lower its value, the closer to 0.3 will be the second term of the sum in Eq. 4. Finally, when $j \in NB$, the closer to the y value, the closer to 0.3 the second term of the sum in Eq. 4.

Algorithm 1 depicts in a function how a quantitative PI is computationally scored. This function always returns a normalized real value between 0 and 1, corresponding to the score of the PI_j carrying value x, according value y desired by the user. Also, this function depends on the function $AttendQt()$, which returns $True$ or $False$ according PI_j attends or not, respectively, the value y desired by the user. Function $type()$ returns the PI_j type (e.g., HB; LB; NB).

Score Qualitative PIs. In spite of numerical values, qualitative PIs (or categorical) have categorical (string) ones. Therefore, qualitative PIs can be ordered or unordered. Comprising the unordered qualitative PIs, or the category is that one the user specified (receiving score 1) or not (receiving score 0). Regarding ordered qualitative PIs, the score depends on the tolerance supported and informed by the user (HT, LT, or HLT) from the PI's value (category) offered by the provider. Categories of higher and/or lower levels to the desired category y can be tolerable to the user and may thus scoring. If nothing is mentioned about it in the input expression it is concluded that there is no tolerance and scoring proceeds in the same way as for unordered qualitative PIs.

Algorithm 1. Scoring a quantitative PI_j according to value y.

1: **function** SCOREQT(PI_j, Number y)   ▷ PI_j mandatorily attends y
2:   **if** $AttendQt(PI_j, y) = True$ **then**
3:     **if** $type(PI_j) = HB$ **then**   ▷ Case HB: $X_{max} \geq value(PI_j) \geq y > 0$
4:       **return** $C_1 + C_2 * [\frac{valor(PI_j) - y}{X_{max} - y}]$
5:     **else if** $type(PI_j) = LB$ **then**   ▷ Case LB: $y \geq value(PI_j) \geq X_{min} > 0$
6:       **return** $C_1 + C_2 * [\frac{y - valor(PI_j)}{y - X_{min}}]$
7:     **else**   ▷ Case NB: $y > 0, valor(PI_j) > 0, t > 0$
8:       **return** $C_1 + C_2 * [\frac{t_j - |y - valor(PI_j)|}{t_j}]$
9:     **end if**
10:   **else**   ▷ PI_j does not attend y
11:     **return** 0
12:   **end if**
13: **end function**

For this work it was defined that the score of tolerable categories will be directly influenced by the disparity between the category specified by the user (y) and that offered by the provider (A). This means the greater the distance of the category in question (A) to the desired one (y) (both given by integers), the lower the score for that PI. Figure 5 presents how the score is influenced by the type of tolerance associated with a qualitative ordered PI, how to specify the categorical levels between the PI categories and how calculate the distance between these levels. The numbers identifying the desired category (y) and the tolerated ones are underlined. The score of a tolerated category is a constant multiplied by the normalized distance between the categories A and y.

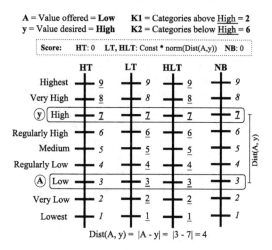

Fig. 5. Relationship between category-value and type of tolerance associated with a hypothetical ordered qualitative PI with 9 distinct categories. (Source [18]).

The score of an ordered qualitative PI will always be a real value between 0 and 1. Therefore, in case of perfect match between the desired category (set by the user in the input expression) and the cloud provider offered category, then that category receives the maximum score 1. When do not occurs a perfect match, categories are scored according Eq. 5. In this case, the desired neighboring categories (above and below) will score C_3 (with $0 < C_3 < 1$) and so on. In this sense, in Eq. 5, $A = value(j)$ is the category under consideration (value of the PI j that is offered by the cloud provider), y the user's desired category and K_1, K_2 and $K_3 = K_1 + K_2$, the total number of tolerable categories, higher, lower to y or both depending on the PI is HT, LT or HLT, respectively. The distance between the categories $value(j)$ and y is the difference between their levels in module: $|level(value(j)) - level(y)|$. To each category is assigned a level value associated with a positive integer from 1 to the total of categories available (for that ordered qualitative PI), in increasing order of graduation (lower levels, lower numbers, higher levels, higher numbers, according to Fig. 5). It is important to note that the bigger the distance between the category $value(j)$ and the desired category y, the smaller the score.

$$Pts(j) = \begin{cases} C_3 * \frac{K_1 - dist(A,y) + 1}{K_1}, & \text{if } j \in HT \\ C_3 * \frac{K_2 - dist(A,y) + 1}{K_2}, & \text{if } j \in LT \\ C_3 * \frac{K_3 - dist(A,y) + 1}{K_3}, & \text{if } j \in HLT \end{cases} \tag{5}$$

The real constant C_3 represents the maximum score that a tolerable category (another category different of the desirable y, but within the tolerances associated with that particular PI) can assume. Therefore, the smaller the value of C_3, more aggressive is the penalty (loss of score) applied to any and every PI j, whose category $value(j)$ diverges from the desired optimal value y. If $C_3 = 0$, then the method punctuates with zero any value different than y, whether the PI is ordered or not. This is an undesirable behavior, since it depreciates suboptimal, and can penalize excessively providers that are also appropriate for the user. If $C_3 = 1$, the method depreciates the importance of reaching the optimal point for a qualitative PI, assigning too much punctuation to sub-optimal ones, encouraging the wrong choice of the best provider(s). For this work it was initially adopted as a starting point $C_3 = 0.7$, that is, a category next to y and within the tolerance will receive a score of 0.7 (70 % of the total score).

Algorithm 2 presents the function that scores a qualitative PI_j based on a user's desired category y. This function returns a normalized real value between 0 and 1. It is worth noting that the greater the distance between the levels of the category A from the PI_j and the desired category y the lower the score. Also, it is noteworthy that function $ScoreQl()$ scores PI_j in case function $AttendQl()$ returns $True$, otherwise it return 0 (meaning PI_j does not attend category y). In this case, function $type()$ returns PI_j type (e.g., HT, LT, HLT).

Algorithm 2. Scoring a qualitative PI_j according to a category y.

1: **function** SCOREQL(PI_j, Category y)
2:   **if** $AttendQl(PI_j, y) = True$ **then**
3:     **if** $Level(PI_j) = Level(y)$ **then**   ▷ Same level = Same category = Max score
4:       **return** 1
5:     **else if** $type(PI_j) = HT$ **then**   ▷ K_1 = Number of categories above y
6:       **return** $C_3 * [\frac{K_1 - |nivel(PI_j) - nivel(y)| + 1}{K_1}]$
7:     **else if** $type(PI_j) = LT$ **then**   ▷ K_2 = Number of categories below y
8:       **return** $C_3 * [\frac{K_2 - |nivel(PI_j) - nivel(y)| + 1}{K_2}]$
9:     **else if** $type(PI_j) = HLT$ **then**
10:      **return** $C_3 * [\frac{K_1 + K_2 - |nivel(PI_j) - nivel(y)| + 1}{K_1 + K_2}]$
11:    **else**   ▷ Without tolerance to category deviations
12:      **return** 0
13:    **end if**
14: **else**   ▷ PI_j does not attend y
15:    **return** 0
16: **end if**
17: **end function**

4.4   Stage 3 – Calculation of the Final Score for Each Cloud Provider and Results Returning

Previous two stages results in four scores for each cloud provider from the list P': one for each priority level: "Essential", "High", "Medium" and "Low", including quantitative and qualitative PIs. The consolidation of these scores in a single one value will be the provider's final score. Therefore, a weighted arithmetic average will be used, where the coefficients (weights) are directly proportional to the importance levels. Equation 6 presents the score to a certain provider i. It is worthwhile to note that the sum of all weights must be 1 ($\alpha_1 + \ldots + \alpha_L = 1$).

$$Pts(i) = \sum_{l=1}^{L}(\alpha_l * Pts_l(i)) \tag{6}$$

The value of each weight (α_l) could be chosen by the user, but a more formal and efficient technique for calculating each coefficient is the use of a judgement matrix. A judgment matrix aims to model relationships (e.g.: importance, necessity, discrepancy, value, etc.) between the judged elements [13]. In this case, the elements to be judged are the PIs' priority levels. Therefore, the judgment matrix is a matrix with dimension L, wherein each row and each column represents a different importance relationship, arranged in descending order of priority (from top to bottom – lines, from left to right – columns). This technique is used several times in the decision-making method called Analytic Hierarchy Process (AHP) [19–21]. To the particular case of this work, the judgement matrix should be composed according the user input data, whenever a new cloud provider selection takes place. This means, the judgement matrix dimension L can vary according to how many priority levels user represents in his input expression. A generic example of a judgment matrix, assuming 4 priority levels ("Essential", "High", "Medium", and "Low") is showed in Table 1.

Table 1. AHP Judgment Matrix: Importance relationship between criteria.

Obj.	Crit.1	Crit.2	Crit.3	Crit.4	(...)	Crit.n
Crit.1	1	a_{12}	a_{13}	a_{14}	...	a_{1n}
Crit.2	$\frac{1}{a_{12}}$	1	a_{23}	a_{24}	...	a_{2n}
Crit.3	$\frac{1}{a_{13}}$	$\frac{1}{a_{23}}$	1	a_{34}	...	a_{3n}
Crit.4	$\frac{1}{a_{14}}$	$\frac{1}{a_{24}}$	$\frac{1}{a_{34}}$	1	...	a_{4n}
(...)	...	...	...	...	1	a_{in}
Crit.n	$\frac{1}{a_{1n}}$	$\frac{1}{a_{2n}}$	$\frac{1}{a_{3n}}$	$\frac{1}{a_{4n}}$	...	1
Col. sum	$\sum a_{i1}$	$\sum a_{i2}$	$\sum a_{i3}$	$\sum a_{i4}$	...	$\sum a_{in}$

The basic rules for keep matrix of judgments' data consistent are:

1. $a_{ij} > 0 \longrightarrow$ Priorities are positive integers;
2. $a_{ii} = a_{jj} = 1 \longrightarrow$ Unit main diagonal;
3. $a_{ij} = \frac{1}{a_{ji}} \longrightarrow$ Reciprocity; and
4. $a_{ij} = a_{ik} * a_{kj} \longrightarrow$ Transitivity.

For all $i, j, k = 1, 2, 3, 4, \ldots, n$, where n is the dimension of the matrix.

Table 2 presents a possible judgment matrix to the four priority levels discussed. The assigned values are based on the scale of Saaty [13]. In this case, the values in the judgment matrix indicate how important is the line element i with respect to the column element j. This importance relationship between priority levels using the Saaty scale, must be provided by the method's user or an expert on his behalf. Thus, following this methodology to build the judgment matrix, we obtain all values in the diagonal equal to 1 and the observed inversions. On the last line, the elements of each column are summed up in order to advance the next step to find the weights, which is the normalization of this judgment matrix.

Following the judgment matrix technique, the judgment matrix normalization takes place. This process takes each column element divided by its Col. sum position, according Table 2. The results can be seen in Table 3, which represents Table 2 normalized.

Finally, at the same Table 3, the weights for each one of the priority levels are resolved summing the values on the priority level line of the normalized matrix and dividing the result by the number of priority levels (L), which is 4 in this case.

Thus, after the consistency checks on the judgment matrix [13, 19, 20], which allowed its normalization and the weights get resolved, we have Eq. 7, where

Table 2. Matrix of judgments: Importance relationships between four different priority levels (Source [18]).

Levels	Essential	High	Medium	Low
Essential	1	2	4	9
High	$\frac{1}{2}$	1	2	6
Medium	$\frac{1}{4}$	$\frac{1}{2}$	1	3
Low	$\frac{1}{9}$	$\frac{1}{6}$	$\frac{1}{3}$	1
Col. sum	1,8611	3,6667	7,3333	19,00

Table 3. Normalized judgment matrix and final weights for each priority level.

Levels	Essential	High	Medium	Low	Final Weights
Essential	0,5373	0,5455	0,5455	0,4737	0,5255
High	0,2687	0,2727	0,2727	0,3158	0,2825
Medium	0,1343	0,1364	0,1364	0,1579	0,1413
Low	0,0597	0,0455	0,0455	0,0526	0,0508

the unknowns α_l of the Eq. 6 are resolved. Therefore, Eq. 7 represents the cloud provider i score.

$$Pts(i) = 0,5255 * Pts_{essential}(i) + 0,2825 * Pts_{high}(i)$$
$$+ 0,1413 * Pts_{medium}(i) + 0,0508 * Pts_{low}(i) \tag{7}$$

It is worth to note that the score of each provider i is normalized between 0 and 1. After scoring all providers, the list of compatible providers is ordered by score in descending order. Then, the proposed method returns the w first providers in that ordered list (highest scores) to the user.

5   Using the Proposed Method

Once the cloud service provider selection method is specified, it is necessary to expose an example of its application on a set of real or hypothetical data in order to show its operation helping to answer questions about its procedure and results. Thus, this Section aims to apply the specified method on a possible data set. Table 4 shows an example of data that can be used for that. It shows 5 fictitious providers, each one with 7 possible interest PIs to the user. This data set represents the information regarding the candidate cloud providers that will be selected using the proposed method.

Several steps compose the proposed method execution. The first step copes with the identification of the nature of each PI and with checking which one attend and which one do not attend the desired values specified by the user. To accomplish that, it is necessary that the proposed method recognizes that the

Table 4. Data set example of PIs to cloud providers. (Source [18]).

PI/Provider	Type	P1	P2	P3	P4	P5
NI	HB	5	3	9	12	10
NOS	NB	1	2	4	8	6
Cost (U$/h)	LB	0,30	0,50	1,00	1,50	1,20
RAM (GB)	HB	4	2	4	8	16
Storage (GB)	HB	10,00	50,00	80,00	15,00	5,00
Avail (%)	HB	99,90	95,00	88,00	99,00	90,00
Sec	HT	M	M	H	L	M
Key
NI: Total types of available Virtual Machines. Integer > 1
NOS: Total available operating systems. Integer > 1
Cost: Average cost of the desired service. Given in U$/h
RAM: Average amount of RAM available. Given in GByte
Storage: Average amount of data storage. Given in GByte
Avail: Availability of the service per year, in average. Given in %
Sec: Estimated level of information security and privacy. It has 3 possible categories: High (H), Medium (M) and Low (L)

PI "NI" is quantitative discrete with utility function HB; "NOS" is quantitative discrete NB; "Cost" is quantitative continuous LB; "RAM" is quantitative discrete HB; "Storage" is quantitative continuous HB; "Avail" is quantitative continuous HB; and "Sec" is qualitative ordered HT. This matching can be done since the cloud provider PIs database is kept updated by experts or by the user of the method, including this information about the PI's nature. Once the PI nature is acknowledged, the user needs to provide an input expression comprising which requirements (PIs), their values (including, eventually, tolerances and their values) as well as their priority levels. This input expression intends to be used by the proposed method to rank the PI attending providers, returning back to the user the w best ranked (when there are w). Table 5 shows an user input data used for this method working example.

Thus, taking into account the PI values provided by the user for this example, Table 6 shows the desirable values (based on the utility functions associated with them) and tolerable values (in accordance with tolerance values associated with utility functions provided by the user) for each PI. Continuing the analysis of the PI values required by the user and those provided by cloud providers, Table 7 shows provider's max/min PI values needed for the final scoring of each provider.

Thus comparing Tables 4, 5 and 6 it is possible to determine if there is incompatible providers to eliminate from the list P (methods's Stage 1). It is incompatible any provider that does not attend all the essential PIs (i.e., "RAM" and "Storage"). A PI attends certain desired value, if its value is in the range

Table 5. Example 1 of data input entered by the user. (Source [18]).

PI	Value	Tolerance	Priority levels
RAM	4 GB	–	Essential
Storage	5 GB	0,5 GB	Essential
Cost	1,00 U\$/h	0,10 U\$/h	High
Avail	90%	0,5%	High
NI	8	1	Medium
Sec	M	H	Medium
NOS	3	1	Low

Table 6. Analysis of the PIs presented in example. (Source [18]).

PI	Desirable values	Tolerable values
RAM	$[4, +\infty)$	–
Storage	$[5, 0; +\infty)$	$[4, 5; 5, 0)$
Cost	$[0; 1, 00]$	$(1, 00; 1, 10]$
Avail	$[90, 0; 100, 0]$	$[89, 5; 90, 0)$
NI	$[8, +\infty)$	7
Sec	Medium	High
NOS	3	2 e 4

Table 7. Max/Min PIs values. (Source [18]).

PI	Max values
RAM	$X_{max} = 16$ GB
Storage	$X_{max} = 80, 00$ GB
Cost	$X_{min} = 0, 30$ U\$/h
Avail	$X_{max} = 99, 90\%$
NI	$X_{max} = 12$
Sec	–
NOS	$t = 1$

of desirable values or at least in the range of tolerable values, both identified in Table 6. On that basis, it was built Table 8, where ($\bullet$) informs that the PI attends the user's value and ($\circ$) that it does not attend.

Observation of Table 8 allows us to conclude that only cloud provider P2 does not attend the essential PI "RAM". This observation is backed up to Table 4 that shows P2 has only 2 GB of RAM, leaving user requirement of 4 GB or more, unattended. Thus, regarding the five PIs used, the only incomparable provider is P2 and, therefore it should be removed from the list of suitable/compatible

Table 8. Provider's attending the user's desired PI values. (Source [18]).

PI/Provider	P1	P2	P3	P4	P5
RAM (E)	●	○	●	●	●
Storage (E)	●	●	●	●	●
Cost (H)	●	●	●	○	○
Avail (H)	●	●	○	●	●
NI (M)	○	○	●	●	●
Sec (M)	●	●	●	○	●
NOS (L)	○	●	●	○	○

providers. Thus, the next stages only will consider the new generated list P' containing all providers (and their PIs), except P2.

Next, on Stage 2, proposed method must score the quantitative and qualitative (Subsect. 4.3) PIs, using Eqs. 4 and 5, respectively, regarding P1, P3, P4 e P5. The score, by priority levels, as requested by user, is calculated according Eq. 3. Table 9 presents the final scores by priority level of the PIs comprising each compatible provider. The constants used are: $C_1 = 0.7$, $C_2 = 0.3$ and $C_3 = 0.7$.

Table 9. Providers' scores by priority level. (Source [18]).

Provider	Priority Levels Score			
	Essential	High	Medium	Low
P1	0,71	1	0,5	0
P3	0,85	0,35	0,7375	0,7
P4	0,77	0,485	0,5	0
P5	0,85	0,35	0,925	0

Next, on Stage 3, final score is calculated and consequently the ranking for each one of the four competing providers. This task is performed to each provider, according to Eq. 7 (Subsect. 4.4). Coefficient values used in the weighted average are the values shown in Table 3. These weights are applied to the scores of each priority level already calculated. Table 10 presents the final score to the cloud providers 1, 3, 4 and 5.

Thus, according to Table 10, it is possible to rank the 4 competing providers in scoring descending order:

1. P1 with 0,7263 points;
2. P3 with 0,6853 points;
3. P5 with 0,6763 points; and
4. P4 with 0,6123 points.

Table 10. Example 1: Providers' final score calculation. (Source [18]).

General formula: (Eq. 7)	
$Pts(i) = 0,5255 * Pts_{essential}(i) + 0,2825 * Pts_{high}(i) +$	
$0,1413 * Pts_{medium}(i) + 0,0508 * Pts_{low}(i)$	
Providers	**Final score**
P1	$0,5255 * (0,71) + 0,2825 * (1,00) + 0,1413 * (0,50) +$ $0,0508 * (0) = 0,7263$
P3	$0,5255 * (0,85) + 0,2825 * (0,35) + 0,1413 * (0,7375) +$ $0,0508 * (0,70) = 0,6853$
P4	$0,5255 * (0,77) + 0,2825 * (0,485) + 0,1413 * (0,50) +$ $0,0508 * (0) = 0,6123$
P5	$0,5255 * (0,85) + 0,2825 * (0,35) + 0,1413 * (0,925) +$ $0,0508 * (0) = 0,6763$

Therefore, P1 is the most suitable to the user in this example. The proposed method can return to the user a list containing the w better ranked/ordered providers. Thus, given $w = 3$, the return would be: {1, P1, 0.7263}, {2, P3, 0.6853}, {3, P5, 0.6763}.

For each different instance of user input, the method recalculates the PIs' priority level weights (using the AHP judgement matrix), score and the ranking of the cloud providers. Depending on the case, users may be not interested in using the "Essential" priority level. Bearing this in mind, and as a way to show the method's flexibility, a new set of weights are calculated and used, according to the expertise and need of the user. In this case, as a second example we used three hypothetical non-essential levels with the following importance relationships: "High" is two times more important that "Medium" and five times more important that "Low". "Medium" is two times more important that "Low". Following the aforementioned rules regarding the construction and use of the AHP judgment matrix, weights can be calculated and used in Eq. 8, which represents the cloud provider final score to be used in this example case, where the "Essential" priority level is not used. It is noteworthy that in this case, there is no scoring for the "Essential" PIs.

$$Pts(i) = 0,5949 * Pts_{high}(i) + 0,2766 * Pts_{medium}(i) + 0,1285 * Pts_{low}(i) \quad (8)$$

Therefore, using the same database (Table 4), same constants ($C_1 = 0.7$, $C_2 = 0.3$ and $C_3 = 0.7$) and user input data in Table 11, the final cloud providers' score is changed. Note that none PI is "Essential" in the user input expression (Table 11). Thus, stage one (removing incompatible providers) is skipped and all five provider can be scored (on stage two) for levels "High", "Medium" and "Low".

In this sense, taking into account the PI values and their tolerances provided by the user (Table 11), it is possible to observe the cloud providers' PIs attendance to the user's desired value (●), or not (○), shown in the same Table 11.

Table 11. Example 2: User data input and provider's PIs attendance.

PI	Value	Tolerance	Priority levels	Providers' PIs attendance				
				P1	P2	P3	P4	P5
RAM	8 GB	–	High	○	○	○	●	●
Cost	0,80 U\$/h	0,20 U\$/h	High	●	●	●	○	○
Storage	10 GB	1 GB	Medium	●	●	●	●	○
Avail	95%	5%	Medium	●	●	○	●	●
NI	5	–	Low	●	○	●	●	●
NOS	2	–	Low	○	●	○	○	○
Sec	L	M,H	Low	●	●	●	●	●

Next, on Stage 2, the method must score the quantitative and qualitative PIs, using Eqs. 4 and 5, respectively, for all providers. Each priority level (High, Medium, Low) is scored according Eq. 3. Table 12 presents the PIs priority levels' final scores comprising each provider.

Table 12. Example 2: Providers' scores by priority level.

Provider	Priority levels score		
	High	Medium	Low
P1	0,500	0,850	0,4667
P2	0,440	0,7857	0,5667
P3	0,290	0,500	0,4071
P4	0,350	0,8331	0,6667
P5	0,500	0,1969	0,5381

Next, on Stage 3, final score is calculated, and consequently the ranking, for each one of the five competing providers. This task is performed to each provider, in this particular case, according to Eq. 8. Coefficient values (weights) used in the weighted average are calculated according to the AHP judgment matrix aforementioned. These values are part of the Eq. 8. Thus, according that equation these weights are applied to the scores of each priority level already calculated. Finally, Table 13 presents the final score to the each cloud provider.

Thus, according to Table 13, it is possible to rank the 5 competing providers in scoring descending order:

1. P1 with 0,5925 points;
2. P2 with 0,5519 points;
3. P4 with 0,5243 points;
4. P5 with 0,4211 points; and
5. P3 with 0,3631 points.

Table 13. Example 2: Cloud providers' final score calculation.

General formula: (Eq. 8)
$Pts(i) = 0,5949 * Pts_{high}(i) + 0,2766 * Pts_{medium}(i) + 0,1285 * Pts_{low}(i)$

Provider	Final score
P1	$0,5949 * (0,500) + 0,2766 * (0,850) + 0,1285 * (0,4667) = 0,5925$
P2	$0,5949 * (0,440) + 0,2766 * (0,7857) + 0,1285 * (0,5667) = 0,5519$
P3	$0,5949 * (0,290) + 0,2766 * (0,500) + 0,1285 * (0,4071) = 0,3631$
P4	$0,5949 * (0,350) + 0,2766 * (0,8331) + 0,1285 * (0,6667) = 0,5243$
P5	$0,5949 * (0,500) + 0,2766 * (0,1969) + 0,1285 * (0,5381) = 0,4211$

Table 14. Example 3: User data input and provider's PIs attendance.

PI	Value	Priority levels	Providers' PI attendance				
			P1	P2	P3	P4	P5
Storage	80 GB	High	o	o	●	o	o
RAM	16 GB	Medium	o	o	o	●	o
Cost	0,30 U\$/h	High	o	●	o	o	o
Avail	99,9 %	Medium	●	o	o	o	o
NI	12	Medium	o	o	o	●	o
NOS	2	Medium	o	●	o	o	o
Sec	H	Medium	o	o	●	o	o

Therefore, P1 is again, the most suitable to the user in this example. If $w = 3$, the return would be: {1, P1, 0.5925}, {2, P2, 0.5519}, {3, P4, 0.5243}.

Now, lets try a more complex case. The database and constants will be the same. The left part of Table 14 presents the input data. There are none "Essencial" PI, none tolerance values and only two specified importance levels: "High" and "Medium". In this case, as there are only two different priority levels, and assuming level "High" is two times more important that "Medium", the final weights calculated using AHP judgment matrix are present in Eq. 9, which represents the cloud provider final score to be used in this example.

$$Pts(i) = 0,6667 * Pts_{high}(i) + 0,3333 * Pts_{medium}(i) \qquad (9)$$

Note that user's desired PI values are the extreme ones offered by cloud providers, which means only one of them is able to attend a particular PI. This can be seen, as the result of the PIs' attendance analysis performed according the method's Stage 1, in the same Table 14, where is shown providers attending the user's PI value (●) and does not attending (o). Table 15 presents the final scores by priority level of the PIs comprising each provider.

Table 16 presents the final score to the cloud providers, according Eq. 9.

Table 15. Example 3: Providers' scores by priority level.

Provider	Priority levels score	
	High	Medium
P1	0,0	0,3333
P2	0,0	0,1667
P3	1,0	0,1667
P4	0,0	0,1667
P5	0,0	0,1667

Table 16. Example 3: Cloud providers' final score calculation.

General formula: (Eq. 9)

$$Pts(i) = 0,6667 * Pts_{high}(i) + 0,3333 * Pts_{medium}(i)$$

Provider	Final score
P1	$0,6667 * (0,0) + 0,3333 * (0,3333) = 0,1111$
P2	$0,6667 * (0,0) + 0,3333 * (0,1667) = 0,0556$
P3	$0,6667 * (1,0) + 0,3333 * (0,1667) = 0,7223$
P4	$0,6667 * (0,0) + 0,3333 * (0,1667) = 0,0556$
P5	$0,6667 * (0,0) + 0,3333 * (0,1667) = 0,0556$

Thus, according to Table 16, it is possible to rank the 5 competing providers in scoring descending order:

1. P3 with 0,7223 points;
2. P1 with 0,1111 points; and
3. P2, P4 and P5 with 0,0556 points.

Therefore, P3 is the most suitable to the user. If $w = 2$, the return would be: { 1, P3, 0.7223 }, { 2, P1, 0.1111 }. Note that in this case, the proposed method behaved like a simple binary matching among the alternatives, since each PI only has been attended by a single provider.

6   Final Considerations

This research effort presented a deterministic scoring and ranking method based on criteria matching to support decision making regarding the selection of the most suitable cloud computing providers. The criteria matching comprises the users desidered and specified cloud computing performance indicators (PI). In this sense, the user input must specify the interest performance indicators, their desired values and priority level of each one meaning the importance of each PI to the accomplishement of the users objectives. The proposed method's simple and intuitive way to match if values of providers' PIs attend user's desired values, as well as the final cloud computing provider scoring based on this matching is a desired added value.

The proposed method is able to deal with whenever PI the user need in order to fulfill its goals. This means the proposed method can score and rank cloud providers using a non fixed set of performance indicators. In this sense, the user can submit as input expression to the method any PI and desired value. It is important to note that, the method utilization examples presented have considered a set of indicators present in five works [8–12].

The proposed method is designed following three stages:

1. filtering (removing) incompatible providers;
2. scoring quantitative and qualitative PIs by priority level and calculating final scores to providers;
3. sorting (ranking) the scored cloud providers and returning results to user.

Two types of PIs are considered: essential and non-essential. The non-essential PIs are considered with different degrees of importance, giving rise to distinct priority levels, thus, the higher the importance, the higher the priority. This priority levels are taken into account in order to final score cloud providers. Thus, higher priority levels have larger weights and consequently they have higher influence on the final score. The final score is a real number between 0 and 1. Therefore, the closer to 1 the final score is, the most suitable is the cloud provider to the user needs.

The proposed method presents high generality and high dimentionality as its main highlights. In other words, it is agnostic coping with any and all available cloud providers' PI regardless being quantitative or qualitative. Moreover, being tight coupled with a database, it can be easily and indefinitely expanded with the adding of new providers and PIs by cloud providers themselves or with the help of third party agents. Furthermore, being simple and intuitive, the proposed method does not require sophisticated mathematical and modelling skills to understand or use it.

On the other hand, the need of a large database of cloud providers with their respective PIs and values as a precondition to the method's operation can pose challenges. On of these challenges is the trust relationship establishment with the cloud providers and/or third parties in order to populate this database. In addition, once obtained the data, it needs to be classified in quantitive (HB, LB or NB) and qualitative (NB, HT, LT or HLT).

The adjustment of parameters C_1, C_2 and C_3 is other factor to be considered comprising the method operation. These factors provide flexibility, however they need to be finely adjusted in order to allow desired method efficiency. These parameters are empirical constants that need several tests to draw more precise conclusions, mainly regarding the ratio of C_1 to C_2. Moreover, these constants must be real values and the following mathematical relations must be obeyed: $C_1 + C_2 = 1$, $C_1 > C_2$ and $C_3 < 1$.

Examples of the utilization of the proposed method were presented, demonstrating its use and the convenience of its adoption.

Future work includes testing the proposed method in realistic settings including the creation of a cloud computing broker that incorporates the developed method. Also, the hydridization of the proposed method comprising addition of non deterministic matching characteristics are scheduled.

Acknowledgment. The authors would like to thank UDESC PROBIC scientific financial programme.

References

1. Hogan, M.D., Liu, F., Sokol, A.W., Jin, T.: NIST cloud computing standards roadmap. NIST Special Publication 500 Series (2013). Accessed Sept 2015
2. Zhang, Q., Cheng, L., Boutaba, R.: Cloud computing: state-of-the-art and research challenges. J. Internet Serv. Appl. **1**, 7–18 (2010)
3. Armbrust, M., Fox, A., Griffith, R., Joseph, A.D., Katz, R., Konwinski, A., Lee, G., Patterson, D., Rabkin, A., Stoica, I., Zaharia, M.: Above the clouds: a berkeley view of cloud computing. Technical report UCB/EECS-2009-28, Electrical Engineering and Computer Sciences Department, University of California at Berkeley (2009)
4. Zhou, M., Zhang, R., Zeng, D., Qian, W.: Services in the cloud computing era: a survey. In: 2010 4th International Universal Communication Symposium (IUCS), pp. 40–46 (2010)
5. Höfer, C.N., Karagiannis, G.: Cloud computing services: taxonomy and comparison. J. Internet Serv. Appl. **2**, 81–94 (2011)
6. Jain, R.: The Art of Computer Systems Performance Analysis: Techniques for Experimental Design, Measurement, Simulation, and Modeling. Wiley, Littleton (1991)
7. CSMIC: Service measurement index framework. Technical report, Carnegie Mellon University, Silicon Valley, Moffett Field, California (2014). Accessed Nov 2016
8. Garg, S.K., Versteeg, S., Buyya, R.: Smicloud: a framework for comparing and ranking cloud services. In: 2011 Fourth IEEE International Conference on Utility and Cloud Computing (UCC), pp. 210–218 (2011)
9. Garg, S.K., Versteeg, S., Buyya, R.: A framework for ranking of cloud computing services. Future Gener. Comput. Syst. **29**, 1012–1023 (2013)
10. Sundareswaran, S., Squicciarin, A., Lin, D.: A brokerage-based approach for cloud service selection. In: 2012 IEEE Fifth International Conference on Cloud Computing, pp. 558–565 (2012)
11. Shirur, S., Swamy, A.: A cloud service measure index framework to evaluate efficient candidate with ranked technology. Int. J. Sci. Res. **4**, 1957–1961 (2015)
12. Baranwal, G., Vidyarthi, D.P.: A framework for selection of best cloud service provider using ranked voting method. In: 2014 IEEE International Advance Computing Conference (IACC), pp. 831–837 (2014)
13. Saaty, T.L.: Decision making - the analytic hierarchy and network processes (ahp/anp). J. Syst. Sci. Syst. Eng. **13**, 1–35 (2004)
14. Wagle, S., Guzek, M., Bouvry, P., Bisdorff, R.: An evaluation model for selecting cloud services from commercially available cloud providers. In: 7th International Conference on Cloud Computing Technology and Science, pp. 107–114 (2015)
15. Achar, R., Thilagam, P.: A broker based approach for cloud provider selection. In: 2014 International Conference on Advances in Computing, Communications and Informatics (ICACCI), pp. 1252–1257 (2014)

16. Wagle, S.S., Guzek, M., Bouvry, P.: Cloud service providers ranking based on service delivery and consumer experience. In: 2015 IEEE 4th International Conference on Cloud Networking (CloudNet), pp. 209–212 (2015)
17. Somu, N., Kirthivasan, K., Shankar Sriram, V.S.: A computational model for ranking cloud service providers using hypergraph based techniques. Future Gener. Comput. Syst. **68**, 14–30 (2017)
18. de Moraes, L.B., Fiorese, A., Matos, F.: A multi-criteria scoring method based on performance indicators for cloud computing provider selection. In: Proceedings of the 19th International Conference on Enterprise Information Systems. ICEIS, INSTICC, vol. 2, pp. 588–599. SciTePress (2017)
19. Sari, B., Sen, T., Kilic, S.E.: Ahp model for the selection of partner companies in virtual enterprises. Int. J. Adv. Manuf. Technol. **38**, 367–376 (2008)
20. Ishizaka, A., Nemery, P.: Multi-Criteria Decision Analysis: Methods and Software. Wiley, United Kingdom (2013)
21. Fiorese, A., Matos, F., Alves Junior, O.C., Rupeenthal, R.M.: Multi-criteria approach to select service providers in collaborative/competitive multi-provider environments. IJCSNS Int. J. Comput. Sci. Netw. Secur. **13**, 15–22 (2013)

Describing Scenarios and Architectures for Time-Aware Recommender Systems for Learning

Eduardo José de Borba[1]($\boxtimes$), Isabela Gasparini[1]($\boxtimes$),
and Daniel Lichtnow[2]($\boxtimes$)

[1] Graduate Program in Applied Computing (PPGCA),
Department of Computer Science (DCC), Santa Catarina State University
(UDESC), Paulo Malschitzki 200, Joinville, Brazil
eduardojoseborba@gmail.com,
isabela.gasparini@udesc.br
[2] Polytechnic School, Federal University of Santa Maria (UFSM),
Av. Roraima 1000, Santa Maria, Brazil
dlichtnow@politecnico.ufsm.br

Abstract. This work investigates the use of Time-Aware Recommender Systems in e-learning systems. In this sense, in the work are defined recommender systems architectures taking into account how the time can be used in recommender systems in the learning domain. For each architecture the main requirements to use the time in a specific way is identified, and some algorithm ideas area presented. Scenarios are presented to illustrate how the proposal architectures can be useful. The results of this work can guide other researches on the field to apply recommender systems techniques in the learning domain.

Keywords: Recommender System · Context-aware · Time · Learning

1 Introduction

The learning management systems, (also called e-learning systems) can be useful tools in the educational process. Using an e-learning system is possible to provide learning objects to students. However, especially when the number of learning objects increases, students can have difficulties to perceive some of these learning objects. Thus, there is a great probability that some learning objects never get studied.

Considering this, the techniques used in Recommender Systems can be useful [1]. Some of Recommender Systems (RSs) take into account the information about the user context to recommend items to users. Context is any information that can be used to characterize the situation of an entity (e.g. location, time, physical conditions, etc.).

Time is an example of contextual information easier to capture than others. Besides, some works have demonstrated that using time information can improve the quality of recommendation [2].

This work aims to identify how Time-Aware RSs (Context-Aware RSs that use time context) can be used in the learning domain. For this purpose, seven categories of

S. Hammoudi et al. (Eds.): ICEIS 2017, LNBIP 321, pp. 366–386, 2018.
https://doi.org/10.1007/978-3-319-93375-7_17

how time can be used in RS are presented, based on previous works in the area [3]. For each of these seven categories, a RS architecture is defined where we present the main technical requirements (e.g., database structure, information to capture, equations, etc.) and recommendation procedure. Also, we present one scenario of use for each category, based on other previous work [4].

This work is: Sect. 2 presents Background of this research; Sect. 3 details the each seven categories of Time-Aware RSs and presents one related work that uses the category; Sect. 4 defines architectures an scenarios for each of the categories introduced in Sects. 3 and 5 presents Conclusions and Future Work.

2 Background

This section presents the main concepts related to Recommender Systems for Learning. Firstly, the definition of Recommender Systems and their traditional approaches is presented. Followed by Context-Aware Recommender Systems and Time-Aware Recommender Systems.

2.1 Recommender Systems

Recommender Systems (RSs) are computational tools that provide personalized suggestions to users [5]. This means that as recommendation each user receives a different set of items based on his/her preferences. In recent years, interest in Recommender Systems applications is growing strongly [6, 7]. Examples of these applications are recommendation of Books, CDs, DVDs, etc., in e-commerce like Amazon or EBAY, recommendation of movies like MovieLens or Netflix; recommendation of songs in music websites like Last.fm or Spotify; friend's recommendations in social networks like Facebook.

Recommender Systems emerged as an independent area in the mid-1990s [6]. Other areas are usually involved with this one, e.g., Information Retrieval, Approximation Theory, Artificial Intelligence, etc.

Recommender Systems are formally represented as follows:

$$F : U \times I \to R \tag{1}$$

Where F is the function that predicts the rating for an unknown item, U represents the users, I represents the items and R denotes an ordered set of predicted ratings.

Traditional approaches of Recommender Systems are [6]: Content-based, Collaborative Filtering, Knowledge-based, Demographic and Hybrid.

Content-based is the approach where the user receives a recommendation of items similar to the ones he/she had interest in, in the past [8]. It usually consists of comparing the description of the items (a set of keywords) to the users' profiles (another set of keywords) and recommending the most suitable item(s). That is why this approach is related with Information Filtering techniques, like TF-IDF or Cosine [6]. The main advantages of Content-based approach are [8]: (1) no dependence on an active community of users and (2) no item cold-start. The main drawbacks of this approach are [8]: (1) user cold-start and (2) overspecialization.

Collaborative Filtering approach recommends items to a user based on what other users - with similar tastes - have interest in [9]. It is the automatization of "word of mouth", where the RS tries to predict item utility to the user based on the utility of this item to users with similar tastes to him/her. The main advantage of this approach is Serendipity [9]. The main drawbacks are [9]: (1) dependence on an active community of users, (2) User cold-start, (3) Item cold-start and (4) Black sheep.

Knowledge-based approach recommends items to users based on the knowledge about how item features matches user needs and how useful this item should be [10]. This approach is usually applied to improve the recommendation precision or in cases where the other approaches have problems. This approach should be chosen where domain allows the representation of knowledge through structures easily read by computers, like ontologies [6]. The main drawback of this approach is that it needs knowledge acquisition [6].

Demographic approach recommends items based on the user's demographic profile, like age, gender, nationality, etc. This approach uses a recommendation by demographic classes, in which users are classified through stereotypes [11]. It considers that different recommendations should be made to different stereotypes. The main advantage of this approach is to recommend items according to users' age, gender, culture, etc. [11]. The main drawbacks are [11]: (1) assuming that users with similar demographics have similar tastes, (2) there are few works in literature about this.

Hybrid approach combines the mentioned approaches to recommend items to users. The objective is to group the advantages of these approaches to improve the recommendation quality with fewer drawbacks [11]. Burke [11] suggests some combinations of the approaches, for example: Weighted, Switching, Cascade and Mixed. In Weighted approach, the predicted ratings of several recommendation techniques are combined and each one has a different weight. In Switching approach, the system changes through different recommendation techniques depending on the current situation. In Cascade approach, one recommender refines the recommendations given by another. In Mixed approach, all combined approaches are used and the results are presented in the same ranking.

2.2   Context-Aware Recommender Systems

Traditional RSs consider only users and items to recommend, but they don't consider the context in which the users are. According to Dey [12], context is any information that can be used to characterize the situation of an entity. In RSs, entities can be the users and the items.

Context-Aware RSs are formally represented as:

$$F : U \times I \times C \to R \tag{2}$$

Where F is the function that predicts the rating of an unknown item, U represents the users, I represents the items, C represents the context and R denotes an ordered set of predicted ratings.

Several authors define different sets of dimensions that could represent context [13–15]. In this work, we follow Schimidt et al. [16] that defines the following dimensions:

- Information on the user, e.g., users' habits, emotional state, etc.;
- Users' social environment, e.g., co-location with other users, social interaction in social networks, etc.;
- Users' tasks, e.g., general goals, whether it is a defined task or random activity, etc.;
- Location, e.g., absolute position, whether the user is at home or office, etc.;
- Physical conditions, e.g., noise, light, etc.;
- Infrastructure, e.g., network bandwidth, type of device, etc.;
- Time, categorical (e.g., Time of the day – Morning, Afternoon, Evening), or continuous (e.g., a timestamp like "June 1st, 2016 at 17:14:36").

Adomavicius and Tuzhilin [17] define three paradigms of context in the recommendation process:

- Contextual Pre-Filtering, where the context filters the data that represents the user and then a traditional RS approach is applied;
- Contextual Post-Filtering, where a traditional RS approach is applied and then the result is filtered according to the context;
- Contextual Modelling, in which the context is applied directly in the recommendation algorithm.

Verbert et al. [18] say that, in e-learning, RSs traditional approaches are not enough to properly recommend items to students, because this domain offers some specific characteristics that are not covered by these approaches. For example, it is much more dangerous to recommend a bad material to a student, which could demotivate him/her to study, than recommend a bad product in an e-commerce system. According to Verbert et al. [18] this application domain requires a major level of personalization.

Using some context dimensions is an alternative to improve the personalization of e-learning environments, properly recommending materials to student current situation, e.g., Learning History, Environment, Timing and Accessible Resources [18].

The next section presents a specific kind of Context-Aware RS that uses time context to recommend. This kind of RS could also be used with other context dimensions.

2.3 Time-Aware Recommender Systems

Among all context dimensions, time has an advantage to be easy to capture, considering that almost every device has a clock that could capture the timestamp when an interaction occurs. Besides that, works in this area showed that the context of time has potential to improve recommendation quality [2]. This kind of RS is called Time-Aware Recommender Systems (TARS).

TARS are formally represented as:

$$F : U \times I \times T \to R \tag{3}$$

Where F is the function that predicts the rating for an unknown item, U represents the users, I represents the items, T represents time context and R denotes an ordered set of predicted ratings.

According to Merriam-Webster dictionary[1], time is "a non-spatial continuum that is measured in terms of events that succeed one after another from past through present to future". This information enables to the system establish an order to time events.

As seen in Sect. 2.2, time may be a continuous or categorical variable. Continuous variables are those that represent the exact time at which items are rated/consumed [2]. Categorical variables are calculated regarding time periods of interest in the recommendation [2]. Also, it can be represented in several time units, e.g., seconds, minutes, hours, days, months, years, etc. Time units are hierarchical, e.g., 1 day has 24 h, 1 h has 60 min, 1 min has 60 s.

3   Time-Aware RS Categories: Definition and Related Works

A Systematic Mapping was conducted in previous work [3], using Peterson et al. [19] methodology, aiming to explore Time-Aware RSs. The main research question defined was: How is time used in Context-aware RSs? To answer the main research question, three secondary research questions were defined: (1) How do recommender algorithms use time? (2) What are the differences about the use of time in different application domains? (3) What other dimensions of context are used to be applied together with the time dimension?

It is important to emphasize that this previous work did not consider only e-learning RSs. After the process of selection of papers, 88 papers were considered to answer the research question. In this previous work, seven categories of Time-Aware RSs were observed. The following subsections present an overview of each category [3] and a related work that uses the category.

3.1   Restriction

In the Restriction category, time is used to restrain which items are recommended. It means that any RS that compares time variables to restrain items to recommend appears in this category. There are, at least, two types of restrictions: (1) the RS matches the user's available time with time required to use the item (e.g., for movies or learning materials) or (2) the RS compares current time with operating hours of items (e.g., for restaurants, museums, etc.).

Anacleto et al. [20] describe a Points of interest recommender that uses time specified by the restriction category (among other context dimensions). In their work, the authors describe a system called PSiS (Personalized Sightseeing Planning System), that has two interfaces [20]: one web that is accessed through a computer, where the user defines his/her preferences and available time and asks for recommendation, and

---

[1] http://www.merriam-webster.com/dictionary/time.

(2) one mobile, where the user sees the recommendations, informs the system whether he/she liked them and can re-plan the initial trip.

On the system described above, recommendations are generated initially based on [20]: user's location; travel direction; speed; weather (for example, if it is raining, the system avoids outdoor points of interest); current time (because if the place is closed it is not worth recommending); and user's rating (in order to understand user's preferences). The system also tracks the user's trip by analyzing if he/she is ahead or behind schedule, and based on the user's availability it may insert or remove points of interest from the trip [20]. For this, the system considers visit duration and travel time for each point of interest.

3.2 Micro-Profile

In the Micro-profile category, the user has distinct profiles for each time. Here, time is usually categorical, so the user has a profile for weekdays and another profile for weekends, or the user has a profile for morning, a profile for afternoon and another for evening. Example: recommend a mobile app to the user on Sunday morning based only in apps used by this user in past Sunday mornings.

Kurihara et al. [21] use the Micro-profile category to recommend suitable applications for mobile device users considering the users' contexts. The authors show what applications a user executes in daily life follows a power law, based on an experiment with three applications (an airline website, a transfer guide website and an e-mail application). By this experiment, Kurihara et al. [21] that the airline website depends only on the time, the transfer guide website depends only on the location and the e-mail application is used anywhere and anytime.

On the work described before, the recommendation considers several micro-profiles for each user. These profiles depend on: (1) the location (captured by GPS), e.g., at home, at work or on the train; (2) time (captured by clock), where a day was divided into 8 periods of three hours. The authors propose an algorithm to predict user ratings called EF-ICF (Event Frequency – Inverse Event Frequency) that is based on TF-IDF and indicates whether the application often appears in the specific context and seldom appears in other contexts [21]. The RS combines this information (about items that are related to some context) with frequently used applications to generate recommendations to the user.

3.3 Bias

In the Bias category, time is the third dimension of the User x Item matrix. This category is more common on Collaborative Filtering RSs, or Hybrid RSs that combine Collaborative Filtering with other approaches. That is because this approach is the one that uses a User x Item to compare most similar users in order to predict ratings to non-viewed items. Time improves the process of finding the k-users more similar to the user that will receive recommendation and the prediction of ratings to non-viewed items.

Vo et al. [22] proposes a task RS that combines collaborative filtering, knowledge-based and utility-based filtering. This work considers that tasks similar to tasks previously accomplished by similar users in similar situations are relevant to the active user [22]. But instead of considering only the interactions that happened on the current situation and ignoring the rest, like it would be if Micro-profile were applied, the authors proposes task-based situation similarity and task-based user similarity calculation that is described below.

Task-based situation similarity considers that two situations are similar if tasks typically accomplished in these situations are similar [22]. **Task-based user similarity** considers that two users are similar if they accomplished similar tasks on similar situations [22]. To calculate these similarities, the RS use a User x Task x Context matrix, as defined by the Bias category, where the context is represented by Time and other context dimensions. Based on similar users, Collaborative Filtering can predict the which tasks to recommend.

3.4 Decay

Time is used as a decay factor, in which old interactions are less important than new ones. This category considers the last items consumed by the user represents best his interests, while items consumed a longer time ago are still important, but in a lesser way. That is why, in this category older interactions are not ignored, but new interactions have more influence on the recommendations.

Wei et al. [23] describe a Collaborative Filtering RS that applies the time-decay factor on users' interactions, as defined by the Decay category. This work proposes a service that recommends advertising in social networks, based on the trust between users. Considering users as nodes and relationships as edges on a social network, the authors define trust as the distance between users [23]. The recommendation algorithm also considers that the relationship fades gradually over time, so a comment made today should have stronger weight than one made last month when evaluating the relationship between two users.

On the system described above, a strategy of Collaborative Filtering is applied with a time-decay function on the relationship between users to find the most similar k-neighbors. Then, Collaborative Filtering predicts user ratings to not-consumed items by combining the k-neighbors' ratings with the time-decay factor on a similarity function and generates a list of recommendations [23]. Also, considering the trust among users the RS generates another list of recommendations that is combined with the former list to provide recommendations to the user.

3.5 Time Rating

In the Time Rating category, time is considered by the RS to infer user's preferences. There are two approaches to capture user's preferences: (1) Explicit, where the RS asks the user, or (2) Implicit where the RS learns from the user behavior. Usually, the RS in this category implements a strategy in which the more the user stays at the item, the more he likes it. It means that time captures user's feedback to an item implicitly, without need of user rating the item. Also, this strategy may be more precise and complete than explicit feedback because more items will have ratings and these ratings are based on user behavior.

Vildjiounaite et al. [24] presents a method that learns users' preferences on a Smart Home from implicit interactions. The proposed RS recommends TV programs, considering the choices which family members make together and separately.

To deduce user interest on TV programs the RS by [24]: (1) percent of time a program was viewed and if it was only a part, (2) indicator derived from physical context, e.g., sound analysis, user appointments (stop of watching because of the appointment does not mean program does not liked). The authors considered that viewing less than 40% of a program denotes lack of user interest and over 80% denotes user interest. And then, based on users' preferences capture with a Time Rating strategy, the RS generates TV program's recommendation.

3.6 Novelty

In the Novelty category, only new items can be recommended. In this category, there are at least two strategies: (1) the RS has a threshold, that depends on the system, and items older than that are not recommended or (2) the RS doesn't ignore old items, but if two items are similar, the newest is recommended. This category is most common in domains where new items tend to be more relevant than old ones (e.g., social networks, news, etc.).

Montes-García et al. [25] presents a news RS for journalists that allows identification of timely and primary information by experts across different sources. The RS takes into account news contextual dimensions (i.e., time, users interests, location and existing trends) combined with traditional recommendation approaches. This work uses time dimension as Novelty and the algorithm is described below.

The RS by Montes-García et al. [25] uses a hybrid approach, that combines Collaborative Filtering and Content-based. Both approaches are applied separately to predict the rating of a non-viewed item (between 0 and 1), and the result of each one is combined to generate the final rating [25]. Collaborative Filtering approach uses several implementations available on Apache Mahout[2]. While Content-based approach considers [25]: (1) relatedness to recent news user shown interest, (2) Recency, that refers to the Novelty factor, (3) Proximity, distance between user's and news position; (4) Trustworthiness, provided by a team of experts.

3.7 Sequence

In the Sequence category, the RS observes items that are usually consumed together, in a certain order. So, when the RS realizes that the user is following some known sequence pattern, it recommends the next items in that sequence to the user. In this category, the RS considers that users tend to follow some behavior pattern while interacting with the system.

Zhang and Liu [26] proposes an approach for recommendation on social networks called TrustSeqMF, that applies information about trust relationships among users and time sequence among items on a model-based Collaborative Filtering algorithm called

---

[2] http://mahout.apache.org/.

Matrix Factorization. Matrix Factorization is a model-based method, i.e., transforms both items and users into the same latent factor space to enable their direct comparison [26].

The RS described above calculates time sequence information by the degree to which one item affects the other. For example, for two items A and B it is calculated dividing the number of users that accessed both items in a certain period of time (e.g., 1 day) by the union set of users who consume item A or B in the same period [26].

4   Time-Aware RS Categories in Learning

In this section, we describe in depth each category described in Sect. 3 and see how each of them could be used in RS for e-learning. Besides we define a recommender system architecture for each Time-Aware RS category on learning domain, we also specify technical requirements and the recommendation procedure. In this section are presented scenarios of use to represent possible interactions of learners with an e-learning system, based on [4], where each Time-Aware RS category is demonstrated in a distinct scenario.

It is important to emphasize that to present the architectures and scenarios in the next sections, we take into account different educational approaches and situations.

In this sense, in e-learning there are courses that are open and do not have schedule to start or to finish (i.e. classes that student can study whenever he/she wants). There are courses where the schedule is restricted (there is a specific date to start and to finish). In face-to-face learning, the e-learning system can be used as complement of the classes, e.g. in the classroom – with technological resources, or out of the class – student's homework, additional study, etc.

4.1   Restriction

Restriction's most appropriate strategy to the learning domain is by matching user's available time with the time needed to consume the learning object. It is important to note that some learning object metadata are necessary here. Taking into account LOM metadata [27] the elements are 4.7 Duration (indicate videos or audios duration) and 5.9 Typical Learning Time (average time that users will spend in the learning object). In the case of text, it is possible to calculate the reading speed to fill Typical Learning Time [28].

A Time-Aware RS that uses this strategy needs an architecture as follows:

- The Learning Object Maintainer Module, that stores and retrieve all learning objects and the average time to consume it, among other information (e.g., description);
- The User interface, that allows user interaction and where the recommendation is shown. Besides the User Interface captures user interaction. One of User Interface responsibilities (in the context of Restriction category) is ask about user's available time, to provide this information to the Recommender Module. It is not necessary to create a new table on the database to save this information, since this information changes constantly, cannot be reused and depends user's current situation. It makes more sense to save this information on user's session, that can be easily accessed and changed and resets on a next user access;

- The Recommender Module, that applies some traditional RS approach and then filters the items to recommend based on user's available time (captured by User Interface) and the average time need to consume it (available on the Learning Object Maintainer Module);

The User Profile that store data about users´ preferences and users' interactions. The sequence of recommendation is as follows:

1. The Recommender Module applies some traditional RS approach (Contend-Based or Collaborative Filtering) and generates a recommendation list (a list of learning objects);
2. Using the User Interface, the user provides information about his/her available time;
3. The Recommender Module filter the recommendation list, i.e., keeps only learning objects that the average time fits the user's available time;
4. The Recommender Module sends the filtered list to User Interface;
5. The User Interface shows the recommendation.

A Scenario of use of this category would be a student Jones who is going to a new subject of this interest. The User Interface asks Jones how much time he intend to study. Jones indicates that he is going to study for 3 h. Thus, after applying a traditional RS approach to select learning objects that fits Jones' available time.

The RS also knows that the learning style of this user is visual, so it tries to recommend only videos to him/her. If no video is available, then the RS recommends other types of items. After applying a traditional RS approach to select the videos that best matches the user profile, the RS filters the list of recommendation, removing all videos that goes over 3 h.

Thus, in scenario 1 Jones watches a video that is 1 h45 min longer. Then, the student has 1 h15 min left. The next time the student asks for recommendations, the RS filters videos that go up to 1 h15 min. This process goes on and on until Jones's available time is over.

4.2 Micro-Profile

To use Micro-profile category on the learning domain, it is necessary to decide how much and which micro-profiles makes sense in this domain, based also on the course and environment where it would be applied. We could use, for example: (1) one profile for weekdays and other for weekends; (2) one profile for mornings, other for afternoons and another for evenings; (3) one profile for vacations and other for the academic year; etc.

A Time-Aware RS that uses this strategy needs an architecture as follows:

- The Learning Object Maintainer Module, that stores and retrieve all learning objects and learning objects metadata (e.g., description);
- The User interface, that allows user interaction and where the recommendation is shown. Besides the User Interface captures user interaction;
- The Recommender Module, that applies some traditional RS approach and then filters the items to recommend based on user's micro profile;
- The User Profile that store data about users' preferences and users' interactions.

For this, the system needs to save user interaction's records relating each interaction with the profile when it happens. A database with the following information would help with this (but it is not the only option) (Figs. 1, 2 and Table 1):

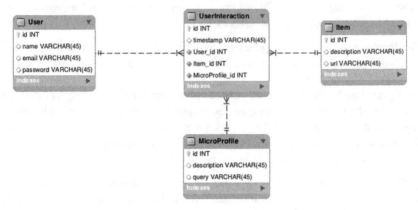

Fig. 1. Micro-profile recommender system database.

We can observe that, in this database proposal, each user interaction is represented by User, Item consumed, Micro-profile related with this interaction and the interaction timestamp. Each Micro-profile has a textual description to defined on its creation and a query. This query is the most important part, because is how Recommender System can identify in which micro-profile the User Interaction fits. A, example of a Micro-profile would be:

Table 1. Micro-profile database record example.

Columns	Values
Id	1435
Description	"Morning"
Query	"WHERE HOUR(timestamp) >=0 AND HOUR(timestamp) < 12"

Based on the query defined on the Micro-profile record, the Recommender System decides if the interaction is related with the profile or not. It also compares the current time with the micro-profile, in order to decide which is the most appropriate. The RS then considers only the interactions that are related to the micro-profile as the current user situation to calculate recommendations.

The sequence of recommendation is as follows:

1. The Recommender Module retrieve the micro profile based on rule base on query;
2. The Recommender Module applies some traditional RS approach (Content-Based or Collaborative Filtering) and generates a recommendation list (a list of learning objects) taking into account the micro-profile;

3. The Recommender Module sends the list of items to User Interface;
4. The User Interface shows the recommendation.

A Scenario of use of this category on the learning domain is presented now. Let's suppose there is a RS in a learning management system that uses Content-based approach. This RS represents students' profile as a set of keywords and each of the items another set of keywords. Student' keywords come from the items he/she liked (rated positively). However, item's keywords are the words that most appeared in the material and it is discovered through an algorithm called TF-IDF (Term Frequency – Inverse Document Frequency) [29].

In this scenario, a teacher uses the learning management system described above to support his/her in-person classes (face-to-face learning). He/she provides papers, presentations, links, games, etc., that may help student while studying.

The RS using Micro-profile strategy could split student's profile in three. One for the time (period) of the classes, other for weekdays (regarding the time out of the class), and other for the weekends. The RS knows what items the student access in each of these time periods. Then, it will recommend items during the face-to-face classes based on items the student accessed during classes, will recommend to him in weekdays out of class based on items accessed in this period and recommend in weekends based on weekend's access, using Content-based approach.

The RS might found out that, for example, one of the students likes to see complementary materials, like presentations while in the classroom to go along with teacher presentation. However, he likes more complete and complex materials to study in depth the subject while on weekdays. Moreover, the student wants short videos in the weekends where he/she will not spend much time studying. These preferences are reflect in each of students' profiles, so the recommender system is going to understand them and improve its recommendations.

4.3   Bias

In order to use Bias category on the learning domain, a Collaborative Filtering RS is required, using user's ratings to learning objects and the timestamp when this rate occurred. Collaborative Filtering without Time Bias uses a 2-dimensional matrix that combines Users and Items and the ratings given by Users to Items. We can see an example of this on Table 2:

Table 2. User x Item matrix example.

Users\Items	Item 1	Item 2	Item 3	Item 4
Bruce	3	2	1	4
Johnson	5	3	3	2
Larson	4	5	4	3
O'Connor	1	2	3	2

To add time Bias category on a Collaborative Filtering, the RS just need to store the timestamp from each rating. Instead of 2-dimensional matrix with Users and Items, Collaborative Filtering would use now a 3-dimensional matrix with Users, Items and Time. It means that, the same user can rate the same item different depending on the current time. This approach allows that the same user rates the same item more than once, if on a different context, and the RS considers both information on the recommendation. For example, we can see Table 3 (we are representing a 3-dimensional matrix by adding a new column time):

Table 3. User x Item x Time matrix example.

User	Time	Item 1	Item 2	Item 3	Item 4
Bruce	Time 1	3	2	5	4
Bruce	Time 2	4	4	3	2
Johnson	Time 1	1	2	4	5
Johnson	Time 2	4	3	4	2

A Time-Aware RS that uses this strategy needs architecture as follows:

- The Learning Object Maintainer Module, that stores and retrieve all learning objects;
- The User interface, that allows user interaction and where the recommendation is shown. The User interface is responsible (on Bias RS) to capture user's ratings for each item (and the timestamp for each rating);
- The User Profile to capture and store data about users' preferences, i.e., the ratings given by the users to items and the timestamp for each rating used by the Recommender Module;
- The Recommender Module, that applies Collaborative Filtering approach on the User x Item x Time matrix, in order to find the k-neighbours with similar taste and predict the ratings for the current user to items he didn't accessed yet.

For this, the system needs to save user interaction's records relating each interaction with the profile when it happens. A database with the following structure is enough for this:

Fig. 2. Bias recommender system database.

The sequence of recommendation is as follows:

1. Using Collaborative Filtering approach, the RS find k-neighbours with similar taste, based on the User x Item x Time matrix. It means that, users are similar if they rate items with similar rating when on a similar context;
2. The RS predicts to the target user the rating given by the user to items not rated yet (in the current context);
3. The learning objects with the highest predicted ratings are recommended to the target user.

In a Scenario of Use for this category, there is an online course, available for six months, and totally non-presential. Despite of there is a schedule to end the course, the system allows students entry at any time. Two users started the course in different times: John started two months ago and Stuart started five months ago. Also, both use to study 2 h by day. Items that Stuart accesses now are probably different of the items John accesses now, because Stuart is forward in the course.

In this case, the RS using time as Bias category compares John's profile today with Stuart's profile of three months ago (when he was also on the second month of the course). When comparing these two profiles, the RS finds out that John and Stuart are similar users, the RS can use Stuart ratings of three months ago to recommend items that John might like. Using this strategy, the RS does not recommend items to John based on what he is studying now, that could be too advanced to him. Instead, recommends items that are probably on the same topic of what John is studying, based in the assumption that these two users are considered similar.

4.4 Decay

Decay category applied on the learning domain would be to give more importance to keywords from learning objects accessed recently than to the ones accessed a long time ago, in a Content-based RS. It means that, instead of just look for learning objects with the same keywords as the ones accessed before, the RS will make some calculation to rank them based on the age of learning object access that originated each keyword.

A Time-Aware RS that uses this strategy needs an architecture as follows:

- The Learning Object Maintainer Module, that stores and retrieve all learning objects and learning objects metadata, mainly the items description and keywords that are used by Content-based RS;
- The User Profile Module that stores data about users' interactions, storing the items accessed and when each item was last accessed, and users' preferences, based on the items accessed. Both information is crucial for the Recommender Module using Decay factor;
- The User interface, that allows user interaction and where the recommendation is shown;
- The Recommender Module, that applies Content-based approach and then rank the items based on the age of learning object access that originated each keyword. For this, is necessary take into account the time.

Each item is represented by a set of keywords. The User profile consists of a set of keywords of items accessed by the user. The similarity between items and the user profile is calculated using TF-IDF [29]. However, the importance of a keyword also depends of the time since it was added to the user profile, i.e., keywords that represents an item accessed/evaluated in the past have lower importance. Combining these two information, the RS generates the recommendations.

The sequence of recommendation would be as follows:

1. The RS generates a list of recommendations, using Content-based approach based on the User profile to a target user;
2. The RS calculates the relevance for each item, based on the similarity between user profile and the items and on the importance of each keyword from the User profile found on the items;
3. The RS recommends to the user the most relevant items.

A Scenario of use of Decay category is following presented. Thus, in scenario 4, student Frank is enrolled in a discipline of Data Structure, that lasts one semester and that has four main topics (stack, queue, list and tree). In this discipline, there are four tests, one for each topic. Also, suppose that the RS in this discipline uses Content-based approach, i.e., recommends items similar to the ones the student accessed.

Before the first test, Frank only studied items about stacks, so he might receive only recommendations about stack. After the first test, Frank starts studying the second topic: queues. If the RS keeps recommending only stacks, the user will probably not like the recommendations he receives.

The RS, using Decay category, gives less weight to the old items that Frank accessed about stacks and gives more weight to the new items about queues. There still possibilities that Frank receives recommendations about stacks, but the RS are going to prioritize the new items about queues to recommend materials.

4.5   Time Rating

In order to apply Time Rating category on the learning domain, it is required from the system that it records how long each student stayed in each item. In a Web site, there are at least two ways to do this: (1) use a JavaScript component to measure the time (in seconds) that the user spent on the item, or (2) track opening and closing objects events to calculate after how long the user stayed on the item. Here we consider that a JavaScript component can be more accurate because it can consider if the user is actually with looking at the material or it is open on another tab and the user is not looking at it.

A Time-Aware RS that uses this category needs an architecture as follows:

- The Learning Object Maintainer Module, that stores and retrieve all learning objects and learning objects metadata;
- The User interface, that allows user interaction and where the recommendation is shown. The interface is responsible on a Time Rating strategy to capture how long the user stayed on each item to provide this information to the User Profile Module;

- The User Profile Module that stores data about users' interactions, calculating user's preference based on how long he stayed on each item;
- The Recommender Module, that applies a traditional RS approach based on the profile provided by the User Profile Module.

The User Profile Module, that calculates user's preferences based on the time the user spent on each item needs to consider that each user has their own behavior, and there are students that usually stays more in times in each item on average, while others have the habits to just take a brief look in each learning object. To treat this problem the RS could be use the following equation to calculate how much the student u like item i:

$$R_{u,i} = \frac{t_{u,i}}{\bar{t}_u} \tag{4}$$

Where $R_{u,i}$ is the rating calculated of user u to item i, $t_{u,i}$ is the time (in minutes) that the user u stayed in the item i, and $\bar{t}_u$ is the average time of user u in the items of the system. This equation expresses that if the user u stays in the item i more than his average, the rating calculated is greater than 1, so this means the user liked it. But, if user u stays in item i less than his average, the rating is between 0 and 1, meaning the user didn't like it.

The sequence of recommendation would be as follows:

1. User Interface captures how long the user stayed on each item;
2. The User Profile Module calculates, based on the equation presented before and the time spent in each item, the ratings given implicitly for the items accessed;
3. The RS applies a traditional RS approach (Collaborative Filtering or Content-based), using the ratings calculated on the previous step;
4. The RS recommends to the user the most relevant items.

A Scenario of use of Time Rating category is following presented. Thus, in scenario 5, there is a RS in an e-learning environment that uses Collaborative Filtering approach. This approach requires an active community of students and requires feedback of the Students to the items. The feedback is usually made through explicit rating, e.g., from 1 to 5 stars.

Suppose that this environment have an active community, but the students rarely rate the items that they access. In this scenario, time is useful to receive implicit feedback about how the student liked this item.

To exemplify, considering two students Anna and Bruce and that all items were created with the same length and therefore the students will spend the same time to use an item. A problem that must be considered by the RS is that some students usually stay more in some items, while others stays less in the same items. Anna has an average time of 30 min per item. Bruce has an average time of 5 min per item. If Anna stays 15 min in the item I, this probably means she did not likes much this item. If Bruce stays 15 min in the item I, this probably means he liked this item.

4.6 Novelty

On a learning domain, do not make sense to disregard materials that were created a long time ago. That's because old items can still be relevant. But, depending on the subject of study, old items should be replaced by new ones. Either because new items tend to be more attractive and helpful for users (e.g., when the teacher updates his material based on experiences) or because the subject is changing and the materials needs to stay up to date.

In order to apply Novelty category on the learning domain, the RS requires the date when items were created to system. Taking into account LOM metadata [27] the element required is 2.2.3 Date, that stores the date when a learning object were first created and indicates how old it is.

A Time-Aware RS that uses this category needs an architecture as follows:

- The Learning Object Maintainer Module, that stores and retrieve all learning objects and learning objects metadata, specially the Date when the learning object were created to provide this information to the Recommender Module;
- The User interface, that allows user interaction and where the recommendation is shown;
- The User Profile Module that store data about users' preferences and users' interactions;
- The Recommender Module, that applies some traditional RS approach and after re-ranking the items based on the creation date.

The sequence of recommendation would be as follows:

1. As on a traditional RS, User Profile captures user's preferences, that depends on the recommendation approach used;
2. The Recommender Module generates a list of items to recommend base on some recommendation approach.
3. The Recommender Module re-ranks the list of items bases on item age (using Date metadata available on the Learning Object Maintainer Module), thus the newest is on the top;

In a Scenario of use, the student Fernando signs-up to an online course about new web technologies, like HTML 5, CSS 3, Angular, etc. This subject is in constant changing, because these actual technologies are been updated and upgraded very frequently. This course is updated every time one of these technologies changes and the course administrator tells the system in metadata when this item was created. The RS, using Novelty category, will recommend (preferentially) items that are new to the system and up-to-date with the technologies.

Finally, when Fernando is interested in a topic about Angular, RS finds two items about this subject, one from 2010 (date of the first Angular release) and other from 2016 (date of Angular 2 release). The Recommender Module would recommend both, if possible, but the newest item (from 2016) is on the above the older one (from 2010).

4.7   Sequence

Sequence category applied on the learning domain considers that there is common sequential access pattern (also called learning path) on learning environments. Then, when the RS identifies that a user's access is matching some of the known learning paths, it uses the next items of the sequence as items to recommend.

A Time-Aware RS that uses this category needs an architecture as follows:

- The Learning Object Maintainer Module, that stores and retrieve all learning objects and learning objects metadata;
- The User interface, that allows user interaction and where the recommendation is shown. The responsibility of the User Interface (for Sequence recommendation) is to capture user's interaction, i.e., which items were accessed and when;
- The User Profile Module that sets up a directed graph for each user based on the item access' order;
- The Sequential Pattern Mining Module, that uses a Sequential Pattern Mining algorithm (e.g., Apriori or GSP) to identify common learning paths;
- The Recommender Module, tries to match user's directed graph with the common learning paths on the system. And if a match is found, the Sequential Pattern found is used to find the next items to be recommended.

The sequence of recommendation would be as follows:

1. User Interface captures all items accessed, together with the timestamp of this interactions;
2. User Profile Module sort all user's interaction by the timestamp and generates a directed graph that represents the user access behaviour;
3. Using all users' graphs, the Sequential Pattern Mining Module apply a Sequential Pattern Mining algorithm to identify common learning paths. The result of this algorithm would probably be a tree with the most common learning paths, in which the root is the system's first page that all users access initially;
4. The Recommender Module tries to match the user's access graph with some of known learning paths. If a match is found, the next items on the sequence are recommended to the user.

In a Scenario of use of Sequence category, there is a short course of Algorithms that occurs one time for semester and lasts a month. This short course has 30 materials numbered from 1 to 30, within papers, links, images, videos, etc.

In the first semester of 2016, 80 students enrolled the short course and Sequential Pattern Mining Module observed that one of the learning path most frequent was:

$$1 \rightarrow 9 \rightarrow 7 \rightarrow 15 \rightarrow 23 \rightarrow 12 \rightarrow 25$$

In the second semester of 2016, the Recommender Module observes that user Norman accessed items 1, 9 and 7, in this order. So, the Recommender Module recommends to Norman the items 15 and 23. This means RS uses the learning path learnt from the last semester to recommend material to new students.

5   Conclusion

In this paper is described architectures and scenarios for Time-Aware RSs for learning, taking into account seven categories of this kind of RS, based in our previous work [3].

For each category, an architecture is proposed based on the technical requirements to implement it on the learning domain. A summary of the time information requirements can be observed on Table 4. It is possible to observe that while some categories only need one type of time information (i.e., Time Rating and Sequence), most of them require more than one (i.e., Restriction, Micro-profile, Bias, Decay and Novelty).

Table 4. Time requirements for each category.

Category	Requirements					
	Interaction timestamp	Current date/time	User's available time	How long user stays on item	Item's date of creation	Time required to consume item
Restriction	No	**No**	Yes	No	No	**Yes**
Micro-profile	**Yes**	Yes	No	No	No	No
Bias	**Yes**	No	No	No	No	No
Decay	**Yes**	Yes	No	No	No	No
Time rating	No	No	**No**	Yes	No	No
Novelty	No	Yes	No	No	**Yes**	No
Sequence	**Yes**	No	No	No	No	No

As said on Sect. 4, Restriction applied in the learning domain only makes sense if we know user's available time and the time required to consume some item (e.g., video length). So, we can match user's available time with the time to consume some item.

For Micro-profile is required the time when each interaction (e.g., user rating, item accessed) happened and the current time it's known. This way we can filter user profile only by similar time to the current (e.g., only consider interactions that happened on weekends if today is a Saturday or Sunday).

Bias only needs the timestamp in which each interaction happened. This information will be incorporated into the User x Item matrix to improve Collaborative Filtering effectiveness and personalization.

In Decay we give a different weight for each interaction according to the difference between the current timestamp and the timestamp in which the supposed interaction happened. That's why the information required for Decay is the current time and the time in which each interaction happened.

Time Rating calculates the implicit feedback to an item based on how long the user stays on it. That's why it is the only information required by this category.

Novelty treats differently an item based on the difference between the current time and the item's date of creation. In this way new items' are more important than old ones. Using this category in the learning domain requires to know the current time and date of creation of all items. Although this category is not applicable in all learning system or courses, since the date of creation is not relevant for a traditional Calculus course, for example, but can be useful for a course on new technologies or politics.

Sequence requires only the timestamp of each interaction. Using only this information is possible to apply different graph algorithms and extract information on user's behavior.

Section 4 presented scenarios that illustrate the Time-Aware RS categories in learning situations and help to better understand their importance and application, based on the scenarios presented on a previous work [4].

As future work, the proposed architectures should be detailed, implemented and tested using a real environment with active users, as well as other combinations between Recommendation approaches and Time-Aware RS categories.

References

1. Brusilovsky, P.: Methods and Techniques of Adaptive Hypermedia. In: Brusilovsky, P., Kobsa, A., Vassileva, J. (eds.) Adaptive Hypertext and Hypermedia, pp. 1–43. Springer, Dordrecht (1998). https://doi.org/10.1007/978-94-017-0617-9_1
2. Campos, P.G., Díez, F., Cantador, I.: Time-aware recommender systems: a comprehensive survey and analysis of existing evaluation protocols. User Model User-Adapt. Interact. **24**, 67–119 (2014)
3. de Borba, E.J., Gasparini, I., Lichtnow, D.: Time-aware recommender systems: a systematic mapping. In: Kurosu, M. (ed.) HCI 2017. LNCS, vol. 10272, pp. 464–479. Springer, Cham (2017). https://doi.org/10.1007/978-3-319-58077-7_38
4. Borba, E.J., Gasparini, I., Lichtnow, D.: The use of time dimension in recommender systems for learning. ICEIS **2**, 600–609 (2017)
5. Ricci, F., Rokach, L., Shapira, B.: Introduction to recommender systems handbook. In: Ricci, F., Rokach, L., Shapira, B., Kantor, P.B. (eds.) Recommender Systems Handbook, pp. 1–35. Springer, Boston (2011). https://doi.org/10.1007/978-0-387-85820-3_1
6. Adomavicius, G., Tuzhilin, A.: Toward the next generation of recommender systems: a survey of the state-of-the-art and possible extensions. IEEE Trans. Knowl. Data Eng. **17**(6), 734–749 (2005)
7. Beel, J., Breitinger, C., Langer, S., Lommatzsch, A., Gipp, B.: Towards reproducibility in recommender-systems research. User Model. User-Adapt. Interact. **26**, 69–101 (2016)
8. Lops, P., de Gemmis, M., Semeraro, G.: Content-based recommender systems: state of the art and trends. In: Ricci, F., Rokach, L., Shapira, B., Kantor, Paul B. (eds.) Recommender Systems Handbook, pp. 73–105. Springer, Boston (2011). https://doi.org/10.1007/978-0-387-85820-3_3
9. Jannach, D., Zanker, M., Felfernig, A., Friedrich, G.: Recommender Systems: An Introduction. Cambridge University Press, New York (2011)
10. Felfernig, A., Friedrich, G., Jannach, D., Zanker, M.: Developing constraint-based recommenders. In: Ricci, F., Rokach, L., Shapira, B., Kantor, P.B. (eds.) Recommender Systems Handbook, pp. 187–215. Springer, Boston (2011). https://doi.org/10.1007/978-0-387-85820-3_6
11. Burke, R.D.: Hybrid recommender systems: survey and experiments. User Model. User-Adapt. Interact. **12**(4), 331–370 (2002)

12. Dey, A.K.: Understanding and using context. Ubiquitous Comput. **5**(1), 4–7 (2001)
13. Schilit, B., Adams, N., Want, R.: Context-aware computing applications. In: Proceedings of the First Workshop Mobile Computing Systems and Applications (WMCSA 1994), pp. 85–90 (1994)
14. Chen, G., Kotz, D.: A Survey of Context-Aware Mobile Computing Research. Technical report (2000)
15. Zimmermann, A., Lorenz, A., Oppermann, R.: An operational definition of context. In: Kokinov, B., Richardson, D.C., Roth-Berghofer, T.R., Vieu, L. (eds.) CONTEXT 2007. LNCS (LNAI), vol. 4635, pp. 558–571. Springer, Heidelberg (2007). https://doi.org/10.1007/978-3-540-74255-5_42
16. Schmidt, A., Beigl, M., Gellersen, G.H.: There is more to context than location. Comput. Gr. **23**(6), 893–901 (1999)
17. Adomavicius, G., Tuzhilin, A.: Context-aware recommender systems. In: Ricci, F., Rokach, L., Shapira, B., Kantor, P.B. (eds.) Recommender Systems Handbook, pp. 217–253. Springer, Boston (2011). https://doi.org/10.1007/978-0-387-85820-3_7
18. Verbert, K., Manouselis, N., Ochoa, X., Wolpers, M., Drachsler, H., Bosnic, I., Duval, E.: Context-aware recommender systems for learning: a survey and future challenges. IEEE Trans. Learn. Technol. **5**(4), 318–335 (2012)
19. Petersen, K., Feldt, R., Mujtaba, S., Mattsson, M.: Systematic mapping studies in software engineering. In: 12th International Conference on Evaluation and Assessment in Software Engineering, vol. 17, no. 1 (2008)
20. Anacleto, R., Figueiredo, L., Almeida, A., Novais, P.: Mobile application to provide personalized sightseeing tours. J. Netw. Comput. Appl. **41**, 56–64 (2014)
21. Kurihara, S., Moriyama, K., Numao, M.: Context-aware application prediction and recommendation in mobile devices. In: Web Intelligence, pp. 494–500 (2013)
22. Vo, C., Torabi, T., Loke, S.: Towards context-aware task recommendation. In: Joint Conferences on Pervasive Computing (JCPC), pp. 289–292 (2009)
23. Wei, C., Khoury, R., Fong, S.: Web 2.0 recommendation service by multi-collaborative filtering trust network algorithm. Inf. Syst. Front. **15**(4), 533–551 (2013)
24. Vildjiounaite, E., Kyllönen, V., Hannula, T., Alahuhta, P.: Unobtrusive dynamic modelling of TV program preferences in a household. In: Tscheligi, M., Obrist, M., Lugmayr, A. (eds.) EuroITV 2008. LNCS, vol. 5066, pp. 82–91. Springer, Heidelberg (2008). https://doi.org/10.1007/978-3-540-69478-6_9
25. Montes-García, A., Álvarez-Rodríguez, J., Labra-Gayo, J., Martínez-Merino, M.: Towards a journalist-based news recommendation system: the Wesomender approach. Expert Syst. Appl. **40**(17), 6735–6741 (2013)
26. Zhang, Z., Liu, H.: Social recommendation model combining trust propagation and sequential behaviors. Appl. Intell. **43**(3), 695–706 (2015)
27. IEEE: Draft Standard for Learning Object Metadata (2002). http://grouper.ieee.org/groups/ltsc/wg12/20020612-Final-LOM-Draft.html
28. Bell, T.: Extensive reading speed and comprehension. Read. Matrix **1**(1), 1–13 (2001)
29. Manning, C.D., Raghavan, P., Schütze, H.: Introduction to Information Retrieval. Cambridge University Press, New York (2008)

Towards Generating Spam Queries for Retrieving Spam Accounts in Large-Scale Twitter Data

Mahdi Washha[1]([✉]), Aziz Qaroush[2], Manel Mezghani[1], and Florence Sedes[1]

[1] IRIT - Paul Sabatier University, Toulouse, France
{Mahdi.washha,Florence.sedes}@irit.fr,
Mezghani.manel@gmail.com
[2] Department of Electrical and Computer Engineering,
Birzeit University, Ramallah, Palestine
Aqaroush@birzeit.edu

Abstract. Twitter, as a top microblogging site, has became a valuable source of up-to-date and real-time information for a wide range of social-based researches and applications. Intuitively, the main factor of having an acceptable performance in those recherches and applications is the working and relying on information having an adequate quality. However, given the painful truth that Twitter has turned out a fertile environment for publishing noisy information in different forms. Consequently, maintaining the condition of high quality is a serious challenge, requiring great efforts from Twitter's administrators and researchers to address the information quality issues. Social spam is a common type of the noisy information, which is created and circulated by ill-intentioned users, so-called social spammers. More precisely, they misuse all possible services provided by Twitter to propagate their spam content, leading to have a large information pollution flowing in Twitter's network. As Twitter's anti-spam mechanism is not both effective and immune towards the spam problem, enormous recherches have been dedicated to develop methods that detect and filter out spam accounts and tweets. However, these methods are not scalable when handling large-scale Twitter data. Indeed, as a mandatory step, the need for an additional information from Twitter's servers, limited to a few number of requests per 15 min time window, is the main barrier for making these methods too effective, requiring months to handle large-scale Twitter data. Instead of inspecting every account existing in a given large-scale Twitter data in a sequential or randomly fashion, in this paper, we explore the applicability of information retrieval (IR) concept to retrieve a sub-set of accounts having high probability of being spam ones. Specifically, we introduce a design of an unsupervised method that partially processes a large-scale of tweets to generate spam queries related to account's attributes. Then, the spam queries are issued to retrieve and rank the highly potential spam accounts existing in the given large-scale Twitter accounts. Our

---

The work described in this paper is an extended version to the published work presented in [1].

S. Hammoudi et al. (Eds.): ICEIS 2017, LNBIP 321, pp. 387–412, 2018.
https://doi.org/10.1007/978-3-319-93375-7_18

experimental evaluation shows the efficiency of generating spam queries from different attributes to retrieve spam accounts in terms of precision, recall, and normalized discounted cumulative gain at different ranks.

Keywords: Twitter · Social networks · Spam query

1   Introduction

With the rapid growth of the user generated content in online social networks (OSNs) such as microblogging sites, a tremendous range of researches and applications such as search engines has begun adopting OSNs as a primary or secondary source of information. OSNs have become the most suitable place for a wide slice of users to share links, discuss, and connect with others. Given the fact that OSNs have easy interactive interfaces with low barriers to publish information in different forms, various information quality (IQ) problems such as rumor, and spam, have been appeared on OSNs. The existence of IQ problems has different side effects, including the obtaining of accurate and relevant information, and maintaining a high performance in the applications that use OSNs information. As a concrete example, Twitter has distinctive services not existing in the same power in other OSNs. Delivering posts (tweets) in a real-time manner, adding hashtags in tweets to group similar tweets to facilitate the search process, inserting URL(s) pointing out to external source(s) of information, and providing a real-time search service to retrieve tweets are different services that Twitter provides [2].

The lack of effective restrictions on the posting action and the openness of OSNs have attracted a special kind of ill-intentioned individuals called as "social spammers". They badly exploit OSNs' services for publishing and spreading misleading, and fake information. Social spammers have different motivations to publish spam content, summarized in [2]: (i) spreading advertisements to generate sales and gain illegal profits; (ii) disseminating porn materials; (iii) publishing viruses and malwares; (iv) creating phishing websites to reveal sensitive information. Unfortunately, propagating spam content may cause problems in different areas such as: (i) polluting search results by spam content; (ii) degrading statistics obtained by mining tools; (iii) consuming storage resources; (iv) and violating user's privacy. The optimal solution for tackling such a problem is filtering out the noisy data to have high quality information. Hence, given the fact that OSNs in general, and Twitter in particular, are not immune towards social spam problem, the most widely acceptable solution is trying to increase the quality of a desired entity (e.g., tweets, Twitter accounts, Facebook posts, etc.). We summarize the increasing information quality process in social networks in three main steps, illustrated in Fig. 1: (i) choosing the data collection (e.g., Facebook accounts, Tweets, Facebook posts) that needs improvement; (ii) determining which noise type (e.g., spam, rumor) should be detected and filtered out; (iii) at last, applying one or more pre-designed algorithms corresponding to the chosen noise type, producing a new noise free data collection.

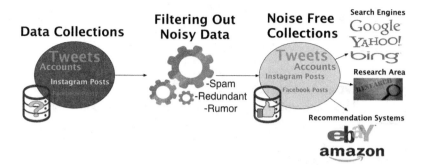

Fig. 1. An overview showing the information quality process to increase the quality of an input data collection.

The Problem. A considerable set of methods [2–13] has been introduced for detecting spam accounts and spam campaigns, with little efforts spent towards spam tweets detection. These conventional methods mainly combine the feature extraction concept with the supervised machine learning algorithms to build predictive models based on an annotated data-set. However, applying these methods on large-scale Twitter data consisting of millions of users (or accounts) is time consuming, which may require months to process such a "crawled" large-scale data. The main source of the time consumption, especially in account and campaign based detection, is the need for retrieving or collecting additional information from Twitter's servers to make the features extractable. Despite of the problem is not in retrieving the information itself, Twitter has its own REST APIs[1] so that the number of calls by those APIs is limited and restricted to a defined number and a time window. Therefore, the exploitation of Twitter's REST APIs is the main responsible about this bottleneck problem, where no alternative solution exists to collect (or retrieve) complete information about users. For instance, collecting additional information for one million accounts with their meta-data, followers, and followees, may take more than 6 months. Hence, inspecting sequentially or randomly each individual account existing in a "crawled" large-scale Twitter accounts or tweets to predict the class label of the account is impractical solution at all, boosting the need for a systematic method that reduces the sequential search space from being millions to thousands.

Spam Queries Generation. The Twitter spam detection methods presented in the literature have been designed to provide the class label, as an output information, of a desired selected entity (account, tweets, campaign). Given the fact that spam content might be partially common in particular information such as username attribute, having a spam searchable information could contribute in making the detection process of spam accounts more systematic and faster. More precisely, based on the information retrieval (IR) concepts, the searchable information corresponds to queries, while the Twitter data are the documents over

---

[1] https://dev.twitter.com/rest/public.

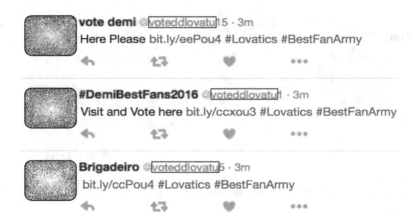

Fig. 2. Illustrative example of spam tweets posted by different users having common screen name pattern "voteddlovatu" [1].

which the retrieval process is taken place. Consequently, generating spam queries in somehow with using them at the retrieval contribute in retrieving accounts having high probability for being spam. As a possible example of spam queries, Fig. 2 shows three correlated spam tweets corresponding to three different spam accounts having almost same screen name attribute value "voteddlovatu". With applying simple information retrieval method on a desired Twitter data with using such a string pattern as a spam query, all accounts that have the string pattern will be retrieved with top ranks. After that the conventional detection methods can be applied on a defined set of the retrieved accounts to produce an accurate class label for each account in the selected set. One important note is that social spammers spend a great effort to avoid random and rubbish names in filling-up the public attributes such as screen name and username because social spammers automate the creation process of Twitter accounts in which the IDs must be unique. To ensure the uniqueness property for some attributes, social spammers fill up those attributes using a unique pattern combined with a systematic simple counting (e.g., "15", "1", and "5") as illustrated in the given example in Fig. 2. Moreover, social spammers must select attractive names in order to lure legitimate users as much as possible and thus using random and rubbish names is not the solution at all.

Contributions. In this paper, we discuss the possibility of using information retrieval concept to retrieve spam accounts existing in large-scale Twitter data. To do so, we introduce an unsupervised method that generates spam queries extracted from different meta-data (e.g., username, and screen name) describing Twitter account object. Specifically, our method processes partially and quickly a subset of tweets exiting in a desired large-scale Twitter data that requires cleaning where those tweets belong to different Twitter accounts. Through a series of experiments, we demonstrate the effectiveness of our method in generating spam queries on a crawled and an annotated data-set containing more than two millions tweets. The experimental results show that the spam queries generated from the screen name and username attributes have superior performance in terms of three different information retrieval metrics (Precision@L, Recall@L, Normalized Discounted Cumulative Gain@L), compared to five different baselines. With the promising results introduced, our method can be leveraged in different ways:

- For a crawled Twitter data, our method can be applied to retrieve the accounts that have high probability for being a spam in a target collection. Then, the conventional detection methods can be used to process the top ranked accounts (e.g., top 1,000), speeding-up the filtration process without needing to examine each account in the given Twitter data.
- Twitter can integrate our spam retrieval method with its anti-spam mechanism to search for spam accounts in a systematic and a fast fashion.

The rest of the paper is structured as follows. Section 2 presents a background and Twitter-based spam detection methods introduced in the literature. Section 3 presents the notations, problem formalization, and the design of an unsupervised method for generating spam queries. Section 4 details the data-set used in experimenting and validating our method. The experimental setup and a series of experiments evaluating the our method are described in Sect. 5. At last, Sect. 6 concludes the work.

2 Background and Related Work

Microblogging Sites. The microblogging is a short broadcast medium which helps users in keeping up with the action of blogging [14]. Specifically, Microblogging sites allow users to exchange images, content, video links and others. Posting users' ideas/opinions in limited number of words is the main feature strongly existing in these sites. As one of many microblogging sites, Twitter is the most popular social Microblogging site dedicated for online news and social networking service. Twitter users can post and interact through messages, so-called tweets, limited to 140 characters.

Social Spam Definition. Social spam is defined as a nonsensical or a gibberish text content appearing in OSNs [15]. Social spam may come in different forms, including profanity, insults, hate speeches, fraudulent reviews, personally identifiable information, fake friends, bulk messages, phishing and malicious links, and porn materials. In the context of information retrieval field, social spam might been viewed as an irrelevant information; however, this view is not accurate. Simply, we justify this misinterpretation through the definition of information retrieval systems [16] in which the relevancy of documents in IR systems is dependent on the input search query. Hence, irrelevant documents w.r.t. an input query are "not" necessary to be a spam content as long as the input query is not a spam.

Social Spammers Facts. Social spammers take the benefits of all legal services provided by OSNs for spreading their spam content. Regardless the targeted social network, there are some interesting facts related to social spammers' behaviors and goals:

- Social spammers are goal-oriented persons aiming at achieving unethical goals (e.g., promoting products). Achieving their goals requires to leverage their smartness to accomplish their spamming tasks in an effective and a quick way.
- Social spammers usually create and launch a bot (group) of spam accounts in a short period (e.g., in one day), to maximize their monetary profit and speedup their spamming behavior.
- Social spammers leverage the APIs that are provided for developers by OSNs to automate their spamming tasks in a systematic way (e.g., tweeting every 10 min). They keep away from using random posting behavior since it may decrease the desired profit and decelerate their spamming behavior.

Twitter's Anti-spam Mechanism. Twitter fights against social spammers through allowing users to report spam accounts by clicking on "Report: they are posting spam" option available on the account page. Once a user gets reported, Twitter's administrators manually review and check the reported user to make a suspension decision. However, adopting such a method for combating social spammers needs significant efforts from both legitimate users and administrators. Moreover, it is not necessary that all reports must be trustworthy, meaning that some reported accounts might belong for legitimate users, not for social spammers. In addition to this manual reporting mechanism, Twitter has introduced some general rules (e.g., posting porn materials is prohibited) for public, targeting to reduce the social spam problem as much as possible with suspending permanently the accounts that violate those rules [17]. However, Twitter's rules are not effective and easy to bypass by social spammers. For instance, social spammers may employ multiple accounts with distributing a desired workload among them to mislead the detection process. Following such a strategy, the separated accounts tend to exhibit an invisible spam behavior. Thus, these shortcomings have motivated various researchers to design more powerful methods for the applications that adopt Twitter as a source of information.

After having a deepen insight into a wide range of scientific research works related to the spam detection methods in Twitter, we build a detailed taxonomy for these methods, illustrated in Fig. 3, based on different criteria, including: (i) type of the detection approach (Machine Learning or Honeypot); (ii) level of detection (Tweet, Account, and Campaign); and (iii) type of features (User, Content, Link, Automation, Graph, and Timing) exploited in the detection methods. Table 1 provides a description for these terminologies. The machine learning axis focuses on detecting social spam in an automated way, while the social honeypot approach requires an intervention from systems' administrators.

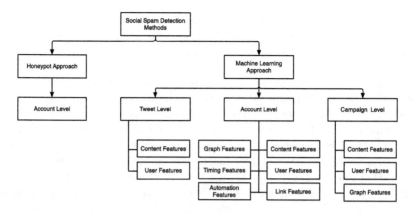

Fig. 3. A taxonomy for social spam detection methods in Twitter. The description of some terminologies is provided in Table 1.

Table 1. A description of different terminologies used in the social spam detection taxonomy.

Terminology	Description
Tweet-Level Detection	Concerning about predicting the class label of tweets (spam or non-spam)
Account-Level Detection	Analyzing deeply the user's profile or account to predict the user of the account whether spammer or legitimate user
Campaign-Level Detection	Taking the collective perspective of accounts so that a group of accounts is deeply examined to judge whether it is a spam campaign or not
User Features	Features extracted from attributes (e.g., username, screen name) existing in the user object, such as account's age, and number of tweets posted by the user
Content Features	Features extracted from the content of one or more tweets, such as number of hashtags, and number of URLs
Graph Features	Features require to build first a bi-directional graph containing user's neighbors to extract features such as local-clustering, node betweenness
Timing Features	Features extracted by analyzing the posting time of a group of tweets posted by a user
Automation Features	Features related to the use of external APIs supported by external websites
Link Features	Features extracted by analyzing URLs posted in user's tweets

Machine Learning Approach. In this approach, researchers built their methods through employing three levels of detection distributed between tweet level detection, account level detection, and campaign level detection.

- *Tweet Level.* Martinez-Romo and Araujo [13] have identified spam tweets using the concept of language modeling widely exploited in IR field. For a given tweet at hand and related to a trending topic, they build two unigram language models; one for the given tweet and the second for all tweets posted in the trending topic. Then, the divergence between the two models is computed using Kullback-Leibler metric. Using statistical features as a representation for the tweet object, Benevenuto [2] has identified spam tweets only by leveraging features extracted from the tweet text such as the number of words and the number of characters. Then, the well-known support vector machine learning algorithm has been applied on a manually created data-set to learn a binary classifier. Washha et al. [18] have introduced an unsupervised probabilistic-based method that performs collaboration with other social networks for filtering spam tweets existing in large-scale Twitter hashtaged tweets. The main strength of some methods introduced at this level of detection is the fast detection from computational time point of view. However, adopting supervised learning approach in some works to have a fixed classification model all the time is not an effective solution because of the high evolving and changing in the spam content.
- *Account Level.* The works of [2,3,5,6,19] have turned their the attention towards working deeply on extracting account-based features, including the number of friends, number of followers, similarity between tweets, and ratio of URLs in tweets. In more dedicated studies, the work proposed in [9] has identified the spam URLs through analyzing the shorten URLs behavior like the number of clicks. However, the ease of manipulation in the account-based features by social spammers have given a strong motivation to extract more complex features using graph theory. For instance, the authors of [7,20] have examined the relation between users using different graph metrics to measure three features, including the node betweenness, local clustering, and bi-directional relation ratio. Exploiting such complex features gives high spam accounts detection rate; however, they are not suitable for detecting spam accounts in large-scale Twitter data because of the considerable amount of information required from Twitter's servers.
- *Campaign Level.* Chu et al. [10] have treated the social spam problem from the collective perspective point of view. They cluster the desired accounts according to the URLs posted in the given tweets, and then a defined set of features is extracted from the clustered accounts to be incorporated in identifying spam campaign using machine learning algorithms. Chu et al. [21] have proposed a classification model to capture the difference among bot, human, and cyborg with considering the content of tweets, and tweeting behavior. Indeed, the major drawback in the accomplished methods at campaign level is the relying intensively on the features requiring too many API calls on Twitter's servers to obtain information like users' tweets and followers. Indeed, this

makes such solutions not scalable for huge number of users (or accounts). Beyond the features design level, [22,23] introduced an optimization framework which uses the content of tweets and basic network information to detect social spammers using efficient online learning approach. However, the main limitations of such works are the need of information about the network, raising the problem of scalability again.

Honeypot Approach. Social honeypot can be viewed as an information system resource that monitor social spammers' behaviors through logging their information such as the information of accounts and any available content [4]. Actually, there is no major difference between Twitter's anti-spam mechanism and the social honeypot approach. Both of them need administration control to produce a decision about the accounts that fall in the honeypot trap. The necessity of administration follow-up is to have more control on the false positive rate problem, as an alternative solution for blindly classifying all users dropped in the trap as spam accounts.

3   Spam Queries Generation Method and Spam Accounts Retrieval Model

In this section, we introduce notations, definitions, and a formalization of the problem that we address. Then, we present the design of our method for generating spam queries, followed by the design of a spam accounts retrieval model.

3.1   Terminology Definition and Problem Formalization

Twitter allows users to post tweets as many they wish, without imposing an obvious constraint at this level. Performing the posting action needs to create first an account on Twitter network. Different attributes (e.g., account description) could be filled to make users' accounts more representative for others; however, relying only on these attributes to speared spam content by social spammers is not effective. Therefore, social spammers tend to post too many tweets since the tweet element is dynamic and effective so that spam content can easily reach legitimate users. Thus, the expected form of a Twitter data is a set of tweets where each tweet has only one user who has posted it. Hence, we model a large-scale of Twitter data that requires a treatment, as a finite set of tweets, defined as $Tweets = \{T_1, T_2, ...\}$, where the tweet element $T_{\bullet}$ is further defined by 3-tuple $T_{\bullet} = <Time, Text, User>$. Given the fact that our method works on a sub-set of tweets for generating spam queries and thus we define the $Working\_Tweets \subset Tweets$ as a finite set of tweets. Each element inside the tweet tuple is described as follows:

- **Time:** It is the posting date of the tweet in *seconds* time unit computed since January 1, 1970, 00:00:00 GMT.

- **Text:** The textual content of the tweet is represented as a finite set of ordered words, $Text = \{w_1, w_2, ...\}$. This set of words is extracted by segmenting the tweet content using the whitespace separator. The word element $w_\bullet$ might be a hashtag, URL, user's account mentioned, and more.
- **User:** Twitter provides a simple meta-data about the user who posted the tweet. Hence, we further represent the user object by 3-tuple of attributes as, $User = (SN, UN, UA)$, where each of which is defined as follows:
  - **Username (UN):** Twitter allows users to name their accounts with a maximum length of 20 characters. Users can use whitespace, symbols, special characters, and numeric numbers in filling their username attribute. This field is not necessary for being unique and thus the users can name their accounts by already used names. We represent this attribute as a set of ordered characters, defined as $UN = \{d_1, ..., d_i\}$, where $i \in \mathbb{Z}_{\geq 0}$ is the character, $d_\bullet \in \{Printable\ Characters\}^2$, position inside the username string.
  - **Screen Name (SN):** This attribute is a mandatory field and it must be filled at the creation time of the account. Users must choose a unique name not used previously by other users, with a maximum length of 16 characters. Twitter also restricts the space of allowed characters to include only the alphabetical letters, numbers, and "_" character. Similar to the username attribute, we represent this field as an ordered set of characters, defined as $SN = \{d_1, ..., d_i\}$, where $i \in \mathbb{Z}_{\geq 0}$ is the character, $d_\bullet \in \{Alphanumeric\ Characters\} \cup \{\_\}$, position inside the screen name string.
  - **User Age (UA):** When a user creates an account on Twitter, the creation date of the account is registered on Twitter's servers without providing any permissions to modify it in the future. We exploit the creation date, as an accessible and available property in user's object, to compute the age of the account. Formally, we calculate the age in *days* time unit through subtracting the current time from the creation date of the account, define as $UA = \frac{Time_{now} - Time_{creation}}{864*10^5}$, where $Time_{now}, Time_{creation} \in \mathbb{Z}_{\geq 0}$ are number of milliseconds computed since January 1, 1970, 00:00:00 GMT.

Problem Formalization. Given a set of large-scale Twitter data, $Tweets$, the main problem is to infer and discover a set of spam queries, SQs, through partially processing the given set of tweets, $Working\_Tweets$, without requiring any prior knowledge in advance such as the relation between users (e.g., followers and followees of users). In a formal way, we aim at designing a function y such that it processes and handles the given set of tweets, $Working\_Tweets$, to generate a set of spam queries, defined as $y : Tweets \rightarrow \{SQ_1, SQ_2, ...\}$ where $SQ_\bullet$ is a set of ordered characters forming a spam query.

---

[2] http://web.itu.edu.tr/sgunduz/courses/mikroisl/ascii.html.

3.2   Spam Queries Generation: The Model Design

Generating spam queries requires a set of tweets so that those tweets have high probability for being attacked by one or more spam campaigns. Also, the process of generating spam queries must be unsupervised as much as possible to be robust towards the dynamic changes in social spammers' behaviors and strategies. Thus, we introduce a design of 5-stage unsupervised method for generating spam queries, illustrated through a detailed example in Fig. 4. For the given *Working_Tweets* set, we extract first a unique users set that has posted the given tweets set. Then, an account age-based clustering is performed on the extracted set of users. After that a community detection stage is applied on each cluster produced by the account age-based clustering stage. For each community resulted, we extract a set of hand-designed community-based features by which we can determine the users of each community are spammers or legitimate users. At last, we generate spam queries from username and screen name users' attributes, using the communities that have been classified as a spam community.

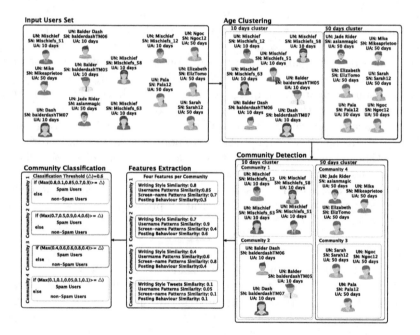

Fig. 4. An example describing the 5-stage unsupervised method designed for generating spam queries from the username and screen name attributes. The generated spam query such as "Mischief" might be leveraged in searching for spam accounts.

Stage 1: Users Set Extraction. We design the clustering and the community detection stages based on leveraging the information available in the users of

Working_Tweets set. Formally, the unique set of users is defined as $Users = \{T.User | T \in Working\_Tweets\}$ where $|Users| \leq |Working\_Tweets|$.

Stage 2: User Age-Based Clustering. Social spammers have the ability to create hundreds and thousands of Twitter accounts in a short period not exceeding few days, for launching their spam campaigns [2,24]. Also, the impact of time has shown its effectiveness in detecting spam accounts so that when a set of accounts has close and recent creation date, the probability of being spam accounts is high. Thus, the creation date of accounts can act as a heuristic for grouping and detecting the spam accounts that might have a correlation among them. According to that, the *Users* set is clustered based on the user age (UA) attribute. In a formal way, let $C_a^{Age} = \{u | u \in Users, u.UA = a\}$ be a day-cluster containing the users who have age equaling $a \in Ages$, where $Ages = \{u.UA | u \in Users\}$ is a set of distinct users ages. Obviously, the number of day clusters is dynamically determined, which exactly equals to the size of the *Ages* set (i.e., $|Ages|$).

Stage 3: Community Detection. Social spammers might create uncorrelated spam campaigns at the same time. In other words, we might have age clusters containing spam accounts belonging to different spam campaigns. Also, many non-spam users daily join Twitter, increasing the probability of having non-spam users created in the same day of spam ones. Therefore, to distinguish among different uncorrelated spam campaigns and non-spam accounts, a community detection stage is performed on each cluster resulted by the age-based clustering stage. We define each spam campaign as a community having high correlation among its users, where the correlation in a given community might be measured over naming accounts level, duplicated tweets content, or similar posting behavior. Hence, in this paper, we exploit the use of non-negative matrix factorization (NMF) method to infer the communities structure because of its outstanding performance in clustering [25]. NMF works through partitioning an information matrix into hidden factor matrices, for an age cluster, C_a^{Age}, $a \in Ages$, defined mathematically as an optimization minimization problem:

$$\min_{H \geq 0} ||\mathbf{X} - \mathbf{HH}^T||_F^2 \tag{1}$$

where $|| \bullet ||_F$ is the Frobenius norm of the considered matrix, $\mathbf{X} \in R^{|C_a^{Age}| \times |C_a^{Age}|}$ is an information matrix representing the strength of social connections between users, $\mathbf{H} \in R^{|C_a^{Age}| \times K}$ is the community structure hidden factor matrix of K communities. More precisely, the entry $X(i,j)$ reflects the strength of the social connection between the $u_i \in C_a^{Age}$ user and $u_j \in C_a^{Age}$ user. The entry $H(i,j)$ in the hidden factor matrix can be interpreted as the confidence degree of user $u_i \in C_a^{Age}$ belonging to the jth community. It is important to mention that each user belongs to one community only, not more than one.

Obviously, inferring the hidden matrix $\mathbf{H}$ requires a formal definition of the information matrix $\mathbf{X}$. For example, $\mathbf{X}$ might be an adjacency matrix representing the social connections or links between the users of the given set C_a^{Age}. However, obtaining the adjacency matrix in our case is not possible because the available information about users are limited to simple meta-data describing the account of each user, without providing information about the followers and followees. Hence, in this paper, we leverage the available and accessible information to estimate social connections among users through proposing three definitions of the information matrix $\mathbf{X}$ denoted as $\mathbf{X}^{SN}$, and $\mathbf{X}^{UN}$, where each of which is formally defined as follows:

– **Screen Name Similarity ($\mathbf{X}^{SN}$):** As the screen name field must be unique, social spammers may adopt a particular fixed string pattern when creating multiple accounts to act as a spam bot. For instance, in Fig. 2, the social spammer has adopted the string "voteddlovatu" as a fixed pattern for the screen name field. Intuitively, the high overlapping or matching in the screen name among users increases the probability of the users to belong to the same community. Therefore, we define the information matrix $\mathbf{X}^{SN}$ to measure the degree of matching in the screen name attribute. More precisely, given two users $u_i, u_j \in C_a^{Age}$, the degree of matching for a particular entry in the matrix $\mathbf{X}^{SN}$ is defined as:

$$\mathbf{X}^{SN}(i,j) = \frac{max\{|m| : m \in Patterns)\}}{min(|u_i.SN|, |u_j.SN|)}$$

$$Patterns = \bigcup_{N \in Max} N - gram(u_i.SN) \cap N - gram(u_j.SN) \qquad (2)$$

where $|\bullet|$ is the cardinality of the considered set, $Max = \{1, ..., min(|u_i.SN|, |u_j.SN|)\}$ is a set consisting of positive integers representing the potential number of characters that have overlapping between the two strings, $N - gram(\bullet)$ is a function that returns a set of contiguous sequence of characters for a given string (set of ordered characters) based on the value of N. For better understanding, the 3-gram (or tri-gram) of this screen name "vote" is $\{$ "vot", "ote"$\}$. The above definition is able to detect the matched string pattern wherever it appears in the screen name attribute. For instance, let "vote12" and "tovote" be screen names for two different users, the degree of matching according to Eq. 2 is around $(\frac{4}{6})66.6\%$ resulting from the use of pattern "vote", regardless the position of the pattern.

– **User Name Similarity ($\mathbf{X}^{UN}$):** Differently from the screen name attribute, spammers can duplicate the entry of user name attribute as many they desire. They exploit representative (not random) names to attract the normal users. Therefore, the full or partial matching among users in such attribute increases the performance of community detection. We define the information matrix $\mathbf{X}^{UN}$ to catch the degree of similarity among users in the user name attribute. Formally, given two users $u_i, u_j \in C_a^{Age}$, the degree of similarity is defined as:

$$\mathbf{X}^{UN}(i,j) = \frac{max\{|m| : m \in Patterns)\}}{min(|u_i.UN|, |u_j.UN|)}$$

$$Patterns = \bigcup_{N \in Max} N - gram(u_i.UN) \cap N - gram(u_j.UN) \qquad (3)$$

where here $Max = \{1, ..., min(|u_i.UN|, |u_j.UN|)\}$.

With these three information matrices, NMF method allows to integrate them together in the same objective function. Thus, the new version of the objective function is defined as:

$$\min_{H \geq 0} ||\mathbf{X}^{SN} - \mathbf{HH}^T||_F^2 + ||\mathbf{X}^{UN} - \mathbf{HH}^T||_F^2 \qquad (4)$$

Obviously, Eq. 4 infers the hidden factor matrix H to represent the consistent community structure of the users.

The objective function is not jointly convex and no closed form solution exists. Hence, we propose the use of gradient descent as an alternative optimization approach. As we have one free variable ($\mathbf{H}$), the gradient descent method updates it iteratively until the variable converge.

Formally, let $\mathcal{L}(\mathbf{H})$ denotes to the objective function given in Eq. 4. At the iteration τ, the updating equation is given as:

$$\mathbf{H}^\tau = \mathbf{H}^{\tau-1} - \eta.\frac{\partial \mathcal{L}(\mathbf{H}^{\tau-1})}{\partial(\mathbf{H})}$$
$$= \mathbf{H}^{\tau-1} - 2\eta\left(6\mathbf{H}^{\tau-1}(\mathbf{H}^{\tau-1})^T\mathbf{H}^{\tau-1}\right.$$
$$- (\mathbf{X}^{SN} + \mathbf{X}^{UN})\mathbf{H}^{\tau-1}$$
$$\left. - ((\mathbf{X}^{SN})^T + (\mathbf{X}^{UN})^T)\mathbf{H}^{\tau-1}\right) \qquad (5)$$

where the parameter η denotes to the gradient descent step in updating the matrix $\mathbf{H}$. We assign the value of η to a small constant value (i.e. 0.05). As the gradient descent method is an iterative process, a stop condition is required in such a case. Thus, we exploit two stop conditions: (i) the number of iterations, denoted as M; (ii) and the absolute change in the H matrix in two consecutive iterations to be less than a threshold, i.e. $|(||H^\tau||_F - ||H^{\tau-1}||_F)| \leq \epsilon$.

Stage 4: Community-Based Feature Extraction. In order to predict the class label (spam or non-Spam) of each community, one or more features must be extracted from each community such that these features can effectively discriminate among spam or non-spam communities. Since social spammers may follow complex and different spamming strategies, no single feature can effectively discriminate between spam and non-spam communities. The design of such features must rely only on the available information in each community to avoid using REST APIs. Thus, we introduce a design of two community-based features extracted from the screen name and username attributes, named as username patterns similarity (**UNPS**), and screen name patterns similarity (**SNPS**) features.

The total number of formed communities is dependent on the number of age clusters ($|Ages|$) beside the number of predefined communities K. Therefore, the final number of communities is $|Ages| \times K$, since the community detection stage is applied on each age cluster. We represent the jth inferred community in the hidden matrix, H, by 4-tuple of attributes $C_j = (Users, UNPS, SNPS, Label)$ where $Users$ is a finite set of the users belonging to the inferred community, and $Lable \in \{spam, non - spam\}$ is the class label of the community, while the rest two attributes are described as follows:

Username Patterns Similarity (UNPS) and Screen Name Patterns Similarity (SNPS). Social spammers may adopt a particular pattern (e.g., "voteddlovatu") in creating their spam campaigns and therefore the probability of having spam communities biased toward a particular pattern used in creating accounts is relatively high. Since there is no prior knowledge about the length and the name of the patterns, we must have a generic and independent way to determine whether the community has a spammy pattern. Thus, we rely on an intuitive and generalized fact, which states that the probability distribution of patterns in non-spam communities is close to the uniform distribution, while the spam communities have the opposite behavior. More precisely, we measure the degree of similarity between string patterns probability distribution extracted from users of a particular community with the uniform probability distribution of the patterns. Formally, let PT^{UN} and PT^{SN} be two finite sets of string patterns extracted from the username and the screen name attributes for the users of the jth community, C_j. Also, let P_D^{UN} and P_D^{SN} be the corresponding probability distributions of the username and the screen name patterns, respectively. For the uniform distribution, let P_{uni}^{UN}, P_{uni}^{SN} be the corresponding uniform distributions of username and screen name patterns, respectively. For instance, for a particular community, let $PT^{SN} = \{$"mischief","isch", "_12", "_14"$\}$ and $P_D^{SN} = \{($"mischief", 0.7$), ($"_15", 0.1$), ($"_14", 0.1$), ($"_12", 0.1$)\}$ be a set of screen name patterns along with its probability distribution, and $\{($"mischief", 0.25$), ($"_15", 0.25$), ($"_14", 0.25$), ($"_12", 0.25$)\}$ be the uniform probability distribution of these patterns.

To extract and catch all string patterns, N-gram method is applied since social spammers may define patterns varying in their length and position. To perform N-gram method, different values of N ranging from three to the length of the string are used, with ignoring low N values (one and two) because they provide meaningless patterns. For the jth community's users, represented as C_j, we extract the string patterns used in the username and screen attributes as follows:

$$PT^{UN} = \bigcup_{u \in C_j \cdot Users} \bigcup_{N \in \{3,...,|u.UN|\}} N - gram(u.UN) \qquad (6)$$

$$PT^{SN} = \bigcup_{u \in C_j \cdot Users} \bigcup_{N \in \{3,...,|u.SN|\}} N - gram(u.SN) \qquad (7)$$

The double unification ($\bigcup\bigcup$) can be viewed as a double "for" loops where the inner unification is responsible about returning all patterns, as a finite set of strings, that a single user have, while the outer unification unifies all sets of users' string patterns to have only one single set of string patterns representing the community itself.

Since the pattern is a categorical random variable in which the string has not a meaningful order of magnitudes, we adopt the Kullback-Leibler divergence [26] (KL) method as a suitable and a fast way to measure the similarity between any two probability distributions of categorical random variables. However, the classical version of KL method cannot be directly exploited in computing similarity among (PT_D^{UN} and PT_{uni}^{UN}) or (PT_D^{SN} and PT_{uni}^{SN}) since the ∞ and 0 values correspond to dissimilar, and similar distributions, respectively. Hence, we perform a few modification on the current version of KL method to inverse the semantic meaning of KL values (i.e., $0 \implies$ dissimilar and $1 \implies$ similar) and taking into account bounding its values. Thus, for the jth community, the value of the $UNPS$ and $SNPS$ features is computed using the customized KL equation as follows:

$$C_j.UNPS = \frac{\log|PT^{UN}| - \sum_{w \in PT^{UN}} P_D^{UN}(w) * min(|\log \frac{P_D^{UN}(w)}{P_{uni}^{UN}(w)}|, \log|PT^{UN}|)}{\log|PT^{UN}|} \tag{8}$$

$$C_j.SNPS = \frac{\log|PT^{SN}| - \sum_{w \in PT^{SN}} P_D^{SN}(w) * min(|\log \frac{P_D^{SN}(w)}{P_{uni}^{SN}(w)}|, \log|PT^{SN}|)}{\log|PT^{SN}|} \tag{9}$$

where $|\bullet|$ is the cardinality (length) of the string patterns set, $P_D^{\bullet}(w)$ is the probability of occurring the pattern w based on the distribution of the considered patterns set, and $P_{uni}^{\bullet}(w)$ is the probability of occurring the pattern w according to the uniform distribution of the considered patterns set.

Stage 5: Community Classification and Spam Queries Generation. We exploit the degree of similarity as a one possible way to label each community as spam or non-spam. However, intuitively, the degree of similarity given here is not a crisp value and thus it is required to define a cut-off point to discriminate among the spam and non-spam communities (bots). Thus, for a given community C_j, we propose the following cut-off point by which the considered community is classified into spam and non-spam.

$$C_j.Label = \begin{cases} spam & C_j.UNPS \leq \Delta || C_j.SNPS \leq \Delta \\ non-spam & otherwise \end{cases}$$

where Δ is a classification threshold value fixed (i.e. 0.1), and determined experimentally for all communities. Spam communities might have low value in one of the two features and thus we check the satisfaction of spam community condition through taking the "OR" operation among the two community-based features.

The last step after determining the class label of each community being inferred is to extract spam queries using the communities that have been classified as a spam. In this work, we generate spam queries from screen name and username attributes where we mainly rely on these attributes in performing community detection stage. As each spam community may provide more than one string pattern in both attributes, we are interested in the longest and frequent pattern. Intuitively, the probability to find the longest pattern in attributes of legitimate users' accounts is quite low. To combine the both properties in generating spam queries, we turn out the problem to a maximization optimization through searching for the string pattern that has the highest value of the multiplication of the pattern likelihood probability with the logarithm of its length, separately defined as follows for username and screen name string patterns:

$$SQ_{UN} = \bigcup_{\substack{j \in \{1,\ldots,|Ages| \times K\} \\ C_j.Label=spam}} \{w^*\} = \max_{w \in PT^{UN}} PT_D^{UN}(w) * \log |w| \qquad (10)$$

$$SQ_{SN} = \bigcup_{\substack{j \in \{1,\ldots,|Ages| \times K\} \\ C_j.Label=spam}} \{w^*\} = \max_{w \in PT^{SN}} PT_D^{SN}(w) * \log |w| \qquad (11)$$

where PT^{UN}, PT^{SN} are the string patterns of username and screen name attributes of C_j community's users, respectively. PT_D^{UN}, PT_D^{SN} are the probability distribution of the string patterns of username and screen name attributes of C_j community's users, respectively. w^* is the optimal string pattern that will be selected as a spam query corresponding to the considered community.

3.3   Spam Accounts Retrieval Model

For a given spam query related to one of the two spam queries set extracted, the next step is to retrieve spam accounts (users) existing in the given collections. We adopt the probability ranking principle to rank accounts for being relevant for a given spam query [27]. Formally, given a user u and a spam query q, we rank the users (or accounts) according the probability of the user being relevant. Mathematically, the scoring probability function is given by

$$P(R = 1|U = u, Q = q) = P(U = u|R = 1) * P(Q = q|U = u, R = 1) \qquad (12)$$

where $R \in \{spam, non-spam\}$ is an indicator random variable that takes value 1 if the user u is relevant w.r.t. query q and 0 if the user u is irrelevant w.r.t. query q, $U \in \{T.User | T \in Tweets\}$ is a random variable that takes value of a user existing in the given collection of Twitter data $(Tweets)$, $Q \in SQ_{SN} \cup SQ_{UN}$ is also a random variable that takes value of a spam query extracted either username or screen name attribute. The probability component $P(U = u|R = 1)$ represents the degree of the user (account) u being a spam, while the $P(Q = q|U = u, R = 1)$ is the probability of the spam query used in creating the account of the current user u. We estimate the prior probability of the user being spam based on the user's account age where the old age user's account has low probability for being a spam account. We adopt Gaussian zero mean probability distribution to compute the probability of the user being spam, formally given as:

$$P(U = u|R = 1) = \frac{1}{\sqrt{2\sigma^2\pi}} e^{-(u.UA)^2/2\sigma^2} \qquad (13)$$

where the variance σ^2 is experimentally determined according to some statistics, and $u.UA$ is the age of the user's account in days time unit. For computing the probability of the account of the given user being created by the given spammy query, q, we leverage the similarity degree between the given query and the value of the selected attribute (username and scree name), using same similarity concept introduced in Eqs. 2 and 3.

4   Data-Set Description and Ground Truth

The data-sets adopted at tweet-level detection [2,13,28] are not publicly available for the research use because of some privacy reasons. When social network based researchers publish a particular data-set, they only provide the target object IDs (e.g., tweets and accounts) to retrieve them then from servers of the desired social network. However, inspired by the nature of the spam problem, providing the IDs of the spam tweets or accounts is not enough because Twitter might already have suspended the corresponding accounts and thus nothing to retrieve from the servers. Hence, we have developed a crawler that uses the Streaming APIs of Twitter. As Twitter offers different basic streaming endpoints, we have adopted the public streaming option which streams of the public data flowing through Twitter network. We have launched our crawler for four months, started since 1/Jan/2015, where millions of tweets have been collected and stored.

As social spammers give a great preference for attacking trending hashtags and topics, we have selected the hashtag as a target entity for studying the effectiveness of our method in generating spam queries. Using the crawled tweets for four months, we have sampled 50 hashtags which had been trending during the crawling period. As each hashtag might have more than one tweet, we extract the unique users (accounts) set which is the main input for our method. The most challenging task is creating an annotated data-set consisting of the true class label of each user extracted, for analyzing the performance of our method. Performing a manual annotation for more than 1.5 million users (accounts) is

Table 2. Distribution of different statistics for social spammers (spam accounts) and legitimate users (non-spam accounts) existing in our data-set.

Statistic name	Social spammers		Legitimate users	
	Value	Rate (per 100 users)	Value	Ratio (per 100 users)
Number of users	134,896 (8.2%)	–	1,520,081 (91.8%)	–
Number of geo-enabled users	10,205 (1.9%)	8 (20%)	514,773 (98.1%)	33 (80.0%)
Number of verified users	0 (0.0%)	0	3,686 (100.0%)	1 (100.0%)
Number of users' followers	103,705,788 (2.7%)	76878 (24.1%)	3,686,545,059 (97.3%)	242522 (75.9%)
Number of users' followees	72,640,728 (3.8%)	53849 (30.1%)	1,829,383,146 (96.2%)	120347 (69.9%)
Number of tweets posted	134,897,419 (0.5%)	100001(5.9%)	24,305,283,191 (99.5%)	1598946 (94.1%)
Number of tweets streamed	608,078 (11.7%)	450 (60.0%)	4,576,143 (88.3%)	301(40.0%)
Number of retweeted tweets	283,663 (10.3%)	210 (56.5%)	2,463,144 (89.7%)	162 (43.5%)
Number of replied tweets	2,930 (4.6%)	2 (33.3%)	60,381 (95.4%)	4 (66.6%)
Number of URLs	181,764 (8.1%)	135 (50.0%)	2,050,215 (91.9%)	135 (50.0%)

time consuming and not practical at all. Hence, we have leveraged a widely followed annotation process in the social spam detection researches [18, 22, 23]. The process checks whether the user was suspended by Twitter. In case of suspension, the user is labeled as a spam one (social spammer); otherwise, we assign non-spam (legitimate user). We have performed this process one year after the crawling of the tweets in order to have a large number of spam users. In total, as reported in Table 2, we have found about 135,000 users (accounts) labeled as social spammer, and about 1,520,000 legitimate users. Also, the number of spam tweets existing in our data-set is more than 608,000 tweets, forming about 11.7% of about 4.5 million tweets. The number of tweets posted is obviously greater than the number of tweets steamed since the former number represents the tweets that have been streamed into the hashtags selected, while the latter number corresponds to the ultimate tweets that have been posted since the creation date of the accounts. As the data-set is not balanced at the class level, we compute the normalized version of the statistics per 100 users to have more fair comparison between social spammers and legitimate users. The normalized version of the number of URLs shows an obvious misusing of URLs in spreading social spammers' content, compared to the legitimate users. It is expected that the number of verified users is zero since having a verified account requires to contact Twitter's administrators and thus the spam accounts are too difficult to be verified.

5   Results and Evaluations

5.1   Experimental Setup

Metrics. Different metrics are used in information retrieval area to evaluate the degree of relevance of documents w.r.t. an input search query. In our work, we exploit three widely used metrics [16]: (i) Precision at L ($P@L$); (ii) Recall at L ($R@L$); (iii) and Normalized Discounted Cumulative Gain at L ($NDCG@L$). $P@L$ is the ratio of *spam* accounts retrieved in the top L retrieved accounts. $R@L$ represents the ratio of *spam* accounts retrieved in the top L w.r.t. the total number of spam accounts in the collection. As the precision metric fails to take into account the position of relevant spam accounts among the top L, $NDCG@L$ metric logarithmically penalizes the late appearance of the spam accounts in the search list, proportional to the position in the list retrieved. For the values, we measure the three performance metrics at two ranks $L \in \{100, 500\}$.

Baselines. We assess the performance of our method in retrieving spam accounts through five simple retrieval baseline methods, which rank accounts of a hashtag according to a particular criteria, summarized in:

- **Random (RN).** RN method ranks the accounts in a random way without biasing toward any account in the set.
- **Recent Age Account (RAA).** This method sorts accounts in an ascending order according to the accounts' creation date (age).

Table 3. Performance results of the five baseline methods evaluated using *Precision@L*, *Recall@L*, and **NDCG@L** metrics and different values of $L \in \{100, 500\}$ [1].

Baseline retrieval method	P@100	P@500	R@100	R@500	NDCG@100	NDCG@500
Random (RN)	7.9%	7.7%	0.5%	1.9%	7.7%	7.7%
Recent Age Account (RAA)	19.9%	20.9%	1.3%	5.8%	19.5%	20.7%
Old Age Account (OAA)	0.6%	1.1%	0.1%	0.3%	0.6%	1.0%
Recent Posted Tweet (RPT)	6.6%	6.9%	0.4%	1.7%	6.3%	6.8%
Old Posted Tweet (OPT)	7.8%	7.0%	0.5%	1.9%	8.0%	7.1%

- **Old Age Account (OAA).** Conversely to **RAA** method, **OAA** sorts accounts in a descending order according to the accounts' creation date (age).
- **Recent Posted Tweet (RPT).** This method ranks accounts according to the publication date of the considered hashtag tweets. Thus, it sorts first the tweets in an ascending order according to the tweets' date and then selects the corresponding accounts in the same order.
- **Old Posted Tweet (OPT).** This method is similar in concept to the **RPT** method; however, it sorts the tweets first in a descending order and then picks the corresponding accounts in the same order.

Parameter Setting. For community detection stage, we set $\eta = 0.001$, $M = 10,000$, and $\epsilon = 0.0001$ as values for the learning rate, number of iterations, and the threshold of absolute change in the hidden matrix $\mathbf{H}$, respectively. For the number of communities K, experiment our method at three different values, $K \in \{2, 5, 10\}$, to study its impact. For the size of information matrices $\mathbf{X}^\bullet$, we consider all distinct users (accounts) of each hashtag without excluding any user available in the testing collection. As an iterative algorithm is used for solving the optimization problem, we initialize each entry of the hidden matrix $\mathbf{H}$ by a small positive real value drawn from an uniform distribution on the interval $[0, 1]$. For the threshold (Δ), we study the effect of this threshold in predicting effective spam queries using different values, $\Delta \in [0.1, 1]$. We set the variance, σ^2, of Gaussian probability distribution to 1 day according to the results introduced in [24].

Experiment Procedure. For each hashtag, we perform the following steps: (i) we extract the users who posted the tweets related to the considered hashtag; (ii) account-age clustering stage is performed on the extracted users set (iii) the community detection method is then performed on each age cluster of users; (iv) afterward, each community is labeled as a spam or non-spam based on the designed objective function for a certain classification threshold (Δ); (v) for each community labeled as a spam, the spam queries are generated using Eq. 10 for username attribute or Eq. 11 for screen name attribute; (vi) for each spam query, we retrieve the accounts that contain the selected query based on the considered attribute (user name or screen name), using all accounts in the data collection; (vii) the retrieval model introduced in Eq. 12 is used to retrieval and rank accounts; (viii) the performance of the considered spam query used in retrieving spam accounts is evaluated using the three metrics described; (ix) the previous two steps is repeated for each spam query generated; (x) in the last step, the performance of all spam queries generated corresponding to the selected attribute (screen name or user name) is averaged for producing the final performance value.

5.2 Experimental Results

In this section, we introduce the results of the five baseline methods, our method introduced in [1], and the new method presented in this paper. Mainly, we divide the results into two parts where the first one shows the performance of the five baseline methods and the second part discusses the results of our original method with the new modification.

We evaluate the performance of the five baseline retrieval methods (**RN**, **RAA**, **OAA**, **RPT**, and **OPT**) by applying each method on each hashtag in our data-set. Averaged over all hashtags, we observe in Table 3 that the recent age account retrieval (**RAA**) method has a superior performance in terms of precision, recall, and NDCG, compared to the rest four baseline methods. For **RAA** method, the 19.9% value of P@100 can be interpreted in two ways: (i) the number of spam accounts retrieved (ranked based on accounts' age) in the top 100 accounts is 20; (ii) or the probability to retrieve a spam account in the top 100 is about 19.9%. The recall@100 values of all baseline methods are not at the same level as precision@100 values. Indeed, the low values of recall are because of the huge number of spam accounts existing in our collection. This interpretation can be ensured by the significant increasing in the recall@500 values of all baselines where more spam accounts can be found at rank 500. However, the recall values of all baseline methods are not satisfactory and adoptable for retrieving all spam accounts in the collection. More precisely, the best recall@500 is obtained by **RAA** method which has retrieved no more than 2,200 spam accounts available in our data-set. The behavior of baseline methods in regards of **NDCG** metric is almost similar to the precision metric. The strength of the **NDCG** metric is in giving weight for each account retrieved based on its position in the list (i.e., top position $\implies$ highest weight). The 19.5% of **NDCG@100** of **RAA** baseline method gives an indication that the spam accounts retrieved are *not* in the top 80 accounts. Overall, the performance results obtained by the five baseline methods draw the following conclusions: (i) the results of **RAA** method ensure the validity of a strong hypothesis that spam accounts are recent in age; (ii) the recall values of the five methods are *not* satisfactory to adopt them in retrieving spam accounts at all.

In producing the experimental results of our method, the procedure described in Sect. 5.1 subsection is performed on each hashtag in the data-set used, with averaging the results over the number of hashtags. We perform two main experiments to provide more insights into the impact of screen name and user name attributes in retrieving spam accounts. In Table 4, we report the evaluation results of the both attributes, experimented at different classification thresholds Δ and at finite set of number of communities K, when excluding the prior probability (i.e., acting as uniform distribution) component of the retrieval ranking

Table 4. Performance results of the screen name and user name attribute-based spam queries for retrieving spam accounts, experimented at various classification threshold (Δ) and at different values of $K \in \{2, 5, 10\}$ as a number of communities, in terms of **P**$recision@L$, **R**$ecall@L$, and **NDCG**$@L$ at $L \in \{100, 500\}$, when excluding the prior probability component in the designed retrieval model [1].

K	Th	Screen-name pattern						User-name pattern					
		P@100	P@500	R@100	R@500	NDCG@100	NDCG@500	P@100	P@500	R@100	R@500	NDCG@100	NDCG@500
2	0.1	55.4%	33.4%	7.8%	19.8%	58.9%	46.4%	48.9%	43.1%	7.1%	23.8%	47.1%	43.8%
	0.2	54.2%	26.3%	7.7%	15.0%	55.9%	37.0%	49.4%	35.3%	7.2%	18.7%	48.4%	37.3%
	0.3	48.7%	19.2%	6.7%	10.9%	55.1%	30.6%	49.4%	33.1%	7.4%	17.5%	48.6%	35.4%
	0.4	45.1%	18.3%	6.0%	9.8%	49.8%	23.5%	46.1%	31.6%	6.9%	16.4%	46.2%	33.9%
	0.5	44.8%	17.2%	5.9%	9.0%	46.9%	22.5%	44.9%	30.1%	6.8%	15.3%	45.0%	32.4%
	0.6	44.4%	15.4%	5.9%	8.9%	46.4%	21.5%	46.7%	29.5%	7.0%	15.1%	46.6%	31.9%
	0.7	42.0%	13.7%	5.5%	8.0%	46.5%	20.0%	43.0%	28.4%	6.5%	14.3%	43.3%	30.6%
	0.8	38.8%	12.5%	5.3%	7.5%	44.6%	18.3%	41.6%	27.5%	6.3%	13.7%	42.1%	29.6%
	0.9	36.0%	10.3%	5.3%	7.0%	41.6%	16.9%	36.9%	25.9%	5.1%	11.8%	37.7%	27.7%
	1.0	36.5%	9.8%	5.4%	6.7%	39.3%	14.6%	37.8%	25.9%	5.2%	11.8%	38.6%	27.9%
5	0.1	59.4%	32.9%	8.2%	18.1%	59.8%	36.9%	48.8%	41.6%	7.1%	22.3%	47.4%	42.6%
	0.2	55.9%	26.1%	7.6%	14.9%	56.9%	30.7%	50.7%	36.9%	7.5%	19.8%	49.5%	38.9%
	0.3	50.9%	19.7%	7.2%	11.6%	52.1%	24.3%	49.8%	34.0%	7.3%	17.8%	48.6%	36.1%
	0.4	39.2%	14.9%	5.3%	8.1%	41.9%	19.0%	44.2%	29.4%	6.3%	14.4%	44.6%	31.7%
	0.5	39.1%	13.6%	5.2%	7.1%	42.2%	18.0%	41.7%	28.1%	5.9%	13.4%	41.8%	30.1%
	0.6	40.4%	12.3%	5.4%	6.9%	44.0%	17.1%	41.2%	26.7%	6.2%	13.0%	42.5%	29.2%
	0.7	42.6%	13.2%	5.4%	7.0%	45.8%	18.1%	42.3%	28.5%	6.2%	14.1%	42.3%	30.5%
	0.8	41.2%	12.2%	5.4%	7.5%	44.1%	16.9%	38.4%	26.6%	5.6%	12.6%	38.8%	28.5%
	0.9	37.9%	10.5%	5.2%	7.0%	40.7%	15.2%	37.7%	26.2%	5.1%	11.8%	38.5%	28.1%
	1.0	37.0%	10.5%	5.0%	7.2%	40.4%	15.0%	38.9%	25.6%	5.5%	11.6%	39.7%	27.7%
10	0.1	60.2%	30.7%	8.3%	15.7%	60.8%	35.0%	50.8%	43.3%	7.5%	23.0%	44.3%	28.9%
	0.2	54.0%	23.3%	7.5%	12.3%	56.0%	28.1%	49.3%	35.5%	7.3%	18.6%	37.7%	24.5%
	0.3	47.0%	18.5%	6.3%	9.5%	48.9%	22.9%	48.4%	32.7%	7.1%	16.8%	35.0%	22.9%
	0.4	43.4%	16.4%	5.7%	.5%	45.7%	20.7%	44.1%	28.9%	6.3%	13.7%	31.1%	20.5%
	0.5	38.9%	13.6%	5.0%	6.7%	41.9%	17.9%	39.4%	27.3%	5.7%	12.1%	29.4%	19.7%
	0.6	34.5%	11.8%	4.4%	5.5%	37.9%	15.9%	38.0%	25.3%	5.7%	11.6%	27.5%	18.7%
	0.7	35.4%	10.0%	4.8%	5.6%	39.5%	14.6%	38.3%	24.6%	5.6%	11.2%	26.7%	18.3%
	0.8	37.2%	10.8%	5.0%	6.1%	41.3%	15.5%	37.4%	24.8%	5.4%	11.4%	27.1%	18.4%
	0.9	35.9%	10.7%	4.4%	6.9%	40.1%	15.2%	36.9%	25.7%	4.9%	11.5%	27.9%	18.8%
	1.0	35.6%	10.0%	4.5%	7.1%	40.0%	14.6%	38.1%	26.1%	5.1%	11.9%	28.4%	19.0%

Table 5. Performance results of the screen name and user name attribute-based spam queries for retrieving spam accounts, experimented at various classification threshold (Δ) and at different values of $K \in \{2, 5, 10\}$ as a number of communities, in terms of $Precision@L$, $Recall@L$, and $NDCG@L$ at $L \in \{100, 500\}$, when including the prior probability component in the designed retrieval model.

K	Δ	Screen-name pattern						User-name pattern					
		P@100	P@500	R@100	R@500	NDCG@100	NDCG@500	P@100	P@500	R@100	R@500	NDCG@100	NDCG@500
2	0.1	**56.0%**	**34.7%**	**7.8%**	**20.2%**	**56.7%**	**38.2%**	48.6%	**42.3%**	7.1%	**23.2%**	47.1%	**43.2%**
	0.2	52.5%	26.0%	7.1%	14.4%	53.3%	30.1%	**49.6%**	38.7%	**7.3%**	20.8%	**48.3%**	40.2%
	0.3	49.5%	20.9%	6.7%	12.0%	51.2%	25.4%	48.9%	34.7%	7.0%	18.1%	48.1%	36.7%
	0.4	45.7%	19.2%	6.0%	9.8%	46.9%	23.2%	47.3%	32.6%	7.0%	16.6%	47.3%	34.9%
	0.5	46.1%	17.2%	6.0%	8.5%	47.8%	21.7%	47.4%	30.9%	7.0%	15.1%	46.7%	33.1%
	0.6	43.5%	14.1%	5.4%	6.9%	46.4%	18.9%	43.8%	29.2%	6.4%	14.0%	44.3%	31.4%
	0.7	42.2%	12.6%	5.3%	6.5%	45.2%	17.5%	42.0%	27.6%	6.4%	13.7%	42.9%	29.9%
	0.8	38.5%	11.2%	4.9%	6.1%	41.6%	15.7%	41.3%	27.2%	6.1%	13.1%	41.6%	29.2%
	0.9	37.2%	10.4%	4.8%	6.0%	40.6%	14.9%	36.8%	26.1%	5.1%	11.8%	37.8%	28.0%
	1.0	37.3%	10.4%	4.9%	6.2%	40.5%	14.9%	36.6%	25.9%	4.9%	11.5%	37.4%	27.7%
5	0.1	**59.8%**	**32.1%**	**8.3%**	**17.2%**	**60.0%**	**36.1%**	49.7%	**41.9%**	7.2%	**22.9%**	47.7%	**42.8%**
	0.2	53.3%	23.7%	7.4%	13.0%	53.9%	28.0%	**50.8%**	37.6%	**7.6%**	19.6%	**49.6%**	39.4%
	0.3	49.7%	21.0%	6.7%	10.8%	51.0%	25.3%	48.5%	34.8%	7.2%	18.1%	47.6%	36.8%
	0.4	42.9%	16.5%	5.5%	8.0%	45.5%	20.8%	45.3%	30.6%	6.7%	15.0%	45.6%	32.9%
	0.5	42.5%	13.2%	5.3%	6.6%	44.0%	17.6%	42.1%	29.0%	6.2%	13.5%	42.3%	31.0%
	0.6	39.7%	12.3%	5.1%	6.6%	41.7%	16.7%	43.8%	28.0%	6.4%	13.2%	43.7%	30.2%
	0.7	41.4%	11.3%	5.4%	6.6%	43.7%	16.0%	42.3%	26.9%	6.3%	12.9%	42.5%	29.1%
	0.8	39.1%	10.7%	5.0%	6.2%	41.7%	15.2%	40.9%	26.6%	6.0%	12.4%	41.3%	28.8%
	0.9	39.6%	11.3%	5.1%	6.9%	42.7%	16.0%	36.2%	25.9%	4.9%	11.5%	37.3%	27.7%
	1.0	36.8%	11.0%	4.4%	6.7%	40.5%	15.6%	38.1%	25.7%	5.0%	11.4%	39.0%	27.8%
10	0.1	**58.5%**	**30.2%**	**7.9%**	**15.6%**	**59.6%**	**34.5%**	49.1%	**41.8%**	7.1%	**22.3%**	47.7%	**42.9%**
	0.2	54.2%	22.5%	7.3%	12.0%	55.7%	27.4%	**50.1%**	38.1%	**7.4%**	20.0%	**48.9%**	39.7%
	0.3	48.9%	18.9%	6.4%	9.7%	51.1%	23.7%	48.3%	33.5%	7.1%	16.9%	47.7%	35.7%
	0.4	43.6%	14.7%	5.8%	7.4%	46.2%	19.4%	46.5%	31.1%	6.8%	15.1%	46.3%	33.3%
	0.5	39.2%	12.4%	5.1%	6.3%	42.2%	16.9%	43.5%	29.8%	6.2%	13.9%	44.0%	32.0%
	0.6	36.7%	10.3%	4.8%	5.8%	39.6%	14.7%	43.5%	27.6%	6.2%	13.1%	44.0%	30.0%
	0.7	39.6%	12.2%	5.0%	6.1%	42.9%	16.8%	42.2%	26.7%	6.1%	12.5%	42.2%	28.9%
	0.8	38.5%	10.5%	5.1%	6.2%	41.1%	14.9%	38.5%	27.3%	5.8%	12.7%	41.4%	29.4%
	0.9	38.5%	10.7%	5.2%	6.5%	40.9%	15.1%	38.9%	27.4%	5.4%	12.3%	39.9%	29.4%
	1.0	35.6%	9.6%	4.4%	5.5%	38.3%	13.8%	39.8%	26.7%	5.2%	11.9%	40.7%	28.9%

model introduced in Eq. 12. The other Table 5 shows the results of our method when considering the prior component probability of the retrieval ranking model. As an external comparison with the baseline methods, our approach has superior performance in retrieving spam accounts either when considering screen name or user name attributes, or when excluding or including the prior probability component. As an internal comparison, there is a complete consistency, in Tables 4 and 5, showing that 0.1 is almost the optimal classification threshold in terms of the performance metrics. We don't report the results of the threshold when be less than 0.1 since no spam community have been identified. The optimal threshold value, 0.1, ensures our hypothesis that the distribution of patterns in a spam community follows non-uniform distribution. Also, we find that increasing the classification threshold implies to classify communities as spam where they are truly not spam ones. Consequently, this misclassification at community level produces spam queries which are non-spam at all. Indeed, this explains the degradation in the performance results when increasing the classification threshold. The effect of number of communities K is obvious in improving precision@100, recall@100, and NDCG@100 metrics. We associate this increasing with the number of spam bots that had attacked the considered 50 hashtags. More precisely, when a hashtag is attacked by 10 different spam bots, the low values of K cannot provide all possible spam queries, and thus not all spam accounts might be retrieved. On contrary, we observe that the increasing in the number of communities decreases the precision@500, recall@500, and NDCG@500 metrics. We explain this behavior because of the existence non-spam accounts having partial matching with the spammy patterns of either screen name or user name attributes.

Obviously, according to the results, none of the both attributes has superior performance compared to each other. For instance, the spammy patterns of screen name attribute perform better than the spammy patterns of user name attribute in terms of precision@100, recall@100, and NDCG@100. The selection among screen name and user name attributes in performing the retrieval process is completely dependent on the size of the list that contains the potential spam accounts (e.g. 100, 500). For instance, user name attribute is preferred when performing the retrieval task to return 500 potential spam accounts.

6   Conclusion

In this paper, we have discussed the possibility of applying information retrieval concept to retrieve and rank a potential set of accounts (users) having high probability for being spam. Thus, we have introduced an unsupervised method that processes a set of users to generate a set of spam queries which they are used for retrieving quickly spam accounts existing in a given crawled large-scale Twitter data consisting of tweets. Our method uses the simple meta-data of a particular set of users posted tweets associated with a topic (hashtag) to spam queries as a searchable information. Our work can be leveraged by Twitter community to search for spam accounts and also for Twitter based applications that work on large collection of tweets to speed up the detection process of social spammers.

References

1. Washha, M., Qaroush, A., Mezghani, M., Sèdes, F.: Information quality in social networks: predicting spammy naming patterns for retrieving Twitter spam accounts. In: Proceedings of the 19th International Conference on Enterprise Information Systems, ICEIS 2017, Porto, Portugal, 26–29 April 2017, vol. 2, pp. 610–622. SciTePress (2017)
2. Benevenuto, F., Magno, G., Rodrigues, T., Almeida, V.: Detecting spammers on Twitter. In: Collaboration, Electronic messaging, Anti-abuse and Spam Conference (CEAS), p. 12 (2010)
3. Wang, A.H.: Don't follow me: spam detection in Twitter. In: Proceedings of the 2010 International Conference on Security and Cryptography (SECRYPT), pp. 1–10, July 2010
4. Lee, K., Caverlee, J., Webb, S.: Uncovering social spammers: social honeypots + machine learning. In: Proceedings of the 33rd International ACM SIGIR Conference on Research and Development in Information Retrieval, SIGIR 2010, pp. 435–442. ACM, New York (2010)
5. McCord, M., Chuah, M.: Spam detection on Twitter using traditional classifiers. In: Calero, J.M.A., Yang, L.T., Mármol, F.G., García Villalba, L.J., Li, A.X., Wang, Y. (eds.) ATC 2011. LNCS, vol. 6906, pp. 175–186. Springer, Heidelberg (2011). https://doi.org/10.1007/978-3-642-23496-5_13
6. Stringhini, G., Kruegel, C., Vigna, G.: Detecting spammers on social networks. In: Proceedings of the 26th Annual Computer Security Applications Conference, ACSAC 2010, pp. 1–9. ACM, New York (2010)
7. Yang, C., Harkreader, R.C., Gu, G.: Die free or live hard? Empirical evaluation and new design for fighting evolving Twitter spammers. In: Sommer, R., Balzarotti, D., Maier, G. (eds.) RAID 2011. LNCS, vol. 6961, pp. 318–337. Springer, Heidelberg (2011). https://doi.org/10.1007/978-3-642-23644-0_17
8. Amleshwaram, A.A., Reddy, N., Yadav, S., Gu, G., Yang, C.: CATS: characterizing automation of Twitter spammers. In: 2013 Fifth International Conference on Communication Systems and Networks (COMSNETS), pp. 1–10. IEEE (2013)
9. Cao, C., Caverlee, J.: Detecting spam URLs in social media via behavioral analysis. In: Hanbury, A., Kazai, G., Rauber, A., Fuhr, N. (eds.) ECIR 2015. LNCS, vol. 9022, pp. 703–714. Springer, Cham (2015). https://doi.org/10.1007/978-3-319-16354-3_77
10. Chu, Z., Widjaja, I., Wang, H.: Detecting social spam campaigns on Twitter. In: Bao, F., Samarati, P., Zhou, J. (eds.) ACNS 2012. LNCS, vol. 7341, pp. 455–472. Springer, Heidelberg (2012). https://doi.org/10.1007/978-3-642-31284-7_27
11. Meda, C., Bisio, F., Gastaldo, P., Zunino, R.: A machine learning approach for Twitter spammers detection. In: 2014 International Carnahan Conference on Security Technology (ICCST), pp. 1–6. IEEE (2014)
12. Santos, I., Miñambres-Marcos, I., Laorden, C., Galán-García, P., Santamaría-Ibirika, A., Bringas, P.G.: (2014) Twitter Content-based Spam Filtering. In: Herrero, Á., et al. (eds.) SOCO 2013-CISIS 2013-ICEUTE 2013. AISC, vol. 239, pp. 449–458. Springer, Cham (2014). https://doi.org/10.1007/978-3-319-01854-6_46

13. Martinez-Romo, J., Araujo, L.: Detecting malicious tweets in trending topics using a statistical analysis of language. Expert Syst. Appl. **40**(8), 2992–3000 (2013)

14. Kaplan, A.M., Haenlein, M.: The early bird catches the news: nine things you should know about micro-blogging. Bus. Horiz. **54**(2), 105–113 (2011)

15. Agarwal, N., Yiliyasi, Y.: Information quality challenges in social media. In: International Conference on Information Quality (ICIQ), pp. 234–248 (2010)

16. Manning, C.D., Raghavan, P., Schütze, H.: Introduction to Information Retrieval. Cambridge University Press, New York (2008)

17. Twitter: The Twitter rules (2016). https://support.twitter.com/articles/18311. Accessed 1 Mar 2016

18. Washha, M., Qaroush, A., Mezghani, M., Sedes, F.: Information quality in social networks: a collaborative method for detecting spam tweets in trending topics. In: Benferhat, S., Tabia, K., Ali, M. (eds.) IEA/AIE 2017. LNCS (LNAI), vol. 10351, pp. 211–223. Springer, Cham (2017). https://doi.org/10.1007/978-3-319-60045-1_24

19. Washha, M., Shilleh, D., Ghawadrah, Y., Jazi, R., Sèdes, F.: Information quality in online social networks: a fast unsupervised social spam detection method for trending topics. In: Proceedings of the 19th International Conference on Enterprise Information Systems, ICEIS 2017, Porto, Portugal, 26–29 April 2017, vol. 2, pp. 663–675. SciTePress (2017)

20. Yang, C., Harkreader, R., Zhang, J., Shin, S., Gu, G.: Analyzing spammers' social networks for fun and profit: a case study of cyber criminal ecosystem on Twitter. In: Proceedings of the 21st International Conference on World Wide Web, WWW 2012, pp. 71–80. ACM, New York (2012)

21. Chu, Z., Gianvecchio, S., Wang, H., Jajodia, S.: Detecting automation of twitter accounts: are you a human, bot, or cyborg? IEEE Trans. Dependable Secure Comput. **9**(6), 811–824 (2012)

22. Hu, X., Tang, J., Liu, H.: Online social spammer detection. In: AAAI, pp. 59–65 (2014)

23. Hu, X., Tang, J., Zhang, Y., Liu, H.: Social spammer detection in microblogging. In: IJCAI, vol. 13, pp. 2633–2639. Citeseer (2013)

24. Washha, M., Qaroush, A., Sèdes, F.: Leveraging time for spammers detection on Twitter. In: Proceedings of the 8th International Conference on Management of Digital EcoSystems, pp. 109–116. ACM (2016)

25. Yang, J., Leskovec, J.: Overlapping community detection at scale: a nonnegative matrix factorization approach. In: Proceedings of the Sixth ACM International Conference on Web Search and Data Mining, WSDM 2013, pp. 587–596. ACM, New York (2013)

26. Kullback, S., Leibler, R.A.: On information and sufficiency. Ann. Math. Stat. **22**(1), 79–86 (1951)

27. He, B.: Probability Ranking Principle, pp. 2168–2169. Springer, Boston (2009)

28. Chen, C., Zhang, J., Xie, Y., Xiang, Y., Zhou, W., Hassan, M.M., AlElaiwi, A., Alrubaian, M.: A performance evaluation of machine learning-based streaming spam tweets detection. IEEE Trans. Comput. Soc. Syst. **2**(3), 65–76 (2015)

Statistical Methods for Use in Analysis of Trust-Skyline Sets

Amna Abidi[1,3]([✉]), Mohamed Anis Bach Tobji[1,2], Allel Hadjali[3], and Boutheina Ben Yaghlane[4]

[1] Université de Tunis, Institut Supérieur de Gestion de Tunis, LARODEC, Tunis, Tunisia
amna.abidi@ensma.fr
[2] Univ. Manouba, ESEN, Manouba, Tunisia
anis.bach@esen.tn
[3] University of Poitiers, ENSMA, LIAS, Poitiers, France
allel.hadjali@ensma.fr
[4] University of Carthage, IHEC, LARODEC, Carthage, Tunisia
boutheina.yaghlane@ihec.rnu.tn

Abstract. Volume and veracity of Resource Description Framework (RDF) data in the web are two main issues in managing information. Due to the diversity of RDF data, several researchers enriched the basic RDF data model with trust information to rate the trustworthiness of the collected data.

This paper is an extension of our previous work in which we extended Trust-Skyline queries over RDF data. We are interested in analyzing the trust-Skyline list. We particularly study the user-defined trust measure (α) problem, which consists in checking the impact of such measure on the resulting list. To this end, we first distinguish between the trust-Skyline points, we propose two main categories, points that enter to the final list after the Pareto-dominance check and points that have trust measures less than α.

Then, we proposed statistical methods to investigate the trust measures dependence. Indeed we used the central tendency measures, and the measures of spread for such analysis. Experiments led on the algorithm's implementations showed promising results.

Keywords: Preference queries · Semantic web · Trust RDF data
Skyline · Statistical measures

1 Introduction

The large adoption of Semantic Web in research and industry has led to the development of a large amount of Resource Description Framework (RDF) data on the Web [2,3,11]. To rate information trustworthiness, new metrics were introduced in RDF representation [10,16,24].

© Springer International Publishing AG, part of Springer Nature 2018
S. Hammoudi et al. (Eds.): ICEIS 2017, LNBIP 321, pp. 413–427, 2018.
https://doi.org/10.1007/978-3-319-93375-7_19

To reason in presence of trust information, we used preference-based queries [7–9,19] that show motivating results to personalize and filter the massive amount of information contained in data. In our previous work [1], we proposed to extend skyline queries, introduced in [4] over RDF data weighted with trust measure.

The aim of this paper is to analyze the results presented in [1]. First of all, we distinguish between the trust-Skyline resulting list. While the points with trust measures less than the user-defined threshold α enter directly to the trust-Skyline list, they are not considered as interesting points. This is due to the non-check of Pareto dominance operator. Then, we opt for separating the two categories of points.

To analyze the results we opt for using statistical methods to investigate the trust measures dependence. Indeed we used the central tendency measures (mean and median standards), and the measures of spread (Quartile measure) for such analysis.

We checked the impact of the trust measure α and the list of the generated trust measures on the resulting trust-Skyline list. The experiments showed interesting results.

The rest of the paper is organized as follows: In the second section, we present our background material. In the third section we review the related work in the literature. In Sect. 4, we recall the trust-Skyline model. For Sect. 5 we analyze our trust-Skyline list. Then, in Sect. 6, we present the proposed methods to check the dependence between trust measures. In Sect. 7, we illustrate our experimental study. Finally, we conclude in Sect. 8.

2   Background Material

2.1   Trust RDF Data

RDF describes Web resources or subject, related via a predicate (property) to other resources (object).

Assume we have an infinite set of RDF URI references (U); an infinite set of Blank nodes (B); and an infinite set of RDF Literals (L). A triple $< Subject, Predicate, Object >$ or (s, p, o) $\in$ (U $\cup$ B) $\times$ U $\times$ (U $\cup$ B $\cup$ L) is called an RDF triple. A set of RDF statements is a graph for representing Meta-Data and describing the semantics of information in a machine-accessible way.

The RDF data are stored as a set `Subject(Node)-Property(Edge)-Object (Node)` triples, often called SPO triples $< s, p, o >$ and represented graphically as a decentralized directed labeled graph as illustrated in Fig. 1. This later is an example of a simplified RDF graph that describes the name and the price (per night) of a given hotel X.

The author in [16] introduces the trust measure to rate the trustworthiness of an RDF information. Indeed, the trust measure quantifies the subject of belief (truth) or disbelief (untruth) of an RDF information.

The trust RDF model was developed in several works such as [10,17,24].

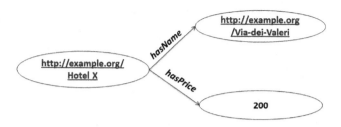

Fig. 1. RDF Graph example.

2.2   Skyline Queries

Skyline Queries have received a lot of attention due to their intuitive query formulation. Based on the concept of Pareto optimality all database objects satisfying different aspects of the query are returned. Specifically, the skyline consists in finding the objects dominated by no other object according to a user-defined criteria.

Definition 1 *Pareto Dominance.*
  Let X and Y be two points in a set of points denoted O with n attributes. A point Y dominates a point X denoted by $Y \succ X$, if $\forall i \in [1, n]$ $y_i \geq x_i$ $\wedge \exists j, y_j > x_j$. The logical dominance concept between two points is modeled as follows:

$$Y \succ X = \bigwedge (\bigwedge_{1 \leq i \leq n} y_i \geq x_i, \bigvee_{1 \leq i \leq n} y_i > x_i)$$

The skyline is a Pareto dominance accumulation, it consists of the set of points that are dominated by no other point. It is defined as follows:

Definition 2 *Skyline.* *Let O be a set of points having n attributes. The skyline of O denoted by S is defined as:*

$$S = \{X \in O / \nexists Y \in O, Y \succ X\}$$

Example 1. We illustrate the well known example presented in [4]. Given a list of hotels with the attributes *price* and *distance* (to the beach), we aim to find the cheapest and nearest hotels to the sea. Figure 2 illustrates the set of all hotels where each point is characterized by a price and a distance. Points in the curve represent the skyline, i.e., the set of hotels dominated by no other one according to the above-mentioned criteria (minimum distance and price) (Table 1).

  The tuple $(H_2, 43, 2)$ is dominated by the tuple $(H_1, 27, 2)$ we recall that the minimum values are the preferred ones. Therefore H_2 is eliminated from the skyline candidate list.

Table 1. Example of hotels properties.

Hotel	Price	Distance
H_1	27	2
H_2	43	2
H_3	55	1.50
H_4	66	1.7
H_5	70	1.40
H_6	70	1.9
H_7	80.12	0.80
H_8	90	1

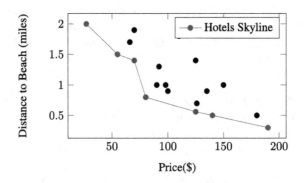

Fig. 2. Hotels' prices and distances to beach [4].

3 Related Work

In this section we present the main works that cope at most with our concern. First, we present several works that tackled the issue of trusted RDF data. Second, we advocate the modeling and computing of skyline queries over RDF data.

Trust is a concept that becomes increasingly important in many domains, such as health applications, E-commerce, social networks, and sensor networks.

Trust measure has been introduced into RDF data by [16] to rate the trustworthiness of RDF data. Many works followed the same field such the work of [10,24]. The authors in [10] presented a formal analysis of RDF data enriched with trust information by focusing on the characterization of its model-theoretic semantics and on the study of relevant reasoning problems that was not advocated in the work of [16]. They studied a number of properties of the trust model related to computational complexity issues. In [24], the authors described a mechanism for representing and reasoning with trust annotated RDF data.

Authors in [12,21] introduced the web of trust. The work of [12] presented an approach to integrate trust, provenance and annotations in semantic web systems.

For [21], authors estimate user believes in statements supplied by any other user and define properties for combination functions for merging trusts. Other works are based on ontologies such as [13] where authors discussed the multi-dimensional networks evolving from ontological trust specifications. An investigation of the applicability of social network analysis to the semantic web has been done.

On the other hand, the only existing work about extending skyline queries over RDF data is the proposal of [6]. The authors presented an approach for optimizing skyline queries over RDF data stored using a vertically partitioned schema model. They proposed an earlier filtering of the skyline candidate subjects using a new mechanism called the *Header Point* which maintains a concise summary of the already visited regions of the data space.

Although the literature is abundant on works about skyline queries over uncertain relational data, such as [5,18,25]. The extension of skyline queries over uncertain RDF has been advocated in our previous work [1] for which we proposed an extension of the skyline to the context of trust RDF data. We introduced a new variant of the skyline, called the trust-Skyline. To this end, semantics of Pareto dominance relationship and (traditional) skyline were redefined.

4   Trust-Skyline Model

This paper is an extension of our previous work [1] where we proposed to extend the classic model of skyline queries to cope with the trust RDF model. We introduced the *Trust-Skyline* in which we extract the set of most interesting resources in a trust RDF dataset. As the skyline query is based on the Pareto dominance operator, we redefined the dominance relationship in the context of trust RDF data. Then, we proposed an appropriate semantics of the *trust-Skyline*. Below, we recall the definition of trust-Skyline queries. In [4], skyline is defined as the set of points dominated by no other point. In such perfect context, dominance is binary. However, in context of trust RDF data [16], dominance is rather quantified with a degree between $[-1, 1]$. Thus, we defined the skyline as the set of database objects dominated by no other object according to a trust threshold α.

Definition 3 Trust-Skyline. *The T-Skyline of a data set D, denoted by $T - Sky^\alpha$, contains each point X in D such there is no point Y that dominates X with a trust degree greater than a user defined threshold $\alpha \in [-1, 1]$.*

$$T - sky^\alpha = \{X \in D / \nexists Y \in D, d(Y \succ X) \geq \alpha\}$$

Example 2. We illustrate an example of five hotels, with two properties each one (Price and Distance). For each property we specify a trust degree to describe the data trustworthiness. Data is stored in an RDF quadruple store representation[1] (Table 2).

---

[1] The physical data model used in this article is an extension of the 3Store model presented in [15,23].

Table 2. Example of hotels candidate list of T-Sky.

Subject	Predicate	Object	Trust
h_1	hasPrice	22	0.5
h_1	hasDistance	5	0.3
h_2	hasPrice	55	0.2
h_2	hasDistance	20	0.6
h_3	hasPrice	52	0.7
h_3	hasDistance	7	0.5
h_4	hasPrice	45	0.1
h_4	hasDistance	2	0.3
h_5	hasPrice	50	0.6
h_5	hasDistance	10	0.4

We want to compute the T-Skyline of the above RDF data set when α is fixed to 0.1.

- $d(h_1 \succ h_2) = 0.2 \ (\geq \alpha)$. As the trust-dominance is asymmetric h_2 does not dominate h_1. We conclude that h_2 could not integrate the skyline. We prune it.
- $d(h_1 \succ h_3) = 0.3$, thus h_3 is also pruned.
- $d(h_1 \succ h_4) = -1$ and $d(h_4 \succ h_1) = -1$. h_1 and h_4 are incomparable, we make no pruning.
- $d(h_1 \succ h_5) = 0.3$, thus h_5 is pruned.

We conclude that the Trust-Skyline list includes h_1 and h_4 which are dominated by no other point.

5   Trust-Skyline List Analysis

In [1] a set of properties have been defined and used to optimize the computation of the T-Skyline list. The first property used is adding directly all points having trust measure less or equal to the threshold α. These points could not be dominated with a degree greater than α. Note that Complexity of this method is $O(n^2)$.

The second method is a combination between the first one and the use of transitivity property. Indeed, there is no need to compare all the pairs of points.

Based on the used methods to compute the T-Skyline list, we can make an analysis of the resulting list. The first category is the list of points having trust values less than α, the second one is the points that are Pareto-dominated by no other point.

5.1 T-Skyline Points with Trust Measure Less Than Alpha

We recall the property presented in our previous work [1] in which we let the points with trust measure less than α enter directly to the T-Skyline list without processing:

Property 1. Given a data set D and its T-Skyline $T - Sky^{\alpha}$ and a point $P \in D$. If $P.t^{-} < \alpha$ then $P \in T - Sky^{\alpha}$.

This category of points could be dominated by no other point with a trust degree greater than α. The search space is considerably pruned because the dominance check between points is reduced, we call this list of points $T - Sky_{<\alpha}$. $T - Sky_{<\alpha}$ points are added to T-Skyline list without considering their property values. Therefore, the list of points is not interested in the T-Skyline final list due to the non-check of Pareto-dominance.

The greater α, the greater the size of the $T - Sky_{<\alpha}$ points. The lower the trust value, the lower the $T - Sky_{<\alpha}$ set and the greater the uncertainty.

5.2 T-Skyline Points with Trust Measure Greater Than Alpha

We call the list of points added to the T-Skyline list after Pareto-dominance check $T - Sky_{>\alpha}$. The list of $T - Sky_{>\alpha}$ are the most interesting points in the result list since they have the best values among all the properties.

The Fig. 3 below present the difference between the two set of points:

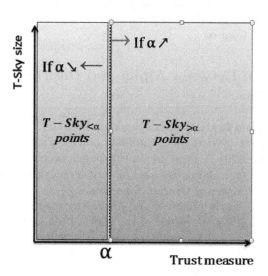

Fig. 3. Trust-Skyline points analysis.

5.3   Great Values of Alpha

We recall the definition presented in our previous work [1] about the trust of a given RDF point.

Definition 4 *Trust of a Point. Given an RDF point P with n properties p_i such that $1 \leq i \leq n$. Each property is associated with a trust value t_i. The trust of a point, denoted by $P.t^-$ is the minimum trust degree among all its properties.*

$$P.t^- = \min_{1 \leq i \leq n} (p_i.t)$$

When α has a great value, the size of the T-Skyline became greater and the algorithms performs better. This is due to the fact that points' trusts are more probably less than α, and thus enter directly to the skyline without processing.

In this case, thanks to proposition 4 in [1] , the search space is considerably pruned. The size of the trust skyline is important, because it is rare to check a dominance between two points, according to a threshold whose value is important.

5.4   Small Values of Alpha

When α has a small value, several points are dominated and so do not enter to the skyline. That is why skyline size is small in this case. The Naive T-Skyline do not benefit from the proposition 4 pruning method, and execution time is very important. However, for TRDF-Skyline algorithm, execution time is very acceptable, since pruning based on the transitivity property is always efficient and doesn't depend from α.

6   Dependence Between Alpha and the Distribution of Trust Values

In this section, we aim to study the dependence between α and the rest of trust values $P.t^-$ of the set of T-Skyline candidate points. There are many methods to describe the variability in data set, in this paper we choose to use statistical methods to organize and summarize a set of trust scores, which are: The *measure of Spread* and the *measure of Central Tendency* [14].

The purpose of central tendency (or central location) is to determine the single value that identifies the center of the distribution and best represents the entire set of scores. The three standard measures of central tendency are the mean, the mode, and the median, we give more explanations in Subsect. 6.1. While, a measure of spread (or of dispersion), is used to describe the variability in a sample or population. From the set of spread measures, we choose to use the quartile method as introduced in Subsect. 6.2.

6.1   Central Tendency Measures

Summarizing the set of trust values can help us understand the data, especially when the dataset is large. There exist multiple measures of Central Tendency that summarize the data into a single value.

There are three main measures of central tendency: The mean, the median and the mode. Each of these measures describes a different indication of the typical or central value in the distribution.

– The mean: This measure is the sum of the value of each observation in a dataset divided by the number of observations. This is also known as the arithmetic average. Looking at the trust values below:

$$0.2, 0.3, 0.4, 0.2, 0.3, 0.8, 0.3$$

The mean is calculated by adding together all the trust values and dividing by the number of observations (Mean of trusts= (0.2+0.3+0.4+0.2+0.3+ 0.8+0.3)/ (7) which equals 0.357.
– The median: is the middle value in distribution when the values are arranged in ascending or descending order. The median divides the distribution in half (there are 50% of observations on either side of the median value). In a distribution with an odd number of observations, the median value is the middle value. We illustrate the same example given in the mean measure, after sorting the trust thresholds: 0.2, 0.2, 0.3, 0.3, 0.3, 0.4, 0.8, the median is 0.3.
– The mode: It is the most commonly occurring value in a distribution. Consider same example shown before, the Table 3 shows a simple frequency distribution of trust measures. The most commonly occurring trust value is 0.3, therefore the mode of this distribution is 0.3.

Table 3. Trust Frequency Distribution.

Trust	Frequency
0.2	2
0.3	3
0.4	1
0.8	1

6.2   Measures of Spread: Quartile Measure

In order to study the dependence between α and the trust set points $P.t^-$ we choose to use the quartile statistical measure.

Quartiles tell us about the spread of a data set by breaking the data set into quarters.

Example 3. For example, consider the price of 11 hotels below, which have been ordered from the lowest to the highest value:

$$6, 7, 15, 36, 39, 41, 41, 43, 43, 47, 49$$

- The first quartile (Q1) is the value of the middle of the first set, for which 25% of the values are least then it and 75% are greater.
- The third quartile (Q3) is the value of the middle of the second set, in which 75% of the values are less than Q3 and 25% are greater.

The first quartile (Q1) lies between the 3rd and 5th price values and the third quartile (Q3) between the 8th and 10th price values, Hence:

- First quartile (Q1) = 15
- Second quartile (Q2) = 43

6.3 Trust Dependence

The use of the quartile measure let as subdivide the generated data set into four parts. Indeed, we can have a global view about the distribution of trust $P.t^-$ of the global set. Such information could be useful for the user in order to know which value of α could fit the best with his query. We illustrate the example below of a set of points with a finite interval of trust each set:

A brief analysis of the Table 4 let as know that if we choose α greater or equal to 0.5, we will have 46 points (46%) of the database will be included directly in the T-Skyline set. However with an α equal to 0.1, only 4 points will be directly included in the T-Skyline list, etc.

The trust assignment allows users to classify resources as trusted or not. For instance, the user is allowed to give more preferences to get the final result [20] such the size of the returned T-skyline points (according to the trust distribution). In case, user wants the most trusted resources, the value of α needs to be not great and vise versa.

Table 4. Example of trust distribution.

Number of points	Interval of trust
54 points	[0.5 ;1]
26 points	[0.3 ;0.5[
16 points	[0.2 ;0.3[
4 points	[0.1 ;0.2[

Another statistical measure is the interquartile range that describes the difference between the third quartile (Q3) and the first quartile (Q1), telling us about the range of the middle half of the values in the distribution. For the Example 3 the interquartile is (43-15=28).

7   Experimental Evaluation

In this section, we evaluate the dependence between the set of trust measures and the user-defined trust value α. Consequently, the experiments we led were about (1) the performance of the methods (time execution), and (2) the size of the skyline (readability of the result). For each measure, we varied (1) the trust threshold, (2) the size of the database. The idea is to understand the effects of these parameters on the execution time and the resulted T-Skyline.

7.1   Experimental Setup

We have presented in our previous work [1] several methods to compute the Trust-Skyline model. Due to the lack of trust RDF databases, we generated synthetic data sets according to the parameters presented in Table 5. For each experiment, we vary one parameter and set the others to the default values (referred in the above-mentioned table). Note that data are generated following the uniform law. We extended the 3Store model presented in [15,22,23], using RDF quadruple store representation to deal with the trust measure. The data generator and the algorithms presented in [1] were implemented in Java. Stored functions were implemented using PL/SQL. All new experiments were conducted under Windows 7 on an Intel(R) Core(TM) i5-2410M CPU with 4GB of RAM.

Table 5. Parameters under investigation.

Symbol	Parameter	Default
D	Number of quadruples	300 K
X	Size of T-Skyline data	-
α	Trust measure	0.2
T	Time execution (ms)	-

7.2   Impact of Trust Threshold Variation and Central Tendency Measures

As we presented previously, this work is an extension of [1], in which we have introduced the Trust-Skyline as the set of points dominated by no other point according to a trust threshold α. In this experiment, we aim to investigate the relation between the user-defined threshold α and the distribution of the set of trust measures $P.t^-$. We start by studying the impact of central tendency measures (We opt for using the mean and the median) and α on the execution time and on the trust skyline, as shown in Fig. 4.

When α has a great value, The TRDF-Skyline algorithm performs quickly. This is due to the fact that $T - Sky_{<\alpha}$ points(defined previously in Sect. 5)

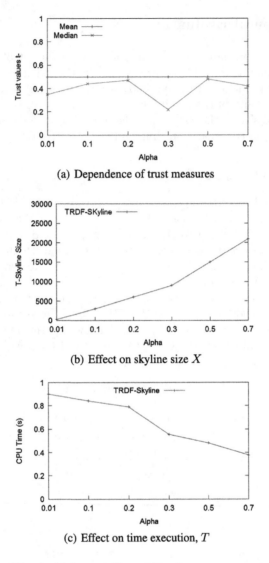

(a) Dependence of trust measures

(b) Effect on skyline size X

(c) Effect on time execution, T

Fig. 4. Alpha and Central Tendency measures.

are huge, and thus enter directly to the skyline without processing with respect to the Property 1. Indeed, the search space is considerably pruned. Size of the trust skyline (Fig. 4(a)) is important, because it is rare to check a dominance between two points, according to a threshold whose value is important. If we check the central tendency measures, for great values of α we found that the median and mod values are less than α. Therefore, the T-Skyline list is huge, and the algorithm performs well. If there is rare dominance-check between points, then we obtain a great number of skyline points.

On the other hand, when α has a small value, The mod and median of the set of points are greater than $alpha$ as shown in Fig. 4. Indeed, the set of $T - Sky_{>\alpha}$ points (defined previously in Sect. 5) is huge, and several points are dominated and so do not enter to the skyline. That is why skyline size is small in this case.

7.3   Impact of Trust Threshold Variation and Quartile Measures

As we presented previously in Sect. 6, we selected quartile measure to study the spread of trust values. Quartiles are less affected by outliers or skewed data set than the equivalent measures of mean and standard deviation. This approach sets upper and lower hit selection thresholds based on number of interquartile ranges above or below $Q1$ and $Q3$ quartiles. In our experiments we studied the $Q1$ and $Q3$ quartiles as shown in Fig. 5.

For low values of α, the quartile range (difference between Q3 and Q1) is greater than α, indeed $T - Sky_{<\alpha}$ list is small. The Q1 quartile represents the most likely points to enter the T-Skyline list without dominance-check, and $Q3$ represents the most likely points to enter this list after dominance-check. We can conclude that the user can use those two measure to specify the value of α, if he wants to have an aggressive pruning of the candidate list, the value of $alpha$ needs to be small and the value of the points in $Q1$ quartile. Another important point is, if the user wants to only let the most interesting points, that we represented with $T - Sky_{>\alpha}$, enter the T-Skyline, the value of $alpha$ needs to be low.

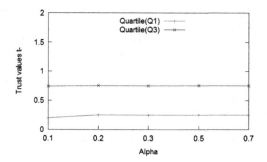

Fig. 5. Alpha and Quartile measure.

8   Conclusion

In this paper, we proposed an extension of our previous work in which we extended the skyline to the context of trust RDF data. Indeed we introduced the trust-Skyline model. We proposed in this paper to analyze the Trust-Skyline resulting list. To this end, statistical methods were used to analyze the dependence between α and the set of generated trust thresholds.

To study the trust-Skyline list, we used two statistical methods that take into account the trust measures to compute the trust-Skyline set. The first method is the central tendency measures, we specifically used the mean and median standards. And the measures of spread that tell us about the spread of a data set by breaking the data set into quarters.

Our experiments showed the impact of the user-defined trust measure α on the T-Skyline list. The T-Skyline list is huge if the trust threshold is medium or high. However, small values of α restrict the entering to this list, only interesting points can be selected.

References

1. Abidi, A., Tobji, M.A.B, Hadjali, A., Yaghlane, B.B.: Skyline modeling and computing over trust RDF data. In: ICEIS 2017 - Proceedings of the 19th International Conference on Enterprise Information Systems, Porto, Portugal, 26–29 April 2017, vol. 2, pp. 634–643 (2017)
2. Antoniou, G., van Harmelen, F.: A Semantic Web Primer. MIT Press, Cambridge (2004)
3. Berners-Lee, T., Fielding, R., Masinter, L.: Uniform resource identifiers (URI): Generic syntax (1998)
4. Börzsönyi, S., Kossmann, D., Stocker, K.: The skyline operator. In: Proceedings of the 17th International Conference on Data Engineering, Washington, DC, USA, pp. 421–430. IEEE Computer Society (2001)
5. Bosc, P., Hadjali, A., Pivert, O.: On possibilistic skyline queries. In: Christiansen, H., De Tré, G., Yazici, A., Zadrozny, S., Andreasen, T., Larsen, H.L. (eds.) FQAS 2011. LNCS (LNAI), vol. 7022, pp. 412–423. Springer, Heidelberg (2011). https://doi.org/10.1007/978-3-642-24764-4_36
6. Chen, L., Gao, S., Anyanwu, K.: Efficiently evaluation skyline queries on RDF databases. In: 8th Extended Semantic Web Conference, ESWC 2011, Heraklion, Crete, Greece, pp. 123–138, May-June 2011
7. Chomicki, J.: Querying with intrinsic preferences. In: Jensen, C.S., Šaltenis, S., Jeffery, K.G., Pokorny, J., Bertino, E., Böhn, K., Jarke, M. (eds.) EDBT 2002. LNCS, vol. 2287, pp. 34–51. Springer, Heidelberg (2002). https://doi.org/10.1007/3-540-45876-X_5
8. Chomicki, J.: Logical foundations of preference queries. IEEE Data Eng. Bull. **34**, 3–10 (2011)
9. Chomicki, J., Ciaccia, P., Meneghetti, N.: Skyline queries, front and back. SIGMOD Rec. **42**(3), 6–18 (2013)
10. Fionda, V., Greco, G.: Trust models for RDF data: semantics and complexity. In: Proceedings of the Twenty-Ninth AAAI Conference on Artificial Intelligence, 25–30 January 2015, Austin, Texas, USA, pp. 95–101 (2015)
11. Frauenfelder, M.: A Smarter Web (2009)
12. Golbeck, J.: Combining provenance with trust in social networks for semantic web content filtering. In: Moreau, L., Foster, I. (eds.) IPAW 2006. LNCS, vol. 4145, pp. 101–108. Springer, Heidelberg (2006). https://doi.org/10.1007/11890850_12
13. Golbeck, J., Parsia, B., Hendler, J.: Trust networks on the semantic web. In: Klusch, M., Omicini, A., Ossowski, S., Laamanen, H. (eds.) CIA 2003. LNCS (LNAI), vol. 2782, pp. 238–249. Springer, Heidelberg (2003). https://doi.org/10.1007/978-3-540-45217-1_18

14. Gravetter, F.J., Wallnau, L.B.: Statistics for the Behavioral Sciences. 5th edn. Wadsworth Thomson Learning, Belmont (2016)
15. Harris, S., Gibbins, N.: 3store: efficient bulk RDF storage. In: Practical and Scalable Semantic Systems, Proceedings of the First International Workshop on Practical and Scalable Semantic Systems (2003)
16. Hartig, O.: Querying trust in RDF data with tSPARQL. In: Aroyo, L., Traverso, P., Ciravegna, F., Cimiano, P., Heath, T., Hyvönen, E., Mizoguchi, R., Oren, E., Sabou, M., Simperl, E. (eds.) ESWC 2009. LNCS, vol. 5554, pp. 5–20. Springer, Heidelberg (2009). https://doi.org/10.1007/978-3-642-02121-3_5
17. Hartig, O.: Towards a data-centric notion of trust in the semantic web (a position statement). In: The Semantic Web: Research and Applications, the 7th Extended Semantic Web Conference, ESWC 2010, May 2010, Heraklion, Greece, pp. 5–20 (2009)
18. Jiang, B., Pei, J., Lin, X., Yuan, Y.: Probabilistic skylines on uncertain data: model and bounding-pruning-refining methods. vol. 38, pp. 1–39. Kluwer Academic Publishers, February 2012
19. Kiessling, W.: Foundations of preferences in database systems. In: Proceedings of the 28th International Conference on Very Large Data Bases, VLDB 2002, pp. 311–322. VLDB Endowment (2002)
20. Kossmann, D., Ramsak, F., Rost, S.: Shooting stars in the sky: an online algorithm for skyline queries. In: Proceedings of the 28th International Conference on Very Large Data Bases, pp. 275–286. VLDB Endowment (2002)
21. Richardson, M., Agrawal, R., Domingos, P.: Trust management for the semantic web. In: Fensel, D., Sycara, K., Mylopoulos, J. (eds.) ISWC 2003. LNCS, vol. 2870, pp. 351–368. Springer, Heidelberg (2003). https://doi.org/10.1007/978-3-540-39718-2_23
22. Sakr, S., Al-Naymat, G.: Relational processing of rdf queries: a survey. ACM SIGMOD Rec. 38, 23–28 (2009)
23. Sakr, S., Al-Naymat, G.: Relational processing of rdf queries: A survey. SIGMOD Rec. 38(4), 23–28 (2010)
24. Tomaszuk, D., Pak, K., Rybinski, H.: Trust in RDF graphs. In: Morzy, T., Härder, T., Wrembel, R. (eds.) Advances in Databases and Information Systems. AISC, pp. 273–283. Springer, Heidelberg (2012). https://doi.org/10.1007/978-3-642-32741-4_25
25. Zhang, Q., Ye, P., Lin, X., Zhang, Y.: Skyline probability over uncertain preferences. In: Proceedings of the 16th International Conference on Extending Database Technology, New York, NY, USA, pp. 395–405. ACM (2013)

Enabling Semantics in Enterprises

André Pomp[(✉)], Alexander Paulus, Sabina Jeschke, and Tobias Meisen

Institute of Information Management in Mechanical Engineering,
RWTH Aachen University, Aachen, Germany
andre.pomp@ima.rwth-aachen.de
http://www.ima.rwth-aachen.de

Abstract. Nowadays, enterprises generate massive amounts of heterogeneous structured and unstructured data within their factories and attempt to store them inside data lakes. However, potential users, such as data scientists, encounter problems when they have to find, analyze and especially understand the data. Possible existing solutions use ontologies as data governance technique for establishing a common understanding of data sources. While ontologies build a solid basis for representing knowledge, their construction is a very complex task which requires the knowledge of multiple domain experts. However, in fast and continuously evolving enterprises a static ontology will be quickly outdated.

To cope with this problem, we developed the information processing platform ESKAPE. With the help of ESKAPE, data publishers annotate their added data sources with semantic models providing additional knowledge which enables later users to process, query and subscribe to heterogeneous data as information products. Instead of solely creating semantic models based on a pre-defined ontology, ESKAPE maintains a knowledge graph which learns from the knowledge provided within the semantic models by data publishers. Based on the semantic models and the evolving knowledge graph, ESKAPE supports enterprises' data scientists in finding, analyzing and understanding data.

To evaluate ESKAPE's usability, we conducted an open competitive hackathon where users had to develop mobile applications. The received feedback shows that ESKAPE already reduced the workload of the participants for getting the appropriate required data and enhanced the usability of dealing with the available data.

Keywords: Semantic computing · Semantic model
Knowledge graph · Internet of Things · Data processing · ESKAPE

1 Introduction

In modern days, most multinational companies attempt to aggregate their data sources from various, previously mostly autonomous factories or production sites. As those data structures have been developed for multiple years with presumably less to no central guidance in the fields of compatibility and standards,

© Springer International Publishing AG, part of Springer Nature 2018
S. Hammoudi et al. (Eds.): ICEIS 2017, LNBIP 321, pp. 428–450, 2018.
https://doi.org/10.1007/978-3-319-93375-7_20

several different kinds of data sources (e.g., operating machines, historical data storages, etc.) with different data models are in place. This can range from a grown IT-infrastructure, where hundreds of heterogeneous data sources exist, to one globally defined and well-maintained format and semantics used for data exchange.

In the context of the (Industrial) Internet of Things (IoT), all available data should be used to enable the companies to provide global quality management and production improvement. For being able to perform the data analysis that is needed to derive answers from the vast amounts of data, all data sets have to be combinable and understandable in one single place by analysts who often do not know the original data sources. Main problems that are arising include finding appropriate data sources in the collected data, combining data from different sources without origin context knowledge of the specific data points and lacking implicit knowledge (e.g., interpretation of proprietary numbers and alphanumeric identifiers) of available data points.

Thus, the common idea of the Internet of Things and various similar industrial and enterprise applications is to enable each participating object, which is part of the system, to collect and exchange data that can be used in multiple domains and sites at the same time [1]. One possible solution for solving this challenge is the standardization of data models, formats and exchanged information. Here, it is necessary to create a fixed standard for each available information that may be recorded by a sensor or produced by an application. An example for standardized sensor readings is SensorML,[1] which provides a model consisting of at least an identifier, a definition and a unit of measurement for each reading, whereby all attributes can be chosen by the user but are fixed afterwards.

However, defining standardized data models leads to different problems. If we want to solve the problem of heterogeneity by using standards and without violating the common idea of IoT, we have to define them in such a way that they comprise all existing concepts. For example, for the concept *Temperature*, a standard also has to define all sub concepts, such as *Indoor, Ambient or Room Temperature*. To allow a common understanding of the general data schema, the standard has to define at least those basic concepts. Here, further problems arise since the usage of those concepts depends on their context. For instance, if a person is located in a room, the room temperature corresponds to the indoor temperature. However, the ambient temperature may either be the temperature outside the room or outside the building. Most of today's data modeling approaches cannot cope with such unpredictable cases.

The example shows that the definition of standards for a common data model among various sensors is already difficult and it becomes more complicated when considering further data sources. For the definition of a corresponding standard to be successful, all software developers and hardware manufacturers would have to accord it and apply it to already rolled out devices or software. While parts of these problems can be simplified by limiting the standard to a specific domain, e.g., smart home or a specific company site, it results in the drawback that

---

[1] http://www.ogcnetwork.net/SensorML.

those devices can then only be used in this domain unless their standard is translated to be compatible with another one. This leads to additional work and is a contradiction to the common idea of connected systems (e.g., Industrial IoT) in which each participant's data should be readable regardless of domain knowledge.

Another frequently proposed solution to the described problems is the use of ontologies, which are for example used in the semantic web. Instead of standardizing data models, we can use ontologies to define the current view of the world. This allows the definition of semantic models based on the ontology, creating an abstraction layer and thus being able to view the data on an information level rather than a data level. This meta level enables the comparability and analysis of data sources with different data models but identical information.

However, ontologies also suffer from various disadvantages. First, the definition of an ontology is a complex task which in advance requires to collect and model all the knowledge that will be required. Second, ontologies suffer from inflexibility. Due to the complex generation, an ontology is usually generated for a specific use case in a specific domain, e.g., medicine. Every annotation that is missing in the ontology will not be available when creating a semantic model later on. Since the (Industrial) Internet of Things is fast and continuously evolving and new devices and sensors are proposed every day, a static ontology will not be able to model each requirement. In addition, covering the complete required knowledge will also be challenging, even within a single enterprise.

To solve the described problems of heterogeneous data sources and the sophisticated definition of static ontologies, we developed the information-based data platform *ESKAPE* (Evolving Semantic Knowledge and Aggregation Processing Engine) for structured as well as unstructured batch and streaming data that is capable of handling data on a semantic information level. To feed data into ESKAPE, users (e.g., data source owners) can add data sources and describe them with a custom semantic model. Instead of generating the model based on a pre-defined ontology, users create the semantic model either by using concepts available in the *knowledge graph* managed by ESKAPE or by defining their own domain-specific concepts leading to an expansion of ESKAPE's knowledge graph. Hence, compared to ontologies created top-down, this knowledge graph is capable of adapting new and unknown concepts and relations bottom-up based on the added data sources and their semantic models. Other users can use the published data sources for analyzing data or developing applications based on it.

We run ESKAPE in a closed enterprise environment, but due to compliance issues of enterprises, we evaluated our approach in an open real-world scenario. We set up a challenge in which teams had to develop smart city applications based on various data sets (batch and streaming data) that we collected from different local providers, such as the local bus or bicycle sharing companies. The evaluation shows that the provided platform features, like a semantic search, information conversion, data format conversion or semantic filtering simplify the development of real-world applications significantly. Hence, ESKAPE forms the foundation for enabling true semantics in the evolving IoT.

This paper is an extended version of [2] and is organized as follows. Section 2 provides a motivating example and Sect. 3 discusses related work. Based on the example and current state of the art, we discuss the concepts of ESKAPE in Sect. 4 as well as its functionality (Sect. 5) and architecture (Sect. 6). Finally, we present the evaluation results in Sect. 7 before we conclude and give an outlook in Sect. 8.

2 Motivating Example

In this section, we provide a motivating example illustrating the necessity for future IoT platforms to consider knowledge about the semantics of data and to offer semantic-based processing. In addition, we discuss why usual ontologies are not sufficient for modeling the semantic knowledge of all data sources in large enterprises.

The scenario consists of a simplified production process. An enterprise e with two production sites ps_1 and ps_2 manufactures products that need to be deformed and painted. Example products may be bicycles or cars. On the production site, different versions of the product are produced in multiple steps by using different production lines and machines.

During the production process, different parts of the involved system generate different kinds of data. For instance, parts of the processes generate live streaming data gathered by sensors (e.g., the current temperature within an oven used for drying paint) whereas other data is recorded manually by employees and stored in an Excel sheet that is uploaded onto a web server.

To be more accurate, we assume that the following data sources are present. The production site ps_1 is equipped with multiple environmental sensors covering three temperature sensors t_1, t_2 and t_3 as well as two humidity sensors h_1 and h_2. All sensors provide a measurement together with a timestamp. For t_1 and t_2 the value of the current temperature is measured in °C whereas t_3 provides the temperature in °F. The timestamp for all three temperature sensors is provided in milliseconds. The humidity sensors provide their values in percentage. However, h_1 provides a timestamp in milliseconds whereas h_2 has a timestamp in seconds. All sensors publish their measured results on an AMQP[2] broker using JSON as data format. The data are then persisted within a NoSQL database.

In addition to the environmental data, the production lines at the production site ps_1 also gather live data from a PLC. Every second, an external system reads the PLC measurements plc_1 and sends them as CSV line via MQTT[3] to a SQL database. For simplicity, we assume that the measurements just contain two temperatures recorded from two ovens on the production line. The temperature readings are measured in °F. Additionally, the ID of the manufactured product and the timestamp in seconds are stored with the corresponding measurements.

---

[2] Advanced Message Queuing Protocol: An open standard application layer protocol.

[3] Message Queue Telemetry Transport: A lightweight publish-subscribe messaging protocol.

Finally, an employee evaluates the quality of the dried paint and stores the qualitative assessment in an Excel sheet es_1 which is uploaded every 24 h onto an FTP server.

Due to varying quality of the dried paint identified by the qualitative assessment, an enterprise's data scientist wants to analyze if the quality of the manufactured product depends on the current environmental situation. For example, she wants to analyze if a higher temperature and a higher humidity lower the quality of the paint. Thus, the data scientist communicates with different departments to get access to the environmental data t_1, t_2 t_3, h_1, h_2, the production line data plc_1 and the data of the department for quality assurance es_1.

By examining the described scenario, you can identify different drawbacks and error-prone process steps. First, the data are distributed among different departments making it challenging to get access to the data. Second, the semantics and underlying structure are most likely unknown to the data scientist. Hence, an exchange of knowledge between the department and the data scientist will be necessary.

Moreover, if the data scientist wants to use the data in this example, she currently has to deal with three different data models in three different formats (JSON, CSV, Excel) available via three different approaches (NoSQL, SQL, FTP) leading to unnecessary implementation overhead. In addition, the data scientist has to deal with information in different units and representation forms. There exist two different temperature units (°C and °F) and two different timestamp representations (s and ms). These heterogeneities again lead to a higher unnecessary implementation overhead.

In addition to the overhead, the different departments that are responsible for the data have to manage the access when the data scientist wants to use the data. Although, if we assume that a common platform exists where the data is stored and the access is granted, the departments still face different challenges. A common platform without semantics will not be able to provide any knowledge about the data. For example, the platform would not be aware of the unit of the temperature and could therefore not convert it into an appropriate unit. If we assume that the platform is already using an ontology for representing information, the ontology would need to cover any concept and relation that will be available in data sets that are added in the future. Otherwise, the platform could not link those unknown data attributes to other data sets containing the same information. While defining a comprehensive ontology may be possible in a closed and controllable environment (e.g., inside a single department of a company), it is very unrealistic for a global company with multiple sites in different countries or in an open scenario where data sources are added over a long time period by multiple independent actors, such as local companies, city administration or private end users. This shows that we are in need of a more generic and evolving approach when dealing with semantics in the (Industrial) Internet of Things.

3   Related Work

In a broad field like the IoT, many other research topics are related to our work. Such topics are data integration and semantic model generation, ontology learning, knowledge representation, community-driven ontology engineering and IoT platforms.

In the area of data integration, multiple approaches focus on solving the problem of heterogeneous data sources, such as query reformulation techniques (Global or Local as View) or ontology-based information integration [3].

The Stanford-IBM Manager of Multiple Information Sources (TSIMMIS) [4] focuses on integrating and accessing heterogeneous data sources by following a Global as View approach. TTIMMIS acts as a translator between data sources and a common data model (CDM) allowing to translate queries to the CDM into data source specific queries and returning the result back to the user in the CDM. By using mediators, TSIMMIS identifies data sources that contain queried information. However, TSIMMIS has the disadvantage that it does not consider additional semantic information, such as relations between data attributes, which enable a more sophisticated information processing.

Knoblock et al. propose in multiple papers [5–8] a platform, called KARMA, which follows the ontology-based information integration approach. This platform allows integrating data of multiple formats (JSON, XML, etc.) based on a pre-defined ontology. Data sources that are attached to Karma use semantic models. For that, Knoblock et al. focus their work on automatically creating semantic models based on a fixed ontology per use case where the ontology does not evolve over time. Another project proposed by Meisen et al. describes a framework for handling heterogeneous simulation tools for production processes by using semantics based on a static ontology [9]. Compared to these approaches, ESKAPE focuses on an evolving knowledge graph that learns from semantic models that were created by users for their provided data sources.

In the area of ontology generation and learning, OntoWiki [10] addresses the problem of the complex ontology generation by crowdsourcing ontologies with the help of community members. In OntoWiki, users create Wiki articles for concepts and describe them in natural language. If a concept is missing, users can create a new article for it. However, the evolving ontology OntoWiki is created by community members where each one can modify the work of the other. Without well-defined processes, the ontology will not achieve stability. Hence, ESKAPE mitigates this problem by supervising the knowledge graph generation using external knowledge databases.

The approaches [11,12] deal with learning ontologies from unstructured text in an automatic fashion for coping with the high effort that arises from creating ontologies by hand. Therefore, the authors use DBPedia as a supervisory tool for guiding a user during the learning of an ontology. Their work is a first attempt to automatically generate ontologies. Xiao et al. focus on learning ontologies from unstructured text where the learned ontology is created based on a fixed corpus of input sources that are not provided by different users whereas ESKAPE's knowledge graph learns from user provided semantic models leading to higher stability and correctness of the learned knowledge graph.

Cochez et al. [13] propose a different approach to represent knowledge. Instead of using common ontologies represented in RDF and OWL, they represent knowledge using prototypes. Compared to ontologies, prototypes do not differentiate between instances and concepts. This increases the flexibility for reusing and sharing knowledge. The concept is similar to ESKAPE's knowledge graph which is also flexible and does not differentiate between pure concepts and named entities. However, Cochez et al. do not address the evolution of prototype ontologies over time whereas ESKAPE's knowledge graph specifically focuses on this issue.

Furthermore, the project Semantic Data Platform (SDP) proposed by [14] uses ontologies and semantic models to enable IoT-based services. They also have the goal to deal with the number of upcoming heterogeneous data sources in the Internet of Things. Palavalli et al. provide a concept to solve the problem by allowing vendors to specify semantic models for their new devices. These models are then used for manually evolving the underlying ontology, which can be used as a common data model. Based on SDP, devices and applications can subscribe to events (e.g., temperature higher than 25 °C) that are obtained from the collected IoT data. This collection is enabled by the use of semantic queries. Palavalli et al. just focus on adding devices with semantic models that were provided by vendors. Their work does not consider other data sources such as applications, that may deliver data with more sophisticated data models, as well as devices where the semantic model may change over time (e.g., modular smart phones). Moreover, the future work presented includes extending the semantic approach to collaboratively evolve IoT data model standard among device vendors whereas our approach does not require to establish a standard.

Similar interest in interoperability of IoT systems has been stated in a new project named 'BIG IoT' [15]. It focuses on the task of offering a single API for multiple IoT applications, bridging the gap between multiple independent data storages. Another project, called Anzo Semantic Data Lake [16], focuses on developing a data lake by adding context to all kinds of data sources. In both projects, the participants do not state how this task can be achieved but describe the need for adding semantics to raw data sources. More concrete examples of semantic data platforms are Mantra [17] and kSpheres [18]. Both projects focus on semantic data processing by enabling use cases like entity extraction or sentiment analysis. Similar to the formerly mentioned projects, there is no statement or explanation how tasks, such as ontology construction or semantic processing, are achieved.

4   Concept

In this section, we will describe the concept behind the platform, specifically the semantic concepts used by ESKAPE. To address the challenges that we identified in the motivating example and in the related work, we are developing ESKAPE,

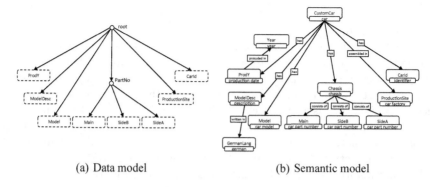

(a) Data model   (b) Semantic model

Fig. 1. Identified data model and respective semantic model for an example data set of cars [2].

an information-based platform that is capable of integrating data from heterogeneous data sources on a semantic level by using a maintained knowledge graph. Common approaches tend to use ontologies for semantic data modeling (cf. Sect. 3) or other static approaches to annotate data sets with semantic information. A drawback of these approaches is the missing ability to adapt to changes in a rapidly changing environment where either new devices are added almost every day or where a data scientist requires a different view on unified data (cf. Sect. 2).

With ESKAPE, we want to provide a new approach of creating semantics for data sources. Using ESKAPE, a user typically starts with a *data model* deducted from a sample data set. The data model contains all data attributes which have been found in the analyzed data points thus representing the structure of the observed input data (Fig. 1(a)). The identified data model then has to be mapped to a semantic representation (*semantic model*). This chapter presents the basics of semantic modeling used by ESKAPE whereas the mapping process is more closely described in Sect. 5.1.

4.1   Semantic Models

ESKAPE extends the technique of matching data source models to (static) ontologies and their vocabulary. The platform uses semantic models to describe single data sources. A *semantic model* is a semantic annotation of a data model adding semantic vocabulary and relations to it. This model gives a semantic representation of the information contained in the raw data points. The model itself is user-maintained and fixed at the time the data integration starts.

A semantic model (cf. Fig. 1(b)) is created by instantiating an *Entity Type* for each data attribute identified during the data analysis which is to be integrated later. Each Entity Type contains a user-defined name for this attribute in this specific semantic model (e.g., 'ProductionSite') and has a semantic concept assigned to it, defining the semantic properties of this attribute (e.g., 'car factory'). The Entity Type is therefore an instantiation of a generic concept for a specific semantic model and is defined by it. Furthermore, the user is not limited to attribute-assigned Entity Types inferred by the source data and can define advanced Entity Types to create more complex models (e.g., 'Chassis'). Those advanced types are not related to a specific data attribute as they resemble a higher order construct, either by combining multiple Entity Types or by specifying an Entity Type in more detail. We require that each Entity Type has a concept assigned to it as well as each concept to be attached to at least one Entity Type for enabling a consistent user and conceptual view on the modeled data. To relate two inferred or created Entity Types, the user can also define *Entity Type Relations* between those two (e.g., CustomCar *has* CarId). An exemplary result of a semantic model for the data model shown in Fig. 1(a) can be seen in Fig. 1(b).

4.2   Knowledge Graph

Upon submission of a final semantic model in ESKAPE, the information contained in the model are added to the *knowledge graph*, which is maintained and supervised by the platform. The knowledge graph cannot be modified directly by users and resembles an auto-generated collection of semantic knowledge from all available semantic models. It consists of three types of core components:

- *Entity Concepts*: Entity Concepts are labeled semantic descriptors which cover and uniquely identify a generic or specific mental concept (e.g., *car*).
- *Entity Concept Relations*: Entity Concepts are connected to other Entity Concepts via Entity Concept Relations which describe invariant connections (e.g., car *has* production date).
- *Relation Concepts*: Relation Concepts are descriptors for kinds of relations, such as *isA*, *producedIn* or *consistsOf* which might be used by Entity Concept Relations and Entity Type Relations. Each Relation Concept contains a name and a set of properties defining the mathematical classes of relations it belongs to like transitive, reflexive, symmetric, etc.

With the availability of an evolving knowledge graph, the creation of a semantic model for a data source is simplified as elements from the knowledge graph can be directly re-used in the annotation process. Re-using elements from the knowledge graph's vocabulary saves the user from defining common concepts and relations multiple times. In addition, it creates links between elements of the newly created semantic model and the knowledge graph. Figure 2 shows an exemplary knowledge graph with three semantic models linked to it. Vertical links indicate Entity Concepts which have been used in Entity Types in the semantic models. Originally re-used Entity Concepts from the knowledge graph, which have been used to built the semantic models, are bold.

Using information already stored in the knowledge graph allows ESKAPE to make suggestions during the modeling process as well as using reasoning based on the previously available knowledge in the knowledge graph, e.g., noticing if a relation is probably used in the wrong direction. However, the user's semantic

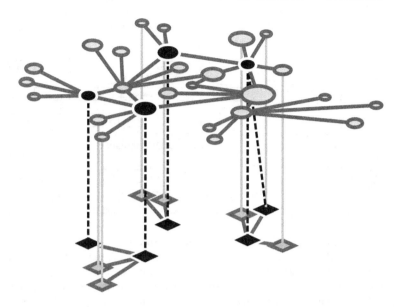

Fig. 2. Knowledge graph (circles) with linked semantic models (squares). Dashed links between concepts of the knowledge graph and types of the semantic model show originally re-used concepts from the knowledge graph.

model can be valid even without elements of the knowledge graph and will not be modified by the system automatically.

The only exception to that is the auto-detection of *probable concepts* during the analysis phase, e.g., concepts which might be a good candidate for a given data attribute. Based on learned patterns for certain concepts, ESKAPE can provide an initial semantic model using only previously known concepts and relations. The system learns about those patterns when data is integrated for a specific semantic model. If concepts of the knowledge graph have been re-used, example values and/or patterns for certain concepts can be identified and analyzed to build patterns.

4.3   Evolving the Knowledge Graph

Upon submission of a new semantic model to ESKAPE, the knowledge graph adapts the newly gathered information by merging a model's concepts and relations into the graph. Re-used elements act as anchor points for matching elements. Previously unknown concepts are matched using heuristics and external resources to detect, e.g., synonyms. If no suitable match is possible, a new Entity Concept is created from the custom concepts and added to the graph using the provided relations to previously known elements of the graph. The same procedure is applied for newly encountered relations, which are converted to Relation Concepts. Entity Concept Relations are deducted from Entity Type Relations

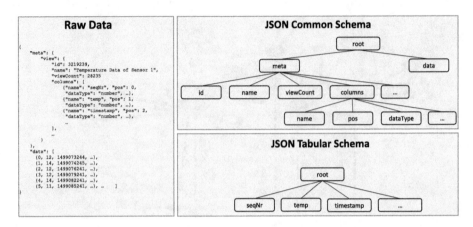

Fig. 3. The example illustrates a raw JSON data snippet and two possible recognized schemas depending on the used format. For the JSON Common Schema, the result schema includes all available JSON properties. In contrast, the result of the schema analysis for the JSON Tabular Schema solely focuses on the important labels for the data and removes the additional meta data which will not be part of the semantic model.

(which implicitly relate Entity Concepts) which occur multiple times, further extending the knowledge graph.

5   Functionality and Implementation

To enable users sharing their data with others, we differentiate between providing data sources to ESKAPE and retrieving and processing the provided data sources from it. The former process includes an initial analysis of the data source (cf. Sect. 5.1), the semantic modeling of the available information (cf. Sect. 5.2) as well as the data integration (cf. Sect. 5.3). After ESKAPE integrated the data, users can start different kinds of processes on the data including data enrichment, transformation or analysis (cf. Sect. 5.4) as well as querying and obtaining data (cf. Sect. 5.5).

5.1   Schema Analysis

When a user connects a data source to ESKAPE for the first time, it collects an example data set and analyzes it to identify a potential schema. Afterwards, ESKAPE presents and visualizes the result to the user to simplify the semantic model creation in the next step. However, gathering and analyzing the raw data schema leads to different challenges.

For analyzing the schema, a sufficient amount of data points is required since a single data point may not contain all data attributes. For batch data, no problems occur as it is a self-contained data set that does not change over time and ESKAPE can just consider each data point to obtain a comprehensive schema. For streaming data, it is unknown if the number of collected data sets and their included data points cover the complete schema. Thus, our current solution observes streaming data for a certain amount of time (configurable by the user). Based on all collected data sets and data points, ESKAPE proposes a comprehensive schema to the user. If the users recognize any flaws, they can refine the schema, e.g., by manually adding missing data attributes that were not covered.

When analyzing the schema, we are not interested in a superficial schema for the data format, but in the relationship between multiple data points and especially the structure of a data point (more precisely, in the relationship between the different data attributes of a single data point). While a data set is available in a fixed format (e.g., CSV or JSON) and follows a pre-defined standard, (e.g., RFC 4180[4] for CSV), the data may be represented in different ways. Depending on the way these formats are used, the semantic of the data attributes and data values inside these formats changes. This might imply whether the data attribute or value is significant or not. The result of this step is a homogeneous representation of all data obtained from this data source.

Thus, the schema analysis does not include all the format specific details, but rather the semantics implied when using the format. Figure 3 depicts an example for data available in the JSON Tabular format recommended by W3C[5] for publishing tabular data as JSON. This schema describes data representing a table consisting of multiple rows and columns, just like a CSV file. However, performing a schema analysis for this data snippet by just considering common JSON format results in the schema shown in the upper left. The resulting schema contains data attributes that do not generate any actual semantic value (e.g., *meta, id, name, viewCount*) and which should not be integrated as data later. Thus, the user should not define a semantic model for those parts of the data.

Hence, when considering the same data using the JSON Tabular format, the schema analysis automatically strips all the data attributes that should not be covered by the semantic model as shown on the bottom right. However, those meta data provide important information that can be used for improving the automatic generation of semantic models, such as proposing Entity Concepts and Relations (cf. Sect. 4).

To increase usability for the semantic model creation (cf. Sect. 4), we examined multiple data sets from different Open Data platforms and partner companies and identified patterns allowing to strip all the unnecessary data attributes. Further identified subtypes of formats are:

- **CSV:** covers all data sets where the values for data attributes are separated by a delimiter.
- **JSON Lines:** covers all data sets where the single data points are in-line separated JSON format.

---

[4] https://www.ietf.org/rfc/rfc4180.txt.

[5] https://www.w3.org/TR/tabular-metadata/.

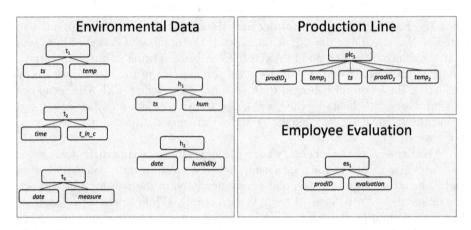

Fig. 4. Different results of the schema analysis for the data described in the motivating example (cf. Sect. 2). The different used labels per data attribute and the missing semantics lead to confusions for a user that is not familiar with these data sets.

- **JSON Tabular:** used for tabular data represented as JSON. This format is recommended by the W3C for tabular data that contain additional meta data.
- **JSON Common:** used for all JSON data sets that are not covered by any other subtype (e.g., JSON Tabular).
- **XML Row:** tabular data represented in XML format.
- **XML Common:** used for all XML data sets that are not covered by any other subtype (e.g., XML Row).
- **XLSX:** covers all Excel-based files that contain data described in tables.
- **Apache Avro:** binary data format for all data that were serialized using the Apache Avro framework.

Since maintaining a schema analysis per subtype leads to high implementation overhead, especially when changing constraints for the analysis, we decide to translate each identified subtype into a platform internal intermediate format (JSON) and perform the schema analysis based on this format. For each subtype, we define an appropriate conversion process which translates the subtype into an equivalent representation in JSON. This allows us to define all schema analysis constraints based on a single format. If constraints for a single subtype change, we just have to adopt the corresponding translation process.

Figure 4 illustrates the result of the schema analysis for the data sources described in the motivating example (cf. Sect. 2). The figure shows the different labels that were present within the data sources.

5.2 Modeling Information of Data Sources

After recognizing a schema for a data source, we present the result to the user who wants to add the data to ESKAPE. Based on the determined schema, the

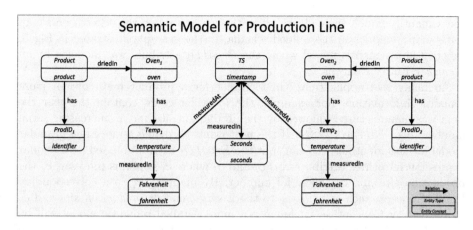

Fig. 5. One possible semantic model for the data set of the production line. For overview reasons, Entity Types and Entity Concepts are combined. Node top: Entity Type (e.g., $ProdID_1$), node bottom: Entity Concept (e.g., *identifier*).

user creates the semantic model using the buildings blocks described in Sect. 4. Following the schema analysis of the production line (cf. Fig. 4), the user creates the semantic model illustrated in Fig. 5. For each data attribute, the user creates an Entity Type ($ProdID_1$, $Temp_1$, Ts, $ProdID_2$, $Temp_2$). For instance, the user creates the Entity Type $ProdID_1$ referencing the Entity Concept *identifier* and assigns it to the attribute $ProdID_1$. In addition, the user defines more complex Entity Types which are not mapped to data attributes directly (e.g., $Oven_1$ referencing the Entity Concept *oven*). By adding more complex Entity Types and defining Relations between them, the user completes the view of the available information and precisely defines characteristic such as the unit of the temperature and the timestamp.

Our approach comes with three novelties allowing to continuously evolve the knowledge graph over time. First, we allow the user to use concepts that are not available in the knowledge graph yet. If the user wants to define an Entity Type, but there is no appropriate Entity Concept available, the user will add this concept to the knowledge graph. To ensure that the concept is added at an appropriate position in the graph, we use external data sources, such as semantic networks (cf. Sect. 4).

The second novelty is that the knowledge graph learns from the semantic model how entities are related to each other. Let us assume that the Entity Concept *oven* was never connected to the Entity Concept *temperature* before the new semantic model was added to ESKAPE. After defining the semantic model and adding it to ESKAPE, the knowledge graph learns that the entity *oven* can also have a *temperature*, which can then be proposed to users which intend to add other data sets containing information about ovens.

Another novelty of our approach is that the data attributes recognized by the schema analysis are not mapped in a one-to-one fashion onto entities of the semantic model. Instead, we allow the user to refine the schema and map the semantic model on the refined schema. In the example illustrated in Fig. 5, we created a semantic model where the $ProdID_1$ attribute was modeled by an *identifier* Entity Concept.

In many real applications, an identifier for a product may contain more semantic information. For example, the identifier could contain the year the item was manufactured followed by the production site and an increasing serial number (e.g., *2017-ps1-4184*). If the user wants to define a more fine granular model for this identifier, she can split the $ProdID_1$ attribute based on a regular expression into three attributes c_1, c_2 and c_3 where c_1 contains the year, c_2 the production site and c_3 the serial number. By mapping c_1 to a corresponding Entity Concept, such as *year*, c_2 to the Entity Concept *production site* and c_3 to the Entity Concept *serial number* a more detailed semantic model will be created. Besides the splitting of a data attribute into multiple ones, we also offer to split lists into multiple lists or single data attributes by using regular expressions and defining repetition cycles. We call fields that are split into multiple ones *composite fields*. Furthermore, we also allow users to remove unwanted data attributes from the schema for integration and publication.

This example shows that the definition of a semantic model is not unique. The user just provides her view of the data even if there might exist more precise semantic models. That means, there will always be a more exhaustive model for the data source. The users define their subjective view to the data which they regard sufficient to understand the observed data points.

5.3   Data Integration

After the user has created the semantic model for a data source, ESKAPE is capable of integrating the data. The main goals of the data integration are:

– Syntactic homogenization
– Splitting composites into single attributes
– Linking specified entity types to the data attributes of the refined schema
– Marking data values that could not be integrated
– Data point homogenization
– Discarding invalid data points

The syntactic homogenization ensures that all data types (text, number, boolean and binary values) are integrated into a unified representation, which simplifies the later handling of the data. For instance, boolean values that occur as *0*, *1* or *F*, *T* are mapped to *False* and *True* and numbers are represented by the American notation. We do not perform a semantic homogenization (e.g., convert all temperatures to a uniform unit such as $°F$) since this information is encoded in the semantic model anyway and can thus be used during processing.

In addition, the integration splits composite fields into multiple data attributes and links all the data attributes to their semantic Entity Type. If, for instance, the splitting or the syntactic homogenization fails (e.g., data type is marked as number but the data value was a string), then the whole data value is marked as invalid. We still store those values, since we do not want to lose information and we do not know the scenario where the data might be used. We only discard complete data points if errors occur that do not allow us to link the data to its semantic type (e.g., parsing errors).

After integrating data sets (batch or streaming), ESKAPE stores the integrated data in our platform specific *Semantic Linked Tree Format*. This format offers the user information about the semantic type, the data value, the syntactic type and if the value was successfully integrated, enabling true semantic interoperability on the data sets. To additionally enable real-time analysis, streaming data are directly forwarded to the next processing step.

5.4   Data Enrichment, Transformation and Analysis

After the successful integration of data sources, the data can be used for data enrichment, transformation and analysis. This step enables the user to perform *heavyweight processing* based on one or more selected data sources, their semantic models and additionally parameters defined by the user. The result is a new data source with its semantic model that again is persisted and can be published on ESKAPE. We explicitly separated this step from the data integration since we define the data integration as a general task while the data processing mostly depends on the use case and the kind of information that is requested.

In processing, we differentiate between *Data Enrichment, Data Transformation* and *Data Analysis*. We define Data Enrichment as the process of extracting and persisting new information by using data attributes that are already available in the data. For instance, a data source could contain a data attribute that holds a description text. A typical data enrichment step would be to determine the language of the description, so we explicitly generate information that is implicitly available and persist it. The information that was added will not change over time and is use case independent.

Opposed to this, *Data Transformation* is the process of transforming or converting data attributes based on knowledge that is offered by the semantic model. Following the motivating example, converting the temperature data attribute $temp_1$ from $^\circ F$ into $^\circ C$ is a data transformation step. Compared to *Data Enrichment, Data Transformation* changes the data depending on the user's use case. Finally, *Data Analysis* involves all tasks that extract new information by, e.g., aggregating multiple data points or joining data sources based on defined criteria. An example is the calculation of the average temperature of the three environmental temperature sensors followed by joining the result with the production line data based on the timestamp.

After the processing of the data was successful, ESKAPE persists the newly created data source on the storage and adds the corresponding semantic model to the knowledge graph. In case of streaming data, the data is directly forwarded to satisfy possible real-time constraints.

5.5   Querying Data and Information

Aside from data integration and processing, users can also extract data from ESKAPE. Since users have different requirements based on the use case, we offer multiple approaches for the data extraction. The user can either trigger the extraction for an available data source on a semantic level by selecting a data source and the semantic parts of it (e.g., selecting the concrete requested entity types) or by actively querying for specific data sets using SQL, which, however, requires the user to consider the semantic model.

For the semantic extraction, we offer the user to perform additional filters and limits on the data and to select a specific data format, such as XML or JSON, in which the data should be extracted. The user can also decide if she wants to receive the data as a stream or as a file. When requesting batch data, a file can be downloaded or emitted as stream for a certain amount of time enabling the simulation of a data stream. For streaming data, the data is sent directly to the user. We do not offer to stream the data, which is persisted by ESKAPE, into a file since it is identical to extracting historic streaming data for a defined time span.

The SQL extraction, on the other hand, addresses expert users who want to perform more sophisticated data extraction by using familiar SQL syntax on a semantic level.

6   Architecture, Technologies and User Interface

To ensure scalability, reliability and performance of ESKAPE, we are using technologies that allow us to distribute tasks among a cluster. Figure 6 provides an overview of the developed architecture and used technologies. The architecture of ESKAPE consists of a data processing back-end (Processing Core), a presentation layer for user interaction and several interfaces using popular data exchange formats. These interfaces allow to feed data into ESKAPE as well as to retrieve queried and streaming data from it.

To store the aforementioned knowledge graph and the semantic models of each data source, we are using the graph database Neo4J[6]. Data storage is handled in a Hadoop[7] cluster. This cluster contains the raw acquired data from gathered data sources and streams as well as the integrated data sets, including enriched data sets and additional data from third-party enhancements, such as text language analysis. The cluster storage concept enables ESKAPE to redundantly store all acquired data sets in the SLTFormat (cf. Sect. 5.3).

ESKAPE performs data processing (cf. Sect. 5) in the Processing Core, which makes up for the largest part of the platform. The Processing Core uses Apache Storm[8] to process data sets in user-defined chains expressed as directed acyclic graphs (DAGs) called *topologies*. A topology consists of spouts, which represent

---

[6] https://neo4j.com/.

[7] http://hadoop.apache.org/.

[8] http://storm.apache.org/.

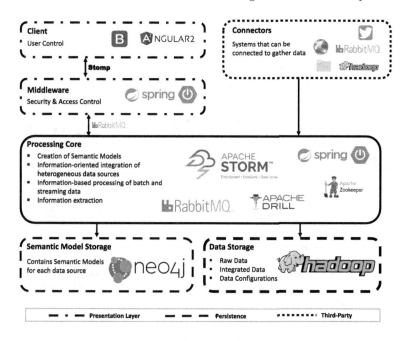

Fig. 6. Overview about the architecture and technologies of ESKAPE.

various data sources, and bolts, which contain processing logic inside the process chain. Combining different spouts and bolts yield a DAG running in the Storm cluster. Figure 7 shows an example of a simple stream processing chain based on our motivating example. Each topology is encapsulated in its own instance but may be distributed over several machines, called nodes. Those topologies are used to form the processing part of any heavy-weight operation as defined in Sect. 5.4. For each specific processing task, a new Storm topology is created by ESKAPE, besides the always present ones handling data integration and export. By design, topologies run infinitely, waiting for new data to be emitted from the spouts, until ESKAPE shuts them down. This is kept to process streaming data, however, on the batch integration part, a topology will be shut down when the source does not yield any more data. Continuous domain-specific data enrichment tasks on integrated data sets defined by users also tend to run indefinitely.

We implemented the communication between the core platform and topologies running on the Storm cluster using RabbitMQ[9], which is an AMQP implementation. It enables the core platform to receive messages, such as errors or status updates from all the topologies.

Data extraction from the Processing Core is done in three ways. To distinguish between those ways, one has to differentiate data extraction and data enrichment. Topologies which are used to enrich data contain a bolt to write the generated data back into the Hadoop storage. In the case of stream pro-

---

[9] https://www.rabbitmq.com/.

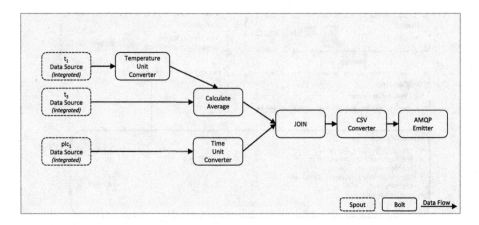

Fig. 7. Example Storm processing chain for combining three heterogeneous data sets from our motivating example. The pipeline calculates the average temperature for two measurements of the sensors t_1 and t_2 that were recorded in a defined time window. Afterwards, the result is joined based on the timestamp with the plc_1 data set, converted to CSV and emitted via AMQP.

cessing, the processed data is stored by default and also forwarded to the aforementioned interfaces providing data exchange technologies. ESKAPE currently supports stream-, HTTP- and file export, where in the case of stream processing RabbitMQ is used.

To allow direct data extraction from the Hadoop cluster (cf. Sect. 5.5), Apache Drill[10] provides an interface to execute a limited set of SQL queries on the integrated data. ESKAPE can then quickly export the queried data from the Hadoop cluster. If any kind of processing is needed, which extends simple operations such as joining and filtering data sets, a new Storm topology is needed to handle those requests.

Beside the processing core, the presentation layer enables users to interact with ESKAPE. The presentation layer consists of a middleware for handling user management, security and access control as well as a web client. The web user interface is based on the common web technologies Bootstrap and Angular. It enables users to add and manage data sources and define semantic models. It also offers users to define the processing steps, e.g., enrichment on selected data sources and query data including visualization of the returned results.

Figure 8 shows parts of ESKAPE's user interface. Figure 8(a) illustrates the identified data model after the schema analysis whereas Fig. 8(b) presents the created semantic model after the modeling process. Users create the semantic model by dragging the desired entity concepts and entity concept relations on the identified data attributes. In addition, they can add more entity types to create a more detailed semantic model.

---

[10] http://drill.apache.org/.

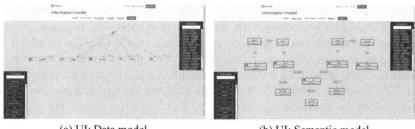

(a) UI: Data model   (b) UI: Semantic model

Fig. 8. ESKAPE's user interface showing the identified data model after the schema analysis for the ps_1 data on the left and the created semantic model after the modeling process on the right. If concepts are missing when creating the semantic model, the user can add them.

7 Evaluation

We run ESKAPE in a closed enterprise environment, but due to compliance issues of enterprises, we evaluated our approach in an open real-world scenario. For evaluating ESKAPE, we set up a hackathon in which teams had to develop mobile applications based on the data that were published on the platform. The goal of this challenge was to get feedback from users to identify potential design flaws as well as missing features.

To provide a sufficient amount of data originating from real-world sources, we teamed up with the local city administration as well as local companies coming from different domains. For example, the local bus company provided real-time data about the delay of approaching buses for each stop via an HTTP API and the regular schedule of each stop as CSV files. Other parties published real-time weather data, the locations of available WiFi spots or the number of free slots at bicycle rental stations. Altogether, nine different parties provided 64 different data sets from which 15 were streaming data and 49 were batch data. All streaming data was published via HTTP APIs, which were polled in different time intervals (min = 1 min, max = 1 day) whereas the batch data sets were published as files (42) or via an HTTP API (7) without any update frequency (one-time polling). From the 64 data sets, 20 were published as CSV, 11 as XLSX (Excel), 2 as JSON Common, 2 as JSON Tabular, 10 as JSON Lines, 3 as PDF, 2 as SHP, 4 as WMS and 10 as XML Common. Since our prototype did not support all formats at the moment, we converted XLSX files manually to CSV and we did not import PDF (not a M2M format) as well as SHP and WMS resulting in 55 available data sets for the hackathon.

For developing applications, 92 persons grouped into 25 teams participated in the hackathon. Each submitted application used at least three different data sets for developing their application. We discovered that mobile applications developed for the Android operating system requested the data as JSON whereas the submitted iOS applications requested the data as XML. Each team that requested data sets with the semantic concept *Temperature* requested a conversion before extracting the data from ESKAPE. Based on interviews with the teams that used such features, we confirmed that the conversion for units as well as formats simplifies the development process for several OS/platforms. However, we also received feedback about missing features, such as an HTTP API (no team liked AMQP extraction) and merging of data directly on ESKAPE (not enabled during the hackathon). Two teams also requested to integrate own processing logic into the processing pipelines, which will be addressed by the analytic layer in the future.

8 Conclusion and Future Work

In this extended paper, we presented the information processing platform ESKAPE for the (Industrial) Internet of Things which facilitates enterprises or other potential operators to deal with various kinds of heterogeneous data sources on different levels by using semantics. We explained the application of ESKAPE based on a motivating example of a simplified manufacturing process.

Compared to current solutions, which either define and apply standards or which use semantics based on static ontologies defined by domain experts, ESKAPE enables, e.g., enterprises to build their own knowledge graph by gathering the knowledge provided by employees who add new data sources to ESKAPE. For each added data source, the employee defines a semantic model using an intuitive drag and drop interface. Based on all these semantic models, ESKAPE's knowledge graph learns how concepts and relations are interrelated and which data is represented by a certain concept.

To simplify the creation of semantic models and to guide the user through the creation process, ESKAPE performs a detailed schema analysis. Instead of considering the raw data schema, this analysis focuses on important parts of a data schema. We therefore identified more fine granular subtypes of data formats that go beyond a standard schema description for formats like JSON or XML. Based on the results of the schema analysis, the user defines a semantic model for the added data source. Here, the user can also refine the data schema allowing the definition of more fine granular semantic models. By combining the results of the schema analysis and the raw data, ESKAPE finally integrates the data, links the defined semantic concepts and the data attributes and stores everything in a unified format.

Integrated data sources can then be used for further processing, such as enriching or transforming data sources, define analytic pipelines or joining and aggregating data from different sources. Finally, the processed data sources can be extracted using different approaches such as querying information using SQL or downloading and subscribing processed data. The latter especially enables the subscription of real-time data sources on a semantic level, enabling true semantics for the (Industrial) Internet of Things.

Future development will focus on improving the general user experience to allow ESKAPE to be usable by a wider range of people. A general improvement of the semantic modeling view (GUI) and the associated access to the knowledge graph should also be available in the near future. This will allow users to create their semantic models with less effort than today, especially when the auto detection of concepts will be in service. This feature will automatically annotate data attributes with likely entity concepts and will provide suggestions on replacements or meta concepts which the user can choose from. To achieve this, the information in the knowledge graph will be used as well as suggestions provided by external sources and machine learning approaches.

To further improve the expansion of the knowledge graph, we are planning to introduce more sophisticated strategies and algorithms for considering the knowledge available by external sources. Here, we especially focus on learning how concepts are represented by their underlying data. In addition, we are planning to introduce strategies for permanently checking the graph for consistency and validity.

Furthermore, we will offer users in the near future the possibility to define their own integration and processing pipelines. By adding self-implemented tasks to the platform, users will be more flexible and can help to extend ESKAPE. In addition, more sophisticated data extraction from the platform is planned to be available utilizing a semantic search for data sources using a sophisticated query language operating on the knowledge graph. Later on, this should also be able to handle natural language to allow non-technical users to fully use the platform as well.

References

1. Internet of Things Global Standards Initiative: Overview of the Internet of Things (2012). http://www.itu.int/ITU-T/recommendations/rec.aspx?rec=y.2060
2. Pomp, A., Paulus, A., Jeschke, S., Meisen, T.: Eskape: Information platform for enabling semantic data processing. In: Proceedings of the 19th International Conference on Enterprise Information Systems. ICEIS, INSTICC, vol. 2, pp. 644–655. ScitePress (2017)
3. Ahamed, B., Ramkumar, T.: Data integration-challenges, techniques and future directions: a comprehensive study. Indian J. Sci. Technol. **9**, 1–9 (2016)
4. Garcia-Molina, H., Hammer, J., Ireland, K., Papakonstantinou, Y., Ullman, J., Widom, J.: Integrating and accessing heterogeneous information sources in TSIM-MIS. In: Proceedings of the AAAI Symposium on Information Gathering, vol. 3, pp. 61–64 (1995)
5. Taheriyan, M., Knoblock, C.A., Szekely, P., Ambite, J.L.: A scalable approach to learn semantic models of structured sources. In: Proceedings of the 8th IEEE International Conference on Semantic Computing (ICSC 2014) (2014)
6. Knoblock, C.A., Szekely, P.: Exploiting semantics for big data integration. AI Mag. **36**, 25–38 (2015)
7. Taheriyan, M., Knoblock, C.A., Szekely, P., Ambite, J.L.: Learning the semantics of structured data sources. Web Semant. Sci. Serv. Agents World Wide Web **37**, 152–169 (2016)
8. Gupta, S., Szekely, P., Knoblock, C.A., Goel, A., Taheriyan, M., Muslea, M.: Karma: a system for mapping structured sources into the semantic web. In: Simperl, E., Norton, B., Mladenic, D., Della Valle, E., Fundulaki, I., Passant, A., Troncy, R. (eds.) ESWC 2012. LNCS, vol. 7540, pp. 430–434. Springer, Heidelberg (2015). https://doi.org/10.1007/978-3-662-46641-4_40

9. Meisen, T., Meisen, P., Schilberg, D., Jeschke, S.: Adaptive information integration: bridging the semantic gap between numerical simulations. In: Zhang, R., Zhang, J., Zhang, Z., Filipe, J., Cordeiro, J. (eds.) ICEIS 2011. LNBIP, vol. 102, pp. 51–65. Springer, Heidelberg (2012). https://doi.org/10.1007/978-3-642-29958-2_4

10. Hepp, M., Bachlechner, D., Siorpaes, K.: Ontowiki: community-driven ontology engineering and ontology usage based on wikis. In: Proceedings of the 2006 International Symposium on Wikis, WikiSym 2006, pp. 143–144. ACM, New York (2006)

11. Xiao, L., Ruan, C., Yang, Zhang, J., Hu, J.: Domain ontology learning enhanced by optimized relation instance in DBpedia. In: Proceedings of the Tenth International Conference on Language Resources and Evaluation (LREC 2016), Paris, France, ELRA (2016)

12. He, S., Zou, X., Xiao, L., Hu, J.: Construction of diachronic ontologies from people's daily of fifty years. In: Proceedings of the Ninth International Conference on Language Resources and Evaluation (LREC 2014), Reykjavik, Iceland, ELRA (2014)

13. Cochez, M., Decker, S., Prud'hommeaux, E.: Knowledge representation on the web revisited: the case for prototypes. In: Groth, P., Simperl, E., Gray, A., Sabou, M., Krötzsch, M., Lecue, F., Flöck, F., Gil, Y. (eds.) ISWC 2016. LNCS, vol. 9981, pp. 151–166. Springer, Cham (2016). https://doi.org/10.1007/978-3-319-46523-4_10

14. Palavalli, A., Karri, D., Pasupuleti, S.: Semantic internet of things. In: 2016 IEEE Tenth International Conference on Semantic Computing (ICSC), pp. 91–95 (2016)

15. Dorsch, L.: How to bridge the interoperability gap in a smart city (2016). http://blog.bosch-si.com/categories/projects/2016/12/bridge-interoperability-gap-smart-city-big-iot/

16. Cambridge Semantics: Anzo Smart Data Discovery (2016). http://www.cambridge semantics.com/

17. ALTILIA Group: Mantra Platform (2015). http://www.altiliagroup.com/platform/mantra-platform/

18. Kinor: kSpheres (2015). http://www.kinor.com/

Human-Computer Interaction

Behavioral Economics Through the Lens of Persuasion Context Analysis: A Review of Contributions in Leading Information Systems Journals

Michael Oduor[✉] and Harri Oinas-Kukkonen

Oulu Advanced Research on Services and Information Systems,
Faculty of Information Technology and Electrical Engineering,
University of Oulu, P.O. Box 8000, 90014 Oulu, Finland
{michael.oduor,harri.oinas-kukkonen}@oulu.fi

Abstract. As technology becomes an integral part of our everyday lives, the more crucial it is to investigate how it can be further harnessed to improve individuals' wellbeing. This involves studying users' interactions with technology, how different design techniques influence their use, and the factors that might lead to sub-optimal use of technology. Such factors include decision biases which are mostly investigated in behavioral economics research. Behavioral economics counters the arguments of standard economic theories and combines psychological theories and economics to study how people actually behave as opposed to how they should behave as rational beings. Thus, this review provides an overview of behavioral economics research in the major IS journals. The aim is to determine the extent of such research within the IS field. An electronic search of the major IS journals was conducted over an 8-year period and the findings were categorized according to the use, user and technology contexts of the persuasive systems design model. The findings reveal the need for awareness of how various behavioral economic principles (or decision biases) influence decision making in technology-mediated settings and the development of strategies to mitigate their influence.

Keywords: Behavioral economics · Persuasive systems design
Information systems

1 Introduction

Increase in the complexity of the environment and its speed of change requires more knowledge about the mechanisms and processes that the economic man uses to relate himself to that environment and to achieve his goals. Normal economic thought is not concerned with individual behavior because it is based on the assumption that the economic actor is rational. Hence, it is thought to be possible to make strong predictions about human behavior without actual observation, and that competition implies only the rational survive [1].

© Springer International Publishing AG, part of Springer Nature 2018
S. Hammoudi et al. (Eds.): ICEIS 2017, LNBIP 321, pp. 453–472, 2018.
https://doi.org/10.1007/978-3-319-93375-7_21

In psychological theories, the motive to act stems from drives and action terminates when the drive has been fulfilled. Furthermore, the conditions for satisfying a drive are not fixed, but may be defined by an aspiration level that itself adjusts upward or downward on the basis of experience and the prevailing situation. What is natural and intuitive in a given situation is not the same for everyone; different cultural experiences favor different intuitions about the meaning of situations, and new behaviors become intuitive as skills are acquired [1, 2]. Behavioral economics examines the factors that influence the consumption of goods and services. It combines psychology and economics to investigate individuals' actual behavior as opposed to how they are expected to behave when considered as perfectly rational beings seeking to maximize their utility [3, 4]. Behavioral economics, organized around experimental findings, counters the arguments of the standard economic theories. It focuses on examining individuals' choices, the motives underlying these choices and increased understanding of a subject's situation at the time of making a choice [5].

The present study, an extension of Oduor and Oinas-Kukkonen [6], analyzes behavioral economics in information systems (IS) research by using persuasion context analysis as described in [7]. Applying behavioral economics methods to study the use and adoption of digital interventions can be a potential avenue for better understanding users' requirements, how users interact with technology and the factors that hinder their adoption and/or use. Many technologies fail, not because of technical problems, but rather due to a lack of careful consideration of human and other nontechnology issues in the design and implementation process of these systems [8]. Therefore, behavioral economics with its focus on how people actually behave [9], has enormous potential to inform and complement IS research. Especially, as there has not been extensive research in the IS field utilizing behavioral economics methods [10].

The objective of the present review is, thus, to examine by applying context analysis [7], behavioral economics research in IS that address how cognitive limitations influence decision-making. The rest of the paper is structured as follows: the following section introduces the theoretical background on behavioral economics and persuasive systems design. Section 3 describes the review process. Section 4 presents the results. The paper then concludes with a discussion summarizing the results, addressing the limitations, directions for future work and the conclusions.

2 Theoretical Background

2.1 Persuasive Systems Design

A large body of research shows that computer-based interventions can be efficacious [11, 12]. Computers can operate as tools, mediums and social actors that increase capability, provide interactive experiences and create relationships [13]. With their increased interactive and persuasive capabilities, computers can, therefore, be used to motivate positive behavior change in users. Especially, as the aim of persuasive communication is to voluntarily change users' attitude and/or behavior without deception or coercion [7, 13].

Behavior modification is important for any type of intervention because behavior is central to the development, prevention and management of preventable diseases and health conditions. Its role in maintaining a healthy lifestyle is substantial and encompasses prevention of diseases, enhancement of health and overall quality of life [14, 15]. Therefore, designing systems to change people's behavior requires a thorough understanding of the problem domain and the underpinning theories and strategies of persuasive systems design [8]. Research by Kelders et al. [16] showed the importance of persuasive systems design in influencing users adherence to web-based interventions.

Oinas-Kukkonen and Harjumaa [7], developed the persuasive systems design (PSD) model; a conceptual framework used to analyze, design, and evaluate the persuasion context and the related techniques for implementing persuasive systems [7, 8]. The model helps to organize thoughts about a persuasive system by mapping persuasive design techniques to the system's requirements [17]. The model outlines the development process of persuasive systems and consists of postulates, persuasion context analysis and the design or evaluation of persuasive systems [7].

The postulates consider the psychological principles behind the design of persuasive systems and they address the neutrality of technology, ease of use of digital interventions, the making and enforcing of commitments, the effective routes to persuasion, the sequential nature of persuasion, the ideal moments for initiating persuasive features and openness of persuasive systems [7].

These postulates are based on social psychological theories on attitude change, influence, learning among others that help explain the factors that influence human behavior in different situations. Such theories include the theory of planned behavior (TPB) [18]. The elaboration likelihood model (ELM) [19] that describes direct and indirect routes to information processing and persuasion. Bandura's [20] social learning and social cognitive theories which describe how people learn new behaviors by studying, observing and then replicating the actions of others. Lastly, Cialdini's [21] studies on influence which show how formulating requests in certain ways can trigger automatic compliance response from individuals.

Persuasion context is where system designers select the behavioral changes that they would like to encourage and the strategies for doing so [17]. A common definition of context was provided by Dey [22], who stated: *"Context is any information that can be used to characterize the situation of an entity. An entity is a person, place, or object that is considered relevant to the interaction between a user and an application, including the user and applications themselves"*. The persuasion context analysis comprises of recognizing the intent, the event, and the strategy [7]. The intent consists of the reasons for developing a system and how the system will be used. Plus, determining who the actual persuader is. The event consists of the context of use, the user, and the technology. The use context refers to characteristics of the problem domain in question, the user context refers to characteristics of the individual user, and the technology context refers to the technical specifications of a system. Finally, the strategy addresses the analysis of persuasive message being conveyed and the route, whether direct or indirect or both [19], that is used to influence the user [7].

2.2 Behavioral Economics

Only in economics is the individual modelled as a logical and consistent set of preferences and certain cognitive facilities [23]. A standard argument in economics and management has been that consumers want to maximize utility and if presented with clear and simple choices that they understand, they will do so. Whereas to behavioral scientists, the real world is so complicated that the theory of utility maximization has little relevance to real choices and even in relatively simple situations, people do not behave in the way predicted by direct application of the utility theory [1]. This stream of research formed the beginnings of behavioral decision research. The 1970s heralded the emergence of behavioral economics with studies investigating judgment under uncertainty, individual's inherent biases and how this influenced their decision making under conditions of risk [24, 25]. Behavioral economics research has shown how, through requests, judgments can be developed and are, consequently, often influenced by factors in the environment in which the judgements are developed [24, 25]. Additionally, research has also demonstrated how differences in formulating a choice of problems cause significant changes in people's preferences. Angner and Loewenstein [26], for example, provide more details on the emergence of behavioral economics.

Behavioral economics acknowledges that human beings: (1) have limited information processing capabilities which lead to their adoption of rules of thumb to aid in problem-solving. (2) do not always make choices that are in their best long-term interest, due to a lack of self-control, and (3) are not always motivated by pure self-interest and their actions can also include altruistic and spiteful behaviors [4]. These traits are explained by psychological principles that consider people's actions in different situations. For example, one's estimates and judgments being biased towards some initial anchor value, preference of the status quo as opposed to changing routines, interventions that help participants pre-commit to future healthy behavior and so forth [4, 27].

Most behavioral economics research mainly focuses on interventions for healthier living [3, 28], strategies for reducing unwanted behaviors [29], environmental sustainability and improving governmental and institutional policies that benefit society [30, 31]. Prince et al. [3], for example, in their review aiming to improve assessment instruments for reducing alcohol involvement among college students, propose improvements to better understand the role of protective behavioral strategies in reducing the use of alcohol and explain why there have been inconsistencies in previous studies and what can be done to enhance future studies. Michie and Williams [28] examine the factors that lead to work-related psychological ill health in different professions and propose solutions that mainly involving training and increased involvement in decision making.

Siva [30] applies lessons in behavioral economics to study how people respond to incentives and the reasons why pay-for-performance programs are flawed and how they can be improved. Lunze and Paasche-Orlow [29] discuss the pros and cons and ethical concerns on the use of incentives in behavioral economics research to promote healthy behavior and reduce health costs. The need for safeguards in the programs to monitor their associated risks and promote fairness in offering the incentives for them to be beneficial is acknowledged [29]. Avineri [31], links travel behavior to psychological theories and shows how individuals' choices in different contexts deviate from the predictions of rational behavior.

In more technical interventions, [32], for example, apply behavioral economics in developing sensor-based interactive systems to initiate change in residential energy consumption. They argue that even though the success of most of the sensor-based power meters and other related residential monitoring devices depends on users responding to the data they generate with appropriate changes in their consumption behavior, most of these devices have not been developed with the end-user in mind. Therefore, a more human-centered process that integrates behavioral insights to determine the effectiveness of sensor-based interactive systems and of interfaces based on cognitive, social and affective frames is proposed [32]. King et al. [33], in their short study on influencing health behavior with games, state that games are designed to influence people's behavior. Whether knowingly or not, insights from behavioral economics which has recognized numerous ways to counter sub-optimal decision making are related to many of the gamification features used to enhance engagement. For example, conditional rewards (points, prizes etc.) are dependent on frequently playing the games and there is a risk of loss if play is not resumed after an interruption or a break from playing (explained by loss aversion) [33].

3 Review Process

A structured literature review is a focused approach to identify relevant articles. Structured reviews provide means to identify and categorize most of the existing literature concerned with the research question(s). The reasons for conducting a review include, but are not limited to summarizing the existing facts about use of technology, creating a firm foundation for advancing knowledge, identifying gaps in current works in order to suggest areas for further analysis, and providing a framework for suitably positioning research interests [34, 35]. Our objective, is to use the PSD model [7] to examine behavioral economics research in IS. This is to enable the identification of any recurring and emerging themes and discern relevant techniques for apply the principles to improve the development of IS.

Kitchenham [35] describes a set of review guidelines a modification of which was used to define the problem, analyze the data and come up with concise conclusions. The steps include: (1) identification of the need for a literature review, (2) formulation of research questions, (3) searching for relevant articles, (4) selecting the primary studies, (5) assessing and recording the quality of included studies, (6) extracting data from the included studies, and (7) synthesizing data and summarizing the results [35].

3.1 Need for a Review of Behavioral Economics in Information Systems

Webster and Watson [34] state that a literature review process stems from (1) scholars need to report progress in a particular stream of research and, (2) from those who have completed a review prior to starting a project and have developed theoretical models from the review. Additionally, there are reviews on mature topics and those on emerging issues that would benefit from exposure to new theoretical foundations ([34].

Behavioral economics has lately been gaining attention in the IS field, and although still relatively new, it has been widely studied in finance and economics, health and wellness and sustainability-related topics.

Vassileva's [36], analysis of the growth of web-based social applications and the approaches they use to motivate user participation, states that most of the applications employ simple techniques that have succeeded in engaging users. Such techniques, though, only ensure that users follow instructions, but are unable to guide the social system(s) towards a desirable overall behavior. For this reason, several future trends related to the application of social psychology, behavioral economics and their convergence with other disciplines are suggested in the design of reward and incentive mechanisms for particular types of communities, persuasive and other user-adaptive systems [36]. Goes [10], further explains how behavioral economic principles can be combined with IS research in areas such as recommendation systems, collective intelligence and gamification. Goes [10], also suggests online social environments as unexplored directions in which the two can travel together.

As the role of information technology (IT) increases in people's daily decision making and experiences, new opportunities to assist people in making self-beneficial choices have arisen [37]. This is important as most studies on persuasive systems and success factors for IS, rarely address the context and the effect it can have on a user's decision-making. Success is also usually measured in terms of changing users' behaviors in ways predetermined by developers or providers of the system [38]. In persuasive systems, information is usually provided for people to better understand certain problems. However, Lee et al.'s [37] research has noted potential disadvantages of using information-centric approaches to motivate behavior change. The emphasis on information-centric approaches rests on the assumption that people are rational actors striving to enhance their utility based on what they know and the available information [38–40]. But people have been shown to be predictably irrational with such behavior being "neither random nor senseless. They are systematic, and since they are repeated again and again, predictable" [9].

Therefore, the is a great need for more understanding about the influence factors on individuals' choices in the context of persuasive and information systems in general [41]. Furthermore, there is an opportunity to combine behavioral economics and IS as these two disciplines both seek to enhance the understanding of the user. Both disciplines emphasize how context and cognitive effects influence decision making–the IS field is mostly about information processing for decision-making [10]. Subsequently, we have examined articles from the top IS journals and have not found a comprehensive review that addresses the research question below regarding the integration of behavioral economic in IS to study the use of technology.

The main research question that guided our review is:

RQ: How can behavioral economics enhance understanding of users and their interactions with information systems?

3.2   Electronic Search

For the present review, a literature search was conducted for the years between 2006 and 2014. The keywords used were behavior(u)ral economics, prospect theory, mental accounting, cognitive bias, choice architecture, nudge, persuasive systems design, persuasive technology, behavior(u)r change, attitudes, and persuasion. This was to ensure that we got a wide variety of articles applying both behavioral economics principles and persuasive techniques.

The above keywords were used to search the metadata related to the top eight IS journals MIS Quarterly, European Journal of Information Systems (EJIS), Information Systems Journal (ISJ), Information Systems Research (ISRe), Journal of Information Technology (JIT), Journal of Management Information Systems (JMIS), Journal of Strategic Information Systems (JSIS), Journal of the Association for Information Systems (JAIS) in Wiley, INFORMS PubsOnline, EBSCOhost, ScienceDirect, Taylor Francis Online, and ProQuest ABI/INFORM.

The search string resulted in 919 articles and after excluding editorials, book reviews and commentaries, and reviewing the abstracts, 63 articles remained, these were further reduced to 15 (Fig. 1) based on the eligibility criteria below.

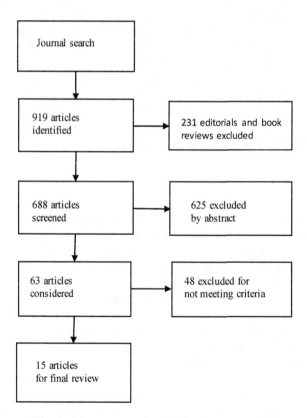

Fig. 1. Literature search and selection process [6].

3.3 Eligibility Criteria

The following inclusion and exclusion criteria were used to select articles for answering our research question. Studies were selected if they, (a) had behavioral economics in the abstract, (b) were full research papers (and not editorials, commentaries), (c) described the persuasive/cognitive stimuli applied, (d) examined the relation between the stimuli and (behavioral) outcome. Articles were excluded, if they: (a) only discussed system implementation; (b) were about either general systems development or systems development to meet organizational/individual needs without a behavioral outcome; (c) only discussed systems benefit(s) to an organization; or (d) were purely on research methodology or systematic reviews not related to the topic.

3.4 Data Extraction and Synthesis

The first author coded all the articles using predefined criteria (devised by both authors) and any uncertainty about a particular article was discussed prior to its inclusion or exclusion based on the eligibility criteria.

Each selected publication was examined for the following elements: Objective of the study and corresponding research question(s); study environment and participants; themes emerging from the study; and, the relevance of the studies' results. This was then followed by a synthesis of the emergent themes and categorization of the articles according to the judgement and decision-making principle studied. To integrate the search results and our conceptualization of behavioral economic studies in IS we applied context analysis as defined by Oinas-Kukkonen and Harjumaa [7] to categorize the articles (Tables 1, 2 and 3) according to the objectives, the cognitive principle(s) studied, the user and technology contexts, and contribution of the study. This categorization is suitable because of the level of abstraction it enables in identifying the effects of the measures used in the reviewed studies.

4 Results

Analysis of these papers was based on the aforementioned objectives and the results reveal a difference in coverage of behavioral economics in the major IS journals. A majority of the articles were from EJIS and ISRe. All but one of the journals produced original results with data, and only two of the articles [42, 43] from ISRe contained behavioral economics as a keyword in their abstracts. While the following analysis is based on the 15 articles that we have labeled as investigating a behavioral economic principle, it is important to note that certain articles [42–51] more strongly considered decision-making and the valuation of presented choices than others (e.g., [52, 53]). Lankron and Luft [54] and Legoux et al. [48] did not include a technical artifact, but analyzed the effects of the behavioral economics principles on investment decisions.

Some articles, while explicitly focused on investigating users' valuation of choices, additionally considered goals and other design issues that may not fall under the realm of behavioral economics. Accordingly, our classification of each of these articles as investigating a behavioral economics principle should be considered with this caution in mind. As further noted in [31], it is important to acknowledge that behavioral economics is not a homogenous field that can straightforwardly be distinguished and there are opposing views as to what counts as behavioral economics. A related discussion can be found in a Q & A with R. Thaler on what it really means to be a "Nudge" [55]. The characteristics of the studies based on the principle examined are presented in Tables 1, 2 and 3.

Analysis of the persuasion context requires an understanding of the occurrences in information processing as the context assists in learning and better understanding user behavior.

4.1   The Intent

Intentions arise from the creators of interactive systems, those who give access to the system, and the individuals using the systems [7, 13]. In the case of the current study, the intent is derived from both the objectives of the reviewed studies. Most of the studies were either Web or mobile-based and involved either experimentation [42, 45] or surveys [44, 46] Six of the studies investigated various aspects of user behavior in online stores. Chiu, Wang et al. [47] apply prospect theory [25] to investigate decision-making under risk and the reasons people continue to buy from an online store. Prospect theory is used to explain decision-making from a value maximizing perspective and how, when one makes a decision, s/he does not take into account the decision's effect on their consumption [47].

Blanco et al. [52] develop mock-ups based on e-commerce practices to investigate the ideal combination of presenting visual and textual information and how various combinations of these affect consumers' cognitive states. Wu and Gaytán [45] discuss a risk-based conceptual framework to help understand the role of seller reviews and product prices on buyers' willingness to pay. Wu and Gaytan [45] apply the buyers' risk perspective to explain conflicting results in previous studies. Adomavicius et al. [43] investigate the influence of recommender systems' ratings on consumers' preferences at the time of consumption by exploring anchoring, timing, system reliability and granularity issues that are related to their impact. Goh and Bockstedt [42] apply behavioral economic principles to examine seller's design choices and how these choices influence consumer behavior. Goh and Bockstedt [42] investigate how framing a multipart pricing scheme can influence consumers perceived value of customizable bundle offers.

Lankton and Luft [54] apply behavioral economic theories to study IT investment valuation and predict the differences between intuitive judgment and real options prescriptions. Ma et al.'s [56] study integrate gambling theory, the availability heuristic, and repeated behavior into a framework that explains online gambling over time. The rest of the studies examine various aspects of human behavior in different environments. These include, the role price and context play in mobile service adoption and the use of location based services in relation to cognitive processes [49, 50] and the role consumer trust in online merchants plays in purchase decisions [57].

4.2   The Event

The event consists of the use, user and technology contexts. These are the issues arising from the problem domain, individual user differences that influence their information processing, and the technologies or strategies employed in computer-human and computer-mediated interaction [7]. The use context was not discussed in detail in any of the studies. This is because they primarily investigated some aspect of user behavior related to valuation of choices and/or how presented information influences users' decisions without going into details on the actual use of the systems or features investigated. As noted in [8] a high abstraction level in systems descriptions makes it difficult to understand the actual interactions taking place through the system and the extent to which any potential outcome(s) are due to the system's intent.

The hypotheses and research design of the reviewed studies provided a clearer picture of the impact and the relevance of the research results. For example, Chiu et al.'s [47] study extended prospect theory and provided additional theoretical reasons why consumers become more risk-seeking or less risk averse in different circumstances. One of the practical implications of their study was a suggestion of how online sellers could attract potential buyers and turn infrequent buyers into frequent ones. This was through delivering guarantees on issues such as security, inspiring customers and keepings customers informed [47].

The studies analyzed were about, (1) Web-based environments which analyzed how users value presented options and make decisions (e.g. [43, 47, 52, 56]), (2) ways of improving user interactions [48], (3) mobile-based services [50], and (4) the decision to use certain systems [49]. Although these studies reported the technology context, as their focus was mostly on studying users' actions, they did not provide a detailed description of the technologies investigated.

4.3   The Strategy

Analysis of the strategy involves identifying the underlying theories applied in the research to examine user behavior, the medium used, and the persuasive techniques that are applied. It is only in the Angst and Agarwal [51] study that there is a mention of the route. The study, investigating privacy concerns, is explicitly about direct and indirect routes to persuasion. The study highlights under which circumstances either or both routes could be used. Unlike previous studies on the ELM where the main focus was on attitude/opinion change, Angst and Agarwal [51] investigated a choice process that could be cognitively taxing.

The message refers to the techniques used to influence or alter users' actions and, in our study, these are the principles (see Tables 1, 2 and 3) applied in or emerging from the reviewed articles. These included: (1) How people make different decisions based on the same set of options depending on how the options are presented (framing) (e.g., [42]). (2) Relying only on information that confirms an initial assumption while discounting opposing information (confirmation bias) (e.g., [46]). (3) How people tend to experience (possible) losses more than (possible) gains, making them risk averse when options are described in terms of gain and risk seeking when they are describe in terms of losses (e.g., [47]). (4) When decision makers begin with an initial value and adjust it

Table 1. Characteristics of studies related to framing [6].

Study	Objective	User context	Technology context	Contribution
[52]	Examine how product presentation affects recall and perceptions on quality (framing)	Graduate and Postgraduate students (N = 108)	Mock websites based on e-commerce practices	Confirmation of the importance of product presentation online, consumer characteristics, and how people perceive and process product information
[42]	Measure whether framing influences consumers' value of customizable bundle offers from online stores (framing)	Behavioral experiments (N = 454)	Online streaming and movie rentals	The technology-driven context of a purchase decision can have significant effects on consumer choices and economic outcomes
[44]	Investigate whether prominence of privacy information influences incorporation of privacy considerations in online purchasing decisions. (Salience, framing, and priming)	Online responses to a concerns survey and a shopping experiment (N = 238)	Shopping search engine interface, Privacy Finder	New insight into consumers' valuations of personal data and evidence that privacy information affects online shopping decision-making
[51]	Investigate whether persuasion can change attitudes and opt-in intentions toward electronic health records even in the presence of significant privacy concerns. (Persuasion and framing)	Participants (attendees to a conference and online survey) (N = 366)	Electronic health records	Even when people have high concerns for privacy, their attitudes can be positively altered with appropriate message framing. These results as well as other theoretical and practical implications are discussed

as needed in order to arrive at decisions. This leads to bias as any decisions made are skewed toward the initial anchor (anchoring) (e.g., [43]). and (5) Applying persuasive principles (explained by information processing-related theories such as the ELM in investigating choice decisions) in Websites to influence users [51].

Table 2. Characteristics of studies related to risk aversion and confirmation bias [6].

Study	Objective	User context	Technology context	Contribution
[47]	Understand reasons for customers' repeat purchase in online retail stores and the effect perceived risk would have. (Risk aversion)	Customers of Yahoo! Kimo in Taiwan (N = 782)	Yahoo! Kimo - online shopping store	The moderating effect of perceived risk, extends prospect theory and provides additional theoretical reasons for risk seeking and risk averseness in consumers
[45]	Apply the buyers' risk perspective to reconcile and explain seemingly conflicting results in previous literature. (Risk aversion and framing)	Undergraduates students (N = 78)	eBay auction site (empirical study)	Customers have different risk preferences and thus select sellers with different risk profiles to match their risk appetites
[46]	Explore the extent investors are subject to confirmation bias in the context of exposure to information on message boards. (Confirmation bias)	Investors in South Korea (N = 502)	Stock message boards	Confirmation bias plays a great role in investment decision-making in numerous contexts e.g., project management
[48]	Investigate how experts' investment decisions are affected by cognitive biases. (Confirmation bias)	Participants from a financial institution (N = 100)	N/A	Prediction accuracy about market reactions to IT investments was hampered by confirmation biases

Table 3. Characteristics of studies related to other biases [6].

Study	Objective	User context	Technology context	Contribution
[43]	Explore how preferences at the time of consumption are influenced by recommender systems' predictions. (Anchoring effects)	Participants N = 216	Recommender systems	Viewers' preference ratings are malleable and can be significantly influenced by the recommendation received
[57]	Explain the role of potential users' trust in creating intention to revisit a website (Bounded Rationality)	Undergraduate MIS students (N = 314)	Website which redirects to 12 other websites	Consumer trust in e-vendor plays a major role in purchasing services

(continued)

Table 3. (*continued*)

Study	Objective	User context	Technology context	Contribution
[50]	Explore the influence of reference situations and reference pricing on mobile service users' behavior. (Reference pricing and Reference situation)	Students and employees in the public sector (N = 74)	Mobile services	The benefits of approaching mobile service adoption and use research in a holistic manner and the importance of considering the reference point on mobile usage behaviors
[56]	Develop and test a model of online gambling that simultaneously takes into account cumulative and recent outcomes, and prior use. (Availability heuristic)	Actual users of a gambling website (N = 22, 304)	Bwin Interactive Entertainment (Internet gambling)	Integration of gambling theory, the availability heuristic, and repeated behavior into a framework that explains online gambling over time
[49]	Investigate how cognitive processes influence information retrieval behavior in location-based services (LBS). (Cognitive processes in decision-making)	Young smartphone users (N = 66)	Location-based services in the German telecommunications market	A new conceptual framework to investigate LBS use and complement existing models in user behavior research
[53]	Extend the effort-accuracy perspective of understanding users' recommendation agents' (RA) acceptance by including trade-off difficulty. (Cognitive aspects of decision-making)	Students at a large North American university (N = 100)	Web-based re-commendation agents	Explains role of preference elicitation methods (PEMs) in assisting users with trade-off difficulty across different decision contexts Perceived effort compared to previous research no longer has a significant influence in the loss condition

(*continued*)

Table 3. (*continued*)

Study	Objective	User context	Technology context	Contribution
[54]	Provide theory-based predictions of how consistency between intuition and normative real options value varies for deferral and growth investment options under differing conditions. (Intuitive judgment and regret theory)	MBA students from a Midwestern public university in the United States (N = 70)	N/A	Techniques by which organizations can limit unwanted effects of regret and overaggressive competitive behavior

5   Discussion

5.1   Contribution and Implications

Psychology offers integrative concepts and mid-level generalizations, which gain credibility from their ability to explain apparently different phenomenon in diverse domains. The impressions that become accessible in any particular situation are mainly determined by the actual properties of the objects of judgment. The judgments that people express, their actions, and their mistakes depend on the monitoring and corrective function of their reasoning, as well as on the impressions and tendencies generated by their intuitions [2]. Decision making is also subject to individuals' bounded rationality, which means their inherent limitations can lead to inaccuracies in evaluating information or estimating the value of a product's utility [1].

Therefore, as users' decision making is not always systematic, it is important to understand how this decision making is affected by different contextual issues. Behavioral economic principles can aid in developing techniques for improved presentation, delivery, and organization of information or services. Behavioral economics also helps to highlight how people are influenced by those they are in close contact with, how their actions and reactions are subconsciously shaped by different heuristics and biases, the need to commit to and be consistent with their promises, and the willingness to reciprocate to acts of kindness experienced from others [2, 4, 9, 27, 58].

The influence of behavior and environment are closely integrated. Some environmental influences are possible through their influence on behaviors (e.g., well-maintained walking and cycling paths in neighborhoods). To further complicate issues, some environmental influences are themselves made up of the behaviors of others (e.g., community norms) [14]. Thus, behavioral economics has the potential to be an important enabler of sustained behavior change, especially in technology-mediated environments. Behavioral economics also offers means to obtain a deeper understanding of how IS and the design of IS can influence users. Primarily because effective persuasive communication is also about correctly interpreting the purpose of an IS. Although, the persuasive communication can be disrupted by the noise sometimes created by people's cognitive biases [9].

As such, the educational approach and the assumption that people are rational actors prevalent in persuasive systems design and most IS-related theories such as the technology acceptance model (TAM) [40] is not the most effective approach to driving (behavior) change [37–39]. Rather, an understanding of people's inherent biases and examining how cues provided by technology influence users' online behavior can be more useful for stimulating change (e.g., [42, 43, 50, 56]). Especially, as results from Adomavicius et al. [43] showed that biased output from recommender systems can significantly influence users' preferences and their ratings of products.

The review asked one main question: "How can behavioral economics enhance understanding of users and their interactions with information systems?" We turned to the major IS journals to examine behavioral studies specific to IS. We were particularly interested in studies investigating behavioral economic principles related to valuation options, how cognitive stimuli influence users' choices, and how these can be explained by use, user and technology contexts outlined in the PSD model [7].

In terms of coverage, the findings suggest that: (1) There is great potential in enhan-cing research in the two fields especially as one considers how cognitive, emotional and environmental factors affect decision-making and the other is about information processing for decision making. This means that designers of intervention programs (whether digital or not) should focus not only on the desired (behavior) change, but also antecedent variables such as saliency, individual beliefs, awareness and so forth [59]. (2) There has been an increase in studies integrating behavioral economic principles in IS in recent years, the majority of which have focused on online retail stores [44, 45, 47] and recommender systems [42, 43, 53]. (3) Considering some of the limitations of IS, behavioral economics in its grounding on cognitive theories as presented in the reviewed studies, offers possibilities to enhance both the design and implementation of IS (including persuasive systems). Considering persuasive design strategies such as goal-setting, self-monitoring, social support have been identified as effective tools in weight management programs [8, 15], integrating these with tech-niques that encourage users to make self-beneficial decisions can enhance self-directed change through digital interventions [12]. Finally, (4) the decision-making process is not consistent. The study of behavioral economics principles in most cases should involve field and/or experimental tests to determine the underlying theoretical rela-tionships in order to enhance the clarity of the studies and the principles applied.

The main IS journals were chosen because major contributions in a particular field are likely to be in the leading journals [34] and studies accepted in these forums are usually concise and comprehensive, detailing all the relevant aspects of the particular phenomena studied. Although, Webster and Watson [34] also suggest searching for articles elsewhere after the initial search in the major journals. In this study, our search was limited to only the basket of eight journals. We concentrated on the major journals because our interest was in studies that primarily focus on IS-related phenomena and the interactions between users and technology. Thus, we excluded from our review behavioral economics studies from other sources such as psychology and marketing (some of these were covered in the background section). Consequently, this review can be considered as the first attempt to synthesize behavioral economics studies from the major IS journals. Furthermore, our study has also considered the limitations of IS (including persuasive systems) research and suggested ways behavioral economics, with its focus on judgment and decision making, can help to mitigate these limitations.

In behavioral economics, the behavioral assumption is that people often act irrationally [9] and not all their actions can be reasonable and/or according to predefined criteria. The prevailing environment and one's emotional state affects decision-making. The persuasive element in behavioral economics lies in the presentation of choices in a way that leverages people's decision making processes; thus, encouraging them to make self-beneficial choices [37]. Consequently, behavioral economics can be used to investigate the scope of decisions regarding finances, health, and dietary choices that people make [9]. Although, it is important that decision biases are controlled given their strengths, especially in technology-mediated settings. If left uncontrolled, they trigger non-rational decision making, which results in sub-optimal decisions that can proactively be exploited to influence users [41]. Therefore, the psychological barriers that prevent desired behaviors should be understood and this knowledge incorporated into systems design. Control over (or even moderating), decision biases in digital interventions enables the enforcement of their persuasive power on a cognitive level [41].

5.2 Limitations and Future Research

For this study, we concentrated only on articles from the major IS journals and as comprehensive as these are, they do represent all the relevant information. Especially, when one considers that behavioral economics is a relatively new field and IS research is itself multidisciplinary so there may be other relevant studies outside the IS realm. For example, examining articles from well-known conferences, other disciplines journals and workshop proceedings. Secondly, our search was meant to produce a large number of articles for review. Therefore, including additional terms in the search string (e.g., known behavioral economic principles (cognitive biases prevalent in judgement and decision-making) such as framing, priming, incentives etc.) and searching in other online libraries and databases, a highly-focused pool of potential articles for review could have been found. Lastly, in persuasion context analysis since the articles did not prescribe to persuasive systems design, interpretive categorization, which may be subjective, was used.

In Sect. 4, we positioned the behavioral economics literature based on context analysis and although there were similarities in approach, the studies analyzed were not about behavior change, which is a key concept in persuasive systems research. Inherently, they do involve change, but the coverage of the change and description of the changing element was limited. Additionally, most of the studies did not consider different user characteristics and how these differences may lead to varied responses to stimuli. Although, the studies on framing (see Table 1) did investigate how framing product or service offerings differently can influences users' choices. Through this, it could be possible to learn the effects of behavioral economic principles on different users if demographic variables that differentiates them are collected. Therefore, in context analysis, as viewed from the persuasive systems domain, not all factors could be applied which has implications for the findings.

Further research to extend the scope of the search is planned and specifically to investigate how behavioral economic principles can be integrated with the principles of persuasive systems design. As most of the studies included in the current review focused on examining the effects of the different stimuli on users' preferences and/or choices, a potential avenue for future research would be to implement some of the principles in actual systems and study the subsequent effects. For example, how varying the allocation and rate of rewards combined with social support in incentive schemes could influence goal achievement. Or how gamification which integrate behavioral elements could be used in systems to encourage collaboration. Furthermore, the reviewed studies were diverse in nature. Some focused on behavioral IS and others on the economics of IS. Future research could examine whether there are any differences in the adoption of behavioral economics between different disciplines and the resulting implications.

6 Conclusions

In IS research, behavioral economics is a field that has been gaining in popularity in the last decade. This study documents a review of behavioral economics in the major IS journals. The purpose was to present an overview of the field and how it has been used to investigate IS-related phenomena in order to identify relevant research issues or unaddressed areas. We analyzed 15 relevant articles from an initial total of 919 articles found in scientific libraries. Based on this, the articles were classified according to context analysis (use, user and technology contexts) and the major behavioral economics principle investigated that were also defined. The main findings from the review are the importance of understanding how various contextual factors influence decision making (especially in IS use context), the factors which lead to sub-optimal decisions and influence how information is processed. The review, although not comprehensive, presented techniques for designing around user biases and represents a step toward understanding decision making in technology-mediated settings and may support the development of (persuasive) strategies that can help mitigate the various biases.

References

1. Simon, H.A.: Theories of decision-making in economics and behavioral science. Am. Econ. Rev. **49**(3), 253–283 (1959)
2. Kahneman, D.: Maps of bounded rationality: psychology for behavioral economics. Am. Econ. Rev. **93**(5), 1449–1475 (2003)
3. Prince, M.A., Carey, K.B., Maisto, S.A.: Protective behavioral strategies for reducing alcohol involvement: a review of the methodological issues. Addict. Behav. **38**(7), 2343–2351 (2013)
4. Thorgeirsson, T., Kawachi, I.: Behavioral economics: merging psychology and economics for lifestyle interventions. Am. J. Prev. Med. **44**(2), 185–189 (2013)
5. Pesendorfer, W.: Behavioral economics comes of age: a review essay on 'advances in behavioral economics'. J. Econ. Lit. **44**(3), 712–721 (2006)

6. Oduor, M., Oinas-kukkonen, H.: Behavioral economics in information systems research: a persuasion context analysis. In: Proceedings of the 19th International Conference on Enterprise Information Systems - Volume 3, ICEIS, pp. 17–28 (2017)
7. Oinas-Kukkonen, H., Harjumaa, M.: Persuasive systems design: key issues, process model, and system features. Commun. Assoc. Inf. Syst. 24(1), 28 (2009)
8. Lehto, T., Oinas-Kukkonen, H.: Persuasive features in web-based alcohol and smoking interventions: a systematic review of the literature. J. Med. Internet Res. 13(3), e46 (2011)
9. Ariely, D.: Predictably Irrational: The Hidden Forces That Shape Our Decisions. HarperCollins Publication, Etats-Unis, New York (2008)
10. Goes, P.B.: Editor's comments: information systems research and behavioral economics. MIS Q. 37(3), iii–viii (2013)
11. Lenert, L., Munoz, R.F., Perez, J.E., Bansod, A.: Automated e-mail messaging as a tool for improving quit rates in an internet smoking cessation intervention. J. Am. Med. Inform. Assoc. 11(4), 235–240 (2004)
12. Lustria, M.L.A., Cortese, J., Noar, S.M., Glueckauf, R.L.: Computer-tailored health interventions delivered over the web: review and analysis of key components. Patient Educ. Couns. 74(2), 156–173 (2009)
13. Fogg, B.J.: Persuasive Technology: Using Computers to Change What We Think and Do. Morgan Kaufmann, Amsterdam (2003)
14. Fjeldsoe, B.S., Marshall, A.L., Miller, Y.D.: Behavior change interventions delivered by mobile telephone short-message service. Am. J. Prev. Med. 36(2), 165–173 (2009)
15. Toscos, T., Faber, A., An, S., Gandhi, M.P.: Chick clique: persuasive technology to motivate teenage girls to exercise. In: CHI 2006 Extended Abstracts on Human Factors in Computing Systems, pp. 1873–1878 (2006)
16. Kelders, S.M., Kok, R.N., Ossebaard, H.C., Van Gemert-Pijnen, J.E.W.C.: Persuasive system design does matter: a systematic review of adherence to web-based interventions. J. Med. Internet Res. 14(6), e152 (2012)
17. Purpura, S., Schwanda, V., Williams, K., Stubler, W., Sengers, P.: Fit4Life: The design of a persuasive technology promoting healthy behavior and ideal weight. In: Proceedings of the SIGCHI Conference on Human Factors in Computing Systems, pp. 423–432 (2011)
18. Ajzen, I.: Theories of cognitive self-regulationthe theory of planned behavior. Organ. Behav. Hum. Decis. Process. 50(2), 179–211 (1991)
19. Petty, R.E., Cacioppo, J.T.: The elaboration likelihood model of persuasion. In: Petty, R.E., Cacioppo, J.T. (eds.) Communication and Persuasion. Springer Series in Social Psychology. Springer, New York, NY (1986). https://doi.org/10.1007/978-1-4612-4964-1_1
20. Bandura, A.: Social Cognitive Theory. In: Annals of Child Development, R Vasta, vol. 6, pp. 1–60 (1989)
21. Cialdini, R.: Descriptive social norms as underappreciated sources of social control. Psychometrika 72(2), 263–268 (2007)
22. Dey, A.K.: Understanding and using context. Pers. Ubiquitous Comput. 5(1), 4–7 (2001)
23. Schelling, T.C.: Self-command in practice, in policy, and in a theory of rational choice. Am. Econ. Rev. 74(2), 1–11 (1984)
24. Tversky, A., Kahneman, D.: Judgment under uncertainty: heuristics and biases. Science 185 (4157), 1124–1131 (1974)
25. Kahneman, D., Tversky, A.: Prospect theory: an analysis of decision under risk. Econometrica 47(2), 263–291 (1979)
26. Angner, E., Loewenstein, G.: Behavioral economics. In: Mäk, U. (ed.) Handbook of the Philosophy of Science: Philosophy of Economic, pp. 641–690. Elsevier, Amsterdam (2012)
27. Thaler, R.H., Sunstein, C.R.: Nudge. Yale University Press, New Haven, Connecticut (2008)

28. Michie, S., Williams, S.: Reducing work related psychological ill health and sickness absence: a systematic literature review. Occup. Environ. Med. **60**(1), 3–9 (2003)
29. Lunze, K., Paasche-Orlow, M.K.: Financial incentives for healthy behavior: ethical safeguards for behavioral economics. Am. J. Prev. Med. **44**(6), 659–665 (2013)
30. Siva, I.: Using the lessons of behavioral economics to design more effective pay-for-performance programs. Am. J. Manag. Care **16**(7), 497–503 (2010)
31. Avineri, E.: On the use and potential of behavioural economics from the perspective of transport and climate change. J. Transp. Geogr. **24**, 512–521 (2012)
32. Crowley, M., Heitz, A., Matta, A., Mori, K., Banerjee, B.: Behavioral science-informed technology interventions for change in residential energy consumption. In: CHI 2011 Extended Abstracts on Human Factors in Computing Systems, pp. 2209–2214 (2011)
33. King, D., Greaves, F., Exeter, C., Darzi, A.: 'Gamification': Influencing health behaviours with games. J. R. Soc. Med. **106**(3), 76–78 (2013)
34. Webster, J., Watson, R.T.: Analyzing the past to prepare for the future: writing a literature review. MIS Q. **26**(2), xiii–xxiii (2002)
35. Kitchenham, B.: Procedures for performing systematic reviews. Keele, UK, Keele Univ. vol. 33(2004), p. 1–26 (2004)
36. Vassileva, J.: Motivating participation in social computing applications: a user modeling perspective. User Model. User-adapt. Interact. **22**(1–2), 177–201 (2012)
37. Lee, M.K., Kiesler, S., Forlizzi, J.: Mining behavioral economics to design persuasive technology for healthy choices. In: Proceedings of the SIGCHI Conference on Human Factors in Computing Systems, pp. 325–334 (2011)
38. Brynjarsdottir, H., Håkansson, M., Pierce, J., Baumer, E., DiSalvo, C., Sengers, P.: Sustainably unpersuaded: how persuasion narrows our vision of sustainability. In: Proceedings of the SIGCHI Conference on Human Factors in Computing Systems, pp. 947–956 (2012)
39. DiSalvo, C., Sengers, P., Brynjarsdóttir, H.: Mapping the landscape of sustainable HCI. In: Proceedings of the SIGCHI Conference on Human Factors in Computing Systems, pp. 1975–1984 (2010)
40. Markus, M.L., Tanis, C.: The enterprise systems experience-from adoption to success. Fram. domains IT Res. Glimpsing Futur. through past, vol. 173, pp. 173–207 (2000)
41. Teppan, E.C., Zanker, M.: Decision biases in recommender systems. J. Internet Commer. **14**(2), 255–275 (2015)
42. Goh, K.H., Bockstedt, J.C.: The framing effects of multipart pricing on consumer purchasing behavior of customized information good bundles. Inf. Syst. Res. **24**(2), 334–351 (2012)
43. Adomavicius, G., Bockstedt, J.C., Curley, S.P., Zhang, J.: Do recommender systems manipulate consumer preferences? a study of anchoring effects. Inf. Syst. Res. **24**(4), 956–975 (2013)
44. Tsai, J.Y., Egelman, S., Cranor, L., Acquisti, A.: The effect of online privacy information on purchasing behavior: an experimental study. Inf. Syst. Res. **22**(2), 254–268 (2010)
45. Wu, J., Gaytán, E.A.A.: The role of online seller reviews and product price on buyers' willingness-to-pay: a risk perspective. Eur. J. Inf. Syst. **22**(4), 416–433 (2013)
46. Park, J., Konana, P., Gu, B., Kumar, A., Raghunathan, R.: Information valuation and confirmation bias in virtual communities: evidence from stock message boards. Inf. Syst. Res. **24**(4), 1050–1067 (2013)
47. Chiu, C.-M., Wang, E.T.G., Fang, Y.-H., Huang, H.-Y.: Understanding customers' repeat purchase intentions in B2C e-commerce: the roles of utilitarian value, hedonic value and perceived risk. Inf. Syst. J. **24**(1), 85–114 (2014)
48. Legoux, R., Leger, P.-M., Robert, J., Boyer, M.: Confirmation biases in the financial analysis of IT investments. J. Assoc. Inf. Syst. **15**(1), 33 (2014)

49. Constantiou, I.D., Lehrer, C., Hess, T.: Changing information retrieval behaviours: an empirical investigation of users' cognitive processes in the choice of location-based services. Eur J Inf Syst 23(5), 513–528 (2014)
50. Blechar, J., Constantiou, I.D., Damsgaard, J.: Exploring the influence of reference situations and reference pricing on mobile service user behaviour. Eur. J. Inf. Syst. 15(3), 285–291 (2006)
51. Angst, C.M., Agarwal, R.: Adoption of electronic health records in the presence of privacy concerns: the elaboration likelihood model and individual persuasion. MIS Q. 33(2), 339–370 (2009)
52. Blanco, C.F., Sarasa, R.G., Sanclemente, C.O.: Effects of visual and textual information in online product presentations: looking for the best combination in website design. Eur. J. Inf. Syst. 19(6), 668–686 (2010)
53. Lee, Y.E., Benbasat, I.: Research note—the influence of trade-off difficulty caused by preference elicitation methods on user acceptance of recommendation agents acrossloss and gain conditions. Inf. Syst. Res. 22(4), 867–884 (2011)
54. Lankton, N., Luft, J.: Uncertainty and industry structure effects on managerial intuition about information technology real options. J. Manag. Inf. Syst. 25(2), 203–240 (2008)
55. Ubel, P.A.: Q & A with R. thaler on what it really means to be a nudge | psychology today (2015). https://www.psychologytoday.com/blog/critical-decisions/201503/q-r-thaler-what-it-really-means-be-nudge. Accessed 15 Apr 2015
56. Ma, X., Kim, S.H., Kim, S.S.: Online gambling behavior: the impacts of cumulative outcomes, recent outcomes, and prior use. Inf. Syst. Res. 25(3), 511–527 (2014)
57. Liu, B.Q., Goodhue, D.L.: Two worlds of trust for potential e-commerce users: humans as cognitive misers. Inf. Syst. Res. 23(4), 1246–1262 (2012)
58. Dolan, P., Hallsworth, M., Halpern, D., King, D., Vlaev, I.: Mindplace: influencing behaviour through public policy (2010)
59. Spittaels, H., De Bourdeaudhuij, I., Brug, J., Vandelanotte, C.: Effectiveness of an online computer-tailored physical activity intervention in a real-life setting. Health Educ. Res. 22 (3), 385–396 (2007)

YouMake: A Low-Cost, Easy for Prototyping, Didactic and Generic Platform for Acquisition and Conditioning of Biomedical Signals

Diego Assis Siqueira Gois$^{(\boxtimes)}$, João Paulo Andrade Lima$^{(\boxtimes)}$,
Marco Túlio Chella$^{(\boxtimes)}$, and Methanias Colaço Rodrigues Júnior$^{(\boxtimes)}$

Computer Department, Sergipe Federal University, Av. Marechal Rondon,
S/n - Jardim Rosa Elze, São Cristóvão, SE, Brazil
diego.se.ita@gmail.com, dm.joaopaulo@gmail.com,
chella@ufs.br, mjrse@hotmail.com

Abstract. The study of cell's electric properties began in XVIII. Since then, several researchers began focusing their studies in biomedical signals, making way for today's high precision tech for modern medicine - expensive and used by professionals. However, the emergence of new research fields in the biomedical area like monitoring of human activity and human-machine interface brought the need to measure biomedical signals through simple devices. In addition, there was a growth of the DIY (do-it-yourself) movement boosted by prototyping platforms such as Arduino and Raspberry-pi. Thus, came the idea to develop YouMake, a platform for acquisition and conditioning of biomedical signals with low cost, easy prototyping, versatile and generic. For evaluation purposes, an experimental study using YouMake with twenty-four participants was divided into two groups, the first consisting of participants with experience in the study area and the latter represented by participants with no experience. Usability and prototyping time of the participants in the prototyping of the platform for the acquisition of three biological signals were evaluated: ECG, EMG and EOG. The usability and prototyping time of the participants were evaluated in the prototyping of the platform for the acquisition of three biological signals: ECG, EMG and EOG. The results were statistically analyzed using the Shapiro-Wilk, Levene and t-student tests, which showed that there was no statistical difference between the means of the experienced and the non-experienced groups. This showed that both experienced and inexperienced people in the study have the same ease in using the platform.

Keywords: Acquisition · Conditioning · ECG · EMG · EOG · Usability

1 Introduction

The Luigi Galvani (1737–1798), Alessandro Volta (1755–1832), George Ohm (1787–1854) and Michael Faraday (1791–1867) researches provided the basis for the understanding of electrical potential and electric current, which helped studies of the electrical properties of cells and tissues, also known as electrophysiology. They have also shown that living tissues have electrical properties [1].

© Springer International Publishing AG, part of Springer Nature 2018
S. Hammoudi et al. (Eds.): ICEIS 2017, LNBIP 321, pp. 473–497, 2018.
https://doi.org/10.1007/978-3-319-93375-7_22

Collura (1993) [1] also claims that the first scientists to focus their work on the electrical phenomena were Carlo Matteucci (1811–1868) and Emil du Bois-Reymond (1818–1896). The first studied the muscle properties of frogs and was the first to observe the potential action that precedes the contraction and the extent reduction of muscle during this contraction. Meanwhile, Du Bois-Reymond built a galvanometer of more than 4000 turns of wire in its coil, increasing its sensitivity. Moreover, Du Bois-Reymond developed non-polarizable electrodes made of clay and understood the importance of their use.

This study and the use of physiological signals increased in the engineering community. Thus, new application fields were born in addition to the more traditional areas of medicine. Such applications range from monitoring of human activity, human-machine interactions in games, and even biometrics, through new systems based on electrocardiography [2].

As the high cost of professional equipment prevents the use of such equipment for engineering students in the field of physiological signals, alternatives to acquisition and conditioning of these signals are necessary.

In practice, it is often necessary to make measurements of different electrical human signals through simple devices. Although there are many bio-amplifiers with excellent precision and multi-channel, these are very expensive for general purpose [3].

Physical computing has grown as a field in its own right field [4] and with the increasing concept of "Do it Yourself" (DIY) various open-source electronics platform emerged, such as Arduino and Raspberry pi.

However, until now, physical computing has been mainly used with equipment designed to meet requirements which are not compatible with the acquisition of physiological signals, such as relatively high noise tolerance and low sampling rate [5]. In addition these requirements, physiological computing requires a circuit for acquisition of biomedical signal, which is not suitible through equipment designed for physical computing.

Thus, equipment commonly used in physical computing such as Arduino or Raspberry Pi are not viable in physiological computing, because they interact with simple actuators and sensors, not having channels for acquisition of biomedical signals and besides having few signals requirements.

Since then, many researchers turned to the study of physiological signals, improving the acquisition and conditioning of signals obtained and making it possible to find high-precision apparatus for use in modern medicine. However, such devices are expensive as they are meant for professional use in hospitals and clinics.

Thus, continuing the "DIY (Do-It-Yourself)" idea, this work presents a platform for acquisition and conditioning of physiological signals with low cost, versatile, generic and easy prototyping. This platform has the characteristics the fact of being composed of interlocking, interchangeable, inter-configurable and reconfigurable boards. It also has a strong documentation, enabling easy prototyping and manipulation.

The evaluation of this tool was made by the SUS scale developed by Brooke (1996) [6] in what concerns the usability of the system. For comparison, it was used the usability of "experienced people" with "less experienced people" in the studied area, and a comparison was made with another work which used the same scale in its context.

The development of a tool such as presented here may be of interest to the Hardware laboratory in the computer department of the Sergipe Federal University (UFS) and other engineering such as electronics or electric, as well as people who work with biomedical engineering. The technology domain enables its flexibility and adaptation in several different surveys, enabling the possibility of integrating hardware with various laboratory equipment, allowing undergraduate and postgraduate students work in biomedical engineering.

The results of this experiment showed that there is no statistical difference between the prototyping time obtained for the "experienced people" and "inexperienced people" groups, also showing the platform usability note with a value A+ (on a scale going from F to a A+). It was also shown that the average usability of the "experienced" group is not different from the average usability of the "no experience" group, thus showing that a person with no experience in the field makes the prototyping with the same ease of a person with experience due to the platform's usability.

The work is divided into eight sections, the first introduction, and the second related work. The third section presents the methodology of the work focusing on describing how the board is designed and assembled. The fourth section contains the experiment planning and the fifth section details the operation of the same. The sixth section presents the results and discussion of the experiment. The seventh section highlights the threats to the validity of the experimental study and eighth section presents the conclusion and future work.

2 Related Works

Due to mismatch between the relevance and timeliness of biomedical engineering and the structure of electrical engineering courses in Brazil [7], a postgraduate team of biomedical engineering institute of UFSC has developed a platform called SPSB-MD (Biomedical Signal Processing System - Teaching Modules) for acquisition and digitalization of electrocardiogram, electromyogram, electrooculogram and electroencephalogram signals, in order to fill the gap in biomedical engineering disciplines in undergraduate and postgraduate in UFSC. Despite the platform developed by Andrighetto et al. (2008) [7] allow user access to analog components, it has distinct modules for acquisition and conditioning of each type of physiological signal. Unlike YouMake that has a module of acquisition and signal conditioning that can be modified by the user through prototyping to the specifications of the signal of interest.

The BITalino, developed by Silva et al. (2014) [5] consists of a hardware card type platform for acquiring physiological signals focused in all in one, low cost. This cost is €149 in a configuration "Board Kit", €159 in the configuration "Freestyle Kit" and 169 euros in the configuration "Plugged Kit" [8]. This platform is for general purpose and able to acquire electromyography signals, electrocardiography, electrodermal activities and accelerometry by fitting sensors blocks in the control block. While BITalino does not allow the change and adjustment of frequency bands and gains in filters and amplifiers, YouMake allows the user to modify these values freely, adapting the platform to the signal of interest. Furthermore, in BITalino it is not possible to connect a sensor block in another sensor block, in order to integrate the filter and improve them.

In YouMake it is possible to connect the boards to integrate filters and gains of the amplifiers. There is still a difference in cost, since the BITalino has estimated cost of between €149 and €169 and YouMake can be mounted with only €3,06.

Babusiak and Borik (2013) [3] developed a four-channel amplifier for measuring the neurophysiological signals of humans, able to acquire the electrocardiogram, electroencephalograms and electrooculogram signals. This amplifier features variable gain and programmable through digital potentiometers, and allows you to change the lead in the measurement, considering the type and characteristics of the signal to be measured. However, in this device it is not possible to learn through prototyping and even interconnection between filters, which can be found in YouMake.

Meanwhile, Zanetti (2013) [9], decided to develop a platform focused in the acquisition of electroencephalogram called RITMUS, having high performance, but because of its robustness, the price is high, around $495.36. Besides the high price, it is not as versatile and general as YouMake.

Finally, much of the work related to the acquisition of biological signals uses it for an application, such works develop a platform specific to acquire the desired signal, this is the case of Silva et al. (2008) [10], which develops a platform to acquire the signals of heart rate, respiration, and galvanic skin response in order to detect anxiety levels. Thus, Vijayprasath, Sukanesh and Rajan (2012) [11] also focused on creating a platform for a specific application. This platform performs the acquisition and amplification of electrooculogram signals in order to use such signals in mouse cursor control through the eyes.

3   Methodology

As this work is to develop a low-cost platform for acquisition and conditioning of biomedical signals, specifically ECG, EOG and EMG, the first step was to design the acquisition and conditioning circuits, paying attention to the use of cheap and commercial components the manufacture of the boards.

With the boards ready and the components purchased, a guide and video was made for the user, in which show how to mount the platform and use it. For evaluation of the work, usability study for the platform was performed, checking the easiness of and the average time spent by users to mount. This usability study was done experimentally and with humans, for this reason, the study was submitted to the ethics committee and approved under the number CAAE: 58536416.6.0000.5546.

The block diagram in Fig. 1 illustrates the YouMake's modules.

The following sections describe how it was designed and assembled the proposed platform.

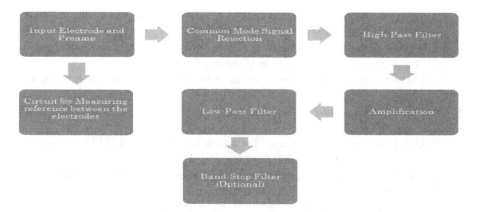

Fig. 1. Platform block diagram. Source: retrieved from Gois et al. (2017) [12].

3.1 Materials

The necessary low-cost materials for the assembly of the platform are:

- Set of printed circuit boards with the project that will be shown in the following sections: each plate cost $1.4 and it took only two plates in this work;
- Integrated circuit LM324: only one was used and cost $0,32;
- Integrated circuit AD620: It was not used in the experiments, but could be used as an option for LM324 in the platform. The average cost is $11,94;
- Integrated circuit LM741: two were used in this work. About $0,32 each;
- Electronic Components: Resistors and capacitors costing a few cents each.

3.2 Supply

The supply of the whole circuit was made with two 9 V batteries connected in series forming a symmetrical source of +9 V and −9 V. However, it can be powered by any source of symmetrical voltage 5 V to 15 V. Special care should be taken, since the maximum voltage of the supply is the maximum value that the signal output voltage can reach, due to saturation of the operational amplifiers.

3.3 Biomedical Signals Acquisition Circuit

Figure 2 shows the schematic of the data acquisition board divided into blocks for better viewing. In addition to the blocks, the terminals were named curtly and standardized so that would fit on the board. The following shows the nomenclature of each terminal:

- IN1.AD: electrode input 1 to the circuit using the AD620 and must be connected to an electrode;
- IN2.AD: electrode input 2 to the circuit using the AD620 and must be connected to an electrode;

- TO.AUX.AD: AD620's circuit output that must be connected to the reference circuit (IN.AUX terminal).
- SAIDA.AD: output of the acquisition circuit formed by AD620 and must be connected at the input of the conditioning plate;
- IN1.LM: electrode input 1 to the circuit using the LM324 and must be connected to an electrode;
- IN2.LM: electrode input 2 to the circuit using the LM324 and must be connected to an electrode;
- TO.AUX.LM: instrumentation amplifier output formed by the LM324 and must be connected to the reference circuit (terminal IN.AUX);
- SAIDA.LM: output of the acquisition circuit formed by the LM324 and must be connected at the input of the conditioning board;
- IN.AUX: reference circuit input and must be connected to TO.AUX.LM terminal if the user is using the acquisition circuit formed by LM324, or TO.AUX.AD terminal if the user is using the acquisition circuit formed by AD620;
- SAIDA.AUX: the reference circuit output and to be connected to an electrode;
- V+ : supply positive voltage;
- V−: supply negative voltage;
- TERRA: supply reference (ground).

Block 1 of Fig. 2 shows AD620 integrated circuit, a circuit suitable for acquisition of biomedical signals. It has three resistors, where R13 and R14 are set to 22 K forming a voltage divider in TO.AUX.AD terminal and a resistor R12 which is the resistor which can be varied to obtain different gain values. The terminal TO.AUX.AD must be connected to IN.AUX in block 4 to use the reference circuit with AD620. The circuit's gain is given by Eq. 1 retrieved from Gois et al. (2017) [12]. Such gain should not be too high, otherwise a significantly increase in gain at this stage may adversely affect the signal with noise. The maximum gain achieved, without much noise, was 100, being advisable a gain smaller than 10 at the early stage. This paper uses a gain of 6.26.

$$R_G = (49.4 \text{ K})/(G—1) \tag{1}$$

The block 2 of Fig. 2 shows the instrumentation amplifier mounted with LM324, where the values of the resistors R2 and R3 were selected to be 47 K (these values enable a wide range of gain variation according to the value of R1). The value of the gain of this amplifier is given by (2) retrieved from Gois et al. (2017) [12], such gain is varied in accordance with the resistor R1 (also called gain resistor) as it can be seen in Fig. 2. This gain must not be too high, since a high gain at this stage may harm the signal with noise. The maximum gain achieved, without much noise, was 8, being advisable not to exceed this value. This paper uses a gain of 7.26.

$$G = 1 + ((R3 + R2)/(R1)) \tag{2}$$

Block 3 of Fig. 2 is rejection circuit for common mode signal, where all resistors have the same value, 10 K (R4 = R5 = R6 = R7 = 10 K). These values mean that there is no gain in this block.

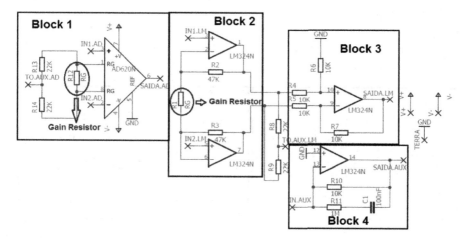

Fig. 2. Acquisition board of biomedical signals. Source: retrieved from Gois et al. (2017) [12].

For acquisition of biomedical signal, a reference is required to measure between IN1 and IN2. This reference is provided by the circuit in block 4, as shown in Fig. 2.

Resistor values in the block 4 were chosen according to the datasheet of AD620: R10 = 10 K and R11 = 1 M. The capacitor C1 has its value set at 100nF. The input circuit (IN.AUX) must be connected to the terminal TO.AUX.LM, which is located at the voltage divider formed by R8 and R9 (both resistors have the 22 K value) if the user decides to use the LM324 circuit. If you want to use the AD620 circuit, the input of the reference circuit (IN.AUX) must be connected to the terminal TO.AUX.AD, which is located at the voltage divider consisting of R13 and R14 (both with 22 K values).

Observing Fig. 2, note that there are two separate and distinct acquisition circuits, one formed by AD620 and another by LM324, and blocks 2 and 3 are connected, because together they form the acquisition circuit through LM324. Thus, when one of the two is chosen to be used, you only need to solder the components referred on the chosen circuit, including the electrodes. Also, the block 4 is shared, so if you are using the acquisition circuit formed by AD620, it is necessary that the input of the reference circuit formed by block 4 is connected with block 1. However, if you are using an acquisition circuit formed by LM324, it must connect the block 4 input to terminal TO. AUX.LM between the blocks 2 and 3.

3.4 Biomedical Signals Conditioning Circuit

Figure 3 shows the schematic of the conditioning board. It is divided into blocks for better viewing. In addition to the blocks, the terminals were named curtly and standardized so that they fit on the board. The following shows the nomenclatures:

- ENTRADA.INVERSOR: inverting amplifier input. Must be connected to the output of the acquisition board;
- S.AMP.I: inverting amplifier output;
- ENTRADA.FILTRO: filter input;

- S.F: filter output;
- V+ : supply positive voltage;
- V− : supply negative voltage;
- TERRA: supply reference.

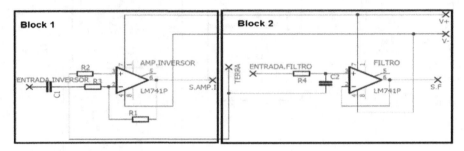

Fig. 3. Conditioning circuit schematic. Source: retrieved from Gois et al. (2017) [12].

Figure 3 shows the schematic of the conditioning board. Block 1 consists of an inverting amplifier formed by a LM741, where the gain can be seen in Eq. (3) retrieved from Gois et al. (2017) [12], for being an amplifier in the inverting configuration, it inverts the input signal. In this block, there is a coupling capacitor C1, since it is positioned at the signal input, it also functions as a high-pass filter with a cutoff frequency defined by Eq. (4) retrieved from Gois et al. (2017) [12].

$$G = -R1/R3 \tag{3}$$

$$F_c = 1/(2 \times \pi \times C1 \times R3) \tag{4}$$

It is in block 1 of Fig. 3 that is applied the largest gain in the signal, in the order of tens or hundreds. Thus, R1 and R3 values are not fixed, and the values depend on the signal gain. The resistor R2 is used to minimize the effect of operational amplifier input bias current, so the resistors R2 and R1 must be equal.

Block 2 of Fig. 3 shows the Butterworth type active low-pass filter and following the Sallen & Key setting that is applied to the signal, this is a first order filter and can be easily changed to a high-pass filter only inverting the position the capacitor with the resistor. R4 and C2 values were not fixed, as these depend on the value of the cutoff frequency of the filter showed in Eq. (5) retrieved from Gois et al. (2017) [12].

$$F_c = 1/(2 \times \pi \times R4 \times C2) \tag{5}$$

4 Experiment Planning

4.1 Objective Definition

The purpose of this experiment is to evaluate, through a controlled experiment, the acquisition platform of biomedical signals using the Brooke systems (1996) [6] usability scale as a measuring tool. This experiment will target two groups of participants, a group with experience and one without experience in electronics.

The goal was formalized using the GQM model proposed by Basili (1984) [13]: analyze the biomedical signals platform in order to evaluate with respect to the usability and time prototyping in the point of view of researchers, students and biomedical signal pickers in the context of undergraduate and postgraduate students and former students, with and without experience in biomedical signs.

4.2 Hypothesis Formulation

In this experiment, we want to answer the research questions RQ1, RQ2 and RQ3:

- RQ1: The group with the most knowledge and experience in the area has an average value of usability higher than the group with less experience and knowledge?
- RQ2: The platform can be used as a low-cost alternative for the acquisition and conditioning of biomedical signals?
- RQ3: The group with the most knowledge and experience in the area has the lowest average value of prototyping time than the group with less experience and knowledge?

To assess these questions, three metrics will be used:

- Average usability of each group (SUS_Valor);
- Overall average value of the usability of the experiment;
- Average time prototyping of each group.

With the research questions and metrics defined, the following hypotheses were defined:

1. Hypothesis 1
- H_{0SUS}: The average usability value of the "experienced" group is equal to the average usability value of the "no experience" group.
- H_{aSUS}: The average usability value of the "with experience" group is higher than the average usability value of the "no experience." group.
2. Hypothesis 2
- H_{0tempo}: The average prototyping time of the "experienced" group is equal to the average prototyping time of the "no experience." group.
- H_{atempo}: The average prototyping time of the "experienced" group is less than the average prototyping time of the "no experience" group.

4.3 SUS Usability Scale

Usability is a quality suitability of any device, for a particular purpose, and their ability to be used in a given context. For being a subjective and complex evaluation, Brooke (1996) [6] developed the Systems Usability Scale (SUS), which is a scale of ten simple, fast and reliable items that provides an overview of subjective usability reviews and is used as a tool to measure the usability of a wide variety of products and systems.

Composed of 10 questions that evaluate the effectiveness, efficiency and satisfaction of the user in relation to a particular product or service, the SUS scale has three characteristics that make it quite attractive in usability measurement. First is a scale with few questions, which makes it quick and easy for both respondents and the research administrator to calculate the values. Secondly, it is a free scale, which can be used without the need for any payment. Third, the SUS is an agnostic of technology, and can be used by a large group of professionals in the evaluation of almost any type of interface or product. Finally, the result is a single score, ranging from 0 to 100, which is relatively easy to understand by people from different study areas [14].

SUS works as follows: the user reads a statement about the system he wants to evaluate and then immediately must choose from a five-point scale ranging from strongly disagree to strongly agree of the statement.

With the questionnaire completed, the user's opinion is converted into a score that represents the system usability for that individual.

4.4   Variables

We describe in this section the independent, intervening and dependents variables of the experiment in this paper.

For independent variables, there are the tool used in case the biomedical signals acquisition and conditioning platform YouMake and its electronic components.

For dependent variables, there are two metrics: the average prototyping time, which was obtained by means of a chronometer and the average usability of SUS scale [6].

As intervening variable, there is the emotional state of the participants, as they might be nervous during of the experiment.

4.5   Participants

Tullis and Stetson (2004) [15] claims the use of SUS scale permit to obtain a system usability mean with a small sample number (8–12). Besides that, the authors assert this sample number has a confidence enough of a good evaluation of how people see your system or product. Thus, it was chosen twenty-four participants for the study.

The question P1 was asked at twenty-four participants, mixed among students and former students of undergraduate and postgraduate in UFS, with the sole purpose to classify the participants into more experienced or less experienced in the study area.

- P1: Have you ever studied electronics?

Thus, the participants were divided into two groups, the group G1, with experience, represented by the people who answered yes and the second group G2 that have only basic knowledge of circuits, represented by those who answered no.

4.6   Pilot Study

Before the experiment, a pilot study was conducted with student with a master in electrical engineering and a degree in electrical engineering. This student has experience in electronic circuits and is currently a Professor of in the Electrical Engineering

Department of the Federal University of Sergipe - Campus São Cristóvão (Sergipe, Brazil). This study was conducted in a laboratory at the Federal Institute of Sergipe - Campus Itabaiana (Sergipe, Brazil). It was given to the participant a user guide and a video showing how to prototype ECG, EMG and EOG. Soon after, the participant performed the experimental work described in the following sections.

The participant got a 12 min prototyping time and 95 points in SUS usability scale. The pilot study was used to better understand the study procedures. It also helped to assess the usability obtained by a person with considerable experience, and the time required to perform the task.

Thus, the pilot study was useful to show that it was possible to prototype the experiment in a timely manner. It also showed that people with enough experience possibly will feel easily in prototyping.

4.7   Experiment Design

ECG Acquisition and Conditioning. For acquisition and conditioning of the ECG, which is the potential heart rate, it is needed to position the surface electrodes that will acquire the signal of the first derivation of the ECG in the chest, just below the shoulder and the reference in the right arm, as shown in Fig. 4. This figure also shows the acquisition circuit using the AD620. Since, with the LM324 it is similar. The electrodes should be connected to IN1, IN2 and SAIDA.AUX terminals as shown in the diagram in Fig. 4. This diagram shows the acquisition format that can be used with both the AD620 and LM324.

With the electrodes connected and the acquisition board made, the output of the acquisition board is connected to the input of the conditioning board, which must be configured with the desired filters and gains, so that the output signal may be easily observed.

In this paper, the ECG is detected through surface electrodes, which requires a passing frequency range between 0.67–40 Hz [16]. Also, one needs a high gain, since the ECG signal amplitude is around 1 mV [3].

As has already been performed several tests in this work, commercial values of components that enable the display the ECG with a good degree of acceptance were found.

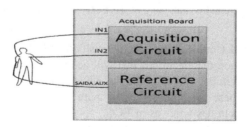

Fig. 4. ECG acquisition schematic.

They are:

- Gain of 6.26 in the acquisition board in case of using the AD620 circuit, also possible with a gain resistor of 6,8 KΩ;
- Gain of 7.26 in the acquisition board in case of using the circuit LM324, this gain is also possible with a gain resistor of 15 KΩ;
- Gain of 150 in the conditioning board through the inverting amplifier in block 1 of Fig. 3, using R1 = R2 = R3 = 1 KΩ 150 KΩ;
- High pass filter of about 0.072 Hz with a 2200 uF capacitor C1 shown in block 1 in Fig. 3;
- Low pass filter of about 34 Hz through a 47 K resistor in R4 and a 100 nF capacitor C2 in block 2 in Fig. 3.

With such passing and gain bands, the obtained signal can be seen in Fig. 5. If the signal appears inverted, there is no problem, since the voltage difference between the inputs is acquired to observe the signal, reverse the electrodes on the chest, placing what was on the left side goes to the right, and what was on the right side goes to the left side. This will make the signal before appeared inverted and it will shown correctly.

In addition to these values, it is possible to vary both the gain and the frequency passband and special care should be taken with the 60 Hz interference from the power grid. For this, it is interesting to acquire the signal away from wires connected to the electricity grid and, if necessary, apply a band pass filter to eliminate the interference (this was not applied in this paper).

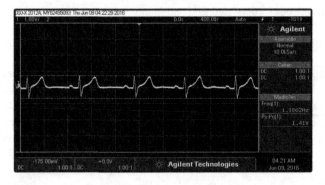

Fig. 5. Acquisition and conditioning of the ECG first derivation with YouMake.

EMG Acquisition and Conditioning. For acquisition and conditioning of the EMG, it is necessary to position the electrodes that will acquire the muscle signal. For this, one electrode is placed in the middle of the muscle and other electrode in muscle base as shown in Fig. 6. These positions serves for both the AD620 and for the LM324, simply connect the electrodes wires as in ECG.

The procedure is equal to ECG, but the passband of the EMG signal with surface electrodes is generally between 2–500 Hz frequency and amplitude between 50 μV and 5 mV amplitude [17].

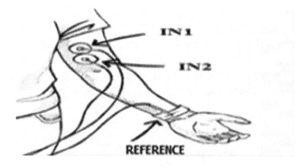

Fig. 6. EMG electrode positioning. Source: retrieved from Gois et al. (2017) [12].

So the cutoff frequency of the low pass filter was changed to 498 Hz and the high pass remained the same, in 0.072 Hz, which had a good answer. The gain in the conditioning board in Fig. 3 was changed to 56, since the EMG signal has higher amplitude than ECG. Thus, the following component values were selected in order to perform this experiment:

- Gain of 6.26 on the acquisition board using AD620. This gain is possible with a 6.8 KΩ gain resistor;
- Gain of 7.26 on the acquisition board using LM324. This gain is possible with a 15 KΩ gain resistor;
- 56-fold gain on the conditioning board, achieved with an inverter amplifier using R1 = R2 = 56 KΩ and R3 = 1 KΩ;
- High-pass filter of approximately 0.072 Hz with 2200 uF capacitor C1;
- Low-pass filter of approximately 498 Hz, achieved with a 47 KΩ resistor R4 and a 6.8 nF capacitor C2.

With such gains and pass bands, the signals are shown in Fig. 7.

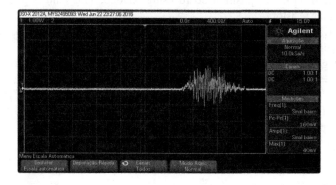

Fig. 7. Acquisition and conditioning of EMG with YouMake.

EOG Acquisition and Conditioning. For acquisition and conditioning of EOG, one needs to position the electrodes that will acquire the small signal of the eye movement.

The positioning depends on which parts of the eye movement is wanted. If it is the signal from moving to the left or to the right, the electrodes are positioned at the side of the right eyebrow and the other at the side of the left eyebrow. If it is the signal from moving up, down, or blinking, the electrodes must be placed as in configuration 2 in Fig. 8. The reference electrode is always at the bone behind the left ear. Such placement serves for both AD620 and LM324, simply connect the electrode wires as in ECG.

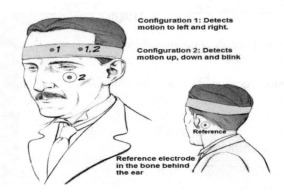

Fig. 8. EOG electrode positioning. Source: retrieved from Gois et al. (2017) [12].

The value of the EOG signal varies from 50 to 3500 µV with a frequency range between 0.001–100 Hz [18]. The procedure is the same as the ECG, but the low pass filter passband changed to 1.5 Hz and the gain to 220 times in the conditioning board in Fig. 3. Although there are frequencies up to 100 Hz in EOG, a 1.5 Hz filter exhibits an acceptable signal. Thus, the following component values were selected in order to perform this experiment:

- Gain of 6.26 on the acquisition board using AD620. This gain is possible with a 6.8 KΩ gain resistor;
- Gain of 7.26 on the acquisition board using LM324. This gain is possible with a 15 KΩ gain resistor;
- 220 fold gain on the conditioning board, achieved through an inverter amplifier using R1 = R2 = 220 KΩ and R3 = 1 KΩ;
- High-pass filter of approximately 0.072 Hz with 2200 uF capacitor C1;
- Low-pass filter of approximately 1.5 Hz, achieved with a 470 KΩ resistor R4 and a 220 nF capacitor C2.

With such gains and pass bands, the signals are shown in Fig. 9.

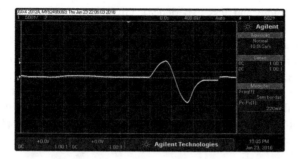

Fig. 9. Acquisition and conditioning of EOG with a movement to the left represented by the upper part of the wave and a movement to the right represented by the lower part of the wave.

5   Experiment Steps

In the following sections, the steps for the operation of the experiment are presented, ranging from preparation and implementation to validation of data.

5.1   Preparation

To prepare the participants for the experiment, a quick assembly guide and a video showing how to prototype EMG, ECG and EOG were provided. Furthermore, a platform with the components (the fixed ones) and connectors at the locations of the variable components were provided already welded.

5.2   Execution

The experiment was conducted in the hardware laboratory of the Federal University of Sergipe - Campus São Cristóvão and in the electronics laboratory at the Federal Institute of Sergipe – Campus Itabaiana. After watching the video, reading the user guide and answered some questions from the participants, the experiment was started. It was the prototyping of the acquisition and conditioning of EMG, ECG and EOG signals, it is worth mentioning the electrodes were placed on the body of the author of this paper.

- Data Collection

  After the experiment, the participants answered the platform evaluation questionnaire (SUS) [6]. In the end, the authors performed the calculations for the SUS usability score (SUS_Valor metric) of each participant.

5.3   Data Validation

For the experiment, it was considered a factor (prototyping of the acquisition and conditioning platform of biomedical signals), and a treatment (prototyping by the participants with more and less experience). Given this context, the average proto-typing time and the mean of SUS usability scale [6] were computed.

To aid the analysis, interpretation and validation, four types of statistical tests were used: Kolmogorov-Smirnov (K-S), Shapiro-Wilk (S-W), Student's t-test (for independent samples), and Levene. K-S and S-W tests were used to verify the normality of the samples. The Student's t-test was used to compare the average of two independent samples, and finally, Levene's test was used to evaluate the homogeneity of variances.

All statistical tests were performed using the SPSS - IBM (2013) [19] tool.

6   Threats to the Experimental Study Validation

6.1   Internal Threat

The internal threat defines if the relationship between treatment and result is casual, without the influence of other factors that may not have been measured. Participants answered the usability scale without supervision, so there is the possibility of them not having understood well some of the issues and may have marked wrongly, besides the scale subjectivity. However, care was taken so that the participants didn't talk among themselves, mitigating the insider threat.

6.2   External Threat

The external threats are the conditions that limit the ability to generalize. The experiments were performed in two different laboratories because the samples have been collected at the IFS and at the UFS and, therefore, in different environments. Moreover, the oscilloscopes (equipment used for signal viewing) used in each laboratory were different in brand and model. Thus, there is the possibility of users answering the questions differently. Although the overall number of samples are sufficient according to Tullis and Stetson (2004) [15], a larger number of samples could better represent the general population of students interested in biomedical signals.

6.3   Construction Threat

The construction threats are related to the design and human factors. Such threat can be characterized by the participants time spent. Perhaps the time is not the best metric, because some users spend more time just viewing the signal than others that are more objective.

6.4   Conclusion Threat

The conclusion threats are related to the ability to reach a correct conclusion about the relationship between about the treatment and the outcome. To avoid hypotheses infringement, we used the normality test, Shapiro-Wilk, and a parametric test, t-test, for data analysis. To reduce the confiability impact to the implementation of the treatment, we followed the same experimental setup in both cases.

7   Results and Discussion

7.1   Experimental Study Results

With the experimental study described in the previous sections, the research questions RQ1, RQ2 and RQ3 may be answered.

Participants were divided into two groups: group G1 representing the participants with experience in the study area and group G2 representing the participants with no experience in the area of study. The values corresponding to the SUS scale of the participants can be seen in Fig. 10 where it shows the values of groups G1 and G2, which are very similar and it leads us to think that all groups can set up an acquisition and signal conditioning system just as easily. This same analysis can also be done by observing the graph of Fig. 11, which shows the times used by the participants to do the experiment, leading us to believe that the times spent by the experienced group is very similar to the time spent by the group with no experience. However, this can not be said without a statistical analysis of the results.

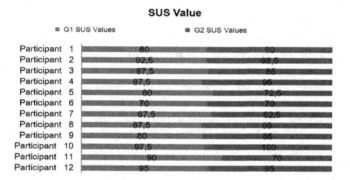

Fig. 10.   Graph of the values acquired by the SUS scale for groups G1 and G2.

The first thing to be considered for the statistical analysis is that the samples are independent, since the participants are evaluated only once and the results are not related [20]. The second thing that needs to be considered is if the sample follows a normal distribution (mathematical function used to describe the variation pattern of a continuous variable). This function involves the mean and the variance as parameters [20].

According to Lopes et al. (2013) [21] a large number of statistical tests assume that the data follows a normal distribution, so the Kolmogorov-Smirnov (KS) tests and the Shapiro-Wilk (SW) test were applied in the sample to evaluate the normality of the sample. However, K-S is more commonly used for samples larger than 30, while S-W is more commonly used for samples smaller than 50 [20]. Thus, for statistical analysis of the sample, it was considered the result of the S-W test for evaluation of its normality and then applied Student's t test for independent samples, such test allows to evaluate the hypothesis that two population means are identical. The t-test was chosen because it was used in small samples. According to Colaço Júnior (2016) [20] the t test

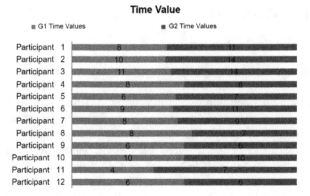

Fig. 11. Graph of the time values acquired during the experiment.

is used for samples smaller than 30, which is ideal for this work where G1 and G2 have 12 samples each. Finally, one of the requirements for application of the test t is that there is homogeneity of variance between the samples [20] and for this reason the Levene test was applied to verify it.

The statistical tests provide a p-value, which can be interpreted as the degree of agreement between the data and the null hypothesis (H_0) [21], the whole experiment being carried out in SPSS with a confidence level of 95% (Significance level $\alpha = 0.05$).

Thus, to answer RQ 1, the normality tests, the t-test and the Levene test were applied. As the samples of this work are less than 30, the S-W was used for analysis. In both the experienced and the non-experienced group the p-value (sig) values were greater than alpha of 0.05. In group G1 the S-W obtained value of 0.425 and in group G2 the S-W obtained value of 0,081. This result shows that the normal distribution is a possible distribution for the set of samples in question, which allows to apply the t test.

The p-value of the Levene test was greater than alpha ($0.107 > 0.05$), which means that there is homogeneity of variance in the samples, therefore the t-test can be applied. In the t-test the sig of 0.964, which is higher than the alpha ($0.964 > 0.05$), may be observed. Thus, there is no evidence to reject H_{oSUS}, which states that the mean of G1 is equal to the mean of G2. From this, it's possible to conclude that the average usability of group G1 is no different than group G2, which answers RQ 1. Thus, there is evidence that a person with no experience in the study area performs the experiment with the same ease as a person with experience due to the usability of the platform.

To answer RQ2, the overall YouMake's usability was compared to the BITalino platform [5], a platform that works by fitting sensor blocks in the main control block, which has an average general usability of 84.62 and was rated A+ in Sauro and Lewis scale (2012) [22], in addition to being characterized, according to the authors, an easy-to-use platform.

In relation to YouMake, it is possible to identify the average general usability of the experiment in the amount of 84.479. With this value of average mean and with the scale constructed by Sauro and Lewis (2012) [22], in that SUS range of 84.1 to 100 means A+ grade, the correlation of the SUS score with is performed. This scale measures the usability in marks ranging from F to A+ , where A+ is the best possible score and F the worst possible grade. According to Sauro and Lewis (2012) [22], a system that receives A or higher marks is a system that people would recommend to their friends.

Comparing the values of average means with the marks in the scale, it is noticed that both YouMake and BITalino have A+ marks, with averages of 84.479 and 84.62 respectively. Thus, by having similar values we can infer that YouMake can be used as a low-cost alternative for acquiring and conditioning biomedical signals, responding RQ2.

To respond RQ3, it is necessary to analyze the time the participants took to run the experiment. As in the case of usability, the normality tests, the Levene test and the t-test were applied. In the results of normality tests, as in the case of SUS, we use S-W values for analysis, and in this the p-value is greater than alpha for both the experienced group $(0.597 > 0.05)$ and no-experience group $(0.110 > 0.05)$. This result shows that the normal distribution is a possible distribution for the set of samples in question, which allows the t test to be applied in the time samples.

The values obtained from the t-test and the Levene test applied in the time samples are observed and the p-value of the Levene test is higher than alpha $(0.155 > 0.05)$. Thus, there is homogeneity of variances in the samples and the t-test can be applied. In the t-test a p-value of 0.201 is seen, which is greater than alpha $(0.201 > 0.05)$. Then, there is no evidence to reject H_{otempo}, which states that the prototyping time of the experienced group would be equal to the prototyping time of the no-experience group. Thus, it can be concluded that the time of prototyping of the experienced group is no different from the prototyping time of the no-experience group, answering RQ3.

7.2 Discussion

The approach used in the YouMake project, to present a didactic solution regarding the acquisition and conditioning of biomedical signals, led to the elaboration of a solution with special features, but transparent to the student, so that he/she is aware of the entire acquisition chain and Signal conditioning. With this, it is possible for the student to design and assemble the whole chain of acquisition and conditioning of the signal of interest, according to their needs through the use of YouMake.

Because it is a didactic platform, one of the concerns was the layout of the board. This was designed for easy understanding and use, so that all usable components are shown on the board itself. In addition, an intuitive design was used in the Biomedical Signal Conditioning Board, and the filters were designed as normally arranged in textbooks as in the book Microelectronics [23].

The choice of an open architecture where the student could follow the signal through the various stages of acquisition and conditioning caused the signal to be affected more strongly by ambient noise such as electromagnetic interference radiated from sources such as fluorescents, radio signals and especially mains. Thus, it is sometimes necessary to use filters that rejects the 60 Hz band depending on the environment in which the student is located. In the results shown in this chapter it can be seen that depending on the frequency range and the type of signal of interest, the use of such a filter may be beneficial in signal visualization. To reduce these interferences, YouMake could have been built in a more compact, closed and isolated way, but this would result in loss of space for writing visual indications on the board and would prevent the use of the board through the student, which would impair the didactic characteristic of YouMake.

Another concern was the cost, since for the proposal of a low cost didactic platform it would require a project that used cheap circuits. That's why YouMake is designed to have a high level of component economics. The LM324 integrated circuit (which is just a set of common operational amplifiers) was then used to make the acquisition circuit together with resistors. There was an initial concern that such an integrated circuit would impede adequate signal collection, since these signals are very low amplitude and require very high common signal rejection, and all the works found in the area used specific integrated circuits to capture biomedical signals such as AD620. In this way, YouMake is also designed to support AD620 (an integrated circuit designed to acquire biomedical signals). However, the results presented in this chapter showed that the use of LM324 was satisfactory and there was no visible difference in the use of AD620, thus allowing a higher level of economy.

Still, as a didactic platform, the concern about the easiness led to the use of first order filters (simpler assembly and understanding). There was also an initial concern about their implementation, since other works found in the area always used second order filters or greater. However, the results obtained showed that the use of first order filters meets the didactic demand of the student with good visualization of the signal of interest. Despite this, it is also possible to mount second order filters with YouMake.

Some platforms for acquisition and conditioning of biomedical signals have already been developed in other works as described in Sect. 2, but they differ from YouMake in some points.

The SPSB-MD [7] was created with the objective of filling an existing gap in biomedical engineering disciplines at UFSC undergraduate and graduate level, so that students can have a set of tools in practical classes. Although the SPSB-MD platform allows user access to analog components, it has very distinct modules for acquisition and conditioning of each type of biomedical signal. Unlike YouMake, which has an acquisition module and a generic conditioning module, which can be freely modified by the user to the specifications of the signal of interest. In addition, no studies on usability were made in SPSB-MD, and it is not possible to say that it is an easy-to-use platform and that students would be able to use it with ease. The cost of SPSB-MD was also not disclosed, and it may not be a low-cost alternative.

Like SPSB-MD, BITalino [5] has very distinct modules for acquisition and conditioning for each type of biomedical signal. This allows only the acquisition of electromyography, electrocardiography, electrodermal activities and accelerometry, made through fixed set of blocks, with their filters and gains fixed and unchanged for the type of signal that may be chosen from the mentioned options. While the BITalino does not allow the change of frequency bands and gains in filters and amplifiers, YouMake allows the user to modify these values freely, adapting the platform to the signal of interest. In addition, in BITalino it is not possible to cascade sensor blocks in order to improve the filters. In YouMake, cascading is possible for improvement of filters and amplifiers gains. There is also a difference in cost, since BITalino has an estimated cost between 149 and 169 euros [8] and YouMake can be assembled with only 3.23 dollars.

Babusiak and Borik (2013) [3] have developed a platform with variable gain by means of digital potentiometers, allowing for changes in measurements of the signal. But in the device in question it is not possible to learn through prototyping with the possibility of measuring the signal after each stage of filtering or amplification and cascading between filters, which can be found in YouMake. Babusiak and Borik (2013) [3] also did not report the price nor did they do any study on usability of their device, so the analysis described for the SPSB-MD can also be made for this programmable gain platform.

Rathke (2008) [24] contributed to the construction of a didactic biomedical engineering platform, developing ECG, EOG and EMG hardware modules for the biomedical signal processing system developed by a group of UFSC graduate students and the other modules were built by Adur (2008) [25], Andrighetto (2008) [7], Possa (2008) [26] and Santos et al. (2007) [27]. Besides that, he developed content for the tutorial on the acquisition of electrocardiography and evaluated the use of the platform in a group of electrical engineering students of the UFSC. This platform has educational objectives such as YouMake, but it uses an integrated circuit AD620 for signal acquisition and second order filters for conditioning, which detracts from both cost and easiness of use. Meanwhile, YouMake uses first order filters with acceptable degree of signal visualization. In order to evaluate the platform developed by Rathke (2008) [24] and his team of graduate students, a questionnaire was prepared by the team itself containing 32 questions, but following a validated system called WebMac SENIOR 4.0 [24]. In this system the student evaluates how much the platform is stimulating, meaningful, organized and easiness of use, being 8 questions for each one of these items. Rathke (2008) [24] collected the gross result of the response of a group of 10 students after they passed through a mini-course of learning the platform, obtaining in their grading scale the score of: 20.2 stimulant, 20.7 significant, 20.4 organized and 19.5 easiness of use. Although the maximum score in each item is 24, it can not be said that the platform is easy to use since these results were not treated statistically and were not compared with a validated grading scale. Unlike YouMake, it followed the standards of a controlled experimental study and had its results subjected to a statistical treatment in order to validate the results. Finally, in the platform of Rathke (2008) [24], it does not allow the students to change the gains and filters, since they are already defined by the designer of the platform.

Although the platforms described before have a more general scope, most of them have the objective of acquiring a single signal or specific signals for some application, such as the RITMUS platform [9], developed for the acquisition of the electroencephalogram. Its high performance comes at a cost: 495.36 dollars. In addition to its high price, it is not as versatile and generic as YouMake and nor can it be said that such platform is easy to use, since the developers have not worried about a usability study. There are also the platforms created by Silva et al. (2008) [10] and by Vijayprasath, Sukanesh and Rajan (2012) [11]. The first one aims to acquire the heart rate signals, respiratory and galvanic response of the skin in order to detect levels of anxiety. The second performs the acquisition and amplification of electro-oculogram signals in order to use such signals in controlling the mouse cursor through the eyes. These two also did not care about usability of their platforms nor the amount spent to produce them. As both were made for specific applications, these platforms does not allow students to modify them.

It is noted that only BITalino [5] and the platform developed by Rathke (2008) [24] are concerned with usability. Nevertheless, they did not follow the standards of an experimental study nor applied a statistical treatment to the results for validation purposes. In YouMake, usability was measured according to the standards of a statistic based experimental study.

Besides that, all mentioned works used second order filters with specific integrated circuits indicated for the acquisition of biomedical signals. This both makes the platform more expensive and makes learning harder for the student. In YouMake, it was used, despite the initial fear of doing different from other works, the LM324 for signal acquisition and first order filters for conditioning.

8   Conclusion and Future Works

It's possible to state that YouMake can be used as a low-cost alternative for acquisition and conditioning of biomedical signals, considering that the average price is only $3.23 using the LM324 and the platform provides good visualization of the signal, be it ECG, EOG or EMG. Also, the experimental usability study showed evidence through statistical tests that the platform has a good level of usability.

Thus, the initial proposal of this work to develop a low cost and didactic platform for acquisition and conditioning of biomedical signals that can contribute to the teachings of subjects related to biomedical engineering in undergraduate and graduate courses was fulfilled.

8.1   Contributions and Limitations

The main contribution of this work is to provide a low-cost and easy to use tool so that students interested in learning biomedical engineering have the possibility to do it more easily. Besides that, the tool is also of great value for students interested in the manipulation of the biomedical signal via software. With YouMake they can acquire the signal quickly, easily and at low cost. In addition, a full paper of this work has already been published in ICEIS 2017 [12].

The main limitations of this platform are related to cost. Because it was designed to be inexpensive, inexpensive components were used to amplify the noise input on the board, for example: the electrode connectors were simple push buttons, the cables were not shielded and the board has an open architecture, which allows for stronger electromagnetic interference. Besides that, because it is a board where the user constantly modifies the components, they are not welded with their body close to the board often. Thus, the component terminals are more exposed to ambient noise. However, despite all these limitations, the results obtained were satisfactory.

8.2   Lessons Learned

The main lesson learned was the possibility of creating a biomedical signal acquisition and conditioning platform using an integrated circuit like LM324, which is just a generic operational amplifier, and first order filters for signal conditioning. This was a challenge, since the works found in the area used integrated circuits suitable for biomedical signals such as AD620 and second order filters, which makes the platform more expensive and makes harder to handle the filters.

Besides that, there was the difficulty of working with a human experiment that required approval by the ethics board.

Finally, the fact that the experiment was done with humans made it difficult to acquire volunteers, since the experiment requires some time for the explanatory video, reading the user guide and executing the experiment. Therefore, several people invited to the experiment refused, claiming that it would be very time consuming.

8.3   Future Works

As a future work it can be mentioned the integration of YouMake with the biomedical signal processing platform being developed in parallel to this work by the graduate João Paulo in the computer department of UFS. This platform has an analog-to-digital converter that can convert the analog signals from YouMake and shows it on a computer screen through software and some treatments for the already digitized signal are also possible. With such integration done, comparisons of the signal acquired by YouMake may be made with some other biomedical signal simulator.

References

1. Collura, T.: History and evolution of electroencephalographic instruments and techniques. J. Clin. Neurophysiol. **10**(4), 476–504 (1993)
2. Guerreiro, J.: A biosignal embedded system for physiological computing, Tese de Doutorado. Instituto Superior De Engenharia De Lisboa (2013)
3. Babusiak, B., Borik, S.L: Bio-Amplifier with programmable gain and adjustable leads. In: 36th International Conference on Telecommunications and Signal Processing (TSP), pp. 616–619. IEEE (2013)
4. O'Sullivan, D., Igoe, T.: Physical computing: sensing and controlling the physical world with computers. Course Technology Press, Cambridge (2004)
5. Silva, H., Guerreiro, J., Lourenço, A., Fred, A., Martins, R.: BITalino: a novel hardware framework for physiological computing. In: Proceedings of the International Conference on Physiological Computing System (PhyCS), pp. 246–253 (2014)
6. Brooke, J.: A quick and dirty usability scale. In: Jordan, P., Thomas, B., Weerdmeester, B., McClelland, I. (eds.) Usability Evaluation in Industry, pp. 189–194. Taylor & Francis, London (1996)
7. Andrighetto, E., Adur, R., Rathke, J., Possa, P., Santos, F., Argoud, F., Azevedo, F., Neto, J.: 'Proposta de uma plataforma didática para o ensino de Engenharia Biomédica em Cursos de Graduação de Engenharia Elétrica: I Os Sinais Bioelétricos'. IV Latin American Congress on Biomedical Engineering 2007, Bioengineering Solutions for Latin America Health, pp. 1108–1112. Springer, Heidelberg (2008)

496   D. A. S. Gois et al.

8. Bitalino (2016). Accessed 30 Jul 2016. http://www.bitalino.com/
9. Zanetti, R.: Desenvolvimento de um Sistema Embarcado Para Aquisição de Sinais Biomédicos. Dissertação de Mestrado. Universidade Federal de Minas Gerais (2013)
10. Silva, M., Martucci, H., Santi, R., Frère, A.: 'Determinação automática da ansiedade por detecção computadorizada de sinais biológicos', IV Latin American Congress on Biomedical Engineering 2007, Bioengineering Solutions for Latin America Health, pp. 118–121. Springer, Heidelberg (2008)
11. Vijayprasath, S., Sukanesh, R., Rajan, S.: Experimental explorations on EOG signal processing for realtime applications in labview. In: IEEE International Conference on Advanced Communication Control and Computing Technologies (ICACCCT), pp. 67–70. IEEE (2012)
12. Gois, D.A.S., et al.: An experiment to assess an acquisition platform and biomedical signal conditioning. In: Proceedings of the 19th International Conference on Enterprise Information Systems. Anais. SCITEPRESS – Science and Technology Publications (2017). Accessed 11 Aug 2017. http://www.scitepress.org/DigitalLibrary/Link.aspx?doi=10.5220/0006293100 750086
13. Basili, V., Weiss, D.: A methodology for collecting valid software engineering data. IEEE Trans. Softw. Eng. **10**(3), 728–738 (1984)
14. Bangor, A., Kortum, P., Miller, J.: Determining what individual SUS scores mean: adding an adjective rating scale. J. Usability Stud. **4**(3), 114–123 (2009)
15. Tullis, T., Stetson, J.: A comparison of questionnaires for assessing website usability. In: Proceedings of UPA 2004 Conference, Minneapolis, Minnesota (2004)
16. Prutchi, D., Norris, M.: Design and development of medical electronic instrumentation: A Practical Perspective of the Design, Construction, and Test of Medical Devices. Wiley, Hoboken (2005)
17. Cohen, A.: Biomedical signals: origin and dynamic characteristics; frequency-domain analysis. In: Bronzino, J. (ed.) The Biomedical Engineering Handbook. 2nd edn. [S.l.]. CRC Press, Boca Raton, (2006). cap. 52
18. Barea, R., Boquete, L., Mazo, M., López, E.: Wheelchair guidance strategies using EOG. J. Intell. Rob. Syst. **34**(3), 279–299 (2002)
19. SPSS: IBM SPSS Statistics 22.0 (2013). Accessed 30 Jul 2016. http://www-01.ibm.com/common/ssi/rep_ca/9/897/ENUS213-309/ENUS213-309.PDF
20. Colaço, Jr., M.: Controlled experiments. In: Lecture Notes of the Discipline Experimental Software Engineering (2016)
21. Lopes, M., Castelo Branco, V., Soares, J.: Utilização dos testes estatísticos de Kolmogorov-Smirnov e Shapiro-Wilk para verificação da normalidade para materiais de pavimentação. Transportes **21**(1), 59–66 (2013)
22. Sauro, J., Lewis, J.: Quantifying the user experience: Practical Statistics for User Research. Elsevier Science, Cambridge, MA (2012). Accessed 30 Jul 2016. https://books.google.com.br/books?id=VKdoO5m5S0sC
23. Sedra, A.S., Smith, K.C.: Microelectronic circuits, 6th edn. Oxford University Press, USA (2009)
24. Rathke, J.E.: 'Sistema de processamento de sinais biomédicos: módulos didáticos de aquisição de ECG, EMG, EOG e conversão analógico-digital de biosinais'. 176 f. Dissertação (Mestrado) – Universidade Federal de Santa Catarina, Florianópolis (2008)
25. Adur, R.: 'Sistema de Processamento de Sinais Biomédicos: Módulo Didático de Eletroencefalograma'. 150 f. Dissertação (Mestrado) – Universidade Federal de Santa Catarina, Florianópolis (2008)

26. Possa, P.R.: 'Sistema de Processamento de Sinais Biomédicos: Módulo Didático de Amplificador de Potenciais Bioelétricos'. 118 f. Dissertação (Mestrado) – Universidade Federal de Santa Catarina, Florianópolis (2008)
27. Santos, F.C., et al.: 'Proposta de Plataforma Didática Para o Ensino de Engenharia Biomédica em Curso de Engenharia Elétrica: V. Ambiente em RV de Eletrocardiografia'. In: XXXV Congresso Brasileiro de Educação e Engenharia (2007)

A Human-Centered Approach for Interactive Data Processing and Analytics

Michael Behringer[(✉)], Pascal Hirmer, and Bernhard Mitschang

Institute of Parallel and Distributed Systems, University of Stuttgart,
Universitätsstraße 38, 70569 Stuttgart, Germany
michael.behringer@ipvs.uni-stuttgart.de

Abstract. In recent years, the amount of data increases continuously.
With newly emerging paradigms, such as the Internet of Things, this
trend will even intensify in the future. Extracting information and, consequently, knowledge from this large amount of data is challenging. To
realize this, approved data analytics approaches and techniques have
been applied for many years. However, those approaches are oftentimes
very static, i.e., cannot be dynamically controlled. Furthermore, their
implementation and modification requires deep technical knowledge only
technical experts can provide, such as an IT department of a company.
The special needs of the business users are oftentimes not fully considered. To cope with these issues, we introduce in this article a human-
centered approach for interactive data processing and analytics. By doing
so, we put the user in control of data analytics through dynamic interaction. This approach is based on requirements derived from typical case
scenarios.

Keywords: Visual Analytics · Human in the loop
Interactive analysis

1 Introduction

In the last several years, more than 90% of all data was produced [1] and its
volume will even double every 20 to 24 months in the future [2]. However, it
must be stated that most of the data is transient and it is no longer a problem
to acquire or store data, but rather to make sense out of it [3]. Unfortunately,
this is anything but trivial – based on studies, only between 0.5% and 5% of
the data is currently analyzed [4,5]. On the one hand, this is the case because
the human perception and analysis capacity remains largely constant while the
data volume has exploded [2]. On the other hand, automatic algorithms lack
human intuition or background knowledge [6] and, therefore, have problems with
semantic correlation. Furthermore, the demand for end user-specific, customized
analyses has to be taken into account since they are usually implemented and
made available by technical experts.

© Springer International Publishing AG, part of Springer Nature 2018
S. Hammoudi et al. (Eds.): ICEIS 2017, LNBIP 321, pp. 498–514, 2018.
https://doi.org/10.1007/978-3-319-93375-7_23

In the last decade, different approaches were introduced to cope with this issue. Famous representatives are Visual Analytics [7] and Self Service Business Intelligence [8]. These approaches both aim at more interactivity in the analysis process and therefore better, i.e., more specific, results, as well as more functionality for non-expert users. They are, however, very different in their characteristics. Visual Analytics exploits the respective strengths of all parties involved and, therefore, combines human perception with huge computational power as described by the *Visual Analytics Mantra "analyze first, zoom and filter, analyze further, details on demand"* [9]. In contrast, the main goal of Self Service Business Intelligence is to *"generate exactly the reports [the users] want, when they want them"* [10] and, as a consequence, to gain faster results through bypassing the IT department. Consequently, the process can be accelerated up to several months.

Furthermore, there are huge differences in the supported functionality. Visual Analytics solutions are mostly designed to solve a specific problem [11], while Self Service Business Intelligence solutions make use of the Visual Analytics principles but are oftentimes limited to selecting parameters, changing attributes, or following a predefined navigation path [10,12]. Hence, these approaches do not provide an acceptable solution to the described problem. Nonetheless, the principle of the *human in the loop*, or nowadays extended to *the human is the loop* [13], is mandatory for both approaches. However, the amount of human interaction is not exactly defined.

Our contribution to tackle the above mentioned issues is an approach towards an *extended* Visual Analytics process, which illustrates all steps from the exploration and selection of data sources, data preparation and cleaning, and data mining, to report and knowledge generation. By doing so, we integrate the basic Visual Analytics principle – the recurring change between visual and automatic methods – in an adjusted Knowledge Discovery in Databases process [14] – a well-established approach for data analysis. We further intend to support domain users by ensuring that they know and understand the characteristics of data during analysis, as well as the complete analysis process itself, i.e., why and how the result is achieved. We evaluate our extended process against requirements derived from an application scenario.

This article is the extended and revised version of the paper entitled "Towards Interactive Data Processing and Analytics" [15] presented at the International Conference on Enterprise Information Systems (ICEIS) 2017.

The remainder of this article is structured as follows: In Sect. 2, we introduce a motivating scenario for our approach. Section 3 describes related work. Section 4 describes several requirements for our approach that were derived from the motivating scenario. In Sect. 5, we present the main contribution of our article: we illustrate and explain an extended Visual Analytics process with strong involvement of the user. In Sect. 6, we introduce a case study our approach can be applied to and, furthermore, we validate our approach based on its requirement. Moreover, we discuss capabilities and limitations. Finally, Sect. 7 summarizes the results of the article and gives an outlook to our future work.

2 Motivating Scenario

In this section, we introduce a real world motivating scenario for our approach, which is depicted in Fig. 1. In this scenario, originating from the manufacturing domain, we assume a domain expert who is responsible for identifying reasons for quality deficiencies in manufactured products. During this identification process, various possible parameters such as, e.g., the temperature in the factory building or the day of the week, have to be considered. In a conventional analysis approach, domain experts define analysis tasks AT_i and create a request R_i for corresponding reports. If a request R_i can be satisfied by an already existing report that fulfills the analysis task AT_i, the results are handed directly to the domain experts (Fig. 1(a)). This conventional approach works great for large amounts of data in combination with precisely specified analysis tasks. However, if no report is available for an analysis task AT_{new}, a new request $R_?$ must be made to the IT department (Fig. 1(b)). However, for the implementation of this analysis in standard software, certain conditions must be fulfilled: (1) sufficient demand for this specific analysis, (2) sufficient prospect of financial returns, and (3) decent capacity in the IT department. If these conditions are fulfilled, this analysis will be implemented as a predefined report for the future (Fig. 1(d)) after negotiations and coordination of various stakeholders (Fig. 1(c)). However, in an exploratory approach, as in our scenario, it is very unlikely that this analysis will be implemented or even would be able to deliver meaningful insights, as it is unclear which parameters are of interest. Based on these considerations, our scenario should support the analysis of multiple data sources, e.g., internal sources, like temperature sensors or quality tests, as well as external sources from the internet. This data has to preprocessed and aggregated, analyzed, and finally, a report must be generated. It is undisputed that this scenario could not be covered by a conventional approach as illustrated above.

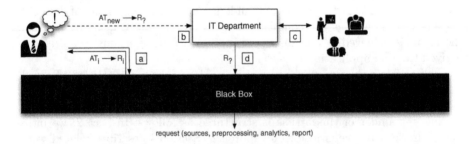

Fig. 1. Motivating scenario: Conventional, predefined analysis process using a black box (based on [15]).

In our approach, we therefore aim for a more flexible, interactive generation of reports to fulfill analysis tasks. By doing so, we minimize the required communication effort between different stakeholders and put the domain expert in control to solve analysis tasks in an interactive manner.

3   Related Work

Highly related to our work is the Knowledge Discovery in Databases process (KDD), originally introduced by Fayyad et al. [14] over 20 years ago. This process describes different steps to gain knowledge from data in a structured way, e.g., by data selection, data cleaning or data mining. The implementation of this process is usually done by technical experts based on background knowledge provided by domain experts. As a consequence, this process oftentimes becomes a black-box to end users unable to communicate the circumstances of pattern recognition and model creation. Furthermore, the background knowledge of the end user, i.e., the analyst, is not considered during the process [6]. Nonetheless, the Knowledge Discovery process can cope with large amounts of data or generic application domains and, therefore, is the way to go for well-understood problems. In contrast, the research area of visualization tackles human perception for a better and faster communication of analysis results. The process to create a visualization is described by the visualization pipeline [16] and contains, e.g., filtering, mapping or rendering. In these steps, data is filtered to receive a subset, which is mapped to shapes and attributes and is oftentimes rendered to an image in order to build a meaningful visualization. This approach can be summarized by the *Information Seeking Mantra "Overview first, zoom and filter, then details-on-demand"* as defined by Shneiderman [17]. Visual Analytics (VA) aims at a combination of these two processes by combining their respective strengths – human perception and the processing power of machines.

The most recent Visual Analytics process by Sacha et al. [18], derived from multiple other processes and integrated to the most extensive one we could find, specifies all stages in which a user could steer the analysis process. Yet, the focus of Visual Analytics is cooperation of visualization and underlying model, while data preprocessing (or more generic the KDD process) is steered by changing parameters. We think that each of these steps should also be supported through ongoing alternation between automatic and visual methods and not only by changing parameters.

For Self Service Business Intelligence (SSBI), the concept of different levels, respecting the task, is common, e.g., access to reports, creating new reports or even creating new information sources [19], while most steps are still undertaken by IT [12]. In principle, this is not surprising, since companies oftentimes use a data warehouse and, thus, a central, managed data storage. As a consequence, in practice, Self Service Business Intelligence is in most cases focused on creating and modifying reports and lacks the possibility for end users to add data sources or to apply data mining algorithms.

Since 2005, when Thomas and Cook [7] introduced the concept of Visual Analytics, different processes to invoke these principles have been published and range from human-centered processes [7,20] to stateful, system-driven processes [3,21,22]. While the former describes how an analyst makes sense (out of data) by creating hypotheses and derive actions, the latter depicts different states, relationships and possible interactions. Sacha et al. [18] combine both components to the currently most extensive Visual Analytics process.

The process is split into a computer part with the characteristic linkage between Visualization and Model, as well as one for the process of human perception. In this article, we focus on the computer part and, therefore, skip the process of human perception. The computer part consists of three major steps, namely Data, Model and Visualization. In short, the data has to be preprocessed and, afterwards, has to be either mapped to visualizations or used to generate models. By doing so, a close coupling between a visual interface and the underlying model takes place which allows users to update and evaluate the model through visual controls.

The above-mentioned integration of the analyst into the analysis is commonly referred to as *"Human in the Loop"* or more recently uncompromising as *"the Human is the Loop"* [13] and shows clearly the central role of the analyst in controlling the analysis process. The integration of the user could be reached on different extends, e.g., in *Enhanced Mining*, *Enhanced Visualization* or *Integrated Visualization and Mining* [21].

4   Requirements for a User-Centric Analysis Process

In this section, we derive different requirement necessary to enable domain experts to verify hypothesis in a scenario like the one introduced in Sect. 2. However, it is important to note that we are limiting the target group for this approach. Thus, we consider a domain expert with basic knowledge in conducting analyses – but no coding experience – who's ability to analyze data is limited to predefined reports, which is neither motivation-promoting nor satisfactory. We assume further that this domain expert has some new hypotheses for profitable analysis which are not met by the available reports and is, therefore, interested in conducting a custom analysis (cf. Sect. 2). For this group of domain experts, it is necessary to accelerate this process by enabling them to conduct their custom analyses on their own. Therefore, it is mandatory to entrust the control over the complete analysis to the domain expert. On this basis, we derive requirements which have to be fulfilled by the user-centric analysis process we aim for:

(R1) Put the User in Charge. The first requirement can be derived directly from our proposed motivating scenario. As described in Sect. 2, conventional approaches are not suitable for this use case since the analysis task cannot yet be defined exactly. The domain experts know about their intentions and expectations and are, therefore, the best authority to steer the process to fulfill their goals. Consequently, it is necessary to give the domain expert full control over each part of the analysis process – from the selection of the data sources to the compilation and interpretation of the results. Furthermore, this may lead to increased development of creativity as well as to exploitation of the implicit background knowledge of the domain expert.

(R2) Explorative Character. In contrast to conventional analysis, the data characteristics can change more often due to countless combinations of data sources or operations. As a consequence, one of the most important factors for a

successful and satisfactory analysis is to have deeper knowledge of the data. This knowledge may determine new ideas for possible analysis goals. Therefore, it is mandatory to explore the data in each step and probe different parameters and settings. In this context, it is important that the primary goal is no longer rapid analysis of data, but much more the generation of new hypotheses.

(R3) Reduction of Complexity. If the target user is not a technical expert, it is necessary to reduce the complexity of utilized algorithms to the core concepts and expected results instead of specifying parameters with unclear effects. By doing so, an abstraction from technical details, such as data formats, data sources, or data analysis algorithms, needs to be provided. This helps non-technical domain experts, with creating analysis they are interested in without any deep knowledge of data processing necessary.

(R4) Balance of Techniques. As mentioned in Sect. 1, different extents of integration between interactive visualization and automatic techniques are possible and should be combined in a way that respects the other requirements. To fulfill this principle, it should be up to the user to decide which extent of automation or integration he prefers. Furthermore, it is mandatory to switch between techniques or algorithms as long as the user is not satisfied with the result.

(R5) Generic Approach. Finally, it is necessary to cope with different domains and data sources and, therefore, a generic approach is required. Consequently, we need generic connectors to data sources and/or a chaining of different operations in data preprocessing, e.g., text mining in a first step to deal with unstructured data. This requires concepts, such as Pipes and Filters [23], common interfaces, or a uniform data exchange format. If a certain domain is completely unsupported, the user should still be able to integrate new visualizations or algorithms to the system on his own and include them in the analysis. We use these requirements as foundation of our extended Visual Analytics process, which can cope with the aforementioned issues and turns the above described black box towards an analysis white box.

5   Interactive Data Processing and Analytics

In this section, we introduce an extended Visual Analytics process to enable user-centric analysis, which is focused on various tasks during the analysis. This does not affect the generality of the Visual Analytics process as the work by Sacha et al. [18] still fits for our process. The central idea of this process is to exploit the basic principle of Visual Analytics: the continuous alternation between interaction in the visual interface, and background recalculation and adaption. This concept – referred to as Visual Analytics principle (VAP) in the context of this article – should not only be used after model building in the knowledge discovery process or visualization pipeline, but rather in each step of the analysis process, from data exploration and selection, up to report generation, which leads to an overarching process model. This is illustrated in Fig. 2. By doing so, the Visual Analytics process is extended with interactive elements and consists of the following main components:

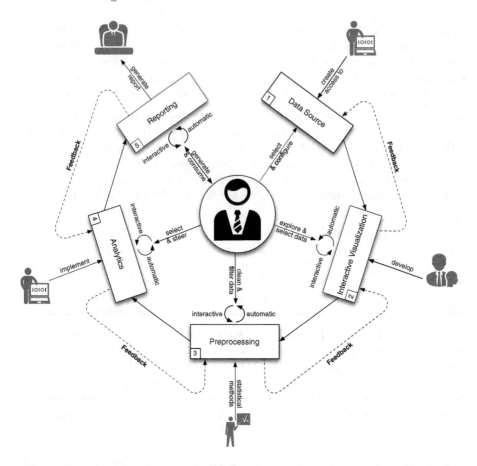

Fig. 2. Data Analytics Process extended with interactive elements (based on [15]).

5.1   Step 1: Data Source Selection

In the first step, users are expected to select either a predefined or configure a custom data source based on their analysis goals. A domain expert is not expected to be able to configure this data source in detail, which is why preliminary work of a technical expert is necessary in this step, e.g., specifying functionality for different file types is done by a technical expert and the selection of the file by the domain expert.

5.2   Step 2: Data Exploration

The exploration of data, stored in corresponding sources, using interactive visualizations, also belongs to the first step of the analysis. In this step, a domain expert is expected to explore different data sources to *get a feeling* for the characteristics of the data set, such as quality, trustworthiness, volume and content.

To fulfill this requirement, we need an appropriate visualization approach, which allows the domain expert to evaluate the contained data, e.g., with respect to correctness, correlation or even trustworthiness based on prior knowledge. Correspondingly, a suitable visualization is required for the respective data source, which in turn is supported by external experts, e.g., psychologists, who contribute their expertise of human perception. Furthermore, various possibilities should be implemented that allow the user to examine the data under different aspects. After this step, the user should, firstly, know whether the data is suitable for the analysis and, secondly, in the best case, can recognize initial patterns.

5.3   Step 3: Data Integration

The third step is targeting the previously selected data. It is undisputed that data has to be preprocessed in regard to the analysis goals. This step should allow the user to create new values by combination as well as recalculation or reshaping, discarding inconsistent attributes, and removing outliers or noise. Furthermore, for subsequent analysis through data mining, usually a single data set is necessary. As a consequence, there is a need for schema matching and integration of different data sources. If necessary, this step could be split even further, e.g., in specialized sub-processes like filtering, cleaning, transformation, or merging. In addition, interactive text mining approaches might be inevitable to structure text data and move on in the analysis. As in the previous steps, external expertise is required, in which case statistical methods can help to identify outliers or to obtain descriptive values for the data set. In this step, the VAP could be implemented, for example, by the use of the *programming by demonstration* [24] concept, which allows the user to work with a small subset of data and use the generated rules on the complete data set. The other way around, automatic methods could be used to notify the user, e.g., about likely incorrect values or conflicts in the data set.

5.4   Step 4: Data Analytics

This step involves all operations to find patterns in the data. For this step, a large collection of different approaches is available either from Visual Analytics or Visual Data Mining, but with focus to a selected application domain. As we need concepts for a generic approach, a possible way to realize this is to present the core idea of the analysis, e.g., clustering, and then utilize different algorithms or parameters to present the user an overview of possible results to evaluate. In the next iterations, the results could be increasingly refined. In this step as well, external experts are needed to implement the algorithms and develop appropriate visualizations. The VAP could be used in the way as classified in [21]. However, we expect that an integrated approach, which has no predominant role of one of the techniques, i.e., visualization or automatic methods, leads to the best results.

5.5   Step 5: Report Generation

After execution of an analysis, the results oftentimes need to be distributed to stakeholders and, therefore, we need a step which creates visualized reports. In this context, we consider different possible scenarios. Firstly, this kind of analysis is expected to fit for personal purposes. Therefore, obtained results could be used to create or extend a personal analysis dashboard. Secondly, report generation for the management is important if there are obtained patterns which are considered relevant for the company. In both these scenarios, the domain expert can use the VAP, e.g., through interactive or more extensively created custom visualizations, like demonstrated in SSBI software. Finally, if the conducted analysis is not only useful for a single user or is often recurring, it could be useful to attract the attention of the IT department to implement this analysis as a predefined report. In this case, the report has to contain every step and all parameters executed during the analysis. This could lead to a knowledge transfer from end users to developers.

5.6   Feedback Loop

As the domain expert is not expected to find an optimal analysis result at the first try, we need to implement a feedback loop and wrangling, the *"process of iterative data exploration and transformation that enables analysis"* [25]. Therefore, it must be ensured that a user is relieved of routine tasks, e.g., if only a change in the analytics step is necessary, all configurations of the precedent nodes have to remain [26]. Hence, we need a *"rule generation system"* for each node, which reapplies the user action on a new pass. Such a rule is generated by analyzing the conducted user actions. In the other direction, a change in the data selection should be continued within the existing processing steps and the user should only be involved in case of a conflict. This concept ensures that a user is only involved in necessary steps while, at the same time, interaction in each step is, in principle, possible.

5.7   Target User and Expert Integration

We are aware that this approach is not suitable for all kinds of users. In the process, we do not differentiate between domain and technical users for generic reasons. However, in practice, we should give the user some help to reduce the complexity without losing functionality. According to Eckerson [10], SSBI users are subdivided into two types: power users and casual users. Both of these user types are domain experts by definition but with different technical knowledge. The above mentioned casual user is usually satisfied with predefined reports or the opportunity to change visualization or analyzed attributes. As a consequence, the power user is the target for our process as this user is limited in current approaches, having basic knowledge about data mining techniques or data characteristics but no programming skills.

Table 1. Integration of experts during the analysis process.

Phase / Role	Data Source Selection	Data Exploration	Data Integration	Data Analytics	Report Generation	Feedback Loop
Domain expert	●	●	●	●	●	●
IT expert	◑	◔	◔	◔	◔	◔
Psychologist	◯	◐	◔	◐	◓	◔
Mathematician	◯	◔	◔	◐	◯	◯
Management	◔	◯	◯	◯	◔	◯

◯ No participation ◔ Low participation ◐ Medium participation ◑ High participation ● Full participation

For this reason, however, this type of user requires a wide range of expert support to achieve an acceptable abstraction level. A rough overview of experts from different research areas, and their participation in the respective steps of the analysis, is given in Table 1. Since, due to the requirements of the process, the participation of the domain expert is easy to understand, this is not discussed separately, but referred to in Sect. 6. Even if the IT department looses relevance for the individual analysis through our approach, it is still eminently important to create the technical foundations. Consequently, IT experts are taking part in each step of the analysis and are, furthermore, highly participating in creating prefabricated and frequently requested data sources. It is undisputed that visualizations offer an immense advantage for the understanding of data. Accordingly, experts and research results from this area, i.e., information visualization and insights from psychologists, are needed to take advantage of this potential, in particular for the steps data exploration, data analytics, and finally, report generation. The last area from which strong support for our process is necessary, is the field of statistics. Algorithms and methods from this field are used, e.g., in the context of data exploration and data integration through outlier detection or sampling. Furthermore, pattern recognition is strongly based on these methods in the sub-step data analysis or data mining. Last but not least, the management is also involved in our approach. On the one hand, the data sources must be made available, either by granting permission or purchasing access rights in case of external data sources. On the other hand, management is most likely the recipient of the generated reports in order to make decisions.

6 Case Study

In Sect. 2, we briefly illustrate a possible case scenario which is used to derive five requirements as described in Sect. 4. These requirements have to be fulfilled to enable the user-centric analysis we aim for in this article. In this section, we describe this scenario in more detail, as well as the application of our approach specific to its challenges. Afterwards, we validate our introduced extended Visual Analytics process against the deducted requirements.

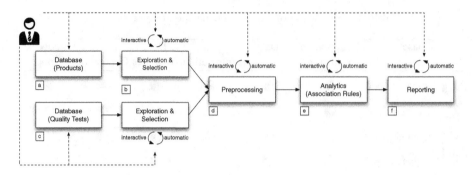

Fig. 3. Extended Visual Analytics process to increase comprehensibility.

6.1   Application Scenario

For our real-world scenario, we consider the following basic assumptions: A medium-sized company produces various products for craftsmanship, which stand for a particularly high quality. To achieve this goal, every product is subjected to extensive quality tests before going to sale. The resulting key figures are stored for future warranty claims. After the opening of another factory hall, however, the complaints are accumulated and the enterprise is concerned about its good reputation. A prefabricated solution is available for analyzing quality issues, which is depicted in Fig. 1 and was explained in Sect. 2. However, as expected, this analysis does not reveal any distinct discrepancies, since the product would otherwise not have been released for sale. Consequently, an exploratory approach is needed outside the standard analyzes in order to find the reason for the increasing complaints. The necessary steps that need to be taken by the domain expert are described in the following:

Step 1: Evaluating Predefined Analysis
In the first step, the domain expert needs to get an understanding of the steps of the predefined analysis, as well as of the characteristics of the data.

By using our extended Visual Analytics process, the black box turns into a white box (cf. Fig. 3). This allows the domain expert to conduct adaptations of different parameters to evaluate the currently applied analysis. The data sources (Fig. 3(a, c)) of the prefabricated analysis are initially retained and examined separately for correctness and conspicuousness (Fig. 3(b)). These sources are then combined, either in an automated and predefined way, or on the basis of changes made by the domain expert. In our scenario, only the correctness of the analysis has to be checked, since disturbance factors, caused by the new factory, are already assumed as the cause. Nonetheless, the domain expert is able to filter and analyze the data according to various aspects and confirm that it is not a fault that can currently be detected by the quality tests.

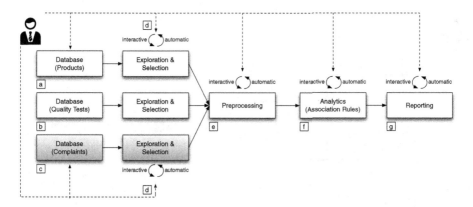

Fig. 4. Dynamic adjustment of data sources and parameters.

Step 2: Find the Defective Part

Since the carried out quality tests do not provide any reason why the number of complaints has suddenly risen, the attention is now directed to the goal of finding the exact error or faulty part. This is depicted in Fig. 4. Our approach provides the domain expert with the possibility to integrate any data sources into the analysis. We therefore assume that a database exists that contains the complaints (Fig. 4(c)). This does not limit the general application of our approach, since this data source can be generated by extraction from workshops or using text mining from web sources in a previous step. In any case, the domain expert has the ability to search for new hints, such as whether a component is affected by errors in particular. This can occur in the first step during the interactive visualization (Fig. 4(d)), or only after integration into a common data set in the subsequent analysis (Fig. 4(e)). In the latter case, the domain expert only needs to make minor adjustments to the predefined analysis, such as parameter adjustments or manual processing through programming-by-example, in the integration step. At the end of this process, the domain expert recognizes that the adhesive bonds for any reason do not withstand the operational loads of daily use.

Step 3: Determine the Reason

Now that the reason for the increased complaint numbers is known, the domain expert must find the cause. An overview of the possibilities and activities in this step can be seen in Fig. 5. Hereby, the first step is the evaluation of data sources to decide which ones are suitable and should be used for further analysis. Several data sources must be considered in our example scenario: First, the databases that contain the produced products (Fig. 5(a)) and the complaints (Fig. 5(b)) are used again. Second, two additional data sources are used as part of the analysis in order to obtain the workers or shifts involved (Fig. 5(c)), as well as various environmental variables recorded by sensors (Fig. 5(d)). It should be noted that the database with the results of the internal quality tests is no longer included in the analysis, since the domain expert could already ascertain in the previous step that no gain in knowledge is to be expected out of this data source. In contrast

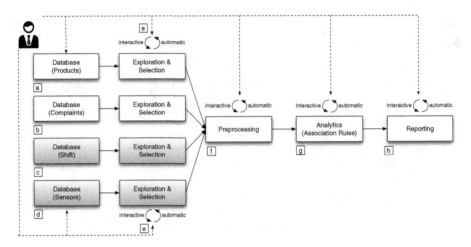

Fig. 5. Resulting analysis flow through adjustments leading to meaningful insights.

to a conventional approach (cf. Sect. 2), the user is obligated to evaluate the data sources in order to obtain reliable analysis results. Using our approach, the data sources can be individually evaluated (Fig. 5(e)). In particular, the use of different visualizations to provide information about characteristics of the data sets is strongly recommended. This enables the proposed better understanding of the data to be analyzed.

In addition, the data quantity can already be reduced in this step by filtering uninteresting attributes or periods directly in the visualization or integration. Thus, these attributes no longer have to be considered for subsequent steps. Hence, different samples can be used to keep the data set transparent to the domain expert as well as to reduce the computation time. This could be achieved, e.g., by a programming-by-example approach in which the data is visualized (most likely as a table view) and the user's attention is led to problematic parts in the data, e.g., to outliers or erroneous entries (Fig. 5(f)).

In the second step of the analysis, the domain expert must now find links between information contained in the new data sources and the resulting defective products. Hereby, an interactive generation of association rules is appropriate (Fig. 5(g)). In this case, parameter adjustments and attribute selection can be used to make changes until abnormalities occur. In our conceived scenario, it quickly becomes clear that neither workers nor the day of the week is responsible. The next cause that our domain expert is considering is the temperature inside the machine or in its environment. For this reason, the data source with the sensor data is now moving into the analyst's focus. During the interactive exploration of the data set, it can already be seen that the temperature is subject to unexpected fluctuations, and therefore, has to be evaluated more precisely. To realize this, the domain expert selects different maximum temperatures and restricts the data set in this way. The system-wide rule-generation system allows the data records to be filtered as desired and analyzed with the same parameters.

Hence, domain experts can approximate stepwise to the maximum temperature at which no abnormality in durability results occur – without having to perform repetitive tasks. In any case, our approach enables the domain expert to rapidly find out that the temperature during production is the cause of quality issues and, consequently, the resulting high number of complaints.

Step 4: Generate a Report
Finally, it is necessary to communicate the created insights (Fig. 5(h)) and how they are retrieved. This is useful in different ways. First, the domain expert can get an overview of accomplished steps and the retrieved results. The latter could also be prepared for management purposes. Second, this could be used to create recommendations for actions of the IT department, e.g., hints about demanded (prospective predefined) reports. In the context of our scenario, this means that different reports must be created with different objectives: firstly, a report on the cause of the issue, as well as suggestions for correcting it. In this case, the high temperature and, as a result, the maximum temperature at which the quality meets the usual requirements. Secondly, a report to the IT department containing the content of the analysis as well as the reasons for it to be implemented in the existing standard solutions.

6.2 Requirement Validation

In this section, we validate the requirements against the described approach.

The first requirement (**R1**) describes the user as central role in the analysis process, which is the core principle we build our extended Visual Analytics process on. In this process, the user has full control over each step – and even in selecting the sequence of execution, e.g., using data mashups [27]. The next requirement is to set the process in the context of exploration (**R2**). We achieve this by integrating the user in each part of the analysis and allow changing parameters and interaction. Furthermore, we can use the rule generation to propagate a change in one step to all dependent steps. This concept is very powerful as it allows the user to perform various analyses over several steps with little effort. The next two requirements are in some kind related. If we put the user in the loop, it is easy to see that the user can control how extensive the combination between automatic and interactive methods (**R4**) is executed. However, this requirement is dependent to a satisfying complexity reduction (**R3**). As our process does not specify how exactly the steps have to be implemented, it is unclear to which extent the complexity of a selected algorithm can be reduced. Finally, if we use a data mashup approach such as the one introduced by Hirmer et al. [28–30] for the process, it is very generic (**R5**) as the user is able to combine single services or algorithms to a comprehensive analysis process.

This approach also allows the user to raise the feedback loop to a new level, e.g., by simply re-executing individual nodes and evaluating the corresponding result immediately. This refined result can afterwards be automatically propagated to subsequent nodes and the user can be involved in case of conflicts. Thus, both the recalculation and the workload of the domain expert can be reduced.

Such an implementation would fit well for implementing the feedback loop of our process, whereby the user must be informed of the current status at all times.

In summary, our process is able to fulfill most of the requirements (**R1, R2, R3, R5**) in an extensive way, while in particular, **R2, R3**, support the domain expert in conducting customized analysis. However, the complexity reduction (**R4**) has to be evaluated for each algorithm applied.

Nonetheless, there are still some limitations in our approach. First, a generic approach could never be as well-fitting as a specialized implementation for a selected domain. Second, it is not a trivial problem to select an appropriate visualization based on generic incoming data. Third, the number of possible interaction techniques and algorithms is unmanageable and leads to a trade-off between functionality and simplicity. Furthermore, we expect mental reservation in IT departments as it is still rather unusual to allow end users to specify their own reports from scratch, even if this is an emerging area as can be seen in Self Service Business Intelligence. Stodder et al. [12] identify possible conflicts, e.g., changes in conventional, project-oriented workflows of an IT department or data security and governance concerns. This could lead to the fact that there is no longer a *Single Point of Truth*, which means that information is only stored in a single location. Last but not least, this kind of analysis process requires more time than a more automated method and depends very strong on the domain expert and his or her discipline in evaluating every aspect of the data. According to Pirolli and Card [20], there is a bias, which means that patterns are ignored or data is selected and filtered to fit for a specific analysis goal.

7   Summary and Outlook

In this article, we introduce a human-centered approach for interactive data processing and analytics. Due to the increasing amount of data and the high complexity of data analytics, insights and interaction of domain experts are important factors to enable high quality results. To enable this, we propose a new extended Visual Analytics process that enables human interaction in each step of the analysis, ranging from data source selection, to data preprocessing, and finally, to the analysis itself. In a first step, we derive requirements from a real world motivating scenario that serves as foundation for our approach. After that, the process itself is introduced and its steps are described. In order to evaluate our approach, we introduce a case study. This case study clearly points out that our process enables the domain expert to speed up the analysis significantly and, as a result, allows to react faster to problem situations. This is expected to lead to a better business result as problems are recognized earlier, as well as potential opportunities to be detected at all.

In our future work, we will investigate the different steps based on our process in an overarching architecture and in more detail. One particular issue is to derive concepts to reduce the conflict potential between domain experts and IT departments as this will directly influence the solution quality.

References

1. IBM: What is big data? http://www.ibm.com/software/data/bigdata/what-is-big-data.html
2. Maimon, O., Rokach, L.: Introduction to Knowledge Discovery and Data Mining. In: Maimon, O., Rokach, L. (eds.) Data Mining and Knowledge Discovery Handbook. Springer, New York (2010)
3. Keim, D., Andrienko, G., Fekete, J.-D., Görg, C., Kohlhammer, J., Melançon, G.: Visual analytics: definition, process, and challenges. In: Kerren, A., Stasko, J.T., Fekete, J.-D., North, C. (eds.) Information Visualization. LNCS, vol. 4950, pp. 154–175. Springer, Heidelberg (2008). https://doi.org/10.1007/978-3-540-70956-5_7
4. Gantz, J., Reinsel, D.: THE DIGITAL UNIVERSE IN 2020: Big Data, Bigger Digital Shadows, and Biggest Growth in the Far East. International Data Corporation (IDC) (2012)
5. EMC Corporation: Digital Universe Invaded By Sensors. Press Release, EMC Corporation (2014)
6. Puolamäki, K., Bertone, A., Therón, R., Huisman, O., Johansson, J., Miksch, S., Papapetrou, P., Rinzivillo, S.: Data mining. In: Keim, D., Kohlhammer, J., Ellis, G., Mansmann, F. (eds.) Mastering the Information Age, pp. 39–56. Eurographics Association, Goslar (2010)
7. Thomas, J.J., Cook, K.A.: Illuminating the Path: The Research and Development Agenda for Visual Analytics. National Visualization and Analytics Center (2005)
8. Imhoff, C., White, C.: Self-Service Business Intelligence. Best Practices Report, TDWI Research (2011)
9. Keim, D.A., Mansmann, F., Schneidewind, J., Ziegler, H.: Challenges in visual data analysis. In: Proceedings of the International Conference on Information Visualisation, pp. 9–16. IEEE (2006)
10. Eckerson, W.W.: Self-Service BI. Checklist Report, TDWI Research (2009)
11. Keim, D.A., Kohlhammer, J., Mansmann, F., May, T., Wanner, F.: Visual analytics. In: Keim, D., Kohlhammer, J., Ellis, G., Mansmann, F. (eds.) Mastering the Information Age, pp. 7–18. Eurographics Association, Goslar (2010)
12. Stodder, D.: Visual Analytics for Making Smarter Decisions Faster. Best Practices Report, TDWI Research (2015)
13. Endert, A., Hossain, M.S., Ramakrishnan, N., North, C., Fiaux, P., Andrews, C.: The human is the loop: new directions for visual analytics. J. Intell. Inf. Syst. **43**, 411–435 (2014)
14. Fayyad, U., Piatetsky-Shapiro, G., Smyth, P.: The KDD process for extracting useful knowledge from volumes of data. Commun. ACM **39**, 27–34 (1996)
15. Behringer, M., Hirmer, P., Mitschang, B.: Towards interactive data processing and analytics - putting the human in the center of the loop. In: Proceedings of the 19th International Conference on Enterprise Information Systems - Volume 3: ICEIS, INSTICC, pp. 87–96. SciTePress (2017)
16. Card, S.K., Mackinlay, J.D., Shneiderman, B.: Information visualization. In: Card, S.K., Mackinlay, J.D., Shneiderman, B. (eds.) Readings in Information Visualization: Using Vision to Think, pp. 1–34. Morgan Kaufmann Publishers Inc., San Francisco (1999)
17. Shneiderman, B.: The eyes have it: a task by data type taxonomy for information visualizations. In: Symposium on Visual Languages, pp. 336–343. IEEE, Washington, DC (1996)

18. Sacha, D., Stoffel, A., Stoffel, F., Kwon, B.C., Ellis, G., Keim, D.A.: Knowledge generation model for visual analytics. IEEE Trans. Vis. Comput. Graph. **20**, 1604–1613 (2014)
19. Alpar, P., Schulz, M.: Self-service business intelligence. Bus. Inf. Syst. Eng. **58**, 151–155 (2016)
20. Pirolli, P., Card, S.: The sensemaking process and leverage points for analyst technology as identified through cognitive task analysis. In: Proceedings of the International Conference on Intelligence Analysis (2005)
21. Bertini, E., Lalanne, D.: Surveying the complementary role of automatic data analysis and visualization in knowledge discovery. In: Proceedings of the ACM SIGKDD Workshop on Visual Analytics and Knowledge Discovery: Integrating Automated Analysis with Interactive Exploration, pp. 12–20. ACM Press, New York (2009)
22. Bögl, M., Aigner, W., Filzmoser, P., Lammarsch, T., Miksch, S., Rind, A.: Visual analytics for model selection in time series analysis. IEEE Trans. Vis. Comput. Graph. **19**, 2237–2246 (2013)
23. Meunier, R.: The pipes and filters architecture. In: Coplien, J.O., Schmidt, D.C. (eds.) Pattern Languages of Program Design, pp. 427–440. ACM Press, New York (1995)
24. Cypher, A. (ed.): Watch What I Do - Programming by Demonstration. MIT Press, Cambridge (1993)
25. Kandel, S., Heer, J., Plaisant, C., Kennedy, J., van Ham, F., Riche, N.H., Weaver, C., Lee, B., Brodbeck, D., Buono, P.: Research directions in data wrangling: visualizations and transformations for usable and credible data. Inf. Vis. **10**, 271–288 (2011)
26. Hirmer, P., Behringer, M., Mitschang, B.: Partial execution of mashup plans during modeling time. Res. Dev. (2017). Springer (to appear)
27. Daniel, F., Matera, M.: Mashups. Concepts, Models and Architectures. Springer, Heidelberg (2014)
28. Hirmer, P., Mitschang, B.: FlexMash - flexible data mashups based on pattern-based model transformation. In: Daniel, F., Pautasso, C. (eds.) RMC 2015. CCIS, vol. 591, pp. 12–30. Springer, Cham (2016). https://doi.org/10.1007/978-3-319-28727-0_2
29. Hirmer, P., Reimann, P., Wieland, M., Mitschang, B.: Extended techniques for flexible modeling and execution of data mashups. In Helfert, M., Holzinger, A., Belo, O., Francalanci, C. (eds.) Proceedings of 4th International Conference on Data Management Technologies and Applications, pp. 111–122. SciTePress (2015)
30. Hirmer, P., Behringer, M.: FlexMash 2.0 - flexible modeling and execution of data mashups. In: Daniel, F., Gaedke, M. (eds.) RMC 2016. CCIS, vol. 696, pp. 10–29. Springer, Cham (2017). https://doi.org/10.1007/978-3-319-53174-8_2

Enterprise Architecture

Understanding Governance Mechanisms and Health in Software Ecosystems: A Systematic Literature Review

Carina Alves[1(✉)], Joyce Oliveira[1,2], and Slinger Jansen[3]

[1] Universidade Federal de Pernambuco,
Centro de Informática, Pernambuco, Brazil
{cfa, japo}@cin.ufpe.br
[2] Universidade Federal de Mato Grosso, Instituto de Engenharia, Cuiabá, Brazil
[3] Department of Information and Computing Sciences, Utrecht University,
Utrecht, The Netherlands
slinger.jansen@uu.nl

Abstract. In a software ecosystem, organizations work collaboratively to remain profitable and survive market changes. For the relationship between these organizations to succeed, it is necessary to participate in the ecosystem software without violating rules of collaboration or to take advantages that destabilize the general health of the ecosystem. The application of governance mechanisms is essential for achieving this balance. Governance mechanisms are employed to define the level of control, rights of decision and scope of owner versus shared ownership in an ecosystem. Selecting appropriate governance mechanisms, organizations can gain strategic advantage over others leading them to better performance and, consequently, to be healthier. In this article, we report a systematic literature review that aggregates definitions of software ecosystem governance and classify governance mechanisms in three dimensions: value creation, coordination of players, and organizational openness and control. Additionally, we propose a research agenda that addresses relevant topics for researchers and practitioners to explore these issues. Initially, we performed a systematic literature review of 63 primary studies. In this extended article, we have included more 26 studies to analyze the relation between health and governance. In total, we reviewed 89 studies. 52 metrics were identified and classified into the three health elements (productivity, robustness, niche creation). Our results suggest that software ecosystems governance determines decision rights between platform owners and extension developers, control mechanisms used by the platform owner, and platform ownership. We posit that ecosystem health is under the direct influence of how governance mechanisms are implemented by ecosystem's players.

Keywords: Software ecosystems · Governance · Health
Systematic Literature review

© Springer International Publishing AG, part of Springer Nature 2018
S. Hammoudi et al. (Eds.): ICEIS 2017, LNBIP 321, pp. 517–542, 2018.
https://doi.org/10.1007/978-3-319-93375-7_24

1 Introduction

In the last decade, a large amount of research has been devoted to investigate the field of software ecosystems from managerial, social, and technological perspectives [1, 2]. Software ecosystems are sets of actors functioning as a unit and interacting with a shared market for software and services, together with relationships among them [3].

Examples of successful software platforms are Apple's iOS, Google Apps, and the Mozilla Firefox browser. The leading firm, typically called the orchestrator (or keystone) firm, must promote the sustainable development of the ecosystem by defining strategies and orchestrating the activities of players. The orchestrator is responsible for managing the evolution of the enterprise architecture [4] and the interactions among all actors within the ecosystem [5]. The governance of software ecosystems requires a careful balance of control and autonomy given to players. Orchestrators that are able to balance their own interests by bringing joint benefits for other players are likely to create healthy ecosystems. Software ecosystems governance has become a crucial managerial aspect for proprietary platform owners and open source communities.

According to Tiwana [6], governance mechanisms are employed to establish the level of control, decisions rights, and scope of proprietary versus shared ownership. There are several models to govern software ecosystems. For instance, GNU Linux is an open source ecosystem with a thriving community of developers. Apple's iOS is a prosperous example of proprietary ecosystem with tight control mechanisms. Google built a lively ecosystem around its Android open source community named the "Open handset Alliance". On the other hand, Nokia's Symbian is an open source operating system that failed to create a vibrant ecosystem due to its inability to attract partners and develop a rich set of apps [7].

The examples above show that choosing the right ecosystem strategies and governance mechanisms are life-or-death decisions for orchestrator organizations. In fact, companies engaging in an ecosystem are mutually dependent on each other for survival [8].

We define software ecosystem governance mechanisms as managerial tools of participants in software ecosystems, i.e., orchestrators and platform extenders that have the goal of influencing an ecosystem's health. Ecosystems are healthy when they exhibit longevity and propensity for growth [9].

Selecting appropriate governance mechanisms is not a trivial task. The challenge is to bound players actions without excessively constraining the desired level of innovation and value creation in the ecosystem. This situation creates fine tension between control and autonomy. Balancing these tensions is one of the main goals of software ecosystem governance. The correct implementation of governance mechanisms can accommodate these tensions towards a sustainable and healthy ecosystem. On the other hand, ineffective governance can result in a declining growth of the ecosystem [10]. The challenge of selecting ecosystem governance strategies that contributes towards the ecosystem health has driven us to conduct a systematic literature review. Our previous review [11] aims at synthesizing the increasing number of studies in the field of software ecosystem governance. In this extended article we include two news research questions to analyze the relationship between health and governance. Therefore, we carried out a new stage of article selection and synthesis.

This article is organized as follows. Section 2 describes the research method. The results of the review are presented in Sect. 3. To discuss the results of our review and propose future areas for investigation, a research agenda containing six areas of interest is proposed in Sect. 4. Then, we discuss threats to validity in Sect. 5. Finally, Sect. 6 concludes this article.

2   Research Method

A Systematic Literature Review (SLR) is a means for answering specific research questions, examining a particular research topic, or phenomenon of interest by systematically identifying, evaluating, and interpreting available relevant research. Our review protocol follows guidelines from Kitchenham and Charters [12]. We undertook the review of studies following these activities: defining research questions, searching relevant studies, applying inclusion/exclusion criteria, assessing the quality of studies, analyzing data, and synthesis.

2.1   Research Questions

We specified four research questions to guide our study:

  (i) RQ1. How is governance characterized in software ecosystems literature?
 (ii) RQ2. What are the mechanisms proposed to govern software ecosystems?
(iii) RQ3. How is health characterized in software ecosystem literature?
 (iv) RQ4. What are the metrics proposed to assess the health of software ecosystems?

In RQ1, we present and discuss available definitions for software ecosystems governance proposed by primary studies. Then, we compare the definitions available and propose an integrated definition for the term. We classify the governance mechanisms based on the data gathered from the primary studies following a thematic analysis approach [13]. Our goal to answer the second question (RQ2) is to identify the mechanisms proposed by current literature to govern software ecosystems. We aim at classifying the governance mechanism adopted both by proprietary and open source ecosystems. Selecting appropriate software ecosystem governance mechanisms can nurture the health of the ecosystem [2]. Then, by answering the third question (RQ3), we examine how the health of a software ecosystem is defined. Finally, in the fourth question (RQ4), we show metrics available to measure its health. These metrics are considered the key performance indicators for managers and indicate how well they are doing regarding the governance of their software ecosystems.

2.2   Search Process

To guide the systematic literature review, a protocol was developed to specify the steps and criteria to undertake the review. The review protocol includes details of how different types of studies will be located, appraised, and synthesized [14]. The strategy to collect studies included the following steps: (i) automatic search of electronic databases (ii) manual search of journals, conferences, and workshops (iii) analysis of reference lists from other secondary studies in software ecosystems. The automatic search was executed on the following databases: ACM Digital Library, IEEE Xplore Digital Library, Science Direct, and SpringerLink. We used two independent search strings: "software ecosystem", "platform ecosystem". We opted to use generic terms to avoid over restricting the search process. In the early stages of our research we tried to use the search string "software ecosystem" AND "governance". However, we considered that using these combined keywords the results retrieved from the search engines were very limited. In addition, we conducted a manual search in the following journals, conferences, and workshops:

- Information and Software Technology;
- Journal of Software Systems;
- International Conference on Software Business;
- International Workshop on Software Ecosystems.

To complement our manual search, we analysed the references of the following reviews in the field of software ecosystems: [1, 5, 15, 16]. Although the scope and research questions of these reviews are different from ours, we examined the list of articles to correct any eventual omission of studies from the other search procedures. 7 studies [S13, S17, S18, S25, S26, S41, S61] were obtained from the analysis of secondary studies described above.

2.3   Inclusion and Exclusion Criteria

We adopted the following inclusion criteria to select articles: (i) studies written in English, (ii) studies that answer at least one research question. The exclusion criteria adopted was: (i) secondary studies (e.g. mapping studies and systematic literature reviews), (ii) technical reports, abstracts, and whitepapers, (iii) duplicate reports of the same study.

The literature collection started with 997 articles returned from the electronic and manual search. The automatic search was conducted on the 5th of January 2016. We did not restrict year range in our search. Then, we excluded articles based on titles and abstract that did not satisfy our inclusion criteria. In practice, we assessed if the title and abstract are likely to answer at least one RQ. Whenever we were in doubt we included the article for further analysis of its full content. After this step, we included 592 studies. Then we read the full content of the articles and selected 67 primary studies. In a last step, a quality assessment [11, 17] of each article was conducted and we finally selected 63 articles [26]. In this extended article, we included 26 new articles that specifically address RQ3 and RQ4, totalizing 89 studies listed in the Appendix.

2.4   Data Extraction and Analysis

We used a database to store data from the selected studies. Two researchers extracted data from the studies. Several discussion meetings were held with all authors to compare extractions, clarify uncertainties, agree on discrepancies, and perform sanity checks. To answer RQ1, we simply searched the term "governance" in the primary studies and checked if the article provided a definition for governance in the context of software ecosystems. To answer RQ2, we used thematic analysis as synthesis method, following the recommended steps proposed by [13]. We identified the relevant codes from primary studies. Then, we merged the codes into key themes. We considered that governance mechanisms were encapsulated in related terms, such as: "manage", "govern", "control", "strategy", "orchestration" and "critical factors". We identified the term "health" in the primary studies to answer RQ3. To answer RQ4, we used productivity, robustness and niche creation definitions [S76, S25, S77] to classify health metrics.

3   Results

3.1   RQ1: How is Governance Characterized in Software Ecosystems Literature?

Our results show that the concept of governance is gaining importance in software ecosystem literature. 9 studies [S1, S4, S20, S21, S28, S32, S51, S54, S62] explicitly define what is software ecosystem governance. Jansen [S34] proposes that governance is one of the key domains of the Open Software Enterprise Model. The study adopts the definition of governance given by Dubinsky and Kruchten [S12], who consider governance as *"the way a responsibilities, and decision-making processes"*. According to Jansen et al. [S32], it also involves the assignment of roles and decision rights, measures, and policies. A fundamental governance decision that orchestrators must make is how much power is given to the community and how much control it keeps for itself. Jansen and Cusmano [S28] and van Angeren et al. [S54] consider that ecosystem governance *"involves the use of strategic procedures and processes to control, maintain, or change the ecosystem"*. Study [S54] also states that software ecosystems governance *"encompasses both technical and managerial aspects, including the management of the software platform and its interfaces, definition of business and partnership models, and establishment of entry barriers"*.

Baars and Jansen [S4] software ecosystems governance as: *"procedures and processes by which a company controls, changes or maintains its current and future position in a software ecosystem on all different scope levels"*. Studies [S1], [S28] and [S62] adopt the same definition. In [S13], the authors do not define what is governance in the context of ecosystems, but they provide a rich discussion on the tensions between open and closed governance models as platforms mature.

Ghazawne et al., [S20] argue that the governance of platform ecosystems involves *"a delicate balance act of the platform owner, trying to keep control of the platform while simultaneously seeking to expand the diversity of potential developers"*. According to Tiwana et al. [S51], governance broadly refers to *"who decides what in an ecosystem"*. Study [S51] states that ecosystem governance *"involves sharing responsibilities and authority, aligning incentives, and sharing stakes"*. Goldbach and Kemper [S21] adopt the same definition of platform governance given by study [S51] to understand how control mechanisms imposed by the platform owner affects the platform stickiness. All primary studies that answer this research question suggest that a key challenge faced by platform owners is balancing their own strategic objectives with the goals and activities of players within the platform. Such delicate balance becomes critical for software ecosystems to thrive.

7 studies [S10, S28, S32, S41, S54, S55, S62] indicate that ecosystem governance influences the health and sustainability of ecosystems. This means that governance strategies and managerial decisions taken by orchestrators will affect the healthy evolution of the entire ecosystem. The primary studies suggest that health metrics provide operational indicators on how software ecosystems are governed. We conclude this section by proposing an integrated definition for software ecosystems governance: *all processes by which a player creates value, coordinates relationships, and defines controls.*

3.2 RQ2: What are the Mechanisms Proposed to Govern Software Ecosystems?

We define software ecosystem governance mechanisms as managerial tools of players in software ecosystems that have the goal of influencing an ecosystem's health. We observed that frequently authors use terms such as "orchestration" and "management" to refer to what can be understood as a governance mechanism. To classify the studies, we propose three main categories of governance mechanisms [11]:

Value Creation – Involve mechanisms to generate and distribute value for the whole ecosystem. Value creation mechanisms are generally proposed and nurtured by the orchestrator (i.e. platform and/or marketplace owner), who must understand how to create value that is appreciated both by partners and customers. In this context, it is important to identify sources of value (such as licenses and revenue models), and stimulate the co-creation of value among players, by means of innovation, investments, and cost sharing. As a result, the ecosystem can attract and retain partners who will mutually benefit from the value distributed within the ecosystem. This category covers all the incentives and benefits that players can gain from a software ecosystem.

Coordination of Players – Describe mechanisms to maintain the consistency and integration of activities, relationships, and structures of the ecosystem, for both customers and partners, leading to a harmonious and effective coordination with players in the ecosystem. We identified mechanisms to stimulate partnership models, define roles and responsibilities for players, improve communication channels within the ecosystem, and nurture collaborations. In addition, primary studies propose mechanisms to manage critical issues, such as: conflicts, resources, risks, and expectations. This category focuses on the coordination aspects of governance, whereas the next focuses on strategic decisions of openness and control.

Organizational Openness and Control – These mechanisms capture the notorious tension between open versus closed organizational models and represent how control will be retained by the orchestrator to guarantee its power position and how autonomy will be given for the community to make their own decisions independently. On the one side, orchestrators can support autonomy, distribute power, and share knowledge regarding technological roadmaps and architectural decisions. On the other side, orchestrators can keep control by defining entry requirements, establishing quality standards, and through certifications.

Table 1 (previously presented in [11]) shows the classification of governance mechanisms proposed by the primary studies. In this extended article, we updated the complete list of primary studies, now it has a total of 89 papers. Therefore, the percentage has changed. We observed that the most cited mechanisms are: attract and maintain partners (28 articles, 31%), share knowledge (20 articles, 22%), promote innovation (25 articles, 28%), manage licenses (21 articles, 23%). We do not claim that these are the most important governance mechanisms, as several studies suggest that the governance must match the specific context and market drivers involved in the ecosystem [S4, S13, S25 S32, S43].

Table 1. Governance Mechanisms in Software Ecosystems presented in [11].

Governance mechanisms		Studies	Number of studies
Value creation	Promote innovation	S61, S7, S32, S50, S40, S48, S52, S9, S47, S3, S7, S45, S10, S8, S35, S27, S18, S17, S19, S61, S38, S57, S24, S43, S44	25
	Manage licenses	S16, S32, S41, S40, S1, S3, S6, S58, S28, S2, S51, S63, S8, S27, S18, S13, S17, S57, S31, S22, S24	21
	Create revenue models	S7, S3, S45, S58, S4, S5, S7S6, S28, S10, S62, S30, S23, S27, S61, S38, S53, S57, S23, S36, S39	20
	Attract and maintain varied partners	S61, S32, S29, S52, S47, S45, S15, S58, S4, S6, S10, S62, S55, S46, S63, S35, S27, S18, S17, S61, S38, S53, S57, S42, S19, S23, S26, S36	28
	Stimulate partner investments and share costs	S61, S56, S3, S45, S8, S27, S22, S23, S43	9
Coordination of players	Create partnership models	S32, S56, S54, S4, 28, S62, S55, S49, S30, S8, S27, S53, S31, S19, S24	15
	Define rules to manage relationships	S32, S40, S29, S56, S52, S9, S3, S4, S5, S46, S2, S63, S35, S27, S57, S42, S36	17
	Establish roles and responsibilities	S41, S50, S40, S56, S3, S15, S4, S5, S49, S46, S51, S63, S27, S13, S42, S26, S37	17
	Enable effective communication channels	S41, S29, S48, S52, S9, S3, S11, S14, 28, S16, S27, S31, S37	13
	Manage conflicts	S32, S52, S15, S8, S27, S57, S31, S42, S19	9
	Manage resources		14

(continued)

Table 1. (*continued*)

Governance mechanisms		Studies	Number of studies
		S1, S52, S9, S47, S3, S15, S10, S46, S20, S35, S42, S26, S36, S44	
	Manage risks	S50, S40, S56, S52, S58, S46, S30, S8, S18, S17, S57, S22, S39, S43	14
	Manage expectations	S47, S49, S16	3
	Nurture collaborations	S61, S50, S52, S46, S58, 28, S62, S55, S49, S46, S35, S17, S42, S44	14
Organizational openness and control	Support autonomy	S7, S50, S52, S3, S48, S4, S7, S46, S20, S51, S35, S18, S17, S61, S42	15
	Share knowledge	S16, S32, S50, S40, S29, S48, S52, S3, S4, S11, S62, S30, S20, S35, S18, S17, S61, S57, S31, S37	20
	Distribute power	S32, S50, S52, S3, S15, S46, S16, S51, S27, S37	10
	Define entry requirements	S54, S45, S4, S28, S62, S30, S18, S38, S53, S24, S36	11
	Share architectural decisions	S16, S29, S48, S1, S52, S9, S47, S3, S5, S58, S28, S62, S2, S51, S27, S11, S14	17
	Share roadmaps	S52, S58, S28, S27, S57, S31	6
	Define quality standards and certifications	S32, S41, S50, S40, S56, S58, S28, S62, S55, S30, S38, S57, S22	13

3.3   RQ3: How is Health Characterized in Software Ecosystem Literature?

Health is a term originally formulated in the field of natural ecosystems. Costanza [S68] defines a healthy natural ecosystem as "*being stable and sustainable, maintaining its organization and autonomy over time and its resilience to stress*". Then, authors from the field of business ecosystems borrowed the term health, such as Den Hartigh, et al. [S10], Iansiti and Levien [S25]. The health concept has been initially proposed by Iansiti and Levien [S25], as a way to measure the performance of business ecosystems. The authors borrowed analogies from biology to explain that similarly as in nature, the health of business networks depends on the intertwined and mutually dependent relationships among ecosystem players. This means that each player may contribute or damage the health of the whole ecosystem.

As suggested by Hansen et al. [18], software ecosystems can be considered a particular type of business ecosystem in which a technological platform intermediates the interactions among players. We observed that primary studies frequently adopt the same definitions from the business ecosystems domain for measuring the health of software ecosystems. In general, platform owners hold a strong responsibility to sustain the performance of the ecosystem. As Iansiti and Levien [S25] points out, platform owners do not promote the prosperity of others for altruistic reasons; they do it because it is a very beneficial strategy. Fotrousi et al. [28] affirm that to create value in a software ecosystem, a platform owner has to ensure that the ecosystem is healthy and sustainable. The overall performance of software ecosystems depends on the actions and decisions taken by each individual player. An ecosystem is healthy when it provides mutual benefits for players [S83]. Sustainability is a closely related concept to ecosystem health. Dhungana et al. [S70] defines sustainable software ecosystem as *"one that can increase or maintain its user/developer community over longer periods of time and can survive inherent changes such as new technologies or new products (e.g., from competitors) that can change the population (the community of users, developers, etc.) or significant attacks/ sabotage of the ecosystem platform"*. To analyze how authors in the field of software ecosystems understand the term health, Table 2 presents different definitions for software ecosystem health proposed in the literature.

Table 2. Definitions for software ecosystem health found in studies.

Definition	Studies	Number of studies
1. Can be measured as productivity, robustness, niche creation.	S41, S64, S65, S82, S54, S71, S44, S28, S10, S62, S55, S47, S30, S21, S25, S76, S89, S77, S83, S66, S57	22
2. Longevity and propensity for growth.	S65, S54, S28, S10, S21, S34, S80, S66, S69	9
3. Can be divided into three components: software component health, software platform health, and software network health.	S41, S65	2
4. The ability of the ecosystem to endure, remain variable and productive over time.	S82, S83, S66, S68	4
5. Provides strategic information on the state and trajectory of ecosystem.	S41, S10, S25	3
6. Is influenced by three forces: actors, software, and orchestration.	S41, S82, S83	3
7. Is mainly defined as the ability to provide durably growing opportunities for its members and for those who depend on it.	S77, S83	2
8. Is a measure that characterizes the performance of an entire ecosystem.	S77, S57, S69	3

3.4   RQ4: What are the Metrics Proposed to Assess the Health of Software Ecosystems?

Measuring the health of software ecosystems inform how the ecosystem is evolving and how effective the governance mechanisms are contributing to the future sustainability of individual players as well as the whole ecosystem. Therefore, we argue that providing an extensive catalogue of health metrics helps players to select the best strategies to survive and obtain benefits from the ecosystem.

In their seminal work, Iansiti and colleagues [S76, S25, S77] defined three critical measures of health for business and biological ecosystems: productivity, robustness, and niche creation. We observed that their studies on ecosystem health have strongly influenced the majority of authors in the software ecosystems domain who investigate this topic. Given the great relevance of Iansiti and colleagues' work to the body of knowledge in the field of software ecosystem health, we adopt their classification to measure ecosystem health by means of productivity, robustness, and niche creation. Following we define each health element:

- Productivity – The ability in which an ecosystem converts inputs into outputs;
- Robustness – The ability of an ecosystem to survive disruptions such as technological and market changes;
- Niche creation – The ability of an ecosystem to increase meaningful diversity by creating valuable resources and niches.

From Table 2 we synthesize the following: ecosystems are healthy when they exhibit longevity and propensity for growth. Software ecosystem health is determined by the capability of an ecosystem to persistently produce meaningful outputs (productivity), survive market disruptions (robustness), and create niches in the ecosystem (niche creation). The health of a software ecosystem is dependent on the health of the platform, the extensions and its extenders, and the network health of extenders surrounding the platform.

A healthy ecosystem attracts and retains players who can create value and innovations for the platform [S54, S38]. Measuring the health can inform the functioning and evolution by predicting changes and future states of an ecosystem [S82]. Mhamdia [S66] extends Iansiti and Levien's three health dimensions by introducing creativity and stakeholder satisfaction dimensions. The study proposes a conceptual model to measure the health of software ecosystems.

In a recent SLR, Manikas [16] concluded that successful governance of software ecosystem must make suitable use of ecosystem resources, enhance productivity, support robustness, and promote the ecosystem health. In [S69], den Hartigh suggest that health measurement can be used as an ecosystem governance instrument. These observations show the relevance of selecting appropriate health metrics because they are operational measures of software ecosystems governance.

A large number of metrics to assess the health of software ecosystems have been proposed in literature. However, previous studies do not provide a comprehensive catalogue of health metrics. Table 3 presents a classification of health metrics proposed by primary studies. In our review, 52 metrics were identified and classified into the three health elements (productivity, robustness, niche creation). By adopting thematic analysis to synthesize evidence, we categorized the metrics identified in the primary studies into groups based on their similar meaning. For example, the measures number of copyrights and number of trademarks proposed by Huang et al. [S24] and Ceccagnoli et al. [S8] were integrated within the metric number of patents. Other variants, such as, number of new developers per month [S80], percentage of developers with partner status [S54] were classified in a more generic metric of active contributors/developers.

In some studies, the authors do not explicitly mention the term metrics to assess the health of ecosystems, but after careful analysis and interpretation we considered some terms as types of metric. For example, West and Wood [S61] use the term "success factors" to present measures that other studies clearly classify as a health metric. Another example is Mizushima et al. [S40] that present a set of mechanism to form a successful OSS community, these mechanisms are clearly types of metrics: events for developers, knowledge sharing.

In short, our procedure to synthesize evidence consisted of starting to fill the table with metrics that were explicitly cited as health metrics by the primary studies. Then, we included data that was closely related to the initially identified health metrics but authors do not describe them as such. To avoid a high granularity of information, we only listed metrics that were cited by at least two studies. In essence, no single metric can cover all constituting aspects of software ecosystem health. It is necessary to select a combination of measures to evaluate the health and resulting performance of software ecosystems.

We also classified the studies that propose health metrics for open source and proprietary ecosystems, as described in Table 4. We identified that 24 studies (26%) present metrics to assess the health of proprietary ecosystems and 25 studies (28%) propose health metrics for open source ecosystems. This finding shows a good balance of research on the health of both proprietary and open source ecosystems. However, as highlighted by Alami et al. [S65], ecosystems may not disclose relevant data related to some metrics. For example, data regarding the metric customer leavers can be considered a sign of an unhealthy ecosystem. In fact, this kind of strategic and sensitive data may not be easily obtained. This situation is a challenge to investigate and establish comparisons regarding the health of ecosystems. Data about open source ecosystems can be acquired using repository mining techniques. This can be an advantage to investigate this kind of ecosystem.

Software ecosystem orchestrators can use information that stem from the health metrics to make well-informed decisions about their strategy. For instance, the governance mechanism attracts and maintains varied partners can be operationalized in terms of the health metrics community building/partnership model, stakeholder/contributor satisfaction, perceived level of intimacy/orchestrator support. By assessing these health metrics, players can make informed decisions on how to improve the attraction and maintenance of varied partners. A key contribution of RQ4 is Table 3. It provides an extensive catalogue of health metrics that can be a useful guide for orchestrators to successfully govern and manage software ecosystems. Therefore, by selecting appropriate health metrics, players can direct the ecosystem towards a sustainable path.

Table 3. Metrics to assess the health of software ecosystems proposed by the studies.

Metrics to assess health		
Productivity	Studies	Number of studies
Total factor productivity	S10, S34, S77, S83, S69	5
Productivity improvement	S84, S73, S10, S34, S76, S77, S83	7
New related projects	S74, S76, S34, S80	4
Events for developers	S40, S56, S71, S3, S28, S62, S30, S34	8
Number and size of commits	S84, S70, S85, S64, S71, S83	6
Orchestration techniques	S41, S29, S58, S83	4
Frequency of releases	S41, S40, S65, S29, S71, S89, S80	7
Line of code	S41, S64, S73, S71, S78	5
Increase Customers/users base	S61, S67, S65, S83	4
Customer leavers	S65, S4	2
Network size and effectiveness	S82, S48, S10, S87, S38, S88	6
Active contributors/developers	S67, S64, S65, S5, S73, S74, S4 S30, S81, S87, S89, S80, S38, S83 S19 S79 S69 S88	18
Number of Apps/projects/extensions	S65, S74, S71, S89, S80, S38	6
Number of Patents	S10, S24, S8, S66, S69	5
Technologies/innovations introduced	S61, S32, S40, S10, S34, S76, S77, S83, S66	9
Responsiveness	S34, S69	3
Return on invested capital	S25	1
Robustness	Studies	Number of studies
Survival rates	S10, S30, S34, S25, S76, S77, S83	7
Persistence of structure	S48, S10, S34, S77, S83	5
Predictability	S10, S34, S77, S83	5
Limited obsolescence	S10, S34, S77, S83	4
Network stability/continuity	S85, S72, S40, S48, S10, S30 S34, S83	8
Artifacts quality and certification model	S32, S72, S67, S50, S65, S29, S54, S30, S34, S38, S83	11
Core network consistency	S74, S34	2
Outbound links to other ecosystems	S85, S32, S34, S80	4
Switching costs	S75, S10, S30, S34	4
Marketing and sales	S84, S70, S32, S40, S47, S28, S62	7
Number of downloads	S8,4 S74, S4, S78, S79, S69	6

(*continued*)

Table 3. (*continued*)

Robustness	Studies	Number of studies
Community building/Partnership model	S84, S32, S67, S64, S29, S54, S47, S4, S28, S62, S30, S81, S87	13
Adaptability	S70, S72, S41, S29, S28, S83	6
Connectedness	S85, S82, S48, S54, S74, S37, S10, S55, S30, S26, S34, S87, S83, S66, S69	15
Density	S54, S55, S26, S69	4
Centralization	S82, S10, S55, S30, S89, S78, S69, S88	8
Market share	S65, S10, S34, S89, S38, S69	6
Platform findability	S32, S65, S89, S69	4
Platform stickiness	S61, S65, S75, S34	4
Number of partners/Community building	S85, S67, S64, S40, S54, S4, S28 S10, S55, S26, S25, S81, S87, S79, S69	15
Stakeholder/Contributor satisfaction	S72, S40, S47, S34, S77, S38, S83 S66	8
Profit growth	S41, S40, S28, S10, S62, S66	6
Revenue increase	S28, S10, S66	3
Niche creation	Studies	Number of studies
Value Creation and innovations	S61, S84, S70, S40, S47, S71, S75, S28, S10, S8, S34, S25, S76, S18, S77, S83, S66	17
Variety	S40, S65, S10, S25, S76, S86 S77, S83	8
Number of new projects	S70, S10, S34	3
Visibility in the market/Reputation	S84, S70, S32, S64, S40, S56, S47, S10, S34, S89, S38	3
Entry barriers	S64, S40, S54, S28, S62, S24, S8, S18, S38, S78	10
Openness/transparency level	S70, S16, S32, S41, S50, S40, S29, S3, S36, S28, S62, S30, S24, S8, S86, S54, S86, S38, S78, S33	20
Average number of supported languages	S65, S80, S38	3
Modularity (creation of sub-communities)	S40, S28, S87, S86, S80, S77, S79, S88	8
Number of markets	S36, S34, S38	3
Perceived level of intimacy/Orchestrator support	S67, S64, S40, S29, S47, S34, S38	7
Sales growth/installed customer base	S40, S24, S8	3
Reciprocity	S86, S79	2

Table 4. Type of ecosystem that health metrics have been proposed.

Type of ecosystem	Studies	Number of studies
Open source ecosystems	S84, S70, S16, S85, S32, S67, S64, S40, S65, S82, S73, S74, S74, S71, S4, S28, S34, S81, S87, S89, S80, S78, S79, S69, S88	25
Proprietary ecosystems	S84, S16, S32, S41, S54, S3, S75, S36, S5 S28, S10, S55, S30, S24, S8, S26, S25, S76, S18, S86, S77, S38, S66, S33	24

4 Discussion and Research Agenda

The following statements can contribute to the overall research agenda on software ecosystems and serve as an addendum to the works of Jansen et al. [3], Barbosa et al. [1], Manikas [16], and Axelsson and Skoglund [19].

1. The Need for a Common Vocabulary in Software Ecosystems Governance – The numbers of publications in this domain emphasize that the field of software ecosystems governance is maturing. Increasing numbers of work take positions on definitions of the concepts central to software ecosystems: health [20], governance (this work), open source ecosystems [S34], developer ecosystems [S33], and quality in software ecosystems [19], each of these concepts is settling in as an established term in the ecosystems discourse. We identified that several studies adopt related terms such as management and orchestration to refer to governance mechanisms. Therefore, we suggest the need to establish a common glossary and conceptual framework that collects these definitions into one tome of ecosystems governance knowledge.

2. The Need for Practical Governance Guidance – Even though there exists an extensive body of knowledge on software ecosystems governance, it is hard for practitioners to extract practical and strategic guidance from the works under study. There is a need for more consumable and practical knowledge for practitioners. Other relevant studies for practitioners interested on creating health ecosystems dashboards, include Goeminne and Mens [21] on GitHub analysis, collecting intelligence on the progress of particular ecosystems. These tools can form the basic groundwork under mature evaluation mechanisms and tools for large open and commercial software ecosystems.

3. The Need for Analyzing the Interplay between Governance Mechanisms and Health Metrics – Our study indicates that health metrics provide operational indicators on how software ecosystems are governed. Therefore, by selecting appropriate health metrics, players can govern the ecosystem towards a sustainable path. A challenge remains on how to implement governance to foster innovation and encourage autonomous behavior for diversity, without undermining the quality of software and accountability of players' actions [S20]. The tension between control and autonomy must be appropriately balanced. Understanding how the implementation of specific governance mechanisms affects the success of ecosystems and the underlying enterprise platform is an exciting problem for scholars in the field.

4. Governance of Developer Ecosystems – The developers' and niche players' impacts in ecosystems are amplified by the success of the ecosystem. Examples like Farmville for Facebook and Angry Birds for iOS illustrate how ecosystems grow immensely through the success of its constituents. The developers are the starting point for any software ecosystem; hence the recent increase of interest in developer ecosystems. There is a need for further understanding developers interests and behaviors [S38]. Barriers to entry, platform stickiness, and developer attraction are factors that require further research. An extension to this perspective is a need for further study of enterprise architecture and delivery mechanisms that enable software ecosystems [S33]. Orchestrators must understand developers' motivations and expectations to adopt appropriate governance mechanisms.

5. The Need for Studying Governance in Open Software Ecosystems – Open source ecosystems exhibit different properties than more traditional closed and commercial ecosystems. The openness of a platform permeates through every aspect of an ecosystem, whether it is about ownership of the code or about mechanisms around supporting tools, such as application stores. These openness questions also play a part in the architecture of a platform itself: without an open platform architecture, extenders cannot extend it. In our SLR, we found no study that presented a comparative analysis of governance mechanisms employed by open source versus proprietary ecosystems. This is a promising line of research.

6. The Need for Understanding the Interactions Between Ecosystems – Even good governance can lead to the demise of an ecosystem due to external factors. When looking at the governance and health of the Symbian ecosystem in 2007, it would have been hard to predict its demise. One can speculate about its poor business support from Nokia and fundamental faults in the business model of Symbian. However, it is hard to ignore the impending doom coming from the iPhone after 2007: its high rate of adoption and superior technology simply blew the Symbian ecosystem away. The challenge for governance research in the next decade will be to analyses and understand the interplay between large ecosystems. As long as standards, age-old ecosystems, and settled industry stacks can be blown away or grow exponentially through the workings of other ecosystems, we must develop governance tools and management practices that focus on the robustness of software ecosystems that can prepare for surviving in such storms. Threats to Validity.

. Our study faced similar validity threats as any other systematic literature review. Two of the main limitations in a review are the bias in selection and data extraction procedures [12]. Software ecosystem is a multidisciplinary field covering studies from software engineering, information systems, organization, and management science. To limit the threat of not including relevant primary studies, we adopted a search strategy with generic keywords to retrieve as many articles as possible that were related to the research topic. We complemented the automatic search with manual searches in the main journals, conferences, and workshops where studies in software ecosystems have been published. In addition, we also analyzed the primary studies of other literature reviews published in the field.

In order to mitigate the impact of selection bias, we defined the review protocol with clear inclusion and exclusion criteria for each selection step. In the first selection step, a large number of irrelevant studies were removed by analyzing title and abstract.

One author performed this task. In the second selection step, two authors screened the content of studies and constantly crosschecked the preliminary selection results. We also analyzed the potential primary studies against a quality assessment checklist. With respect to bias in the data extraction, we had some problems to extract relevant information from primary studies. This problem was more critical to answer RQ2. We observed that studies use different terminologies to describe aspects related to governance mechanisms and metrics to operationalize health. This specific limitation of the software ecosystem literature was discussed on item 1 of our research agenda presented in Sect. 4. In several occasions, we had to interpret the subjective information provided by the articles. To minimize interpretation bias, we conducted a very careful reading and had several discussion meetings among the authors during the data extraction phase.

5   Comparison with Other Reviews in the Field

The field of software ecosystems has received a number of literature reviews in the last years. Some studies cover the area of software ecosystems in general, such as [1, 5, 16, 22]. Other reviews focus on specific aspects of software ecosystems research, for instance quality assurance [19], quality models [15], key performance indicators [23], open innovation [24], and health [25].

Barbosa and Alves [22] published the first mapping study in software ecosystems. The study analyzed 44 primary studies and the results brought a general perspective of the field by identifying benefits, challenges, and the main areas of investigation in software ecosystems. In Barbosa et al. [1], the authors extended the review by analyzing software ecosystems from a three-dimensional perspective: technical, business, and social.

Manikas and Hansen [5] published a systematic literature review covering the whole field of software ecosystems. They analyzed 90 primary studies and addressed general research questions. The main contributions included a comparison of definitions for software ecosystems and a description of the most common actors found in literature. In the review that covered studies between 2007–2012, the authors recognized that the field was still immature due to a lack of analytical models and industrial studies.

In [16], Manikas updated the review to cover 231 studies published until 2014. This study is the most recent review that analyzes the software ecosystems field as a whole. In Table 4, we identified that primary studies describe health metrics for open and proprietary ecosystems in quite similar proportion as Manikas. However, it is worth noting that the scope of our studies is different. Manikas [16] cover the whole field of software ecosystems while ours focus specifically on governance issues.

An important result from Manikas [16] is the confirmation that the field obtained a fast increase in the number of publications and a growing number of empirical studies. These results could be interpreted as a sign of field maturity. Nevertheless, Manikas concludes that the field still lacks theories to explain specific phenomena in the field of software ecosystems.

Hyrynsalmi et al. [25] conducted a SLR of 38 primary studies to characterize software ecosystem health. The authors obtained a similar result as ours by confirming that the most adopted definition for health is provided by Iansiti and Levien [8] [S25]. Our review is more complete than the work by Hyrynsalmi et al. [25] because we performed an extensive classification of metrics to operationalize the three health elements (productivity, robustness, and niche creation). While the authors simply listed how primary studies define software ecosystems health and analyzed the factors that affect the health of ecosystems. Therefore, our review provides an updated and comprehensive synthesis of health metrics as described in Table 3. We consider it is a novel contribution.

Axelsson and Skoglund [19] mapped the literature of quality assurance in software ecosystems. The authors only identified six primary studies. The findings are quite superficial and the analysis of studies is very descriptive. The primary studies were simply summarized in the review. The main contribution of this mapping study is a research agenda to address the challenges in this specific area of software ecosystem research.

Franco-Bedoya et al. [15] conducted a superficial SLR, based on 17 primary studies, with the purpose of identifying measures to evaluate the quality of OSS ecosystems. The main contribution of the review is the proposal of a quality model called QuESO that organizes the quality measures found in literature into several quality characteristics. The model covers three aspects of OSS ecosystems: platform, community, and network. Our study is more complete because we synthesize a comprehensive list of health metrics for proprietary and open source ecosystems.

Fortrousi et al. [23] executed a mapping study to provide an overview on the use of Key Performance Indicators (KPI) for managing software ecosystems. The study analyzed 34 articles. The authors identified that ecosystem objectives supported by KPI embrace business improvement, interconnectedness improvement, growth and stability, quality improvement, and sustainability. A key contribution of the review is the classification of measurement attributes. Again, the results presented in our review, such as in Table 3, are more complete than the results from [23].

Finally, Papatheocharous et al. [24] performed a mapping study on ecosystems and open innovation for embedded systems, in which 260 studies were identified. An important limitation of the study [24] is the lack of a complete list of primary studies. This type of information is essential for other researchers to compare secondary studies and assess the reliability of the review performed. The research questions are very generic. In fact, the review does not provide a clear discussion on the main overlaps between ecosystem and open innovation areas.

Our review differs from the previously described secondary studies in that we address a specific area of software ecosystem research – the governance of software ecosystems.

6 Conclusion

Governance is a well-established concept primarily associated with the needs to protect investment and ensure the sustainability of businesses through time [26]. Governance involves a set of principles to direct the distribution of rights and responsibilities among stakeholders. Traditional corporate governance mechanisms include monitoring actions, policies, and decisions by aligning the interests of different stakeholders.

In our SLR we provide an in-depth analysis of the field by characterizing what ecosystem governance means (RQ1), by classifying 20 governance mechanisms found in literature as value creation, coordination of players, and organizational openness and control (RQ2), by defining software ecosystem health (RQ3) and describing catalogue with a large variety metrics proposed to assess the health of software ecosystems (RQ4).

We concluded that software ecosystems governance is all processes by which a player creates value, coordinates relationships, and defines controls. We derive from the literature that software ecosystem health is determined by the capability of an ecosystem to persistently produce meaningful outputs (productivity), survive market disruptions (robustness), and create niches in the ecosystem (niche creation). Therefore, we understand that our article brings a novel contribution to synthesize the body of knowledge in software ecosystems governance that has a relevant scientific impact.

Practitioners can use our results to understand the concept of ecosystem governance. The catalogue of metrics also will be useful for practitioners to create operational indicators and improve the governance of software ecosystems.

Presently we are developing a conceptual model that represents a holistic view of the elements to be governed in SECO and their relations. The model is building from the assumption that understanding the governance elements of a software ecosystem and governing them based on the relationships they have with one another increases the chances of survival of a software ecosystem. The conceptual model will be evaluated by a survey with researchers and through case studies of open and proprietary software ecosystems. In future research, we aim to analyze the interplay between governance mechanisms and health metrics.

Appendix

S1. Albert. B.E., Santos, R.P., Werner, C.:. Software ecosystems governance to enable IT architecture based on software asset management. In Proceedings of the 7th IEEE International Conference on Digital Ecosystems and Technologies (2013).

S2. Alspaugh, T.A., Asuncion, H. U., Scacchi, W.: The Role of Software Licenses in Open Architecture Ecosystems. In proceedings of the 1st International Workshop on Software Ecosystems (IWSECO'09), pp. 4–18 (2010).

S3. Axelsson, J., Papatheocharous, E., Andersson, J.: Characteristics of software ecosystems for Federated Embedded Systems: A case study. Information and Software Technology, Volume 56, Issue 11, pp. 1457–1475 (2014).

S4. Baars, A., Jansen, S.: A framework for software ecosystem governance. In Proceedings of the Third International Conference on Software Business (ICSOB'12), pp. 168–180 (2012).

S5. Bosch, J., Bosch-Sijtsema, M.P.: Esao: A Holistic Ecosystem-Driven Analysis Model. In Proceedings of the 5 th International Conference on Software Business (ICSOB 2014), Springer Verlag, pp. 179–193 (2014).

S6. Burkard, C., Widjaja, T., Buxmann, P.,. Software ecosystems. Business & Information Systems Engineering, volume 4, Issue. 1, pp. 41–44 (2012).

S7. Campbell, P., Ahmed, F.: A three-dimensional view of software ecosystems. In Proceedings of the Fourth European Conference on Software Architecture: Companion Volume (ECSA '10), CarlosE. Cuesta (Ed.). ACM, New York, NY, USA, pp. 81–84 (2010).

S8. Ceccagnoli, M., Forman, C., Huang, P., Wu, D.J.: Co-creation of value in a platform ecosystem: The case of enterprise software. MIS Quarterly, Forthcoming (2011).

S9. Che, M., Perry, D.E.: Architectural Design Decisions in Open Software Development: A Transition to Soft/ware Ecosystems. In Proceedings of the 23rd Australian Software Engineering Conference, pp. 58–61 (2014).

S10. Den Hartigh, E., Tol, M., Visscher, W.: The health measurement of a business ecosystem. In proceedings of the European Network on Chaos and Complexity Research and Management Practice Meeting. pp. 1–39 (2006).

S11. Dittrich, Y.: Software engineering beyond the project – Sustaining software ecosystems. Information and Software Technology, Volume 56, Issue 11, pp. 1436–1456 (2014).

S12. Dubinsky, Y., Kruchten, P.: Software development governance (sdg): report on 2nd workshop. ACM SIGSOFT Software Engineering Notes, Volume 34, pp. 46–47 (2009).

S13. Eisenmann, T.R., Parker, G., M.W.; Van Alstyne, M.W.: Opening platforms: how, when and why? In Platforms, Markets and Innovation. Gawer A (ed). Edward Elgar: Cheltenham, UK, pp. 131–162 (2008).

S14. Eklund, U., Bosch, J.: Introducing software ecosystems for mass-produced embedded systems. In Software Business. Springer Berlin Heidelberg, pp. 248–254 (2012).

S15. Fricker. S.: Requirements Value Chains: Stakeholder Management and Requirements Engineering in Software Ecosystems. In proceedings of Requirements Engineering: Foundation for Software Quality (REFSQ'10), volume 6182, pp. 60–66 (2010).

S16. Fricker, S.: Specification and Analysis of Requirements Negotiation Strategy in Software Ecosystems. In proceedings of Workshop on Software Ecosystems, pp. 19–33 (2009).

S17. Gawer, A., Cusumano, M.A.: Industry platforms and ecosystem innovation. Journal of Product Innovation Management, Volume 31, Issue 3, pp. 417–433 (2014).

S18. Gawer, A., Henderson, R.: Platform owner entry and innovation in complementary markets: Evidence from Intel. Journal of Economics & Management Strategy, Volume 16, Issue 1, pp. 1–34 (2007).

S19. Gawer, A., Cusumano, M.A.: Platform leadership: How Intel, Microsoft, and Cisco drive industry innovation. Harvard Business School Press, pp. 29–30 (2002).

S20. Ghazawne, A., Henfridsson, O.: Governing third-party development through platform boundary resources. In proceedings of International Conference on Information Systems (ICIS' 10), AIS Electronic Library (AISeL), pp 1–18 (2010).

S21. Goldbach, T., Kemper, V.K.: Should I Stay or should I go? the effects of control mechanisms on app developers´ intention to stick with a platform. In proceedings of European Conference on Information Systems (ECIS'S3) (2014).

S22. Haile, N., Altmann, J.: Value creation in software service platforms. Future Generation Computer Systems, Volume 55, pp. 495–509 (2016).

S23. Hyrynsalmi, S., Suominen, A., Makila, T., Jarvi, A., Knuutila, T.: Revenue models of application developers in android market ecosystem. In M. Cusumano, B. Iyer, N. Venkatraman, eds.: ICSOB 2012. Number 114 in Lecture Notes in Business Information Processing. Springer Heidelberg (2012).

S24. Huang, P., Ceccagnoli, M., Forman, C., Wu, D.J.: Appropriability mechanisms and the platform partnership decision: Evidence from enterprise software. Management Science, Vol 59, Issue 1 (2013).

S25. Iansiti, M., Levien, R.: Strategy as ecology. Harvard business review. Vol 82, Issue 3 (2004).

S26. Iyer, B., Lee,C.H., Venkatraman, N.: Managing a small world ecosystem: Some lessons from the software sector. California Management Review, Volume 48, Issue 3, pp. 28–47 (2006).

S27. James, W.P., and De Meyer, A.: Ecosystem advantage: how to successfully harness the power of partners. California Management Review, Volume 55, Issue 1 (2012): 24–46 (2012).

S28. Jansen, S., Cusumano, M.:. Defining Software Ecosystems: A Survey of Software Platforms and Business Network Governance. In Proceedings of the 4th International Workshop on Software Ecosystems (IWSECO '12), pp. 41–58 (2012).

S29. Jansen, S., Finkelstein, A., Brinkkemper, S.: A sense of community: A research agenda for software ecosystems. In Proceedings of the 31st Conference on Software Engineering, pp. 187–190 (2009).

S30. Jansen, S., Brinkkemper, S., Finkelstein, A.:. Business Network Management as a Survival Strategy: A Tale of Two Software Ecosystems. In proceedings of the 1st International Workshop on Software Ecosystems (IWSECO'09). pp. 34–48 (2009).

S31. Jansen, S., Brinkkemper, S., Souer, J., Luinenburg, L.: The open software enterprise model: how open is my software business? In Software Ecosystems: Analyzing and Managing Business Networks in the Software Industry. UK: Edward Elgar Publishing, pp. 159–186 (2013).

S32. Jansen, S., Brinkkemper, S., Souer, J., Luinenburg, L.: Shades of gray: Opening up a software producing organization with the open software enterprise model. Journal of System and Software. Volume 85, Issue 7, pp. 1495–1510 (2012).

S33. Jansen, S.: Opening the Ecosystem Flood Gates: Architecture Challenges of Opening Interfaces Within a Product Portfolio. In proceedings of European Conference on Software Architecture (ECSA'15), Springer International Publishing, pp. 121–136 (2015).

S34. Jansen, S.: Measuring the health of open source software ecosystems: Beyond the scope of project health. Information and Software Technology, Volume, 56, Issue 11, pp. 1508–1519 (2014).

S35. Kapoor, R., Lee, J.M.: Coordinating and competing in ecosystems: How organizational forms shape new technology investments. Strategic Management Journal, Volume 34, Issue 3, pp. 274–296 (2013).

S36. Kim, H.J., Kim, L., Lee, H.: Third-party mobile app developers' continued participation in platform-centric ecosystems: An empirical investigation of two different mechanisms. International Journal of Information Management, Volume 36, Issue 1, pp. 44–59 (2016).

S37. Knauss, E., Damian, D., Knauss, A., Borici, A.: Openness and requirements: Opportunities and tradeoffs in software ecosystems. In Proceedings of the IEEE 22nd International Requirements Engineering Conference (RE'S3), 2014, pp. 213–222 (2014).

S38. Koch, S., Kerschbaum, M.: Joining a smartphone ecosystem: Application developers' motivations and decision criteria. Information and Software Technology, Volume 56, Issue 11, pp. 1423–1435 (2014).

S39. Manikas, K., Klaus, M.H., and Kyng, M,K.: Governance mechanisms for healthcare apps. In Proceedings of the 2014 European Conference on Software Architecture Workshops. ACM, p. 10 (2014).

S40. Mizushima, K., Ikawa,Y.: A structure of cocreation in an open source software ecosystem: A case study of the eclipse community. In Proceedings of Technology Management in the Energy Smart World (PICMET'11). pp. 1–8 (2011).

S41. Monteith, J.Y., McGregor, J.D., Ingram, J.E.:. Proposed metrics on ecosystem health. In Proceedings of the 2014 ACM international workshop on Software-defined ecosystems (BigSystem'S3), ACM, pp. 33–36 (2014).

S42. Mukhopadhyay, S., de Reuver, M., and Bouwman, H.: Effectiveness of control mechanisms in mobile platform ecosystem. Telematics and Informatics, Volume 33, Issue 3, pp. 848–859 (2016).

S43. Olsson, H., and Bosch, J. Strategic Ecosystem Management: A multi-case study on challenges and strategies for different ecosystem types. In proceedings of Software Engineering and Advanced Applications (SEAA'15), pp. 398–401 (2015).

S44. Pilinkienė, V., Mačiulis, P.: Comparison of Different Ecosystem Analogies: The Main Economic Determinants and Levels of Impact. Procedia – Social and Behavioral Sciences, Volume 156, Issue 26, pp. 365–370.

S45. Popp, K.M.: Goals of Software Vendors for Partner Ecosystems – A Practitioner's View. In proceedings of First International Conference on Software Business (ICSOB'10). Springer: pp. 181–186 (2010).

S46. Sadi, M.H., Yu, E.: Designing Software Ecosystems: How Can Modeling Techniques Help?In proceedings of Enterprise, Business-Process and Information Systems Modeling. Springer International Publishing, pp. 360–375 (2015).

S47. Sadi, H., Yu, E.: Analyzing the evolution of software development: From creative chaos to software ecosystems. In Proceedings of the IEEE Eighth International Conference on Research Challenges in Information Science (RCIS'S3), pp. 1–11 (2014).

S48. Santos, R., Werner, C.: Treating social dimension in software ecosystems through ReuseECOS approach. In Proceedings of the 6th IEEE International Conference on Digital Ecosystems Technologies (DEST'12), pp. 1–6 (2012).

S49. Schönberger, A., Elsner, C.: Modeling Partner Networks for Systematic Architecture Derivation in Software Ecosystems. In: Linnhoff-Popien, Claudia; Zaddach, Michael; Grahl, Andreas (Ed.): Marktplätze im Umbruch – Digital e Strategien für Services in Mobilen Internet. Springer Berlin Heidelberg, pp. 655–665 (2015).

S50. Schultis, K.B., Elsner, C., Lohmann, D.: Architecture challenges for internal software ecosystems: a large-scale industry case study. In Proceedings of the 22nd ACM SIGSOFT International Symposium on Foundations of Software Engineering (FSE'S3), ACM, pp. 542–552 (2014).

S51. Tiwana, A. Konsynski, B. Bush, A.: Platform evolution: Coevolution of platform architecture, governance, and environmental dynamics. Information Systems Research. Volume 21, Issue 4, pp. 675–687 (2010).

S52. Valenca, G., Alves, C., Heimann, V., Jansen, S., Brinkkemper, S.: Competition and collaboration in requirements engineering: A case study of an emerging software ecosystem. In Proceedings of the IEEE 22nd International Requirements Engineering Conference (RE'S3), pp. 384–393 (2014).

S53. van Angeren, J., Kabbedijk, K., Popp, K., Jansen, S.: Managing software ecosystems through partnering. In Software Ecosystems: Analyzing and Managing Business Networks in the Software Industry. Cheltenham, UK: Edward Elgar Publishing, pp. 85–102 (2013).

S54. van Angeren, J., Alves, C., Jansen, S.: Can We Ask You To Collaborate? Analyzing App Developer Relationships in Commercial Platform Ecosystems. Journal of Systems and Software, Volume 113, pp. 430–445 (2016).

S55. van Angeren, J., Jansen, S., Brinkkemper, S.: Exploring the relationship between partnership model participation and interfirm network structure: An analysis of the office365 ecosystem, In Proceedings of Software Business (ICSOB'S3). Springer, pp. 1–15 (2014).

S56. Ven, K., Mannaert, H.: Challenges and strategies in the use of Open Source Software by Independent Software Vendors. Information and Software Technology, Volume 50, Issues 9–10, pp. 991–1002 (2008).

S57. Viljainen, M., Kauppinen., M.: Framing Management practices for keystones in platform ecosystems. In Software Ecosystems: Analyzing and Managing Business Networks in the Software Industry. Cheltenham, UK: Edward Elgar Publishing, pp. 121–137 (2013).

S58. Viljainen, M., Kauppinen, M. Software Ecosystems: A Set of Management Practices for Platform Integrators in the Telecom Industry. In proceedings of 2nd International Conference on Software Business. Springer Berlin Heidelberg, pp. 32–43 (2011).

S59. Wareham, J., Fox, P.B., CanoGiner, J.L. Technology ecosystem governance. Organization Science Volume 25, Issue 4, pp. 1195–1215 (2014).

S60. West, J., and Wood, D.: Creating and Evolving an Open Innovation Ecosystem: Lessons from Symbian Ltd. Available at SSRN Working Paper Series (2008).

S61. West, J., and Wood, D. Tradeoffs of Open Innovation Platform Leadership: The Rise and Fall of Symbian Ltd. In proceedings of Social Science and Technology Seminar Series (2011).

S62. Wnuk, K., Manikas, K., Runeson, P., Lantz, M., Weijden, O., Munir, H.: Evaluating the governance model of hardware-centric software ecosystems: a case study of the axis ecosystem. In proceedings of 5th International Conference on Software Business, pp. 212–226 (2014).

S63. Yu, E., Deng, S.:. Understanding Software Ecosystems: A Strategic Modelling Approach. In International Workshop on Software Ecosystems (IWSECO'10) (2010)

S64. Aarnoutse, F., Renes, C., Snijders, R., and Jansen, S.: The Reality of an Associate Model: Comparing Partner Activity in the Eclipse Ecosystem. In Proceedings of the 2014 European Conference on Software Architecture Workshops (ECSAW '14), ACM, pp. 6–8. (2014).

S65. Alami, D., Rodríguez, M., and Jansen, S.: Relating Health to Platform Success: Exploring Three E-commerce Ecosystems. In Proceedings of the 2015 European Conference on Software Architecture Workshops (ECSAW '15), ACM, p. 43. (2015).

S66. Ben Hadj Salem Mhamdia, A.: Performance measurement practices in software ecosystem. International Journal of Productivity and Performance Management, Volume 62, Issue 5, pp. 514–533. 2013.

S67. Cardoso, J.L., Barbin, S.E., and Silva Filho, O.S.: The public software ecosystem: exploratory survey. In Proceedings of the Fifth International Conference on Management of Emergent Digital EcoSystems (MEDES '13), ACM, pp. 289–296 (2013).

S68. Costanza, R.: Toward an operational definition of ecosystem health. Ecosystem health: New goals for environmental management, Island Press, pp. 239–256 (1992).

S69. Den Hartigh, E., Visscher, W., Tol, M., and Salas, A.: Measuring the health of a business ecosystem. In Software Ecosystems: Analyzing and Managing Business Networks in the Software Industry. Cheltenham, UK: Edward Elgar Publishing, 221–246 (2013).

S70. Dhungana, D., Groher, I., Schludermann, E., and Biffl, S.: Software ecosystems vs. natural ecosystems: learning from the ingenious mind of nature. In Proceedings of the Fourth European Conference on Software Architecture: Companion Volume (ECSA '10), Carlos E. Cuesta (Ed.). ACM, New York, NY, USA, pp. 96–102 (2010).

S71. Eckhardt, E., Kaats, E., Jansen, S., and Alves, C.: The Merits of a Meritocracy in Open Source Software Ecosystems. In Proceedings of European Conference on Software Architecture Workshops (ECSAW '14), ACM, p. 7 (2014).

S72. Eklund U., and Bosch, J.: Using architecture for multiple levels of access to an ecosystem platform. In Proceedings of the 8th international ACM SIGSOFT conference on Quality of Software Architectures (QoSA '12), ACM, pp. 143–148 (2012).

S73. German, D, M., Adams, B., Hassan, A. E.: The Evolution of the R Software Ecosystem. In Proceedings of the 17th European Conference on Software Maintenance and Reengineering (CSMR'13), pp. 243–252 (2013).

S74. Hoving, R., Slot, G., Jansen, S.: Python: Characteristics identification of a free open source software ecosystem. In Proceedings of the 7th IEEE International Conference on Digital Ecosystems and Technologies (DEST'13), pp. 13–18 (2013).

S75. Hyrynsalmi, S., Seppänen, M., Suominen, A.: Sources of value in application ecosystems. Journal of Systems and Software, Volume 96, pp. 61–72 (2014).

S76. Iansiti, M., and Richards, G.L.: Information technology ecosystem: Structure, health, and performance. The Antitrust Bull., Volume 51, p. 77 (2006).

S77. Iansiti, M., and Levien, R.: Keystones and Dominators: Framing Operating and Technology Strategy in a Business Ecosystem. Harvard Business School, Working Paper, p. 03–061 (2004).

S78. Kabbedijk, J., and Jansen, S.: Unraveling Ruby ecosystem dynamics: a quantitative network analysis. In Software Ecosystems: Analyzing and Managing Business Networks in the Software Industry. Cheltenham, UK: Edward Elgar Publishing, pp. 322–332 (2013).

S79. Kilamo, T., Hammouda, I., Mikkonen, T and Aaltonen, T.: Open source ecosystems: a tale of two cases. In Software Ecosystems: Analyzing and Managing Business Networks in the Software Industry. Cheltenham, UK: Edward Elgar Publishing, pp. 276–206 (2013).

S80. Lucassen, G., van Rooij, K., Jansen, S.: Ecosystem health of cloud paas providers. In Software Business. From Physical Products to Software Services and Solutions. Springer Berlin Heidelberg, pp. 183–194 (2013).

S81. Lundell, B., Forssten, B., Gamalielsson, J., Gustavsson, H., Karlsson, R., Lennerholt, C., and Olsson, E.: Exploring health within OSS ecosystems. In proceedings of the First International Workshop on Building Sustainable Open Source Communities (OSCOMM' 09) (2009).

S82. Manikas, K., and D., Kontogiorgos, D.: Characterizing Software Activity: The Influence of Software to Ecosystem Health. In Proceedings of the 2015 European Conference on Software Architecture Workshops (ECSAW '15), ACM, p. 46 (2015).

S83. Manikas, K and Hansen, K.M. Reviewing the Health of Software Ecosystems-A Conceptual Framework Proposal. In proceedings of the 5th International Workshop on Software Ecosystems (IWSECO'13), in ICSOB, pp. 33–44 (2013).

S84. McGregor, D. J.: A method for analyzing software product line ecosystems. In Proceedings of the Fourth European Conference on Software Architecture: Companion Volume (ECSA'10), Carlos E. Cuesta (Ed.). ACM, New York, NY, USA, pp. 73–80. 2010.

S85. Spauwen, R., and Jansen, S.: Towards the roles and motives of open source software developers. In Proceedings of the 5th International Workshop on Software Ecosystems (IWSECO'13), p. 62 (2013).

S86. Stefi, A., Berger, M., and Hess, T.: What Influences Platform Provider's Degree of Openness?–Measuring and Analyzing the Degree of Platform Openness. In proceedings of Software Business. Towards Continuous Value Delivery. Springer International Publishing, pp. 258–272 (2014).

S87. Syed, S and Jansen, S.: On Clusters in Open Source Ecosystems. In proceedings of International Workshop on Software Ecosystems (IWSECO'13), in ICSOB, pp. 19–32. (2013).

S88. Teixeira, J., Robles, G., González-Barahona, J.M.: Lessons learned from applying social network analysis on an industrial Free/Libre/Open Source Software ecosystem. Journal of Internet Services and Applications, Volume 6, Issue 1, pp. 1–27 (2015).

S89. Van Lingen, S., Palomba, A., and Lucassen, G.: On the software ecosystem health of open source content management systems. In proceedings of the 5th International Workshop on Software Ecosystems (IWSECO 2013), p. 38 (2013).

References

1. Barbosa, O., Santos, R., Alves; C., Werner, C., Jansen, S.: A systematic mapping study on software ecosystems through a three-dimensional perspective. In: Software Ecosystems: Analyzing and Managing Business Networks in the Software Industry, pp. 59–81. Edward Elgar Publishing, UK (2013)

2. Bosch, J., Bosch-Sijtsema, P.: ESAO: a holistic ecosystem-driven analysis model. In: Lassenius, C., Smolander, K. (eds.) ICSOB 2014. LNBIP, vol. 182, pp. 179–193. Springer, Cham (2014). https://doi.org/10.1007/978-3-319-08738-2_13

3. Jansen, S., Finkelstein, A., Brinkkemper, S.: A sense of community: a research agenda for software ecosystems. In: Proceedings of the 31st Conference on Software Engineering, pp. 187–190 (2009)

4. Iyer, B., Dreyfus, D., Gyllstrom, P.: A network-based view of enterprise architecture. Handbook of Enterprise Systems Architecture in Practice, pp. 500–525 (2007)

5. Manikas, K., Hansen, K.M.: Software ecosystems – a systematic literature review. J. Syst. Softw. 86(5), 1294–1306 (2013)

6. Tiwana, A., Konsynski, B., Bush, A.A.: Platform evolution: Coevolution of platform architecture, governance, and environmental dynamics. Inf. Syst. Res. 21(4), 675–687 (2010)

7. West, J., Wood, D.: Creating and Evolving an Open Innovation Ecosystem: Lessons from Symbian Ltd. Available at SSRN Working Paper Series (2008)

8. Iansiti, M., Levien, R.: Strategy as ecology. Harvard Bus. Rev. 82(3), 68–81 (2004)

9. den Hartigh, M., Visscher, W.: The health measurement of a business ecosystem. In: proceedings of the European Network on Chaos and Complexity Research and Management Practice Meeting. pp. 1–39 (2006)

10. Wareham, J., Fox, P.B., Cano Giner, J.L.: Technology ecosystem governance. Organ. Sci. 25(4), 1195–1215 (2014)

11. Alves, C., Oliveira, J.A., Jansen, S.: Software ecosystems governance: a systematic literature review and research agenda. In: 19th International Conference on Enterprise Information Systems (ICEIS) (2017)
12. Kitchenham, B., Charters, S.: Guidelines for Performing Systematic Literature Review in Software Engineering. EBSE Technical Report, 2.3, Keele University (2007)
13. Cruzes D., Dybå, T.: Recommended steps for thematic synthesis in software engineering. In: Proceedings of International Symposium on Empirical Software Engineering and Measurement (2011)
14. Brereton, P., Kitchenham, B., Budgen, D., Turner, M., Khalil, M.: Lesson from applying the systematic literature review process within the software engineering domain. J. Syst. Softw. **80**(4), 571–583 (2007)
15. Franco-Bedoya, O., Ameller, D., Costal, D., Franch, X.: Queso a quality model for open source software ecosystems. In: Proceedings of the 9th International Conference on Software Engineering and Applications (ICSOFT-EA'S3), pp. 209–221 (2014)
16. Manikas, K.: Revisiting software ecosystems research: a longitudinal literature study. J. Syst. Softw. **117**, 84–103 (2016)
17. Brhel, M., Meth, H., Maedcher, A.: Exploring principles of user-centered agile software development: a literature review. Inf. Soft. Technol. **61**, 163–181 (2015)
18. Hansen, G., Dyba, T.: Theoretical foundations of software ecosystems. International Workshop on Software Ecosystems (2012)
19. Axelsson, J., Skoglund, M.: Quality assurance in software ecosystems: a systematic literature mapping and research agenda. J. Syst. Softw. **114**, 69–81 (2016)
20. Manikas, K., Hansen, M.K.: Reviewing the health of software ecosystems - a conceptual framework proposal. In: Proceedings of the 5th International Workshop on Software Ecosystems (IWSECO 2013), in ICSOB, pp. 33–44 (2016)
21. Goeminne, M., Claes, M., Mens, T.: A historical dataset for the Gnome ecosystem. In: Proceedings of the 10th IEEE Working Conference on Mining Software Repositories (2013)
22. Barbosa, O., Alves, C.: A systematic mapping study on software ecosystems. In: Proceedings of the Third International Workshop on Software Ecosystems (IWSECO 2011) (2011)
23. Fotrousi, F., Fricker, Samuel A., Fiedler, M., Le-Gall, F.: KPIs for software ecosystems: a systematic mapping study. In: Lassenius, C., Smolander, K. (eds.) ICSOB 2014. LNBIP, vol. 182, pp. 194–211. Springer, Cham (2014). https://doi.org/10.1007/978-3-319-08738-2_14
24. Papatheocharous, E., Andersson, J., Axelsson, J.: Ecosystems and open innovation for embedded systems: a systematic mapping study. In: Proceedings of the 6th International Conference on Software Business (ICSOB 2015), pp. 81–95 (2015)
25. Hyrynsalmi, S., Seppanen, M., Nokkala, T., Suominen, A., Jarvi, A.: Wealthy, Healthy and/or Happy — What does 'Ecosystem Health' Stand for? ICSOB 2015, pp. 272–287. Springer, Heidelberg (2015)
26. Hoogervorst, J.A.P.: Corporate governance. Enterp. Governance Enterp. Eng. **3**(1), 3–11 (2009). Springer

Exploring the Ambidextrous Analysis of Business Processes: A Design Science Research

Higor Santos[(✉)] and Carina Alves

Centro de Informática, Universidade Federal
de Pernambuco, Pernambuco, Brazil
{hrms, cfa}@cin.ufpe.br

Abstract. Traditionally, business processes are analyzed in a qualitative or quantitative form with the purpose to exploit, reduce or eliminate existing problems in the processes, such as bottlenecks, financial or resources waste, cycle time and handworks. Business process analysis is an important phase of the Business Process Management (BPM) lifecycle because it provides a critical examination of problems and potential improvements of business processes. However, few studies have been conducted to provide novel analysis techniques and methods to explore external and future opportunities, in addition to satisfying clients' expectations, needs and experience. In this context, we used the Design Science Research approach to build the Ambidextrous Analysis of Business Process (A2BP) method, which enables process analysts to balance exploration and exploitation thinking. We defined the problem and the research questions through a systematic literature mapping. Then, we empirically evaluate the proposed method through an expert opinion survey and an observational case study to assess the usefulness and ease-of-use of the method. Overall, the participants of the empirical study evaluated the method positively and suggested feedbacks to refine it.

Keywords: Business Process Management · Business process analysis
Organizational ambidexterity · Design thinking

1 Introduction

Business Process Management (BPM) is a holistic management approach that has grown substantially in the last decades. BPM has a strong focus on information technology advances [1]. BPM is considered an assembly of techniques to support the continuous and iterative improvement of business processes in an organization [2]. Examples of techniques normally used are Ishikawa Diagram, SWOT Analysis, Cycle Time Analysis, Risk Analysis, and Gap Analysis.

However, [3] affirms that BPM as a managerial discipline does not seem to be sufficiently capable to harvest the potential of a dynamic and opportunity-rich environment. One main reason is that current BPM capabilities are largely following an 'inside-out' paradigm, also called analytical thinking. This paradigm addresses management through exploitation techniques that repeat themselves continuously over time [4].

© Springer International Publishing AG, part of Springer Nature 2018
S. Hammoudi et al. (Eds.): ICEIS 2017, LNBIP 321, pp. 543–566, 2018.
https://doi.org/10.1007/978-3-319-93375-7_25

The planning and analysis phases of business processes, contained in the BPM lifecycle, are the moments in which techniques are used to collect and analyze data in order to improve the business process incrementally or radically [5, 6]. In this regard, [7] suggest that it is necessary to complement a traditional BPM approach with the 'outside-in' paradigm, also called intuitive thinking. Intuitive thinking uses exploration techniques. It is centered in the convergence and divergence of ideas by using creativity, originality, and innovation techniques [4].

Ambidextrous organizations have capabilities to manage both analytical and intuitive thinking. It encompasses two profoundly different features of businesses - those focused on exploiting existing capabilities for incremental improvements and those focused on exploring new opportunities for growth. As Table 1 indicates, the two features require very different strategies, structures, processes, and cultures [8, 9].

Table 1. Alignment for ambidextrous features by [8].

Alignment of:	Exploitative	Exploratory
Strategic intention	Cost, profit	Innovation
Critical tasks	Operations, efficiency, incremental innovation	Adaptability, new products, breakthrough innovation
Competencies	Operational	Entrepreneurial
Structure	Formal, mechanistic	Adaptive, loose
Controls, rewards	Margins, productivity	Milestones, growth
Culture	Efficiency, low risk, quality, customers	Risk taking, speed, flexibility
Leadership role	Authoritative	Visionary

By deploying the idea of ambidextrous organizations to the Business Process Management discipline, [3] proposes the concepts Exploitative BPM and Explorative BPM. Exploitative BPM is aiming towards running and incrementally improving business processes. Exploitative analysis capabilities are dedicated to assessing current processes with the aim to identify and quantify process problems. Exploitative BPM serves well industries and organizations with largely static market conditions (e.g., banking back-offices, shared service providers, and mass production).

On the other hand, [3] affirms that Explorative BPM is a significant future opportunity, and challenge for the BPM community. Explorative BPM is about crafting process visions that are so compelling and transformational that they motivate staff and customers, involved to explore how to make a desired future state via a sequence of transition states a reality, and by doing this turns the current process obsolete. This is in sharp contrast to exploitative BPM, which develops new (to-be) processes in light of current shortcomings.

The balance between exploitation and exploration, or between incremental and radical organizational change has been a consistent theme across several approaches to research in organizational adaptation [8, 10, 11]. Design thinking is a well-established approach that follows the 'outside-in' paradigm. [12] emphasize that instead of focusing on surface adoption of new customer experience methods and techniques, design thinking forces BPM teams to think about process problems from a completely different perspective. This allows teams to be more effective in their interactions with executives, line-of-business owners, and stakeholders when focused on improving and optimizing for customer experience.

Despite the high number of studies promoting the use of design thinking to create innovative products and services [4, 13, 14], few studies in the BPM area propose an integrated use of exploitative and explorative techniques to support designing and innovation of business processes models aligned to expectation, experience and satisfaction of customers [3, 12, 15, 16].

Traditionally, business processes are analyzed in a qualitative or quantitative form with the purpose to exploit, reduce or eliminate existing problems in the processes, such as bottlenecks, financial or resources waste, cycle time and handworks [5, 17]. Business process analysis is an important phase of the BPM lifecycle because it provides a critical examination of problems and potential improvements of business processes. However, few studies have been conducted to provide novel techniques and methods for the business process analysis phase [7, 18].

This paper aims to contribute to the emerging area of ambidextrous BPM. In particular, our research focuses on the phase of business process analysis. Motivated by this scenario, the main research problem of this study is to investigate: *how to exploit internal problems and explore external opportunities of the business process?* This paper aims to investigate the following research questions:

(RQ1) What are the features of a method that supports the ambidextrous analysis of business processes?

(RQ2) How is the ease-of-use and usefulness perceived by process analysts of the proposed method for ambidextrous analysis of business processes?

The main contribution of this paper is to design a method to support the ambidextrous analysis of the business process. The method was evaluated through an expert opinion survey and an observational case study at an organization with experience in BPM.

The rest of the paper is organized as follows. Section 2 presents the background of our research. Section 3 outlines the research method. Section 4 describes the proposed method called A2BP. Section 5 presents the results of the empirical study. Finally, Sect. 6 discusses the conclusions and presents directions for future work.

2 Background

Business process analysis is considered an important phase of the BPM lifecycle [5, 6]. According to the International Institute of Business Analysis (IIBA), business analysis is the set of activities and techniques used to serve as a link between stakeholders in order to understand the structure, policies and operations of an organization and to recommend solutions that allow the organization to achieve its goals. In addition, this phase involves understanding how organizations work and achieve their purposes, and defining the capabilities an organization must have to provide products and services to external stakeholders [19].

In this context, the analysis of business processes should be seen as a means to propose value for the organization [5]. In a BPM initiative, this value is transformed into improvement opportunities for the process itself, for the organization and for its customers. As discussed in the introduction, improvement opportunities can be identified, analyzed, and explored through 'inside-out' and/or 'outside-in' paradigms.

According to [3], the 'inside-out' paradigm takes into account a much more reactive approach to existing problems and bottlenecks in order to make the organization mature and consistent with its business processes. On the other hand, the 'outside-in' paradigm seeks to proactively identify problems and innovation opportunities not yet explored in order to create new products, services and business processes. Figure 1 illustrates the conflict between these two paradigms in the BPM context.

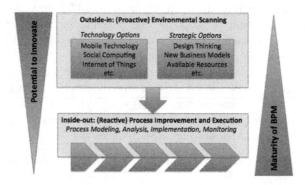

Fig. 1. The maturity-innovation conflict in BPM by [3].

Given this conflict, organizations need to balance their capabilities and abilities to continuously improve as well as to be attentive to market changes so as to innovate their processes, products and/or services. Organizational ambidexterity refers to the ability to manage complex and contradictory components such as flexibility and efficiency, continuous improvement and radical innovation, alignment and adaptation, exploit problems and explore opportunities [8]. Although it is difficult for organizations to balance their capabilities, [11] highlight that exploration and exploitation need not always be competing activities, but can and should be complementary. In this regard, [4 p. 15] states that "the most successful businesses in the years to come will balance analytical mastery and intuitive originality in a dynamic interplay that I call design thinking".

According to [20], design thinking is an approach to support innovation and that aims to align analytical with intuitive thinking. Design thinking generates an environment highly interactive and promotes innovation through the following steps: empathize, define, ideate and prototype. In the context of this research, we use concepts and practices of organizational ambidexterity and design thinking to organize and systematize the business process analysis phase. In the next section, we describe the research method used to build and evaluate the proposed method for ambidextrous of business process analysis.

3   Research Method

Given that our goal is to create a useful artifact, we purposefully chose a Design Science Research (DSR) approach. [21] propose that DSR artifacts are defined as constructs (vocabulary and symbols), models (abstractions and representations), methods (algorithms and practices) and instantiations (systems or prototypes).

The DSR approach is suitable to address our research objective and questions because it emphasizes the investigation of a method artifact with a problem context in order to improve the business process analysis in organizational context. Moreover, DSR guides us through an iterative, yet structured process of building and evaluating the artifact. In sum, this approach provides a well-suited base to build an artifact of high utility, closely connected to extant knowledge and a relevant, real-world problem [21, 22].

As presented in Fig. 2, our study adopts the DSR framework suggested by [22]. The social context contains the stakeholders who may affect the project or may be affected by it. In our case, the stakeholders are business process analysts, business specialists, internal stakeholders and customers of the organization. The knowledge context consists of existing theories from science and engineering, useful facts about currently available products. Our research was grounded in the following areas of knowledge: BPM, Design Thinking, Organizational Ambidexterity and Design Science Research.

Initially, we defined the problem and the research questions through a systematic literature mapping. In order to investigate the research problem stated in Sect. 1, automatic searches were conducted in the digital libraries of the Association for Computing Machinery (ACM), the IEEE Computer Society, Emerald Insight, Science Direct and Springer Link. We also used the pearl growing research strategy cited by [23]. This strategy is similar to snowball sampling strategy, but its focus is to investigate the references used by the most relevant articles of the main authors of the area.

Then, we designed the artifact called A2BP method, which aims to investigate how to exploit internal problems and explore external opportunities of the business process. A core feature of the Design Science Research is the empirical evaluation of the artifacts in the appropriate environment. Thus, an expert opinion survey with seven participants was conducted in order to analyze the ease-of-use and usefulness of the proposed method A2BP before evaluating it in an organization. According to [22], expert opinion is the simplest way to validate an artifact. The design of an artifact is submitted to a panel of experts, who imagine how such an artifact will interact with problem contexts imagined by them and then predict what effects they think this would have. The experts are used as instruments to "observe", by imagining, a validation model of the artifact.

To conduct the expert opinion, an e-mail was sent explaining the context of the research to experts. It included the time needed for evaluation, a link to the website where the artifact is available (i.e. the A2BP method) and a link to the evaluation survey. After the critical analysis of the proposed artifact, experts answered the semi-structured questionnaire. It was categorized as follows: perceived ease-of-use, perceived usefulness, suggestions, and criticisms. The survey contained eight open questions and five closed questions. The closed questions were written in the assertive

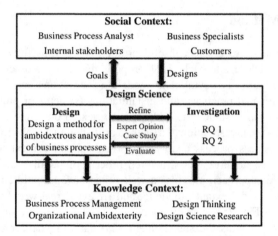

Fig. 2. Instantiation of the DSR framework [22] in the context of our research by [16].

form and their responses ranged from Strongly Disagree to Strongly Agree to the five-point Likert scale [24]. Only closed questions were mandatory. The results of the expert opinion are presented in Sect. 5.1.

The artifact was adjusted according to the recommendations of the experts. Then, we carried out an observational case study in a public-sector organization with the goal to conduct an empirical evaluation of the proposed method. [22] highlights that observational case studies are a useful research method for implementation evaluation and problem investigation, where the researcher investigates the real world.

The case organization conducts a BPM initiative for five years and has a Business Process Management Office (BPMO) that plans and manages several organization-wide business process improvement projects. The criterion to select this case was intentional, which as defined by [25], it is suitable for research of a qualitative nature, aiming at the selection of a context that is meaningful to the studied phenomenon. The specific objective of this case study is to evaluate the ease-of-use and usefulness of the A2BP Method to support the needs of an ambidextrous analysis of business processes by an organization. In addition, the case study provided a rich feedback for us to further improve the proposed method.

The case study participants included one BPM manager and two analysts as the team responsible for the ambidextrous business analysis process. The BPMO coordinator participated in some meetings and activities in order to appraise the A2BP method. One researcher was present during the whole case study to observe and make notes in a diary about everything that happened.

We also provided a journal for participants to write their experiences and provide critical reflections on the use of the A2BP method. Furthermore, they reported their experiences regarding each method phase, tasks and activities conducted by them. Finally, we designed a semi-structured questionnaire and applied to the BPMO coordinator, the BPM manager and the two process analysts. This questionnaire was similar to the instrument of the expert opinion survey. After finishing the case study, a new version of the artifact was generated based on the suggestions provided by participants. The results of the case study are described in Sect. 5.2.

4   A2BP: A Method for Ambidextrous Analysis of Business Process

In this section, we describe the artifact characterized as a method according to Design Science Research. The proposed method seeks to answer the research problem: *how to exploit internal problems and explore external opportunities of the business process?* Our aim is to support the phase of business process analysis by means of a novel method that stimulates both analytical and intuitive thinking. [21] state that a method is "a set of steps required to perform a given task". It can be graphically represented or encapsulated in specific algorithms and heuristics. Methods promote both the construction and representation of the needs for improvement of a phenomenon in a given context.

Aiming to design a new business process model that addresses the characteristics of operational efficiency and organizational innovation, the phase of business process analysis should be conducted differently from the conventional form [18]. To identify new opportunities, understand customers' needs and generate creative solutions, it is necessary the inclusion of design and innovation concepts in the process analysis phase [3].

In order to systematize the analysis of business processes, our method is categorized into phases, steps, activities, tasks, techniques and expected results. Figure 3 presents an abstraction of these elements proposed by the A2BP method. This categorization was developed based on PMBoK, which the phases refer to the process groups (initiating, planning, executing, monitoring and closing); the tasks are the inputs; the techniques are the tools; and the expected results are the outputs [26].

The A2BP method is available on the website (https://goo.gl/3r1HYW) to facilitate its application during the empirical study. As shown in Fig. 3, we divided the business process analysis into planning, executing and closing phases. The planning phase aims to create the analysis plan to guide the entire execution. In this way, this phase will assist: in the definition of the team that will participate in the ambidextrous analysis of

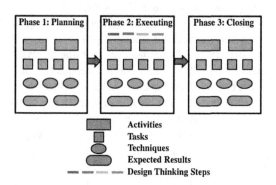

Fig. 3. Abstraction of A2BP method by [16].

the business process and the roles of each one of those involved; in the holistic understanding about the business environment; in the scope establishment; and in the development of process analysis plan. The following analytical techniques are suggested in this phase: meeting with stakeholders, interviews, desk research. As intuitive techniques, brainstorming and/or brainwriting are suggested to establish the scope of the business process analysis. Figure 4 presents the planning phase.

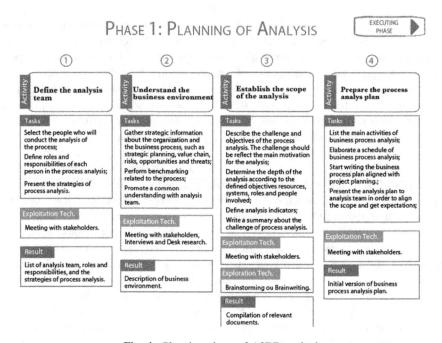

Fig. 4. Planning phase of A2BP method.

The executing phase will guide participants throughout the ambidextrous analysis of the business process. It is categorized in steps (Fig. 5) according to design thinking approach [20]: empathize, define, ideate and prototype. We suggest that exploration techniques are used in combination with exploitation techniques. The exploration techniques suggested by our method are available in [27].

In the empathize step (Fig. 6), the goal is that the analysts learn everything involved in the business process. From the customer perspective, it is important to note that the business process begins when the client is deciding which product or service to request. Furthermore, expectations and customer experience about the process are important variables to improve the product and/or service offered.

This step will assist those stakeholders: in reviewing the scope and understanding of the business process; in the preparation of the data collection according to the environment to be researched, the actors and client's profiles to be approached, as well as the guidance and materials that will be used; in learning about the current model of the business process according to the perspective of actors, clients, experts and similar

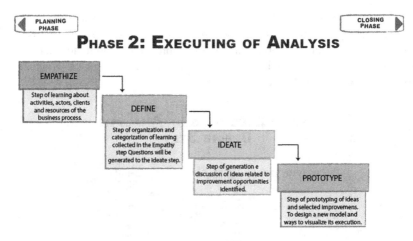

Fig. 5. Executing phase of A2BP method.

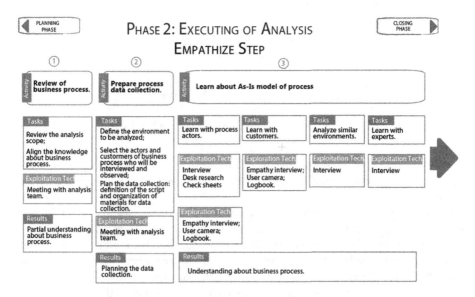

Fig. 6. Empathize step of the executing phase of A2BP.

environments. Exploration techniques such as empathy interview and user camera can assist in this regard. Desk research and check sheets are exploitation techniques that support analysts to identify reworks, alternatives for activities automation, among other aspects related to existing bottlenecks and problems in the process.

After the analysts have collected data on how the process happens through different perspectives, the define step (Fig. 7) will allow the team to share learning through documentation and discussion among the participants of the analysis, categorize those learnings, and list improvements and actions to be discussed at the ideate step. Thus, analytical reports containing the main problems and bottlenecks related to time, cost and quality are derived from the documents and interviews. Through the support of exploration techniques, such as empathy map, insights cards, personas and user journey, it is possible to increase opportunities for improvement throughout the business process. These techniques enable process analysts to look beyond the organizational boundary and explore subjective data.

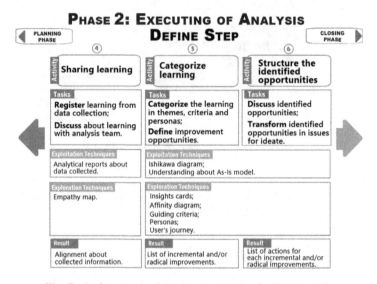

Fig. 7. Define step in the executing phase of A2BP by [16].

The discussion of ideas and documentation are part of the business process analysis. The ideate step (Fig. 8) is responsible for selecting the best ideas generated according to the feasibility and obstacles.

At this step, the team will organize the environment for the ideation, select the best ideas, check the feasibility of each one, list the obstacles, discuss new ideas and describe the ideas generated. The 5W2H (exploitation technique) is often used to define actions on what will be done in terms of improvement, why, where, when, who, how and how much the implementation of these actions. In parallel, exploration techniques can be used to explore new opportunities and organize them according to the personas identified above, such as brainstorming, brainwriting, menu ideas and positioning matrix.

Finally, the prototype step (Fig. 9) aims to facilitate an initial preview of how the selected ideas can be transformed into a new process model (to-be model) to support the final documentation of ambidextrous analysis of the business process. It is important to highlight that the prototype step within the analysis phase is characterized differently to the process design, the next phase of the BPM cycle. In the design phase, for example, the analysis documentation will be used to define all the business rules, metrics and more robust simulations. In addition, the to-be model should be prepared more accurately and analysts should provide details to represent how the process is going to be performed after its implementation. Therefore, the goal of the prototype step in the analysis phase is to develop early versions of the to-be business process for

PHASE 2: EXECUTING OF ANALYSIS
IDEATE STEP

PLANNING PHASE   CLOSING PHASE

⑦   ⑧

Activity — Generate ideas   **Activity** — Refine ideas

Tasks
Select the issues to be discussed;
Prepare the environment to ideation;
Realize the ideation to generate incremental and radical improvements;
Select best ideas.

Tasks
Verify ideas viability;
List obstacles;
Explore and discuss new ideas;
Describe the ideas.

Exploitation Tech.
5W2H

Exploration Tech.
Brainstorming, Brainwriting, Ideas menu, Decision matriz.

Result
Documentation of ideias to be prototyped.

Fig. 8. Ideate step of the executing phase of A2BP.

PHASE 2: EXECUTING OF ANALYSIS
PROTOTYPE STEP

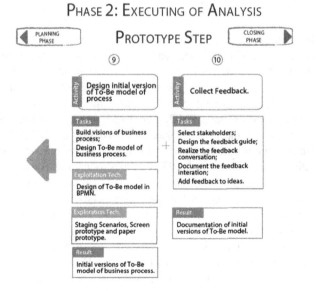

PLANNING PHASE   CLOSING PHASE

⑨   ⑩

Activity — Design initial version of To-Be model of process   **Activity** — Collect Feedback.

Tasks
Build visions of business process;
Design To-Be model of business process.

Tasks
Select stakeholders;
Design the feedback guide;
Realize the feedback conversation;
Document the feedback interation;
Add feedback to ideas.

Exploitation Tech.
Design of To-Be model in BPMN.

Exploration Tech.
Staging Scenarios, Screen prototype and paper prototype.

Result
Documentation of initial versions of To-Be model.

Result
Initial versions of To-Be model of business process.

Fig. 9. Prototype step in the executing phase of A2BP.

quick and minimal test the improvement opportunities identified by analysts, stake-holders and customers. Business process views should be developed through story-boards, paper and screen prototypes or by the process modeling to be presented to stakeholders and collect feedback.

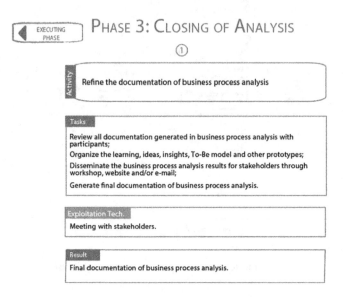

Fig. 10. Closing phase of A2BP.

Finally, the closing phase (Fig. 10) involves the review of the data collected, the organization of learning, insights, ideas and prototypes in order to generate the final documentation of business process analysis. This documentation will assist in the design of the new business process model by using techniques that stimulate the explorative and exploitative thinking. We suggest the use of the method by any organizational unit, such as the BPMO. The BPM manager and analyst team can conduct the method during the analysis phase of the BPM cycle.The A2BP method has as main input the model of the current business process (*as-is model*). The main output is a documentation that will support the BPM team responsible to design a new process model (*to-be model*) by using techniques of analytical and intuitive thinking. As intuitive thinking takes into account the outside-in perspective, we consider that the method is more suitable for processes that begin and finish in the customer organi-zation, (i.e. end-to-end process).

Our intention is that business process analysts can use the A2BP method as a complementary approach of their BPM methodology. However, we believe that the depth and quality of outcomes depend on professional experience. Furthermore, the high number of techniques and the time required to perform the method will also depend on the size and complexity of the process being analyzed. We emphasize that the main reason to include exploration techniques and practices include the capability to stimulate divergent and convergent thinking to generate ideas to make the business process aligned with customer expectations.

As there are different types of goals to analyze a business process, the techniques proposed by the method are presented as suggestions to analysts according to the expected results of the tasks to be performed. Exploration techniques are more present in the execution phase because it was organized under the structure of design thinking approach. Thus, it is important to note that the method proposes exploitation or exploration techniques for certain tasks.

According to [3], nowadays, process analysts are unaware of the design thinking approach and may never experienced the use of exploration techniques in the context of BPM. Even though, there are a number of exploration techniques, we suggest 16 exploration techniques so that the understanding and application of the A2BP method does not become over exhausting and complex for the analysts. Otherwise, they would spend a lot of time learning how to use several existing exploration techniques. In the website of the method, we provide a specific menu that presents the techniques and recommended flow to be followed along the ambidextrous analysis of business process, as presented in Fig. 11.

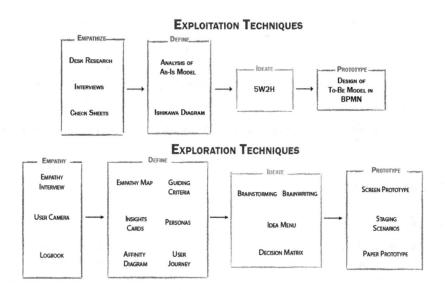

Fig. 11. Exploration and exploitation techniques suggested in A2BP.

By clicking on the title of the desired technique, the user is directed to a page, such as Table 2, that details what is the technique, why to use it, how to use it and the participants who can carry it out.

It is important to note that it is not the scope of this research to investigate what are the best techniques for each proposed step of the method. Just as there are many consolidated exploitation techniques, several exploration techniques have been developed by academia and industry. However, the application of exploration

Table 2. Example of exploration technique – empathy map.

Empathy map technique	
What	The analysis team needs to deeply understand the users (actors and customers) of the business process in order to design improvements for them. Empathy Map is a technique to assist synthesize collected data and extract unexpected insights according to what users say, do, think, and feel. Unexpected insights may arise primarily from inferences about what users think and feel. For these are two variables that can not be directly observed
Why	This technique is useful in the definition phase of the process analysis. Its use will help the analysis team to reflect on the learning obtained in the data collection of the Immersion Phase. This technique is better applied integrated with the Insights Cards technique
How	1. Write short sentences in the technique template: What do users say about the process/product/service (Speak)?; 2. What actions and behaviours do you perceive in users (Do)?; 3. What are users thinking or what do they talk about (think)? What emotions are users feeling (Feeling)? What do users hear (Hear)? What do users see (See)?; 4. Identify the pains, obstacles, weaknesses, fears and frustrations of users; 5. Identify needs in the form of verbs. Needs are activities and desires with which your users can be helped. Realize the contradictions that may exist between what they say and what they do, for example; 6. Identify the insights according to the Insights Cards technique
Participants	This technique should be performed with the participation of the analysis team

techniques in analyzing and improving business processes is still an emergent topic in the literature [12, 15].

5 Empirical Study

5.1 Expert Opinion

As described in Sect. 2, design science research cycle includes the design and evaluation of an artifact that has the theory as a foundation and has a business context for which it should have a practical use. After designing the artifact, an expert opinion was held. Briefly, the profile of each participant is described in Table 3.

As the proposed artifact aims to be applied by BPM professionals and organizations that want to analyze and improve their business processes, we invited experts who have experience in business and/or IT with solid knowledge in BPM. Just one expert reported to have participated in a project involving design thinking but said that his experience in this matter is low. The others only read about it or never had contact. This profile was chosen because it is similar to what is found in organizations that will apply A2BP method.

Table 3. Experience of experts by [16].

Experts	Experience
Expert 1	Has a MSc in BPM, worked as business analyst for 2 years, structuring the BPMO of a public organization. Since 2013, he acts as a manager in a research agreement between a University and a public institution, whose main activity is the conduction of process improvement projects
Expert 2	Has over 10 years of experience in the IT field, is a consultant in management activities, systems analysis, requirements analysis, negotiation and BPM. He also has experience in the use of BPM practices for business process modeling and knowledge in BPMS tools
Expert 3	Has worked for over 20 years in IT, having worked as Manager, Business Analyst and Data Architect. He is Project Management Professional (PMP) and Certified Business Process Professional (CBPP) and Certified Scrum Master (CSM)
Expert 4	Has 23 years of professional experience in IT and organizational consulting, has experience as BPM analyst in public and private companies. Has a MSc and PhD in the BPM area and owns PMP and CBPP certifications
Expert 5	Is a master in computer science and works in the implementation of tools for organizational competitiveness and efficiency in the areas of Project Management, BPM, Digital Quality and Audit. It has the PMP and CBPP certifications
Expert 6	Is a University lecturer and conducts research in the BPM area. Has experience in BPM projects in various companies. He has worked with modeling, analysis, design and automation of processes with the integration of services with *web service* and SOA (*Service-Oriented Architecture*)
Expert 7	Has a MSc in BPM and has experience as consultant and team manager of process analysts in several companies through improvement projects and process automation for nearly 9 years

The following sections describe the results of the expert opinion survey to answer RQ2. Here we analyzed the expert's perceived ease-of-use and usefulness of the A2BP method.

Perceived Ease-of-Use

The first question addressed the ease of understanding and use of the phases, flow activities and tasks proposed by the A2PB. Four experts said they strongly agree and three marked that agree with the assertion of the first question.

The second question of the survey was open. The experts suggested ways to improve the understanding and execution of the phases, activities and tasks of the method. We present below two recommendations given by experts:

- "Joining the last two tasks of the activity 2 of empathize step. Place a broader term, something like 'To plan data collection'";
- "Develop a glossary to explain terms that are not self-explanatory, such as, 'partial alignment of understanding'";
- "Change the name of the 'prototype process' to the 'initial version of the to-be model' so as not to confuse the user with more jargon";

- "Increase the size of the box of activity 3 of the empathize step to make it clear that everything below belongs to it".

The third question was assertive on the clear understanding of how to use the exploitation and exploration techniques proposed by the method. As results we had that: one expert does not agree, one was undecided, four agree and one strongly agree that the method provided clear instructions on how to use the exploitation and exploration techniques.

The fourth question asked if the description of the techniques could be improved to facilitate their understanding. The suggestions given by the experts are listed here:

- "For me, the how to use the techniques is not so didactic. I think it would be interesting to number the steps. For a first version, as a whole, the work is very good";
- "The method should make explicit who are the mandatory and desirable participants to apply the techniques";
- "Can improve the image of the 'guiding criteria' technique. The images should bring the idea of the expected result";
- "Make it clear in the techniques page what participants are obligatory and desirable".

The fifth question asked suggestions for improvements to the method website layout taking into account the colors, fonts, images, layout of text, templates, etc. All the experts who answered this question praised the layout and organization of the site. The only recommendation was to design the website with better look and feel.

Perceived Usefulness

The sixth question asked if the phases, activities and tasks are appropriate to carry out an ambidextrous business analysis process. One expert marked as undecided, five agreed and one strongly agreed with the statement.

The seventh question asked suggestions to increase or change the phases, activities and tasks to make the method more useful for ambidextrous analysis of the business process. The experts recommended the method should provide more explicit advice on when to use or make optional the execution of any activity, task and/or technique.

The eighth question addresses whether the experts consider the exploitation and exploration techniques appropriate to perform incremental and radical improvements of business processes. One expert was undecided, five agreed and one strongly agreed with the assertion. The ninth question asked for suggestions to experts on the inclusion or exclusion of any technique. There was no suggestion given to this question.

In order to better illustrate how to use the A2BP method, we created a fictitious project of an ambidextrous analysis of a pizzeria business process improvement. In this documentation, users can observe the results of the application of the techniques present in the proposed method. Therefore, the question tenth asked if the pizzeria example helps in use of the techniques. As a result, an expert disagreed, two were undecided and four fully agreed with the assertion. The question eleventh asks for suggestions to improve the pizzeria example. Two suggestions were given to make the example more simple and straightforward.

Expert Experience and Criticisms
In order to understand the perception of experts regarding the proposed method, the final question asked experts to comment their experience in general. Five experts reported their experiences:

- "I think it's a rich experience by using creative techniques";
- "I agree that it is interesting, certainly putting it to test on a real project, I believe that the results would be very interesting";
- "I found quite interesting, but seemed a little" 'heavy' if considered at all steps/techniques";
- "I found it interesting and curious because I saw the junction of several good practices";
- "I had a very good experience. The use of exploration techniques stimulates us to think beyond what we are used to".

Finally, we also asked how the method could be improved. Experts suggested the following improvements:

- "Develop an explanatory video about the method in general";
- "Experience report about the difficulties and facilities found in the use of the method";
- "A model of evaluation with indicators established to monitor the adherence of the method".
- "Include information from a real case study".

Method Refinement
According to the DSR [21], after conducting the first cycle of empirical evaluation, we must refine the method artifact. The following feedbacks from experts were taken into account to improve our A2BP method:

1. We adjusted the nomenclature of some tasks to facilitate understanding;
2. We integrated some tasks that have similar results;
3. We developed a glossary to explain terms that are not self-explanatory;
4. We improved the images of some techniques;
5. We developed a video that contextualizes the method in general.

5.2 Observational Case Study

After refining and improving the A2BP method with feedback from experts, as discussed in the previous section, we carried out a case study to evaluate the applicability of our method in an organization with experience in BPM. The case study was conducted between July and October 2016. The following section describes the organization in which the method was applied. Then, we also evaluated the method by means of the perceived ease-of-use and usefulness, as well as suggestions and critics of the participants.

Case Description

The organization chosen to implement the A2BP Method has the function of assisting the Legislative in the external control of the Public Administration. It performs the monitoring and auditing of public accounts. Because the method is suitable for business processes that start and end on the customer, we chose the complaint process. This process aims to investigate information about irregularities in the administrative, financial, budgetary and balance of government agencies, including indirect administration or those who executed any public expenditure.

The complaint process has the following phases: formalization, investigation, judgment and publication. Initially, the citizen delivers a petition to the protocol sector. It can be an individual or legal person. Then, the admissibility requirements are checked and the protocol sector forwards it to the counselor to authorize the formalization of the process. To be formalized, the process goes to the investigation to audit.

The auditor writes a report with the outcome of the investigation confirming or rejecting the facts alleged by the complainant. Concluded the case to judgment, the counselor's office provides the preparation of the vote and submit the case to judgment by the collegiate based on the audit report. Following the decision, the process proceeds to the implementation of the resolutions included in the decision and its result are published in the official journal of the State.

As described in Sect. 4, the application of the A2BP method has as input the as-is process model. The participants of the case study were a BPM team of the case organization comprised of one manager and two process analysts. During the case study, one researcher participated as observer of all activities conducted by the team to apply the A2BP method.

To start the study, the team created the as-is model of the complaint process by obtaining information through interviews with three staff responsible for the formalization phase, six staff of the investigation, three staff involved in the judgment and two in the publication. In total, fourteen interviews were carried out to create the as-is model.

With the input of the as-is model of the complaint process, the case study began with the activities of A2BP method **planning phase**. Initially, the team collected information related to the complaint process through the exploitation technique of desk research. Among some documents searched, are the Organic Law No. 12,600 of 2004 and Resolution 008/2006 regarding the complaint process.

To establish the scope of the analysis, the team invited three stakeholders responsible for the complaint process who had roles of managers of their functional areas. The team presented the as-is model to stakeholders. They discussed problems and opportunities with the brainstorming technique. After the meeting, two Improvement Opportunities (IO) to be explored during the analysis:

- IO1: there are two procedural rules that do the same activities and are handled differently (special audit and complaint). That causes rework and waste of time;
- IO2: complainants write information on the application form in very different manners. This causes confusion and delays in the complaint formalization sector.

Based on that, the first version of the analysis plan was drawn up containing the main activities to be carried along with a schedule. Then the team started the **executing**

phase of A2BP method comprises the steps of empathize, define, ideate and prototype. During the **empathize step** the team carried out a review of the complaint process (Activity 1) and conducted a preparation to learn with the actors and customers of the complaint process (Activity 2).

Activity 3 of the empathize step includes learning more about the as-is process. Therefore, the team conducted empathy interviews with a customer and two employees of the protocol sector, who are responsible to receive the petition with the complainant (i.e. the customer of the process). Through the technique of empathy interview, the team identified that the customer does not receive any estimate of when the facts will be investigated. After entering the complaint letter, the complainant receives a protocol number to track its progress through the organization's website. However, from the period when he enters the petition until its formalization, the complainant does not receive any information about the progress of his request. Thus, beyond the two problems identified in the planning phase, the team included another Improvement Opportunity:

- IO3: the complainant cannot follow the progress of his denunciation until it is formalized.

The team noted this problem causes customer frustration due to the lack of process visibility. It is also evidence that the organization is not taking into account customer satisfaction. After the empathy interviews, the **define step** started. In Activity 4, the team shared what they learned about the IO of the complaint process. They reported the interviews and filled the empathy map (explorative technique).

Then, the Activities 5 and 6 were performed to categorize these learnings and to structure opportunities identified. At that moment, the team used the Ishikawa diagram (exploitation technique) as well as insights cards, affinity diagram, and user journey (exploration technique). During this step, the team categorized three new Improvement Opportunities for the process, such as:

- IO4: a guideline on how to write a complaint is not available for customers;
- IO5: there are no standard procedures for the auditors on how to formalize petitions as a complaint;
- IO6: the information on the organization's website regarding the reports of each sector is not easy to understand for the customer because they contain many acronyms and jargons used internally by the organization.

Considering the six Improvement Opportunities identified by analysis team, four were prioritized to be further analyzed in the **ideate step**. The prioritized IO were: IO1, IO2, IO3, IO4. For each IO, several ideas were generated (Activity 7) and refined (Activity 8) by using 5W2H (exploitation technique) and brainstorming (exploration technique).

After the team carried out discussions and documented the ideas generated, in the **prototype step**, they prototyped possible solutions for each IO according to the Activities 9 and 10 of the A2BP method. For IO1, the team investigated how other similar organizations handle modalities of different processes as a unique process. The team noted that it would be feasible to implement this solution. For IO2, a new version of the application form has been generated in order to standardize all data concerning the complaint process.

Regarding IO3, the idea chosen for prototyping was to improve the traceability of the process through notifications to the complainant whenever their complaint letter change status within the organization. This notification can be received by SMS and/or e-mail according to customer choice. To contemplate the IO4, the team decided to provide guidelines at the organization's website on how to fill in the complaint letter to avoid misunderstanding and disagreements.

Finally, the team refined all the documentation generated during the analysis of the complaint process using the A2BP method. A meeting was held with stakeholders in order to present the results of the analysis. After the **closing phase**, the application of A2BP method was completed and the team conducted discussions about the design of the to-be model of the complaint process.

After application of the A2BP method, a semi-structured questionnaire was conducted with the analysis team and the BPMO manager to assess the perceived ease-of-use and usefulness, experience of use and criticism of the method. Four participants answered the questionnaire. These results are presented in the following sections.

Perceived Ease-of-Use

The first question addressed the ease of understanding and use of the phases, flow activities and tasks proposed. One participant said he was undecided, two partially agreed and strongly agreed that the method was easy to use. The second question asked for suggestions to facilitate the understanding of the phases, activities and tasks of the method. Two participants gave their opinions:

- "The method could make it clear that it is intended to be used integrated with the existing BPM methodology of the organization";
- "The description of the activities and techniques was easy to understand... The figure representing the steps of Design Thinking was very good too";
- "It was not clear for me if I could perform again, the activities already were done".

The third question was an assertion on the clear understanding of how to use the exploitation and exploration techniques suggested in the method. One participant disagreed, two partially agreed and one strongly agreed that it was clear on how to use the techniques. In the fourth question, it was asked how the description of the techniques could be improved to facilitate their understanding. The suggestions are listed below:

- "The templates of the techniques available were not fully used because they do not look good when printed";
- "The sequence of exploration techniques was not clear when the technique was required or optional".

There was no answer to the fifth question, which asked if they have suggestions for improvement in the website layout of the A2BP method. Two participants praised the website layout.

Perceived Usefulness

The sixth question asked if the phases, activities and tasks are appropriate to carry out an ambidextrous business analysis process. One participant marked as undecided and three agreed with the statement. The seventh question asked for suggestions to make the method more useful, but there was no answer to that question.

The eighth question addressed whether the case study participants consider the exploitation and exploration techniques appropriate to perform incremental and radical improvements in the business processes of the organization. One participant was undecided, two agreed and one strongly agreed with the assertion. The ninth question asked for suggestions on the inclusion or exclusion of any technique. One participant suggested the method should include fewer exploration techniques.

The tenth question asked if the example of the pizzeria process helped in the learning on how to use the techniques. As a result, one participant did not agree, two agreed and one strongly agreed with the statement. In question eleventh, the only suggested improvement was to improve the details of the results of the planning phase.

Expert Experience and Criticisms

In order to understand the experience of the participants on the use of the proposed method, the last question asked how was their experience in general. The participants evaluated the method positively:

- "Overall, the experience was very enriching. I believe that using the method can bring a gain for the organization, mainly by combining techniques that make us stop to think and act not only mechanically";
- "I can say I learned innovative ways to analyze a process. The idea of mapping for empathy, personas, and user journey are important to know how the idea of improvement is accepted or not by the people who actually are working on the process daily";
- "For me, it was very good. I felt a good organization and focus to understand, analyze and improve process".

Method Refinement

The following feedbacks from participants of the case study were taken into account to improve our A2BP method:

1. In the description of the method, we should make more explicit that it contemplates only the analysis phase of the BPM lifecycle;
2. We adjusted the templates of the techniques that had problems of understanding and visualization;
3. We described in the method that exploitative and exploratory techniques are all desirable and their application depends on the context and nature of the business process to be improved.

After performing these refinements, we will be able to continue the DSR cycle to further improve our proposed artifact – the A2BP method.

6 Conclusions

In this paper, we investigated organizational ambidexterity and design thinking practices during the phase of business process analysis. The literature has evidenced that the traditional BPM practices and techniques are not enough to identify new business opportunities or to explore clients' expectations, emotions and feelings. In this way, a recent trend is to adopt more exploration techniques in the BPM cycle, such as design thinking. Exploration techniques allows analysts to improve incrementally with focus on the efficiency of operations as well as to innovate their business processes, generating greater adaptability and creation of new products and services. Despite the possibility of applying design thinking throughout the whole BPM lifecycle, we focused on the process analysis phase because it is a moment of reflection and critical investigation of the as-is business process model. During the analysis phase, we propose the use of several techniques to identify, generate improvements and design to-be business process model.

In this context, this paper presents an empirical research whose main contribution is the development of a new method called Ambidextrous Analysis of Business Process (A2BP). We have adopted a design science research approach as a methodological framework to address our research objective and questions. After conducting the systematic literature mapping, we designed the A2BP method artifact, which aims to investigate how to exploit internal problems and explore external opportunities of business process.

Regarding the RQ1 (What are the features of a method that supports the ambidextrous analysis of business processes?), the main feature of A2BP refers to the capability to empower stakeholders to think in an intuitive and analytical way in the understanding, organization, reflection, and identification of improvement opportunities (both incremental or innovation) for business process. In addition, the A2BP method uses concepts and practices from outside-in and inside-out paradigms, as well as from organizational ambidexterity and design thinking. The exploitation and exploration techniques suggested in the method were developed by academia and industry and are widely used. The method was organized in phases, steps, activities, tasks, techniques and expected results according to PMBoK.

In relation to RQ2 (How is the ease-of-use and usefulness perceived by process analysts of the proposed method for ambidextrous analysis of business processes?), we also conducted empirical studies by means of expert review and observational case study to evaluate the method proposed. Both studies evaluated the perceived usefulness, ease-of-use and obtained suggestions and criticisms to improve the method. In particular, the purpose of the expert opinion was to achieve the first round of refinement of the method. According to their experience, experts envisioned how to apply the method in their own contexts. Then, with the case study, we were able to verify the method's applicability in a real BPM initiative. We observed the difficulties experienced by the participants and collected new opportunities for improving the method.

According to the results of the empirical studies, we perceived that both experts and participants of the case study assessed the A2BP method as easy-of-use and useful to exploit internal problems and explore external opportunities. In the case study, six

Improvement Opportunities were discovered. Of which, four IO were problems identified internally and two IO emerged based on the interactions with the customer of the complaint process through the use of exploration techniques.

According to the case study participants, probably these two IOs would not be identified if the team used only traditional exploitation techniques for business process analysis. Therefore, we conclude that the exploration techniques proposed by the A2BP method enriched the analysis of the complaint process. As practical contribution, the A2BP method is available for organizations conducting BPM initiatives that aim to explore innovative ways to continuously improve their business processes.

Despite the methodological rigor adopted in our research method, our empirical studies face some limitations. The main limitation is related to a low generalization of results because we applied the method in only one BPM project at the case organization. Another limitation lies in the nature of expert opinion survey that our findings are based on the perception of only a limited number of participants.

As future work, we plan to conduct longitudinal case studies at other organizations to evaluate the practical utility of the A2BP method. Furthermore, we suggest the conduction of a quasi-experiment to compare the results of two business process analysis teams (one using the A2BP method and the other using traditional analysis techniques). We also plan to conduct another round of expert review to further refine the A2BP method.

References

1. van der Aalst, W.M.P.: A decade of business process management conferences: personal reflections on a developing discipline. In: Barros, A., Gal, A., Kindler, E. (eds.) BPM 2012. LNCS, vol. 7481, pp. 1–16. Springer, Heidelberg (2012). https://doi.org/10.1007/978-3-642-32885-5_1
2. OMG: Business Process Management with OMG specifications. http://www.bpm-consortium.org/literature.htm. Accessed 20 June 2017
3. Rosemann, M.: Proposals for future BPM research directions. In: Ouyang, C., Jung, J.-Y. (eds.) AP-BPM 2014. LNBIP, vol. 181, pp. 1–15. Springer, Cham (2014). https://doi.org/10.1007/978-3-319-08222-6_1
4. Martin, R.: The Design of Business: Why Design Thinking is the Next Competitive Advantage, 3rd edn. Harvard Business Review, Boston (2009)
5. ABPMP: BPM CBOK - Guide to the Business Process Management Common Body of Knowledge, vol. 2 (2013)
6. Malinova, M., Brina, H., Mendling, J.: A framework for assessing BPM success. In: Twenty Second European Conference on Information Systems, Tel Aviv, pp. 1–15 (2014)
7. Kohlborn, T., Mueller, O., Poeppelbuss, J., Roeglinger, M.: Interview with Michael Rosemann on ambidextrous business process management. Bus. Process Manage. J. 20(4), 634–638 (2014)
8. O'Reilly, C.A., Tushman, M.L.: The ambidextrous organization. Harv. Bus. Rev. 1–7 (2004)
9. He, Z.-L., Wong, P.-K.: Exploration vs. Exploitation: an empirical test of the ambidexterity hypothesis. Organ. Sci. 15(4), 481–494 (2004)
10. Bauer, M., Leker, J.: Exploration and exploitation in product and process innovation in the chemical industry. R&D Manage. 43(3), 196–212 (2013)

11. Chen, E., Katila, R.: Rival interpretations of balancing exploration and exploitation: Simultaneous or sequential? In: Shane, S. (ed.) Handbook of Technology and Innovation Management, vol. 1. Wiley, New York (2008)

12. Richardson, C., Leaver, S., Cullen, A., Keenan, J.: Design for Disruption: Take An Outside-In Approach to BPM. Forrester Research, Cambridge (2013)

13. Brown, T.: Change by Design: How Design Thinking Transforms Organizations and Inspires Innovation. Harper Business, New York (2009)

14. Chasanidou, D., Gasparini, A., Lee, E.: Design thinking methods and tools for innovation in multidisciplinary teams. In: Workshop Innovation in HCI, NordiCHI 2014, Helsinki, Finland, pp. 27–30, (2014)

15. Luebbe, A., Weske, M.: Bringing design thinking to business process modeling. In: Meinel, C., Leifer, L., Plattner, H. (eds.) Design Thinking. Understanding Innovation, pp. 181–195. Springer, Heidelberg (2011). https://doi.org/10.1007/978-3-642-13757-0_11

16. Santos, H., Alves, C.: A2BP: a method for ambidextrous analysis of business process. In: Proceedings of the 19th International Conference on Enterprise Information Systems, vol. 3. ICEIS (2017)

17. Jeston, J., Nelis, J.: Business Process Management, Practical Guidelines to Successful Implementations, 2nd edn. Elsevier Ltd, Oxford (2008)

18. Vergidis, K., Tiwari, A., Majeed, B.: Business process analysis and optimization: beyond reengineering. IEEE Trans. Syst. Man Cybern. **38**(1), 69–82 (2008)

19. IIBA: A Guide to the Business Analysis Body of Knowledge (BABOK Guide), vol. 2. International Institute of Business Analysis, Toronto (2009)

20. Brown, T., Wyatt, J.: Design Thinking for Social Innovation. Open Knowledge Repository (2010). https://openknowledge.worldbank.com/handle/10986/6068. Accessed 15 July 2017

21. Hevner, A., March, S., Park, J., Ram, S.: Design science in information systems research. MIS Q. **28**(1), 75–106 (2004)

22. Wieringa, R.: Design Science Methodology for Information Systems and Software Engineering. Springer, Heidelberg (2014). https://doi.org/10.1007/978-3-662-43839-8

23. Ramer, S.: Site-ation pearl growing: methods and librarianship history and theory. J. Med. Libr. Assoc. **93**(3), 397–400 (2005)

24. Brown, J.D.: What issues affect Likert-scale questionnaire formats? JALT Test. Eval. SIG **4**, 27–30 (2000)

25. Merriam, Sharan B.: Qualitative Research and Case Study Applications in Education, 2nd edn. Jossey-Bass, San Francisco (1998)

26. PMI: A Guide to the Project Management Body of Knowledge (PMBOK® Guide), 5th edn. Project Management Institute (PMI), Sylva (2013)

27. DSCHOOL: Bootcamp Bootleg (2009). https://dschool.stanford.edu/wp-content/uploads/2011/03/BootcampBootleg2010v2SLIM.pdf. Accessed 10 June 2017

Toward an Understanding of the Tradeoffs of Adopting the MEAN Web Server Stack

Steve Kitzes, Eric DeMauro, and Adam Kaplan[✉]

California State University Northridge, Northridge, CA 91330, USA
steven.kitzes@gmail.com, erickdemauro@gmail.com,
akaplan@csun.edu

Abstract. In the past decade, the performance of web services has been enhanced via scale-up and scale-out methods, which increase available system resources, and also by improvements in database performance. As cloud technology continues to rise in popularity, storage and compute services are reaching unprecedented scale, with great scrutiny being turned to the performance tradeoffs of the web application server stacks. In particular, the MEAN (MongoDB, Express.js, AngularJS, and Node.js) web server stack is increasingly popular in the computing industry, yet has largely escaped the focus of formal benchmarking efforts. In this work, we compare MEAN to its more entrenched competitor, the LAMP (Linux, Apache, MySQL, PHP) web server stack, the most widely distributed web platform in production. We herein describe the design, execution, and results of a number of benchmark tests constructed and executed to facilitate direct comparison between Node.js and Apache/PHP, the web server applications of these stacks. We investigate each web server's ability to handle heavy static file service, remote database interaction, and common compute-bound tasks. Analysis of our results indicates that Node.js outperforms the Apache/PHP by a considerable margin in all single-application web service scenarios, and performs as well as Apache/PHP under heterogeneous server workloads. We extend our understanding of the MEAN stack's performance potential by exploring the performance and memory tradeoffs of Angularizing the Mongo-Express web application, a database administration dashboard for MongoDB. We find that porting Mongo-Express to MEAN's AngularJS provides up to a 4x improvement in document read bandwidth and up to almost 2.2x improvement in collection read bandwidth, at a cost of roughly double the client memory footprint.

Keywords: Web server · Lamp · Mean · Benchmark · Cloud technology

1 Introduction

Cloud technologies and their proliferation have revolutionized the ways in which we live our lives [30]. Service domains that have come to rely on the cloud include retail commerce, entertainment, and business functions across the board, including, in a circular fashion, software development itself. Many service and research domains would not be possible at current scale without the cloud. These include contemporary social networks and big-data analytical science. These domains leverage massive amounts of

© Springer International Publishing AG, part of Springer Nature 2018
S. Hammoudi et al. (Eds.): ICEIS 2017, LNBIP 321, pp. 567–590, 2018.
https://doi.org/10.1007/978-3-319-93375-7_26

instantly-accessible data which can be collected, moved, and analysed upon a flexible collection of computing resources deployed across the world.

A need has arisen to assess the various popular web frameworks, and to produce an understanding of their performance characteristics. In the absence of such understanding, a web-service company may find itself under- or over-provisioning resources, and/or poorly utilizing developer effort. For a modern technology company developing a web-service product, an ideal design includes a thorough analysis of existing web-stack technologies, such that their strengths and weaknesses can be identified and their performance capabilities estimated. Such an analysis can guide selection of the most promising technology stack upon which to host a given service.

Existing research has focused on *scaling up* the hardware on which cloud technologies are hosted, by upgrading or expanding hardware resources to become more performant [2], or to *scaling out* the host hardware by adding more computational resources upon which to distribute compute workloads [7]. Investigations have also targeted database performance [23], resulting in extensive database benchmarking standards [29]. These standards may guide web-service architects through the database design space.

However, less focus has been paid to the comparative performance of the web application software being run on these hardware platforms. This software is often deployed on numerous load-balanced machines, and facilitates business logic for thousands of concurrent users or more [3]. In our work, we investigate the performance of these web application service engines as they compare under concurrent user load when run on the same hardware [12]. We specifically focus attention on Node.js in conjunction with the Express.js framework, together part of an increasingly popular, recently deployed web application server stack known as MEAN [17]. We compare Node.js to its more entrenched competitor, namely the Apache web server in conjunction with PHP, which together form part of the famous LAMP stack, still the most widely distributed web platform in production [21].

It is worth noting that Node.js functions as a complete platform that allows developers to write server-side software and web applications using JavaScript. By comparison, Apache does not contain an engine for executing PHP code, but rather integrates with the PHP interpreter and serves the resultant output of a given script to the requesting client as appropriate. Node.js is special in this regard, because an application can be written in JavaScript that handles all aspects of an application's duties, from serving client requests, to database interaction, to executing server side JavaScript code. Since Node.js is capable of managing static file hosting, handling business logic, serving dynamic content, and handling database and file I/O, this platform has proven to be an attractive solution, in some cases winning a place over other popular frameworks in the development environments of industry leaders including eBay, LinkedIn, PayPal, Uber and many others [8]. To these early adopters, Node.js provides tremendous community support and a broad selection of libraries made available both officially and unofficially via the NPM (Node Package Manager) system; as well as the ability to code entire web applications from front to back entirely in a single programming language (JavaScript).

Also attractive to Node.js users is the enticing possibility of superior web application performance [3]. The attention Node.js has attracted from the community and from industry leaders generates the confidence that this is a framework that is worthy of further performance investigation, especially in direct comparison against the current industry leader, Apache/PHP.

To further understand the performance potential of the MEAN stack, we also explore the performance impact of using the AngularJS client-side framework, which comprises the "A" from MEAN. AngularJS differs from other popular JavaScript libraries, such as jQuery, in that is it an entire framework for building single-page applications. This allows the user to continue interacting with the single page of the web application in the client browser while asynchronous HTTP requests are made from client to server. The results of these requests then update the content of the web page in real time, providing the responsiveness of an interactive Desktop application.

We investigate the performance of AngularJS by porting (*Angularizing*) a popular MongoDB database administration tool named Mongo-Express [19] from its traditional build to one that employs AngularJS. We run benchmark tests against Mongo-Express operations that read and write a document, as well as read an entire collection, and profile Mongo-Express's request bandwidth and memory usage both with and without Angularization.

The remainder of this paper is organized as follows. In Sect. 2, we provide a background description of the Node.js and Apache runtime architectures, and discuss porting Mongo-Express to an Angularized (AngularJS) version. In Sect. 3 we discuss the most closely related work in web service benchmarking. In Sect. 4, we detail our experimental methodology for comparing Node.js and Apache, as well as for profiling the performance and memory consumption of Mongo-Express with AngularJS. Section 5 provides experimental results over multiple contemporary web-service benchmarks, as well as a bandwidth and memory consumption comparison between the original and Angularized Mongo-Express. Finally, in Sect. 6, we provide concluding remarks and a brief discussion of future work.

2 Background

2.1 Node.js (The "N" of the MEAN Stack)

Node.js employs an event loop, executed on a single thread, to carry out execution of all user defined program code, as shown in Fig. 1 [12]. However, only the management of the event loop and the tasks placed upon it are executed by this single thread. Many other threads are involved in the process of managing a full Node.js instance. Node.js is built upon a bedrock of supporting technologies, most importantly Google's V8 Runtime and the libuv support library. V8 allows JavaScript to be run efficiently on server side hardware whereas libuv provides the asynchronous event handling structure which holds the promise of enhanced application performance [13].

At a high level, libuv's architecture can be described as follows. An event is placed into the Node.js event queue by a client request, and the event loop will process this event. The client request will then be handled by user code. In cases requiring asynchronous operations, such as database or file system interaction, the user code will invoke Node.js (or third party) function calls for these tasks.

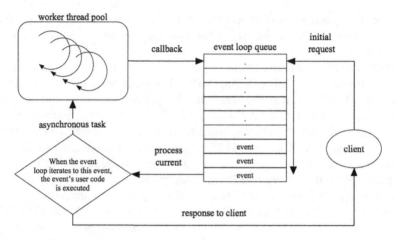

Fig. 1. The node.js event loop.

These function calls spawn asynchronous processes on one of several worker threads running in a thread pool behind the scenes. Node.js, as well as third party library developers, provide this asynchronous behavior by default, and implicitly encourage its use.

Otherwise, as asynchronous tasks execute upon separate worker threads, the event loop thread continues serving other pending requests, invoking callbacks, or spawning additional asynchronous tasks upon worker threads as needed. Asynchronous tasks, once completed, return control to the application developer via callbacks, which are placed on the end of the event queue as new events, and wait their turn to be handled by the Node.js event loop as appropriate.

For performance reasons, it is critical that users take care to avoid introducing computationally heavy code, or other synchronous tasks, into either request handlers or callbacks that are executed on the event loop thread, as these block execution of the event loop. In fact, programmers must explicitly specify when and if they wish to use a synchronous version of a given operation, as any synchronous implementation will block the event loop until its task completes [28]. However, if the asynchronous functionality that comes packaged with Node.js is employed, and the event loop remains unburdened with synchronous operations, then the load of processing each individual item on the event loop queue remains relatively light, and chiefly consists of spawning an asynchronous task on a worker thread.

2.2 Apache (The "A" of the LAMP Stack)

As Fig. 2 demonstrates, Apache employs a configurable multi-process, multi-threaded solution to concurrency [12]. This modern Apache architecture represents a departure from the original Apache engine, which was designed at a time when concurrency was not a severely limiting factor for most use cases. The contemporary Apache maintains a thread pool (in varying patterns by version, configuration, and host operating system) for handling request service operations in parallel [18]. However, as mentioned above, while these processes are carried out in true parallel fashion on multiple threads – and possibly even on multiple processors – each individual thread will block in its own right while waiting on outstanding operations that might take long stretches of time, such as database or file system access. Moreover, the construction, tear-down, and context switching of these threads can be costly in and of itself. We aim to mitigate the computational overhead of Apache/PHP's management of many parallel threads, each of which may individually block as it handles a single user request. We compare against the aforementioned Node.js event queue model, where a single thread responds to multiple requests and multiple responses using the same single queue, and farms subtasks to a pool of worker threads.

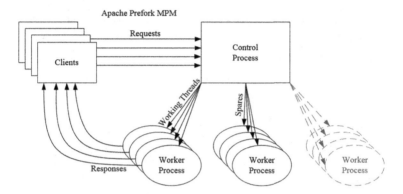

Fig. 2. The apache prefork multi-processing module.

2.3   AngularJS Port of Mongo-Express

In Fig. 3 we illustrate both the traditional Mongo-Express application (herein referred to as *Mongo-Express Implementation*) and the AngularJS port of Mongo-Express (herein referred to as *AngularJS Implementation*). Mongo-Express behaves as a traditional web application, sending an HTTP request to the Node.js server which in turn queries the MongoDB database. The results of the database query are then sent back to the Node.js web server and returned to the client as HTML.

In the AngularJS port of Mongo-Express, the client-facing site has evolved into a single-page application. With AngularJS, a client will still send an initial synchronous HTTP page request. However, the client only receives HTML in the initial request along with assets for AngularJS. All of the future requests are sent asynchronously (via AJAX) and all responses return JSON-formatted data instead of HTML.

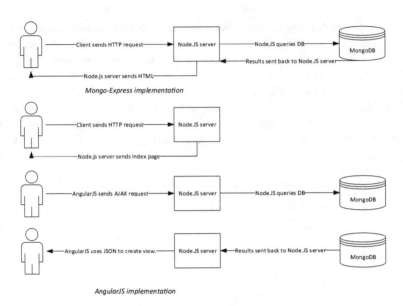

Fig. 3. Mongo-Express and AngularJS implementations.

3   Related Work

The first efforts to provide web benchmarks include SPECweb and SPECjbb from the Standard Performance Evaluation Corporation. Although SPECjbb, specific to Java servers and JVMs, continues to be supported with a 2015 release [26], SPECweb's collection of server-side applications implemented in JSP, PHP, and ASPX has retired as of 2012 [27]. Although these benchmarks have been used to compare web server implementations before, including power characteristics [6] and maximum concurrent users [20], the underlying architecture of these servers has changed in recent years, and the applications are no longer representative of the feature-set nor asynchronous APIs provided by modern web services. Studies using WebBench or other traffic generators to load-test Apache and other web-servers have measured server performance when accessed by tens of simultaneous clients [11], rather than the hundreds or more expected on contemporary services.

Prior work has also investigated the performance of JavaScript virtual machines on different mobile platforms [4], or have compared the benchmarks offered by JavaScript engines to the execution of JavaScript on the websites of famous web applications [25]. Both of these studies limit performance analysis of JavaScript to client-side execution, either measured coarsely over the application duration, or by analysing fine-grain events recorded by instrumented client browsers. Although these studies compare different browsers and/or different client hardware, they do not demonstrate the scaling advantages of JavaScript when executed on the server side.

One recent study in particular measures the server-side execution of Node.js in comparison to Apache/PHP and Nginx, another open source web server competitor [3]. The results found that for most purposes, under concurrency stress testing, Nginx performed better at scale than Apache/PHP, but also that Node.js outperformed both, except in the case of static file hosting, where Nginx was the winner. The ultimate performance solution proposed by Chaniotis et al. [3] was to develop a hybrid system in which Nginx was used to serve static files and Node.js was used for all other purposes. However, it was also acknowledged that Node.js as a singular web server environment bore other advantages, including the fact that an entire web application could be developed, front to back, all in JavaScript, a single language.

To refresh and enhance the results of prior investigation into server-side performance, we focus on the server-side benchmarking process in particular, using a number of operations commonly employed by contemporary web services. Beyond the results reported by the most recent web-server measurements [3], other contemporary studies focus on database benchmarking [23], and cloud scaling techniques [7]. Moreover, the web workloads employed by Chaniotis et al. are limited to static file retrieval, hashing operations, and basic client/server I/O [3]. Thus, investigation into web application framework performance remains relatively quiet at the time of this writing. In this work, we extend the efforts of prior art by developing more extensive benchmarks that allow us to directly exercise, measure, and compare the performance of Node.js and Apache/PHP as they fare in typical client-server interactions. Furthermore, we exercise these servers with heterogeneous workloads comprised of multiple simultaneous combinations of different operations. These workloads are more representative of the diverse set of functions executed on-demand by modern web service APIs.

4   Methodology

4.1   Benchmarking the Apache/PHP and Node.js Web Servers

Three physical machines were employed as nodes for this study. A Lenovo X230 ThinkPad with 8 GB of RAM and a 64-bit 2.60 GHz Intel i5 processor hosts a pair of virtual servers. The guest virtual machines thereon run atop Oracle VM VirtualBox, and feature a dual-core configuration with 4 GB of RAM powering an installation of 32-bit Ubuntu 14.04. The server versions of Apache and Node.js are 2.4.18 and v5.6.0 respectively. Apache Bench was executed upon a client desktop machine boasting a six-core 64-bit AMD Phenom II clocked at 3.0 gigahertz and running Windows 7 on 4 GB of RAM. Finally, our MySQL server was executed upon a desktop machine featuring a six-core 64-bit AMD FX clocked at 3.3 GHz and running Windows 10 on 8 GB of RAM.

Using Apache Bench [1], we execute several tests against both Apache/PHP and Node.js. These tests vary load, in terms of total requests made; as well as concurrency, in terms of requests sent to the server concurrently by Apache Bench. In this work, we generate up to 8192 concurrent requests for our simplest benchmark in Sect. 5.1.

To provide a direct "apples-to-apples" comparison, each benchmark is implemented both in PHP and Node.js using the APIs available in each framework. In Sect. 5.5, we employ child processes in both frameworks to measure the impact of this programming practice on workload performance.

We address performance variability in our measurements by testing each reported level of concurrency 10 times, and averaging these results into a single value represented by each bar (measurement) in the figures of Sect. 5. Put differently, for each benchmark, we executed each web server configuration 10 times at each concurrency level, and average these 10 executions to provide the single reported result per concurrency level per benchmark.

The metric *concurrent mean* is defined by Apache Benchmark as the mean time per request "across all concurrent requests." This refers to the amount of time spent on each individual request, as a calculated mean value [1]. If a given test executes N requests, at some constant concurrency level, for a total execution time of T, the concurrent mean is defined in concurrent mean $= T/N$ (1) as follows.

$$concurrent\ mean = T/N \tag{1}$$

In our work, we employ the concurrent mean metric to represent how much time on average a server spends working on each single request [12].

4.2   Angularizing the Mongo-Express Application

To measure the performance of Mongo-Express with and without AngularJS, we employed Apache Bench running against a Node.js server returning both HTML (traditional Mongo-Express) and JSON-formatted (Angularized Mongo-Express) data. The Node.js server is hosted on a physical computer running CentOS 6.7 with an eight-core CPU and 16 GB RAM. Node.js, MongoDB, and Apache Benchmark are all installed on the aforementioned machine. By keeping these applications installed on the same single machine, we remove network latency as a confounding factor in these tests.

We derived our Apache Benchmark concurrency and total request parameters by locating the threshold at which Node.js would crash and dialing our parameters back to ensure stability. The Node.js server, when running on a single process, was incapable of consistently handling more than one hundred concurrent read requests. Thus, for read requests, we execute 5000 total requests with a concurrency level of 100 using a varying degree of Node.js server processes, namely one, two, three, four, and eight processes.

While Node.js running on a single process could serve one hundred concurrent requests performing read operations, it could not reliably serve more than twenty-five concurrent requests when performing write operations. Thus, for write operations, we perform tests with 25 concurrent requests and 5000 total requests.

Read operations consist of both reading a single document and reading an entire collection of documents from MongoDB. Each collection consists of 1000 documents. Document read operations consist of reading a document with two values: an id and a string. Write operations consist of writing a single document with two key-value pairs to MongoDB.

Each test for each number of processes was executed five times, and all reported results are averages of these five executions. As result variability did not present an obstacle to measuring the impact of AngularJS on Mongo-Express, we omit error bars from these results.

Figure 4 illustrates what a single document in each of our tests consists of. As mentioned earlier, each document consisted of two key-value pairs with one pair holding a unique object id and the second pair holding a username field with a string value. In our collection tests, the collection holds 1000 documents with this exact structure.

```
{
    "_id" : ObjectId("579bd2a536c4ee327227613e"),
    "username": "testing"
}
```

Fig. 4. Example of a MongoDB document.

To handle the creation of multiple processes, we employed a process manager for Node.js applications named PM2 [22]. We chose to use PM2 because of its popularity in the industry, with companies such as PayPal and Intuit using it with their production servers [13]. PM2 simplifies creating any number of processes and monitoring their status. From PM2, we are able to track memory usage and processor utilization of each process in real time.

In order to measure the impact of using AngularJS, we used Chrome DevTools to profile memory-usage [5]. Chrome DevTools allows us to inspect the performance of our most-used functions and to determine how AngularJS performs during runtime. Further, it also allows us to see how network performance is impacted by using AngularJS. We determined that it would be best to have the Node.js server on a separate machine from the one running Chrome DevTools. The purpose of using a separate machine is to remove any inconsistences that may arise from having to share the resources on the same machine. Chrome version 54.0.2840.99 was used for testing since it was the most up-to-date version at the time. Furthermore, we ensured that all tests were ran in Incognito mode to remove any external variables.

For the process of porting the Mongo-Express application to a full MEAN-stack implementation with AngularJS, we attempted to match current standard industry practice by employing Gulp, Protractor, and Karma as described hence.

Gulp. Automated task runners are deployment tools frequently used by businesses for application development These richly configurable deployment tools represent a refinement of the traditional shell-script approach to moving and managing source files. At the time of this writing, the most popular task runner for JavaScript applications is Gulp [8, 9]. We use Gulp was used to lint all JavaScript files, enforce code style guidelines, compile ECMAScript 6 into ECMAScript 5, maintain and reload our web server, and to copy files to their deployment locations.

Protractor. Protractor was used to run all end-to-end tests. Protractor is a testing framework created using Node.js specifically to test AngularJS applications [24]. Protractor uses Selenium WebDriver to run a web server against which automatic tests can be executed.

Karma. Karma was used run all non-end-to-end tests. Karma is a JavaScript test runner developed by Google [13]. Karma is a tool which spawns a web server and executes tests against the web server. Since Karma is a testing-framework agnostic, we chose to use Jasmine since that is the same syntax used in Protractor.

In order to minimize unintended effects, the porting process retained as much of the existing code as possible. The majority of the changes to the existing code resulting in returning JSON-formatted data to the client rather than the HTML data returned by Mongo-Express. Furthermore, the index page was altered to all of the AngularJS assets in addition to the original ones and an area to bootstrap the AngularJS application. All routing was shifted over to AngularJS using the Angular UI Router library [16]. Finally, all of the Mongo-Express routes were converted to API routes to reflect this change. To ensure that the ported application worked as intended, an entire suite of tests was written and executed using Protractor and Karma.

5   Experimental Results

5.1   Web Service Baseline Measurement

Our initial test determines the maximum possible performance of which our server frameworks are capable. To measure their performance potential, we execute the "no-op" benchnark on each server. This is a simple call-and-answer test employing a single-packet constant response string, representing the smallest possible amount of server work per request. In Fig. 5 we compare the bandwidth (requests handled per second) of Node.js and Apache under the "no-op" scenario. This will serve as a baseline against which we consider other bandwidth results from a variety of scenarios. The results of this simple test, measuring the number of requests served per unit time at exponentially increasing levels of concurrency, demonstrate a clear advantage in favor of Node.js for the "no-op" scenario. For this test, both executions of Apache Benchmark make 10000 total requests. In this test, we begin at concurrency level 2, meaning 2 requests outstanding from clients at any given moment, and ramp concurrency up by powers of 2 through concurrency level 8192.

At low concurrency levels, and as concurrency begins to ramp up slowly, Apache/PHP bandwidth wavers near 300 requests/second, before collapsing to a plateau level, so named as performance levels-off beyond (to the right of) this point. Node.js, on the other hand, performs similarly to Apache under testing conditions of up to concurrency level 256, but only wavers slightly near the plateau level of Apache/PHP. Positive results for Node.js persist longer than expected, and far beyond the concurrency level at which performance for Apache/PHP drops off.

In Fig. 6, mapping mean request time against longest request service time for both Node.js and Apache/PHP at exponentially increasing levels of concurrency (the x-axis of the chart), we begin to see the effects of high concurrency as it taxes both of our server stacks. We see a number of interesting results surfacing from this particular manifestation of the data. First, we see that mean time and longest time do not deviate far from each other for either technology set. Next, we observe that Node.js appears to enjoy a tremendous advantage over Apache/PHP, although this is partially an illusion created

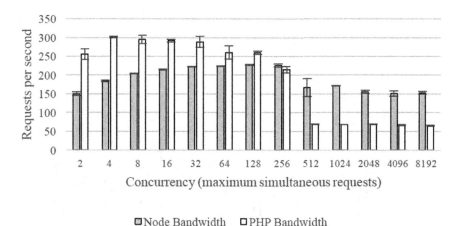

Fig. 5. Bandwidth for the Baseline "No-Op" (in requests per second).

by our charting methodology. If the same chart were presented with a logarithmically scaled Y-axis we would see that the performance for our two technologies, with respect to mean and longest times, actually tracks linearly with respect to concurrency, and that the performance difference between the two technologies likewise tracks linearly. This result suggests that across all levels of concurrency, Node.js can be expected to maintain a considerable lead over Apache/PHP.

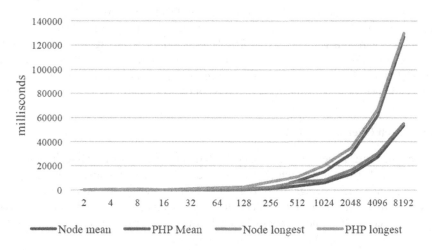

Fig. 6. Mean vs longest request time for baseline "No-Op" (in ms).

In Fig. 7 we observe the concurrent mean across all concurrent requests. Here again, the x-axis represents concurrency, or maximum simultaneous requests. As might be predicted based on the results shown above in Fig. 5, we see the average time per request rising precipitously from approximately 4 to 15 ms for Apache/PHP at the plateau level beyond 256 concurrent requests. The average time per request for Node.js remains relatively flat, showing no significant rise as concurrency crosses the plateau level for Apache/PHP.

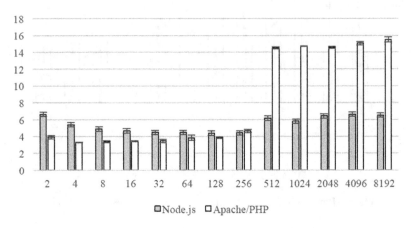

Fig. 7. Concurrent mean for the baseline "No-Op" (in ms).

Note that each of the accompanying bar and line charts includes the measurements themselves for the averages across all results for the test being illustrated, as well as an additional bracket for each individual average, illustrating the confidence interval (or CI) for that average. The confidence interval bracketing illustrates the range of measurement values within which 95% of test results fell for that particular test. For the purposes of this study, we calculate our confidence interval across test batch averages. This limitation results from our use of Apache Benchmark, which aggregates the results of its test batches. In other words, for each test described, we ran 5 batches of test runs, each yielding an average (reported by Apache Benchmark) across that batch. We then calculated the confidence interval across this set of 5 averages.

5.2   Search Over Large Strings

Our next test is designed to stress the computational efficiency of each technology. To that end, we devise a test in which a very large body of text is searched using regular expressions for target strings of various length and frequency. Again, this test was run at exponentially increasing levels of concurrency, beginning with 2 and ramping up 64. Due to time constraints and the computational cost of large string searches, we are herein prevented from testing at concurrency levels beyond 64.

Figure 8 shows the concurrent means for the large body string search tests. We see that concurrency for this particular test had no noticeable impact on performance overall, but we do see Node.js outperforming Apache/PHP in dramatic fashion, again, by a constant factor. Differences in our Node.js results are nearly indiscernible across the board in this test. The same is true for Apache/PHP, which takes a near-constant factor of 5 times longer than Node.js per request.

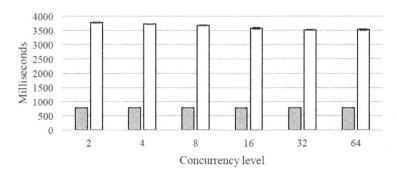

Fig. 8. Concurrent mean for the string search service (in ms).

Monitoring system performance during our tests at various concurrencies, we have observed that over all of our test runs, Node.js used 100% of all available processing resources on a single core, and Apache/PHP used 100% of all computational resources on both of the cores available to our virtual machine. In the case of Node.js, this took the form of one, single process, occupying 100% of the processor to which it had access, whereas Apache/PHP spawned many processes, each of which divided all available computational resources among themselves. In other words, when Apache/PHP received two concurrent requests, our performance monitors report two Apache/PHP processes, each occupying 99% of computational resources (effectively 100% of all resources not demanded by the operating system). Note that this totals 198% of resources, this being due to the fact that our performance monitor reports the percentage of a given processor core's utilization that is being used by a process, not the percentage of all system-wide processor availability. (This is why we know that Node.js only occupied a single core, but did occupy the entirety of that core's computational resources, based on the 99% utilization drawn by a single process.)

When Apache/PHP received four concurrent requests, we saw reported four Apache/PHP processes, each utilizing approximately 49.5% of computational resources (again, totaling 198%, meaning 99% of each of two cores). When Apache/PHP received eight concurrent requests, we observed eight Apache/PHP processes, each utilizing approximately 24.7% of computational resources, and so on. This reinforces our understanding of the Apache/PHP model of handling multiple concurrent client requests by dedicating one process to each. Despite that, and the verification at the system level that Apache/PHP was successfully processing requests in parallel, Node.js still managed to outperform Apache/PHP by a near constant factor of more than 5 over tests at all concurrency levels.

We attempt to explain this surprise in our results as follows. First, it is possible that Node.js's string search and regular expression engine is far more efficient for this particular type of task than Apache/PHP's. It is also likely that the cost to Apache/PHP of building up and tearing down threads and processes to carry out this parallelization is damaging to its overall performance. The constant and costly context switching among

Apache processes is potentially a contributing factor as well. Regardless, the evidence suggests that, for this particular type of computationally intensive task, Node.js performance is superior to Apache.

We note that in this test, performance is not impacted by increasing concurrency. We observe that the performance of this test is not bound by the efficiency of concurrency management, but by the computation of the task itself. Even if we reduce our concurrent load to a single outstanding request, the server would still require approximately the same time to service that single request, since it is the string search itself that produces a response delay.

5.3   Serving Large Static Files

Static file service is another application domain that we investigate with respect to the performance of our two web application engines under heavy concurrent load. The goal in testing this particular scenario was to evaluate whether Apache/PHP would continue to be outperformed by Node.js in this service domain, as in prior work [3]. Our strategy in designing this test is to stress the servers by making requests for large static files. For this test, we selected a JPEG file of approximately 3.2 MB in size, representing the common transfer of profile pictures and other photos in social media and similar web service scenarios.

In Fig. 9, we observe a more pronounced effect on performance with increased concurrent load for this test, as opposed to the results of the string search results in Fig. 8. However, the results for both of our servers tracked more closely to each other than in any other test. This close tracking indicates that the server platform hosting our application has less impact on performance in this scenario than limitations of the host hardware. Figure 9 shows that Node.js has a small performance advantage at a concurrency level of 32 simultaneous requests and beyond, beating Apache/PHP by more than 100 ms per request (on average) at a concurrency level of 128. In this test, we were forced to limit the number of requests both in total, and under heavy concurrency, due to the amount of time required to serve static files of this size. We believe that a similar

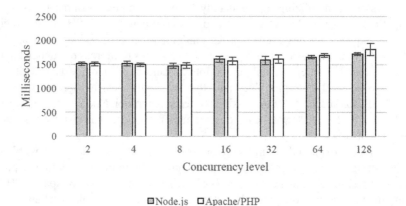

Fig. 9. Concurrent mean for the static files (in ms).

test with much smaller static files would yield results that highlight the performance benefits and limits of our servers themselves, rather than the hardware hosting them, and we consider this a prime candidate for future work.

5.4   Database Operations

The final benchmark used to compare Apache/PHP to Node.js measures their performance in fielding client requests for database operations. These requests demand little computation from the web-server itself, but require a tremendous amount of database communication by the servers to satisfy client requests. We anticipated this test would stress our server memory utilization, since state would need to be maintained on outstanding database requests, and in very large quantities as our concurrency level ramped up into the thousands. We intentionally designed the database queries to perform relatively high-latency work, such as complex join functions, in order to force our servers to hold onto request state longer.

Figure 10 displays the concurrent means results for this database scenario, and shows a pattern very similar to that observed during our "no-op" testing in Sect. 5.1. Performance for both platforms improves early on as concurrency begins to ramp up, then levels off. Later, when concurrency ramps beyond 256 simultaneous client requests, we see Apache/PHP take a precipitous dive in performance, falling down to a plateau level very much like the one we saw during "no-op" testing. Once we reach our plateau level of 512 concurrent requests, the concurrent means for Apache/PHP skyrocket beyond 14 ms per request. Node.js continues to perform admirably by comparison, despite some heavy turbulence in results near the same concurrency level where Apache/PHP performance drops. Node.js performance hovers around 6 ms per response as seen at lower concurrency, even as Apache/PHP experiences a sudden performance drop. The reason for this plateau level cropping up in multiple test scenarios for Apache/PHP, and the reason for turbulence in Node.js's results pattern at the same point in its curve on our graphs, is a chief target for future work, as discussed in our conclusion.

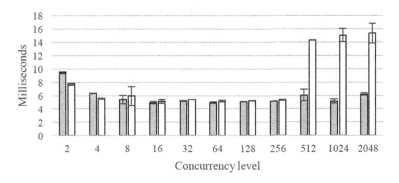

Fig. 10. Concurrent mean for the database ops (in ms).

5.5 Heterogeneous Workloads

Our final test employs a heterogeneous mix of concurrent requests, generated by three simultaneously instantiations of Apache Bench – one to make requests that require heavy computation, one to make static file requests, and one to make requests necessitating heavy database interaction with the server. Instead of performing a single test multiple times at varying levels of concurrency, we ran three tests simultaneously at constant concurrency levels. These include (for both Node.js and Apache/PHP) 10,000 database interaction requests at a constant concurrency level of 64, 30 computationally heavy requests at a constant concurrency level of only 1, and 30 large static file requests at a constant concurrency level of only 1.

Since it is known to be poor practice to make the event loop responsible for time consuming computation, we employ better (if more complex) practices by moving that computation off of the Node.js event loop. This allows us to explore the impact of good programming practice on Node.js performance under a heterogeneous request load.

We accomplish this by taking advantage of child processes, which are supported by first-party libraries in both Node.js and Apache/PHP. To begin, we implemented a standalone version of our time consuming, computationally intensive large string search that could be executed from the command line. We implemented this as a standalone string- search script in PHP. Next, we adjusted our server scripts (both Node.js and Apache/PHP) so that incoming requests for this heavy computation would be handled by child processes spawned by our servers, rather than in code executed by the web servers themselves. Also, by implementing the string-search script in PHP, we remove any potential advantage that Node.js may realize via better regular expression implementation.

Of particular note is that in Node.js, the function that kicks off a child process is implicitly asynchronous, meaning that Node.js spawns the process, allowing it to run in parallel on the operating system, then receives the result packaged as a new callback event on the event loop. Thus, we anticipated that Node.js would handle our computationally heavy task in a dedicated process, freeing the event loop to handle lighter requests quickly in parallel, just as Apache/PHP does by default at scale (for better or worse). In Fig. 11, we compare concurrent mean results for heterogeneous workloads with and without child processes, for both Apache/PHP and Node.js. In this heterogeneous workload, Node.js trails behind Apache/PHP with respect to database operations per second, but with the use of child processes, the margin of difference can be reduced from a gap of over 15% (without child processes) to less than 2% (with child processes). In this workload, Node.js with child processes takes the lead over Apache/PHP for static file requests, with a narrow advantage of less than 0.1 requests per second. However, without employing child processes, Node.js falls behind Apache/PHP by approximately 0.2 requests per second. Interestingly, though both Node.js and Apache/PHP are spawning identical PHP child processes to perform the string search task, Node.js performs slightly worse than Apache on this workload, losing the entire advantage it had when executing the regular expression in its own engine (without child processes).

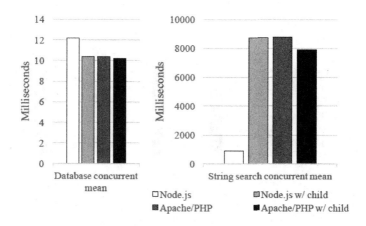

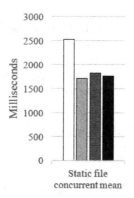

Fig. 11. Concurrent mean for heterogeneous workloads with and without child processes (in ms).

In Fig. 11 we observe that the mean time for concurrent database interactions is nearly indistinguishable between Node.js and Apache/PHP with child processes, though Apache/PHP does have a slight advantage (barely lower time per request) [12]. The mean time per static file request tracks very closely between our two applications with child processes, with Node.js eking out a narrow lead here. Comparing the mean time per string search request, however, shows a more dramatic advantage of nearly 10% for Apache/PHP with child process. This margin of victory is particularly large as the performance bottleneck for this task lies in a separate child process executing in parallel to our web applications. Moreover, this 10% advantage amounts to nearly a full second of time per request, which is significant.

We identify two potential reasons for this result. First, it is possible that the libraries used by Node.js to spawn child processes, and pass data between the Node.js context and the context of a child process itself, is itself slow, resulting in the lag time of nearly a full second when compared to Apache/PHP with child processes in Fig. 11. Second, this may be an artefact of implementing the child processes in PHP, as the Apache server already has the PHP engine loaded to handle other service requests when the child

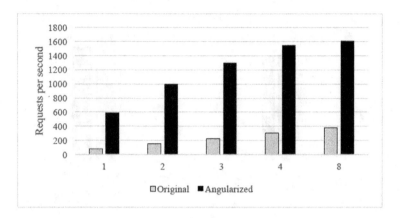

Fig. 12. Bandwidth comparison of Read Document operation in Mongo-Express (original and Angularized).

process is spawned. Thus, the ready availability of the PHP engine may save time creating the child process context, as caches and other system resources are warmed-up and ready for the child code to execute. By comparison, Node.js must spin up this PHP engine from scratch when the child process is executed. This may account for the nearly full second of lag time between the two engines.

5.6   Evaluating AngularJS with the Mongo-Express Web Application

Database Operation Performance. Figure 12 contains the results of a throughput test run against Mongo-Express using 1, 2, 3, 4, and 8 server processes (Mongo-Express running upon Node.js). This test was run using a concurrency level of 100 with 5000 total requests. Each client request performs a Read Document operation, which results in Node.js reading and returning a single document (see Fig. 4) from the MongoDB database. We find that Node.js has far higher throughput on an Angularized Mongo-Express client than in its original non-Angular form, maintaining a nearly 4.3x bandwidth improvement even scaled to 8 server processes. This improvement may result from passing more succinct data in the form of JSON rather than in the original bulkier HTML document.

In Fig. 13 we examine the same conditions, except with each client performing a Write Document operation, resulting in writing a single document in the MongoDB database. This test was run using a concurrency level of 25 with 5000 total requests. In the case of a document write, the original and Angularized versions of Mongo-Express track very closely, with the Angularized version performing the same or better than the original in response bandwidth at each level of concurrency. Notably, both versions of Mongo-Express scale moderately well as server instances increase, each version performing roughly 2.6x better on 8 server processes than on a single instance.

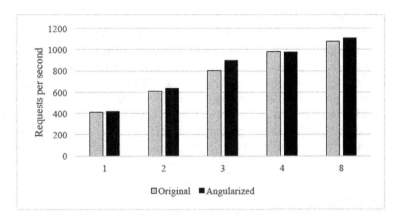

Fig. 13. Bandwidth comparison of Write Document operation in Mongo-Express (original and Angularized).

In Fig. 14 we examine the case where each client request performs a Read Collection operation, which reads a collection of (1000) documents in the MongoDB database. This test was run using a concurrency level of 100 with 5000 total requests, against up to 8 server instances as before. In all cases, the Angularized version of Mongo-Express performs approx. 2x better than the regular version.

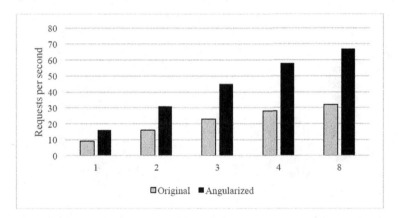

Fig. 14. Bandwidth comparison of Read Collection operation in Mongo-Express (Original and Angularized).

These results point to a shift in responsibility from the back-end Mongo-Express web service to the front-end AngularJS code. Whereas the original Mongo-Express responds with an HTML document containing the collection, the Angularized Mongo-Express service responds with a more succinct collection of JSON data, which the AngularJS front-end parses to manage the HTML page-content and forms.

Memory Consumption. We next investigate the cost of adding AngularJS to the front-end code, in the form of memory consumption on the client browser. As mentioned in Sect. 4.2, we employ Chrome DevTools [5] to profile the memory consumption within the client browser, and to determine the overall usage of browser memory by data type. We examine memory consumption at two points of Mongo-Express execution: first, at the window.load event of the Mongo-Express homepage (in Fig. 15), and after loading a collection of 1000 documents (in Fig. 16). In each of the figures, a pie chart is shown representing the browser's memory profile by variable type. Each pie slice is labeled by the tuple: variable type, number of kilobytes used, and percentage of overall memory.

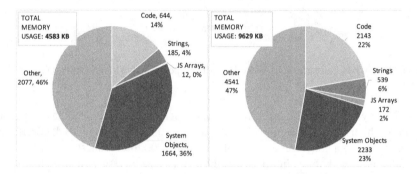

Fig. 15. Memory usage comparison by type of homepage of original (left) vs Angularized (right) Mongo-Express.

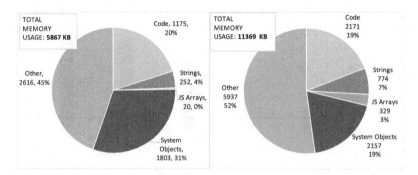

Fig. 16. Memory usage comparison by type of collection page of original (left) vs Angularized (right) Mongo-Express.

The load event of the main homepage takes approx. 1.6 s with AngularJS vs 0.7 s in the original Mongo-Express. This indicates that AngularJS spends about 2.3x the time (an overhead of almost a second) loading its resources. Once the load event fires, we see in Fig. 15 that AngularJS client code consumes over 2.1x the memory as the original Mongo-Express, and that JS Code, Strings, and JS Arrays comprise a greater percentage of this memory footprint in the AngularJS version.

Figure 16 depicts the profile of browser memory at the time that a 1000-document collection is loaded into the browser. At this time, the AngularJS client code is still consuming nearly 2x (more precisely 1.93x) the resources that the original Mongo-Express code does. In the AngularJS version, this memory consumption is more largely comprised of Strings (3x the amount of String storage as the original Mongo-Express, 7% of the overall memory rather than 4%) and JS Arrays (16.5x the amount of array storage as the original Mongo-Express, now 3% of the memory rather than 0.3%). The contribution of "Other" data types, which are partially comprised of miscellaneous AngularJS objects, has also substantially increased, from 45% of memory to 52%. These miscellaneous objects consume 2.3x the amount of memory that they did in the original Mongo-Express.

6   Conclusions

In this study, we design and execute a number of benchmark tests against Node.js and its most popular competitor and predecessor, Apache/PHP. These benchmarks are designed to determine which of these web application engines is best suited to a variety of common server-side tasks. We identify three major types of server tasks for examination, these being database interaction, heavy computation, and static file service. We compare these against a baseline "no-op" benchmark, wherein the web server always responds with a short constant string literal.

We have found that database interactions considerably favor Node.js, as do computationally heavy tasks (as represented by pattern matches on a long string). No distinguishable difference in performance was experienced between Apache and Node.js engines when serving large static files, although Node.js enjoys a modest lead at higher levels of concurrency.

We further benchmark our server engines by employing a heterogeneous mixture of request types – database, static file, and heavy computation– all being executed concurrently by each of our server stacks. In this scenario, Node.js demonstrates sensitivity to good coding practices, as computationally heavy tasks will block the synchronous event loop unless child worker processes are employed.

With the Node.js event loop freed from burden of heavy computation, Node.js falls behind Apache/PHP in performance with respect to the management of string search tasks in child processes, but manages to nearly match the performance of Apache/PHP on database interactions, and maintains a modest performance edge in static file service.

Our conclusion from the generated test data is that Node.js is the clear winner in homogeneous workload cases, i.e. wherein the web-server performs the same type of work repeatedly for numerous clients. In some tests, Apache/PHP outperforms Node.js at very low levels of concurrency, though in such cases the difference in performance between the two server stacks was insignificant. At higher concurrency levels, the advantages enjoyed by Node.js become apparent.

Finally, we port the popular Mongo-Express database administration tool for MongoDB to AngularJS, to explore performance potential of other services in the MEAN stack. We find that employing AngularJS gives us a tremendous increase in read bandwidth, with single documents being served over 4x as quickly and entire 1000-docu-ment collections being served nearly 2.2x as quickly as the original Mongo-Express. Document-write bandwidth is nearly unaffected by the change. However, the tradeoff of using AngularJS is a doubled memory footprint inside the browser, and a 2.3x increase in page-load time (approx. an additional second) due to the overhead of AngularJS code.

Although the MEAN stack enjoys growing community support and a rich repository of ready source code, PHP has a long history and a breadth of existing libraries and open templates that can be leveraged by industry adopters, Moreover, the LAMP stack is still very well-deployed, offering an abundance of administrative and developer experience with which to support new and legacy installations. We note that if abundant legacy code is an issue, or a team consists of developers with a strong background in one language or framework and no experience with another, then performance may not be the sole factor on which to base the selection of a server stack technology. However, all other things being equal, we can report that Node.js is the more performant server when compared with Apache/PHP. We have shown that Apache/PHP is capable of very slightly outpacing Node.js under certain types of light load, but we have also shown that Node.js is capable of keeping pace with – and sometimes dramatically outshining – its most popular competitor.

Moreover, we have shown that Angularizing a web page provides more than a compelling single-page user experience, but can also realize incredible server bandwidth improvements due to reduced communication and reduced data-management responsibility on the server itself. This attractive boost in performance and usability comes with a memory and performance cost on the client side, which may prove tolerable as most of the communication between client and server happens asynchronously, as the user continues to interact with the page.

Further investigation is warranted into the results of fine-tuning the Apache and Node.js server configurations. For example, we could utilize multi-processing modules other than the prefork execution model in Apache, or we could tinker with server cache settings. Moreover, exploration of this configuration space may yield custom tuning of these server engines to best suit each application type. In future work we also aim to characterize the "plateau level" exhibited by Apache/PHP, at which point performance drops and levels off with increasing concurrency. By exploring the shape of the perform-ance curve in the neighbourhood of this plateau level, we aim to better understand Apache's behaviour at this level of concurrency, and gain further insight about its performance when hosting contemporary web services.

References

1. Apache Software Foundation: ab – Apache HTTP server benchmarking tool (2016). http://httpd.apache.org/docs/2.2/programs/ab.html
2. Appuswamy, R., Gkantsidis, C., Narayanan, D., Hodson, O., Rowstron, A.: Scale-up vs scale-out for Hadoop: time to rethink? In: 4th Annual Symposium on Cloud Computing. ACM (2013)

3. Chaniotis, I., Kyriakou, K., Tselikas, N.: Is Node.js a viable option for building modern web applications? A performance study. Computing **97**(10), 1023–1044 (2015)
4. Charland, A., Leroux, B.: Mobile application development: web vs. native. Commun. ACM **54**(5), 49–53 (2011)
5. Chrome: Chrome DevTools (2017). https://developers.google.com/web/tools/chrome-devtools/
6. Economou, D., Rivoire, S., Kozyrakis, C., Ranganathan, P.: Full-system power analysis and modeling for server environments. In: Proceedings of the International Symposium on Computer Architecture (ISCA). IEEE (2006)
7. Ferdman, M., Adileh, A., Kocberber, O., Volos, S., Alisafaee, M., Jevdjic, D., Kaynak, C., Popescu, A.D., Ailamaki, A., Falsafi, B.: Clearing the clouds: a study of emerging scale-out workloads on modern hardware. In: ACM SIGPLAN Notices, vol. 47, no. 4, pp. 37–38. ACM, March 2012
8. Github: Projects, Applications, and Companies Using Node (2016). https://github.com/nodejs/node/wiki/Projects,-Applications,-and-Companies-Using-Node
9. Github: Who uses Gulp? Issue #540 (2016). https://github.com/gulpjs/gulp/issues/540/
10. Gulp: Gulp.js (2016). http://gulpjs.com/
11. Haddad, I.: Open-source web servers: performance on a carrier-class Linux platform. Linux J. **2001**(91), 1 (2001)
12. Kitzes, S., Kaplan, A.: Stack wars: the node awakens. In: Proceedings of the 19th International Conference on Enterprise Information Systems (ICEIS), INSTICC (2017)
13. Jina, V.: Testacular – Spectacular Test Runner for JavaScript (2012). https://testing.googleblog.com/2012/11/testacular-spectacular-test-runner-for.html
14. Joyent: Node.js at PayPal (2014). https://www.joyent.com/blog/node-js-on-the-road-sf-node-js-at-paypal/
15. Libuv: Design overview – libuv API documentation (2016). http://docs.libuv.org/en/v1.x/design.html
16. McKeachie, C.: UI-Router: Why many developers don't use AngularJS's built-in router (2014). http://www.funnyant.com/angularjs-ui-router/
17. MEAN.JS: MEAN.JS – Full-Stack JavaScript Using MongoDB, Express, AngularJS, and Node.js (2014). http://meanjs.org
18. Menasce, D.A.: Web server software architectures. IEEE Internet Comput. **7**(6), 78–81 (2003)
19. Mongo-Express: Web-based MongoDB admin interface, written with Node.js and express (2012–2016). https://github.com/mongo-express/mongo-express
20. Nahum, E., Barzilai, T., Kandlur, D.D.: Performance issues in WWW servers. IEEE/ACM Trans. Netw. (TON) **10**(1), 2–11 (2002)
21. Netcraft: September 2015 Web Server Survey (2015). http://news.netcraft.com/archives/2015/09/16/september-2015-web-server-survey.html
22. PM2: PM2 – Advanced Node.js process manager (2016). http://pm2.keymetrics.io/
23. Pokorny, J.: NoSQL databases: a step to database scalability in web environment. Int. J. Web Inf. Syst. **9**(1), 69–82 (2013)
24. Protractor: Protractor – end-to-end testing for AngularJS (2016). http://www.protractortest.org/
25. Ratanaworabhan, P., Livshits, B., Zorn, B.G.: JSMeter: comparing the behavior of JavaScript benchmarks with real web applications. WebApps **10**, 3 (2010)
26. SPECjbb: SPECjbb®2015 (2015). https://www.spec.org/jbb2015/
27. SPECweb: SPECweb2009 (2009). https://www.spec.org/web2009/
28. Tilkov, S., Vinoski, S.: Node.js: using JavaScript to build high-performance network programs. IEEE Internet Comput. **14**(6), 80–83 (2010)

29. Transaction Processing Performance Council. About the TPC (2016). http://www.tpc.org/information/about/abouttpc.asp
30. Welke, R., Hirschheeim, R., Schwarz, A.: Service oriented architecture maturity. IEEE Comput. **47**(2) (2011). IEEE

Recognition of Business Process Elements in Natural Language Texts

Renato César Borges Ferreira[1], Thanner Soares Silva[1], Diego Toralles Avila[1], Lucinéia Heloisa Thom[1(✉)], and Marcelo Fantinato[2]

[1] Institute of Informatics, Federal University of Rio Grande do Sul,
Av. Bento Gonçalves 9500, Porto Alegre, Brazil
[2] School of Arts, Sciences and Humanities, University of São Paulo,
Rua Arlindo Bettio 1000, São Paulo, Brazil
{renato.borges,thanner.silva,dtavila,lucineia}@inf.ufrgs.br,
m.fantinato@usp.br

Abstract. Process modeling is a complex and important task in any business process management project. Gathering information to build a process model needs effort by analysts in different ways, such as interviews and document review. However, this documentation is not always well structured and can be difficult to be understood. Thus, techniques that allow the structuring and recognition of process elements in the documentation can help in the understanding of the process and, consequently, in the modeling activity. In this context, this paper proposes an approach to recognize business process elements in natural language texts. We defined a set of 32 mapping rules to recognize business process elements in texts using natural language processing techniques and which were identified through an empirical study in texts containing descriptions of a process. Furthermore, a prototype was developed and it showed promising results. The analyses of 70 texts revealed 73.61% precision, 70.15% recall and 71.82% F-measure. Moreover, two surveys showed that 93.33% of participants agree with the mapping rules and that the approach helps the analysts in both the time spent and the effort made in the process modeling task. This paper is a reiteration and an evolution of the work presented in Ferreira et al. [1].

Keywords: Process models · Natural language processing
Process element · Business Process Management
Business Process Model and Notation · Process modeling

1 Introduction

To ensure better interaction with your customers and business partners, organizations need to offer high quality products and services. Furthermore, they seek to achieve high standardization and efficiency in the performance of their business processes (referred in this text as processes), as their automation provides greater control over the costs, time, errors and redundancy during their execution [2,3].

© Springer International Publishing AG, part of Springer Nature 2018
S. Hammoudi et al. (Eds.): ICEIS 2017, LNBIP 321, pp. 591–610, 2018.
https://doi.org/10.1007/978-3-319-93375-7_27

A business process is a "collection of events, activities, and decision point actions, involving a number of actors and objects, which collectively lead to results that bring value to the customer" [4]. Business Process Management (BPM) is defined as a set of methods, techniques and tools to discovery, analyze, redesign, implement and monitor business processes [4,5]. Through BPM, organizations can flexibly adapt in a continuously changing business environment [6], since it provides many benefits, such as the modeling of processes, their improvement and the quick execution of their activities [2,3].

Process modeling is a very complex and important task in any BPM project. It consists of elaborating a comprehensive description of the process as performed in an organization. Among the main reasons that lead to process modeling are understand the process and share the understanding of the process with the people who are involved with the process [4]. In addition, a wrong business process modeling can lead to problems in understanding, improvement and automating a process.

The process modeling task is performed by a BPM analyst (referred in this text as process analyst). To accomplish process modeling, the process analyst searches for information about a process in different sources, such as workshops, interviews and text documents (e.g. manuals, e-mail messages, reports, forms, letters, surveys, systems knowledge management, business policies, textbooks, event data of information systems, web pages). In fact, studies report that 85% of the information in companies is stored in an unstructured way, especially as text documents [7]. Moreover, this information is growing at a faster rate than conventional structured data [8].

In this context, being able to extract business process information from text documents would greatly assist in the process modeling task, especially as the amount of documents increases to the point of becoming impractical for standard modeling. In practice, several works [9–11] have demonstrated that the extraction of process models from natural language texts can minimize the effort of the process analyst.

In a previous work [1] we proposed a semi-automatic approach based on mapping rules to recognize process elements in Natural Language texts. This approach seeks to assist process analysts in the discovery of process elements in natural language texts and, thus, to minimize their effort in the modeling process. In addition, a prototype based on Natural Language Processing (NLP) techniques and tools was implemented according to these mapping rules.

Furthermore, this work was validated in three ways: (i) a first survey which verified if process modelers agree with the mapping rules, (ii) a second survey that verifies the effectiveness of the mapping rules to minimize the effort of the process analyst in extracting process elements, (iii) a comparison of the results of a prototype to those of expert modelers.

The present paper is a reiteration and an evolution of the work presented in Ferreira et al. [1]. In addition, this evolution was also featured in the paper published by Ferreira et al. [12]. In particular, this paper presents the original approach with the complete and updated set of mapping rules. Further, this paper also presents both surveys that validate this approach with a more in-depth explanation of their motivation and planning. Finally, a new test of the prototype was performed based on a increased sample of texts.

This paper is structured as follows. Section 2 provides related works. Section 3 shows the complete and updated set of the mapping rules for the proposed approach. Section 4 shows the evaluation and analysis of results, with more details about how and why they were performed. Finally, Sect. 5 concludes the paper.

2   Related Works

The state of the art related to natural language processing and BPM can be separated in two related categories: (i) the extraction of process models from natural language text and, (ii) text generation from process models. Table 1 provides an overview of the identified state of the art.

Table 1. The state of the art related to NLP and BPM (Source: Ferreira et al. [1]).

Categories	
Process Model Extraction from Text	Text Generation from Process Models
• Generate process models from text	• Generate text from process models
– Friedrich et al. [9]	– Leopold et al. [15]
– Chueng et al. [10]	– Meitz et al. [16]
	– Leopold [6]
• Process mining from natural language text	• Inconsistencies between process models and text
– Santoro et al. [13]	– van der Aa et al. [17]
– Jiexun et al. [14]	– van der Aa et al. [18]
– Gonçalves et al. [11]	
	• Text Structuring
	– Heinonen [19]
	– Hearst [20]
	– Hearst [21]
	– Hynes and Bexley [22]

Regarding the process model extraction from natural language texts, we considered works that propose to generate process models by analyzing texts that describe a process. In this category, we identified two main aspects. The first aspect is related to generate process models from texts. In this aspect, Friedrich et al. [9] proposed an approach for the extraction of process models from textual descriptions that considers three outlooks: (i) syntactic analysis, determination of a syntax tree and grammatical relationships between the parts of the sentences; (ii) semantic analysis, extraction of the meaning of words or phrases; (iii) anaphora resolution, identifying concepts that are referenced using pronouns *(we, he* and *it)* and articles *(this, that)*. In this work, the texts analyzed for the generation of process models need to be grammatically correct in the English language. Furthermore, the text must not contain questions and needs to be described sequentially. We performed an introductory approach to solve this problem [23], in which it was concluded that a natural language text must be processed before extracting process models (generating an intermediate model defined as process-oriented text). Furthermore, Chueng et al. [10] describe that the source of information from text are heterogeneous information sources (e.g., corporate documentation, web-content, code etc.).

The second aspect refers to process mining from natural language texts. Santoro et al. [13] and Gonçalves et al. [11] explore the use of narrative techniques for extracting process models from group stories. In this approach, each story relates the point of view of one teller. As a consequence, the paper shows that miscommunications can occur, e.g. each author represents their individual point of view within the stories, there is always a possibility of multiple workflows for the same business process [24]. Therefore, the source of information can have ambiguities. Moreover, Jiexun et al. [14] proposed a process mining framework named policy-based process mining (PBPM) for the automatic discovery of process models based on business policies. Considering that policy texts is a new topic in BPM research and text mining, the approach requires additional research efforts to be entire validated and produce practical solutions. Thus, there is a small training set and a small portion of positive examples in the approach.

Regarding text generation from process models, we consider works that seek to construct a natural language text from an existing process model. In this category, we identified three main aspects. The first aspect is related to generate text from process models. In this aspect, Leopold [6] described an approach for generating natural language texts from process models. In this approach, the author describes challenges to generate texts from process models such as text planning; sentence planning; surface realization and flexibility. The limitations of this work refer to the fact that the sentences generated are comparatively short and elementary. Another limitation is to ensure a stable level of complexity of the texts created manually so it would be necessary to train the text classifiers.

The second aspect is related to the inconsistencies between process models and texts. In this aspect, van der Aa et al. [17,18] describe an approach that seeks to identify inconsistencies, such as ambiguous or contradictory information, between process models and their textual descriptions. In addition, this approach can be used to identify process models in a collection that are likely to diverge from their accompanying textual descriptions.

Finally, the third aspect is related to the techniques for structuring texts that allow to reduce the inconsistency and ambiguity of natural language texts extracted from process models. Many researches seek to identify how to optimally structure natural language texts using paragraphs. Similarity metrics such as the semantic relatedness between words to compute the lexical cohesion between the sentences of a text are implemented by many methods [20, 21, 25]. Therefore, a text can be heuristically subdivided into multiple paragraphs. More approaches seek to use the similarity distribution for identifying the optimal fragment boundaries [19]. Hynes and Bexley [22] shows that paragraphs containing more than 100 words are less understandable than paragraphs with fewer words.

3   An Approach to Recognize Process Elements in Natural Language Texts

In our previous research [1, 23], we present a method of recognizing process elements in natural language texts. That research serves as the foundation for the approach presented in this paper. In this section we reiterate the original approach and present the complete and updated set of mapping rules.

This approach consists of four main steps executed sequentially (see Fig. 1). This main steps are: (i) input data, (ii) text syntactic analysis, (iii) text logic analysis, (iv) output.

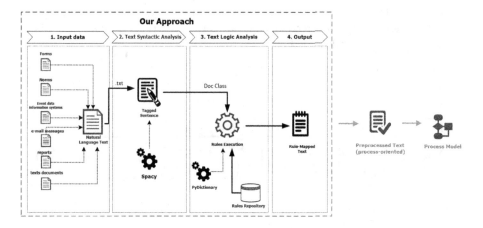

Fig. 1. A semi-automatic approach to identify process elements in natural language texts (Source: Ferreira et al. [1]).

The first step of this work is related to the input data. The input data refers to texts in natural language that are stored in *.txt* format and can be obtained from different sources, such as: forms, norms, event data of information systems, e-mail messages, etc.

In the second step, a syntactic analysis parsing is performed in order to obtain a tagged sentence, which makes it possible to determine the structure of the input text. Per Allen [26], to perform the syntactic analysis, three things are necessary:

- A lexicon of legal words and their part of speech (e.g., *verb, adverb, adjective, subject, direct object, indirect object* etc.).
- A grammar which has a set of rules that a parser can use.
- A parser which has a sentence as input and produces an analysis.

Part of speech tags provides significant information about the role of a word in its context. It may also provide information about the inflection of a word [27]. There are many tools that can classify words by their parts of speech (POS-taggers), such as the Brill tagger [28], the GATE[1], the RASP system [29], and the NLTK[2].

For our approach, we use Spacy[3]. Spacy is an open-source library for natural language processing on Python and it was chosen due to its good execution time among its equivalents (according to our tests), its overall accuracy (90,53% average) [30] and its support for all the requirements for the development of our prototype.

An overview of how a tagged sentence is generated is depicted in Fig. 2. In short, for each sentence in a text, Spacy generates a syntactic tree containing all words related to morphological classes. Subsequently, the parser generates a *DOC class*, which represents a vector containing an object for each word of the sentence. This object has the information about the features of the word (e.g., tokenization, sentence recognition, part of speech tagging, lemmatization, dependency parsing, and named entity recognition).

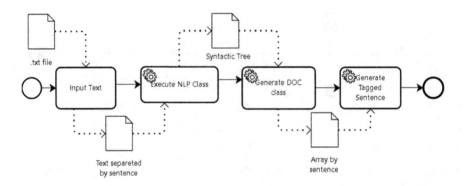

Fig. 2. A overview of the syntactic analysis (Source: Ferreira et al. [1]).

---

[1] https://gate.ac.uk/; last accessed 2017-10-02.
[2] http://www.nltk.org/; last accessed 2017-10-02.
[3] https://spacy.io/; last accessed 2017-10-02.

After the syntactic analysis, the each tagged sentence is analyzed according to a set of mapping rules and word correlations in such a way that process elements may be recognized from those sentences. The types of process elements used for this were selected from the Business Process Model and Notation (BPMN). The BPMN is an official notation supported by the Object Management Group [31] and is a graphical representation for specifying business processes in a business process model. As BPMN 2.0 is the most used and stable version, we relied on its set of elements for mapping the rules in process elements. However, considering that BPMN defines a large number of process elements, many which are not used frequently, the mapping rules were limited to just the most common elements (i.e. activities, events, swimlanes, parallel gateways (AND) and exclusive gateways (XOR)). Despite having significant use, inclusive gateways (OR) were excluded since they present structural and semantic problems [32–34], including semantic ambiguities [35].

Table 2. Rules for identification of activities (Source: Ferreira et al. [1]).

Rules	Description	Activities
		Sentence example
Rule 1	*<subject>+ <verb>+ <object>*	*The Support Officer* <subject> *updates* <verb> all *group calendars* <object>
Rule 2	*<subject>+ <aux>+ <verb>+ <object <in the future>>*	*The secretary* <subject>*will* <aux>*send*<verb>*to dispatch* <object.>
Rule 3	*<verb>+<article>+ <object>*	- *choose* <verb>*a* <article>*document* <object>. - it *do* <verb>*a* <article>*order* <object>.
Rule 4	*<subject>+<verb>+ <object>+ <conjunction>+ <verb>+ <object>*	*A client* <subject>*calls* <verb>*the help desk* <object>*and* <conjunction>*makes* <verb>*a request* <object>.
Rule 5	*<object>+<subject>+ <verb>*	*The severity* <object>*of the claimant* <subject>*is evaluated* <verb>.
Rule 6	*<verb>+ <conjunction>+<verb>+ <object>*	*The first activity is to check* <verb>*and* <conjunction>*repair* <verb>*the hardware* <object>.
Rule 7	*<subject>+<subject>+ <verb>+ <subject>*	*Department of engineering* <subject>*and sell* <subject>*are informed* <verb>*by Manager* <subject>.
Rule 8	*<verb>+ <subject>+ <object>*	- *...eat* <verb>*your* <subject>*pizza* <object>. - *...wait* <verb>*until your* <subject>*pizza* <object>*comes*.
Rule 9	*<object>+ <verb>+ <indirect object>*	*...the forms* <object>*are sent* <verb>*to the claimant* <indirect object>*...*

The mapping rules were defined after a search for patterns on example texts found in the works of Dumas et al. [4] and Weske [5]. In this context, three styles of patterns were identified in the text: verbal tense verification; identification of signal words; identification of subjects and indirect objects.

Regarding verbal tense verification, we observed that the sentences containing verbal tenses in the present or in the future represent activities. On the other hand, verbal tenses in the past or present perfect represent events. According to Mendling [36,37], the activity labels should be composed of a *verb* and an *object*, describing the action taken and the business object of that action as for example *"Inform Complainant"*. In relation to event labels, Mendling [37] and Leopold [6] describe that the event labels should be represented by the *object* of the sentence and followed by a *verb* in the present participle like *"Invoice Created"*.

As an example of recognizing activities in sentences, in the phrase "The secretary will send to dispatch" we can find a sequence of *subject* followed by an *aux*, then by a *verb in the future tense* and afterward by an *object in the future*. The recognition of this sequence of elements would become one task with the label "Send to dispatch". On the other hand, in the phrase "After the agent has confirmed the claim to the clerk" we can find a sequence of *subject*, followed by a *verb in the past tense* and then by an *object*. The recognition of this sequence of elements would become one event with the label "The claim is confirmed".

Table 3. Rules for identification of events (Source: Ferreira et al. [1]).

	Events	
Rules	**Description**	**Sentence example**
Rule 1	<*subject*>+ <*verb*>+ <*object*>	After the agent <**subject**>has confirmed <**verb**>the *claim* <**object**>to the clerk.
Rule 2	<*subject*>+ <*verb*>+ <*agent*>+ <*object*>	The *SCT physical* <**subject**>file was *stored* <**verb in the past**>*by* <**agent**>the *Back office* <**object**>. (passive voice)
Rule 3	<*subject*>+ <*verb*>+ <*object*>+ <*conjunction*>+ <*object*>	After the customer <**subject**>has chosen <**verb**>several products *and* <**conjunction**>*services* <**object**>.
Rule 4	<*object*>+ <*verb* <*past*>> + <*subject*>	...a *message* <**object**>was *generated* <**verb**>to the *customer*<**subject**>.
Rule 5	<*object*>+ <*verb*>+ <*adjective*>	Once the *forms* <**object**>are returned, they were *checked*<**verb**>for *completeness* <**adjective**>.
Rule 6	Temporary event - <*Time*>+ <*preposition*>+ <*Time*>	...it may take *thirty minutes*<**Time**>to <**preposition**>an *hour* <**Time**>
Rule 7	<*signal word*>+ <*Time*>	If we are not contacted *within* <**signal word**>2 *weeks* <**Time**>...
Rule 8	<*subject*>+ <*object*>+ <*verb* <*past*>>	The *claimant* <**subject**>was informed that *claim* <**object**>must be *rejected* <**verb**>.
Rule 9	<*object*>+ <*verb* <*present perfect*>>+ <*subject*>	... *Urgent document* <**object**>has been *received* <**verb**>by the *Manager* <**subject**>

For the recognition of both exclusive and parallel gateways, the rules make use of words that indicate the existence of the control flow. These words are denominated as *signal words* and they describe either a condition that must be checked before deciding what further actions must be done (for exclusive gateways) or the parallelism of the proceeding actions (for parallel gateways). These words are depicted in Table 7. In order to recognize synonyms of these *signal words*, we implemented a Python module called *PyDictionary*[4] that allows to retrieve synonyms from the *thesaurus*[5] database.

For example, in the phrase "It first checked whether the claimant is insured by the organization" the signal word "whether" allows us to recognize a exclusive gateway that is decided through question "Is claimant insured?".

Finally, we observed that *subject* or *indirect object* of these rules are likely to be swimlanes of the process model. Furthermore, the *subject* can be a human being, equipment, system or something that practices the action.

Table 4. Rules for identification of exclusive gateway (XOR) (Source: Ferreira et al. [1]).

	Exclusive gateways (XOR)	
Rules	**Description**	**Sentence example**
Rule 1	*<verb>+<signal word>+ <subject>+ <object>*	It first checked **<verb>**whether **<signal word>**the claimant **<subject>**is insured **<object>**by the organization.
Rule 2	*<signal word>+ <Condition>+ <task/event>+ <alternative signal word>+ <task/event>*	If **<signal word>**the claimant requires two or more forms **<Condition>**, the Department of customer select the forms **<task>**. Otherwise **<alternative signal word>**, Department of customer it requires documentation **<task>**.
Rule 3	*<task/event>+ <signal word>+ <Condition>*	After that they enter into a firm commitment to buy the stock and then offer it to the public **<task>**, when **<signal word>**they haven't still found any reason not to do it **<Condition>**.
Rule 4	*<task>+ <signal word>+ <Condition>+ <alternative signal word>+ <task>*	The clerk checks **<task>**whether**<signal word>**the beneficiary's policy was valid at the time of the accident **<Condition>**. If not **<alternative signal word>**, it send to Department of the intelligence **<task>**.
Rule 5	*<signal word>+ <Condition>+ <conjunction>+ <Condition>+ <task/event>*	If **<signal word>**Department of sell send the document **<Condition >**and **<conjunction>**notify the department of engineering **<Condition>**, the document is processed **<task/event>**.
Rule 6	*<signal word>+<task/event>+ <task/event>*	If **<signal word>**the agent has completed his additional support and the clerk has issued the money order **<task/event>**, the claim is closed**<task/event>**.
Rule 7	*<alternative signal word>+ <task/event>*	If not **<alternative signal word >**, it send to Department of the intelligence **<task/event>**.

[4] https://pypi.python.org/pypi/PyDictionary; last accessed 2017-10-02.
[5] thesaurus.com.

Table 5. Rules for identification of parallel gateways (AND) (Source: Ferreira et al. [1]).

Parallel Gateway (AND)		
Rules	**Description**	**Sentence example**
Rule 1	*<task/event>+ <signal word>+ <task/ event>*	*Forward the document* **<task/event>**, *In parallel with this* **<signal word>**, *the RCC shall also notify the Executive Board* **<task/event>**.
Rule 2	*<signal word>+ <task/event>+ <conjunction>+ <task/event>+ <task/event>*	*In parallel with this* **<signal word>** *Department of sell send the document* **<task/event>** *and* **<conjunction>** *notify the department of engineering* **<task/event>**. *Then, the document is processed* **<task/event>**.
Rule 3	*<signal word>+ <task/event>*	*In the meantime* **<signal word>**, *the engineering department prepares everything for the assembling of the ordered bicycle* **<task/event>**.
Rule 4	*<signal word>+ <task/event>+ <alternative signal word>+ <task/event>*	*The ongoing repair consists of two activities, which are executed, in an parallel order* **<signal word>**. *The first activity is to check and repair the hardware* **<task/event>**, *whereas* **<alternative signal word>** *the second activity checks and configures the software.* **<task/event>**.

Table 6. Rules for identification of swimlanes (Source: Ferreira et al. [1]).

Swimlanes		
Rules	**Description**	**Sentence example**
Rule 1	**The subject of the sentence.**	*<subject>* perform *<task/event>*
Rule 2	*<task>+<indirect object>*	*She then submits an order* **<task>** *to the customer* **<indirect object>**.
Rule 3	*<event>+<indirect object >*	*The Manager forwarded the form* **<event>** *to Official* **<indirect object>**.

The complete set includes 32 mapping rules. From these, nine refers to activities (Table 2), nine to events (Table 3), seven to exclusive gateways (XOR) (Table 4), four to parallel gateways (AND) (Table 5) and three to swimlanes (Table 6).

Finally, the last step is output from the text mapped by the rules. This text serves as a prerequisite for a generation of the preprocessed text depicted in Fig. 1. Such text is defined as a structure that allows to recognize: the participant associated with an activity; swimlanes associated with each pool; interaction between pools (*message flow*); events (*start*, *intermediate* and *end*) and control flows (*parallel gateways*, *inclusive gateways* and *exclusive gateways*). It is expected to generate a template of how the text should be structured for the extraction of process models from the text. In other words, our approach is a prerequisite for generating preprocessed text (process-oriented).

Table 7. Signal words.

Type of signal word	Signal words		
Signal words that refer to parallelism (AND)	While Concurrently In the meantime Simultaneously	Meanwhile Meantime In addition to At the same time	In parallel Whereas In parallel with this
Signal words that refer to the start of an exclusive choice (XOR)	If Or Till Otherwise	Whether Either Until (unless) Only if	If not Only In case [of] When
Signal words that refer to choices in an exclusion (XOR)	But Or Otherwise Unless	Then Without Other	Else Either If its is not

4 Evaluation

After constructing the mapping rule set, we needed to verify the feasibility of the approach, by testing its the correctness, its effectiveness and its usability. This means that we needed to verify that the rules are considered correct, that the approach works well in real life situations (e.g. large amount of sentences, unstructured texts) and how much the marked-up text helps the analysts in the process of process modeling.

To achieve this goal, three different experiments were conducted. The first experiment refers to the validation of mapping rules from the user point of view. We did a survey with potential users, especially users who were considered experienced with modeling. The second experiment sought to perform a research to verify the contribution of the mapping rules in the process modeling activity. Finally, the third experiment was a validation of a prototype constructed based on the mapping rules. This prototype allowed us to verify the ability of the approach to recognize process elements in natural language texts. The description and results of each of the experiments will be presented in the next subsections.

4.1 Survey for Validation of the Mapping Rules

To validate the correctness of our mapping rules, we collected the opinions of expert analysts about the rules, by presenting them with descriptive texts accompanied with their respective specific process models and asking if they considered the model to be a correct representation of the text. To collect these opinions, we used an online survey which was divided in three steps.

For the first step, it was indispensable to collect the participants background, seeing that this test relies heavily on the expertise of the analysts. The questions on this step were of multiple choices and were intended to identify characteristics that could influence the survey's results. According to [38–41], such characteristics influence the results of modeling. The complete set of questions are:

1. Profession
2. Education
3. Experience in BPM
4. Amount of experience time in BPM
5. Experience in BPMN
6. Amount of experience time in BPMN
7. Knowledge in process modeling guidelines
8. Knowledge in the grammar of the English Language

In the second step, the goal was to get opinions on the participants about the recognition of which process elements could be recognized in the sentence considered in the survey. The purpose of this step was to enable the agreement of the answers according to the mapping rules created for process element shown in the sentence. The sentences are:

1. *A customer brings a defective computer and the CRS checks the defect and hands out a repair cost calculation back.*
2. *If the customer decides that the costs are acceptable, the process continues, otherwise, she takes her computer home unrepaired.*
3. *The ongoing repair consists of two activities, which are executed, in a parallel order. The first activity is to check and repair the hardware, whereas the second activity checks the software and configures the hardware.*

In the third step, our goal was to get an opinion of the participants about the process modeling shown in the survey. Thus, six process models were created from sentences shown in the survey, and only two process models were modeled according to the mapping rules. The rest of the process models were purposefully modeled incorrectly. The reason is to verify whether the participants' answers are in accordance with the mapping rules for such sentence.

The survey was applied using *Google Forms*[6]. The form was available from Oct 20 to Nov 10, 2016. We advertised it in social networks and websites and, consequently, 43 answers were collected from participants, including process experts, software developers, students, among others.

The evaluation conducted in this survey demonstrated encouraging results (Figs. 3, 4 and 5). From the 43 answers, we filtered the results to get all the opinions given by process experts. To do this, we have selected a total of 22 participants based on the following characteristics:

1. Process experts
2. Experience in BPMN
3. More than two years of experience in BPMN
4. Experience in process modeling
5. More than two years of experience in process modeling

---

[6] https://www.google.com/forms/about; last accessed: 2016-11-17.

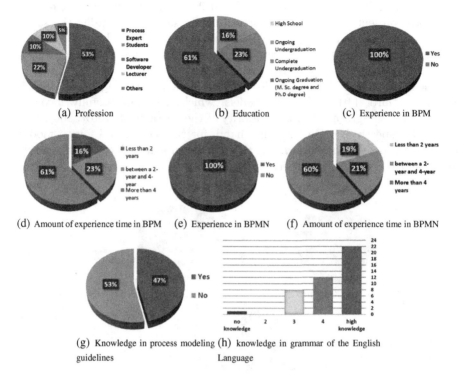

Fig. 3. Results obtained from the first step of the first survey with all participants. (Source: Ferreira et al. [1]).

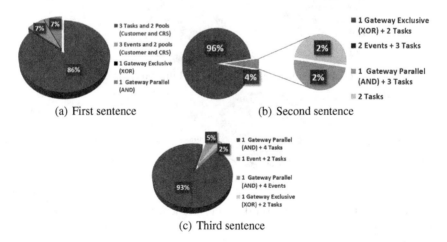

Fig. 4. Results obtained from the second step of the first survey with 22 participants. (Source: Ferreira et al. [1]).

The second step of the survey shows that 90% of the participants agree with the model presented in the first sentence of the survey. Regarding the second sentence 100% of the participants agree with the modeling while 90% agree with the modeling in the third sentence. All sentences were modeled based on the proposed modeling rules by our approach.

The third step of the survey also demonstrates encouraging results (Fig. 5). The first, third, fifth and sixth models, which were purposefully incorrect, obtained the disagreement of the majority of the participants (90%, 100%, 95% and 77% respectively). On the other hand, for the second and fourth models, which were correct, the majority of the participants agreed with the proposed modeling (68% and 81% respectively).

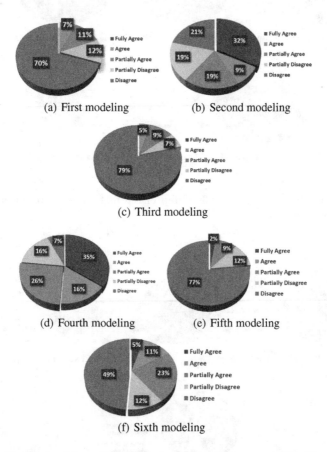

(a) First modeling   (b) Second modeling

(c) Third modeling

(d) Fourth modeling   (e) Fifth modeling

(f) Sixth modeling

Fig. 5. Results obtained from the third step of the first survey with 22 participants. (Source: Ferreira et al. [1]).

4.2   Survey on the Contribution of the Mapping Rules in the Process Modeling Activity

To verify the contribution of the mapping rules, we conducted a second survey to check the response of modelers to the aid of the mapping rules. The main objective was to evaluate the difference of modeling process when the modelers use rule-mapped text compared to the modeling done by the same modelers without this additional aid. We focused on measuring the time spent to complete the modeling task and the effort necessary as perceived by the modeler. The survey was divided into four steps.

The first step of this survey was to gather information about participants' experiences. For this reason, this first part is similar in form and purpose to the first step of the survey presented in Sect. 4.1, with the main difference being the removal of questions 7 and 8, since they were not adequate for the purpose of this survey.

The second step had the objective of measuring the estimated modeling time and measure the difficulty level of such modeling. We provided a text in English describing a process model and asked the participants to model this process in BPMN. Initially, the source of the text and the activities to be developed are presented to the participant. Shortly after, the text to be modeled is displayed. Subsequently, the participant would answer the amount of time it took to finish this task and how difficult it was, which was based on the five-point Likert scale, ranging from very easy to very difficult.

In the third step we also had a modeling task with similar questions at the end, but text provided was different, containing tags highlighting the process elements created according to the mapping rules, while maintaining similar length and complexity to the previous text.

Finally, the last step was subjective in nature, seeking to capture the user's satisfaction and experience with the recognition of process elements in the text. This step was composed of four questions:

1. Which of the texts had more details of process modeling?
2. Justify your answer.
3. Do you agree that the recognition of business process elements in Text 2 helped to model such elements described in the text?
4. Do you agree that recognizing business process elements in natural language text will help and minimize the effort required by process analysts in the modeling step?

The form was available from Jan 11 to Jan 30, 2017. As the first survey, this survey was also widely disseminated on social networks, websites, mailing lists, and other means. The survey attained answers from 21 participants including process specialists, software developers, students, among others.

For the selection of participants, the same criteria for filtering presented in the first survey were used. Also, because we could not guarantee that the process models created by the participants were correct, we removed the answers from participants which were *quick and wrong*. This filtering reduced the number of participants to 12, representing 57.14% of the total. These answers are depicted in Figs. 6, 7 and 8.

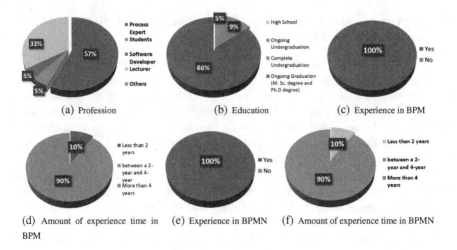

(a) Profession   (b) Education   (c) Experience in BPM

(d) Amount of experience time in   (e) Experience in BPMN   (f) Amount of experience time in BPMN
BPM

Fig. 6. Results obtained from the first step of the second survey with all participants.

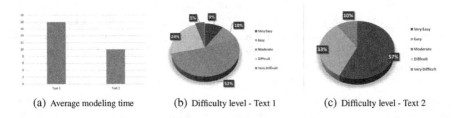

(a) Average modeling time   (b) Difficulty level - Text 1   (c) Difficulty level - Text 2

Fig. 7. Results obtained from the second and third step of the second survey with 12 participants.

Comparing the results, the average modeling time spent by the participants was 17 min for the plain text, which is higher than the average time of 10 min that the participants took to model a text with the highlighted process elements. In the case of the difficulty perceived by the participants, the plain text scored an average of 3.25, also higher than the average score of 1.33 for the enhanced text. This suggests that the mapping rules may contribute in reducing the time, the effort and, consequently, the cost spent on the modeling phase.

In the last step, the first question showed that 100% of the participants selected agree that text 2 had more details for process modeling. In the third question, which sought to verify if the recognition of process elements in the text aided the process modeling, 91.66% of the participants agree that recognition of process elements in the texts actually helped the modeling. Finally, the fourth question demonstrated that 100% of the selected participants agreed that the recognition of process elements would actually minimize the effort of the analysts.

4.3 Prototype Validation Based on NLP Tools

We conducted one experiment to demonstrate the feasibility of applying our approach to a large collection of tests. A prototype we created was used in this

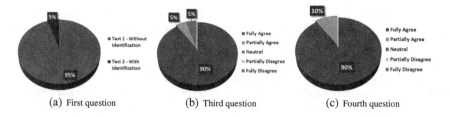

(a) First question   (b) Third question   (c) Fourth question

Fig. 8. Results obtained from the fourth step of the second survey with 12 participants.

experimental study to analyze natural language texts from six sources, which in total contain 417 sentences from 70 texts:

1. BMW owner's Manuals & Documents[7].
2. Immigrant Visa Process[8].
3. Federal Network Agency of Germany[9].
4. Vista Project Office Documentation Plan[10].
5. BPMN modeling and reference guide [42].
6. Queensland University of Technology (QUT).

We used the standard machine learning evaluation metrics and measures for information retrieval (i.e. precision, recall and F-measure) [43–45] to evaluate the performance of our prototype for each process element considered (activities, events, parallel gateways and exclusive gateways). Table 8 summarizes the performance of our prototype. In general, our prototype achieves good performance.

Table 8. Results of performance of our prototype proposed by our approach (Source: Ferreira et al. [1]).

Class	Found	Precision	Recall	F-Measure
Activities	140	75.48%	70%	73.12%
Events	106	81.81%	72.26%	76.74%
Exclusive gateway (XOR)	98	65.47%	73.95%	69.60%
Parallel gateway (AND)	43	71.69%	64.40%	67.85%
Total	387	73.61%	70.15%	71.82%

5   Conclusion

In this paper, we presented a reiteration and an evolution of a semi-automatic approach to recognize process elements in natural language texts. To achieve

---

7 https://goo.gl/REUmu6; last accessed 2016-11-12.
8 https://goo.gl/rPLqXE; last accessed 2016-11-12.
9 https://goo.gl/KuQOBw; last accessed 2016-11-12.
10 https://goo.gl/MxzAAH; last accessed 2016-11-12.

this goal, we have created 32 mapping rules to recognize process elements in the texts. Moreover, we have developed a prototype to semi-automatically recognize process elements in texts. The evaluation of our approach was made through two surveys and one experiment to demonstrate the feasibility of our prototype. The validation through the survey demonstrated that 93.33% of the participants agree with the mapping rules. Moreover, both the time spent by the participants in the modeling process and the difficulty level defined by the participants was decreased. Furthermore, the prototype experiment was presented 73.61% precision, 70.15% recall and 71.82% F-measure. Thus, our approach minimizes the effort of the process analyst to capture business process elements from natural language texts and indicates completeness of the texts based on BPMN rules.

Despite these promising results, one limitation of our approaches refers to the automatically generation of rules. Hence, we intend to generate them through artificial intelligence. With the objective of expanding the set of process elements, in future works we will explore the creation of mapping rules for other BPMN process elements, such as message flows, sub-processes, exception flows, data object, sequence flow and inclusive gateways (OR), etc. In addition, Fig. 1 shows the next step in this approach, described as preprocessed text (process-oriented). It is expected to generate a template of how the text should be structured for the extraction of process models from text. Our approach can be considered as a prerequisite for generating preprocessed text (process-oriented).

References

1. Ferreira, R.C.B., Thom, L.H., Fantinato, M.: A semi-automatic approach to identify business process elements in natural language texts (2017)
2. Thom, L.H.: Gerenciamento de Processos de Negócio e Aplicabilidade na Saúde e na Robótica. Biblioteca Digital Brasileira de Computação (2012)
3. Thom, L., Reichert, M., Iochpe, C.: Activity patterns in process-aware information systems: basic concepts and empirical evidence. Int. J. Bus. Process Integr. Manag. (IJBPIM) **4**, 93–110 (2009)
4. Dumas, M., Rosa, M.L., Mendling, J., Reijers, H.A.: Fundamentals of Business Process Management. Springer, Heidelberg (2013). https://doi.org/10.1007/978-3-642-33143-5
5. Weske, M.: Business Process Management: Concepts, Languages, Architectures. Springer, Berlin (2007). https://doi.org/10.1007/978-3-642-28616-2
6. Leopold, H.: Natural Language in Business Process Models. Springer, Switzerland (2013). https://doi.org/10.1007/978-3-319-04175-9
7. Blumberg, R., Atre, S.: The problem with unstructured data. DM Rev. **13**, 62 (2003)
8. White, M.: Information overlook. vol. 26, p. 7 (2003)
9. Friedrich, F., Mendling, J., Puhlmann, F.: Process model generation from natural language text. In: Mouratidis, H., Rolland, C. (eds.) CAiSE 2011. LNCS, vol. 6741, pp. 482–496. Springer, Heidelberg (2011). https://doi.org/10.1007/978-3-642-21640-4_36
10. Chueng, A., Koliadis, G., Ghose, A.: Process discovery from model and text artefacts. In: 2007 IEEE Congress on Services, pp. 167–174 (2007)
11. Goncalves, J.C.A., Santoro, F.M., Baião, F.A.: Let me tell you a story - on how to build process models. J. Univers. Comput. Sci. **17**, 276–295 (2011)

12. Ferreira, R.C.B., Thom, L.H., de Oliveira, J.P.M., Avila, D.T., dos Santos, R.I., Fantinato, M.: Assisting process modeling by identifying business process elements in natural language texts. In: de Cesare, S., Frank, U. (eds.) ER 2017. LNCS, vol. 10651, pp. 154–163. Springer, Cham (2017). https://doi.org/10.1007/978-3-319-70625-2_15

13. Santoro, F.M., Goncalves, J.C.A., Baiao, F.A.: Business process mining from group stories. In: International Conference on Computer Supported Cooperative Work in Design, pp. 161–166 (2009)

14. Jiexun, L., Wang, H.J., Zhang, Z., Zhao, J.L.: A policy-based process mining framework: mining business policy texts for discovering process models. Inf. Syst. E-Bus. Manag. **8**, 169–188 (2010)

15. Leopold, H., Mendling, J., Polyvyanyy, A.: Supporting process model validation through natural language generation. IEEE Trans. Softw. Eng. **40**, 816–840 (2014)

16. Meitz, M., Leopold, H., Mendling, J.: An approach to support process model validation based on text generation. **33**, 7–20 (2013)

17. van der Aa, H., Leopold, H., Reijers, H.A.: Detecting inconsistencies between process models and textual descriptions. In: Motahari-Nezhad, H.R., Recker, J., Weidlich, M. (eds.) BPM 2015. LNCS, vol. 9253, pp. 90–105. Springer, Cham (2015). https://doi.org/10.1007/978-3-319-23063-4_6

18. van der Aa, H., Leopold, H., Reijers, H.A.: Dealing with behavioral ambiguity in textual process descriptions. In: La Rosa, M., Loos, P., Pastor, O. (eds.) BPM 2016. LNCS, vol. 9850, pp. 271–288. Springer, Cham (2016). https://doi.org/10.1007/978-3-319-45348-4_16

19. Heinonen, O.: Optimal multi-paragraph text segmentation by dynamic programming. In: Proceedings of the 36th Annual Meeting of the Association for Computational Linguistics and 17th International Conference on Computational Linguistics - Volume 2, ACL 1998, pp. 1484–1486. Association for Computational Linguistics, Stroudsburg (1998)

20. Hearst, M.A.: Multi-paragraph segmentation of expository text. In: Proceedings of the 32nd Annual Meeting on Association for Computational Linguistics, ACL 1994, pp. 9–16. Association for Computational Linguistics, Stroudsburg (1994)

21. Hearst, M.A.: TextTiling: segmenting text into multi-paragraph subtopic passages. Comput. Linguist. **23**, 33–64 (1997)

22. Hynes, G., Bexley, J.: Understandability of banks' annual reports. In: 69th Association for Business Communication Annual Convention, Albuquerque, pp. 1–11 (2003)

23. Ferreira, R.C.B., Thom, L.H.: An approach to generate process-oriented text from natural language. In: XII Brazilian Symposium on Information Systems, p. 77 (2016)

24. WfMC: Wfmc: Process definition language: XPDL 2.0, p. 164 (2005)

25. Morris, J., Hirst, G.: Lexical cohesion computed by thesaural relations as an indicator of the structure of text. Comput. Linguist. **17**, 21–48 (1991)

26. Allen, J.: Natural Language Understanding. Benjamin-Cummings Publishing Co., Inc., Redwood City (1995)

27. de Kok, D., Brouwer, H.: Natural Language Processing for the Working Programmer (2011)

28. Brill, E.: A simple rule-based part of speech tagger. In: Proceedings of the Third Conference on Applied Natural Language Processing, ANLC 1992, pp. 152–155. Association for Computational Linguistics, Stroudsburg (1992)

29. Briscoe, T., Carroll, J., Watson, R.: The second release of the RASP system. In: Proceedings of the COLING/ACL on Interactive Presentation Sessions, COLING-ACL 2006, pp. 77–80. Association for Computational Linguistics, Stroudsburg (2006)
30. Choi, J.D., Palmer, M.: Guidelines for the Clear Style Constituent to Dependency Conversion. Technical report 01–12, University of Colorado Boulder (2012)
31. OMG: Business process modeling notation (BPMN). versão 2.0.2 (2013)
32. Mendling, J., Neumann, G., van der Aalst, W.: Understanding the occurrence of errors in process models based on metrics. In: Meersman, R., Tari, Z. (eds.) OTM 2007. LNCS, vol. 4803, pp. 113–130. Springer, Heidelberg (2007). https://doi.org/10.1007/978-3-540-76848-7_9
33. Figl, K., Recker, J., Mendling, J.: A study on the effects of routing symbol design on process model comprehension. Decis. Support Syst. **54**, 1104–1118 (2013)
34. Kossak, F., Illibauer, C., Geist, V.: Event-based gateways: open questions and inconsistencies. In: Mendling, J., Weidlich, M. (eds.) BPMN 2012. LNBIP, vol. 125, pp. 53–67. Springer, Heidelberg (2012). https://doi.org/10.1007/978-3-642-33155-8_5
35. Kindler, E.: On the semantics of EPCs: resolving the vicious circle. Data Knowl. Eng. **56**, 23–40 (2006)
36. Mendling, J., Reijers, H.A., van der Aalst, W.M.P.: Seven process modeling guidelines (7PMG). Inf. Softw. Technol. **52**, 127–136 (2010)
37. Mendling, J.: Managing structural and textual quality of business process models. In: Cudre-Mauroux, P., Ceravolo, P., Gašević, D. (eds.) SIMPDA 2012. LNBIP, vol. 162, pp. 100–111. Springer, Heidelberg (2013). https://doi.org/10.1007/978-3-642-40919-6_6
38. Mendling, J., Strembeck, M., Recker, J.C.: Factors of process model comprehension : findings from a series of experiments. Decis. Support Syst. **53**, 195–206 (2012)
39. Mendling, J., Reijers, H.A., Cardoso, J.: What makes process models understandable? In: Alonso, G., Dadam, P., Rosemann, M. (eds.) BPM 2007. LNCS, vol. 4714, pp. 48–63. Springer, Heidelberg (2007). https://doi.org/10.1007/978-3-540-75183-0_4
40. Schrepfer, M., Wolf, J., Mendling, J., Reijers, H.A.: The impact of secondary notation on process model understanding. In: Persson, A., Stirna, J. (eds.) PoEM 2009. LNBIP, vol. 39, pp. 161–175. Springer, Heidelberg (2009). https://doi.org/10.1007/978-3-642-05352-8_13
41. Reijers, H., Mendling, J.: Modularity in process models: review and effects. In: Dumas, M., Reichert, M., Shan, M.-C. (eds.) BPM 2008. LNCS, vol. 5240, pp. 20–35. Springer, Heidelberg (2008). https://doi.org/10.1007/978-3-540-85758-7_5
42. White, S.A.: BPMN Modeling and Reference Guide: Understanding and Using BPMN. Future Strategies Inc., Lighthouse Point (2008)
43. Japkowicz, N., Shah, M.: Evaluating Learning Algorithms: A Classification Perspective. Cambridge University Press, New York (2011)
44. Forbes, A.D.: Classification-algorithm evaluation: five performance measures based onconfusion matrices. J. Clin. Monit. **11**, 189–206 (1995)
45. Manning, C.D., Raghavan, P., Schütze, H.: Introduction to Information Retrieval. Cambridge University Press, New York (2008)

An Interface Prototype Proposal to a Semiautomatic Process Model Verification Method Based on Process Modeling Guidelines

Valter Helmuth Goldberg Júnior[1], Vinicius Stein Dani[1], Diego Toralles Avila[1],
Lucineia Heloisa Thom[1(✉)], José Palazzo Moreira de Oliveira[1],
and Marcelo Fantinato[2]

[1] Department of Informatics, Federal University
of Rio Grande do Sul, Porto Alegre, Brazil
{vhgjunior,vsdani,dtavila,lucineia,palazzo}@inf.ufrgs.br
[2] School of Arts, Sciences and Humanities, University of São Paulo, São Paulo, Brazil
m.fantinato@usp.br

Abstract. The design of comprehensible process models is a very complex task. In order to obtain them, process analysts usually rely on process modeling guidelines. This is specially true when dealing with collections counting up to hundreds of process models, since querying or organizing such a collection is not easy. In this paper we report a method presented in an earlier work to verify if a process model is following process modeling guidelines. In addition we propose an interface prototype to display which process models are not following which guidelines. A collection of 31 process models were used to validate the identification method and the results shows that 23 of these process models contains at least one guideline violation.

Keywords: Business process · BPMN · Ontology
Process model quality · Modeling guidelines · Information visualization

1 Introduction

Organizations seek continuously to enhance the quality of their business processes (henceforth namely processes, for the sake of simplicity) with Business Process Management (BPM). However, studies analyzing models of industry processes reveal that many of them contain issues that hamper their quality, such as control flow errors, poorly designed structures and layouts or incorrect labeling [1,2]. With the process modeling being a key part of BPM, it is important to prevent these issues if we expect processes with better quality standards.

The demand for the assessment of process models in terms of their quality has been increasing. The assessment task is not trivial and requires time and effort to be performed. This is especially true when this assessment must be performed

© Springer International Publishing AG, part of Springer Nature 2018
S. Hammoudi et al. (Eds.): ICEIS 2017, LNBIP 321, pp. 611–629, 2018.
https://doi.org/10.1007/978-3-319-93375-7_28

among a large amount of process models. In this situation, a proper tool to automate part of this assessment by identifying and displaying deficiencies in the design of process models within a collection is vital to correct them. Considering these facts, we have two problems to solve: the identification of the quality issues in a process model and a manner to display this information in the context of a collection of process models.

Quality issues of process models usually occur due to the difficulty of process modeling [3]. The expertise or the guidance of an experienced modeler may highly influence resultant process model's correctness and its comprehensibility. When this expertise or guidance is missing, it is common that process models embody errors and become poorly designed, which may restrain an organization from accomplishing its objectives. It is important to consider that, while the use of process modeling tools can help in this regard, they cannot guarantee that the modeler won't make mistakes.

To deal with the issue of correctness, we can use a process model ontology which is the study of the nature of being and pursues to represent the world as entities, categories and relations [4,5]. In a more practical description, an ontology provides an approach to define types, properties and relations. It is possible to use an ontology to represent BPM process models as a meta-model with inference capability to verify a process model's correctness.

In the case of comprehensibility, the expertise of experienced modelers can be consolidated in process modeling guidelines which support a user in reducing the complexity and the amount of errors in a process model by preventing an unsuitable use of modeling elements. Many guidelines have been proposed by both practitioners [6–8] and researchers [9–12]. Once a process model is verified that it is following a set of guidelines, we can presume that it is comprehensible.

In terms of displaying information, visualization tools help people in situations where viewing a data set in detail is better than seeing only a brief summary of that data (i.e., in cases where it is desired to confirm patterns that are assumed to exist in the data or to discover new patterns). There are many possible different combinations in terms of information visualization in order to obtain a good result regarding the design of a visualization [13]. In this sense we aim to define the most suited design for our approach.

In a previous work [14] we proposed a semiautomatic process model verification method, based on process modeling guidelines, to identify quality issues within process models. In this paper, we reiterate this previous work and extend it by proposing a first draft of an interface prototype to display which process models are not following which guidelines.

This paper is organized as follows: Sect. 2 presents reviews of previous works related to the verification of process models. Section 3 introduces the basic concepts used in this paper. Section 4 explains the context chosen to work with and the method developed. Section 5 presents the application study and the results. Section 6 proposes an interface prototype to display the results from the previous section. Section 7 closes the paper with conclusions.

2   Related Works

Many researchers addressed the subject of verification of process models concerning issues of correctness (e.g., in [5] the author proposes two different approaches aiming the verification of soundness of a process model drawn using Event-driven Process Chains).

The evaluation and diminishing of complexity within a process model is not a trivial task, since it is not possible to be done directly. Different authors [15–18] propose candidate solutions to solve this problem indirectly through metrics, evidenced by statistical experiments where process models are judged by the metrics and by people with varying levels of modeling experience [19,20].

In the study [21] the support of popular BPMN process modeling tools to guidelines usage was tested based on 27 guidelines that were described in the overview of Moreno-Montes de Oca et al. [22]. According to this study, the Signavio[1] tool provides better support for modeling processes using guidelines.

A literature study of various areas that relates to managing large collections of business process models was made by [23]. To name two of these areas that most relates to the present work we have querying and collection organization. Querying can be used to identify process models that do or do not satisfy a set of given standards [24]; and, collection organization can be used to keep the overview of the collection so the users can easily find the processes they are looking for through crossing the relations that the different process models have with each other [25].

While the referenced works are built upon important process modeling concepts, none of them provide an approach to certify the comprehensibility of process models nor to display which processes violate guidelines within a collection of processes modeled with BPMN. The present work reiterates the explanation of the development of a method and how to adapt each concept for an ontological approach that allows the verification of the process models in a semi-automatic way, and proposes an interface to display the results of this verification within a set of processes.

3   Background

The notation used to the modeling task of BPM is often the Business Process Model and Notation (BPMN). BPMN was developed by the Business Process Management Initiative (BPMI) and nowadays is maintained by the Object Management Group (OMG), with the purpose of consolidating the many existing notations for process models in a single standard. This standard should ease understanding of the notation to all stakeholders [26].

BPMN has many different types of elements to represent a process, each with different purposes. In this paper we cover basically five main types (Fig. 1):

---

[1] www.signavio.com.

- **Activities and Sub-processes:** activities are called *tasks* when it can be seen as a single unit of work; otherwise, if it's required many steps, we call it an *activity*. Sub-processes contains multiple elements of a process inside a single element;
- **Events:** correspond to things that happen with no duration and may be basically of three types: *start, intermediate* or *end events*;
- **Gateways:** also called *decision points*, are used to split (or join) the flow of actions performed along the process and may be of three types: (i) *XOR gateways*, for exclusive choices; (ii) *AND gateways*, for concurrency; and (iii) *OR gateways*, for inclusive choices;
- **Sequence Flows:** responsible for linking two elements together, forming the paths that may be taken during the execution of a process;
- **Pools and Swimlanes:** the pools group together elements that belongs to a single organization (e.g., a university). Swimlanes divide a pool to identify different resources of that organization (e.g., departments).

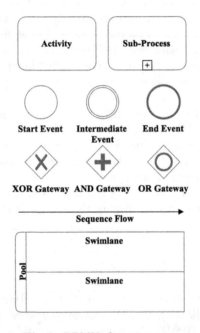

Fig. 1. BPMN element types.

It is difficult to achieve quality in BPMN process models since BPMN does not appropriately teach modelers how to use its elements to create meaningful and expressive process models. Many frameworks were created to handle this difficulty by means of defining what are the quality types that may help building a high quality process model. To cite a few examples of these there are: the SEQUAL Framework [27], the Guidelines of Modeling (GoM) [28] and the SIQ

Framework [29]. This last framework is used as guidance to the present work, due to its simplicity and its widespread use in the literature surrounding the quality of process models. It defines process model quality as composed of three basic quality types (Fig. 2): (i) syntactic quality, which concerns to the correct use of elements in terms of its notation' syntax. To check the static and behavioral properties of a process model is called verification; (ii) semantic quality, which concerns to the connection between a process model and its real world process representative. To check if all elements of the process model corresponds to its real world process representative is called validation; (iii) pragmatic quality, characterizes the comprehensibility of a process model. To check if a user's interpretation of a process model is equal to the real world process is called certification.

According to the SIQ Framework, it is not reasonable to consider the pragmatic nor the semantic quality of a process model if it is not syntactically correct. Any knowledge extracted from an incorrect process model has its validity compromised as at the same time that the model is readable some doubt may exists about the modeler intended representation [29]. Therefore, syntactic quality can be considered to be the basis for the other two qualities, as seen in Fig. 2. As a result, the verification of a process model must be done before its validation and its certification. This verification may be done by using an ontology. More specifically, we can use an ontology design to serve as a meta-model for a process modeling notation. When dealing with BPMN there is the *BPMN Ontology* [30], which supports mapping of a BPMN process model into elements of the ontology, while maintaining the relations and structures between the BPMN elements. Using this ontology makes possible to apply an inference engine to verify the mapped process model, checking if the static properties of BPMN model (i.e., its structure) are correct according to the BPMN syntax.

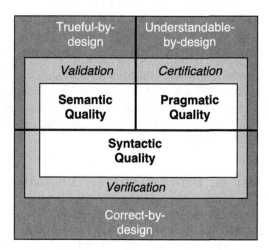

Fig. 2. The SIQ Framework, adapted from [29]. Source: Goldberg et al. [14].

Assuming the process model is syntactically correct it is possible to try to ensure its pragmatic quality, which is done by checking it via the use of the process modeling guidelines. Mendling et al. [3, p. 3] propose seven process modeling guidelines (7PMG) which are *"thought to be helpful in guiding users towards improving the quality of their models, in the sense that these are likely (1) to become comprehensible to various stakeholders and (2) to contain few syntactical errors"*. These guidelines have been built upon empirical insights and provide a short, yet meaningful, set of rules which encouraged their use at an academic level to teach beginner modelers about process models quality. The seven process modeling guidelines are as follows:

G1 Use as Few Elements in the Model as Possible. Large process models tend to be more difficult to understand and more error prone;

G2 Minimize the Routing Paths per Element. It is harder to understand a process model containing elements with a high total of incoming and the outgoing arcs;

G3 Use One Start and One end Event. Models that satisfy this requirement are easier to understand and less likely to have errors;

G4 Model as Structured as Possible. A process model well structured, i.e. to every split connector there is a matching join connector of the same type, tends to be easier to understand;

G5 Avoid or Routing Elements. The use of OR gateways difficult the comprehension of the process model;

G6 Use Verb-object Activity Labels. According to the literature, the verb-object style is less ambiguous and more useful than other labeling styles, like action-noun;

G7 Decompose a Model if it has More than 30 Elements. Like G1, a high number of elements makes the process model less understandable and more error-prone. For models with more than 30 elements it is recommended to split the process model into smaller models, either by creating new ones or by gathering a group of process model elements and replacing them with a sub-process.

It is important to note that these guidelines do not concern with the semantics of the process model. Whether a model of a specific process follows or not these guidelines it should not imply in a change of the behavior of the modeled process. All that the 7PMG rules change is the comprehensibility of the process model reducing the possibility of modeling errors [3].

4   Guideline-Driven Process Model Verification

To fulfill the objective of this paper, we specified six steps that, with the assistance of an ontology, allows us to certify a process model's pragmatic quality by checking whether it follows the seven process modeling guidelines [14].

There are different process models notations and each one has its own manner to represent a process model within a file. In this paper we decided to work with

Table 1. Indicators tested for each guideline from 7PMG. Source: Goldberg et al. [14].

7PMG	Indicators and comparisons
G1	Number of elements > 30
G2	Maximum connector degree > 5
G3	Number of start events > 1 Number of end events > 1
G4	Number of splits ≠ Number of joins
G5	Number of OR gateways > 0
G6	Wordnet
G7	Number of elements > 30

Table 2. BPMN ⇒ Ontology Mapping. Source: Goldberg et al. [14].

BPMN	Ontology	Example
Element type	OWL class	Activity, gateway
Element instance	Individual named	Task 1: Submit report
Attribute	Object property	Label= "Name"
Attribute value	Data property	Name:String= "Task 1: Submit report"

BPMN version 2.0, which may be exported to an interchangeable format defined by OMG and consists basically of a XML file with a specific schema and a ".bpmn" extension [26]. From such file it is possible to map elements from a process model to an ontology, via the *BPMN Ontology*.

We have also established a way to check whether a guideline is being followed or not by a process model, by expressing it as a binary, yes or no, question. Previous works [5,18,31,32] studied process model indicators to produce empirically validated thresholds for each guideline with the objective of alerting the process modeler about the existence of any issues that may affect a process model's comprehensibility. In this sense, we used these indicators and their optimal thresholds, as presented in Table 1, to check if the process model violates or not each guideline.

Two guidelines turned out to be problematic in this context and were left aside in this work:

1. G1 is redundant with G7, since they are expressed by the same indicators and thresholds. When considering their application, G1 is more suited for when a process model is in development, as opposed to G7 which is more useful when the model is finished. Therefore, we chose to keep G7;
2. G6 excels the scope of this work, once it is strongly related to the complexity of checking the language of each label through Natural Language Processing (NLP) [33].

We also determined how an ontology will be loaded and edited. For this task we used the ontology editor *Protégé*[2] which is able to verify the integrity of ontologies using an inference engine and can be extended using plugins. Such extensibility was explored so we could build our method.

With these decisions made, we specified a method to certify the pragmatic quality of process models based on 7PMG, verifying a process model' syntax using the ontology and its associated inference engine. The first step of the method is to configure *Protégé* for instantiating BPMN models. The BPMN ontology is loaded to support the mapping of elements from BPMN to the ontology by serving as the meta-model containing the structuring rules of BPMN so each element from the BPMN models can be extracted and instantiated into the ontology by a Java plugin (capable of reading the ".bpmn" file), which extracts from the process models its tasks, gateways, sequence flows and messages. After this, the same plugin uses the OWL-API to create individuals for each element, mapping and instantiating them as each type described by the BPMN Ontology (Table 2 presents this mapping in a concise way).

Table 3. Recommended Actions for each tested guideline. Source: Goldberg et al. [14].

7PMG	Recommended action
G2	Reduce the number of sequence flows connected to a single element
G3	Restructure the process model to reduce the number of Start and End events
G4	Restructure the process model to have the same number of Split and Joins
G5	Restructure the process model to remove the OR Gateways
G7	Decompose the process model

With the entire process model instantiated in the ontology, *Protégé* verifies if the model is syntactically correct with its inference engine, by checking the integrity of the ontology. If the integrity is assured, according to BPMN Ontology, we can say that the BPMN model is syntactically correct.

The final step of this method is to check the process model according to the 7PMG and recommending modeling alternatives based on the results. Another Java plugin checks the process model's indicators and, for each violated guideline, recommends actions according to Table 3, displaying it initially through the system console. In the Sect. 6 we propose a better way to show these informations alongside with which are the guidelines violated by each process model.

This method' sequence of steps (Fig. 3) are more concisely listed below:

1. Load the BPMN Ontology in *Protégé*;

---

[2] http://protege.stanford.edu/.

2. Extract each Individual Element from a BPMN Model;
3. Instantiate Each Extracted Element in *Protégé* via OWL-API and using the BPMN Ontology;
4. Use *Protégé*'s Inference Engine to Verify the Integrity of the New Ontology;
5. Check if the Process Model's Indicators Obey the Limits Defined by the Modeling Guidelines;
6. Recommend Modeling Alternatives to the Process Model for Each Guideline not Followed (Table 3).

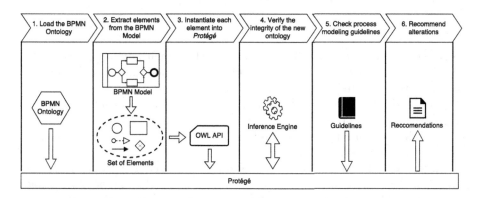

Fig. 3. Steps to verify process models based on process modeling guidelines. Source: Goldberg et al. [14].

Table 4. Statistics for the indicators related to the guidelines G2, G3, G5, G7. Source: Goldberg et al. [14].

	Maximum connector degree	N° of start events	N° of end events	N° of OR gateways	N° of elements
Average	3.7097	1.871	1.9355	0.2903	23.4194
Std. Deviation	0.9379	0.8848	0.892	0.8638	13.458
Minimum	2	1	1	0	6
Maximum	6	4	4	4	76
Median	3	2	2	0	21

5   Application Study and Results

We used a collection of 31 BPMN models representing the processes of an university to validate our method. These models were created by BPM students (using

Table 5. Statistics for the indicators related to the guideline G4. Source: Goldberg et al. [14].

	Splits - Joins difference		
	AND	XOR	OR
Average	0.129	0.4839	−0.0968
Std. Deviation	0.3408	1.3873	0.3962
Minimum	0	−2	−2
Maximum	1	4	0
Median	0	0	0

the Bizagi[3] modeler tool), verified and corrected by their adviser and semantically validated by the processes' stakeholders. Bizagi does not offer support for the guidelines we tested [21].

Associated indicators were extracted for statistical analysis for each one of the guidelines used in our method (as seen in Tables 4 and 5), so that we could try to predict whether the majority of process models of this collection violate or not these guidelines.

The statistics for maximum connector degree, associated with guideline G2, shows that the highest value found was 6, which is above the suggested threshold value of 5 for this guideline. It is unlikely, assuming a normal distribution, the average of 3.7097 and the standard deviation of 0.9379, that a random process model picked from our collection will surpass this recommended limit. Consequently, it is possible to anticipate that the majority of the process models from the collection will follow this guideline.

As the number of both start and end events has a high average (being almost 2) compared to the suggested threshold of one event for each of these types, it's possible to infer that most process models from the collection have multiple start and end event, therefore they do not follow this guideline.

The analysis of guideline G4 is more intricate. In this case we need to determine whether the process model is structured or not from the measure of the difference between the number of splits and the number of joins. But not only that, we also need to measure the difference for each type of gateway. The closer to zero this balance is and the lower is the standard deviation then it is more likely that the process model is structured. It's possible to see that there is an imbalance of the number of XOR splits versus the number of XOR joins, according to the average of 0.4839 for this indicator. Beyond that, the high standard deviation of 1.3873 for the XOR gateway reveal that most process models in the collection are not structured. In other words, many process models do not follow this guideline.

G5 is similar to the analysis made regarding G2. Since the average number of OR gateways is low, but not zero, and the standard deviation is almost 1,

---

[3] http://www.bizagi.com.

implying that a few process models do use OR gateways (up to the maximum of 4), it is possible to infer that the majority of process models follows this guideline.

Finally, statistics for guideline G7 are somewhat unclear. At the same time we can see a high average for the measure of the number of elements, suggesting that this guideline is followed; and, we can see a high standard deviation which shows a hint that at least some process models do not follow this guideline (i.e., are constituted of more than 30 elements).

With this data in mind, we expect that most process models violate guidelines G3 and G4, while do not violate guidelines G2 and G5; guideline G7 will have a few violations.

Table 6. Number of violations per guideline. Source: Goldberg et al. [14].

	Total violations	Percent of total
G2	1	3.23%
G3	1	3.23%
G4	22	70.97%
G5	4	12.90%
G7	6	19.35%

The comparison of these conclusions with the results of the applied method (as shown in Table 6) shows that the predictions for guidelines G2, G4, G5 and G7 matches the expected. However, results for guideline G3 is unexpected but, after further analysis, we found the reason for this behavior: many process models of the collection have multiple pools or sub-processes; both of which require, according to the notation, a new start and a new end event, leading to a distortion of the number of events within each process model. Nonetheless, we must consider this distortion for the statistical analysis.

6   An Interface Prototype Proposal

Information visualization techniques make it possible to build tools that support people in situations where viewing a dataset in detail is better than viewing just a brief summary of the data. These tools can be useful to exploring, analyzing and interpreting sets of data that would otherwise require a lot of time (or even be unfeasible) to work with if they were, for example, drawn by hand [13].

Considering that, we applied information visualization techniques to assist with the analysis and interpretation of a set of business process models based on the process modeling guidelines, presented in Sect. 3. As a result, we propose an interface, for later validation and use by process analysts and professors, to help identifying which process models do not follow process modeling guidelines. In addition, which are the most recurrent guidelines not followed by the processes.

There are many different approaches for information visualization. In order to obtain a visualization design prototype, we used an analysis framework presented by Munzner [13] that asks three questions to ease the process of thinking systematically about design choices:

- **What Data does the User See?** A set of process models and their respective guidelines violations;
- **Why does the User Intend To Use the Visualization Tool?** To see which models are not following one or more guidelines and which are the most guidelines not being followed;
- **How are Visual Encoding and Interaction Languages Built in Terms of Design Choices?** Through a "Focus + Context" approach, as proposed by [34], which gathers the overview (or the context, i.e. a subset of the collection of business process models) and the partial view (or focus, i.e. information regarding which guidelines are not followed within each process model) in the same representation.

Combined to this, we used the "4-level nested model", proposed by Munzner [35], which divides the nontrivial visualization design problem into 4 cascaded levels and provides a framework of analysis that allows to deal with different concerns separately:

- **Domain Problem Characterization:** the specific situation of the domain is described, which encompasses a group of target users, their domain of interest, their questions and their data;
- **Data/Operation Abstraction Design:** we abstract the domain-specific questions and data from the previous level to a more general representation;
- **Encoding/Interaction Technique Design:** it is decided specifically how to create and manipulate the visual representation of the abstract data defined in the previous level, guided by the tasks - also defined in level 2;
- **Algorithm Design:** the algorithms are created to represent what was defined in level 3.

The output of a more external level is the input to the subsequent innermost level (see Fig. 4). Each one of these levels and how they are used in this interface prototype proposal are detailed in the following subsections.

6.1   Domain Problem Characterization

This level describes the specific situation of the domain, which includes:

- **A group of Target Users:** process analysts and/or professors;
- **The Domain of Interest:** a collection of business process models containing information about which are the guidelines they are not following;
- **The Questions:** which process models not follow one or more guidelines? What guidelines are the most not followed ones?;
- **The Data:** the result of the guideline-driven verification of a collection of process models (as presented in Sect. 4).

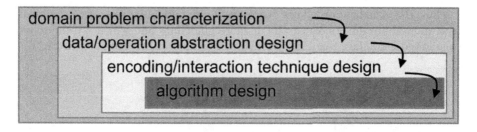

Fig. 4. Model of visualization creation with four nested layers as proposed by [35].

6.2   Data/Operation Abstraction Design

There are two tasks to be done in this layer: the characterization of data and the abstraction of tasks.

In this work we handle basically two types of data, provided by our method [14], to generate the visualization proposal: guidelines violations, which are binary yes or no questions for each guideline; and the model unique identifier. These data comes from the Java plugin implemented by Goldberg et al. [14] and, based on the work by Balieiro [36], its possible to define the data characterization (as presented on Table 7). In this case, the process model's identifiers are discrete quantitative data (i.e., those in which the set of possible outcomes is finite and enumerable) and guidelines violations, expressed by binary yes or no questions, are the categorical nominal ones (i.e., those which can not be put into order but can be compared by difference).

Table 7. Characterization of the data used in this proposal.

Data	Value	Type
idModel	Any integer	Discrete quantitative
G2, G3, G4, G5 e G7	yes or no	Nominal categorical

The abstraction of tasks aims to enable the visualization to be clear displaying the desired data. There are several works [37,38] providing different approaches to support the determination of task abstractions. Based on Shneiderman [39], because of its clarity and objectivity, we chose three task abstractions:

1. **Overview:** reached through the possibility of having an overview of the collection of business process models, see Fig. 6;
2. **Filtering:** reached through a feature which makes possible to see models that are not following any guideline, Fig. 7(a); or, see any subset of models (e.g., the ones that follows only guidelines G2 and G3, Fig. 7(c), or even models that follows no guideline);
3. **Details on Demand:** reached through the possibility of clicking on a certain model and viewing, for example, the model itself, Fig. 10.

Thus, the visualization allows process analysts and/or professors to visualize which models are not following one or more guidelines and which are the most not followed guidelines (see Fig. 5, which will be used as an increment to Fig. 6).

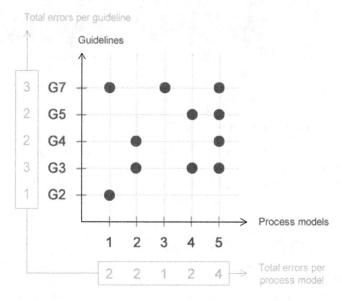

Fig. 5. Multi dotted chart presenting totals of errors per guideline and per process model.

6.3   Encoding/Interaction Technique Design

Figures 6 and 8 illustrate the idea of "Focus + Context" as show by the initial view that presents to a user the process models in a "card format", along with the guidelines not followed. In another perspective (Fig. 9(a)), all guidelines not followed by each process model are presented and may be reordered by the user (Fig. 9(b)). This reordering aims to make visually explicit how many guidelines were not followed by each process model, and it's achieved by grouping the guidelines not followed (at the bottom of the Fig. 9(b)) and the ones followed (at the top of the Fig. 9(b)) separately. These visualizations would represent the "overview", in addition to the visualization presented on Fig. 6. By clicking on any process model, independently of these views, the user should be taken to another screen (see Fig. 10) showing even more detailed information about the process model like the descriptions of the guidelines not followed alongside with recommended actions that should be performed aiming its correction and the process model itself.

6.4   Algorithm Design

In order to develop this interface prototype, we intend to implement algorithms using HTML, CSS and JavaScript, so that this contribution can easily be reused

Fig. 6. Example of a collection of process models and its respective guidelines not followed.

(a) Filters set to display processes presenting any guideline violation.

(b) Filters set to display only processes violating guidelines G2 and G3.

Fig. 7. Examples of the process model's guideline violation filters.

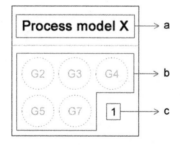

Fig. 8. Card containing information about a given process model. Wherein (a) holds process model's identification and modeler identification; (b) represents each guideline. In this case, all are disabled; which means no guideline is being followed; (c) shows the total of guidelines not followed by the process model.

by anyone interested in these visualizations. The base input file format used shall be the "CSV" (Comma-Separated Values) and it will be composed of columns based on the Table 7.

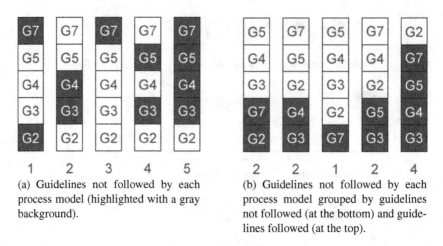

(a) Guidelines not followed by each process model (highlighted with a gray background).

(b) Guidelines not followed by each process model grouped by guidelines not followed (at the bottom) and guidelines followed (at the top).

Fig. 9. Before and after grouping guidelines by not followed and followed per process model.

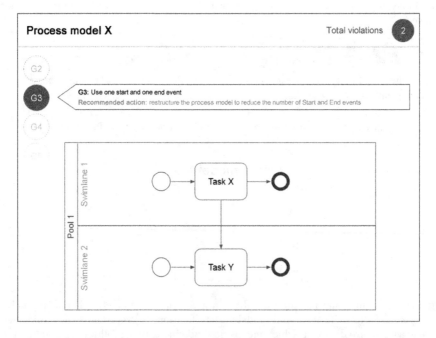

Fig. 10. Example of screen showing more detailed information about the process model like the descriptions of the guidelines not followed alongside with recommended actions that should be performed aiming its correction and the process model itself.

7   Conclusion

Through this study we could see that modelers with less experience in process modeling often makes at least one mistake relatively to the comprehensibility aspect of the process model. There were 13 models with one violation to guidelines; 9 with two violations; and 1 with three violations. It is noticeable that beginner modelers need help in creating process models with high quality. Such help may only be accomplished if more support is provided by modeling tools. The work of an organization may even be enhanced when modelers achieve better process modeling with such support.

In this paper we demonstrate that it is possible to semi-automatically verify process modeling guidelines with the assistance of BPMN ontology, analyzing the process models and recommending solutions to increase its pragmatic quality. It was developed a plugin to identify which of the seven process modeling guidelines proposed by [3] were being violated with the hope of assisting beginner modelers with identifying modeling mistakes which injure a process model's comprehensibility. Further, with the interface proposal, our objective was to make clearer which process models are not following the process modeling guidelines from the context of analyzing an entire collection of process models.

In future works, we intend to validate this interface and further improve it based on the feedback from real users. We hope that this work brings attention to the necessity of an accurate tool support for creating process models with high comprehensibility and better information gathering from a collection of process models. We also believe that our work will provide a basis for future works in these areas.

References

1. Mendling, J., Verbeek, H., van Dongen, B., van der Aalst, W., Neumann, G.: Detection and prediction of errors in EPCs of the SAP reference model. Data Knowl. Eng. **64**, 312–329 (2008)
2. Leopold, H., Mendling, J., Gunther, O.: Learning from quality issues of BPMN models from industry. IEEE Softw. **33**, 26–33 (2016)
3. Mendling, J., Reijers, H.A., van der Aalst, W.M.P.: Seven process modeling guidelines (7PMG). Inf. Softw. Technol. **52**, 127–136 (2010)
4. Guizzardi, G.: Ontological foundations for conceptual modeling with applications. In: Ralyté, J., Franch, X., Brinkkemper, S., Wrycza, S. (eds.) CAiSE 2012. LNCS, vol. 7328, pp. 695–696. Springer, Heidelberg (2012). https://doi.org/10.1007/978-3-642-31095-9_45
5. Mendling, J.: Metrics for Business Process Models. In: Metrics for Process Models, vol. 6, pp. 103–133. Springer, Heidelberg (2008). https://doi.org/10.1007/978-3-540-89224-3_4
6. Silver, B.: BPMN method and style: a levels-based methodology for BPM process modeling and improvement using BPMN 2.0 (2009)
7. White, S.A., Miers, D.: BPMN Modeling and Reference Guide (2008)
8. Allweyer, T., Allweyer, D.: BPMN 2.0 : introduction to the standard for business process modeling. Books on Demand GmbH (2010)

9. Becker, J., Rosemann, M., von Uthmann, C.: Guidelines of business process modeling. In: van der Aalst, W., Desel, J., Oberweis, A. (eds.) Business Process Management. LNCS, vol. 1806, pp. 30–49. Springer, Heidelberg (2000). https://doi.org/10.1007/3-540-45594-9_3

10. Mendling, J., Neumann, G., van der Aalst, W.M.P.: On the correlation between process model metrics and errors. 26th International Conference on Conceptual Modeling, pp. 173–178 (2007)

11. Vanderfeesten, I., Reijers, H.A., Mendling, J., van der Aalst, W.M.P., Cardoso, J.: On a quest for good process models: the cross-connectivity metric. In: Bellahsène, Z., Léonard, M. (eds.) CAiSE 2008. LNCS, vol. 5074, pp. 480–494. Springer, Heidelberg (2008). https://doi.org/10.1007/978-3-540-69534-9_36

12. Correia, A., Abreu, F.B.E.: Adding preciseness to BPMN models. Procedia Technol. **5**, 407–417 (2012)

13. Munzner, T.: Visualization Analysis and Design. CRC Press, Boca Raton (2014)

14. Júnior, V.H.G., Heloisa, L., Jos, T.: A semiautomatic process model verification method based on process modeling guidelines (2017)

15. Vanderfeesten, I., Cardoso, J., Mendling, J., Reijers, H.A., van der Aalst, W.M.P.: Quality metrics for business process models. BPM and Workflow, pp. 1–12 (2007)

16. Mendling, J.: Metrics for Process Models, vol. 6. LNBIP. Springer, Heidelberg (2008)

17. Gruhn, V., Laue, R.: Complexity metrics for business process models. In: 9th International Conference on Business Information ... (2006)

18. Sánchez-González, L., García, F., Ruiz, F., Mendling, J.: Quality indicators for business process models from a gateway complexity perspective. Inf. Softw. Technol. **54**, 1159–1174 (2012)

19. Cardoso, J.: Process control-flow complexity metric: an empirical validation. In: IEEE International Conference on Services Computing, SCC 2006 (2006)

20. Sánchez-González, L., García, F., Mendling, J., Ruiz, F., Piattini, M.: Prediction of Business Process Model Quality Based on Structural Metrics (2008)

21. Snoeck, M., Moreno-Montes de Oca, I., Haegemans, T., Scheldeman, B., Hoste, T.: Testing a selection of BPMN tools for their support of modelling guidelines. In: Ralyté, J., España, S., Pastor, Ó. (eds.) PoEM 2015. LNBIP, vol. 235, pp. 111–125. Springer, Cham (2015). https://doi.org/10.1007/978-3-319-25897-3_8

22. Moreno-Montes de Oca, I., Snoeck, M.: Pragmatic guidelines for Business Process Modeling, p. 70 (2014)

23. Dijkman, R.M., La Rosa, M., Reijers, H.A.: Managing large collections of business process models-current techniques and challenges. Comput. Ind. **63**, 91–97 (2012)

24. Beeri, C., Eyal, A., Kamenkovich, S., Milo, T.: Querying business processes. In: Proceedings of the 32nd International Conference on Very Large Data Bases, VLDB Endowment, pp. 343–354 (2006)

25. Hipp, M., Mutschler, B., Reichert, M.: Navigating in process model collections: a new approach inspired by google earth. In: International Conference on Business Process Management, pp. 87–98. Springer (2011)

26. OMG (Object Management Group): BPMN Specification - Business Process Model and Notation (2015)

27. Krogstie, J.: Model-Based Development and Evolution of Information Systems. Springer, London (2012)

28. Schuette, R., Rotthowe, T.: The guidelines of modeling – an approach to enhance the quality in information models. In: Ling, T.-W., Ram, S., Li Lee, M. (eds.) ER 1998. LNCS, vol. 1507, pp. 240–254. Springer, Heidelberg (1998). https://doi.org/10.1007/978-3-540-49524-6_20

29. Reijers, H.A., Mendling, J., Recker, J.: Business process quality management. In: Handbook on Business Process Management 1, pp. 167–185. Springer, Heidelberg (2015). https://doi.org/10.1007/978-3-642-00416-2_8
30. Rospocher, M., Ghidini, C., Serafini, L.: An ontology for the Business Process Modelling Notation. In: Garbacz, P., Kutz, O., (eds.) Formal Ontology in Information Systems - Proceedings of the Eighth International Conference, FOIS 2014, 22–25 September, 2014, Rio de Janeiro, Brazil, vol. 267, pp. 133–146. IOS Press (2014)
31. Recker, J.: Evaluations of process modeling grammars: ontological, qualitative and quantitative analyses using the example of BPMN. Springer (2011)
32. Mendling, J., Sánchez-González, L., García, F., La Rosa, M.: Thresholds for error probability measures of business process models. J. Syst. Softw. **85**, 1188–1197 (2012)
33. Gassen, J.B., Mendling, J., Thom, L.H., de Oliveira, J.P.M.: Business process modeling. In: Proceedings of the 32nd ACM International Conference on the Design of Communication CD-ROM - SIGDOC 2014, pp. 1–10. ACM Press, New York (2014)
34. Cockburn, A., Karlson, A., Bederson, B.B.: A review of overview+detail, zooming, and focus+context interfaces. ACM Comput. Surv. **41**, 2:1–2:31 (2009)
35. Munzner, T.: A nested model for visualization design and validation. IEEE Trans. Vis. Comput. Graph. **15**, 921–928 (2009)
36. Balieiro, J.C.D.C.: Introdução à estatística (2008)
37. Wehrend, S., Lewis, C.: A problem-oriented classification of visualization techniques. In: Proceedings of the 1st Conference on Visualization1990, pp. 139–143. IEEE Computer Society Press (1990)
38. Zhou, M.X., Feiner, S.K.: Visual task characterization for automated visual discourse synthesis. In: Proceedings of the SIGCHI Conference on Human Factors in Computing Systems, pp. 392–399. ACM Press/Addison-Wesley Publishing Co. (1998)
39. Shneiderman, B.: The eyes have it: a task by data type taxonomy for information visualizations. In: Proceedings of the IEEE Symposium on Visual Languages, pp. 336–343. IEEE (1996)

Author Index

Printed in the United States
By Bookmasters